D0593610

THE STORY OF THE IRISH RACE

The Story of the Irish Race

A Popular History of Ireland

By

Seumas MacManus

Assisted by Several Irish Scholars

Third Edition

CHARTWELL
BOOKS

This edition published in 2018 by Chartwell Books,
an imprint of The Quarto Group
142 West 36th Street, 4th Floor
New York, NY 10018 USA
T (212) 779-4972 **F** (212) 779-6058
www.QuartoKnows.com

Chartwell Books titles are also available at discount for retail, wholesale, promotional, and bulk purchase. For details, contact the Special Sales Manager by email at specialsales@quarto.com or by mail at The Quarto Group, Attn: Special Sales Manager, 401 Second Avenue North, Suite 310, Minneapolis, MN 55401, USA.

10 9 8 7 6 5 4 3 2 1

ISBN: 978-0-7858-3641-4

Printed in China

This Book is Inscribed

TO THE HALOED MEMORY OF ONE WHO, PONDERING THE HEROIC RECORDS OF HER RACE, DEDICATED HER LIFE TO IRELAND'S HOLY CAUSE, AND IN UNDYING STRAINS SANG THE GLORIES THE SORROWS AND RADIANT HOPES OF HER LAND BELOVED—

Eire's Queen of Song,
ETHNA CARBERY.

Contents

Foreword

This is an attempt to sketch a rough and ready picture of the more prominent peaks that rise out of Ireland's past—the high spots in the story of our race.

The story is developed with the object of interesting and informing the man who can not, or will not, afford the time to read studiously. Yet it is earnestly hoped that it may whet the appetites of many, and stimulate them to go browsing in broader and richer pastures—in anticipation of which there are set down, at ends of chapters or periods, titles of some of the more important books dealing with the subject just treated of.

The writer was impelled to the compilation of this story of our race by the woeful lack of knowledge on the subject which he found in the four corners of America, among all classes of people, alike the intelligent and the ordinary. With the vast majority of America's intellectual ones he found Ireland's past as obscure as the past of Borneo. On three occasions he was asked by educated women who were pillars in their Societies, Has Ireland got a history?

To a large extent the blame for American ignorance of Ireland's story rests upon the ignorance of our own exiles, and the children of those exiles. Were these possessed of a general knowledge of Ireland's past, and the proper pride that must come of that knowledge, the good Americans around them would catch information by contagion. The writer hopes that even this crude compendium may put some of the necessary knowledge and pride in the minds and hearts of his people—and also the incentive to seek out and study the history of the country that endowed them with the rare riches, spiritual and mental, that characterises the far-wandered children, and children's children, of the Gael.

Also it is to be hoped that many of the general American public, ever sympathetic toward Ireland, may, through the aid of this rough record, graduate from a state of instinctive sympathy and love to the beginning of an intelligent one.

In making this compilation, the political narrative common to all Irish histories is given briefly. But, non-political phases of our race's history—often far more important than the political, and usually omitted or only hinted at—are gone into more largely: such as the ancient customs, laws, learning, literature, scholars, teachers, saints, missionaries—and in more modern times the spiritual struggles and sufferings of our people.

In spelling the ancient Irish proper names the Gaelic form is usually employed—except in cases where a modern form has been popularised. For sake of readers who know nothing of Irish pronunciation, the confusing aspirate has been, in most cases, omitted—except with *g* or *c* where the aspirate is, to English speakers, a help rather than a hindrance. The Gaelic reader will know where to supply the missing aspirates.

For the inquiring reader's benefit it may be useful to quote here a passage from an article on The Ancient Language, History and Literature of Ireland, which Dr. Douglas Hyde kindly contributed for this volume—but which was unfortunately received too late for inclusion.

Says Dr. Hyde: "The numerous Irish annals in which the skeleton of Irish history is contained, are valuable and ancient. We have of course no outside testimony by which we can verify their statements, but there is abundance of *internal* testimony to show the accuracy with which they have been handed down. The Annals of Ulster, to take one of several compilations of a like character, treat of Ireland from about the year 444, and record numerous natural phenomena as they occurred. If it could be proved that these phenomena actually took place upon the very date ascribed to them in the annals, we should be able to conclude with something like certainty that they were actually written down at the time and recorded by eye-witnesses. The illustrious Bede in recording the great eclipse of the sun which took place only eleven years before his own birth is two days astray in his date, while the Irish annals give correctly not only the day but the hour. This proves that their compiler had access either to the original record of an eye-witness, or to a copy of such a document. These annals contain, between the end of the fifth century and the year 884, as many as eighteen records of eclipses, comets, and such natural phenomena—and modern science by calculating backwards shows that all these records are absolutely correct, both as to the day and hour. From this we can deduce without hesitation that from the fourth or fifth century the Irish annals can be absolutely trusted."

The compiler expresses his earnest thanks to the Irish scholars and writers who generously aided his work.

The fine chapter on the Danish period[1] is contributed by one eminently well versed on the subject, Dr. Joseph Dunn, translator of the Táin bo Chuailgne, and Professor of Celtic and Lecturer on Romance Philology at the Catholic University of America.

The noted worker in Irish history, biography, archaeology, and literature, "Sean-Ghall"—whom Arthur Griffith characterised as "the greatest living authority on Irish history"—gives us the fruit of years of research in the picture which he contributes of the obscure period from after the advent of Shane *Buide* to the eve of Shane O'Neill.[2]

Miss L. MacManus, the admired author of "The Silk of the Kine" and other fine Irish historical novels, and an authority upon the periods of which she has here treated, supplies the chronicle of Ireland during the Wars of Elizabeth, and during those of William of Orange.[3]

The bright chapter on the Wild Geese,[4] and the record of those momentous decades of Irish militancy 1782–1803[5] have been treated by another of the distinctive Irish writers, Helena O'Concannon (Mrs. Thomas O'Concannon), author of "The Book of Irish Womanhood," and several other valuable works.

Rev. Tomás O'Kelly of the National University (Galway), whose writing both in Irish and in English is not yet as well known as it ought to be, tells the story of the Parnell period.[6]

Another of the new generation, one who is making a name in fiction, essay, and poetry (Gaelic and English) Aod de Blacam, author of "Holy Romans," and "Towards the Republic" contributes the informing chapters on Gaelic literature, and those on the Sinn Fein period.[7]

Seumas MacManus
of Donegal

[1] Chap. XXX.
[2] Chaps. XXXVII–XLI.
[3] Chaps. XLII–XLV and Chap. LII.
[4] Chap. LIV.
[5] Chaps. LVI–LIX and Chap LXI.
[6] Chaps. LXXII–LXXVI.
[7] Chaps. LXXVII–LXXIX.

CHAPTER I

Early Colonisations

The Irish Race of today is popularly known as the Milesian Race, because the genuine Irish (Celtic) people were supposed to be descended from Milesius of Spain, whose sons, say the legendary accounts, invaded and possessed themselves of Ireland a thousand years before Christ.[1]

But it is nearly as inaccurate to style the Irish people pure Milesian because the land was conquered and settled by the Milesians, as it would be to call them Anglo-Norman because it was conquered and settled by the twelfth century English.

The Races that occupied the land when the so-called Milesians came, chiefly the Firbolg and the Tuatha De Danann,[2] were certainly not exterminated by the conquering Milesians. Those two peoples formed the basis of the future population, which was dominated and guided, and had its characteristics moulded, by the far less numerous but more powerful Milesian aristocracy and soldiery.

All three of these races, however, were different tribes of the great Celtic family, who, long ages before, had separated from the main stem, and in course of later centuries blended again into one tribe of Gaels—three derivatives of one stream, which, after winding their several ways across Europe from the East, in Ireland turbulently met, and after eddying, and

---

[1] Many scientific historians deny this in toto. See Chapter III.

[2] De Jubainville denies a De Danann race to Ireland. He asserts they were mythological. MacNeill agrees with him. But many students of the question disagree with both of these able men. The fact that myths grow around great people must not lead us to conclude that the people were mythical. Fortunately Fionn and his Fian fell within historical time when actual facts, countering the myths that have gathered around them, were set down; otherwise, by the same process of reasoning, they might have been classed with the De Danann as an entirely imaginary people.

surging tumultuously, finally blended in amity, and flowed onward in one great Gaelic stream.

Of these three certain colonisations of Ireland, the Firbolg was the first. Legend says they came from Greece, where they had been long enslaved, and whence they escaped in the captured ships of their masters.

In their possession of Ireland the Firbolgs were disturbed by the descents and depredations of African sea-rovers, the Fomorians, who had a main stronghold on Tory Island, off the Northwest Coast.

But the possession of the country was wrested from the Firbolgs, and they were forced into partial serfdom by the Tuatha De Danann (people of the goddess Dana), who arrived later.

Totally unlike the uncultured Firbolgs, the Tuatha De Danann were a capable and cultured, highly civilized people, so skilled in the crafts, if not the arts, that the Firbolgs named them necromancers; and in course of time both the Firbolgs and the later-coming Milesians created a mythology around these.

The great Irish historiographer, Eugene O'Curry, says: "The De Danann were a people remarkable for their knowledge of the domestic, if not the higher, arts of civilized life"—and he furthermore adds that they were apparently more highly civilized than even their conquerors, the Milesians.

In a famed battle at Southern Moytura (on the Mayo-Galway border) it was that the Tuatha De Danann met and overthrew the Firbolgs. There has been handed down a poetical account of this great battle—a story that O'Curry says can hardly be less than fourteen hundred years old—which is very interesting, and wherein we get some quaint glimpses of ancient Irish ethics of war (for even in the most highly imaginative tale, the poets and seanachies of all times, unconsciously reflect the manners of their own age, or of ages just passed). The Firbolgs, only too conscious of the superiority of the newcomers, used every endeavour to defer the fatal encounter. When the armies were drawn up in seeming readiness, the Firbolgs refused to begin battle. And they coolly replied to the impatient enemy that they could not say when they would be ready to begin. They must have time to sharpen their swords, and time to put their spears in order, to furbish their armour, and brighten their helmets. The Tuatha De Danann had better restrain their impetuosity. Tremendous things hung upon the outcome of this fight, and they, wisely, were not going to be rushed into it until the last rod in the last (wickerwork) shield was perfect.

Moreover, they observed that their opponents had a superior kind of light spear: so time must be given them to get like weapons made. And they magnanimously pointed out to the Tuatha De Danann that, on the other hand, as they, the Firbolgs, had the advantage of possessing *craisechs,* heavy spears that could work great destruction, the De Danann needed to provide themselves with *craisechs.* Anything and everything to stave off the dread matching of courage and skill. Altogether they most skilfully managed to keep the enemy fretting and fuming with impatience for a hundred days and five before the great clash resounded to the heavens.

But the De Danann gained an important point also. For, as the Firbolgs were possessed of overwhelming numbers, the strangers demanded that they eliminate their majority and fight on equal terms, man for man—which the laws of battle-justice unfortunately compelled the reluctant Firbolgs to agree to.

The battle raged for four days. Then the Firbolgs, finding themselves beaten, but pretending not to know this, proposed that the doubtful struggle be ended by halting the great hosts and pitting against each other a body of 300 men from each side. So bravely had the losing ones fought, and so sorely exhausted the De Danann, that the latter, to end the struggle, were glad to leave to the Firbolgs that quarter of the Island wherein they fought, the province now called Connaught. And the bloody contest was over.

The Firbolgs' noted King, Eochaid, was slain in this great battle. But the greatest of their warriors, Sreng, had maimed the De Danann King, Nuada, cutting off his hand—and by that stroke deposed him from the kingship. Because, under the De Danann law (and ever after in Eirinn) no king could rule who suffered from a personal blemish.

The great warrior champion of the De Danann, Breas (whose father was a Fomorian chief) filled the throne while Nuada went into retirement, and had made for him a silver hand, by their chief artificer, Creidné.

Breas, says the legend, ruled for seven years. He incensed his people by indulging his kin, the Fomorians, in their depredations. And he was finally deposed for this and for another cause that throws light upon one of the most noted characteristics of the people of Eire, ancient and modern. Breas proved himself that meanest of all men, a king ungenerous and inhospitable—lacking open heart and open hand—"The knives of his people" it was complained, "were not greased at his table, nor did their breath smell of ale, at the banquet. Neither their poets, nor their bards, nor their satirists, nor their harpers, nor their pipers, nor their trumpeters, nor their jugglers, nor their buffoons, were ever seen engaged in amusing them in the assembly at his court." So there was mighty grumbling in the land, for that it should be disgraced by so unkingly a king. And the grumbling swelled to a roar, when, in the extreme of his niggardliness, he committed the sin, unpardonable in ancient Ireland, of insulting a poet. Cairbre, the great poet of the time, having come to visit him, was sent to a little bare, cold apartment, where a few, mean, dry cakes upon a platter were put before him as substitute for the lavish royal banquet owed to a poet. In hot indignation he quitted the abode of Breas, and upon the boorish king composed a withering satire, which should blight him and his seed forever. Lashed to wrath, then, by the outrage on a poet's sacred person the frenzied people arose, drove the boor from the throne, and from the Island—and Nuada. *Airgead Lam* (of the Silver Hand) again reigned over his people.

Breas fled to the Hebrides, to his father, Elatha, the chief of the Fomorians, where, collecting a mighty host of their sea-robbers, in as many ships as filled the sea from the Hebrides to Ireland, they swarmed into Eirinn—and gave battle to the De Danaan at Northern Moytura, in Sligo. In this, their second great battle, the De Danann were again victorious. They routed their enemy with fearful slaughter, and overthrew the Fomorian tyranny in the island forever. The famous Fomorian chief, Balor of the Evil Eye, whose headquarters was on Tory Island, off the Northwest coast, was slain, by a stone from the sling of his own grandson, the great De Danann hero, Lugh. But Balor had slain King Nuada before he was himself dispatched.

This famous life and death struggle of two races is commemorated by a multitude of cairns and pillars which strew the great battle plain in Sligo—a plain which bears the name (in Irish) of "the Plain of the Towers of the Fomorians."

The De Danann were now the undisputed masters of the land.

So goes the honored legend.

CHAPTER II

The Tuatha De Danann

Over the island, which was now indisputably De Danann, reigned the hero, Lugh, famous in mythology. And after Lugh, the still greater Dagda—whose three grand-sons, succeeding him in the sovereignty, were reigning, says the story, when the Milesians came.

Such a great people were the De Danann, and so uncommonly skilled in the few arts of the time, that they dazzled even their conquerors and successors, the Milesians, into regarding them as mighty magicians. Later generations of the Milesians to whom were handed down the wonderful traditions of the wonderful people they had conquered, lifted them into a mystic realm, their greatest ones becoming gods and goddesses, who supplied to their successors a beautiful mythology.

Most conquerors come to despise the conquered, but here they came to honor, almost to worship those whom they had subdued. Which proves not only greatness in the conquered, but also bigness of mind and distinctiveness of character in the conquerors.

The De Danann skill in the arts and crafts in course of time immortalised itself in beautiful legends among the Milesians. Lugh was not only the son of a god (of Manannan MacLir, the sea-god), and the greatest of heroes, but tradition gave him all the many mortal powers of his people, so that he was called Sab Ildanach, meaning Stem of all the Arts. When the De Danann had first arrived in Ireland Lugh went to the court of Eochaid, the Firbolg king at Tara, and sought an office. But no one was admitted a member of this court unless he was master of some art or craft not already represented there. The doorkeeper barring Lugh's way demanded on what ground he sought to be admitted. Lugh answered that he was a *saer* (carpenter). No, they had a good *saer* in the court already. Then he said he was a good smith.

They had an able smith, also. Well, he was a champion. They already had a champion. Next, he was a harper. They had a wonderful harper, too. Then a poet and antiquarian. They had such—and of the most eminent. But he was a magician. They had many Druids, adepts in the occult. He was a physician. They had the famous physician, Diancecht. He was a cupbearer. They had nine. Then, a goldsmith. They had the famous Creidné.[1] "Then," said Lugh, "go to your king, and ask him if he has in his court any man who is at once master of all these arts and professions. If he has, I shall not ask admittance to Tara."

Eochaid, the King, was overjoyed. He led in the wonderful Lugh, and put him in the chair of the ard-ollam, the chief professor of the arts and sciences.

The Dagda, who reigned just before the coming of the Milesians, was the greatest of the De Danann. He was styled Lord of Knowledge and Sun of all the Sciences. His daughter, Brigit, was a woman of wisdom, and goddess of poetry. The Dagda was a great and beneficent ruler for eighty years.

---

[1]The old traditional tales say that the Creidné mentioned was a very famous worker in the precious metals. The basic truth of these traditions seems evidenced by the reference in very ancient manuscripts to Bretha Creidné, "The Judgments of Creidné," a body of laws dealing with fine scales, weights and measures, and the precious metals. There is still preserved part of a very old poem, which says that Creidné was drowned, returning from Spain with golden ore.

CHAPTER III

THE MILESIANS

The sixteenth-century scholar, O'Flaherty, fixes the Milesian invasion of Ireland at about 1000 B.C.—the time of Solomon. Some modern writers, including MacNeill, say that they even came at a much later date. There are, however, philologists and other scientific inquirers, who to some extent corroborate O'Flaherty's estimate.

It is proven that the Celts whencesoever they came, had, before the dawn of history, subjugated the German people and established themselves in Central Europe. At about the date we have mentioned, a great Celtic wave, breaking westward over the Rhine, penetrated into England, Scotland, and Ireland. Subsequently a wave swept over the Pyrenees into the Spanish Peninsula. Other waves came westward still later.

The studies of European scholars have shown that these Celts were an eminently warlike people, rich in the arts of civilized life, who subdued and dominated the ruder races, wherever they went on the Continent. They were possessed of "a high degree of political unity, had a single king, and a wise and consistent external policy." Mostly, however, they seem to have been a federation of patrician republics. At various times they had allied themselves with the Greeks to fight common enemies. They gave valuable service to, and were highly esteemed by Philip, and by his son, the great Alexander. In an alliance which they made with Alexander, before he left on his Asiatic expedition, it was by the elements they swore their fealty to the pact—just as we know they continued to swear in Ireland, down to the coming of Christianity in the fifth century.

They piqued Alexander's pride by frankly telling him that they did not fear him—only feared Heaven. They held sway in Central Europe through long centuries. A Celtic cemetery discovered at Hallstatt in upper

Austria proves them to have been skilled in art and industries as far back as 900 B.C.—shows them as miners and agriculturists, and blessed with the use of iron instruments. They invaded Italy twice, in the seventh and in the fourth centuries before Christ. In the latter time they were at the climax of their power. They stormed Rome itself, 300 B.C.

The rising up of the oppressed Germans against them, nearly three centuries before Christ, was the beginning of the end of the Continental power of the Celt. After that they were beaten and buffeted by Greek and by Roman, and even by despised races—broken, and blown like the surf in all directions, North and South, and East and West. A fugitive colony of these people, that had settled in Asia Minor, in the territory which from them (the Gaels) was called Galatia, and among whom Paul worked, was found to be still speaking a Celtic language in the days of St. Jerome, five or six hundred years later. Eoin MacNeill and other scientific enquirers hold that it was only in the fifth century before Christ that they reached Spain—and that it was not via Spain but via north-western France and Britain that they, crushed out from Germany, eventually reached Ireland. In Cæsar's day the Celts (Gauls) who dominated France used Greek writing in almost all their business, public or private.

The legendary account of the origin of the Gaels and their coming to Ireland is as follows:

They came first out of that vast undefined tract, called Scythia—a region which probably included all of Southwest Europe and adjoining portions of Asia. They came to Ireland through Egypt, Crete, and Spain. They were called Gaedhal (Gael) because their remote ancestor, in the days of Moses, was Gaodhal Glas. When a child, Moses is said to have cured him of the bite of a serpent—and to have promised, then, that no serpent or other poisonous thing should infest the happy western island that his far posterity would one day inhabit. Niul, a grand-son of Gaodhal, who had been invited as an instructor into Egypt by one of the Pharaohs, married Pharaoh's daughter Scota—after whom Ireland was, in later ages, called Scotia. And the Irish Scoti or Scots are the descendants of Niul and Scota. In Egypt Niul and his people grew rich and powerful, resented the injustice of a later Pharaoh, were driven from the land, and after long and varied wanderings, during succeeding ages, reached Spain. When, after they had long sojourned in Spain, they heard of Ireland (perhaps from Phœnician traders) and took it to be the Isle of Destiny, foretold for them by Moses, their leader was Miled or Milesius, whose wife also was a Pharaoh's daughter, and named Scota. Miled's uncle, Ith, was first sent into Ireland, to bring them report upon it. But the Tuatha De Danann, suspecting the purpose of his mission, killed Ith.

Miled having died in Spain, his eight sons, with their mother, Scota, their families and followers, at length set out on their venturous voyage to their Isle of Destiny.[1]

In a dreadful storm that the supposedly wizard De Danann raised up against them, when they attempted to land in Ireland, five of the sons of Milesius, with great numbers of their followers, were lost, their fleet was

---

[1] Inisfail, one of many ancient names for Ireland, signifies Isle of Destiny. Of "The Coming of the Milesians," Moore sang:

They came from a land beyond the sea,
  And now o'er the western main
Set sail in their good ships, gallantly,
  From the sunny lands of Spain.
"Oh, where's the isle we've seen in dreams,
  Our destin'd home or grave?"
Thus sang they, as by the morning beams,
  They swept the Atlantic wave.

And lo, where afar o'er ocean shines
  A sparkle of radiant green,
As though in that deep lay emerald mines
  Whose light through the wave was seen,
'Tis Inisfail—'tis Inisfail!
  Rings o'er the echoing sea;
While, bending to heaven, the warriors hail
  That home of the brave and free.

Then turned they unto the Eastern wave
  Where now their Day-God's eye
A look of such sunny omen gave
  As lighted up sea and sky.
No frown was seen through sky or sea,
  Nor tear o'er leaf or sod,
When first on their Isle of Destiny
  Our great forefathers trod.

Here let us understand that the ancient historical legends of Ireland are, generally speaking, far from being baseless myths. The Irish people are a people who eminently cling to tradition. Not only were the great happenings that marked great epochs enshrined in their memory forever, but even little events that trivially affected the history of their race, were, and are, seldom forgotten. We know that away back to the remotest antiquity, the *seanachie* (shanachy, the historian) and the poet were honored next to the king, because of the tremendous value which the people set upon the recording and preserving of their history. The poet and the *seanachie* following the fashion of the time, took advantage of their artist privilege to color their narrative to an extent that to the modern mind would seem fantastic. But it was with the details of the story that they were granted this liberty. The big, essential facts had to remain unaltered. The things of importance no poet of repute, however highly he might color, could or would dare to falsify.

dispersed and it seemed for a time as if none of them would ever enjoy the Isle of Destiny.

Ancient manuscripts preserve the prayer that, it is said, their poet, Amergin, now prayed for them—

> "I pray that they reach the land of Eirinn, those who are riding upon the great, productive, vast sea:
>
> "That they be distributed upon her plains, her mountains, and her valleys; upon her forests that shed showers of nuts and all fruits; upon her rivers and her cataracts; upon her lakes and her great waters; upon her spring-abounding hills:
>
> "That they may hold their fairs and equestrian sports upon her territories:
>
> "That there may be a king from them in Tara; and that Tara be the territory of their many kings:
>
> "That noble Eirinn be the home of the ships and boats of the sons of Milesius:
>
> "Eirinn which is now in darkness, it is for her that this oration is pronounced:
>
> "Let the learned wives of Breas and Buaigne pray that we may reach the noble woman, great Eirinn.
>
> "Let Eremon pray, and let Ir and Eber implore, that we may reach Eirinn."

Eventually they made land—Eber with the survivors of his following landing at Inver Sceni, in Bantry Bay; and afterwards defeating a De Danann host under Queen Eiré but losing their own Queen Scota in the fray—and Eremon with his people at Inver Colpa (mouth of the Boyne).

When they had joined their forces, in Meath, they went against the De Danann in general battle at Taillte, and routed the latter with great slaughter. The three kings and the three queens of the De Danann were slain, many of them killed, and the remainder dispersed.

The survivors fled into the remote hills and into the caves. Possibly the glimpses of some of these fugitive hill-dwellers and cave-dwellers, caught in twilight and in moonlight, by succeeding generations of Milesians, coupled with the seemingly magical skill which they exercised, gave foundation for the later stories of enchanted folk, fairies, living under the Irish hills.

Though, a quaint tale preserved in the ancient Book of Leinster says that after Taillte it was left to Amergin, the Milesian poet and judge, to divide Eirinn between the two races, and that he shrewdly did so with technical justice—giving all above ground to his own people, and all underground to the De Danann!

Another pleasant old belief is that the De Danann, being overthrown, were assembled by their great immortal Mannanan at Brugh of the Boyne, where, after counselling together, it was decided that, taking Bodb Derg, son of the Dagda, as their king, and receiving immortality from Mannanan, they should distribute themselves in their spirit land under the happy hills of Ireland—where they have, ever since, enjoyed never-ending bliss.[2]

Of the Milesians, Eber and Eremon divided the land between them—Eremon getting the Northern half of the Island, and Eber the Southern. The Northeastern corner was accorded to the children of their lost brother, Ir, and the Southwestern corner to their cousin Lughaid, the son of Ith.

An oft-told story says that when Eber and Eremon had divided their followers, each taking an equal number of soldiers and an equal number of the men of every craft, there remained a harper and a poet. Drawing lots for these, the harper fell to Eremon and the poet to Eber—which explains why, ever since, the North of Ireland has been celebrated for music, and the South for song.

The peace that fell upon the land then, and the happiness of the Milesians, was only broken, when, after a year, Eber's wife discovered that she must be possessed of the three pleasantest hills in Eirinn, else she could not remain one other night in the Island. Now the pleasantest of all the Irish hills was Tara, which lay in Eremon's half. And Eremon's wife would not have the covetousness of the other woman satisfied at her expense. So, because of the quarrel of the women, the beautiful peace of the Island was broken by battle. Eber was beaten, and the high sovereignty settled upon Eremon.

---

[2] Here is the ancient story-teller's description (from the Táin Bo Cuailgne) of the cavalcade of Bodb Derg, in after ages, coming from his palace under Sliabna-mban to pay a visit to the De Danann chief, Ochall Oichne, who resided under Cruachan (in Roscommon)—"Seven score chariots and seven score horsemen was their number. And of the same colour were all their steeds; they were speckled; they had silver bridles. There was no person among them who was not the son of a king and a queen. They all wore green cloaks with four crimson pendants to each cloak; and silver cloak-brooches in all their cloaks; and they wore kilts with red interweavings, and borders or fringes of gold thread upon them, and pendants of white bronze thread upon their leggings or greaves, and shoes with clasps of red bronze in them. Their helmets were ornamented with crystal and white bronze; each of them had a collar of radiant gold around his neck, with a gem worth a newly calved cow set in it. Each wore a twisted ring of gold around him, worth thirty ounces of gold. All had white-faced shields, with ornamentations of gold and of silver. They carried flesh-seeking spears, with ribs of gold and silver and red bronze in their sides; and with collars (or rings) of silver upon the necks of the spears. They had gold-hilted swords with the forms of serpents of gold and carbuncles set in them. They astonished the whole assembly by this display."

It was in his reign, continues the legend, that the Cruitnigh or Picts arrived from the Continent. They landed in the southwest, at the mouth of the River Slaney (Inver Slaigne). A tribe of Britons who fought with poisoned arrows were at the time ravaging that corner of the Island. The Picts helped to drive out the marauders, and in reward were granted a settlement there, from Crimthann, the chief of that quarter. Afterwards they had an outfall with Crimthann—and it was decided that they should be passed into Alba (Scotland).[3] The three Pictish chiefs were given Irish wives to take to Alba with them, on condition that henceforth their royal line should descend according to the female succession—which, it is said, was henceforth the law among the Alban Picts.

Eremon's victory over Eber had slight effect in fixing on his lineage the succession to the overlordship: for, through many hundreds of years afterward, the battle had to be refought, and the question settled once more—sometimes to the advantage of the Eremonians, sometimes to that of the Eberians. A warlike people must have war. Occasionally, during the reigns of the early Milesian kings, this want was filled for them by the Fomorians, who, though disastrously defeated by the De Danann at Northern Moytura, were far from being destroyed. Irial, the prophet, the grandson of Eremon, and third Milesian king of Ireland, had to fight them again. And at many other times the Island suffered from their depredations.

Names of a long list of kings, from Eremon downward, and important particulars regarding many of them, were preserved by the historical traditions—traditions that were as valuable, and as zealously guarded, as are the written State Records of modern days.[4] The carefully trained filé, who was poet, historian, and philosopher, was consecrated to the work—and, ever inspired with the sacredness of his trust, he was seldom known to deviate from the truth in anything of importance—however much he confessedly gave his imagination play in the unimportant details. And, much as the people reverenced him, they reverenced the truth of history more; and it was the law that a filé, discovered falsifying, should be degraded and disgraced.

The Scottish historian Pinkerton, who was hardly sympathetic, admits: "Foreigners may imagine that it is granting too much to the Irish to allow

[3] MacNeill holds that the Picts came to Ireland ahead of the Gael: and that, as distinct tribes, portions of them inhabited many parts of it, down till historic times. They also occupied large part of Scotland.

[4] Many notable scholars deny the complete authenticity of this list. But undoubtedly the greater part of the names are the real names of real kings who held sway over the Northern or the Southern half, if not over all, of Ireland.

them lists of kings more ancient than those of any other country of modern Europe. But the singularly compact and remote situation of that Island, and the freedom from Roman conquest, and from the concussion of the Fall of the Roman Empire, may infer this allowance not too much."

And the British Camden, another authority not partial to Ireland, but sometimes hostile, says: "They deduced their history from memorials derived from the most profound depths of remote antiquity, so that compared with that of Ireland, the antiquities of all other nations is but novelty, and their history is but a kind of infancy."

Standish O'Grady in his "Early Bardic History of Ireland" says: "I must confess that the blaze of Bardic light which illuminates those centuries at first dazzles the eye and disturbs the judgment . . . (but) that the Irish kings and heroes should succeed one another, surrounded by a blaze of Bardic light, in which both themselves and all those who were contemporaneous with them are seen clearly and distinctly, was natural in a country where in each little realm or sub-kingdom the ard-ollam was equal in dignity to the King, as is proved by the equivalence of their *eric.* The dawn of English history is in the seventh century—a late dawn, dark and sombre, without a ray of cheerful sunshine; that of Ireland dates reliably from a point before the commencing of the Christian Era—illumined with that light which never was on sea or land—thronging with heroic forms of men and women—terrible with the presence of the supernatural and its over-reaching power."[5]

---

[5] D'Arcy McGee sang of

THE CELTS

Long, long ago beyond the misty space
Of twice a thousand years,
In Erin old there dwelt a mighty race,
Taller than Roman spears;
Like oaks and towers they had a giant grace,
Were fleet as deers
With winds and waves they made their 'biding place,
These western shepherd seers.

Their ocean-god was Mannanan MacLir,
Whose angry lips,
In their white foam, full often would inter
Whole fleets of ships;
Crom was their day-god, and their thunderer,
Made morning and eclipse;
Bride was their queen of song, and unto her
They prayed with fire-touched lips.

Great were their deeds, their passions, and their sports;
With clay and stone
They piled on strath and shore those mystic forts,
Not yet o'erthrown;
On cairn-crowned hills they held their council-courts;
While youths alone,
With giant dogs, explored the elks' resorts,
And brought them down.

Of these was Fin, the father of the Bard,
Whose ancient song
Over the clamor of all change is heard,
Sweet-voiced and strong.
Fin once o'ertook Grania, the golden-haired,
The fleet and young;
From her the lovely, and from him the feared,
The primal poet sprung.

Ossian! two thousand years of mist and change
Surround thy name—
Thy Finian heroes now no longer range
The hills of fame.
The very name of Fin and Goll sound strange—
Yet thine the same—
By miscalled lake and desecrated grange—
Remains, and shall remain!

The Druid's altar and the Druid's creed
We scarce can trace,
There is not left an undisputed deed
Of all your race,
Save your majestic song, which hath their speed,
And strength, and grace;
In that sole song, they live and love and bleed—
It bears them on thro' space.

Oh, inspired giant! shall we e'er behold,
In our own time,
One fit to speak your spirit on the wold,
Or seize your rhyme?
One pupil of the past, as mighty souled
As in the prime,
Were the fond, fair, and beautiful and bold—
They, of your song sublime!

CHAPTER IV

Some Notable Milesian Royalties

The popular traditions give details regarding many notable Milesian royalties in the decade of centuries before the Christian Era.

Within the first century after Eremon, is said to have reigned the distinguished Tighernmas (seventh of the Milesian line) who, they say, first smelted gold, and introduced gold ornaments, and gold fringes on dress. He also introduced various colours into dresses. Sometimes to him, sometimes to his successor, Eochaid, is credited the ancient ordinance which distinguished the various classes and professions by the colours in their dress. A King or Queen might wear seven colours; a poet or Ollam six; a chieftain five; an army leader four; a land-owner three; a rent-payer two; a serf one colour only.

Tighernmas and two-thirds of his people were wiped out when they were assembled in the plain of Magh Slecht in Brefni, at worship of Crom Cruach—a great idol which St. Patrick in his day destroyed.

All the stories say that the greatest king of those faraway times was the twenty-first Milesian king, known to fame as Ollam Fodla (Ollav Fola) who blessed Ireland in a reign of forty years, some seven or eight centuries before the Christian Era. His title, Ollam Fodla, Doctor of Wisdom, has preserved his memory down the ages. The legends indicate that he was a true father to his people, and an able statesman. He organised the nation for efficiency—divided it into cantreds, appointed a chief over every cantred, a brugaid (magistrate) over every territory, and a steward over every townland. Some traditions say that he established a School of Learning. And as crowning glory he established the celebrated Feis of Tara, the great triennial Parliament of the chiefs, the nobles, and the scholars of the nation, which assembled on Tara Hill once every three years to settle the nation's affairs.

This great deliberative assembly, almost unique among the nations in those early ages, and down into Christian times, reflected not a little glory upon ancient Ireland.

One queen, famous and capable, whom early Ireland boasted was Macha Mong Ruad (the Red-haired), who reigned over the land about three hundred years before Christ. Her father, Aod Ruad was one of a triumvirate—the others being Dithorba and Cimbaoth—who by mutual agreement took seven-year turns in reigning. Aod Ruad was drowned at Eas-Aod-Ruad (Assaroe), now Ballyshanny. And when came round again the seven-year period which would have been his had he lived, his daughter, Macha, claimed the crown. But for it she had to fight her father's two partners—which she did, killing Dithorba; and first defeating, and afterwards marrying, Cimbaoth—and making him king.

For many, the reign of Cimbaoth—which synchronises with that of Alexander the Great—marks the beginning of certainty in Irish history—because of the famed remark of the trusted eleventh century historian, Tighernach, that the Irish records before Cimbaoth were uncertain.

When Cimbaoth died this able woman took up the reins of government herself, becoming the first Milesian queen of Ireland. But the record above all others by which this distinguished woman lives to fame, is her founding of the ancient and much-storied stronghold—named after her—of Emain Macha, which henceforth, for six hundred years, was to play a most important part in the fortunes of Uladh (Ulster) and of Ireland.

Macha's foster-son, Ugani Mor (the Great), who succeeded her, led his armies into Britain, and had his power acknowledged there. After bringing a great part of Britain to obedience, some traditions say that his ambition led him on the Continent, where he met with many successes also, giving basis for the ancient seanachies styling him, "King of Ireland and of the whole of Western Europe as far as the Muir Torrian" (Mediterranean Sea).

All the leading families of Ulster, Leinster and Connaught trace their descent from Ugani Mor—the common father of the royalties of the three provinces. The origin of the name of Leinster is ascribed to the activities of Ugani Mor's great grandson, Labraid Loingsech. Labraid's grandfather (Ugani Mor's son), Laegaire Lorc, was killed for sake of his throne, by his brother, Cobtach. His son was killed at the same time: and the grandson, Labraid Loingsech, only spared because he was dumb, and consequently could not rule. Labraid Loingsech was reared up in secret, under the joint fosterage and tutorship of a celebrated harper, Craftine, and a celebrated poet and philosopher, Feirceirtne. Getting a blow of a caman once, when playing caman (hurley) with other boys, he suddenly found the use of speech. When he grew up and Cobtach discovered that he no longer had the disabling blemish, and was moreover held in high esteem, he drove him out. The young man was received with honor at the King's court in Gaul—whence after some time he returned, with an army of over two thousand Gauls, armed with broad spears to which the Irish gave the name of Laighen. On his arrival in Ireland, he learnt that Cobtach, with thirty princes, was holding an assembly in Dinn Righ. There Labraid marched, and destroyed them all. He attacked and burned the Dinn and its guests—and won his grandfather's throne—and incidentally supplied the plot for one of the most famous of old Irish tales, "The Burning of Dinn Righ." From the Laighen of the Gauls, whom he settled in this southeastern part, Leinster, it is said took its name.[1]

The story of Cobtach and Labraid is to some extent curiously paralleled in that of the next Irish monarch of much note, Conaire Mor, who reigned within the century before, or at the time of, Christ: and who, in establishing his strong rule over Ireland, putting down lawlessness and making himself and his rule respected and feared, drove out his own foster-brothers, the four sons of a chieftain of Leinster. These returned after a time with a great body of Britons, under Ingcel, son of a British king. They destroyed and burned Meath, and then attacked Conaire Mor and his retinue in the Bruighean of DaDerga (one of the six public houses of hospitality that

---

[1] About this Labraid Loingsech grew the myth (closely paralleled in the Greek) of his being cursed with the ears of a horse.

He always wore a golden helmet, says the legend, to conceal his horrible secret. Because the barber who cut his hair was ever chosen by lot, and put to death immediately after he had performed his task, a dread fear was on the whole nation, of some awful mystery that their king concealed from them.

Once the barber's lot fell upon the son of a poor widow. The woman's broken-hearted supplications so moved Labraid that he promised to spare her son's life, on his taking a solemn oath of secrecy. His terrible discovery, which he must now carry forever, a festering secret in his mind, so preyed upon the young man that he lost his sleep, lost his health, and was on the verge of losing his reason. He consulted a wise Druid, asking what he should do to save himself. The Druid's advice was that he must travel to a place where four roads met, and then tell to the nearest growing tree the dread secret which he must not give to any living being. He did this, and was instantly relieved, and grew hale, with a mind at ease, once more.

Now it was a willow tree to which he told the secret. In course of years this tree was cut down, and a harp made of it for Craftine, the king's harper. And to, when Craftine touched the strings of his new harp, in the hall of the king, the instrument sang: "The ears of a horse has Labraid Loingsech! The ears of a horse has Labraid Loingsech!" Over and over again, "The ears of a horse has Labraid Loingsech!"

The court was horror-stricken, the king dumbfounded. Filled with remorse, and humiliated, but brave as a king should be, he bowed his head, and before the whole court, removed his golden helmet—thus ending the dreadful mystery forever.

Ireland then boasted) destroyed it, and killed Conaire and his retinue. This tragic incident gave us the equally famous and remarkably beautiful tale, The Bruighean DaDerga.

Some of the historians say that it was Conaire Mor who reigned in Ireland when Christ was born. But others make the reigning monarch then Crimthann Niad Nair (Abashed Hero)—a king famous in ancient story for his foreign expeditions—from one of which we are told he brought back, among the booty, a gilt chariot, a golden chess-board inlaid with 300 transparent gems, a sword entwined with serpents of gold, a silver embossed shield, and two hounds leashed with a silver chain.

During Crimthann's reign occurred a notable return of Firbolgs from the Western Islands of Alba (Scotland) whereto their forefathers had been driven, long ages before. Now a colony of them, led by the four sons of the chief, Umor, with the eldest son, Angus, at their head, took refuge in Ireland from the persecution of the Picts, and by the high king were granted lands in Meath. They soon however found him as oppressive as the Picts had been coercive. And on a night they fled Westward from their Meath possessions. They crossed the Shannon into Connaught, which was still largely inhabited and dominated by their Firbolg kin. There, the celebrated Queen, Maeve, and her husband, Ailill, gave them lands in South Connaught, where they settled once more.

But they were pursued by the two great Ulster warriors and heroes of the Red Branch, Cuchullin and Conal Cearnach, who had gone security to the high king for their good behaviour—who here fought them a battle wherein great numbers of the Umorians were slain, including Angus' three brothers, and his son, Conal the Slender. A great cairn, known to this day as Cairn Chonaill, was erected on the battlefield to commemorate him and them. Angus with his own people then settled in the islands of Aran, in Galway Bay, where he built the wonderful fortress still standing there and known as Dun Angus.

At the time of Christ, the celebrated Conor (Conchobar) MacNessa reigned over Ulster.

CHAPTER V

Ireland in the Lore of the Ancients

Scotia (a name transferred to Alba about ten centuries after Christ) was one of the earliest names of Ireland—so named, it was said, from Scota, the daughter of Pharaoh, one of the ancient female ancestors of the Milesians—and the people were commonly called Scotti or Scots[1]—both terms being frequently used by early Latin historians and poets.

Ireland was often referred to—by various names—by ancient writers both Latin and Greek. Plutarch testifies to the nation's antiquity by calling it Ogygia, meaning the most ancient.

One of its ancient titles was Hibernia (used by Cæsar)—which some trace from Ivernia, the name, it is said, of a people located in the south of the Island; but most trace it from Eber or Heber, the first Milesian king of the southern half; just as the much later name, Ireland, is by some traced from Ir, whose family were in the northeastern corner of the Island. Though it seems much more likely that this latter name was derived from the most common title given to the Island by its own inhabitants, Eiré—hence Eire-land, Ireland. It was first the Northmen and then the Saxons, who, in the ninth and tenth century began calling it Ir-land or Ir-landa—Ireland.

In the oldest-known foreign reference to Ireland, it was called Ierna. This was the title used by the poet Orpheus in the time of Cyrus of Persia, in the sixth century before Christ. Aristotle, in his Book of the World, also called it Ierna. In the first half of the first century Pomponius Mela refers to it as Iuvernia.

---

[1] MacNeill thinks the term Scot (and then Scotia) was derived from an old Irish word which signified a raider. He thinks they earned the title from their frequent raiding in Alba and in Britain in pre-Christian times. The conjecture is to the present writer unconvincing.

It was usually called either Hibernia or Scotia by the Latin writers. Tacitus, Cæsar, and Pliny call it Hibernia. Egesippus calls it Scotia—and several later Latin writers did likewise. A Roman, Rufus Festus Avienus, who wrote about the beginning of the fourth century of this era called it "Insula Sacra"—which leads us to suppose that in the very early ages, it was, by the pagans, esteemed a holy isle. In a noted geographical poem of his occur the lines

> "This Isle is Sacred named by all the ancients,
> From times remotest in the womb of Chronos,
> This Isle which rises o'er the waves of ocean,
> Is covered with a sod of rich luxuriance.
> And peopled far and wide by the Hiberni."

And the fourth century Istrian philosopher Ethicus in his cosmography tells how in his travels for knowledge he visited "Hibernia" and spent some time there examining the volumes of that country—which, by the way, this scholarly gentleman considered crude.

That travellers' tales were about as credible in those far-away days as they are in days more recent, is evident from some of the curious things related about this Island by the early Latin writers—oftentimes grotesque blends of fable and fact. The Latin writer, Pomponius Mela (who was a Spaniard and flourished near the middle of the first century of the Christian Era), says in his cosmography books: "Beyond Britain lies Iuvernia, an island of nearly equal size, but oblong, and a coast on each side of equal extent, having a climate unfavourable for ripening grain, but so luxuriant in grasses, not merely palatable but even sweet, that the cattle in very short time take sufficient food for the whole day—and if fed too long, would burst. Its inhabitants are wanting in every virtue, totally destitute of piety."

The latter sentence is quite characteristic of the Latin writers of that day, to whom the world was always divided into two parts, the Roman Empire with which exactly coincided Civilisation and the realm of all the Virtues, and the outer world which lay under the black cloud of barbarism.

But Strabo, who wrote in the first century of this era, does even better than Pomponius Mela. Quoting Poseidonios (who flourished still two centuries earlier), he informs us that the inhabitants of Ierne were wild cannibals who considered it honourable to eat the bodies of their dead parents! But he blends sensational picturesqueness with caution; for he adds: "But the things we thus relate are destitute of witnesses worthy of credit in such affairs." He suspected he was setting down wild fiction, but evidently could not resist the temptation to spice his narrative for the sensating of his readers.[2]

Solinus (about 200 A. D.), as naïve as any of his fellows, has the inhabitants of Juverna (as he names the Island) "inhuman beings who drink the blood of their enemies, and besmear their faces with it. At its birth the male child's foot is placed upon its father's sword, and from the point of the sword it receives its first nourishment!" He, however, also heard of, and records, the account of Juverna's luxuriant grasses, which he says injure cattle. And the true statement that there is no snake in the Island he counterbalances by the misstatements that there are few birds in it, and that the inhabitants are inhospitable!

Seemingly forgetful of the fact that even the early Christians were accused of eating human flesh, St. Jerome accused the Irish of cannibalism. And a reason suggested for his making the wild accusation was because he smarted under the scathing criticism of the Irish Celestius—"an Alban dog," as the good sharp-tongued Father calls him, "stuffed with Irish porridge."

The careful Ptolemy, in the second century, gives a map of Ireland which (from a foreigner in that age of the world) is remarkable for the general correctness of the outline, and more noteworthy features. He names sixteen "peoples" (tribes) inhabiting it (the names of half of them being now recognised), and he mentions several "cities"—probably royal residences.

With the exception of Ptolemy who, in all likelihood, derived his knowledge from the trading Phœnicians, the early Greek and Latin writers only knew of Ireland that it was an island sitting in the Western ocean, and remarkable for its verdure. Yet the Phœnicians were probably well acquainted with its ports. Tacitus says, "The Irish ports in the first century were well known to commerce and merchants."

The great antiquity of Ireland, incidentally acknowledged by foreign writers of olden time, is, as might be expected, sometimes fantastically exaggerated by ancient native writers.

We have the legend set down by several early Irish writers that a Greek, Partholan, with his people came here a few hundred years after the flood. The Island of Inis Saimer, in the mouth of the River Erne, at Ballyshanny, is named after Partholan's favourite hound. A plague exterminated the Partholanians.

---

[2] An English clergyman with the Cromwellian troops in Ireland vouched for the fact that every man in a garrison which they captured was found to have a tail six inches long. Some of the English still believe it.

But, not to be outdone in antiquity, by any European nation, some very ancient Irish poets people their country even before the flood—when, they say, in a well-known legend, that the Lady Cesair came with her father Bith, a grandson of Noah, and their following to Ireland, hoping to escape the flood—but in vain.[3]

[3] Yet another legend, of much later origin, tells that one of the Lady Cesair's party did escape, namely, Finntann, a grandson of Bith, who kept afloat during the deluge—and lived afterwards, seemingly immortal, at Dun Tulcha in southwestern Kerry. Finntann reappeared in Irish history, on a notable occasion some thousands of years later, when, in the reign of Diarmuid MacCarroll, in the sixth century of our Era, this veteran, turned up at Tara to settle, by testimony taken from his long memory, a dispute about the limits of the Royal Demesne. Great was the awed wonder at the King's palace, when the old man arrived, preceded by nine companies of his own descendants, and followed by another nine. To prove the fitness of his memory, for testifying what had or had not been from the founding of Tara downward, he gave the wondering king and people some little idea of his age, by telling them the following story: "I passed one day through a wood in West Munster: I brought home with me a red berry of the yew tree, which I planted in the garden of my mansion, and it grew there until it was as tall as a man. I then took it out of the garden, and planted it in the green lawn of my mansion; and it grew in the centre of that lawn until an hundred champions could fit under the foliage, and find shelter there from wind, and rain, and cold, and heat. I remained so, and my yew remained so, spending our time alike, until at last it ceased to put forth leaves, from old age. When, afterwards, I thought of turning it to some profit, I cut it from its stem, and made from it seven vats, seven keeves, seven stans, seven churns, seven pitchers, seven milans and seven medars, with hoops for all. I remained still with my yew-vessels, until their hoops all fell off from decay and old age. After this I re-made them, but could only get a keeve out of the vat, and a stan out of the keeve, a mug out of the stan, a cilorn out of the mug, a milan out of the cilorn, and a medar out of the milan—and I leave it to Almighty God that I do not know where their dust is now, after their dissolution with me, from decay."

CHAPTER VI

Conor Mac Nessa

At the time of Christ, as said, there reigned over Ulster—residing at Emain Macha (Emania)—a king noted in ancient song and story, Conor MacNessa.

He was a great grandson of Rory Mor, a powerful Ulster ruler who had become monarch of Ireland, and who was the founder of the Rudrician line of Ulster kings.

The memory of Conor MacNessa is imperishably preserved in the tale of The Sons of Usnach and in the greater tale of The Táin Bo Cuailgne (Coolney)—not by any means with honour, in the former.

Emain Macha was the headquarters of the famed Knights of the Royal Branch—now more commonly known as the Knights of the Red Branch. And it was in the days of Conor, and at his court, that these warrior champions reached the climax of their fame. For he was himself a doughty champion, an able leader, and a great man—inspiration sufficient for such band of chivalrous warriors as now rallied around him. In one of the tales of The Táin there is given by the herald MacRoth, a poetic description of this king, which at least tallies with what we would wish to think such royal king must be. Detailing to Queen Medb (Maeve) of Connaught and her courtiers, a description of what he saw at the enemy Ulster camp, MacRoth says: "A tall graceful champion of noble, polished, and proud mien, stood at the head of the party. This most beautiful of the kings of the world stood among his troops with all the signs of obedience, superiority, and command. He wore a mass of yellow, curling, drooping hair. He had a pleasing, ruddy countenance. He had a deep, blue, sparkling, piercing eye in his head and a two-branching beard, yellow, and curling upon his chin. He wore a crimson, deep-bordered, five-folding tunic; a gold pin in the tunic over his bosom; and a brilliant white shirt, interwoven with thread of red gold, next his white skin."

The deeds of the Red Branch Knights in Conor's day, over and over again chronicled by succeeding generations of poets and chroniclers, have not been, and never will be, forgotten. And Conor MacNessa was part of it all.

His first wife was the Amazonian Medb (Maeve) just mentioned, a daughter of Eocaid, the Ard-Righ (High King) of Ireland. Afterwards, as queen of Connaught and the instigator of the great Connaught-Ulster war (commemorated in The Táin Bo Cuailgne) she, too, was destined to become immortal. From her—who needed a husband to whom she could be both master and mistress—Conor had to separate. He found his happiness with her sister, Ethne, whom he took to wife then, and who proved to be all that was indicated by her name—Ethne, that is "sweet kernel of a nut."

Conor was not only a warrior and a patron of warriors, but a patron of scholars and poets, also. His Ard-filé (chief poet) was the great Ferceirtne—to whom some writers of a thousand years ago were wont to ascribe a rude grammar of the Gaelic language, one of four books of ancient grammar, preserved in the Book of Leinster. "The place of writing this book," says the prefatory note to the grammar, "was Emania; the time was the time of Conor MacNessa, the author was Ferceirtne, the poet: and the cause of composing it was to bring the ignorant and barbarous to true knowledge."

Conor, patron of poetry and the arts, was a practical man who is said to have struck from learning the oppressive shackles of tradition that hitherto had cramped and bound it. Till his day the learned professions, both for sake of monopoly and of effect upon the multitude, used an archaic language that only the initiated understood, and that awed the mass of the people. Once, however, the young poet, Néide, son of Ferceirtne's predecessor at Conor's court, having just won his poetic laurels, came to the court of Conor, where finding the poet's mani-colored *tuigín* (mantle)—made of the skins and wings of birds—lying on the poet's chair, he assumed the mantle, and took the poet's seat. When Ferceirtne discovered this, he, highly indignant, rebuked Néide, commanding him to resign both the chair and the *tuigín.* King Conor, to whom the matter was referred, commanded that it should be decided by a learned controversy between the two poets. The occasion of the controversy, in the presence of the king, the court, and the general public, was a great one. But to every one's disappointment, though the two scholars disputed long, and no doubt learnedly, no one there—with the possible exception of the two principals—was any wiser at the end than at the beginning. For they had used the obsolete language of the scholars.

Conor, provoked and disgusted, at once ordered that the professions should not henceforth remain in the hereditary possession of the ancient learned families—but should be thrown open to all, irrespective of family or rank.

Yet Conor's reverence for poets was such that he saved them from expulsion, when, once they were threatened with death or exile, because, having grown so vast numbers, and got to be lazy, covetous, tyrannous, they had become an almost unbearable burden upon the multitude. O'Curry, indeed, says that in Conor's time so far had the taste for learning of all kinds, in poetry, music, Druidism in particular, seized on the mind of the nation, that more than one-third of the men of Eirinn had then given themselves up to the unproductive sciences. Conor gathered twelve hundred poets, it is said, into his dominion, and protected them there for seven years, till the anger of the people had abated, and they could scatter themselves over Ireland once more.

The famous story of Deirdre and the Sons of Usnach, however—though it be a legend splendidly elaborated by the poet, but yet, we may well suppose, based upon facts—would show that King Conor, for all his kingliness, was sometimes no better than kings are supposed to be. According to it, he betrayed the immortal Naoisi and his brothers, and drove the beautiful Deirdre to her death. The sorrows of Deirdre as told in the story of The Sons of Usnach is one of the Three Sorrows of Irish story-telling.[1]

---

[1] Deirdre was the daughter of Conor's story-teller, Feidlimid, and was born on a night when Conor was at the house of Feidlimid. Conor's Druid there and then foretold that this babe would be the cause of misfortunes untold coming upon Ulster.

To prevent this, Conor took charge of the babe. Had her confined in a fort where she should be reared up, without seeing any one except a nurse and a tutor, and Conor's spokeswoman—and when she should reach maturity, he would make her his wife.

As a young maiden, however, she managed to see Naisi, eldest of the three sons of Usnach, and immediately fell in love with him, and asked him to elope with her. Accompanied by Naisi's two brothers, Andli and Ardan, they fled to Alba. After a time they had to leave Alba, because the king had seen the rare beauty of Deirdre and coveted her. So they went off upon one of the islands.

Conor's nobles, pitying the distress and sufferings of the wandering lovers, pleaded for their forgiving and recall. Conor appeared to consent to all this. Deirdre and the three sons of Usnach returned joyfully to Emania. On the green of Emania a body of Conor's friends, led by Eogan, fell upon the three sons of Usnach and slew them, and Conor then took the broken-hearted Deirdre to himself.

For his treachery Fergus MacRigh whose honor Conor had pledged for the safety of the sons of Usnach, led a fierce assault upon Emania, in which Conor's son was slain, and 300 of his people, Emain itself pillaged and burned.

It is recorded that the Danes made descent upon Ireland in King Conor's day. They are said to have besieged, about this time, a stronghold on the site where now stands Dublin. The ancient seanachies tell in particular of one battle, fought at Emain Macha against the Danes, under their commander, Daball, the son of the King of Lochlinn (Denmark)—whereat Conor, having only youths to put in the field against the invaders, had the youth's faces dressed with wool, so that their enemies, instead of being heartened to victory by knowing that an army of youngsters was coming against them, were instead disheartened by the idea that they were meeting battle-tried veterans.

Conor died by a brain-ball that sunk into his skull—fired by the hand of Cet MacMagach, the Connaught champion, whom he had pursued after a Connaught cattle raid.

The legend attached to Conor's death is curious. The brain-ball fired by Cet did not directly kill him. It sank into his skull—and his doctor, Faith Liag, would not remove it, because that would cause instant death. With care, Conor might live long, carrying the brain-ball. Henceforth, however, he must be moderate in all things, avoid all passion, all violent emotion and lead such a life of calm as kings in those days rarely knew.

Under Faith Liag's wise care Conor contrived to live and enjoy life for seven years. But, one time, his court was thrown into consternation by finding broad day suddenly turned into blackest night, the heavens rent by lightning, and the world rocked by thunder, portending some dread cataclysm. Conor asked his Druids and wise men for explanation of the fearful happening. The Druid Bachrach, a noted seer, told him that there had been in the East, in one of the many countries under the dominion of Rome, a singular man, more noble of character, more lofty of mind, and more beautiful of soul, than the world had ever before known, or ever again would know—a divine man, a God-man, who spent his life lifting up the lowly, and leading the ignorant to the light, and giving new hope to a hopeless world—one, too, who loved all mankind with a love that surpassed understanding—one, the touch of whose gentle hand gave speech

---

Deirdre was with Conor for a year, during which time she was never once seen to raise up her head, or smile. No amusement or kindness had any effect upon her, neither wit nor mirth could move the lowness of her spirit.

Incensed at her attitude, Conor at the end of the year, gave her to Eogan, the chief of Fernmach, the man who for him had done the base deed to the sons of Usnach.

As they took her away from Conor's residence to the residence of Eogan, she wildly leaped from the chariot, her head struck a sharp rock, and she was killed.

Fergus MacRigh and his companions with 3,000 followers quitted Ulster after Conor's treachery, and went into Connaught where they took service in the army of Medb.

to the dumb, sight to the blind, life to the dead. He was the noblest, greatest, most beautiful, most loving of men. And now the heavens and the earth were thrown into agony because on this day the tyrant Roman, jealous of his power over the people, had nailed him high upon a cross, and between two crucified thieves, had left the divine man to die a fearful death.

Fired to rage by the thought of the terrible injustice meted out to such a noble one, Conor MacNessa, snatching down the sword that had not been unsheathed for seven years, and crying, "Show me the accursed wretches who did this base deed!" burst through the restraining ring of courtiers, leapt into the storm, dashed through a grove of trees, fiercely hewing down their bending branches and shouting, "Thus would I treat the slayers of that noble Man, could I but reach them."

Under the strain of the fierce passion that held him the brain-ball burst from King Conor's head—and he fell dead.[2]

---

[2] Some say that it was a Roman Consul, Altus, who informed Conor of the death of Christ. Still others say it was the Royal Branch champion, Conal Cearnach—who had been a prisoner with the Romans, and who had been taken by them to the limits of their Empire, in the course of which expedition, he was in Jerusalem on the day of days, and witnessed the Crucifixion. "A representative of every race of mankind," says the legend, "was on the Hill of Calvary at the dreadful hour." Conal Cearnach represented the Gael. The beautiful story of Conal Cearnach at the Crucifixion is related by Ethna Carbery in her book "From the Celtic Past."

CHAPTER VII

Cuchullain

Those days when Conor MacNessa sat on the throne of Ulster were brilliant days in Ireland's history. Then was the sun of glory in the zenith of Eire's Heroic period—the period of chivalry, chiefly created by the famous Royal or Red Branch Knights of Emania. Though, two other famous bands of Irish warriors gave added lustre to the period—the Gamanraide of the West (who were Firbolgs), and the Clanna Deaghaid of Munster led by Curoi MacDaire.

All three warrior bands had their poets and their seanachies, who chanted their deeds in imperishable song and story which, down the dim ages, have since held spell-bound the clan of the Gael.

But the greatest, the most belauded, and the most dazzling of all the heroes of that heroic age was undoubtedly Cuchullain, of whose life and wondrous deeds, real and imaginary, hundreds of stories still exist.[1]

No cycle of Irish story with the one possible exception of the Finian cycle (whose time is a couple of centuries later) can at all compare with the wondrously rich, and extensive, Cuchullain cycle. And in the legendary literature of the whole world, by few other cycles is it surpassed.

Cuchullain was a foster-son of King Conor. "I am little Setanta, son to Sualtim, and Dectaire your sister," he told the questioning king, when, as a boy, in whose breast the fame of the Red Branch warriors had awaked the thirst for glory, he came up to the court of Emania. When he arrived there the youths in training were playing caman upon the green. And having

---

[1] The name of Cu-chullain, Cullan's hound, he took because once, as a little lad, when he approached the house of Cullan and was ferociously attacked by the smith's great watch-hound, Setanta tore the hound asunder—and then pitying the bereaved Cullan said, "I shall henceforth be your hound, O Cullan."

taken with him from home his red bronze hurl and his silver ball, the little stranger, going in among them, so outplayed all the others, that the attention of the court was drawn to him. And it was then that the little stranger gave the above reply to the question of the admiring King.

The eager attention of the warriors of the Red Branch was drawn to this bright lad, and they foresaw great things for him, when they heard him express himself nobly and wonderfully, on the day that, in Emania, in the Hall of Heroes, he took arms.

When a youth had decided to take up the profession of arms, a certain day was appointed for the solemn ceremony that dedicated him thereto. The day of dedication chosen by Cuchullain was disapproved of by the Druids, who having read the omens, pronounced that the youth who took arms on this day would be short-lived, though he should win great fame, so his friends would dissuade the eager youth from taking arms today. In answer to them, the youth, standing up in the Hall of Heroes, with spear in one hand, and shield in the other, exclaimed: "I care not whether I die tomorrow or next year, if only my deeds live after me."

And in his after career he amply fulfilled the rich promise that lay in his words. He was to become his country's immortal hero.

And the memory of this hero has run the gauntlet of strange vicissitudes in Ireland—the greatness of the man excessively stimulating the imagination of the poet, in the course of centuries, causing his reality to be lost in legend; and in the course of further centuries, the greatness of the legendary Cuchullain creating for him a new reality in the minds of the Irish people.

His legendary history is recounted in many stories in the greatest of Irish epics, "The Táin Bo Cuailgne"—the Cattle-raid of Cuailgne. The plan of the very great, very ancient, epic of The Táin Bo Cuailgne is roughly this: Queen Medb (Maeve) of Connaught, who was daughter of the Ard-Righ of Ireland, Eochaid Feidlech, and was first the wife of Conor MacNessa, King of Ulster, secured for herself the kingdom of Connaught, through a second marriage. And by a third marriage she had Ailill, of Leinster, as her consort and understudy. Once this queen Maeve and her King Ailill got counting and matching their worldly possessions. Throughout long and detailed reckoning of these possessions, it was found that neither one had any advantage over the other in worldly wealth—until, at length, it was discovered that Ailill, in his herds, had one precious bull which Maeve in her herds could not equal. Furthermore, in all Ireland, there was no bull to equal him, with the single exception of the celebrated brown bull of Cuailgne (in the present County of Louth). To the chief of Cuailgne Maeve sent a courier, to request the loan of his valuable animal, so that her herd might surpass Ailill's. And since it was natural that he might not wish to let out of his sight this precious bull, the chief was invited to come with the bull to the Connaught court, and there be royally entertained as long as the bull remained on loan.

The request was readily granted; but unfortunately Maeve's courier in his cups that night had vaunted that if the bull had been denied to Maeve, she and her forces would have come and taken it anyhow. The account of the boasting was carried to the Cuailgne chief, who immediately ordered Maeve's courier back to Connaught—without the bull.

Then Maeve, enraged and determined, mobilised a great army for the invasion of Ulster (which was enemy-ground, anyhow) and for the forcible carrying off of the brown bull of Cuailgne. She had all the Connaught forces, chief among them the Fir Domnainn Knights, under their leader, Ferdiad; and she had a splendid body of Ulster malcontents, under Fergus MacRigh (cousin to King Conor MacNessa), who were eager to revenge themselves upon Conor and their native province. And she had also the armies of her allies, from the other three-fifths of Ireland.

With this mighty army she marched upon Ulster—in the gap of which province they were met by the redoubtable Cuchullain—who standing in the gap of Ulster, and defending it against Maeve, and the four-fifths of Ireland, is henceforth the hero and the great central figure in the Táin.

Not only are his wonderful deeds in this wonderful fight here recorded, but frequently the palpitating narrative is suspended, to give the seanachie time to recite some deed, relate some incident, or give us some glimpse, of the great hero's earlier career.

The greatest, most exciting, portion of this great and exciting epic is the account of our hero's fight with his friend, Ferdiad, at the ford, where, single-handed, he is holding at bay the forces of Connaught. Ferdiad is the great Connaught champion, chief, as said, of the Connaught Knights of the Sword, the Fir Domniann and a dear friend and comrade of Cuchullain, since, in their youth, they were training for the profession of arms. And it is now sore for Cuchullain to fight the soul-friend whom the Connaught host has pitted against them. He would dissuade Ferdiad from fighting, by reminding him of their comradeship, when they were together learning the art of war from the female champion, Scathach, in Alba.

"We were heart companions,
We were companions in the woods
We were fellows of the same bed,

Where we used to sleep the balmy sleep.
After mortal battles abroad,
In countries many and far distant,
Together we used to practise, and go
Through each forest, learning with Scathach."[2]

But Ferdiad had not the tenderness of Cuchullain, and would not let fond memories turn him from his purpose. Indeed lest he might yield to the weakness of temptation, he forced himself to answer Cuchullain's tenderness with taunts, so as to provoke the combat. And fight they finally did.

"Each of them began to cast spears at the other, from the full middle of the day till the close of the evening; and though the warding off was of the best, still the throwing was so superior, that each of them bled, reddened, and wounded the other, in that time. 'Let us desist from this, now O Cuchullain,' said Ferdiad. 'Let us desist,' said Cuchullain.

"They ceased. They threw away their arms from them into the hands of their charioteers. Each of them approached the other forthwith, and each put his hands around the other's neck, and gave him three kisses. Their horses were in the same paddock that night, and their charioteers at the same fire; and their charioteers spread beds of green rushes for them, fitted with wounded men's pillows. The professors of healing and curing came to heal and cure them, and they applied herbs and plants of healing and curing to their stabs and their cuts and their gashes, and to all their wounds. Of every herb and of every healing and curing plant that was put to the stabs and cuts and gashes and to all the wounds of Cuchullain, he would send an equal portion from him westward over the ford to Ferdiad, so that the men of Eirinn might not be able to say, should Ferdiad fall by him, that it was by better means of cure that he was enabled (to kill him).

"Of each kind of food, and of palatable, pleasant, intoxicating drink that was sent by the men of Eirinn to Ferdiad, he would send a fair moiety over the ford northwards to Cuchullain because the purveyors of Ferdiad were more numerous than the purveyors of Cuchullain."

---

[2] This, and following excerpts, descriptive of the fight, are from O'Curry's translation.

On the evening of the second day, after a terribly fierce combat—

> "They threw their arms from them into the hands of their charioteers. Each of them came towards the other. Each of them put his hands round the neck of the other, and bestowed three kisses on him. Their horses were in the same enclosure, and their charioteers at the same fire."

When the fight reaches its third day the worn and wounded Ferdiad, by his irritable temper, and testy, taunting words, shows that he is getting the worst of it. On their meeting, Cuchullain notices the sad change that has come over Ferdiad's darkened countenance: "It is not from fear or terror of thee that I am so disdained," said Ferdiad, "for there is not in Eirinn this day a champion that I could not subdue." And again he says vauntingly of himself: "Of none more valiant have I heard, or to this day did I ever meet."

Cuchullain replies to his boasting:

> "Not one has yet put food unto his lips,
> Nor has there yet been born,
> Of king or queen, without disgrace,
> One for whom I would do thee evil."

Cuchullain's persistent tenderness backs up the tide of Ferdiad's bad humour, and gives outlet for a time to his better nature. He replies:

> "O Cuchullain of the battle triumph,
> It was not thee, but Medb that betrayed me.
> Take thou victory and fame,
> Thine is not the fault."

Cuchullain's reply:

> "My faithful heart is a clot of blood,
> From me my soul hath nearly parted,
> I have not strength for feats of valour
> To fight with thee, O Ferdiad."

But the weariness of the long, long struggle had so sorely told upon both of them that there is bitterness in their fight today as well as fierceness, till the hour of even's close.

> "'Let us desist now from this, O Cuchullain,' said Ferdiad.
>
> "'Let us desist, now, indeed, if the time hath come,' said Cuchullain. They ceased.
>
> "They cast their arms from them into the hands of their charioteers. Though it was the meeting—pleasant, happy, griefless, and spirited of two (men), it was the separation—mournful, sorrowful, dispirited, of two (men) that night.
>
> "Their horses were not in the same enclosure that night. Their charioteers were not at the same fire."

As will have been noticed from the references, the Red Branch Knights and other famous knights of their day used chariots and frequently fought from them.

Cuchullain's charioteer, Laeg, is, too, clothed in immortality, because of the frequent references to him in The Táin. Laeg's usefulness to Cuchullain did not end with his superb ability as a charioteer: he was worth gold, for abusing and taunting his master into hotter ire and fiercer effort, whenever in the course of a fight his master relaxed, or weakened, or was being worsted.

For instance, on one day of the fight, Ferdiad who evidently knew a little psychology and profited by his knowledge, took occasion, before the fight began, and within sight of Cuchullain, to practise himself in some of his most startling sword feats. The display had its desired effect.

> "I perceive, my friend, Laeg" (said Cuchullain), "the noble, varied, wonderful, numerous feats which Ferdiad displays on high, and all these feats will be tried on me in succession, and therefore it is that if it be I that shall begin to yield this day, thou art to excite, reproach, and speak evil to me, so that the ire of my rage and anger shall grow the more on me. If it be I that prevail, then shalt thou laud me, and praise me, and speak good words to me, that my courage may be the greater."
>
> "It shall so be done, indeed, O Cuchullain," said Laeg.

And it was so done, indeed. When Cuchullain was getting the worst of it that day, the fourth and last, the faithful Laeg came to his rescue.

> "Alas, indeed," said Laeg, "the warrior who is against thee casts thee away as a lewd woman would cast her child. He throws thee as foam is thrown by the river. He grinds thee as a mill would grind fresh malt. He pierces thee as the felling axe would pierce the oak. He

> binds thee as the woodbine binds the tree. He darts on thee as the hawk darts on small birds, so that henceforth thou hast not call, or right, or claim to valour or bravery to the end of time and life, thou little fairy phantom."

Laeg's abusive efforts are fruitful. Cuchullain rallies to the fight more fiercely, more terribly, more overpoweringly than ever, and at length gives to his friend, Ferdiad, the *coup de grace.*

> "'That is enough now, indeed,' said Ferdiad. 'I fall of that. But I may say, indeed, that I am sickly now after thee. And it did not behove thee that I should fall by thy hand.'
>
> "Cuchullain ran toward him after that and clasped his two arms about him, and lifted him with his arms and his armour.
>
> "Cuchullain laid Ferdiad down then; and a trance, and a faint, and a weakness fell on Cuchullain over Ferdiad there."

Laeg called upon Cuchullain to arise, because the Connaught host would be so frenzied by the fall of their champion that forgetting the ethics of combat, they would throw themselves upon Cuchullain.

> "'What availeth me to arise, O servant,' said Cuchullain, 'after him that hath fallen by me.'"

Cuchullain deplores what he calls the treachery and abandonment played upon Ferdiad by the men of Connaught, in pitting Ferdiad against himself who is invincible. And he sang this lay:

"O Ferdiad, treachery has defeated thee.
Unhappy was thy last fate,
Thou to die, I to remain,
Sorrowful for ever is our perpetual separation.

"When we were far away, in Alba
With Scathach, the gifted Buanand,
We then resolved that till the end of time
We should not be hostile to each other.

"Dear to me was thy beautiful ruddiness,
Dear to me thy comely, perfect form,

Dear to me thy grey clear-blue eye,
Dear to me thy wisdom and thy eloquence.

"There hath not come to the body-cutting combat,
There hath not been aroused by manly exertion,
There hath not held up shield on the field of spears,
Thine equal, O ruddy son of Daman.

"Never until now have I met,
Since I slew Aife's only son,
Thy like in deeds of battle—
Never have I found, O Ferdiad.

• • • • • • • •

"There has not come to the gory battle,
Nor has Banba nursed upon her breast,
There has not come off sea, or land,
Of the sons of Kings, one of better fame."

After long wars and doughty deeds done on both sides, Medb gets the coveted brown bull, and fights her way back to Connaught with the rare prize. Yet, does he make Connaught, in its very short possession of him, sorely rue his carrying away.

As the account of Cuchullain's fighting gives us an idea of the remarkable chivalry of the fighters in ancient Eire—at least the chivalry of that very ancient time in which the poet wrote, if not of that time in which the hero fought—so the account of his courtship gives us some impression of the quality and character of the women of Eire in the faraway time, and the loftiness of men's ideals regarding them.

When Cuchullain, chariot-driven by his faithful Laeg, went upon his famous courting journey, to woo the Lady Emer, the beautiful daughter of Forgaill the Brugaid (Hospitaller) of Lusc, the spectacle was impressive to all the wondering ones who beheld it. When he arrived at her father's Bruighean, the honoured Lady, modest as she was beautiful, was on the Faithe (lawn) sewing, and teaching sewing among a group of maidens, daughters of the neighbouring farmers. The hero was not only smitten by her beauty and her modesty, but captivated by her womanly accomplishments.

For Emer was possessed of the six womanly gifts, namely, "the gift of beauty of person, the gift of voice, the gift of music, the gift of embroidering and needlework, the gift of wisdom, and the gift of virtuous chastity."

When, to her maidenly confusion, she learns the purpose of Cuchullain's visit, she, with magnificent modesty, and as noble-hearted generosity, urges upon her wooer the prior and superior claims of her elder sister, thereby involuntarily making herself doubly desirable. Beyond all doubt she is and must be the one woman in all the Island suited to mate with and make happy, Eire's champion most renowned. And eventually she did make him happy.

Cuchullain died as a hero should—on a battlefield, with his back to a rock and his face to the foe, buckler on arm, and spear in hand.

He died standing, and in that defiant attitude (supported by the rock) was many days dead ere the enemy dared venture near enough to reassure themselves of his exit—which they only did when they saw the vultures alight upon him, and, undisturbed, peck at his flesh.

CHAPTER VIII

Two First Century Leaders

The first century of the Christian Era saw two remarkable movements in Ireland—wherein the whole national structure was forcibly turned upside down by one remarkable man—and then as forcibly re-adjusted by another man even still more remarkable.

These two great leaders were the usurper, Carbri Cinn Cait, and the monarch, Tuathal the Desired.

It was early in the first century that occurred the great Aithech Tuatha revolution. The Aithech Tuatha meant the rent-paying peoples. They were probably the Firbolgs and other conquered peoples—who had been in bondage and serfdom to the Milesians for hundreds of years.

Among these serfs arose an able leader, chief of one of their tribes in Leinster, named Carbri Cinn Cait—which some translate "cat-head," a term of derision applied to him by the Milesians—but which Sullivan (introduction to O'Curry) more reasonably interprets "head of the unfree ones."

Amongst these people who by the Milesian law were excluded from every profession, art and craft that carried honour, and ground down by rents and compulsory toil, this remarkable man succeeded in spreading a great, silent conspiracy. When they were ripened for revolution, the Aithech Tuatha invited all the royalties and all the nobility of the Milesians to a great feast, on a plain in the County Galway, which is now called Magh Cro, or the bloody plain, and there treacherously falling upon their guests, slew them. After which, the rent-payers, for five years, governed the land with Cinn Cait as their monarch. The Four Masters say of Carbri's reign, "Evil was the state of Ireland: fruitless her corn, for there used to be only one grain on the stock; fruitless her rivers; milkless her cattle; plentiless her fruit, for there used to be but one acorn on the stalk."

On the death of Carbri, his son Morann, who had become noted as a lawgiver and who was surnamed "the Just," refused the crown, and said that it should be given to the rightful one. Now Baine, wife of the slain King of Connaught, and daughter of the King of the Picts, who was pregnant, and visiting her father in Alba at the time of the great massacre, had borne a son, Feradach. And Feradach Finn-feactnach, the Fair Righteous One, now recalled from Pict-land, became King of Ireland.

But his reign was a troubled, unhappy one. For the unruly elements were reluctant to settle down, after having tasted revolution and rapine. Even the so-called legitimate chiefs who had come to their own again were restless and rebellious. In the reign of Fiacha of the White Cows, occurred another revolution—in which the provincial Milesian kings and the Aithech Tuatha seem to have been banded together. They overturned the reigning house, slew Fiacha, and placed on the throne Elim of Ulster—who, by repressing the Legitimists, and holding the favour of the Aithech Tuatha, managed to hold to his insecure position during a stormy reign of 20 years.

But the favour shown the Aithech Tuatha, and the power they were permitted to exercise, so angered and aroused the Milesian classes that they recalled from his exile (in Britain) Tuathal Feachtmar—that is to say, Tuathal the Desired—the son of Fiacha (and sixth in descent from Eochaid Feidlech, the father of Medb). A great portion of the nation joyfully hailed the Desired and rallied to his standard. And at the Hill of Scire in Meath he overthrew Elim, who was killed in the battle. But before he felt secure upon the throne of Ireland, Tuathal had to fight 133 battles!

Tuathal broke up the tribes of the Aithech Tuatha and scattered and redistributed them over the land in such way that they could not easily combine and conspire again.

This was a man of strong character, marked ability, and great moral power, whose reign influenced the future of Ireland. He established order in a land that had been for half a century in chaos. He fostered trade, and instituted laws for its protection and propagation. He made a new and important fifth province of Meath—which became fixed henceforward as the Ard-Righ's (High-King's) province. Before his day the other provinces met at the hill of Uisnech in that part of Ireland which is now called West Meath. From each of these he cut off a portion, which, attached to the former small domain of Meath made an important, rich, and royal Meath—enlarged from its former one *tuath* to eighteen *tuatha*. From a little district Meath then became an important province—the province of the Ard-Righ or High King of all Ireland. In each of the four cut off portions, moreover, he erected a royal residence—at the famous location where the four great provincial fairs were held, namely, at Tlachtga in Leinster; at Uisnech in Munster; Cruachan in Connacht; and Taillte in Ulster. Tuathal also re-organised the great National Fairs of Ireland, and re-established the interrupted Feis or Parliament of Tara.

And thus did the country and the Milesian dynasty recover, under this strong man from the staggering revolution of the Aithech Tuatha.

One other most notable happening in this king's reign was the laying upon Leinster of the famous Boru tribute—a crime which, for long centuries, was to be the cause of bloody wars that should shake the Island.

This was the origin of the Boru tribute: Of Tuathal's two beautiful daughters, Dairine and Fithir, the former wedded King Eochaid of Leinster. After some time, however, either tiring of her or coveting the beauty of her younger sister, Eochaid put Dairine away, and confined her in a tower. Giving out that she was dead, he went in mourning to the court of Tara, to seek consolation. Tuathal gave him that, by presenting to him Fithir for wife. Eochaid took Fithir with him to the court of Leinster, where, after a time, and through an accident, the two sisters met face to face, thus discovering a hidden, horrible truth. The shocking discovery of the double shame he had put upon them overwhelmed with mortification and grief the two sisters; and they died, broken-hearted.

When their father, the High King, learnt how that Eochaid had brought about his daughters' dishonour and death, he rallied auxiliaries to his aid, and marched into Leinster, ravaging it as he went. The province and its king were saved only by Eochaid's humiliated submission, and his binding the province to pay to the High King at Tara, every alternate year for an indefinite period, the tremendous tribute which came to be known as the Boru or cow-tribute—five thousand cows, five thousand hogs, five thousand cloaks, five thousand vessels of brass and bronze, and five thousand ounces of silver.

This crushing tribute was henceforth laid upon Leinster, by the High King of Tara from the time of Tuathal forward till the reign of Fionnachta, a period of five hundred years—but in most cases having to be lifted with steel hands. It caused more bloody history than did almost any other festering sore with which Ireland was ever afflicted. During these five centuries hardly a High King sat upon the throne of Tara, who did not have to carry the bloody sword into Leinster again and again, forcibly to hack his pound of flesh from off that province's palpitating body. And only sometimes was the fight fought between Meath and

Leinster alone. Often, through alliances, mutual sympathies, antagonisms, hopes, or dangers, half of Ireland, and sometimes all of Ireland was embroiled. So, together with much that was good Tuathal left to his country a bloody legacy.[1]

---

[1] Tuathal's son, who succeeded him, Feidlimid Rechtmar, the Lawgiver, successfully pursued his father's policy of making the laws respected,—and the better to achieve the noble purpose, devoted himself first to making them just—according to his lights. He established the Lex Talionis—the law of an eye for an eye—a rude and severe justice, which held thereafter in Ireland until the coming of Patrick. With the more lenient spirit of Christ, which he introduced, Patrick ended the reign of Feidlimid's Lex Talionis.

For still one other thing Feidlimid's name is somewhat memorable. The old seanachies quaintly record of him that "he died on his pillow," a phrase which indirectly throws a flood of light upon the abrupt manner in which the kings (of all countries) in those days usually made their exit from the world.

CHAPTER IX

Conn of the Hundred Battles

The celebrated Conn of the Hundred Battles was a son of Feidlimid, the son of Tuathal—though he did not immediately succeed Feidlimid. Between them reigned Cathair Mor, who was the father of thirty sons, among whom and their posterity he attempted to divide Ireland, and from whom are descended the chief Leinster families.

And we may pause to note that Cathair Mor is immortalised in Irish history by reason of a famous ancient will ascribed to him—a will that is of value because of the light it sheds upon many things of prime historical interest in early days. In this will we read, for instance, that he left to Breasal, his son, five ships of burden; fifty embossed bucklers, ornamented with border of gold and silver; five swords with golden handles; and five chariots. To Fiacha-Baiceade, another son, he left fifty drinking cups; fifty barrels made of yew-tree; and fifty piebald horses, the bits of the bridles made of brass. He left to Tuathal-Tigech, son of Maine, his brother, ten chariots; five play tables; five chess-boards; thirty bucklers, bordered with gold and silver; and fifty polished swords. To Daire Barach, another of his sons, he left one hundred and fifty pikes, the wood of which was covered with plates of silver; fifty swords of exquisite workmanship; five rings of pure gold; one hundred and fifty billiard-balls of brass, with pools and cues of the same material; ten ornaments of exquisite workmanship; twelve chess-boards with chess men. To Mog-corf, son of Laogare Birnbuadach, he left a hundred cows spotted with white, with their calves, coupled together with yokes of brass; a hundred bucklers; a hundred red javelins; a hundred brilliant lances; fifty saffron-coloured great-coats; a hundred different coloured horses; a hundred drinking cups curiously wrought; a hundred barrels made of yew-tree; fifty chariots of exquisite workmanship; fifty chess-boards; fifty tables used by wrestlers; fifty trumpets; fifty large copper boilers, and fifty standards; with the right of being a member of the council of state of the king of Leinster. Lastly, he bequeathed to the king of Leix, a hundred cows; a hundred bucklers; a hundred swords; a hundred pikes, and seven standards.

Cathair Mor was succeeded by Conn who overthrew him in a great battle in Meath. As Conn's title suggests, his reign was filled with battling. Conn's strenuous militancy and the suggestive title that it won for him, made him famed beyond worthier men—famed through the generations and the centuries—so that it was the greatest pride of some of the noblest families of the land a thousand years and more after his time to trace back their descent to him of the Hundred Battles.

But against Mogh Nuadat of Munster many of his most notable battles were fought. And in Mogh, Conn had an opponent worthy of his mettle.

The Southwestern province, Munster, used to be reigned over, says Keating, alternately by the two races that inhabited it, the Ithians, descendants of Milesius' uncle, Ith, who occupied the extreme Southwestern angle, comprising the remote corners of the modern counties of Cork and Kerry—and the Eberians, descendants of Milesius through Eber, who occupied the remainder of the province. There was an amicable arrangement between these two races that each in turn should rule Munster. And when one race supplied the king, the other supplied the chief judge, and vice versa.

This arrangement lasted till about half a century before the Christian Era, when there came South a portion of the Northern warlike Earnaan, from their late territory along Loch Erne, whence they had been forced out by the jealous Rudricians, the royal race of Rory, who ruled Ulster. By King Duach, who then ruled in Munster, the Earnaan were granted a settlement in Kerry. But, lustful of power, dominant and aggressive, they imposed themselves as rulers upon Munster, when King Duach died. Their great leader, Deagad (from whom that portion of the Earnaan were afterwards called Deagades), became king of Munster. And for more than 200 years after, these Northern intruders held the Munster kingship in their tribe—to the complete exclusion and subjection of both Ithians and Eberians.

It was in the time that Conn reigned in Meath as Ard-Righ, that Mogh Nuadat, an Eberian, roused his fellow Munstermen to battle for freedom from the tyrannical Earnaan. The monarch, Conn, jealous of the

Munstermen, and sympathetic toward his fellow Northerners, the Earnaan, gave his aid to the latter. Nevertheless, the power of the Earnaan in Munster was overthrown, and Mogh Nuadat took the sovereignty of the province.

Mogh Nuadat then, confident of his might, went against Conn himself. But the tide of success, that had been with him, at last turned; and Mogh had to flee the country. To Spain he went, remained there nine years, and wedded Beara, daughter of Heber Mor, king of Castile. Then his father-in-law, the Spanish King, gave him 2,000 troops under command of his own son, wherewith to return and battle for the monarchy of Ireland. Returning with these Spaniards, he rallied to his standard his former subjects, and once again boldly invaded Conn's territory.

Conn, with his allies, the Degades, was defeated in ten battles—till at length, for peace sake, he had to grant to Mogh one-half of Ireland—the southern half, henceforth to be known as Leth Mogha, Mogh's half—dominion over which was claimed by Mogh's successors, through almost ten centuries following. The northern half, which he retained under his own rule is since known as Leth Cuinn, Conn's half.

Unfortunately, the brave Mogh soon repented making peace for the reward of only one-half of Ireland, when, as he felt, he was powerful enough to have had the whole. The Spanish adventurers with him, having found peace unwelcome to their roving, warring nature prodded his ambition—till he declared war against Conn once more.

Mogh Nuadat marched to Moylena in the midlands, where he pitched his camp, challenging Conn. Conn went against him with a great army of the North, and the Fian of Connaught, under the command of their hero chieftain, Goll MacMorna. Conn and the leaders of his army planned to attack Mogh Nuadat in the night—and did so—all except Goll and his Fian. For Goll had vowed that he would never attack an enemy in the night, or by surprise, or take him at any disadvantage. He had never broken his vow, and would not do so now.

Such a capable leader was Mogh and so brave his men, that, despite the night surprise, they were not only not overcome but, after long fighting in the darkness, were wearing down and repulsing the army of the North. Fortunately for Conn he was able to hold out till day dawned. Then the chivalrous Goll, going to his assistance, gave a new spirit to Conn's army. Goll himself slew Mogh Nuadat, and Fraech, the son of the King of Spain. And following that, the Southern army wavered, were routed, and destroyed.

When Mogh Nuadat was slain, the Northerners took up his body upon a stretcher and triumphantly bore it up and down in view of both armies—till

Goll MacMorna, seeing this, rebuked them, saying: "Lay him down. He died as a hero should."

Conn, in his triumph, displayed both discretion and marked ability by the adroitness with which he converted enemies into friends. For while he gave to his ally, Mogh Lama, leader of the Deagades, his daughter Saraid in marriage (the son of which pair, Conaire, was to succeed Conn in the kingship), he married his second daughter, Sabia (who was then widow of MacNiad, late chief of the Ithians), upon Oilill Olum, the only son and heir of the slain chieftain, Mogh Nuadat. He thus drew together, by family tie, the Ithians, the Eberians, the Deagades, and his own people, the Eremonians.

Moreover, because Mogh Nuadat was unfairly slain, Conn, accepting the arbitration of the judges upon the crime, paid *eric* (fine) for it—his own ring of gold, his own precious carved brooch, his sword and shield, 200 driving steeds, and 200 chariots, 200 ships, 200 spears, 200 swords, 200 cows, 200 slaves, and his daughter Sadb in marriage. So says the old "Book of Munster."

Oilill Olum then became king of all Munster, both of the Eberian and of the Ithian sections—the first king of all that province. And thereafter (except in the one instance of Oilill's successor, the Ithian MacNiad) the kingship of Munster was reserved to the Eberians alone, and handed down in Oilill Olum's family. He willed—and his will was observed for long centuries—that the crown of Munster should henceforth alternate between the descendants of his two eldest sons, Eogan Mor and Cormac Cas—from the former of whom is the race of the MacCarthys, and from the latter, the race of the O'Briens.

Conn's reign and life were ended by his assassination at Tara. Fifty robbers hired by the King of Ulster, came to Tara, dressed as women, and treacherously despatched the Monarch.

Conn's son-in-law, Conaire II, who succeeded him as monarch—for his son Art was then but a child—is famed as father of the three Carbris, namely Carbri Musc, from whom was named the territory of Muskerry, Carbri Baiscin, whose descendants peopled Corca-Baiscin in Western Clare, and, most notable of them, Carbri Riada, who, when there was a famine in the South, led his people to the extreme Northeast of Ireland, and some of them across to the nearest part of Scotland, where they settled, forming the first important colony of Scots (Irish) in Alba, and driving there the edge of the Irish wedge which was eventually to make the whole country known as the land of the Scots (Irish). The Irish territory which Carbri Riada's people settled, the Northeast of Antrim, and the territory opposite to it in Alba, into which his people overflowed, became known as the two Dal Riada. And though divided by sea, these two territories were, for many centuries, to be as one Irish territory, administered and ruled over by the one Irish prince.

CHAPTER X

Cormac Mac Art

Of all the ancient kings of Ireland, Cormac, who reigned in the third century, is unquestionably considered greatest by the poets, the seanachies, and the chroniclers. His father Art was the son of Conn of the Hundred Battles, and was known as Art the Lonely, because, the story goes, that from the time he lost his brothers, Connla and Crionna—both slain by their uncles (though another famous story has it that Connla sailed away to Fairyland and never returned), he was pitifully solitary, and silent ever after till life's end[1]—the day of Moy Mocruime (in Galway) at which great battle he was killed, fighting the foreign forces which his exiled nephew Lugaid MacCon had brought back with him from his exile among the Picts, and the Britons. Lugaid, having won at Moy Mocruime, established himself as Ard-Righ of

---

[1] ART THE LONELY

The berried quicken-branches lament in lonely sighs,
Through open doorways of the *dun* a lonely wet wind cries;
And lonely in the hall he sits, with feasting warriors round,
The harp that lauds his fame in fights hath a lonely sound.

The speckled salmon, too, darts lonely in the pool,
The swan floats lonely with her brood in shallows cool,
His steeds—the swift and gentle—are lonely in their stall,
The sorrow of his loneliness weighs heavy over all.

For in the house of Tara three shadows share the feast,
Conn sits within the High-King's place, against the East,
And Crionna whispers to his hound some memory of the chase,
While Connla to the harping turns a joyous listening face.

—Ethna Carbery in "The Four Winds of Eirinn."

Eirinn. A rude, ill-tempered, domineering man was this Lugaid, who won little heart-loyalty from the people, and was but little mourned when he died. He was stabbed to death by a Druid, at Gort-an-Oir, as he was bestowing golden gifts on the poets.

It was at the court of this Lugaid at Tara, that Cormac first distinguished himself, and gave token of the ability and wisdom, which were, afterwards, to mark him the most distinguished of Eirinn's monarchs.

From his exile in Connaught, Cormac, a green youth, had returned to Tara, where, unrecognised, he was engaged herding sheep for a poor widow. Now one of the sheep broke into the queen's garden, and ate the queen's vegetables. And King Lugaid, equally angry as his queen, after he heard the case, ordered that for penalty on the widow, her sheep should be forfeit to the queen.

To the amazement of Lugaid's court, the herd-boy who had been watching the proceedings with anxiety, arose, and, facing the king, said, "Unjust is thy award, O king, for, because thy queen hath lost a few vegetables, thou wouldst deprive the poor widow of her livelihood?"

When the king recovered from his astoundment, he looked contemptuously at the lad, asking scathingly: "And what, O wise herd-boy, would be thy just award?"

The herd-boy, not one little bit disconcerted, answered him: "My award would be that the wool of the sheep should pay for the vegetables the sheep has eaten—because both the wool and the green things will grow again, and both parties have forgotten their hurt."

And the wonderful wisdom of the judgment drew the applause of the astounded court.

But Lugaid exclaimed in alarm: "It is the judgment of a King."

And, the lad's great mind having betrayed him, he had to flee.

He returned and claimed the throne when Lugaid was killed, but at a feast which he gave to the princes whose support he wanted, Fergus Black-Tooth of Ulster, who coveted the Ard-Righship, managed, it is said, to singe the hair of Cormac—creating a blemish that debarred the young man temporarily from the throne. And he fled again from Tara, fearing designs upon his life.

Fergus became Ard-Righ for a year—at the end of which time Cormac returned with an army, and, supported by Taig, the son of Ciann, and grandson of the great Oilill Olum of Munster, completely overthrew the usurper in the great battle of Crionna (on the Boyne) where Fergus and his two brothers were slain—and Cormac won undisputed possession of the monarchy.

Taig was granted a large territory between Damlaig (Duleek) and the River Liffi, since then called the Ciannachta. He became the ancestor of the O'Hara's, O'Gara's, O'Carroll's, and other now Northern families.

"A noble, illustrious king," says a tract preserved in the Book of Ballymote, "now took sovereignty and rule over Eirinn, namely, Cormac, the grandson of Conn. The world was replete with all that was good in his time: the food and the fat of the land, and the gifts of the sea were in abundance in this king's reign. There were neither woundings nor robberies in his time, but every one enjoyed his own, in peace."

And another ancient account says: "A great king, of great judgment now assumed the sovereignty of Eirinn, i.e., Cormac, the son of Art, the son of Conn of the Hundred Battles. Eirinn was prosperous during his time, and just judgments were distributed throughout by him, so that no one durst attempt to wound a man in Ireland, during the short jubilee of seven years."

Cormac rebuilt the palace of Tara, with much magnificence. He built the Teach Mi Chuarta, the great banqueting hall, that was 760 feet by 46 feet, and 45 feet high. Until quite recently, the outline of the foundations of this great hall with the traces of its fourteen doorways, were still to be observed on Tara Hill. He also built a grianán (sun-house) for the women—and the House of the Hostages, and the House of a Thousand Soldiers. He gave to the office of Ard-Righ a magnificence that it had not known before.

Amergin MacAmlaid, the scholar-bard of King Diarmaid MacCarroll, in the seventh century, gives a poetic account of Cormac's princely household, in which he says his hall had a flaming lamp, and 150 beds; and 150 warriors stood in the king's presence when he sat down at the banquet; there were 150 cup-bearers; 150 jewelled cups of silver and gold; and 50 over 1000 was the number of the entire household.

In the Book of Leinster is related, "Three thousand persons each day is what Cormac used to maintain in pay; besides poets and satirists, and all the strangers who sought the king; Galls, and Romans, and Franks, and Frisians, and Longbards, and Albanians (Caledonians), and Saxons, and Cruithnians (Picts), for all these used to seek him, and it was with gold and with silver, with steeds and with chariots, that he presented them. They used all to come to Cormac, because there was not in his time, nor before him, any more celebrated in honour, and in dignity, and in wisdom, except only Solomon, the son of David."

And to the Feis of Tara he gave a new dignity and importance that helped to make its decisions and decrees respected in every corner of the land.

From the Book of Ballymote is taken this interesting description of Cormac at that Feis:

> "His hair was slightly curled, and of golden colour; he had a scarlet shield with engraved devices, and golden hooks and clasps of silver; a wide-flowing purple cloak on him, with a gem-set gold brooch over his breast; a gold torque around his neck; a white-collared shirt, embroidered with gold, upon him, a girdle with golden buckles, and studded with precious stones, around him; two golden net-work sandals with golden buckles upon his feet; two spears with golden sockets, and many red bronze rivets, in his hand; while he stood in the full glow of beauty, without defect or blemish. You would think it was a shower of pearls that were set in his mouth; his lips were rubies; his symmetrical body was as white as snow; his cheek was like the mountain ash-berry; his eyes were like the sloe; his brows and eye-lashes were like the sheen of a blue-black lance."

The noted 17th century Irish scholar and historian, O'Flaherty, says: "Cormac exceeded all his predecessors in magnificence, munificence, wisdom, and learning, as also in military achievements. His palace was most superbly adorned and richly furnished, and his numerous family proclaim his majesty and munificence; the books he published, and the schools he endowed at Temair (Tara) bear unquestionable testimony of his learning. There were three schools instituted,[2] in the first the most eminent professors of the art of war were engaged, in the second, history was taught, and in the third, jurisprudence was professed."

He sought not to confine the benefits of his rule to Eirinn, but wanted to extend them to Alba also. The Four Masters record under the year 240, that the fleet of Cormac sailed across Magh Rian, the Plain of the Sea, and obtained for him the sovereignty of Alba.

Cormac, for all his greatness, was not invariably just. He carried an unjust war into Munster—and was punished therefor. Once Tara ran short of provisions—which to befall king or commoner in ancient Ireland, at whose residence guests might any moment arrive, was almost the unpardonable sin. On this occasion, Cormac's high steward advised him that the great province of Munster which, by its size and wealth, ought to pay two-fifths of the tribute of Ireland to the high-king, only paid one-fifth, and

[2] O'Curry says he can find no authority for this statement.

should now be called on to provision Tara. Cormac, impressed by the argument, made demand upon Munster—which Fiacha, the son of Eogan Mor, the son of Oilill Olum, promptly refused. Cormac immediately marched into that kingdom, at the head of his army, to collect what he considered his due. Fiacha, with the Munstermen met him at the place which is now called Knocklong, in Limerick, gave brave battle to, and completely routed, the High-King's army, pursued them into Ossory, and humiliatingly compelled Cormac to give him securities and pledges, and to promise to send him hostages from Tara.

O'Halloran says that there was at Tara in Cormac's time, a house of virgins who kept constantly alive the fires of Bel or the sun, and of Samain, the moon. It became historic from the fact that Dunlaing MacEnda, King of Leinster, once broke into this retreat, and put the virgins to the sword—for which Cormac decreed death to the scoundrel; and compelled his successors to send to Tara, every year, 30 white cows with calves of the same colour, 30 brass collars for the cows, and 30 chains to hold them while milking.

Historians record that the first watermill was introduced into Eirinn by Cormac. It was to spare toil to his concubine, Ciarnat, the daughter of the king of the Picts, that he did it. She was said to have surpassed all women in beauty. The men of Ulster had carried her off from Alba. From them Cormac obtained her; and his wife Ethni, jealous of her, made Ciarnat her slave, compelling the woman to grind by the quern every day nine pecks of corn. Cormac, it is said, brought craftsmen from Alba—where water-mills had been introduced from the Romans—to construct the mill—for sparing of Ciarnat.

A new classification of the people is said to have been made by the assembled nobles and scholars, at the Feis of Tara, in Cormac's time—being ranked according to their mental and material qualifications.

When Cormac found himself advanced in years, he resigned the throne and its cares. Some say he had to resign, because he lost an eye—lost it in his own hall, one time that his son, Cellach, who had insulted a woman of the Desi was thereinto pursued by the avenger of the Deisi, the chieftain, Aengus, who killed Cellach in his father's presence, and in the scuffle, put out the eye of the monarch also.

Aengus, it is worth noting here, was not summarily slain by Cormac's order. This philosophic and just king called him to answer before a court of justice. And, for his double crime, Aengus and his clan were exiled from Meath, where they (of the Southern Ciannachta) had their patrimony. They sojourned for a while in Leinster, and afterwards went onward to Munster, of their own kindred. There they helped the Munster King (Aengus of Cashel) to wrest from Leinster large territory in Tipperary and Waterford—and in reward there was settled on them part of the new territory—in Waterford, where their country is to this day known as the Deisi.

Cormac, as said, resigned the High-Kingship, thus ending one of the most fruitful as well as illustrious reigns that ever blessed the Island. "He was the greatest king," says one of the old historians, "that Ireland ever knew. In power and eloquence, in the vigour and splendour of his reign, he had not his like before or since. In his reign no one needed to bolt the door, no one needed to guard the flock, nor was any one in all Ireland distressed for want of food or clothing. For of all Ireland this wise and just king made a beautiful land of promise."

He retired to Cleite Acaill, on the Boyne, where he gave himself to study and good works.

Three great literary works are, by various ancient authorities, ascribed to him in his retirement—namely, Teagasc an Riogh (Instructions of a King), The Book of Acaill, and The Psaltair of Tara. Teagasc an Riogh taking the form of a dialogue between Cormac and his son Cairbre whom he is instructing for the duties of his position as Ard-Righ, is one of the works that some old writers claim to have originated with him—though it is more likely to be a literary product of several centuries later.[3]

---

[3] Of whatever ancient age they are, these Precepts form a rather remarkable, very wise, code of ethics—of which some samples are here pieced together—(chiefly from Kuno Meyer's version).

"O grandson of Conn, O Cormac," said Cairbre, "what is best for a king?"

"Not hard to tell," said Cormac. "Best for him—firmness without anger, patience without strife, affability without haughtiness, guarding of ancient lore, giving justice, truth, peace, giving many alms, honoring poets, worshipping the great God.

" . . . Let him attend to the sick, benefit the strong, possess truth, chide falsehood, love righteousness, curb fear, crush criminals, judge truly, foster science, improve his soul, utter every truth. For it is through the truth of a ruler that God gives all.

"Let him restrain the great, slay evil-doers, exalt the good, consolidate peace, check unlawfulness, protect the just, confine the unjust.

"He should question the wise, follow ancient lore, fulfil the law, be honest with friends, be manly with foes, learn every art, know every language, hearken to elders, be deaf to the rabble.

"Let him be gentle, let him be hard, let him be loving, let him be merciful, let him be righteous, let him be patient, let him be persevering, let him hate falsehood, let him love truth, let him be forgetful of wrong, let him be mindful of good, let him be attended by a host in gatherings, and by few in secret councils, let his covenants be firm, let his levies be lenient, let his judgments and decisions be sharp and light. . . . For it is by these qualities, kings and lords are judged."

"O grand-son of Conn, O Cormac," said Cairbre. "What were your habits when you were a lad?"

"Not hard to tell," said Cormac.

"I was a listener in woods,
I was a gazer at stars,
I was unseeing among secrets,

A second book attributed to Cormac is the Book of Acaill so named from his place of retirement. It is a book of the principles of Criminal Law, which is supposed to have been developed and enriched by later lawgivers and commentators—in particular by the eminent lawgiver, Ceann Falad, who died in 677. The Book of Acaill is found annexed to a law treatise of Ceann Falad's. Both are preserved and form a part of the Irish Brehon Laws.

I was silent in a wilderness,
I was conversational among many,
I was mild in the mead-hall,
I was fierce in the battlefield,
I was gentle in friendship,
I was a nurse to the sick,
I was weak toward the strengthless,
I was strong toward the powerful,
. . . .
I was not arrogant though I was wise,
I was not a promiser though I was rich,
I was not boastful though I was skilled,
I would not speak ill of the absent,
I would not reproach, but I would praise,
I would not ask, but I would give—

For it is through these habits that the young become old and kingly warriors."

"O grandson of Conn, O Cormac," said Cairbre, "what is good for me?"

"Not hard to tell," said Cormac, "if you listen to my teaching—

"Do not deride the old, though you are young;
Nor the poor, though you are wealthy;
Nor the lame, though you are swift;
Nor the blind, though you are given sight;
Nor the sick, though you are strong;
Nor the dull, though you are clever;
Nor the foolish, though you are wise.
. . . .
Be not too wise, be not too foolish;
Be not too conceited, be not too diffident;
Be not too haughty, be not too humble;
Be not too talkative, be not too silent;
Be not too harsh, be not too feeble.
If you be too wise, they will expect (too much) of you;
If you be too foolish, you will be deceived;
If you be too conceited, you will be thought vexatious;
If you be too humble, you will be without honor;
If you be too talkative, you will not be heeded;
If you be too silent, you will not be regarded;
If you be too harsh, you will be broken;
If you be too feeble, you will be crushed."

The prolegomenon of the Book of Acaill says: "The place of this book is Acaill close to Teamair (Tara), and its time is the time of Cairbre Lifechair, the son of Cormac, and its author, Cormac, and the cause of its having been composed was the blinding of an eye of Cormac by Aengus Gabuidech, after the abduction of a daughter of Sorcer, the son of Art Corb, by Cellach, the son of Cormac."

The scholars differ regarding the authenticity—but several of them conclude that the foundations of it at least are Cormac's. All of them agree that it is a noteworthy product of a very ancient lawgiver. Archbishop Healy, however, says its authenticity "is proven beyond doubt."

The third great work attributed to Cormac is the Psaltair na Tara. This is no longer in existence, and is known only by the frequent references to it of ancient chronologists, genealogists, seanachies, and poets—which references prove that it was a rich mine of very ancient historic and genealogic information, and that it was regarded as the greatest and most reliable authority of the very early days. The Book of Ballymote records that it contained "the synchronisms and genealogies as well as succession of the kings, the battles, etc., of antiquity, and this is the Psaltair of Tara, which is the origin and the fountain of the historians of Eirinn from that period, down to the present time."

The learned O'Curry thinks the Psaltair was in existence a long time before Cormac, and that Cormac altered and enlarged it to bring it up to his time. He further says: "We have reason to believe that the age of writing existed here, long before Cormac's reign." And Healy in talking about that remarkable monument of ancient lore says: "It proves to a certainty that in the third century of the Christian Era, there was a considerable amount of literary culture in Ireland."

O'Flaherty says of Cormac, "His literary productions, still extant, show him a wonderful legislator and antiquarian."

This remarkable king died in the year 267—more than a century and a half before the coming of St. Patrick. By reason of his extraordinary wisdom, the righteousness of his deeds, judgments and laws, he is said to have been blest with the light of the Christian faith seven years before his death. There is an ancient tract called Releg na Riogh preserved in the Book of the Dun Cow, which records—"For Cormac had the faith of the one true God, according to the law; for he said he would not adore stones, or trees, but that he would adore Him who made them, and who had power over all the elements, i.e., the one powerful God, who created the elements: in Him he would believe. And he was the third person who had believed in Erin, before the arrival of St. Patrick. Concobar MacNessa to whom Altus had told concerning the Crucifixion of Christ, was the first; Morann, son of Cairbri Cinncait (who was surnamed MacMaein), was the second person; and Cormac was the third; and it is possible that others followed on their track, in this belief."

O'Curry, however, records a fourth pagan who was said to have got the faith by inspiration—Art, the father of Cormac, and son of Conn of the Hundred Battles, who, tradition says, believed on the eve of the battle of Magh Mocruime—the great battle in which he was to be overthrown and slain by Lugaid MacCon.

The traditions about Cormac also state that having been inspired by the faith he made dying request that he should be buried, not with the other pagan kings at their famous burying ground, Brugh-na-Boinne, but at Ros na Riogh looking toward the East, whence would dawn the holy light that should make Eirinn radiant. Disregarding his dying wish, the Druids ordered that he should be interred with his ancestors at Brugh of Boyne. But when, in pursuance of this, the bearers were bearing his body across the river, a great wave swept it from their shoulders, down the stream, and cast it up at Ros na Riogh, where, according to his wish, he was then buried.

CHAPTER XI

TARA

Tara, which attained the climax of its fame under Cormac, is said to have been founded by the Firbolgs, and been the seat of kings thenceforth. Ollam Fodla first gave it historic fame by founding the Feis or triennial Parliament, there, seven or eight centuries before Christ. O'Curry says it was under, or after, Eremon, the first Milesian high-king that it, one of the three pleasantest hills in Ireland, came to be named Tara—a corruption of the genitive form of the compound word, Tea-Mur—meaning "the burial place of Tea," the wife of Eremon, and daughter of a King of Spain.

In its heyday Tara must have been impressive. The great, beautiful hill was dotted with seven duns, and in every dun were many buildings—all of them, of course, of wood, in those days—or of wood and metal.

The greatest structure there was the Mi-Cuarta, the great banqueting hall, which was on the Ard-Righ's own dun. There was also the House of a Thousand Soldiers, the ancient poets tell us. Each of the provincial kings had, on Tara, a house that was set aside for him when he came up to attend the great Parliament. There was a Grianan (sun-house) for the provincial queens, and their attendants. The Stronghold of the Hostages was one of the structures. Another was the Star of the Bards—a meeting-house for the poets and the historians, the doctors and judges. This latter was built by Cormac. He also rebuilt the great banqueting hall, the Mi-Cuarta, wherein at the great triennial Feis, all the kings, and chiefs and nobles, the Ollams or doctors, the Brehons or judges, the Files or poets, and the Seanachies or historians, were seated according to rank.

There every warrior sat under his own shield, which hung upon the wall above the place reserved for its owner. The upper end of the hall was reserved for the Ollams, the Brehons, the Filés, the Seanachies, the Musicians, and other professors of learned arts and sciences. The lords of territories occupied one side of the hall, and the captains of armies, the other side.

When a banquet was spread in the Hall of Mi-Cuarta or when a session of the Feis was to begin, the following was the form gone through.—The Hall was first cleared of all but three, a genealogist, a marshal, a trumpeter. Then, at a word from the marshal, the trumpeter sounded his horn, in response to which came the shield-bearers of the chiefs and nobles, gathering at an open door. The marshal took the shield of each, and under the direction of the genealogist, hung it in its proper place, above the seat that was thereby reserved for its owner. A second time the trumpeter sounded his horn—which now brought to the door the shield-bearers of the captains. Then the marshal, under the direction of the genealogist, hung the warriors' shields in order. Again the trumpeter blew a blast. And to this third blast answered the nobles and the warriors, who filed in, and took each his place beneath his own shield—"so that there was neither confusion nor contention for places among them."

The great Feis was held at Samain (Hallowday). It lasted for three days before Samain and three days after. But the Aonach or great fair, the assembly of the people in general, which was a most important accompaniment of the Feis, seems to have begun much earlier.

At the gathering in the Mi-Cuarta, the Ard-Righ of Eirinn sat mid-way of the hall, facing West, the King of Ulster sat at his right hand, the King of Munster at his left, the King of Leinster faced him, and the King of Connaught sat behind him. Naturally, at such state assemblies the participants arrayed themselves in such splendour as those ages sanctioned. Cormac MacArt's appearance at the Feis of Tara is thus colourfully described by one of the ancient poets:

> "Splendidly does Cormac come into this great assembly; for the equal of his form has not appeared, excepting Conaire Mor, son of Eidersgeal; or Concobar, the son of Cathbad; or Aengus, the son of the Daghda.
>
> "Beautiful was the appearance of Cormac in that assembly. Flowing, slightly curling, golden hair, upon him. A red buckler, with stars and animals of gold and fastenings of silver, upon him. A crimson cloak in wide descending folds upon him, fastened at his breast by a golden brooch set with precious stones. A neck-torc of gold around his neck.[1] A white shirt, with a full collar, and intertwined

> with red gold thread, upon him. A girdle of gold inlaid with precious stones around him. Two wonderful shoes of gold, with runnings of gold, upon him. Two spears with golden sockets in his hand, and with many rivets of red bronze. And he was, besides, himself symmetrical and beautiful of form, without blemish or reproach."

At this Feis the ancient laws were recited and confirmed, new laws were enacted, disputes were settled, grievances adjusted, wrongs righted. And in accordance with the usual form at all such assemblies, the ancient history of the land was recited, probably by the high-king's seanachie, who had the many other critical seanachies attending to his every word, and who, accordingly, dare not seriously distort or prevaricate. This constant and continual repetition, down through the ages, of the ever lengthening history—repeated, too, almost always in the presence of many critics—fixed the facts of the past story, and familiarised them to all the people. And while plenty of poetic colouring and artistic exaggeration was undoubtedly permitted to the poet-historian, the basic truths, ever had to be, preserved inviolate. This highly efficient method of recording and transmitting the country's history, in verse, too, which was practised for a thousand years before the introduction of writing, and the introduction of Christianity—and which continued to be practised for long centuries after these events—was a highly practical method, which effectively preserved for us the large facts of our country's history throughout a thousand of the years of dim antiquity—when the history of most other countries is a dreary blank.

Every prince had his own seanachie, a man who, having studied twelve years under masters, was well versed in the history of Ireland in general and in the history of his own principality, in particular. For more easy memorising and thus familiarising the multitude with the facts and the more surely to guard against incorrect repetition, all Irish histories and chronicles were, in these early ages, cast in verse. For the seanachie had to make the studies of a poet as well as of an historian, and to have intimate acquaintance with the hundreds of kinds of Irish verse.

---

[1] That the wonderful, remarkable description of Tara's ancient greatness, glory, and luxury is not any figment of the fancy of the hundreds of ancient poets who sang its praises, is evidenced in many ways, not the least noteworthy of which is the silent testimony of the valuable and rarely beautiful ornaments which in recent times have been dug up there—amongst others, two splendid gold torcs (bands of twisted gold worn around the neck), one of them being five feet seven inches in length, weighing twenty-seven ounces, and the other of large size also, and weighing twelve ounces. Both of them are beautifully wrought.

And since, at all minor assemblies, and even at small gatherings, the seanachie was constantly requisitioned for the purpose of reciting passages of history, all of the people down to the humblest had that pride of race, of clan, and of family, which results from familiarity with their great achievements. Their marvellously organised methods of recording and transmitting history signalises the Gael among the peoples of ancient time—just as their ancient Parliament signalised them.

As from the great heart and centre of the Irish kingdom, five great arteries or roads radiated from Tara to the various parts of the country—the Slighe Cualann, which ran toward the present County Wicklow; the Slighe Mor, the great Western road, which ran via Dublin to Galway; the Slighe Asail which ran near the present Mullingar; the Slighe Dala which ran Southwest; and the Slighe Midluachra, the Northern road.

Great, noble and beautiful truly was our Tara of the Kings.[2]

---

[2] Another much storied, very ancient royal residence was Ailech in Inishowen, said to have been founded by the Dagda, and where, long afterwards, but still in very ancient times, a wonderful, beautiful residence was said to have been erected by a famous builder, Frigrind, who had eloped with Ailech, the daughter of the King of Alba. It was for her that he built within the great stone fort of Ailech (which fort still stands a monument to the pre-historic builders) this beautiful house which a poet of the far-off days says was of red hue, carved and emblazoned with gold and bronze, and so thick-set with shining gems that day and night were equally bright within it. It was in the beginning of the fourth century the legend says, that Frigrind erected this notable structure. Two centuries earlier Ptolemy, the Egyptian geographer, had properly located this royal residence upon his map of Ireland.

At the famous Western royal residence of Rath-Cruachain, the house of Medb and Ailill is poetically pictured by another of the ancients, in the very old tale of the Tain Bo Fraich:—"The manner of that house was this: There were seven companies in it; seven compartments from the fire to the wall, all round the house. Every compartment had a front of bronze. The whole was composed of beautifully carved red yew. Three strips of bronze were in the front of each compartment. Seven strips of bronze from the foundation of the house to the ridge. The house from this out was built of pine. A covering of oak shingles was what was upon it on the outside. Sixteen windows was the number that were in it, for the purpose of looking out of it and for admitting light into it. A shutter of bronze to each window. A bar of bronze across each shutter; four times seven ungas of bronze was what each bar contained. Ailill and Medb's compartment was made altogether of bronze; and it was situated in the middle of the house, with a front of silver and gold around it. There was a silver band at one side of it, which rose to the ridge of the house, and reached all round it from the one door to the other. The arms of the guests were hung up above the arms of all other persons in that house; and they sat themselves down, and were bade welcome."

This Rath was a circular stone fort of dry masonry, with wall thirteen feet thick at the base, and surrounded by five concentric ramparts, traces of three of which are still to be seen.

CHAPTER XII

The Fairs

The holding of the Feis of Tara was the occasion also for holding a great Aonach or fair. Almost all the great periodic assemblages of ancient Ireland had fairs in their train.

After that of Tara the most famous of these periodic assemblies were those held at Tlachtga, Uisnech, Cruachan and Taillte—the three royal residences in those three portions of the royal domain of Meath, which had been annexed from Leinster, Munster, Connaught and Ulster, respectively. Also the Fair of Emain Macha (in the present county of Armagh), the Fair of Colmain on the Curragh of Kildare, and the famous Fair of Carman (Wexford).

As mentioned, some of the fairs originated as accompaniment to serious state or provincial representative assemblages. Many fairs, however, had their beginning in commemorative funeral games, at the grave of some notable—as the Fair of Emain Macha was instituted in memory of the great Ulster queen.

In the case of a fair which was not instituted as the accompaniment of a Feis, a Feis usually developed as an accompaniment of the fair.

For at all such fairs the chiefs, the judges, the scholars, and other leading ones held deliberative assemblies, on a certain day or days, during the fair's progress. Also it was an invariable part of the pleasure and the profit of the fair gathering, that the best seanachies, poets, and genealogists in attendance should gather the crowds, and recite to them portions of the history of the country, province, or tuath (district); the deeds of the great ones gone before; the praises of the great ones who still walked the land; the legends and traditions; and the genealogies of the principal families.

There were certain two of these gatherings, those of Emain Macha and Cruachan, whereat an important concern was the selection and examination of candidates for the various crafts, and the certificating the successful ones. As described by Keating, the candidates presented themselves before a board constituted of the King, the Ollams, chiefs and nobles, who examined and passed upon each, giving him the right to practise the craft or trade that he ambitioned.

At Emain and Cruachan, as well as at Tara, the assemblages were primarily political. They were conventions of representatives from all parts, for the purpose of discussing national affairs—and were presided over by the king.

The yearly Fair of Taillte (now Telltown) in Meath, was mainly for athletic contests—and for this was long famous throughout Eirinn, Alba, and Britain. In the course of time, too, Taillte acquired new fame as a marriage mart. Boys and girls, in thousands, were brought there by their parents, who matched them, and bargained about their *tinnscra* (dowry)—in a place set apart for the purpose, whose Gaelic name, signifying marriage-hollow, still commemorates its purpose. The games of Taillte were Ireland's Olympics, and, we may be sure, caused as keen competition and high excitement as ever did the Grecian. These Tailltin games took place during the first week of August—and the first of August, to this day, is commonly called Lugnasad—the games of the De Danann Lugh, who first instituted this gathering in memory of his foster-mother, Taillte. Another great assemblage for games and sports was held by the Ulstermen during the three days of Samain—on the plain of Muiremne (in Louth).

The last Fair of Taillte was celebrated in the year in which the first English invaders came into Ireland—in 1169. It was held by order of the High-King, Roderic O'Connor—and is recorded by The Four Masters, who state that the horses and chariots, alone, carrying people to this Fair, extended from Taillte to near Kells, a distance of six miles.

The great fairs and Feisanna were regarded as of such overwhelming national importance that special and exceptional laws and ordinances were instituted to insure their proper carrying out. For such occasion the king's peace was proclaimed for all. During its continuance all fugitives from justice walked free men amongst free men. At the fair, going to it, and returning from it, no oppressed debtor could be molested, arrested, or distrained for his debt. On the eve of a feis or fair all personal ornaments, rings, bracelets, or brooches, that had been pawned to relieve financial distress, or impounded for debts overdue, must, for the time of the assemblage, be released to their owners. The creditor who refused to release them was heavily fined for the mental suffering caused those who were forced to the disgrace of appearing without adornment at the great festive gatherings, whereat all the nation appeared in its richest, most beautiful, and best.

Another wise law provided for the peace of gatherings where mingled friend and foe, where heads and hearts were light, and where blood ran high. Any man royal or simple, who broke the king's peace, was to be punished with death. In the days of Colm Cille, even the saint's privilege of sanctuary failed to save a king's son who had disturbed the peace of the Fair. The law of the Fair was inflexible. Says an ancient writer, "They were carried out without breach of law, without crime, without violence, without dishonour. There was one universal Fair truce."

Surely, highly commendable was the spirit, and highly creditable the prudence, of the ancient lawmakers, which hedged with wise precautions these beautiful days of jubilee provided for a highly sociable and gregarious, but clannish and quick-tempered people, who equally loved sporting and battling, the matching of power in games, civil or warlike.

Joyce points out that there were three objects fulfilled by these great gatherings. Here the people learnt their laws, their rights, the past history of their country, the warlike deeds of their ancestors. Here also they got their relaxation and enjoyment, in the music, the poetry, the fun, the games, and the sports, provided for them. And here, likewise, were their markets[1] for buying, selling and exchanging. It should be added that a fourth most important function of the fairs was the opportunity they provided for mating and marrying the young, and thereby drawing closer the relationship of families and clans who had been distant, or at enmity.

Studying the account of "the fun at the fair" in those faraway days one is struck by the slightness of the change which the lapse of a couple of thousand years has effected. Besides athletic feats and racing of horses and chariots they had there—we quote from the poem on the Fair of Carman:

> "Trumpets, harps, wide-mouthed horns;
> Cruisechs, timpanists, without fail,
> Poets, ballad singers and groups of agile jugglers,
> Pipers, fiddlers, banded men,

---

[1] They had three different markets there—

> "A market for food, a market for live cattle,
> The great market of the foreign Greeks
> In which are gold and noble raiment."

Bow-men and flute players,
The host of chattering bird-like fliers,
Shouters and loud bellowers,
These all exert themselves to the utmost."

The fame of the great fair of Carman is perpetuated by an ancient poem, preserved in the Book of Ballymote and in the Book of Leinster. The description of the Carman fair given in this poem may well convey to us a general picture of all those ancient Irish fairs. Here are set down some excerpts from the version given in the Appendix to O'Curry:

"Listen, O Lagenians of the monuments!
Ye truth-upholding hosts!
Until you get from me, from every source,
The pleasant history of far famed Carman.

"Carman, the field of a splendid fair,
With a widespread unobstructed green
The hosts who came to celebrate it,
On it they contested their noble races.

"The renowned field is the cemetery of kings,
The dearly loved of noble grades;
There are many meeting mounds,
For their ever-loved ancestral hosts.

"To mourn for queens and for kings,
To denounce aggression and tyranny,
Often were the fair hosts in autumn
Upon the smooth brow of noble old Carman.

• • • • • • • • •

"Heaven, earth, sun, moon, and sea,
Fruits, fire, and riches,
Mouths, ears, alluring eyes,
Feet, hands, noses, and teeth—

"Steeds, swords, beautiful chariots,
Spears, shields, human faces,
Dew, fruits, blossoms, and foliage,
Day and night, a heavy flooded shore—

"These in fulness all were there,
The tribes of Banba without lasting grief,—
To be under the protection of the fair,
Every third year, without prohibition.

"The gentiles of the Gaedhil did celebrate,
In Carman, to be highly boasted of,
A fair without (breach of) law, without crime,
Without a deed of violence, without dishonor.

"On the Kalends of August without fail,
They repaired thither every third year;
There aloud with boldness they proclaimed
The rights of every law, and the restraints."

The forbidden things are enumerated:

"To sue, to levy, to controvert debts,—
The abuse of steeds in their career,
Is not allowed to contending racers,—
Elopements, arrests, distraints—

"That no man goes into the women's Airecht,
That no women go into the Airecht of fair clean men;
That no abduction is heard of,
Nor repudiation of husbands or of wives—

"Whoever transgresses the law of the assembly—
Which Benen with accuracy indelibly wrote,—
Cannot be spared upon family composition,
But he must die for his transgression."

The music at the fair:

"There are its many great privileges;—
Trumpets, Cruits, wide-mouthed horns,
Cuisigs, Timpanists without weariness,
Poets and petty rhymesters."

The literary entertainment provided consisted of stories, philosophy, history, and so forth.

"Fenian tales of Find,—an untiring entertainment,—
Destructions, Cattle-preys, Courtships,
Inscribed tablets, and books of trees,
Satires, and sharp edged runes;

"Proverbs, maxims, royal precepts,
And the truthful instructions of Fithal,
Occult poetry, topographical etymologies,
The precepts of Cairbri and of Cormac;

"The Feasts, with the great Feast of Teamar,
Fairs, with the fair of Emania;
Annals there are verified,
Every division into which Erin was divided;

"The history of the household of Teamar—not insignificant—
The knowledge of every territory in Erin,
The history of the women of illustrious families,
Of Courts, Prohibitions, Conquests;

"The noble Testament of Cathair the Great
To his descendants, to direct the steps of royal rule
Each one sits in his lawful place,
So that all attend to them to listen, listen.

"Pipes, fiddles, chainmen,
Bow-men, and tube-players,
A crowd of babbling painted masks,
Roarers and loud bellowers.

"They all exert their utmost powers
For the magnanimous king of the Barrow;
Until the noble king in proper measure bestows
Upon each art its rightful meed.

"Elopements, slaughters, musical choruses,
The accurate synchronisms of noble races,

The succession of the sovereign kings of Bregia,
Their battles, and their stern valour.

"Such is the arrangement of the fair,
By the lively ever happy host;—
May they receive from the Lord
A land with choicest fruits."

CHAPTER XIII

FIONN AND THE FIAN

It is only recently that we have realised the all-important part played by legendary lore in forming and stamping a nation's character. A people's character and a people's heritage of tradition act and react upon each other, down the ages, the outstanding qualities of both getting ever more and more alike—so long as their racial traditions are cherished as an intimate part of their life. But the people's character gets a new direction on the day that there comes into their life any influence which lessens their loving regard for the past.

Than the Gaelic, the world has known but few races that were enriched with a richer heritage of legend—poetic, romantic, heroic, idealistic, wondrous, humorous—which in ancient ages sprang from the souls of the nation's noblest, and through all subsequent days nurtured the minds and souls of the multitude. In these wonderful traditions every ancient great poet and teacher lives, and leads his listening people, for all time.

Of all the great bodies of ancient Irish legendary lore, none other, with the possible exception of the Red Branch cycle, has had such developing, uplifting, and educational effect upon the Irish people, through the ages, as the wonderful body of Fenian tales—in both prose and verse, rich in quality and rich in quantity.

Fionn MacCumail (Finn MacCool), leader of the Fian (Fenians), in the time of Cormac MacArt, is the great central figure of these tales. Fionn and the Fian were not figments of the ancient poets' fancy—as think some who know of this lore only by hearsay. The man Fionn lived and died in the third century of the Christian Era. The Four Masters chronicle his death on the Boyne, under A.D. 283—though he must have died some years earlier. Fionn's father Cumal, was chief of the Fian, in his day; and his grandfather, Treun-Mor, chief before that. In contrast to the Red Branch which was of Ulster, the Fian was of Munster and Leinster origin.[1] Connaught with its Clan na Morna contributed largely to the body, later.

It was in the reign of Conn, at the very end of the second, or beginning of the third century that was founded the Fian—a great standing army of picked and specially trained, daring warriors, whose duty was to carry out the mandates of the high-king—"To uphold justice and put down injustice, on the part of the kings and lords of Ireland—and to guard the harbors from foreign invaders." From this latter we might conjecture that an expected Roman invasion first called the Fian into existence.

They were soldiers in time of war, and a national police in time of peace. We are informed that they prevented robberies, exacted fines and tributes, put down public enemies and every kind of evil that might afflict the country. Moreover they moved about from place to place, all over the island. During the summer and harvest, from Beltinne to Samain—May first till November first—they camped in the open, and lived by the chase. During the winter half-year they were quartered upon the people.

But Fionn, being a chieftain himself in his own right, had a residence on the hill of Allen (Almuin) in Kildare. An old poem (quoted by O'Mahony) pictures it as a very palatial residence, indeed:

"I feasted in the hall of Fionn,
And at each banquet there I saw
A thousand rich cups on his board,
Whose rims were bound with purest gold.

"And twelve great buildings once stood there,
The dwellings of those mighty hosts,
Ruled by Tadg's daughter's warlike son,
At Alma of the noble Fian.

"And constantly there burned twelve fires,
Within each princely house of these,
And round each flaming hearth there sat
A hundred warriors of the Fian."

---

[1] Fionn's clan, Clan na Baoiscne (which was the heart of the Fian) belonged in North Munster.

The Fianna[2] recruited at the great fairs, especially at Tara, Uisnech, and Taillte. The greatest discrimination was used in choosing the eligible ones from amongst the candidate throng—which throng included in plenty sons of chieftains and princes.

But no candidate would be considered unless he, his family, and clan, were prepared philosophically to accept for him life or death, all the daily hazards of a hazardous career—and that his family and his clan should, from the day he joined the Fian, renounce all claims to satisfaction or vengeance for his injuring or ending. His comrades must henceforth be his moral heirs and executors, who would seek and get the satisfaction due if he were wounded or killed by any means that violated the code of honor and justice. And, it should here be remarked that the high ethical code of the Red Branch Knights in the days of Christ was not any more admirable than the code of justice and of honor observed now, two centuries after, by the Fian.

Many and hard were the tests for him who sought to be of the noble body.

One of the first tests was literary: for no candidate was possible who had not mastered the twelve books of poetry. With this condition in mind one will no longer wonder that the Fian bequeathed to posterity ten thousand fragrant tales.

In a trench, the depth of the knee, the candidate, with a shield and hazel staff only, must protect himself from nine warriors, casting javelins at him from nine ridges away.

Given the start of a single tree, in a thick wood, he has to escape unwounded from fleet pursuers.

So skilful must he be in wood-running, and so agile, that in the flight no single braid of his hair is loosed by a hanging branch.

His step must be so light that underfoot he breaks no withered branch.

In his course he must bound over branches the height of his forehead, and stoop under others the height of his knee, without delaying, or leaving a trembling branch behind.

Without pausing in his flight he must pick from his foot the thorn that it has taken up.

In facing the greatest odds the weapon must not shake in his hand.

When a candidate had passed the tests, and was approved as fit for this heroic band, there were four *geasa* (vows of chivalry) laid upon him, as the final condition of his admission:

---

[2] Fianna, meaning bodies of the Fian, is the plural of the collective noun, Fian.

1. He shall marry his wife without portion—choosing her for her manners and her virtues.

2. He shall be gentle with all women.

3. He shall never reserve to himself anything which another person stands in need of.

4. He shall stand fight to all odds, as far as nine to one.

Hard, then, was the task of him who entered the ranks of the noble Fian. But in the ensuing life of beauteous adventure, the fortunate one was recompensed an hundred-fold.

Roaming and roving from end to end of the Island, hunting and fighting, feasting and love-making, the Fian made legend every day of their lives. New romance dawned for them with the dawning of each new day. Adventure and poetry marched with them, on either hand. They lived exciting history; they breakfasted with song, supped with entrancing story, and, on their three beds of branches, rushes and moss, bedded with rare dreams of yesterday's pleasuring and the morrow's daring. Their own warrior-poets chanted for them their own heroic deeds; their own musicians carolled, and their own *sgeuladoirs* (story-tellers) charmed their leisure hour with blithesome tale. They left lasting impression on every hill, and vale, and stream from North to South, from East to West, of the Island. They hung rare tales of themselves on every rowan-tree, and ten thousand great grey rocks that stud the Island's face, are monuments immortal, proclaiming to the wondering generations, "Here passed Fionn and his Fian."[3]

There were three cathas (battalions) of the Fian—three thousand in each catha. This, in time of peace. In time of war, the quota was seven cathas. And twenty-one thousand such men, trained in agility and in

---

[3] The sceptic who is eager to discount the singular pre-eminence, physical, spiritual, and intellectual, of the ancient Gael says: "Ah, but all those fine things are the fictions of far-away poets!" Even if we gratuitously discard the compelling pile of contrary evidence, supplied by the poems and the histories, by the ancient legends and the ancient laws, and thoughtlessly assume with him that the fineness of ancient Gaelic character is a fiction of the old-time poets,—then such beautiful fictions of such beautiful ideals, by themselves presume and prove a beautiful-souled people, capable of appreciating lofty ideals. The greatest poet is never more than a hand's breadth higher than his people. And if the song he sings lives after him forever, that is proof conclusive that the people who cherished it, and passed it on to future ages, could see his visions, speak his language, and hear with him the music of the spheres. In any age, and of any race, the visions (fictions) of the poet, are only the reflections from the mirror of heaven's dome of the souls of his people. So for the purpose of constructing for us of today a true picture of our forefathers, their thoughts, their deeds, their character, their height, their depth, and limitations, every merest myth and legend is a fact four-square, ready for the building.

strength, and in marvellous feats of arms, by their mode of life hardened against all hardships, accustomed to reckless daring, and familiar with death, must have been a formidable weapon in the hands of the High King, and insured respect for him, for his laws and his commands, in the hearts of all men in the remotest corners of the country.

Keating says they ate only one meal a day, the evening meal. When the chase was ended at the day's end, they encamped in a pleasant place, and dug their dinner-pits, at the bottom of which they built fires that made the dinner-stones red hot. On the stones they laid the meat, wrapped in green rushes, and buried it while it broiled. They repaired to the nearby stream to bathe—then combed and plaited their hair—after which they were eager for their great meal. When they had eaten, they seated themselves on the ground, in circle around a big log-fire, while one or other of their myriad gifted bards and story-tellers entertained them with poem, with story, with history and with legend, till sleep stole over their tired limbs, and they couched them beneath fragrant branches—on "the three beddings of the Fian"—first green boughs, over that green moss, and finally green rushes.

Although the Fianna were supposed to uphold the power of the Ard-Righ, their oath of fealty was not to him, but to their own chief.

And in course of time, in the reign of Cairbre Lifeachar, son of Cormac, they revolted against the Ard-Righ—Fionn and his Fian joining Breasil, king of Leinster, in resisting Cairbre's levying of the Boru tribute. Cairbre met with overwhelming defeat at the battle of Cnamros—where he is said to have left nine thousand dead upon the field.

One reason for their revolt was because Cairbre had favoured the Clan na Morna, the Connaught branch of the Fian, from whom Fionn had formerly usurped power and favour for his own branch, the Clan na Baoscni. Cairbre had put away the latter, and made the former, under their leader Aedh the Comely, his *buannacht* (paid soldiers).

Also, from enjoying too much power too long, the Clan na Baoscni had got arrogant. Amongst other privileges which they came to claim as their right was that no maiden in the land, of any rank, should marry outside the Fian unless she was first offered in marriage to the eligible in their ranks. And when at length they demanded gold tribute from Cairbre himself, because, without asking their approval, he chose to marry his beautiful daughter, Sgeimsolas (Light of Beauty) to a chief of the Deisi, the final break befell. They allied themselves with the King of Munster, Mogh Corb, whose mother, Samair, was a daughter of Fionn, and whose father, Cormac Cas, was son to the great Oilill Olum, son of Mogh Nuadat. Since it was Goll

MacMorna who had slain Mogh Nuadat on the field of Moylena, the Munstermen had double reason for allying with the Clan na Baoscni against the Clan na Morna and their master, Cairbre.

In the year 280 A.D., both sides met in death grapple at the battle of Gabra—one of the fiercest fights of ancient times. Oisin, the son of Fionn (who was now dead), led the Fian. Oisin's son, Oscar, the most powerful fighter of the Fian, was killed in single combat by Cairbre. And the Fianna, who had so long filled such a shining part in Ireland's history, were annihilated.[4] Though Cairbre's army and the Clan na Morna under Aedh, won, they had but little to boast of—and not a large number of them were left to boast. Cairbre carried himself out of the battle, but, as he returned to Tara, was killed by one of his own kin. Aedh the Comely survived; and Mogh Corb escaped. These two leaders afterwards renewed the fight in Muskerry, where Aedh killed Mogh.

But the Fian na h-Eireann were gone forever.

Yet, though dead, they live. The lays of Oisin, the Dialogue of the Ancients, and innumerable other Finian poems and tales have kept, and will keep, their name and their fame imperishable.[5] Not only is the Fian in general immortalised, but the names, the qualities, and the characteristics of every one of Fionn's trusted lieutenants—Oscar who never wronged bard or woman, Gol the mighty, Caoilte the sweet-tongued, Diarmuid Donn the beautiful, the bitter-tongued Conan, and the rest of them, have lived and will live. Even their hounds are with us, immortal. Bran, Sgeolan, and their famed fellows still follow the stag over the wooded hills of Eirinn, and wake the echoes of our mountain glens, by their bay melodious.

> "The two hounds which belonged to Fionn,
> When they were let loose through Glen Rath;
> Were sweeter than musical instruments,
> And their face outwards from the Suir."

In every corner of Ireland to the remotest headland, the stories of the Fian awake the admiration, and excite the emulation of our people. Round every hearth, in every cottage, on every hillside in Eirinn, the Fian is the enchanted word with which the seanachie awakes the instant interest and

---

[4] One old tale has it that Oisin and Caoilte were the only ones of the Fian who escaped with their lives from the battle.

[5] Legend says they had four leading poets—Fionn, his two sons, Oisin and Fergus Finnbeoil, and Caoilte.

for as long as he likes holds the spellbound attention of man and child, of learned and simple, rich and poor, old and young.

The best of the stories of the Fian are preserved to us in the poems of Oisin, the son of Fionn, the chief bard of the Fian, in the Agallamh na Seanorach, and many other fine poems of olden time.

The Agallam na Seanorach (the Colloquy of the Ancients), by far the finest collection of Fenian tales, is supposed to be an account of the Fian's great doings, given in to Patrick by Oisin and Caoilte—more than 150 years after.

After the overthrow of the Fian, Caoilte is supposed to have lived with the Tuatha De Danann, under the hills—until the coming of St. Patrick. Oisin had been carried away to the Land of Youth, under the western ocean. Both of them return to their mortal existence, and to Ireland, when Patrick is in the land, winning it from Crom Cruach to Christ. Patrick meets and converts each of them. They attach themselves to his company, and travel Ireland with him. When the Saint is wearied from much travelling and work, or, as often happens, from the perversity of the people he has to deal with, Oisin or Caoilte refresh and beguile him with many a sweet tale of the Fian—all of which, says the tradition, the pleased Patrick had his scribe Breogan write down and preserve for posterity. These tales make the Agallam na Seanorach.

The tired Patrick would say:

"Oisin, sweet to me is thy voice!
A blessing on the soul of Fionn—
And relate to us the great deer-hunt
That day in Sliab-nam-Ban-Fionn."

Often however Oisin, old, blind, and bitterly remembering the happy long-gone days, was far from sweet in tongue or temper.

"Oh, Patrick, sad is the tale,
To be after the heroes, thus feeble;
Listening to clerics and to bells,
Whilst I am a poor, blind, and old man.

"If Fionn and the Fenians lived,
I would abandon the clerics and the bells;
I would follow the deer from the glen,
And would fain lay hold of his foot."

He was ever longing for by-gone joys—

"The warbling of the blackbird of Litir Lee,
  The wave of Rughraidhe lashing the shore;
  The bellowing of the ox of Magh-maoin,
  And the lowing of the calf of Gleann-da-maoil.

"The resounding of the chase on Sliab g-Crot,
  The noise of the fawns around Sliab Cua;
  The sea-gulls scream on Lorrus, yonder,
  Or the screech of the ravens over the battlefield.

"The tossing of the hulls of the barks by the wave,
  The yell of the hounds at Drumlish;
  The cry of Bran at Cnoc-an-air,
  Or the murmur of the streams about Sliab Mis.

• • • • • • • • •

"Oh, delight to Fionn and the heroes
  Was the cry of his hounds afar on the mountain;
  The wolves starting from their dens,
  The exultation of his hosts, that was his delight.

And Oisin could never comprehend why Fionn and the Fian should, or could, now be in Hell—

"What did Fionn do to God,
  Except to attend on hosts and schools;
  A great while bestowing gold,
  And another while delighting in his hounds.

"Were the Clanna Morna within [in Hell]
  Or the Clanna Baoiscne, the mighty men;
  They would take Fionn out,
  Or would have the house to themselves.

"If Faolan and Goll lived,
  Diarmuid the brown haired and Oscar the noble;
  In any house that demon or God ever formed,
  Fionn and the Fenians could not be in bondage.

"Were there a place, above or below,
Better than Heaven;
'Tis there Fionn would go,
At the head of his Fianna."

Sometimes his boasting and his perversity provoked to ire the quick-tempered Patrick—

"Misery attend thee, old man,
Who speakest the words of madness;
God is better for one hour,
Than all the Fians of Eire."

This would elicit retort in kind from Oisin—

"O Patrick of the crooked crozier,
Who make me that impertinent answer;
Thy crozier would be in atoms,
Were Oscar present.

"Were my son Oscar and God
Hand to hand on Cnoc-na-Fiann
If I saw my son down,
I would then say God was a stronger man."

But the ardent Patrick would insist on impressing this old heathen that in power, might, and all good qualities, God was infinitely beyond all mortals. This was very hard for Oisin to comprehend or admit—

"Hadst thou seen, O chaste cleric,
The Fenians one day on yonder Southern strand;
Or at Naas of Leinster of the gentle streams,
Then the Fenians thou wouldst greatly have esteemed.

"Patrick, enquire of God,
Whether he recollects when the Fenians were alive;
Or hath he seen East or West,
Men their equal, in the time of fight.

"Or, hath he seen in his own country,
Though high it be above our heads;

In conflict, in battle, or in might,
A man who was equal to Fionn."

Moreover, these old comrades of his, from whose example, and from the admiring of whom, Patrick strove to turn him—possessed those very virtues which, according to Patrick's preaching, should have won them Heaven—

"We (the Fenians) never used to tell untruth,
Falsehood was never attributed to us;
By truth and the might of our hands,
We came safe out of every conflict.

"There never sat a cleric in a church,
Though melodiously ye think they chant psalms,
More true to his word than the Fian,
Men who never shrank from fierce conflicts.

"A cleric never sat in a church,
O Patrick mild of the sweet voice!
More hospitable than Fionn himself;
A man who was not niggardly in bestowing gold.

"Fionn never suffered in his day
Any one to be in pain or difficulty;
Without redeeming him, by silver or gold,
By battle or fight, till he got the victory.

"All that thou and thy clerics tell,
According to the laws of Heaven's king;
These (qualities) were possessed by the Fian of Fionn,
And they are more powerful in God's kingdom.

"Great would be the shame for God,
Not to release Fionn, from the shackles of pain;
For if God himself were in bonds,
The chief would fight on his behalf."

But desire for Oisin's delightful tales of these brave Pagans would overcome in Patrick the zest for theological controversy—

"Oisin, sweet to me is thy voice,
And a blessing, furthermore, on the soul of Fionn!
Relate to us how many deer
Were slain at Sliabh-nam-Ban-Fionn."

And, Oisin, mollified, forgiving and forgetting Patrick's strictures on his Fian fellows, would forthwith launch into another of his rare tales.

CHAPTER XIV

THE BREAK OF ULSTER

Of the line of Ir, son of Milesius, to whom Ulster had been apportioned, that Branch called the Clan na Rory (after its great founder, Rory, who had been King of Ulster, and also High-King of Ireland) now had ruled the province for nearly 700 years, namely, for more than 300 years before the Christian Era, and more than 300 years after. And their capital city and the King's seat had been at Emain Macha. During practically all of this time, from that fort's first founding by Queen Macha, the Royal Court of Ulster had been a court of splendour, and ever noted as a centre of chivalry and the home of poetry.

And the power, and might, and courage of Ulster had ever acted as a brake on the ambitions of their neighbouring royal depredators, and especially the royal aggressors of Connaught, who were made to fear Ulster's name.

But in the beginning of the fourth century, Ulster's power was irrevocably broken, and by far the greater portion of her territory wrested from her—her people driven into miserably narrow bounds from which, ever after, they can hardly be said to have emerged.

It was when Muiredeach Tireach, grandson of Carbri of the Liffey, was High-King of Ireland, that Ulster was despoiled and broken by his nephews, the three Collas, who, on the ruins of the old kingdom of Uladh, founded a new kingdom—of Oirgialla (Oriel)—which was henceforth for nearly a thousand years to play an important part in the history of Northern Ireland.

Muiredeach's father, Fiacha (son of Carbri), was reigning High-King at Tara in the beginning of the fourth century. Muiredeach, a young man of exceeding ability, was made King of Connaught (for during some centuries now the Ard-Righship was in possession of the Connaught royal family) and the throne of Connaught was usually the stepping-stone to the high throne at Tara. Yet because of the general Irish custom which alternated the headship of a kingdom or a chieftainry between two collateral branches of a paramount family, King Fiacha's nephew, Colla Uais (the Noble), ambitioned the Ard-Righship in succession to Fiacha.

Now, at a time when Muiredeach was in Munster, fighting his father's battles with great success and bright renown Colla Uais saw himself eclipsed, and popular feeling leaning to the victorious Muiredeach as the proper successor to his father, Fiacha. So Colla Uais, and his two brothers, Colla Da-Crioch and Colla Maen, gathered an army of their own adherents, formidably augmented it by seducing from their allegiance a large portion of Ard-Righ Fiacha's army, and giving battle to Fiacha, at Taillten in Meath, overthrew and slew him.

They seized the throne for Colla Uais who reigned Ard-Righ for four years. At the end of that time he, in turn, was overthrown by Muiredeach, and fled with his two brothers and their followers, to Alba, to the King of the Picts, who was his mother's father.

Then Muiredeach became Ard-Righ of Ireland, and reigned for 27 years.

But in the third year of Muiredeach's reign the three Collas returned. The story says, a Druid at the court of the king of the Picts divined that should they return to Ireland, and Muiredeach take the life of one of them, the Irish crown should fall to the survivors. And on the Druid's disclosure, they, keenly covetous of the Ard-Righship, promptly acted.

They sailed for Ireland, went to Tara, and into the presence of the King. Muiredeach was naturally surprised to find his father's slayers audaciously present themselves before him; but, being a man of superior qualities, he surprised them by his kindly greeting. Then he asked what news they brought. They, determined to provoke this good man, replied, tauntingly: "We killed your father."

"That," said Muiredeach calmly, "is not news to me."

"Then," they said, with bravado, "you want your revenge—and may have it."

"Yes," said the great man, "I want my revenge—so, you are all three forgiven your crime."

The three Collas were at first dumbfounded by a great-mindedness incomprehensible to them. But they were not to be turned from their object. This dull man must be baited to vengeance. They said, "You take the way of a coward."

And the great Muiredeach, far from resenting the insolent taunt again surprised and dumbfounded them by a noble, gentle reply—which completely won their hearts to him, and filched from their minds the foul ambition. They thereupon professed their profound sorrow, and swore fealty to him.

But the keen-minded Muiredeach knew that these bold youths were not meant to loll at court, and that if he did not find fitting trouble for them, they would, themselves, in all certainty find trouble which might be in no way welcome to him. So he directed them to face North and win swordland for themselves from the Ultach (Ulstermen)—on which direction they promptly acted.

The ostensible cause of their attack upon Ulster was the ancient grudge borne that province because many generations before, the Ulster king, Tiobraide, had sent to Tara fifty robbers disguised as women, who had slain Conn of the Hundred Battles—and because, a generation later, the Ulster prince, Fergus Blacktooth, had, by setting fire to his hair at a feast, put a blemish upon Cormac MacArt, which, for a time, debarred him from the throne which Fergus then usurped.

But the Callas first went to their kin in Connaught and there gathered a great army for the invasion of Ulster. On the plain of Farney in Monaghan they met the Ulstermen under their king, Fergus, and on seven successive days broke battle upon them, finally slaying Fergus and putting the Ultach to complete rout. Then they ravaged and destroyed famed and ancient Emain Macha, and drove the Ultach east of the Uri River and Loch Neagh—from the great expanse of their olden kingdom, hemming them into the straitened limits of the new kingdom, which comprised only parts of the present two counties of Antrim and Down. Of the conquered portion of Ulster, from Louth in the south to Derry in the north, and from Loch Neagh to Loch Erne, the Collas made themselves the new kingdom of Oirgialla (Oriel), which was possessed, afterwards, by their descendants, the MacMahons, O'Hanlons, O'Carrolls, and MacGuires.

CHAPTER XV

Niall of the Nine Hostages

Niall of the Nine Hostages was the greatest king that Ireland knew between the time of Cormac MacArt and the coming of Patrick. His reign was epochal. He not only ruled Ireland greatly and strongly, but carried the name and the fame, and the power and the fear, of Ireland into all neighbouring nations. He was, moreover, founder of the longest, most important, and most powerful Irish dynasty. Almost without interruption his descendants were Ard-Righs of Ireland for 600 years. Under him the spirit of pagan Ireland upleaped in its last great red flame of military glory, a flame that, in another generation, was to be superseded by a great white flame, far less fierce but far more powerful—and one which, unlike this one, was to shed its light far, far beyond the bounds of neighbouring nations—to the uttermost bounds of Europe. That is the great flame that Patrick was to kindle, and which was to expand and grow, ever mounting higher and spreading farther, year by year, for three hundred years.

And Niall's career was full of drama—romantic and tragic.

Niall was a grandson of Muiredeach Tireach. His father, Eochaid Muigh-medon, son of Muiredeach, became Ard-Righ midway of the fourth century. By his wife, Carthann, daughter of a British king, Eochaid had the son Niall. By another wife, Mong-Fionn, daughter of the King of Munster, Eochaid had four sons, Brian, Fiachra, Ailill, and Fergus. Mong-Fionn was a bitter, jealous and ambitious woman, who set her heart upon having her son, Brian, succeed his father as Ard-Righ. As Niall was his father's favourite, Mong-Fionn did not rest until she had outcast him and his mother, Carthann, and made Carthann her menial, carrying water to the court. The child was rescued by a great poet of that time, Torna,[1] who reared and educated him.

When he had reached budding manhood, Torna brought him back to court to take his rightful place—much to his father's joy. Then Niall, showing strength of character, even in his early youth, took his mother from her menial task, and restored her to her place.

Of Niall's youth there are many legends, but two in particular show the working of his destiny.

One of these legends tells how, on a day, the five brothers being in the smith's forge when it took fire, they were commanded to run and save what they could. Their father, who was looking on (and who, say some, designedly caused the fire, to test his sons), observed with interest Niall's distinctiveness of character, his good sense and good judgment. While Brian saved the chariots from the fire, Ailill a shield and a sword, Fiachra the old forge trough, and Fergus only a bundle of firewood, Niall carried out the bellows, the sledges, the anvil, and anvil-block—saved the soul of the forge, and saved the smith from ruin.

Then his father said: "It is Niall who should succeed me as Ard-Righ of Eirinn."

The other legend tells how, on a day when the five brothers were hunting, and all of them sorely thirsted, they at length discovered a well, in the woods, which, however, was guarded by a withered and ugly, repulsive, old hag, who granted a drink only to such as should first kiss her. Thirsty as they were, neither one of Niall's four brothers could muster enough resolve to pay the price. But Niall unhesitatingly went forward and kissed the ugly old hag—from whom the rags immediately dropped, and the age and witheredness also, disclosing a radiantly beautiful maiden, who was in reality the symbol of sovereignty. Then, before Brian, Fiachra, Ailill, and Fergus were permitted to quench their raging thirst all four of them had to yield to Niall their chances for the kingship—and to swear loyalty to him.

But Mong-Fionn schemed so well that, when Eochaid died at Tara, she had her brother, Crimthann, take the crown, to the exclusion of Niall—with the intention that Crimthann should wear it until her son, Brian, came of age. To her bitter wrath, however, Crimthann, instead of acting as a *roi faineant,* merely filling a gap, threw over Mong-Fionn's control, and made himself a real king, and a powerful, not only ruling Ireland but mak-

[1] Torna was also fosterer of Corc, king of Cashel—one of the three Kings who is said to have been on the board with St. Patrick, at the revision of the laws.

ing successful expeditions abroad against the Picts in Alba, and against the Britons and Romans both in Britain and in Gaul, meeting great success, inspiring respect for his might, and from his foreign campaigns bringing back to Eirinn great booty.

During his almost twenty years' reign the evil and designing, covetous Mong-Fionn never ceased planning for her son Brian's enthroning through the downfall of Crimthann. In her main object she failed. She, however, succeeded in killing Crimthann by poison, but at the cost of her own life; for, to induce him to believe the poison cup harmless—she herself had to drink from it first. To attain her ambition she gave her life—in vain.[2]

Niall's first foreign expedition was to Alba, to subdue the Picts. The little Irish (Scotic) colony in that part of Alba just opposite to Antrim had gradually been growing in numbers, strength, and prestige—until they excited the jealousy and enmity of the Picts, who tried to crush them. Niall fitted out a large fleet and sailed to the assistance of his people. Joined then by the Irish in Alba, he marched against the Picts, overcame them, took hostages from them and had Argyle and Cantire settled upon the Albanach Irish.

After obtaining obedience from the Picts, his next foreign raid was into Britain. When Maximus and his Roman legions were, in consequence of the barbarian pressure upon the Continental Roman Empire, withdrawing from Britain, Niall, with his Irish hosts and Pictish allies, treaded upon their hurrying heels. Yet did the Romans claim victory over Niall. For it is said his was the host referred to by the Roman poet, Claudian, when in praising the Roman general, Stilicho, he says Britain was protected by this bold general.

> "When Scots came thundering from the Irish shores,
> And ocean trembled struck by hostile oars."

Such rare booty was to be got from the retreating Romans that Niall who had had a fleet with him, and had it coast around Britain, crossed the English Channel, and pursued the Romans into Gaul. He had laid Britain helpless, and in the maritime parts of Armorican Gaul must have worked wide devastation.

---

[2] Not only did the Ard-Righship of Eirinn pass from Brian, but the kingship of Connaught, also. This latter fell to Fiachra and his posterity, who, for 700 years after, held it, to the exclusion of Brian and his posterity. The Ard-Righship fell to the more worthy Niall. That was in the last quarter of the fourth century.

Gildas, the ancient British (Welsh) historian, records three great devastations of Britain by the Scots (Irish) and Picts, of which this invasion led by Niall was probably the first.

Niall must have made many incursions into Britain and probably several into Gaul. He carried back hostages, many captives, and great booty from these expeditions. Yet how often out of evil cometh good. It was in one of these Gallic expeditions that the lad Succat, destined under his later name of Patrick to be the greatest and noblest figure Ireland ever knew, was taken in a sweep of captives, carried to Ireland and to Antrim,[3] there to herd the swine of the chieftain, Milcho. Many and many a time, in Alba, in Britain, and in Gaul, must Niall have measured his leadership against the best leadership of Rome, and pitted the courage and wild daring of his Scotic hosts against the skill of the Imperial legions. Yet his fall in a foreign land was to be compassed, not by the strategy or might of the foreign enemy, but by the treachery of one of his own.

He fell on the banks of the River Loire, in France, by the hand of Eochaid, the son of Enna Ceannselaigh, King of Leinster, who, from ambush, with an arrow, shot dead the great king.

Eochaid, coming in the train of Gabran, king of the Alban Dal-Riada, had probably come purposely to France for this chance. The old sore of the Boru Tribute imposed by the Ard-Righ of Tara upon the King of Leinster was, of course, aback of this tragedy. The evils begotten of that deep sore were the immediate cause. Enna Ceannselaigh, King of Leinster, had several times put defeat upon Ard-Righ Eochaid, the father of Niall. Niall himself, since he had become Ard-Righ, had had trouble with the Leinster royal family. And, once, this Eochaid, son of King Enna, taking advantage of Niall's absence on a British expedition, had actually attempted to seize Tara. On Niall's return he punished Leinster for the bold outrage, took Eochaid, and held him at Tara as a hostage. But Eochaid, in the course of time, escaped, and fled for his father's realm. On his way home, near the Liffey, he came to the residence of Laidcenn who was a poet at the court of Niall. Here he wreaked his ire upon the poet's son, killing him. For this unholy violation of the sanctity of a poet's house, even his royal father with all the forces of Leinster would not be able to save him from vengeance sure and swift—which must fall, if he remained in Ireland. Eochaid fled from Ireland, and sheltered him at the court of Gabran, king of the Scottish Dal Riada.

---

[3] Probus' life of Patrick sets him down in Mayo by Croagh Patrick.

The sorrowing poet-father took his own revenge upon Leinster. For a full year, it is said, he satirised that country, and its king and its people, till, in accordance with the ancient belief in the fearful power of a poet's satire "neither corn nor grass, nor other green things, grew there."

When Niall was about to set out upon his final expedition into Britain and Gaul, he had sent command to Gabran to join him with his forces—which gave Eochaid the opportunity of dogging Niall's footsteps abroad, and taking his revenge. Eochaid hid himself in a grove on the banks of the Loire just opposite Niall's camp—and at favourable opportunity speeding an arrow to the great man's heart, ended a notable career.

The victorious host of the Irish, now a sorrowing multitude, had to turn their backs upon victory and Gaul, and bearing the body of their worshipped chief, return to their island, crying loud their lamentations instead of chanting long anticipated pæans of joy.

The slain warrior was laid to rest at Ochain—the honoured place, getting its name, says an old historian, from the mighty sighing and lamentations made by the men of Eirinn at the hiding in earth of their greatest and best.

Niall's reign and life ended in the year 404 A.D.

By two wives Niall is said to have had fourteen sons—eight of whom founding families, and it may be said founding principalities and dynasties, lived to history.

"He was a man," says Gratianus Lucius, "very valiant, most skilled in war. He overcame in several engagements the Albanians, Picts and Gauls, and carried off great numbers of prisoners and of cattle."

Four of these sons, namely, Fiacaid the ancestor of the MacGeoghegans and O'Molloys, Laegaire the ancestor of the O'Quinlans, Conal Crimthanni ancestor of the O'Melaghlains, and Mani ancestor of the MacCatharnys, settled in Meath and adjoining parts, and are since known to history as the Southern Ui Neill (or y Neill). His son, Conal Gulban—against the will and command of his father—led his brothers, Eogan, Carbri, and Enna Fionn to found kingdoms in the northwest of the Island. The instigation of Conal Gulban's disobedient march of conquest was the slaying of his tutor by the Connaughtmen. From Connaught he then conquered the northwest of the Island—the present counties of Donegal and Tyrone, and parts of Derry, Fermanagh, Leitrim, and Sligo. Tir Conal (Donegal) Conal Gulban reserved for himself. Tir Eogan (Tyrone) became the domain of Eogan. The northeast of Sligo and North Leitrim went to Carbri. And Enna Fionn was settled in the southern shoulder of Tir Conal.

Eogan became ancestor of the royal house of O'Neill of Tyrone, and Conal Gulban of the royal house of O'Donnell, of Donegal. Although in later centuries the Kinel Conal and the Kinel Eogan developed a fierce rivalry, so great was the affection between the brother founders of the two families that when Conal Gulban was killed in 464 by a clan of the Firbolgs, on the Plain of Magh Slecht, in the present county of Cavan, his brother, Eogan, within a year after, died of grief.

As was mentioned before, even the kingship of Connaught did not fall to Niall's half-brother, Brian,[4] the favourite of Mong-Fionn. That overlordship went to Fiachra, and was continued to his posterity thenceforward to the 12th century.

Now on the death of Niall, his brother Fiachra's son, Dathi, became Ard-Righ—and followed in Niall's footsteps, leading his armies abroad for foreign conquest, and for the bringing home of foreign spoils. He set out on his career of conquest at the age of seventeen—after a Druid at Tara had told him that he would be conqueror of Alba and impress his power on other foreign lands. He first brought Alba to submission—fighting and overcoming Feredach Finn, King of the Picts. (Conal Gulban, son of Niall, seized hold of that king and killed him against a pillar stone.) Then, as Niall had followed upon the heels of Maximus in his evacuation of Britain, Dathi followed up and hastened the later retreat of Constantine with his Roman legions from that kingdom. He followed them into Gaul—where he was killed by lightning. If it be true, as recorded by the ancient historian, that it was at the foot of the Alps he met his death, we must conclude that Dathi was both a bold and powerful prince.[5]

Dathi's body, too, was borne home over land and sea and was buried in the great cemetery of the Connaught kings, at Cruachan.

From Niall's day onward to the 11th century, this Dathi and his son, Ailill Molt, were the only Ard-Righs that Connaught gave to Tara and Ireland. All the other kings of Tara, for the space of 600 years, were of the family of Niall—usually taken alternately from the Northern Ui Neill and the Southern Ui Neill.

---

[4] Brian is ancestor of the Connaught O'Conors, the O'Reillys, O'Rorkes, O'Flahertys, MacDermotts, and MacDonoughs. Fiachra is the ancestor of the O'Dowds, O'Kevans, O'Hynes, O'Shaughnessys, O'Clerys.

[5] The Abbe MacGeoghegan, chaplain to the Irish brigade in the service of France, and noted Irish historian, says that in his day there still existed in Piedmont a tradition of the invading Irish king being there, and of his having spent a night at the castle of Sales—which latter fact, the Abbe says, was recorded in an ancient registry in the archives of the House of Sales.

The final cancelling of Connaught's claim to the throne of Tara came in the last quarter of the 5th century in about the 20th year of the reign of the aforesaid Ailill Molt—when Lugaid, the son of Laegaire and grandson of Niall, aided by Murchertach MacErca of the Northern Ui Neill, and by the King of Ulad and the King of Leinster, completely overthrew Ailill Molt and the Connaught forces, at the great battle of Ocha. And henceforth, for long centuries the paramount lords of the land were of the family of the great Niall of the Nine Hostages.

CHAPTER XVI

Irish Invasions of Britain

In spite of their apparently isolated position the Irish, from the earliest times, seem to have kept up a fair intercourse with foreign countries—being intimate with Alba (Scotland) and Britain, and somewhat less intimate with France, and with other Continental countries. The ancient traditions of all lands naturally reflect the true manners and customs of those countries, and echo truly the old-time happenings. The ancient Irish tales bristle with references to the aforementioned intercourse, and with evidence that foreigners of diverse races were frequently entertained in Irish courts, foreign mercenaries sometimes employed in Irish wars, and foreign matrimonial alliances occasionally contracted by Irish royal families.

Labraid Loingseach in very distant, pre-Christian days, was said to have brought back from his exile in France two thousand Gallish soldiers, by whom he avenged his grandfather's murder, and put himself upon the throne. The very ancient poetical account of the Battle of Ross-na-ri says that Conor MacNessa (who reigned in Ulster at the beginning of the Christian Era) sent an embassy to some foreign country, and that Cano, a foreigner, went as pilot, to teach them their way over the surface of the sea. The Táin tells us that Queen Maeve (Conor's contemporary) had a number of Gallish mercenaries in her army when she went against Ulster.

British and Pictish visitors are frequent in the old tales—and even the Northmen—these latter almost always as enemies. Saxo Grammaticus says that the Northmen besieged Dublin—or some great fort that stood there—in the first century. Cuchullain, in the old tale, is made to fight a Scandinavian, Swaran, the son of Starno. And the Fianna in the legends had many an encounter with the Northmen. At the battle of Magh

Mochruime (in the final years of the second century), we are told that MacCon had in the army which he led against Art the Lonely many foreigners whom he had gathered with him on his travels—Franks, Saxons, Britons, and Albans. That great old tale, the Bruidean da Dearga, shows Saxons at the court of Conari Mor (in the century before Christ).

Although the Irish were not a sea-going people—in this respect bearing not the remotest comparison with the Northmen—and probably because, unlike the Northmen, their country was so rich and fruitful as not to make sea-going a necessity—yet they seem to have been moderately well equipped for sea-travel and moderately expert in the art. They certainly sailed as far as France, and several of the stories would indicate that they sailed to Spain. But this is highly doubtful. Yet the Book of Rights (said to have been first compiled in the early third century, under direction of Cormac MacArt) informs us that ten ships with beds was part of the yearly tribute paid from the king of Cashel to the Ard-Righ. Part of the Book of Acaill (also said to have been compiled by Cormac MacArt) contains Muir-Brethra, Sea-laws, and defines the rights and duties of foreign trading vessels.

The Annals of Tighernach tell us that in the year 222 Cormac's fleet sailed over the sea for three years. We are told that Niall took his fleet with him when he invaded Britain; that he had it sail around the British Coast, and then convey his army to France. And Cormac's Glossary says that Breccan, grandson of Niall, had a trade fleet of 50 currachs sailing between Ireland and Scotland—which were swallowed up by the whirlpool off Rathlin Island—ever since called Coire-Breccain after him who met disaster there.

There is a tale of how Conal Cearnach, once, at the instigation of Fraech, went over the sea eastward into Britain, over the Muir Nicht to the Continent, over Saxony to the North of Lombardy till he reached the Alps—to recover plunder.[1]

In Patrick's time we find the slave-boy, quitting his slavery, arrive at the sea just in time to catch a ship about to sail for foreign lands. And a little later still, when that troublesome Irish agitator and denouncer of royal vice, Columbanus, is ordered to be deported from France to his own country, they readily find a ship at Nantes, just about to sail for Ireland. These historic happenings imply that there must then have been fairly intimate intercourse between Ireland and other lands.

---

[1] It is scarcely necessary to repeat that the evidential points taken from tales are not set down as facts—but as the probable or possible echoes of facts.

Of course in the pre-Christian days practically all Irish foreign military expeditions were into Alba and Britain.

The Romans, though they valued and held Britain a long time, and even penetrated deep into Alba, never once ventured into Ireland—though it is recorded that at one time they were collecting their forces in the Northeast of Britain, to attempt the Irish conquest. And the Roman general, Agricola, who, in the year 80 A.D. finished the conquest of Britain, evidently considered the conquering of Ireland. His historian son-in-law, Tacitus, mentions how he frequently talked with Agricola on that subject; that Agricola had had an Irish prince (an exile, or a prisoner) from whose talk he concluded that the conquest of Ireland might be accomplished by one Roman legion, and a small number of auxiliary troops. Undoubtedly he formed this conclusion from learning that Ireland (as an ancient Latin historian puts it) contained "sixteen different nations"—by which he meant different tribes. Having successfully won the rule of Britain, by assaulting separately the many tribes of that country, it was a natural conclusion that tribal Ireland should as easily fall into the Roman net. And his conjecture was probably correct. The want of a strong and permanent autocratic central authority in Ireland, commanding the respect and obedience of the various sub-kingdoms and unifying Ireland's power, always left the nation open to the great danger of foreign conquest. Tacitus says that two tribes of the Britons could rarely be got together against the foreign foe. The self-same was always the weakness of Ireland and of all tribal nations.

Yet the Romans never launched their attack against Ireland's independence; though oftentimes they must have been sorely provoked so to do, because of the frequent harassing attacks of the Irish upon their territories in Britain. Their discovery of the fierceness of Irish fighters may have played a part in dissuading them from the Irish venture. The recklessness and persistency of Irish fighting taught them to respect Irish fighters, and Irish commanders. Continental records show that the Romans recruited, anyhow one, and possibly many, Irish regiments, for Continental service. Latin inscriptions have been found on the Rhine front showing that the "Primi Scotti" (First Scots) regiments safeguarded the Roman Empire there. The Emperor Diocletian appointed as Commander in Gaul an Irishman of distinguished ability. This was Carausius, who had charge of the defence of the maritime parts. Eventually they broke with him—and broke him—because, they say, of his greed of gold. However, considering himself as good as his masters, he went into Britain, and set up opposition to them there. He assumed the kingship of the Britons, and as he was an able statesman as well as fine fighter, ruled Britain well for the space of seven years. Carausius was native of an Irish city which the Roman historian calls "Menapia[2] in Ireland." It was in the reign of Carbri Lifeachar over Ireland that this, his brother Irishman, was ruling over Britain.

Of course various kings of Ireland were, at various times, styled kings of Britain also. And parts of Britain, if not all of it, paid tribute to these Irish overlords. Cormac's Glossary tells that the first lap-dog was brought into Ireland by Irish envoys who were collecting the Irish tribute from south-western England. "For at that time," says the Glossary, "the sway of the Gaels was great over the Britons. They divided Alba between them, and each one knew the habitation of his friends." (Which is to say that the various resident Irish lords or deputies in Britain, were thickly located, in touch one with another.) "And," it continues, "the Gaels did not carry on less agriculture at the east of the seas, than at home in Scotia. And they erected habitations and regal forts there."

Roman coins, some probably taken in tribute, some in war booty, and some in trade, have been found in various parts of Ireland. Gold coins of the times of Theodosius and Valentinian, and copper coins of Nero, have been found in Meath, Antrim, and Derry, respectively.

Though, because of the independent tribal system and consequent want of cohesion, the Irish nation was weak for defence, yet was it strong for offence—and could, and did, again and again, brave the best of the Roman legions. It was their wonderful discipline and their weight of numbers that enabled the Romans to overcome the bold Irish attacks in Britain. And when at length Rome, threatened by the invading hordes nearer home, had to call back from her island outposts, legion after legion of her soldiers, and that her army in Britain was weakened, the Irish (Scots, as they were always called by the Roman historians) in alliance with the Picts, helped to push south the garrisons that were left and eventually to crowd them off the island.

Britain was then left at the mercy of her northern and western neighbours, and as the British had grown effete under Roman occupation, and were no longer fighters, they suffered fearfully from these invasions.

It was after the destruction of Emania (A.D. 331) that the Irish and Pictish invasions of Britain assumed their most serious phase. The Connaught royal house and its kin was then securely established over the greater part of Ireland—and probably because of this easy security at

[2] Ptolemy, a couple of centuries earlier, also mentions this Irish city. It has not been identified by our historians.

home the Irish fighters had both time and inclination to look abroad for that excitement and adventure which was the breath of their nostrils. Soon, so successfully and so threateningly did they carry on their British operations that in 343 the Emperor himself, Constantine, had to take personal charge of repelling them.

Marcellinus records another invasion of the Picts and Scots in the year 360—when they proved a terror to the Romans—and still another in 364, at the inconvenient time when Gaul was being ravaged by Continental enemies of the Empire—and yet again in 368. He always refers to them as the Scots. (The country which we now call Scotland was then inhabited by the Picts in the North, and by the Caledonii in the South. The colony of Scots from Ireland which later gave the country its name, was still an insignificant tribe clinging to the islands and headlands opposite Antrim.)

Probably this latter invasion, as well as some subsequent ones, was conducted by the Ard-Righ Crimthann, uncle of Niall. Irish records say that Crimthann the Great reigned over Britain (meaning, of course, a chief part of Britain) for 13 years, from 366 to 379. The Roman general, Theodosius, father of the Emperor of that name, led the Roman legions against this victorious Irish king, and finally drove him out. The Roman poet, Claudian, says: "And Theodosius, following the Scots through all windings, broke the waves of the Hyperborean Sea with his adventurous oars." From references in the writings of the Romans, it is evident that the Irish and the Picts had at various times made treaty with them. Ammianus Marcellinus, speaking of the invasion of 360, says that those nations "had broken the agreed peace in the British provinces."

In 386 the invaders, successfully fighting their way, had almost reached the gates of London. Theodosius overcame and drove them back.

The British historian Gildas, records three great invasions of the allied fighters, the Picts and the Scots—in 396, 418 and 426. For their attacks had then grown fiercer—as the Roman garrison in Britain had been depleted for much needed service against the Continental invaders of the Empire. Each time the Britons had to beg their Roman conquerors to return and protect them. They sent embassies to Rome thus entreating. By command of the Romans they made the great dike across their Northern boundary from sea to sea, to keep out the invaders. But the Romans were scarcely gone when the invaders came flying over the dike. And the Britons had once more to cry out for Roman protection. The next time that the Romans returned to free them from their oppressors, they ordered the Britons to put up a defence of solid masonwork across their country. And in consequence was built the great Roman wall, 12 feet high and 8 feet thick—extending from sea to sea.

But walls were useless against these persevering and indomitable invaders. The Britons tediously had to appeal to Rome again. In their appeal they said that their "barbarian" enemies drove them upon the sea, and the sea threw them back upon the barbarians, so that they were either slaughtered or drowned.

In the year 450 the Britons, to save themselves from their enemies, chose as their king a strong man, Vortigern, who, it is claimed by some, was Irish, his proper title being Mor-Tigearna (high-lord).

Finally, to free themselves from the yoke of their neighbours, the British in 474 invited over Hengis and Horsa with their Saxon host. They readily came, cleared the country of the Picts and Scots, and then appropriated it for themselves. The poor harried Britons had exchanged one yoke for another.

A long while after, the Irish were still dominating Wales. One particularly important Irish invasion of Wales, an account of which is contained in an ancient Welsh manuscript, was conducted by an Irish commander, whom they named Ganfael, which probably stands for Ceannfaelad—and who may have been Ceannfaelad, son to King Blathmac, mentioned by the Four Masters under date 670. After this conquest of Wales, the Welsh account says that the Irish ruled there for 59 years. They were driven out by Caswallawn.

Sullivan, in his introduction to O'Curry, says that for a long time Wales was ruled by chiefs who were not only Irish but probably owed allegiance to Irish kings.

The Christian faith which the whole Irish people imbibed so readily from Patrick during the fifth century caused a radical change in their character. After that century, there is not, with the exception of the presumed Welsh conquest, any other recorded instances of military raids abroad. If we compare the history of Ireland in the 6th century, after Christianity was received, with that of the 4th century, before the coming of Christianity, the wonderful change and contrast is probably much more striking than any other such change in any other nation known to history.

CHAPTER XVII

General Review of Pagan Ireland

Before quitting the story of the Race in its pagan days, let us see definitely just what stage of civilisation the Irish people had now reached.

In the centuries before St. Patrick the keen and inquiring, intellectual, ones at the Irish courts must have had a fair general knowledge of what was transpiring in the intellectual and commercial world around the Mediterranean. And in turn that world must have had a general knowledge of Ireland and its circumstances. Ptolemy's second century map of Ireland with its good, general outline of the shape and proportions of the Island, and of its coastline, and the generally correct details marked upon it, is a surprise to those who took it for granted that Hibernia or Ierna was little more than a name to the learned of Greece and Rome in the first century of the Christian Era. The general correctness, for instance, with which Ptolemy traces the River Shannon, and other rivers and lakes, is significant—as well as his properly locating such royal sites as Ailech, and Emain Macha.

Marcianus Heracleota, in the third century, was acquainted with sixteen different Irish clans, and records that there were in Ireland eleven cities of note. These assemblages of habitations which he called cities were not of course those commerical centres which the Romans usually knew as cities. They were evidently the great assemblages of habitations that gathered around a royal court. When we note that Tara had twenty acres of raths, that these raths were covered with residences of the leading ones, and that we might naturally expect, in addition, other many hundreds of residences—habitations of the common people—upon the plain and around the foot of the hill, we may well understand the meaning of Marcianus' "eleven cities of note." (We may here add that the chief structures then were almost always built of wood—with some bronze—while the habitations of the general mass of the people were constructed of upright poles supporting walls of wicker work, or else were simple bothies.)

But in the first century of the Christian Era, Tacitus tells us that the Irish ports were well known to commerce and to merchants. The Phœnicians undoubtedly carried on a fair trade between the Mediterranean and Ireland. The very fertile island, fruitful in soil, and not poor in minerals, had much to give to the Mediterranean traders, and much to get from them. When their ships sailed into the various Irish ports, we can readily see the Phœnician agents travelling thence, at head of bands of burdened slaves, white, and brown, and black, bent under the rich merchandise of Tyre and Sidon—penetrating the country, to the various inland royal courts, to the duns of the chiefs and brughaids, and to the many great fairs, for which Ireland was then distinguished. And we can see them returning, laden with the wealth of Ireland's woods and vales, and of her earth—pelts and metals and ores, and corn; rare products, too, of her weaver's shuttle; fancy ones of her women's needle; and delicate work of her craftsmen. Around the big blazing fire, at the Court, in the evening, we can hear these merchants, mellowed by Irish mead, enchanting the king, the king's scholars, his warriors and visitors, with account of the works and the wars, and the laws and the lore, the statesmen, the orators, the poets and historians, of their far fascinating world. And we can furthermore see occasional ambitious natives—with that roving disposition for which a few centuries later they became noted, if not notorious, on the Continent—some thirsting for knowledge, and some for adventure, returning with the merchants to their ships, and sailing away to the far lands that seemed haloed in glory. Most of these adventurers were eventually swallowed up in oblivion, so far as concerned the land and the kin that they left; though it is certain in later years there were not a few citizen ornaments of the far-flung proud Roman Empire, who, if from them were torn the toga, would stand revealed exiles of Eirinn—such, for instance, as the great Latin poet Sedulius (Seadhal), the Christian Virgil, and the noted Roman lawyer and famous heresiarch Celestius (Cellach), of whom we shall treat in a future chapter.

Undoubtedly Ireland was then rich in metals, and the hands of its unsurpassed craftsmen deftly wrought from them not only the utilitarian article, but also ornaments whose beauty astonishes connoisseurs today. From the common sickle of the far-away bronze age to the delicately beautiful spear of days only a little less ancient, and to the beautiful, spiral-decorated bronze ornaments—of all of which, rare specimens still exist—Ireland can show samples of pre-Christian metalwork which in perfectness are paralleled by the productions of few of the most ancient countries.

The Céird or metalworker, in ancient Ireland, was ever a highly-honoured craftsman, who, because of the beauty and excellence of his work, ranked among the nobles. And the soil of Ireland is still wealthy with the buried evidences of his superb artistry.

Here may be mentioned, too, the very ancient art of enamelling, in which the early Irish artists excelled. Philostrates, a Greek teacher in the Imperial Palace in Rome at the time of Septimus Severus (about 200 A.D.) is supposedly referring to the Irish, when he describes, as a new art to him, enamels which he examined on the horse trappings of "barbarians who live in the ocean." (To the egotistical Roman all who lived beyond Roman influence and did not adopt Roman culture, were "barbarians.") Very beautiful examples of this Irish enamel work can be seen on those two venerable and beautiful treasures, the Ardach chalice, and the Cross of Cong. And though these articles are hoary with antiquity, the enamel craftsmanship shown on them, was in its turn hoary when they themselves were new.

Ireland was rich in gold. It was the one country above all others in Western Europe that was distinguished for its gold wealth. Professor Mentelius says that the ancient gold of Scandinavia came chiefly from Ireland "which during the bronze age was one of the lands in Europe richest in gold."[1] The ancient gold ornaments preserved in the National Museum in Dublin weigh 570 ounces; while in the British Museum the total gold ornament collection from England, Wales and Scotland combined, is only 50 ounces.

The ancient seanachies in the olden tales constantly convey to us an impressive sense of the lavishness with which the precious metals were, in those times, used. In quoting from the tale of the Bruidean Da Dearga the poetic description of the maiden Edain, dressing at the fountain, O'Curry says that the old writer might well be charged with too extravagant fiction, if we did not still have, in proof of its accuracy, the combs, the gracefully carved caskets of gold, the clasps and the fastenings, and the gold balls in which the ends of the ladies' flowing locks were anciently inserted.

> "There was of old an admirable illustrious king over Eirinn, whose name was Eochaid Fedleach. He on one occasion passed over the fair-green of Bri Leith, where he saw a woman on the brink of a fountain, having a comb and a casket of silver, ornamented with

---

[1] In the year 1796 nuggets of native gold weighing 7 ounces, 9 ounces, 18 and 22 ounces were picked up in a mountain stream that flows between Wicklow and Wexford.

> gold, washing her head in a silver basin with four birds of gold perched upon it, and little sparkling gems of crimson carbuncle upon the outer edges of the basin. A short, crimson cloak, with a beautiful gloss, lying near her; a brooch of silver, inlaid with sparkles of gold, in that cloak. A smock, long and warm, gathered and soft, of green silk, with a border of red gold, upon her. Wonderful clasps of gold and silver at her breast, and at her shoulder-blades, and at her shoulders in that smock, on all sides. The sun shone upon it, while the men (that is the king, and his retinue) were all shaded in red, from the reflection of the gold against the sun, from the green silk. Two golden-yellow tresses upon her head, each of them plaited with four locks or strands, and a ball of gold upon the point of each tress. The color of that hair was like the flowers of the bog fir in the summer, or like red gold immediately after receiving its coloring. And there she was disentangling her hair, and her two arms out through the bosom of her smock."

Silver and bronze ornament, also, were plentifully used then. The old story-teller is of course idealising some realities that must have been in themselves both rich and beautiful, when he gives a description of the dun, which Cormac MacArt entered in the Land of Promise. "He saw there a very large house with its rafters of bronze, and its wattling of silver, and a thatch of the wings of white birds. And he saw too a sparkling well within the lis, and five streams issuing from it, and the hosts around drinking the waters of these streams."

The reader will remember that at the Feis of Cruachan and of Emain Macha were held examinations for the various kinds of craftsmen. Sixty persons of each craft were selected at each feis, and assigned each to his own district. But even then, before he could practice in that district, the chosen craftsmen had to be finally examined and approved by the Saoi-re-Céird or master mechanic of his own craft, in that district.

Speaking of two pieces of a Pagan Irish bronze ornament preserved in the Petrie Museum, Miss Stokes says: "If they are not the finest pieces of casting ever seen, yet, as specimens of design and workmanship they are, perhaps, unsurpassed." And she quotes the authority Kemble, the author of "Horae Ferales," who says of them: "For beauty of design and execution, they may challenge comparison with any specimen of bronze work that it has ever been my fortune to see." Those few words from these two eminent authorities, more strikingly impress upon us the wonderful advance of art in pre-Christian Ireland than could volumes written upon the subject.

Evidence of beautiful Irish art, in days more ancient still, is found in the delicately ornamented burial urns of beautiful form, that have been dug up out of ancient raths, and taken out of the very ancient Irish sepulchres. Some of these urns are pottery, some are stone—evidencing the forwardness of the Irish mind in the remote and supposedly primitive Stone Age. Also, the great dome-roofed sepulchres of the royal cemeteries on the Boyne, wherein the beautiful urns containing the ashes of the dead were preserved, are admirable evidences of the singular advancement of ancient Ireland among the countries of the West—as also are the much later, but still very ancient, pre-Christian, gigantic stone forts like those of Dun Aengus on the island of Aran, and Ailech in Inishowen, with their great walls of marvellously fine construction.

Apropos of modes of burial in pre-Christian days, of interest is Caoilte's description of one. In an ancient tale in the Book of the Dun Cow, this old Fenian warrior, returned to earth from his long sojourn in the enchanted palaces of the Tuatha De Danann, is called upon to settle a dispute about a happening which was now history, but which befell during his former days on earth—the death of King Eochaid Airgtech (who was slain in battle in Antrim, A.D. 280). Caoilte says: "There is a chest of stone about him there in the earth; there upon the chest are two bracelets of silver, and his bunne-do-ats (ancient ornaments) and his neck torque of silver. And by his tomb there is a stone pillar, and on the end of the pillar that is in the earth is an Ogham which says: 'Here Eochaid Airgtech. Caoilte slew me in an encounter against Finn.' "

It is generally assumed that, for making short, important records, the early Irish used the ogham style of writing, represented by numbers of straight lines upon both sides of the edge-angle of a flag or tablet of wood. The ogham letters are named for trees. They follow in an order totally different from the order of the letters in all other alphabets. The Irish call this alphabet Beth-luis-nion—the three syllables of which word are the three first letters (b, l, n) of that alphabet. Great numbers of ogham stones have been found in Ireland, and the form of the language used on them points to the conclusion that these stones are mainly from pre-Christian times. Though it is the opinion of some noted scholars that ogham was introduced into Ireland at or immediately after the coming of Christianity. Anyhow, the ogham writing continued to be used down to the sixth and even the seventh century. The Continental Celtologist Zeuss who was profoundly impressed with the great antiquity of it, found ogham among the glosses on a copy of Priscian, which emanated from the Swiss-Irish school and monastery of St. Gall—glosses that were written by

Irishmen in the 7th or 8th century. He concluded that the Irish in pagan days wrote only in ogham.

Several leading scholars agree, however, that books were written in Ireland for a long time before the coming of Patrick. Says Dr. Todd: "That a pagan literature existed in Ireland before Patrick, and that some of it is preserved, is highly probable." He points out that some fragments found in the Brehon Laws show internal evidence of pagan origin, and of high antiquity. O'Curry says that St. Patrick found the country teeming with men distinguished for their acquirements in the native language and literature, if not in other languages; philosophers, Druids, poets, judges. "Even at that remote period," he says, "we were a nation not entirely without a native literature, and a national cultivation sufficient to sustain a system of society, and an internal political government so enlightened that, as our history proves, Christianity did not teach us to subvert, but rather endeavored to unite with it; a system, moreover, which had sufficient vitality to remain in full force through all the vicissitudes of the country, even till many ages after the intrusion of the Anglo-Normans, in the twelfth century—who themselves indeed found it so just and comprehensive that they adopted it in preference to the laws of the countries from which they came."

There is foreign evidence, too, of a pre-Christian Irish literature. In the fourth century of the Christian Era there was produced on the Continent a work, *Cosmographia Aethici Istrii*, compiled by a Christian philosopher of that time, in which are recorded the observations of Aethicus of Istria on his travels in various countries. He tells of visiting Ireland and remaining there some time, examining the books of the Irish, about which he, in egotistical Latin way is scornful. From Orosius' history Joyce quotes the terse account of his visit to Ireland—"He hastened (from Spain) to Hibernia and remained there some time examining their volumes; and he called them (*i.e.*, the Irish sages) *ideomochos* or *ideohistas*, that is, unskilled toilers or uncultivated teachers."

The hard-headed Scotch-Englishman, Fergusson, concludes that from the time of Cormac MacArt (middle of the third century) the Irish had books. In his View of the State of Ireland, Edmund Spenser (who so frequently derides the Irish people among whom he spent days both pleasant and profitable) says: "It is certain that Ireland hath had the use of letters very auncientlY and long before England. Whence they had those letters it is hard to say . . . but that they had letters auncientlY is nothing doubtful, for the Saxons of England are said to have their letters and learning, and learned them from the Irish, and that also appeareth by the likeness of the character, for the Saxon character is the same with the Irish."

After the Seanchus Mor was compiled by a council of the learned ones under direction of St. Patrick—a collection of the old laws expurgated and Christianised—various accounts agree in stating that he committed to the flames a pile of old pagan volumes—some say up to two hundred. But it is probable that this conclusion about Patrick burning the pagan books may, by the old authorities, have been arrived at rather by inference than instance.

In both the Book of Ballymote and the Book of Lecan there is an ancient Irish grammar, in four parts, in which the Gaelic language is elaborately compared with the Latin, and occasionally with the Greek and Hebrew. The first three parts of this grammar are attributed to pre-Christian Irish scholars, and only the fourth to an ante-Patrician scholar, the celebrated Ceann Faelad—a remarkable man in many ways. Some who believe that he is rightly credited with part four of the book, also think that he revised, or rewrote, or was himself the author of, the other three parts.

There is an ancient metrical life of St. Patrick attributed to Fiacc—who, when Patrick came, had been a disciple and pupil of the court poet, Dubtach, and whom Patrick converted and chose as one of his disciples. It contains one hundred and thirty-six lines in the most ancient style, idiom, and rhythm of the Gaelic. The oldest existing copy is contained in a remarkable collection, that is more than a thousand years old, the Liber Hymnorum. Several noted antiquarians express their belief that this remarkable hymn or poem is the genuine work of him to whom it was attributed. If the work be really Fiacc's, then, though it was written in Christian days, it is obviously the fruit of pagan culture.

The same, of course, is true of the Seanachus Mor, that wonderful code of laws compiled under Patrick. Sullivan, in his introduction to O'Curry, treating of the Brehon Laws, proves that the fundamental principles of them belong to very early pagan times—and says that the latest period at which those institutions could have attained their *full* development was in the seventh or eighth century.

Among shining lights of pagan Ireland, Keating enumerates—a famous wise Brighitt of whom survives the phrase "Briathra Brighdi," the Sayings of Brighitt; Conla of the Mild Judgments, a Connaught sage; the two Senchans; Morann, the son of Maen; Fercertni, the poet; Neidi, the son of Adna; Athairni; Fergus, his son; Feradach the Just; Fithil the Sage; Fergus, the poet; Dubthach O'Lugair; and Rossa, the son of Tirchin (the last three of whom laid the old laws before St. Patrick). And he points out on ancient authority, that in pagan times in Ireland so high was the ethical standard that no one could hold the rank of Ollam ri-Seanchus, or Doctor of History, who once falsified a fact, and that no one could hold the rank of Brehon, or Doctor of Law, who had once given a corrupt judgment.

Finally, it is to be remembered that the late Professor Zimmer (of the University of Berlin) most eminent of recent Celtologists on the Continent, concludes that Irish schools had begun to be known on the Continent before the coming of Patrick—by the end of the fourth century.

Altogether, the mass of evidence is strongly in favour of the supposition that Ireland was in the enjoyment of letters long before the introduction of Christianity.

While there is much evidence to show that the pagan Irish indulged in the sun worship which their ancestors brought with them from the East, there is also some little ancient evidence, including a sentence from the pen of St. Patrick himself, betraying that some idol worship must have been practised there, likewise. Though it is quite possible that this idol worship may have pertained not to the Milesian but to one or other of the subject races on the Island.

The idol, Crom Cruach, which stood on the plain of Magh Slecht (near Ballymagauran, in Cavan) before which the ancient Tighernmas and his host, long centuries before Christ, were stricken with sudden death, on the eve of Samain (Hallow Eve) was destroyed, it is said, by Patrick. The image or the pillar of Crom Cruach was said to be of gold and silver (probably covered with these metals) and around it were twelve other images or pillars of brass or bronze.

Before St. Patrick's time O'Curry says the instruction of youth seems to have been in the hands of the Filés (philosophers) and the Druids. The instruction was sometimes given indoors, but oftentimes in the open air. And frequently the teaching was carried on as the master and his pupils travelled from place to place over the country.

The Druid is frequently mentioned in the old Irish tales and poems. The Irish word Draoi is used—which, by general acceptance, is rendered Druid. However, there seems to have been very great ceremonial difference at least between the Druidism of Ireland (if it was Druidism) and the Druidism of Wales and Gaul. But to the Irish, as to the Continental Druid, fire and water were sacred elements. The holy wells of all Christian days, from Patrick's time to the present, were still holy in pagan times. And the festive bon-fires still lighted on all hills of Ireland on Midsummer Night (which term we apply to the night of June 23rd) with torches from which, even in the present generation, the sacred circle of fire was drawn around the growing crop to insure both its protection and its fruitfulness—and through the embers of which the cattle were, for their blessing, driven—

these bon-fires are assuredly of pagan origin, marking a great sun feast, on that day on which the Sun-god was supposed to be longest above the horizon. The Irish name for May-day, Baltinne, meaning the fire of Bal, or the sun, commemorates another of the great sun festivals of our forefathers. And the title Bal given to the sun-god is the same title which the faraway ancestors of the Milesians knew and reverenced in the far Eastern land, before their chronicled wanderings began. Patrick had to preach against this sun worship—"All those who adore it," he says in his Confession, "shall in misery and wretchedness be given unto punishment."

That frequent and much reverenced character, the Draoi, is said, by some, including John D'Alton, to have been, not at all a Druid priest, but a wiseman and instructor. There were two of these, namely, Luchru and Lugad the Bald, who, at the court of King Laegaire, met, encountered, and tried to overthrow Patrick, when he first appeared there. Other two of them, Mal and Caplait, were at the royal palace of Cruachan, instructing the two beautiful daughters of the king, Eithne the Fair and Fedelm the Ruddy.

Most famous of Irish Druids was Mogh Ruith, a great Munster magician—of whom is the legend that after having exhausted all the secret knowledge of these islands, he went with his clever daughter, Tlachtga, to Italy, to Simon Magus, to assist him in his contention with the Apostles. With the aid of Simon Magus they constructed a dread, magical wheel, the Roth Ramach, Rolling Wheel—which rolled along the skies, blinded all who saw, and killed all who touched it.

In these pre-Christian days the paradise of the Gael, to which went the good and the heroic, was beneath the hills, or far off under the sea. It is variously named—Magh Mell, the Plain of Pleasure: Tir-Tairnigri, the Land of Promise; I-Breasil, the Isle of the Blessed; or Tir na n-Og, the Land of Perpetual Youth—"a land wherein there is not save truth, and where is neither age nor decay, sorrow nor gladness, nor envy nor jealousy, hatred nor haughtiness."

Midir, a chief immortal of the immortal Tuatha De Danann whose paradise was under the hill of Bri Leith, in Longford, very finely describes this paradise, in his poetic address to Queen Edain, when he surprised her, with her fifty beautiful maidens, bathing at Inver.

"O Befind! wilt thou come with me
　To a wonderful land that is mine,
Where the hair is like the blossom of the golden *sobarche*,
　Where the tender body is as fair as snow.

"There shall be neither grief nor care;
White are the teeth, black the eyebrows,
Pleasant to the eye the number of our host;
On every cheek is the hue of the foxglove.

"Crimson of the plain is each brake,
Delightful to the eye the blackbird's eggs;
Though pleasant to behold are the plains of Inisfail,
Rarely wouldst thou think of them after frequenting the Great Plain.

"Though intoxicating thou deemest the ales of Inisfail,
More intoxicating are the ales of the good land—
The wonderful land—the land I speak of,
Where youth never grows to old age.

"Warm sweet streams traverse the land,
The choicest of mead and wine;
Handsome people without blemish,
Conception without sin, without stain.

"We see every one on every side,
And no one seeth us;
The cloud of Adam's transgression
Has caused this concealment of us from them.

"O lady, if thou comest to my valiant people,
A diadem of gold shall be on thy head;
Flesh of swine, all fresh, banquets of new milk and ale,
Shalt thou have with me there, O Befind!"[2]

Many of the noted heroes of old were borne away in the body to the pagan paradise. Oisin, it will be remembered, was taken there, and his comrade-in-arms, Caoilte: and Conla, the son of Conn, was by a fairy maiden carried there in a crystal boat. The famous Voyage of Bran, one of the finest of ancient Irish stories, gives an account of Bran's search, over the

[2] Translated by Dr. Joyce.

Among modern poets who have described the enchanted land, one of the many beautiful descriptions is by Ethna Carbery in her "Four Winds of Eirinn"—

western wave, for that coveted land. He found the happy isles of paradise—and sailed among them for hundreds of years. At last venturing home to Kerry one of his company jumped on shore, and became a heap of dust. Laegaire of Connaught with fifty men reigns in Magh Mell—jointly with Fiachna who had gone before him.

The voyage of St. Brendan, too, was in search of this Land of Promise.

For that enchanted land did not fade away before the light of Christianity. Even to many of the spiritual-minded, present-day dwellers on the Western margin of Ireland, Tir n'an-Og or I-Breasil, exists under the sea, just at the horizon's rim. Some rarely blessed people still alive, have, on

---

I-BREASIL

There is a way I am fain to go—
To the mystical land where all are young,
Where the silver branches have buds of snow,
And every leaf is a singing tongue.

It lies beyond the night and day,
Over shadowy hill, and moorland wide,
And whoso enters casts care away,
And wistful longings unsatisfied.

There are sweet white women, a radiant throng,
Swaying like flowers in a scented wind;
But between us the veil of earth is strong,
And my eyes to their luring eyes are blind.

A blossom of fire is each beauteous bird,
Scarlet and gold on melodious wings,
And never so haunting a strain was heard
From royal harp in the Hall of Kings.

The sacred trees stand in rainbow dew,
Apple and ash and the twisted thorn,
Quicken and holly, and dusky yew,
Ancient ere ever grey Time was born.

The oak spreads mighty beneath the sun
In a wonderful dazzle of moonlight green—
Oh, would I might hasten from tasks undone,
And journey whither no grief hath been!

Were I past the mountains of opal flame,
I would seek a couch of the king-fern brown,
And when from its seed glad slumber came,
A flock of rare dreams would flutter down.

occasion, seen it on a beautiful summer's eve rise over the sea, in all its intoxicating, indescribable, beauty. And more than once have courageous fishermen tried to reclaim it for mortal man—but ever in vain—and sometimes, also, with dire result to the adventurous one.[3]

But I move without in an endless fret,
  While somewhere beyond earth's brink afar,
Forgotten of men, in a rose-rim set,
  I-Breasil shines like a beckoning star.

The Irish scholar O'Flaherty in 1684 in his "Iar Connacht" tells: "There is now living Morrogh O'Ley, who imagines he was himself personally in O'Brazil,"—he went there from Aran—and came back to Galway 6 or 8 years later and began (as a result) to practise "both chirurgery and phisick, and so continues ever since to practise, tho' he never studied or practised either all his life time before, as all we that knew him since a boy can averr." Hardiman says the story now is that the Book of O'Brazil was given him there—but he was not to open it for seven years.

O'Flaherty relates that about 20 years before he wrote, a boat out of the Owles, blown west by night, next day about noon spied land so near that they could see sheep grazing on shore—yet dared not touch shore, imagining it was O'Brazil. They were two days coming back toward home.

In the early 17th century Leslie of Glasslough, Co. Monaghen (ancestor of the present Leslie family there) secured a grant of I-Breasil when it should be recovered—such recovery or disenchantment being considered imminent then (as it was in every generation). Hardiman in his "Irish Minstrelsy" reprints a letter sent from W. Hamilton of Derry in 1674 to a friend in London advising him of the discovery, a few weeks before, and practical recovery, of I-Breasil, by the Captain of a Killybegs schooner. The curious account is given in most circumstantial detail—and Hamilton asks his friend to inform young Leslie of the good news, that he may claim the land under his father's patent.

[3] Sometimes the spiritual Celt even in those pagan times had a paradise here on earth. Such was the case in the reign of Geide Ollgotach, Geide of the great voice, so called, says the Book of Leinster, because of the peaceful, harmonious character of his reign, when the people heard each other's words and voices, with the same delight as if they had been the strings of the melodious harp of Ben-Crotta.

SELECTION OF WORKS DEALING WITH THE VARIOUS PERIODS AND PHASES OF PAGAN IRELAND

Carbery, Ethna: In the Celtic Past (Stories of Ancient Ireland).

D'Alton, John: Prize Essay on Irish Hist. (Proc. R. I. A.).

Henderson, Geo., M.A., Ph.D.: Fled Bricrend, the Feast of Briciu, Irish Text, Translation and Notes.

Hull, Miss Eleanor: The Cuchullin Saga in Irish Literature.

Hyde, Douglas, LL.D.: A Literary History of Ireland, from the Earliest Times to the Present Day.

Jones, the Rev. Wm. Basil, M.A.: Vestiges of the Gael in Gwynedd (North Wales).

Joyce, P. W.: Social History of Ancient Ireland.

Jubainville, H. D'Arbois de: Le Cycle Mythologique Irlandais et la Mythologie Celtique. Cours de Litterature Celtique.

Keating's History of Ireland (Translated by Jno. O'Mahony).

Meyer, Kuno: The Courtship of Emer, Translation (without Text) Archaeol. Rev., 1888.

MacGeoghegan Abbé: History of Ireland.

MacNeill, Eoin: Some Phases of Irish History.

Nutt, Alfred: The Voyage of Bran: Essays on the Irish "Other World" or Pagan Heaven and on the Celtic Doctrine of Re-birth.

—— Ossian and the Ossianic Literature.

—— Cuchulainn, the Irish Achilles.

O'Curry, Eugene: Manuscript Materials of Irish History.

—— Manners and Customs of the Ancient Irish.

O'Donovan, Jno., LL.D.: Annals of the Four Masters (Translation and Notes).

O'Halloran's History of Ireland.

Ossianic Society: Transactions of.

Petrie, Geo.: On the History and Antiquities of Tara Hill.

Rhys, Jno., M.A., D.Litt.: Early Irish Conquests of Wales and Dumnonia: in Proc. Roy. Soc. Antiq., Ireland, 1890–91.

Stokes, Whitley, D.C.L., LL.D.: Bruden Da Derga: the Destruction of Da Derga's Hostel; Rev. Celt. XXII.

Sullivan, W. K., Ph.D.: Introduction to O'Curry's Manners and Customs of the Ancient Irish.

—— Tain bo Chuailnge (The Táin).

Wakeman, Wm. F.: Handbook of Irish Antiquities: Pagan and Christian.

Wilde, Sir Wm., M.D.: Catalogue of Irish Antiquities.

——— The Boyne and Blackwater.
Wood-Martin, Col. W. G.: Pagan Ireland.
——— Traces of the Elder Faiths of Ireland, 1902.
——— Rude Stone Monuments.

CHAPTER XVIII

Irish Christianity Before St. Patrick

While St. Patrick was unquestionably the evangeliser of Ireland, there is now hardly a doubt remaining in the minds of the scholars that Christianity had foothold on the Island before he came—and long before, think some.

In A.D. 431, a year before the coming of Patrick on his Christian mission, Palladius (who, by one authority, John Sichard, is even said to have been himself an Irishman) was sent by the Pope "ad Scotos in Christum credente"—to the Irish believing in Christ—which words clearly show Rome to have been impressed with the fact that the Irish Christians then were of some numerical importance.

"It is universally admitted," says George Stokes, "that there were Christian congregations in Ireland before Palladius came."

It is an interesting curiosity to find told among the ancients—as recorded by Eusebius and Nicephorus—that some of the apostles visited the Western Islands. Julian of Toledo says that James addressed a canonical letter from Ireland to the Jews in Spain. And Vincentius of Bauvais says that James, the son of Zebedee, preached in Ireland and that when he returned to Jerusalem—where he was martyred—he took with him seven Irish disciples.

Usher quotes Nicephorus' Ecclesiastical History as saying that Simon Zelotus brought the Gospel to these islands, and was crucified in Britain.

St. Paul is also mentioned as having been in these Western lands.

Reference has been made to the tradition of Conal Cearnach's visit to Jerusalem. Richardson (Prael. Ecc. History) says he brought back the faith to Conor MacNessa, and others of the Ultach, and that several Irish went to Jerusalem to be baptised.

While the foregoing are set down as interesting curiosities, it is still an easy matter to conclude, as a result of the frequent intercourse between Ireland and the Romanised possessions of both Britain and Gaul, and of the interchange of war captives and refugees likewise, and the coming and going of travellers, that the doctrines of Christianity, which in the early centuries were promulgated with such ardour and spread to the earth's ends with such amazing rapidity, must have been conveyed to Ireland from many sources, and through many channels—and that these new strange doctrines must have been many times examined and frequently debated by the scholars at the Irish courts, ever eager to discuss the doings of the outside world.

Although Christianity did not obtain a hold upon the minds of the mass of the British people until Augustine, to some extent, and the Irish missionaries, in the main, carried the doctrines of Christ to them, it is known that there was Christianity in Britain in the latter half of the first century of the Christian Era—obviously conveyed there by ardent Continental Christians in the Roman legions. And at the Council of Arles (in the year 314) a few British bishops were in attendance.

Bollandus says that Palladius probably found in Ireland more Christians than he made. And that some Irish Christians figured prominently on the Continent of Europe in the pre-Patrician days is fairly well established by Continental records. "It is evident," says Dr. Todd, "there were Irish Christians on the Continent of Europe before the mission of St. Patrick, some of whom had attained to considerable literary and ecclesiastical eminence." He refers to, among others, Mansuy or Mansuetus of Toul, and says that in all probability he was an Irishman, distinguished as an eminent Christian missionary about a century before Patrick. Mansuy was sent from Rome to be first Bishop of Toul (in Lorraine). His tenth century metrical biographer, the abbot Adso, shows that Mansuy's Irish nativity was then taken for granted:

> "Insula Christicolas gestabat Hibernia gentes,
> Unde genus, traxil, et satus inde fuit."
> (Hibernia's soil was rich in Christian grace;
> There Mansuy saw the light, there lived his noble race.)

Near Toul more than half a century before Patrick's day, in the time of the apostate Julian, and, say some, in the presence of Julian, was martyred St. Eliphius, with his brother, Eucharius, and their sisters—who, says Peter Merss, were Hibernians of royal blood. Rupert of Luitz, in his

"Life of St. Eliph," says, too, that he was son of the King of Scotia (Hibernia). Mt. St. Eliph where he is buried still commemorates him. St. Eliph did great missionary work in the city of Toul, suffered imprisonment, and afterwards converted four hundred people.

Usher states that St. Florentinus who was imprisoned by Claudius, and converted and baptised ninety-six men and women fellow prisoners as well as his jailer, Asterius, "was a glorious confessor of Christ, born in Ireland." It is by no means certain, however, that Florentinus flourished before Patrick.

The poet, St. Sedulius (in the Irish, Siadal), is asserted to be Irish by many authorities, from Trithemius who called him "Scotus Hybernienses," down to present day scholars. Dr. Sigerson says it was this poet and Irishman who first introduced into Latin poetry the Irish rhyme and assonance, which, at that time, were cultivated only in Ireland. His most noted work, "Carmen Paschale," earned for him the title of the Christian Virgil. Sedulius travelled much in Southern Europe and in Asia. He dedicated a work to the Emperor Theodosius.

By far the most brilliant Continental celebrity claimed for Ireland before the days of St. Patrick, is undoubtedly Celestius, the disciple of Pelagius, who drew world-wide attention to himself in the very first years of the fifth century. This noted man's nationality is disputed, but amongst those who have gone into the subject there is fair consensus of opinion that he was at least Irish in blood if not also Irish by birth—either Irish of Ireland, or Irish of the Irish colony in Scotland. For those who would deny his Scotic (Irish) origin there is no way of getting around the allusions in St. Jerome's abuse of him, where once he calls him a "stupid fellow, loaded with the porridge of the Scots," and again, "a huge and corpulent Alban dog who can do more with his claws than with his teeth, for he is by descent of the Scotic nation." He was a well-known lawyer in Rome about the year 400 when he began espousing the heretical doctrines of Pelagius, so warmly, persistently and aggressively, that he overshadowed his master. Those who would argue that he is not Irish have to admit that he showed the eloquence, persuasiveness, aggressiveness of a true Irishman. He went to Carthage to preach against St. Augustine. He spoke before the Patriarch in Constantinople and before the Pope in Rome. Both by Imperial and Ecclesiastical decree he was expelled again and again from both Rome and Constantinople. But this only increased his vigour, his ardour, and his militancy. He is said to have won over to his side Pope Zosimus in 416—whom it took all the powers of Augustine and Jerome to win back again. This man who would not be downed, turned up at the Council of

Ephesus in 431, espousing, against the Pope, the cause of the patriarch, Nestorius, in the great Nestorian controversy. He was excommunicated by the Ephesian Council. He had been condemned by the Senate of Carthage twenty years earlier—but that had not dampened his ardour or dulled the edge of his word.

There is mention made by Gennadius of three epistles said to have been written by this fighter, "to his parents in Ireland"—before he espoused the cause of Pelagius.

It is Dr. Douglas Hyde's conclusion that the Scot whom St. Jerome abuses is not Celestius, but his heresiarch master, Pelagius. He says: "Pelagius was an Irishman, descended from an Irish colony in Britain."

Lanigan concludes that Celestius "of Pelagius, the most able favourite," surely seems Irish. Usher, O'Connor, Petrie and Stokes hold the same opinion. And Dr. Todd sums up his conclusion in the following words: "Be this as it may, it must suffice to observe that St. Jerome manifestly speaks of an Irishman who was a professor of Christianity, engaged in the controversies of that day. This is unquestionable evidence that there was at least one Irishman on the Continent of Europe at that early period who was a Christian."

Pelagius was the genius, and Celestius the brilliant talent, of the great Pelagian controversy.

The brothers Moroni, who wrote the life of the Irish evangeliser, and patron saint, of their city Tarentum, St. Cataldo (Irish, Cathal), say that he came there in the second century—but other evidence, which we may treat of later, would show that he was ante-Patrician.

So much for the claims of Continental Irish Christians before St. Patrick. Now to return to the claims made for Irish Christians living in Ireland. Many of the old Irish authorities, and indeed a few of the modern, urging that Christianity had not a disputed, but firm, foothold in some parts of the South, say that four of the well-known Irish saints flourished and preached to native congregations before Patrick began his mission—Saints Ailbe of Emly, Declan of Ardmore, Ibar of Beg Eri, and Ciaran of Saighir. Colgan indeed says that not only were these four pre-Patrician, but eight or nine other old Irish saints, also.

It is Hyde's opinion that the pre-Patrician claims made for Declan and Ailbe are substantiated. "We have it from the most ancient Acts of our Saints," says Colgan, "written one thousand years ago and up, that there were in Ireland not only many believers of Christ, but also many distinguished for sanctity, before Patrick and Palladius came." There is a tradition of Ailbe that in the beginning of the fifth century, returning with fifty companions from Rome, he preached to the Gentiles and baptised many and built a monastery for them.

This is what an ancient Life of St. Declan says upon the subject of the four bishops, his alleged forerunners, making their submission to Patrick:

> "The four Bishops aforesaid, who were in Ireland before St. Patrick, having been sent from Rome, as he also was, namely, Ailbe, Declan, Ciaran and Ibar, were not of the same mind as St. Patrick, but differed with him; nevertheless, in the end they came to an agreement with him. Ciaran, indeed yielded all subjection, and concord, and supremacy to Patrick, both when he was present and absent. But Ailbe, seeing that the great men of Ireland were running after Patrick, came to St. Patrick in the city of Cashel, and there, with all humility, accepted him as his master in presence of King Aongus; this, however, had not been his original intention. For those Bishops had previously constituted Ailbe their master, and therefore he came to St. Patrick before them, lest they, on his account, should resist Patrick. But Ibar, by no argument could be induced to agree with St. Patrick or to be subject to him. For he was unwilling to receive a patron of Ireland from a foreign nation; and Patrick was by birth a Briton, although nurtured in Ireland, having been taken a captive in his boyhood. And Ibar and Patrick had at first great conflicts together, but afterwards, at the persuasion of an angel, they made peace, and concord, and fraternity together. Declan, indeed, was unwilling to resist St. Patrick because he had before made fraternity with him in Italy: but neither did he think of becoming his subject, inasmuch as he also had the apostolic dignity: but having been at length admonished by an angel, he came to Patrick to do his will."

Talking of the claims made for St. Ciaran of Saighir, MacNeill urges that southwest Cork, being, as shown by historical incidents, in touch with foreign lands, might well have got Christianity before Patrick came.

Usher agrees with Colgan regarding the four first mentioned. But such keen thinkers as Lanigan and Todd decisively deny their pre-Patrician claims—and by some it is alleged that these claims made for the four southern saints were cunning inventions of the 11th and 12th centuries, when there was being waged a struggle for the spiritual supremacy of the Munster See of Cashel over the old Primatial See of Armagh.

Archbishop Healy thinks that Ibar was probably pre-Patrician. He, anyhow, became a disciple of Patrick. He retired to the Island of Beg-Eri,[1] in Wexford Harbor, about fifteen years before the fifth century's end, and died in the last year of the century.

The dates of the deaths of these men, as recorded in the Annals, and pretty generally agreed upon, tend to prove that they could not possibly have been pre-Patrician, unless we suppose them to have far outstayed the ordinary span—for all of them lived into the sixth century, with the exception of St. Ibar who, as mentioned, died on the threshold of that century.

At all events it is a safe conclusion that there were groups of Christians in Ireland when Palladius, preceding St. Patrick, came.

Palladius landed in the southeast of the Island. He stayed only a short time, yet—and this is additional evidence of his having found Christians there—he had erected three churches before he left. He departed in the same year—some say driven out by a Leinster chieftain, Nathi—and went to Alba, where he died. It was on the news reaching Rome of his departure from Ireland and his death that permission was given to Patrick to follow his heart's desire, and, answering the cries which he had heard in his dream from the children of Focluit Wood, go to the evangelising of the people whom he loved.

Lannigan, Rev. John, D.D.: Ecclesiastical History of Ireland.
Hyde, Douglas, LL.D.: A Literary History of Ireland.
Stokes, the Rev. Dr. Geo. T.: Ireland and the Celtic Church.
MacGeoghegan, Abbe: History of Ireland.
Keating's History of Ireland.
Healy, the Most Rev. Jno.: Ireland's Ancient Schools and Scholars.
—— St. Patrick.

[1] Says the tradition, when Patrick threatened Ibar that if he did not make submission, he would not suffer him to remain in Eire, Ibar answered, "If I will not be in Eire, it will be Eire where I am"—hence "Beg-Eri" (little Ireland).

CHAPTER XIX

St. Patrick

The coming of Patrick to Ireland marks the greatest of Irish epochs.

Of all most momentous happenings in Irish history, this seemingly simple one had the most extraordinary, most far-reaching effect. It changed the face of the nation, and utterly changed the nation's destiny. The coming of Patrick may be said to have had sublime effect not on Ireland alone, but upon the world. It was a world event.

The man himself proved to be a world figure—one of the massive giants who tower distinct and sublime above the dense mists of dim antiquity—one, too, of whom it may truly be said that the more intimately you approach him and the nearer you view him, the greater he grows. He was one of the greatest of Celts, became one of the greatest of Irishmen, and one of the very great among men.

Patrick first came to Ireland—as a captive—in the year 389, in the reign of Niall. It was forty-three years later, in the year 432, the reign of Laoghaire, that he came upon the mission which was so miraculously to change the Island's destiny. An ancient Pagan prophecy attributed to Conn of the Hundred Battles says: "With Laoghaire the Valiant will the land be humbled by the coming of the Tailcenn (i.e., Patrick): houses across (i.e., churches): bent staffs which shall pluck the flowers from their high places."

In the period of Patrick's coming the great Roman Empire was crumbling, while Ireland, with fleets on the sea and armies in foreign lands, had reached the pinnacle of her political power—a time that would seem the least propitious for winning men to the meek and abnegatory doctrines of Christ. Yet was it, in His own mysterious way, God's chosen time for sending His chosen man.

There is endless dispute as to where exactly was the birthplace of Patrick, which, in his Confession he appears to tell us was in "Bannaven of Taberniae."[1] Many authorities hold that it was near Dumbarton, in the most Northern Roman province of Celtic Britain. Others hold that it was in the Celtic province of Brittany in France. In his Confession are pieces of internal evidence that sustain either theory. The fact that St. Martin of Tours was his maternal uncle is one of the strong points in favour of his Continental origin. His father, Calporn held municipal office in the Romanised town (of Britain or Brittany) which was his native place—was a Decurion, a kind of magistrate, there. His mother, Conchessa, was niece of St. Martin. He himself was christened Succat, signifying "clever in war."

Wherever he was born it seems to have been from Brittany, from the home of his mother's parents, where he was visiting, that at the age of sixteen he was taken captive, with his two sisters, Darerca and Lupida. It was in a raid made by the men who sailed on a fleet of King Niall, says Keating. They were borne to Ireland, and his sisters said to have been placed in Muirthemne (Louth) while he was sold to an Antrim chieftain named Miliue, who set him herding his flocks in the valley of the Braid, around the foot of the mountain, Sliab Mis.[2]

His occupation as a herd upon a mountainside was fine probation for the holy career that was to be Patrick's. He confesses in his biography that in his wayward youth at home he had forgotten God, and from Him wandered into the ways of sin. Alone with his herd upon Sliab Mis during the day and the night, the months and the seasons, his spirituality was reawakened. And God guided his feet to the path of duty again. "I was always careful," he says, in the affecting picture which he paints of the herdboy's wonderful days on the mountains, "to lead my flocks to pasture, and to pray fervently. The love and fear of God more and more inflamed my heart; my faith enlarged, my spirit augmented, so that I said a hundred prayers by day and almost as many by night. I arose before day in the snow, in the frost, and the rain, yet I received no harm, nor was I affected with slothfulness. For then the spirit of God was warm within me."

And thus did he spend seven years in human slavery, working out, with God, his spiritual freedom. And his human freedom followed. In a dream

---

[1] Though strictly speaking the only assurance to be found in that sentence of the Confession is that he was there taken captive.

[2] One of his biographers, Probus, says that it was into the country of Tirawley, in Mayo, that Patrick was sold—and on the mountain of Croagh Patrick herded his flocks. There is grave doubt as to whether Darerca and Lupida were sisters (other than sisters in religion) of his.

that came to him he was told to travel to the seashore at a certain place two hundred miles distant, where he should find a ship on which he would make his escape. He found the ship and was taken on board—after first getting a refusal and being turned away by the captain—and in the seventh year of his captivity he sailed away from Ireland.

And be it noted that the Irish land which he had entered as a foreigner, he now left as an Irishman. For, as he was destined to give a new faith and new soul to Ireland, Ireland had given a new faith and new soul to him. He had found himself and found God in that land to which he was destined to bring God. In his seven years' slavery the Irish tongue had become his tongue, and his spirit was the Irish spirit, which at that impressionable age he had imbibed. So, to make him truly one of the people to whom he was to carry God's word, God had wisely ordained his slave service among them during the very six or seven years in which men's characters are stamped with the qualities of those amongst whom they move. For it is not where a man is born, or spends the careless years of childhood, but where and among whom he spends the plastic and absorbent years of youth, that determines his true nationality. So the Irishman, Patrick, now sailed away from his own land, whereto had arrived, several years before, an alien Patrick.

A three days' voyage brought him to the land from which he had been carried captive—after which a distressing journey of twenty-eight days through deserts and wilds brought him to his home, where the lost one was welcomed with great rejoicing.

Yet, though his people resolved never to let him from their sight again, and though it gladdened him to be with his kin, his heart could find no peace for thinking of the country and the people that had grown into his soul, and had become his. There were centred the thoughts of the day, the dreams of the night.

Till at length he had a vivid night vision, in which there came to him a man, Victor, from Ireland, bearing letters which were marked, "Vox Hibernionacum"—which, however, he could not read understandingly, for keen pathetic cries filled his ears, from the people of Focluit Wood beseeching him to come to them. "And there I saw a vision during the night, a man coming from the west; his name was Victoricus, and had with him many letters; he gave me one to read, and in the beginning of it was a voice from Ireland. I then thought it to be the voice of the inhabitants of Focluit Wood, adjoining the western sea; they appeared to cry out in one voice, saying, 'Come to us, O holy youth, and walk among us.' With this I was feelingly touched, and could read no longer: I then awoke."

After this he could not rest inactive. He must prepare himself for the task of carrying the Gospel of Christ to the people of his heart. And despite the tears and entreaties of his own relatives, he bade good-bye to them and home, and travelled away to study for the ministry.[3]

But, finally, having been consecrated Bishop, Pope Celestine commissioned him to carry the gospel to the land of his love—and conferred on him the Roman noble name Patricius.

He reached Ireland in 432 in the fourth year of the reign of Laoghaire, son of Niall, High-King.[4]

---

[3] A tantalising vagueness settles over the history of his Continental travels in search of learning and ordination. And very many conflicting accounts of his travels and studies are given. In 396, he is said to have entered the monastery of Marmoutiers, near Tours, a foundation of his uncle, St. Martin. Here he remained till Martin's death, which occurred, some say in 397, some in 402. And here had St. Martin given him the monastic habit and the clerical tonsure.

Some (doubtful) accounts show him studying next (in 403) with the students of St. John of Lateran in Rome. He visited and sojourned in many holy places and studied under many holy men—in monasteries and in hermitages, in Italy and in Mediterranean islands. He is said to have spent many years in a monastery on the Isle of Lerins, under St. Honoratus and St. Maximus. Afterward, many years seem to have been spent at Auxerre under St. Germanus, the Bishop, a man of great culture as well as piety.

In the year 430 St. Patrick turned up at Auxerre again, his age being now thirty-eight. He had long sought to be commissioned to Ireland. At this time again, backed by the influence of Germanus, he preferred his request to Rome—but was refused because Palladius had then been sent. When finally came the news of the failure and of the death of Palladius, Patrick journeyed to Rome, to Pope Celestine, carrying with him a letter from Germanus. Celestine now granted his request, and consecrated him Archbishop for the Irish mission. Also twenty priests and deacons were ordained, to be his companions in the undertaking. And at his consecration, says a tradition, three choirs answered: to wit, the choir of Heaven's household, the choir of the Romans, and the choir of the children of the Wood of Focluit, all singing: "Hiberniensis omnes clamant ad te, tuer."

Celestine also conferred upon him his new name, Patricius—an ancient title of the highest honour among the Romans.

It was on his last journey from Germanus to Rome that, tradition says, he got his famous Bachaill Iosa, Staff of Jesus—his pastoral staff, which is still preserved. Sailing to Rome, he stopped at a house on an island in the Tyrrhenian Sea, says the story, a new house of a young married couple, who had children and grandchildren, old and decrepit. The *lanamain,* the young couple, had been married in the time of Jesus, who passed that way immediately after they were married, and received their hospitality—for which He blessed them and their house, and said that they and it should remain new and young till the Judgment Day. In their care He left His Staff, with injunction that it should be kept for Patrick against the day that he, too, passing that way, should there be entertained. "And God hath enjoined thee," said the young man to Patrick, "to go and preach in the land of the Gael. And Jesus left with us this staff to be given to thee."

Then, the desire of his life being crowned, he, at the age of sixty, with buoyant soul and gladdened heart, amid his rejoicing company, set forward from Rome, upon his momentous mission. On his way he stopped with Germanus, who presented him with vestments, chalices, and books, and gave him advice and blessing.

[4] He is said to have first landed near Vartry in the County Wicklow—at about the same place at which Palladius before him, had arrived. There he preached and baptised, and like Palladius, was driven out. He sailed northward, and into Strangford Loch in Down, where landing he was again attacked.

On the eve of Easter, Patrick's party encamped at Slaine, on the left bank of the Boyne, opposite to and in sight of Tara; and Patrick lighted in front of his tent a fire which was visible at the king's court. Now a great festival was beginning at Tara, coincident with the beginning of Patrick's Easter festival. And it was a gross violation of royal and ancient order that on this eve any fire should be lighted before the court Druids should light their sacred fire upon the royal Rath. Accordingly, when Laoghaire's astounded court beheld in the distance the blazing of Patrick's fire before the Druid fire had yet been lit, great was their consternation and high and hot their wrath.

Dichu, a chieftain of the Dal Fiatach, taking Patrick and his company to be a band of British pirates, descended upon them. But Dichu was so struck with respect and veneration when Patrick faced him, that he lowered his arms, hearkened to the words of the apostle, and finally, with his family, was baptised. Patrick afterwards built a church on this spot, commemorating this first conversion of his, in the north. The place has since been called Sabhall Padraic—or corruptly, Saul.

But Patrick craved to bring to Christ his old master, Miliuc. Forth then he fared toward the country of his captivity and the house of his master. But Miliuc is said to have grown furious when intelligence was brought him that Succat, his former slave, was journeying hence, bent on converting him to a new faith—and that he was winning all to whom he preached by the way; for the new faith's appeal, voiced by Succat, no man could resist. Rather than submit to the mortification of being converted by his swineherd, the determined old pagan set fire to his house, and immolated himself in the flames.

But a son of the old pagan was saved, and two daughters. They were converted, moreover, and the son lived to become a bishop, and the two daughters nuns.

When Patrick arrived and found what had happened, and that his old master had removed himself from the reach of Christ, he is said to have shed floods of tears. He wended his way back to the territory of Lecale where he had first landed, and there did successful missionary work, converting and baptising Dichu's people. And having ordained priests for them, he sailed again southward, and landed at the mouth of the Boyne—with intention of proceeding to the court of the High King, Laoghaire, at Tara. He left his nephew, Luman, with some sailors in charge, in the boat, while he travelled inland—toward the royal Court.

On his journey to Tara he won the love and the faith of a little lad who was destined to shine as the brightest and greatest of his disciples. He had stopped to rest and be refreshed at the house of the chieftain, Sesgne, and falling asleep in his seat beneath a tree, after he had eaten, a little son of Sesgne, Benin, whose love had gone out to him, now approached the resting warrior of Christ, and was strewing wild flowers over him—till he was stopped and rebuked. But Patrick, awaking, said, "Molest him not, for that youth shall yet heir my kingdom." And when, later, Patrick was entering his chariot to go forward, the little Benin, pressing through the surrounding throng, took hold of his hand crying: "Let me go, too." And Patrick added to his company the gentle and beautiful, sweet-voiced little Benin whose love he had won. The goodness and loveliness of the gentle-natured boy won all hearts to him—won for him even the love of the beautiful Ercnat, daughter of King Daire, of Ulster—which love he could not return, since he was bent upon giving himself to Christ. The sweet-voiced boy became Patrick's psalmist. Later, in Armagh, he became Patrick's coadjutor. And finally he heired and worthily filled Patrick's primatial chair in Armagh, and headed the school of Armagh, as well as ruled the church. And to the learned Benin (Benignus) is now attributed, by many scholars, the authorship of the great and valuable ancient Irish book, The Book of Rights. Others hold that Benin only re-wrote and revised this important work, which, they say, was compiled by Cormac MacArt, 200 years earlier.

"What audacious miscreant," demanded the king, "has dared to do this outrage?" The Druids answered him that it was indeed the Tailcenn of the old prophecy, come to supersede his rule, and their rule, in Eirinn. "Moreover," they said, "unless the fire on yonder hill be extinguished this very night, it shall never more be extinguished in Eirinn. It will outshine all fires that we light, and he who lit it will conquer us all: he will overthrow you, and his kingdom overthrow your kingdom: he will make your subjects his, and rule over them all forever."

Then King Laoghaire, a splendidly determined old pagan, of like nature with Miliuc, angrily demanded that the transgressor should be dragged before him, with all the other foreign intruders who were supporting him.

Then Patrick's camp was raided by Laoghaire's soldiers, and he and his companions ordered to march to Tara.

An old tradition has it that, as, on Easter morning, the missionaries proceeded in processional order, toward the king's court, they chanted the sacred Lorica, called the Faed Fiada, or Deer's Cry, specially composed by Patrick for their protection. It is said that as the minions of the Druids lay in ambush to intercept and kill them as they came to court, these evil ones now saw not Patrick and his companions pass, only saw pass a harmless herd of gentle deer, a doe followed by her twenty fawns. Hence the hymn's title, the Faed Fiada—Deer's Cry. And through all the centuries since, the Faed Fiada—which many old authorities pronounce to be Patrick's own work, and the first hymn written in Gaelic—has been used by the Irish Race as a lorica for protection.[5]

---

[5] I

I bind me today,
God's might to direct me,
God's power to protect me,
God's wisdom for learning,
God's eye for discerning,
God's ear for my hearing,
God's word for my clearing.

II

God's hand for my cover,
God's path to pass over,
God's buckler to guard me,
God's army to ward me,
Against snares of the devil,
Against vice's temptation,
Against wrong inclination,
Against men who plot evil,
Anear or afar, with many or few.

III

Christ near,
Christ here,
Christ be with me,
Christ beneath me,
Christ within me,
Christ behind me,
Christ be o'er me,
Christ before me.

IV

Christ in the left and the right,
Christ hither and thither,
Christ in the sight,
Of each eye that shall seek me,
In each ear that shall hear,
In each mouth that shall speak me—
Christ not the less
In each heart I address.
I bind me today on the Triune—I call,
With faith in the Trinity—Unity—God over all.

This, Dr. Sigerson's rendering of the hymn is in the same measure, metre, and rhythm of the original.

And having been carried safe by the Lord through the ambushes prepared for them, Patrick led his host into the king's presence, chanting: "Let them that will, trust in chariots and horses, but we walk in the name of the Lord."

To impress and awe these foreigners, King Laoghaire with his queen and court, sat aloft in state, while his warriors, in silence, sat around in a great circle, with the rims of their shields against their chins. Laoghaire, evidently apprehensive of the secret power of the Tailcenn, had warned his court that none of the marks of respect which were the due of a stranger, should be shown to this bold aggressor. But so impressive was Patrick's appearance that immediately he came into their presence, Dubthach, the King's Ollam poet, arose, in respect for him; as also a young noble, Erc—who afterwards became Bishop Erc. And these two were Patrick's first converts at Tara.

In the presence of King and court Patrick was first confronted with the Druids, who, it was hoped, would quickly confound him. But matching his miracles against their magic he showed to all that his powers far transcended theirs. He dispelled a darkness, which they, by their magical powers had produced, but were powerless to dissipate—"They can bring darkness," he significantly said, "but cannot bring light." He preached Christ to the assembly, and won to his Master the queen and several prominent members of the court. And, though Laoghaire's pagan faith was unshaken, he was so far won by the man Patrick that he gave him the freedom of his realm to preach the new faith where and to whom he would.[6]

---

[6] Laoghaire, we may here mention, died a pagan—killed by lightning. The Leinstermen had defeated him in the battle of Athgara, and taken him prisoner, at a time when he had gone to demand from them the Boru Tribute. They compelled him to take oath, by the sun, moon, and stars, that he would never again demand the tribute. But he broke his oath and went against them once more. Then Heaven's lightning, it is said, visited vengeance on him, for the breaking of the oath. He was buried in one of the old pagan fashions—in standing attitude, fully accoutred, and facing Leinster and his enemies.

Among the many distinguished converts whom Patrick made at Tara on that occasion was a young noble, Fingar, who, because he had accepted and would not recant the new faith, was, by his father, Clito, driven into exile. With several other nobles who had become Christians he sailed to Brittany. When his father died, he returned to Ireland, and after renouncing his heritage, he took with him his sister, Fiala, and seven hundred men, including seven bishops, all of whom sailed away to devote themselves to religion, to enjoy Christ themselves, and give Christ to those other lands that had Him not. But the whole party was massacred in Cornwall by the Cornish King, Theodoric.

The life of Fingar, written by St. Anselm, Archbishop of Canterbury, and preserved in Paris through long years, was finally published there, in the seventeenth century.

Patrick's next great preaching was to the vast assembly of the men of Eirinn, who had gathered at the Fair of Taillte. Though at these national fairs the multitude always anticipated hearing and seeing many wonderful things—scholars, historians and poets of their own nation addressing them, sometimes scholars and travellers from far countries, as well as, always, foreign merchants bringing rare merchandise—the Fair of Taillte at the Lammas of 432 furnished to the expectant multitude a rare sensation. When they beheld the procession of foreign clerics, all clad in strange garments, and headed by a beautiful and venerable man, arrive chanting strange new chants, there surely was startling commotion—even at that Fair where sensations and commotions were many. Astonishing must have been the crush, and vast the crowd, of the tens and hundreds of thousands of fair-goers who now pushed and pressed to get nearer sight of this wonderful procession of chanting strangers—to learn who they were and whence, and what was their object in Eirinn. And when the venerable one who headed the procession addressed the seething crowds telling them that he was the ambassador of the King of the world's kings, describing to them his King's kingdom, telling them of the infinite love of his King for all of them, of His yearning desire to have them know Him, and to enter into and enjoy the kingdom whose beauties and whose pleasures, and whose riches and whose bliss, infinitely exceeded all that the mind of man had ever before conceived or man's imagination in its powerfulest flight ever pictured, of His sending His own Son as His messenger to mankind, of the beauty and goodness, meekness and lovableness of that Son, and then of His sufferings, His torture and death, at the hands of those whom He came to invite to the enjoyment of His Father's kingdom—how the bearded warrior throngs, and even the eager youths there must have been impressed, inspired, fired and melted; how the wild ones must have felt themselves tamed; and the haughty humbled; and the scornful sweetened; and the strenuous soothed; as eventually the mightily moved multitude—including a Prince, Conal, son of Niall, whose heart was there reached by the grace of God—bowed for the Tailcenn's blessing.

He spent the next year preaching throughout Meath and Leinster. He went into the province of Connaught in 434. On his way there he visited the Plain of Magh Slecht, where stood the great idol Crom Cruach, before which, in the ancient time, Tighernmas and his worshipping thousands had been slain by Heaven—and threw down this idol, along with the twelve others that stood around it.

He met and converted King Laoghaire's two beautiful daughters, Ethni the Fair, and Fedelm the Ruddy, who were at the Connaught Palace of Cruachan, under the tuition of the two Druids, Mal and Coplait.[7]

On top of the mountain of Croagh Patrick in Connaught, he spent the forty days of Lent, watching, and fasting, and praying. And the tradition goes, as recorded by the Monk Jocelin that it was from this mountaintop he commanded all the serpents and venomous things in Ireland, driving them into the ocean, and ridding Ireland of all viperous things forever.[8]

The Saint at length reached the Wood of Focluit dear to his memory—reached it at the time of a great assemblage of people and there preaching to those children of Focluit Wood, whose cries he had heard in his dream, he converted, it is told, the seven sons of the chieftain, Prince Amalgaid, and twelve thousand people.

In 441 after seven years in Connaught, he proceeded by the narrow way between Benbulbin and the sea, into Ulster, where he spent four years travelling, preaching, baptising and church-building.

After that he preached through Leinster—on the way to which, the Dubliners, it is said, came out in crowds to meet him. And then on through Munster. At royal Cashel in Munster, he converted the king, Aongus.[9]

---

[7] He had to measure his power with these Druids, as with the Druids at Tara. To prevent his finding the palace of Cruachan, they, by their Druidic art, brought down upon the plain, for many miles around, a thick darkness which enveloped Patrick, his companions, the castle and all within the plain of Magh Air—a darkness which held that region for the space of three days and three nights. Then Patrick, in the name of Christ, blessed the plain, so that the Druids alone remained in darkness, while the blessed light was restored to all others there. Finally Mal and Coplait were convinced and converted—along with their charge, the beautiful princesses.

[8] Some centuries before, Solinus, the Roman writer, recorded that there were no snakes in Ireland—which belies the honoured tradition. The tradition, however, persists, and will always persist in the popular belief. There is a second legend in some parts of Ireland which says that one serpent, either through a fortunate slothfulness or some other cause, was not cast out with the others. Patrick, being later informed of this, induced the dilatory fellow to go down into the deep waters of Loch Neagh, on the promise, more ingenious than ingenuous, that he should be released therefrom "on the morrow." Since that time children living in the neighbourhood of Loch Neagh can hear the prisoned fellow raising his head above the waters, at the dawning of each new day, to inquire, "Is this day the morrow? Is this day the morrow?" But alas for him—for him, and for all unfortunates who wait for the morrow which never comes!

[9] When about to baptise the king, Patrick thrust his pastoral staff, by its sharp iron point, into the earth—as he thought. But it was through the foot of Aongus he thrust it. He discovered his grave mistake only when the ceremony was finished. "Why did you not tell me this?" he cried to the king. And Aongus answered simply. "Because I thought it part of the ceremony."

Twelve sons and twelve daughters of the heroic Aongus were consecrated to God. Aongus ordered that henceforth a capitation tax from his people should be paid to St. Patrick and to his successors in Armagh. It was paid every third year, by the kings of Munster, down to the time of Cormac MacCullanan in the tenth century.

Patrick convened a Synod at Cashel, where he met his southern rivals, Saints Ailbe, Declan, Ciaran and Ibar, and after much argument got their obedience. Ibar was the most obstinate and last to yield. For he was unwilling, says an account, that any one but a native of Ireland should be acknowledged the ecclesiastical patron of the country.

After completing his work in Munster the Saint returned north again through Leinster into Ulster, where he was to spend six years more, visiting the churches, organising congregations and ordaining priests.

He then founded Armagh—where was to be his See[10]—built his church, his monastery, and school. He made it the primatial city of the island. But, through the work and the fame of the great schools which were to develop there, it was to become, within a few centuries—to quote words of a great Continental scholar (Darmesteter)—"not only the ecclesiastical capital of Ireland but the capital of civilisation."

His favourite disciple, Benignus (Benin), the herdboy, he put into his See of Armagh, to administer it for him, while he spent these years of his old age for the most part in tranquillity, sometimes in Armagh and sometimes in his first church of Saball.

In all likelihood it was during these tranquil years, when now his hardest work was over, that Patrick directed the compilation of the laws, known as the Senchus Mor. He got the law-givers to lay before him all the old laws, and, to codify and purge them, called into council upon them

---

[10] The Hill of Armagh on which he founded his Archiepiscopal city was given him by Daire, the chief of that district. Tradition says that Patrick saved the life of Daire; and as a token of his thanks, Daire sent to Patrick, by messenger, a brazen cauldron. When the messenger returned, the chieftain, desiring to have pictured to him the overwhelming gratitude which he had anticipated Patrick would display, asked what Patrick had said. And the messenger replied that the good man had said, "Gratias agam." "Gratchacam!" exclaimed Daire, "that's a poor reward for a good cauldron. Go take it from him again!" When the messenger returned with the cauldron, Daire once more asked what Patrick had said when the cauldron was taken. The messenger answered that he had said, "Deo gratias!" "Gratchacam again!" exclaimed Daire. "Gratchacam is the first word with him, and gratchacam the last. Gratchacam when giving it to him, and gratchacam when taking it away. The word must be good!" With his wife he then went to Patrick, and bestowed on him not only the cauldron but also the Hill of Armagh, for the building of his primatial city. Says the Four Masters, under the year 457: "Ard Macha was founded by St. Patrick, it having been granted to him by Dari, son of Finneadh, son of Eogan, son of Niallan. Twelve men were appointed by him for building the town. He ordered them in the first place to build an archbishop's city there, and a church for monks, for nuns, and for the other orders in general; for he perceived that it would be the head and chief of all the churches in Ireland." It is related that when he went with his men to mark out the city lines upon the hill, he came upon a doe that had just given birth to a fawn which the men would kill or roughly drive away. But Patrick lifted the helpless fawn tenderly in his arms, and bore it off where it could remain undisturbed—while its mother meekly and trustingly followed, like a pet sheep.

three kings, three bishops, three ollams, and they got a poet "to throw a thread of poetry around them."

Now also it probably was that he wrote his famous Confession; and possibly also during this period his second most famous work, his Epistle to Coroticus—works which after fourteen hundred years, still live—and will live.[11] They were written in the rather poor Latin of which Patrick was master, the provincial Latin of the Roman provinces. For, as he humbly stated again and again, he was not of the very learned; and he was profusely apologetic for his temerity in writing what would be read and criticised by the really learned ones, his contemporaries.

"I, Patrick the sinner, unlearned, no doubt," he humbly begins his Epistle to Coroticus, a British prince, who making a raid into Ireland, slaughtered many there, and carried off with him many captives—among them some of Patrick's newly baptised children of the Church. "With mine own hand," he says, "have I written and composed these words, to be given and handed to, and sent to, the soldiers of Coroticus." "On the day following that on which the newly baptised in white array were anointed with the chrism, it was still gleaming on their foreheads, while they were cruelly butchered and slaughtered with the sword."

In this intense document Patrick first gives utterance to that cry against British oppression which the agonising heart of Ireland has echoed every year of the past seven hundred and fifty years. "Is it a crime," he cries out, "to be born in Ireland? Have not we the same God as ye have?" He boldly demands return of the captives, and mercilessly castigates the tyrant who sacrilegiously carried them off.

But of course Patrick's *magnum opus,* which will live forever, is his Confession. To others, Fathers of the faith, he had been calumniated. One whom he had held to be a dear friend turned disloyal to him and endeavoured to injure him in the eyes of these, his brethren. Amongst other things he informed them of a false step Patrick had taken in his youth. And he evidently had accused him of presumption and egotistical ambition, in assuming to himself the task of converting Ireland. The Confession was written for the purpose of defending himself against the false charges.

Timidly, and with characteristic humility, but still with a great calm, he opens this famous document:

---

[11] These, his works, were preserved in the ancient Book of Armagh, into which they were copied by the scribe Firdomnach, about the year 810—there, too, copied, as Firdomnach states from the manuscript in Patrick's own handwriting.

> "I, Patrick, a sinner, the most rustic and the least of all the faithful, and in the estimation of very many deemed contemptible, had for my father Calpornius, a deacon, the son of Potitus, a presbyter, who belonged to the village of Bannaven Taberniae; for close thereto he had a small villa, where I was made a captive.
>
> "At the time I was barely sixteen years of age, I knew not the true God; and I was led to Ireland in captivity with many thousand persons according to our deserts, for we turned away from God and kept not His commandments, and we were not obedient to our priests who used to admonish us about our salvation. And the Lord brought us the indignation of His wrath, and scattered us amongst many nations even to the utmost part of the earth, where now my littleness may be seen amongst strangers.
>
> "And there the Lord opened the understanding of my unbelief so that at length I might recall to mind my sins and be converted with all my heart to the Lord, my God, who hath regarded my humility and taken pity on my youth and my ignorance, and kept watch over me before I knew Him, and before I had discretion, and could distinguish between good and evil; and He protected me and consoled me as a father does his son."

The part of the Confession which many authorities adduce as testimony that Patrick, with his moderate learning, found himself in Ireland in the midst of very learned ones and great critics, is this:

> "For this reason I have long been thinking of writing, but up to the present I hesitated; for I feared lest I should transgress against the tongue of men, seeing that I am not learned like others, who in the best style therefore have drunk in both laws and sacred letters in equal perfection; and who from their infancy never changed their mother tongue; but were rather making it always more perfect.
>
> "My speech, however, and my style were changed into the tongue of the stranger, as can easily be perceived in the flavour of my writings how I am trained and instructed in languages, for as the wise man saith: 'By the tongue wisdom will be discerned, and understanding, and knowledge, and learning of the truth.'"

Both his humility and his testimony to the scholars—a scornful one this time—are read out of the following passage of the Confession:

"Whence I, at first a rustic and an exile, unlearned and surely as one who knows not how to provide for the future—yet this I do most certainly know, that before, I was humble, I was like a stone which lies in the deep mire, and He that is mighty came and in His mercy lifted me up, and placed me on the top of the wall. And therefore I ought to cry out and render something to the Lord for these benefits so great both here and for eternity, that the mind of man can not estimate them.

"Wherefor, be ye filled with wonder both small and great, who fear God, and ye too, lordly rhetoricians, hear and search out. Who was it that exalted me, fool though I be, from the midst of those who seemed to be wise and skilled in the law, and powerful in word and in everything else? And me truly despicable in this world He inspired beyond others, though being such, that with fear and reverence, and without blame I should faithfully serve the nation to whom the love of Christ transferred me and bestowed me for my life, if I should be worthy—that in humility and truth I should serve them."[12]

Out of some later sentence in the Confession is taken apparent substantiation of Britain's claim on his nativity where he says:

"Wherefore, however, I might have been willing to leave them, and go into the Brittaniæ, as to my country and relatives, and not only so but also to the Galliæ, to visit my brethren."

"Again after a few years I was in the Brittaniæ with my parents."

This evidence, while colourable, is far from being positive, in favour of his British birth. For one thing, Brittany may well have been called one of the Brittaniæ—which it was; and in the next place, even if he referred to Britain proper, it does not follow that because his family, of which the father was a Roman official, was then in that particular province of the Roman Empire, he and his had been there at the time of Patrick's birth.

The Confession testifies to idol worship in Ireland where it says:

"Whence Ireland, which never had the knowledge of God, but up to the present always adored idols and things unclean—how are

[12] In neither of the foregoing instances, however, can we feel sure that he refers to Irish "rhetoricians," or learned ones.

they now made a people of the Lord, and are called the children of God? The sons of the Scots and the daughters of their chieftains are seen to become monks and virgins of Christ."

And again his humility—and also a hint of the accusations made against him—in the following extracts:

"And behind my back they were talking among themselves and kept saying: 'Why does he expose himself to danger, amongst enemies who know not God?' Not for malice sake, but because they did not approve it, as I myself can testify, and understand, on account of my rusticity. . . . But though I be rude in all things, still I have tried to some extent to keep watch over myself. . . . Or when the Lord ordained clergy everywhere by my mediocrity, and I gave them my ministrations gratis, did I ask from any of them so much as the price of a sandal? Tell it against me and I shall restore you more.

"Sufficient is the honour that is not seen but is believed in the heart. And He that promised the faithful, He never lies. But I see that in this present world I am exalted above measure by the Lord. And I was not worthy, nor am I such that He should grant this to me, since I know for certain that poverty and affliction become me better than riches and luxury. Nay, Christ the Lord was poor for our sake. But I, poor and wretched, even should I wish for wealth I have it not, nor do I judge myself, for daily I expect either a violent death or slavery, or the occurrence of some such calamity. But I fear none of these things on account of the promises of Heaven! I have cast myself into the hands of the Almighty God, for He rules everything. As the prophet saith: 'Cast thy cares upon the Lord, and He Himself will sustain them.' . . . Lo, again and again, I shall in brief set out the words of my Confession. I testify in truth and in the joy of my heart before God and His holy angels that I never had any motive except the Gospel and its promises in ever returning to that nation from which I had previously with difficulty made my escape."

And the final paragraph—of the great Confession from which these few excerpts are taken:

"But I pray those who believe and fear God, whosoever will have deigned to look on this writing which Patrick, the sinner and unlearned no doubt, wrote in Ireland, that no one shall ever say it was my ignorance (did it), that I have done God's will; but think ye, and let it be most firmly believed that it was the gift of God. And this is my Confession before I die."

This powerfully appealing and magnificently simple document breathes in its every line the rare fragrance of a great and sincere, meek and beautiful heart, reverently bowed down in the palpable presence of God. The faultiness of the language in which it was originally written fails to mar this precious piece of the old world's literature. Patrick's Confession is a great picture of a great soul, painted by one who, scorning to give art one thought, was a great natural artist. He swept art aside—and despising it, triumphed over it, and by that very means triumphantly attained art's goal.[13]

After a full life, rich with great labours greatly done, and by Christ crowned with success, thrice blessed by seeing the fruit ripen from the seed he sowed, Patrick passed away, at Down, in about the year 460—leaving behind him a grief-stricken people who had made this man one of their own, and learnt to love him almost to the point of worship. The twelve days of his wake are known as Laithi na Caointe, the Days of Lamentation, when a whole nation whom he had brought to Christ, bewailed the most mournful loss a nation had ever known.

---

[13] Another work of Patrick's which is lost, is referred to, by his biographer Tirechan, under the title of Commemmoratio Laborum.

In the noted work, The Book of Rights, ascribed to his disciple Benignus, is found the Blessing of St. Patrick, which some think is one of Patrick's poems:

"The Blessing of God upon you all,
Men of Erin, sons, women,
And daughters; prince-blessing,
Meal-blessing, blessing of long life,
Health-blessing, blessing of excellence,
Eternal blessing, heaven-blessing,
Cloud-blessing, sea-blessing,
Fruit-blessing, land-blessing,
Crop-blessing, dew-blessing,
Blessing of elements, blessing of valour,
Blessing of dexterity, blessing of glory,
Blessing of deeds, blessing of honour,
Blessing of happiness be upon you all,
Laics, clerics, while I command
The blessing of the men of Heaven;
It is my bequest, as it is a Perpetual Blessing."

"And for the space of twelve nights to wit the time during which the elders of Ireland were watching him with hymns and psalms and canticles, there was no night in Magh Inis, but an angelic radiance therein. And some say that angelic radiance abode in Magh Inis till the end of a year after Patrick's death. And so night was not seen in the whole of that region during the days of lamentation for Patrick. The odour of the divine grace which came from the body, and the music of the angels, brought sleep and joy to the elders of the men of Ireland who were watching the body."

"Patrick, son of Calphronn, son of Potaide, Archbishop, first Primate, and Chief Apostle, of Ireland," say the Four Masters, "whom Pope Celestine the First had sent to preach the Gospel, and disseminate religion and piety among the Irish, was the person who separated them from the worship of idols and spectres, who conquered and destroyed the idols which they had for worshipping, who expelled demons and evil spirits from among them, and brought them from the darkness of sin and vice to the light of faith and good works, and who guided and conducted their souls from the gates of hell to which they were going, to the gates of the kingdom of heaven. It was he that baptised and blessed the men, women, sons and daughters of Ireland, with their territories and tribes, both fresh waters and sea inlets. It was by him that many cells, monasteries and churches were founded throughout Ireland, seven hundred churches was their number. It was by him that bishops, priests, and persons of every dignity were ordained, seven hundred bishops and three thousand priests was their number. He worked so many miracles and wonders, that the human mind is incapable of remembering or recording the amount of good which he did upon the earth. The body of Patrick was afterwards buried at Dunda-leth-glas, with great honour and veneration. And during the twelve nights that the religious seniors were watching the body, with psalms and hymns, it was not night in Magh-Inis, or the neighbourhoods, as they thought, but as if it were the full undarkened light of day."

And says the ancient Tripartite Life of Patrick:

"Now after founding churches in plenty; after consecrating monasteries; after baptising the men of Ireland; after great patience and after great labour; after destroying idols and images and after rebuking many kings who did not his will, and after raising up those

> who did his will; after ordaining three hundred and three score and ten bishops, and after ordaining three thousand priests and folk of every grade in the church besides; after fasting and prayer; after mercy and clemency; after gentleness and mildness to the sons of Life; after love of God and his neighbours, he received Christ's body from the bishop, from Tassach, and then he sent his spirit to Heaven. His body, however, is here still on earth, with honour and veneration. And though great be the honour to it here, greater will be the honour to it on Doomsday, for it will shine like a sun in Heaven, and then it will give judgment on the fruit of his preaching, even as Peter and Paul. It will abide thereafter in the union of patriarchs and prophets, in the union of the saints and holy virgins of the world, in the union of the apostles and disciples of Jesus Christ, in the union of the church both of Heaven and earth; in the union of the nine ranks of Heaven that transgress not, in the union of the Godhead and manhood of God's son, in the union that is nobler than any union, the union of the Trinity, Father and Son and Holy Ghost."

Thus passed away one of the greatest, perhaps the greatest, that Ireland ever knew, or ever will know—still more, one of the dominant personalities of world history, whose influence will end only with the final running out of the sands of Time. What Confucius was to the Oriental, Moses to the Israelite, Mohammed to the Arab, Patrick was to the Gaelic race. And the name and the power of those other great ones will not outlive the name and the power of our Apostle.

> "A righteous man, verily, was this man. With purity of nature, like the patriarchs. A true pilgrim like Abraham. Mild, forgiving from the heart, like Moses. A praiseworthy psalmist like David. A shrine of wisdom, like Solomon. A joyous vessel for proclaiming righteousness, like Paul the Apostle. A man full of the grace and the favour of the Holy Ghost, like John the child. A fair herb-garden with plants of virtues. A vine-branch with fruitfulness. A flashing fire with the fervour of the warming and heating of the sons of Life, for kindling and for inflaming charity. A lion for strength and might. A dove for gentleness and simplicity. A serpent for prudence and cunning as to good. Gentle, humble, merciful unto the sons of Life. Gloomy, ungentle to the sons of Death. A laborious and serviceable slave to Christ. A king for dignity and power as to binding and loosing, as to liberating and enslaving, as to killing and quickening life."

One of the secrets of the wonderful power he has wielded over the Irish, and one of the secrets of his world-popularity, was the rare combination in him of the spiritual with the human. Among saints, Patrick is eminently saintly, and very, very human among human beings. His shining virtues make him kin of the angels, while his human frailties—Celtic frailties—his passionateness, his impetuosity, his torrential anger against tyrants, his teeming fierceness against sinners in high place, his biting scathe and burning scorn, made men feel that he was a brother to all men—especially to all Irishmen. More surely did these qualities win the Irish Celt when they found in him combined the terror of a warrior with the tenderness of a woman; the ferocity of a tiger, with the gentleness of a lamb. The same Patrick who had tenderly lifted on his shoulders and carried to safety the fawn of Armagh Hill later thundered denunciations at the plundering, murdering Coroticus and his men—"fellow-citizens of demons," "slaves of hell," "dead while they live," "patricides, fratricides, ravening wolves, eating up the people of the Lord like breadstuffs!" It was only a man of such terrible passion and such ineffable tenderness who could have gained, as quickly as Patrick did, complete moral ascendancy over the Irish nation—so amazingly compelling their allegiance, obedience, faith, belief and trust as in one generation to work that wondrous change which called forth the testimony by the old poet (put into the mouth of the returned Caoilte): "There was a demon at the butt of every grass-blade in Eirinn before thy advent; but at the butt of every grass-blade in Eirinn today there is an angel."

And that Caoilte's figure of speech finds its justification in the historical records of those days we shall admit, when we contrast the two widely differing natures of the Irish people who before Patrick were carrying the ruthless law of the sword far over sea and land, and that very different Irish people who, after Patrick, left the conquering sword to be eaten by rust, while they went far and wide again over sea and land, bearing now to the nations—both neighbouring and far off—the healing balm of Christ's gentle words. All histories of all countries probably could not disclose to the most conscientious searcher another instance of such radical change in a whole nation's character being wrought within the lifespan of one man.

An unquenchable burning desire for bringing souls to Christ was the passion of Patrick's life. And he pursued his passion with an unremitting perseverance, with a greatness of mind and a grandeur of soul that has infrequently been paralleled in missionary annals, and seldom surpassed.

And this singularly great man was, as we have seen, steeped in humility: "I was a stone, sunk in the mire till He who is powerful came, and in His mercy, raised me up." He was possessed of that great humility and sublime simplicity which is attained never except by moral giants.[14]

It is of interest to note that the traditions of Patrick which linger down the ages represent him not merely as a saint, law-giver, statesman, and a brother of the common people, but ever, also, as an admirer of the literary men, scholars, and poets of the nation, and an ardent lover of their profane literature. In the Ossianic tales are many evidences of this. The Colloquy of the Ancients again and again shows the old poets building upon Patrick's love of the national lore. This love, indeed, is so strong in him, that he fears it may be sinful—until he questions his guardian angel, and gets his approval for the delightful indulgence of harkening to Caoilte's fascinating stories of the Fenians. And he is so charmed with them that he orders them to be written down, so as to preserve them for the delight of future generations of the noble men of Eirinn.

"Palm of eloquence on thee, my son," Patrick says to Caoilte, "and let every third word uttered by men of thine art seem melodious to every hearer, and let one of them possessed of the skill always be a king's bedfellow and the torch of every assembly."

In recent times several ingenious people have demonstrated to their own complete satisfaction that Patrick was a Protestant, a Methodist, a Presbyterian, a Baptist—a Jew even—almost everything except what he was—and that he founded in Ireland an independent church which they call the Celtic Church. These absurd contentions are set at rest—if they needed setting at rest—by the Canon of St. Patrick, preserved in the old Book of Armagh—which was finished by the scribe Firdomnach in 807—a

---

[14] This singular humility of his as well as his characteristic impetuosity, are both well illustrated in the account given us of the origin of Sechnall's Hymn—made in Patrick's honour and published to him with fear and trembling of the author. Sechnall made the hymn by way of amends for having angered Patrick by an imprudent criticism. For, Patrick did not please all his fellow-workers, by reason that he asked not sufficient contributions from the faithful for the support of himself and his fellows. So Sechnall once said: "Patrick is a good man, were it not for one thing, that he preaches charity so very little." When this came to Patrick's ears he, in a holy rage, got into his chariot, and set out for Sechnall, whom he drove his chariot against—some say drove it over—"What is that one thing thou saidst I did not fulfil? For if I fulfil not charity, I am guilty of breaking God's commandment." He added: "It is for sake of charity that I preach not charity: for other good men will come after us, who, more than we, will need the support of the faithful."

Sechnall made his hymn as a peace offering, and brought it to Patrick. "What is it that you have there?" Patrick asked. "A hymn," replied Sechnall: "that I made for a certain son of Light. I desire you to listen to it." Patrick answered: "I welcome the praise of a man of God's household." And Sechnall held Patrick's ear and won approval and praise from him by artfully hiding, till he came to the end, the fact that Patrick himself was the subject.

Canon which those very learned Protestant Irish scholars, Usher and Whitley Stokes, accept as proof of his Roman authority and affiliation.[15]

> "Moreover, if any case should arise of extreme difficulty, and beyond the knowledge of all the judges of the nations of the Scots, it is to be duly referred to the chair of the Archbishop of the Gaedhil, that is to say, of Patrick, and the jurisdiction of this bishop (of Armagh). But if such a case as aforesaid, of a matter at issue, cannot be easily disposed of (by him), with his counsellors in that (investigation), we have decreed that it be sent to the apostolic seat, that is to say, to the chair of the Apostle Peter, having the authority of the city of Rome.
>
> "These are the persons who decreed concerning this matter, viz.: Auxilius, Patrick, Secundinus, and Benignus. But after the death of St. Patrick his disciples carefully wrote out his books."

Healy, The Most Rev. Jno.: St. Patrick.
Stokes, Whitley, D.C.L., LL.D.: The Tripartite Life of St. Patrick.
Lannigan, Rev. Jno., D.D.: Ecclesiastical History of Ireland.
Keating's History of Ireland.
Bury, J. B., LL.D.: Tirechan's Memoir of St. Patrick; printed in Eng. Hist. Rev. for 1902.
Todd, James Henthorn, D.D.: Memoir of St. Patrick.
Jocelyn: Life of St. Patrick.
O'Curry, Eugene: Manuscript Materials of Irish History.

[15] Even if, by straining of the imagination, we should suppose this document to be forged by Firdomnach—without any conceivable reason for forging it then—it shows that, at the time Firdomnach wrote it, the See of Armagh, the centre of the church in Ireland, was subordinate to the Pontiff.

Again within the Century after Patrick we find the great Columbanus, when submitting to Pope Gregory the question of his dispute with the Gaulish ecclesiastics, saying, "We Irish . . . are bound to the Chair of Peter."

CHAPTER XX

The Brehon Laws

We may here take a glimpse at those marvellous institutes, the old Irish laws which Patrick is credited with codifying—and the study of which, in these later days, throws a flood of light upon both the intellectual and the social condition of early Ireland.

Marvellous they are—and have excited the wonder and admiration not of laymen only, but of eminent jurists deeply versed in law codes both ancient and modern. It has proved amazing to modern scholars in other countries to find such a great and such a just and beautiful judicial structure reared up, in dim centuries of antiquity, in one little island seated on the waters of a wide ocean, far off on the rim of the world.

Of the great body of ancient Irish law literature still existing, five large volumes have been printed—the principal part of these being the Senchus Mor, supposed to be the fruits of Patrick's endeavour—and their ordinances appropriately called after him Cáin Padraic, that is, the Statute Law of Patrick. When we reflect that these five volumes are but a portion of what came down to the twentieth century, and that what came to the twentieth century was necessarily but a small fraction of the ancient Irish Cana or ordinances, we get some impression of the vastness of the law literature of ancient Ireland. When it is stated that in the ancient glosses upon the Senchus Mor citations are made from no less than fourteen different books of civil law; and that Cormac in his later Glossary (about tenth century) quotes from five law books only one of which is among the fourteen of the Senchus glosses, that also will give the reader a little idea of the multitude of law books that there must have been prior to the tenth century in which the scholar Cormac wrote.

And realising the vastness of the body of the old Irish laws, the reader will not wonder to learn these laws covered almost every relationship, and every fine shade of relationship, social, and moral, between man and man.

The ancient Irish laws are now popularly termed, "The Brehon Laws"—from the Irish term Brehon which was applied to the official lawgiver.[1] The Brehon was an important officer at all royal Courts, from the most remote times of which we have any shred of record, historical or even legendary. The precepts and maxims of famous law givers, men and women, of legendary days are quoted to us through famous successors who just came within the horizon of history. Even a famous woman law-giver of pre-historic times is thus commemorated in Briathra Brigid, or the judgments of a very ancient wise Brigid, cited by the earliest writers.

---

[1] Instead of filling the position of judge (as usually supposed) the Brehon was rather a legal expert who devoted himself to arbitration—and sometimes to advising—and was paid a fee from his client—a fee that in case of an award was about one-twelfth of the amount awarded. In studying for the profession the Brehon had not only to make himself master of the ancient legal records, and of the very complicated legal rules, the abstruse technical terms, and all the intricate forms in which the law was purposely entangled, but he must also be a genealogist and historian.

Though the Brehon was but an arbitrator, so scholarly was he, so skilled in the laws and so wise and weighty in his solemn judgments, that, sitting at a Dal, where two witnesses were needed to prove a fact, his words were venerated and his awards sacredly respected—as though they were the awards of a judge consecrated to the judgment seat, and rare was it to find any person hardened enough to evade or reject them.

But it should be recorded that there were lawyers, or law arguers—advocates—of a very much lower status, much less learned and much less honoured than the Brehon—men who were paid to argue cases before the Brehon. It is some of those lawyers—not unlike many of our own day—whom Cormac raps in the ancient "Instructions of a King"—

"O Cormac, grandson of Conn," said Carbery, "what is the worst pleading and arguing?"

"Not hard to tell," said Cormac.

"Contending against knowledge,
Contending without proofs,
Taking refuge in bad language,
A stiff delivery,
A muttering speech,
Hair-splitting,
Uncertain proofs,
Despising books,
Turning against custom,
Shifting one's pleading,
Inciting the mob,
Blowing one's own trumpet,
Shouting at the top of one's voice."

One of the most famous of ancient historic personages celebrated as a law-giver, was, as mentioned heretofore Cormac MacArt, in the third century. Cormac's chief judge, too, Fithal the Wise, wrote his name on fame's honour-roll. But some centuries earlier, in the time of Christ, flourished Irish law-givers, who are still known to fame. Senchan, the son of Ailill was then chief judge of Ulster, at Conor MacNessa's court. The venerated Morann the son of Maen (or of Cairbre), lived then. Athairne, the bitterest of ancient satirists, was also a lawyer at the court of King Conor. Ferceirtne, Conor's chief poet, was famed in law, likewise. But up to the era of Ferceirtne the poet-brotherhood held a monopoly of all legal knowledge. It has already been described how this monopoly was, by the indignant Conor, shattered—after he and his court had, non-understandingly, harkened to the famous dispute, Agallam na da Suach (the Contest of the two Sages), between Ferceirtne and Neide—some say between Aithairne and Neide—contending for the poet's *tuigin.* For in order to shut out the laity from the legal profession, and also for purpose of duly impressing the said laity with their dazzling erudition, the lawyers wrapped the law in a phraseology so obsolete that none but the initiated could understand the legal language. Conor, in his wrath, on this occasion, deprived the poet order of their exclusive right to legal knowledge and practice, and opened the field to everybody.

Yet, notwithstanding this supposed great reform of Conor's at the beginning of the Christian Era, the lawyers of a couple of centuries later were again indulging their vanity and their exclusiveness, concealing their legal wisdom under obsolete verbiage. We find, for instance, that though the Senchus Mor was profusely glossed by law students some centuries later, and after some further centuries the gloss itself glossed to bring it within the range of legal understanding of that day, O'Curry, learned student though he was in ancient glosses, still had the most infinite difficulty in picking out the meaning of the greater part of the work, and had to be content with giving the probable meaning of many passages, and leaving in their primitive obscurity, some things that utterly baffled him.[2]

This Brehon law remained the law of three-quarters of Ireland for several centuries after the coming of the English—was in fact adopted by a large portion of the English settlers themselves, to the exclusion of the Anglo-Norman code—and it may be said not to have gone out of existence as living law till the sixteenth century.

---

[2] Of course part of the difficulty—but not all—arose from progress of language.

The advancement of civilisation in early Ireland was such that the legislative and the judicial functions were separated at a period before the dawn of history. While the Brehon administered the law, the king, the nobles, and the professors of the various branches of learning, were responsible for originating it. Even for the making of a local law called Nos Tuaighe—literally "the Nine knowledge of a territory," the aggregate wisdom of nine leading representatives was necessary—all of whom had to agree to its institution, and all of whom had to sanction its abolition. The nine needed for the making of a local law were the chief, poet, historian, brugaid (hospitaller), bishop, professor of literature, professor of law, Aire Forgaill (a noble) and Archinnech (lay-vicar).

The local traditional, or customary, law of particular territories was called Urradus, as distinct from national law which was Cáin law. And be it noted that when the Cáin or national law conflicted with the Urradus, or local traditional law, the traditional territory law was acknowledged as annulling the national.

Of the many collections of ancient Irish laws the most famous known to scholars, are the Meill Brethra, or Mild Judgments, said to have been written at Tara in the time of Conn, and which had to do with regulations for juvenile sports (and of which only the name now remains): second, the Cáin Fuirthime, a body of Munster laws in twelve books, compiled by Amergin, for King Finghin of Munster (who died in 694), which, like the Meill Brethra, have been lost also: third, the Crith Gablach (which O'Curry thinks was a part of the Cáin Fuirthime), which is still preserved: fourth, the Book of Acaill (third century) still preserved: and fifth, the Senchus Mor, still preserved. The last three named are included in the five volumes of the Brehon Laws which were recently printed by the Brehon Law Commission.

The Crith Gablach defines the rights and privileges of the various ranks of society. O'Curry says it undoubtedly belongs to the middle or end of the seventh century, and thinks it probable that it was part of the Cáin Fuirthime.

The Book of Acaill is attributed to King Cormac MacArt and brought up to a later date by that famous scholar and most remarkable man, Ceannfalad, who flourished in the seventh century. As usual in the ancient Irish books, the Book of Acaill starts by telling the place, the time, and the cause of its writing, and the author. It says: "The place of this Book is Acaill close to Temhair, and its time is the time of Coirpre Lifechair, son of Cormac, and its author is Cormac, and the cause of its having been composed was the blinding of the eye of Cormac by Aengus

Gabuaidech after the abduction of the daughter of Sorar son of Art Corb, by Cellach son of Cormac. And Ceannfalad did part of it." The Book of Acaill is chiefly a record of criminal law and laws relating to personal injuries.

The Senchus Mor is the most monumental and remarkable record of ancient Irish law. In contradistinction to the Book of Acaill, it deals entirely with civil law. This is believed to have been the great work of Patrick. He called together all the professors of legal law, with their many law records, and he had Dubthach (one of his first converts), "a vessel full of the grace of the Holy Ghost" and the great scholar at Laeghaire's court, interpret them to him. (For Patrick had blessed Dubthach's mouth, and the grace of the Holy Ghost alighted on his utterance.) Then he had a board of three kings, three bishops and three scholars (a philosopher, a historian and a poet) sit upon them for three years, codifying and correcting them, taking out of them the pagan eye-for-an-eye doctrine, toning down their pagan severity, and weeding out from them whatsoever was inconsistent with the new law of Christ, which he had brought to them.

O'Curry (in his Manuscript Material of Irish History) says the recorded account of this great revision of the body of the laws of Erin is as fully entitled to confidence as any other well-authenticated fact in history.

The very ancient introduction to the Senchus Mor finely describes how the work was produced.[3]

> "It was then that all the professors of the sciences in Erin were assembled, and each of them exhibited his art before Patrick, in the presence of every chief in Erin.
>
> "It was then Dubthach was ordered to exhibit the judgments and all the poetry of Erin, and every law which prevailed among the men of Erin, through the law of nature, and the law of seers, and in the judgments of the island of Erin, and in the poets.
>
> "Now the judgments of true nature which the Holy Ghost had spoken through the mouths of the Brehons and just poets of the men of Erin, from their occupation of this island, to *the reception* of the faith, were all exhibited by Dubthach to Patrick. What did not

---

[3] It also tells us where the work was done:

"It was Teamhair in the summer and autumn on account of its cleanness and pleasantness during these seasons; and Rathguthaird was the place during the winter and spring, on account of the nearness of its firewood and water, and on account of its warmth in the time of winter's cold."

clash with the Word of God in the written law and in the New Testament, and with the consciences of the believers, was confirmed in the laws of the Brehons by Patrick and by the ecclesiastics and the chieftains of Erin; for the law of nature had been quite right, except the faith, and its obligations. And this is the Senchus Mor."

The Senchus Mor as it has been preserved to us today is composed of four parts—namely, the introduction describing when and how it came to be written; then the original text, written in a large hand, and with very wide spaces between the lines; third, commentaries on the text, written in a much smaller hand, just beneath the lines of the original; and fourth, glosses or explanations of the words and phrases in the text, written under the commentaries, and in a hand still smaller. The text is more archaic than the commentaries, and the commentaries more so than the glosses. The sentences in the original text are so skeleton-like, terse and suggestive, that it is considered they are mere headings meant to be expounded and extended in courses of oral instruction.

The laws in the Senchus Mor, like all the old Brehon Laws, were rarely legislative enactments. Some few undoubtedly, were enacted, but most of them were laws of user, which obtained their force from public opinion. And a vast body of the laws were precedents and commentaries of venerated law-givers of earlier times.

The whole superstructure of the ancient Irish civil law (as again and again proclaimed) rested upon the foundation of the sanctity of verbal contract. "For," says the old law-giver, "the world would be in confusion if verbal contracts were not binding."

O'Curry pointedly and succinctly tells us of these contract provisions in the Senchus Mor:

"The Senchus Mor contains a system of law respecting Contracts, in which every species of contract, bargain, or engagement is defined, and the competency or incompetency, and the rights and duties, of the contracting parties made clear; by which a penalty is incurred for the non-performance of every separate kind of contract; false and fraudulent contracts annulled, and fraud punished; and under which judges and officers are provided to decide all disputes concerning contracts, the decisions of such judges being in all cases enforced by the power and authority of the state. It is curious to remark that, under this ancient system, neither the judge nor the advocate—of the latter of whom there were, it appears, three grades or classes,—was held harmless in cases of false or corrupt judgments, or faulty or incompetent advocacy."[4]

Although O'Curry again and again says that there was an executive power attendant upon the judicial—that the state enforced the Brehon's decision—there is the best reason to believe that the executive power was, not official, but that greatest of all powers, especially in Ireland, the moral power of public opinion. Everybody considered it his bounden business to see that the pronouncement of their venerated Brehons were observed to the letter, and the verdict summarily executed. And despite the *sean-fhocal* that everybody's business is nobody's business, we know that, so far as concerned carrying out the judgments of the Brehons, everybody's business was truly the business of each.

---

[4] O'Curry gives a highly interesting enumeration of the various kinds of law that are embodied in this marvellous record—a list that will surprise those who hitherto knew little about the subject of ancient Irish law. He shows that the Senchus Mor includes:

The laws defining all the different species of Bargains, Contracts, and Engagements between man and man.

The laws respecting Property entrusted or given in charge by one man to another; and the Liability of the person trusted, in case of loss or damage, whether by accident or design.

The laws respecting Gifts and Presents, and respecting Alms and Endowments.

The laws as to Waifs and Strays, Derelictions, and the Abandonment and Resumption of Property.

The law of Loans, Pledges, Accommodations, and Securities.

The law of Prescription, or lapse, and of the Recovery of Possession of Property.

The laws concerning the relation of Father and Son, and the legal and illegal contracts of the son as connected therewith.

The laws respecting illegitimate Children; as to Affiliations, and the Adoption of children.

Laws minutely regulating the Fees of Doctors, Judges, Lawyers, and Teachers, and of all other professional persons.

A series of laws concerning the varied species of Industry: such as Weaving, Spinning, Sewing, Building, Brewing, etc.; concerning Mills and Weirs; concerning Fishing; concerning Bees, Poultry, etc.

Laws with respect to Injuries to Cattle; by neglect, by over-driving, etc.

Laws concerning Fosterage, and the relative duties of Parents and Children, Foster-fathers and Foster-mothers; including details of a very curious kind, respecting the training, food, clothing, etc., of all foster-children, from the king to the peasant.

A very complicated, yet clearly defined series of laws for Landlord and Tenant, and Master and Servant; explaining the different species of lords and masters, of tenants and of servants; and the origin and termination of Tenantry and Service.

Laws concerning Trespass and Damage to Land, whether by man or beast.

A curious series of laws concerning Co-Occupancy of Land; and concerning the dividing, hedging, fencing, paling, ditching and walling, and the ploughing and stocking of land.

Laws of Evidence; of Corroborative Testimony; and of Compurgation.

The law of Distress and Caption; including most minute details, which appear to embrace almost every possible point that could be made concerning the legality or illegality of a Distress or Seizure.

The laws of Tithes and First Fruits; and concerning the relations of the Church with the state or nation (a law, doubtless introduced at the direct suggestion of St. Patrick).

As a sample of judicial procedure in civil law we set down the usual course followed in recovering for a debt. A *fasc* (summons) was first served upon the debtor, in which were entered the details of the claim, and demand for payment made according to law. A certain number of days of grace was then allowed the debtor, after which, if the debt was not paid, a *gabail* (distress)[5] was laid upon some portion of his property—almost always on his live-stock. For this purpose the creditor took with him a law agent and seven witnesses, and attached, but did not then carry off, the seized goods. There was an *anad* (stay) of a day or days—to give the debtor a second chance of paying. If he did not pay within the *anad,* the distrained goods were lifted—the cattle, say, driven off, and placed in a pound. An *apad* (notice) was then served upon the debtor, telling him that the cattle were taken, and informing him just where they were impounded. Then followed a *dithim,* another stay, to give the debtor yet another chance for redeeming his property. If, when the *dithim* had expired, the debtor had not redeemed his property, the next stage, the *lobad* (wasting) began; that is, instead of selling all of the seized property for the immediate and complete satisfying of the debt, it was sold in portions—out of still further regard for, and mercy toward, the debtor.

But if, when the creditor with his agent and witnesses first went to distrain, the debtor denied the claim, and demanded trial of the case—or if he agreed to pay after the expiration of a certain time—he got a stay of execution on giving pledge *(gell),* or giving bail. If, then, the debtor did not fulfil

---

Laws concerning the regulation of Churches and the tenants of Church lands, and the servitors of Churches and Ecclesiastical establishments.

In Criminal Law; complete laws respecting Manslaughter and Murder, distinguishing accurately between principals and accessories before and after the act.

Laws concerning Thefts, and the receiving and recovery of stolen property; in the greatest possible detail.

Laws concerning the infliction of Wounds and the shedding of Blood; and with regard to the commission of violence by insane as well as by same persons.

And lastly, laws concerning Accidental Injuries; as from sledges, hammers, flails, hatchets, and other implements connected with peaceful labour.

After perusing that wonderful list of only one collected portion of the laws of Ireland in the early centuries of the Christian Era, the reader can, for himself, hazard a guess at the very advanced state of early Irish civilisation which evolved and called forth such laws—and which evolved, too, a professional body of highly-trained law-givers. Overtrained indeed Brehons often came to be, and so steeped in, and saturated with, their science, that, passing beyond the love of law for justice sake, many of the noted ones, as shown by their rulings, their commentaries, and anecdotes of them, came at length to pursue law for law's sake, and loved to indulge themselves, and dazzle the multitude, by elaborate quibblings, and the working out of fantastically far-fetched legal problems.

[5] Sullivan, in his introduction to O'Curry derives the word gaol from gabail (pron., *gow-ail*), which originally meant a distress by the body.

the conditions of the stay of execution, the pledge, or the bail, was forfeited, and the levying of the distress proceeded. Sometimes he gave his own son in pledge. In that case the services of the son were forfeit, if the conditions were not fulfilled—the son became the bondsman of the creditor, till the debt was worked out. If he had been bailed the *athire* (bailsman) became the creditor's bondsman, in the same case, if he could not meet the liabilities of him whom he had bailed. If the debtor was superior in rank to the creditor, the latter had to try fasting upon his debtor before he could seize his goods.[6]

---

[6] This fasting upon a debtor, or upon a wronger, which is an Eastern custom still or till recently practised in some parts of India, was a common enough practice in olden times in Ireland. A creditor wanting payment of his debt from a superior, or a wronged person demanding justice, or any one demanding any right to which he was entitled, sat him down by the door of the dishonest or unjust one, and, while the sympathetic world looked on, and its indignation daily grew greater against the wronger who had forced the wronged to take this extreme course, the latter tasted of no food. In short it was a plain hunger-strike for compelling justice from the powerful.

If he who was fasted upon, felt that he had not been unjust, that he was wrongly accused and exposed, by the hunger-striker at his door—or if, knowing that he was unjust, he wished to make the world believe otherwise, he in turn adopted the fast against his accuser. Naturally he who could longest hold out in suffering—which usually meant the man whose conscience supported and inspired him—won out.

In the ancient tale of the sons of O'Corra is an account of how Conal Dearg O'Connor and his wife fasted against the devil, that he might bless them with children—and succeeded. In the Book of Lismore is the account of three young clerics, who had pledged themselves to say between them a certain total of prayers, daily. One of them died, leaving a heavier task on the other two. Then a second died, leaving still greater task to the survivor—whereupon last of them—upon which he began fasting against God for the injustice of taking away the other two and leaving their burdens to him. Also, one of the Irish legends tells how Adam, in the Jordan, after he had been expelled from Paradise, and Eve in the Tigris, fast against God, to compel forgiveness; and request the beasts and the fishes to fast with them.

There were a few special laws bearing upon the subject of debtor and creditor which are interesting to note in passing.

One law justly provided that "no one must be oppressed when in difficulty."

To those who had pledged personal ornaments for debt (as has been stated in a previous chapter), the pledged object had to be released on the occasion, and during the term, of any of the great Aonachs (fairs), which the debtor, like the people in general, was expected to attend. If the creditor neglected to release the ornaments on such occasion he was under liability to pay to the debtor a blush fine for the embarrassment incurred by the debtor in appearing before the gay and richly-decked crowds on festive occasions without his personal ornaments.

Moreover, as general jubilee was proclaimed during the term of the great fairs, it was the law that during such festive time the creditor must rid his mind of debt memories. A debtor could not be arrested, or annoyed, for debt at the Aonach, or going to, or coming from it.

Furthermore, the laws against debtors were suspended during the official period of grief following the death of the Primate of Armagh, or the Ard-Righ of Ireland. Both these grave occasions were the cause of proclaiming a twelve months' moratorium. On the death of the king of one of the provinces all debtors had a three months' exemption: and one month on the death of a chieftain of a tuath (territory).

The most notable way in which Patrick deprived the ancient law of its severity was his substitution of eric-law for the Lex Talionis. Under the new law a graduated system of money fines, called *eric,* was substituted for the eye-for-an-eye ordinance of the old. Only, when the criminal or his family or tribe did not pay his eric, the law sanctioned his personal punishment—which, moreover, might even then, instead of following the old method, take the form of his being sold as a bondman. Or, again, he might become the bondman of any one, outside his *fine* (his own relatives), who paid the *eric* for him.

The *eric* for killing one of the bond-class was twenty-one cows. Forty-two cows was the eric for killing a freeman. This, however, was only the standard when the homicide was one of the plain people. If a noble were guilty of killing he had to pay the ordinary *eric* plus a *log-enach,* or honour price, graduated in the scale according to his rank: the higher his rank the higher was the honour price which he had to add to the ordinary *eric.*[7]

The Senchus Mor established it that half a noble's *log-enach* was lost to him the first time he was found guilty of false judgment, false witness, fraudulent security, false information, false character-giving, bad stories, lying, criminal wounding, betrayal, or refusal of food. On commission of the third such offence he was deprived of his honour-price complete.

In the old Irish laws then, the sword of Justice had ever two edges sharpened for punishing people of rank. From those to whom much was given, much was to be expected. The democracy of those laws was shown in dozens of other ways. The king carrying building material to his castle had the same and only the same claim for right of way as the miller carrying material to build his mill. The poorest man in the land could compel payment of a debt from a noble—could levy a distress upon the king himself, through the person of the king's steward. The man who stole the needle[8] of a poor embroidery woman was compelled to pay a far higher fine than the man who stole the queen's needle.

[7] The *log-enach* or honour price, not merely made for the democratic justice of the law, which recognised that the fine laid upon a poor man or an ignorant, did not suffice to punish a noble, or a learned man—but it likewise placed in the hands of the law another unique and powerful instrument for the punishing of men in high place. This power lay in the fact, which will at first seem strange, that if a man of rank (social or intellectual) was found guilty of a degrading act, his honour price—the extra fine he should pay for his misdeed—was thereby reduced: thereafter, he paid for his crimes the smaller fine of a man of lower rank. The dramatic justice of this usage is plain to us, when we consider that the reducing of his honour price had the moral effect of degrading him henceforth to lower rank.

[8] A needle then was a prized possession—value for a year-old calf.

One of the seven things forbidden by law was for a poor man to give service or rent to a noble who demanded an excess of either; while the noble was mulcted for making the unjust demand. The king himself was bound by law to do justice to his meanest subject: for the law, while enumerating and acknowledging his rights, very distinctly and definitely points out to him that he had duties also. "The king must not exact his rights," says the law, "by falsehood, nor by force, nor by despotic might. His fostering care must be perfect to all, both weak and strong." And this sacred regard for rigid justice is well exemplified in the judgment given (in the case of the killing of Patrick's charioteer) by Dubtach, King Laoghaire's Ollam, in the presence of the King and the court, and of Patrick, when, unlike the degenerate courtiers of later days, he boldly proclaimed:

> "Let every one die who kills a human being;
> Even the king . . .
> Who inflicts red wounds intentionally."

The king, too, was threatened with degradation by these impartial laws. Four dignitaries who may be degraded are, "a false-judging king, a stumbling bishop, a fraudulent poet, and an unworthy chieftain." One special privilege accorded the king, however, was that only men of three specified ranks could reply to him at law; namely, a bishop, an ollam, and a pilgrim.

Running through all the laws for all the ranks, impartiality was the salient characteristic. Always the Irish law expected most from those who had most received from God. The laws bearing upon ecclesiastics, again, well exemplify this. For instance, while there was a certain fine imposed upon laymen for neglecting to honour a summons to court, an ecclesiastic was fined double for the same offence. And, whereas, for certain offences, lay people of rank were deprived of half their honour-price the first time, and all their honour-price the third time, clerics for the very first offence were condemned not only to lose all their honour-price, but likewise to be degraded. Pursuing stern justice still farther—while ordinary clerics could, by doing penance and suffering punishment, win back their grade, he of higher rank, the Bishop, not only lost his honour-price and was degraded for the first offence, but could never again regain his position. He must go out from the abodes of men and henceforth live a hermit.[9]

---

[9] It may here be noted that, in the sight of the law, in the same rank with the bishop was the king, the chief poet, and the brugaid or public hospitaller: a like *dire* fine or eric was payable for the killing of either of the four.

That the impartiality of the law persisted even toward its own professors is exemplified in the ordinance which discriminated against law advocates being paid a blush fine. Blush fines were payable for insults offered to all persons of all ranks, with a few notable exceptions. The ne'er-do-well, the squanderer, the idler, and the lazy man, could not claim blush-fine. Neither could the selfish, earthy one who thought only of his cows and his fields; the druth or the clown who distorted himself before crowds at a fair; the Cáinte or Satirist who himself made a trade of insulting others, and, finally—the lawyer! "A man who is paid to abuse others," says the law, "is not entitled to claim damages when abused himself."

For the Brehons who framed the laws showed no leniency toward their own order. "Every judge," says the Book of Acaill, "is punishable for his neglect. He has to pay eric-fine for his false judgment." Another law, too, ordered that for false judgment he should be degraded.

And the old law's fairness is again shown, and its chivalry, in the stipulation that every alien who came into the country to pursue a suit at law against a native, was entitled to his choice of the Brehons of Eirinn. And paralleling this was the ordinance that every outsider who came into any territory for purpose of suing a subject in that territory, had his choice of the Brehons of the territory.

But, the thoughtful wisdom of the ancient law-makers is everywhere exemplified. There were laws prescribed for the care of the poor, the aged and the sick—with detailed instructions in each case. For the sick, the doctor was bound to provide plentiful ventilation—so that, through open doors or windows, the patient could be seen from all four sides, by one outside the house. A running stream of fresh water must flow through his hospital. For neglect, or blunder, or mismanagement of an operation, the doctor was fined. If he failed, through ignorance, to effect a cure he could claim no fee.

Knowing the exacting nature of those who depended upon the charity of others, this law thoughtfully provided that the official who looked after the poor should have no recourse at law against the abusiveness of those under his charge. He or his family could not claim blush-fine for insult hurled at him by the creatures whom he helped.

Minute details are given of what must be provided for the dependent aged person; details of the house; the furnishings of the house; the supplies necessary; details of the old person's care—as for instance, how often he must be bathed, how often have his head washed, and so on.

There is found in the Yellow Book of Lecan, and also in the *Leabar Breac* a curious *Cáin Domnach,* Law of Sunday, which was said to have been brought over from Rome by St. Conall, a sixth-century Donegal saint. During the Sabbath, which in ancient Ireland extended from sunset on Saturday to sunrise on Monday, the Cáin Domnach forbids all labour outdoor or indoor. It forbids sweeping or cleaning the house, combing, shaving, clipping the hair or beard; it forbids games of all kinds, buying, selling, washing, bathing, cutting, sewing, churning, fishing, boating, grinding corn, cooking, splitting firewood, riding on horseback, journeying of travellers. Wherever the evening of Saturday descended on a traveller, there should he pause in his journey, and resume it only on Monday morning.

In quitting the subject of the old laws, after this brief glimpse at a broad field, we may agree with Patrick when he indicated that even the Pagan law-givers were inspired by the Spirit. He considered that they spoke, as he asked Dubtach, when giving judgment, to speak—"What God will give you for utterance, say it. It is not you that speak but the spirit of the Father which speaketh in you."

Ginnell, Lawrence: The Brehon Laws.
Joyce, P. W.: Social History of Ancient Ireland.
Brehon Laws: The Ancient Laws of Ireland.
Maine, Sir Henry: Dissertations on Ancient Law.
Sullivan, W. K., Ph.D.: Introduction to O'Curry's Manners and Customs of the Ancient Irish.
O'Curry, Eugene: Manuscript Materials of Irish History.
—— Manners and Customs.

CHAPTER XXI

St. Bridget

For four centuries after the Bishop Patrick, setting foot in the country, began scattering far and wide the seeds of the Gospel, the history of the Irish race hangs upon the history of the holy men and women, and the scholars, who continued Patrick's work, at home in Ireland and afar on the Continent of Europe.

And by far the greatest woman in this work was Bridget.

When Patrick rested from his labours it was on Bridget that the seeding sheet was bound. And over the hills and the dales of Ireland then went she, sowing the fruitful words of the new Master to whom Ireland had learnt to bow. And a worthy successor to Patrick was she—Bridget the beloved, Bridget of Eirinn, the Mary of the Gael! In the centre of the trinity of Irish patron saints Patrick, Bridget and Colm Cille, she stands, crowned, the spiritual queen of the race. And warmly and fondly as the memory of the other two great ones is treasured in the Irish heart, it is doubtful if their names evoke the deep, sweet and tender, overwhelming affection that is breathed with the name of Bridget.[1]

---

[1] Oh, she was fair as a lily,
And holy as she was fair,
The Virgin Mary of Erin—
Brigid of green Kildare.
She came to earth when the snow drops
Were starring the rain-drenched sod,
The sweetest blossom among them,
From the far-off gardens of God.

O Brigid, so high and holy!
So strong in womanly grace,
Look down from the sills of heaven

But not in Ireland alone is it a living thing, that intimate devotion to her, the woman patron saint of the Gael, but wherever they go and wherever they are they bear in their breast a little flame of the perpetual fire of Kildare. And devotion to her is as sweet and ardent among the simple islanders of Highland Scotland's fjords as it is in the Western Aran, or on the Currach of Kildare. The bare-footed maiden in Uist of Hebrides, driving the cows to pasture, still chants—but in melodious Gaelic:

> "The protection of God and Columba,
> Encompass your going and coming,
> And about you be the milk-maid of the smooth white palm,
> Bridget of the clustering hair, golden brown."

Bridget was born just twenty years after the coming of Patrick, about the year 450, at Fochart, near Dundalk. She met and heard Patrick preach. According to an ancient tradition she slept a mystic sleep once, during his preaching at Clogher, and had a symbolic dream in which was shown her

---

Today on your olden race.
'Tis over the world we're scattered,
And your land is a land of woe,
But we're holding you as a lodestar,
Whatever the roads we go.

For you are our pledge in heaven,
With Padraig and Colm Cille,
For the Faith by our foes unbroken,
And the hopes that they could not still;
For the surge of our prayers unceasing,
For the depth of our love unpriced,
For our agony in earth's garden,
And our crucifixion with Christ.

And we cry to you, holy Brigid,
'Tis you have the right to pray
For us in the land of Erin,
In the hour of our need today.
We breathe your name as a symbol,
Like the lamp on your altar set,
That God is an unforgetting God,
And will stand for our righting yet.
Yea, He who so long has tried us
In the flame of His purging fire,
Will give to the race of Brigid
The crown of their souls' desire.

—Teresa Brayton.

the future triumphs, and the future trials of the faith in Ireland. Another tradition has it that she aided in making his winding-sheet.

It is the universal Irish claim upon Bridget which has called forth legends giving every quarter of Ireland a proprietary right upon the national treasure. So some traditions would have her born in the house of a Druid, at the court of the chieftain of Tir-Conaill, of a Munster father and Connaught mother, while her future home was to be Leinster.

Bridget's mother appears to have been a bond-maid in the house of Bridget's father,[2] Dubtach, who was of royal descent, tenth from King Feidlimid the Lawgiver. And the tradition goes that just before Bridget's birth, her mother, like Hagar, was, through the jealousy of the wife of Dubtach, driven forth upon the world. She was sold into the service of a Druid—in whose house Bridget was born, and in whose service she is said to have lived to free her mother.

The Druid, when he had acquired the bond-maid and learnt the cause of her selling foretold to Dubtach: "The seed of thy wife shall serve the seed of the bond-maid, for the bond-maid will bring forth a daughter conspicuous, radiant, who will shine like a sun among the stars."[3]

---

[2] Concubinage was, in ancient times, common in Ireland, as in almost all countries.

[3] As Bridget grew up she became both a shepherd and a dairy-maid on the Druid's farm—a dairy-maid, sweet, gentle and beautiful, with a disposition that was perpetual sunshine in her clean white dairy, or in the woods with her sheep. In these days Bridget's heart went out to all living things, to God's beasts and birds as well as His mankind—on all which she lavished her love. And all in return loved her. God, too, sent His blessing upon her and her work. "Everything to which her hand was set," says the Book of Lismore, "used to increase. She tended the sheep; she satisfied the birds; she fed the poor."

Bridget cared for the milk of twelve cows. And when she took the butter she made it into twelve equal parts and one large part, in memory of Christ and the apostles. And the large portion she gave to the poor and to the stranger—for she used to say, "Christ is in the person of every faithful guest."

And one of the legends of the Book of Lismore tells how, once, the Druid and his wife learning that great quantities of their butter were being given away by the dairy-maid came to the dairy to see for themselves, and to demand from Bridget a hamper of butter for their own use. "Of butter, what has thou?" the Druid demanded. Now it happened that Bridget, because of her generosity, had only as much left as should come off one and one-half churning. Yet when her master and mistress demanded a full hamper, she cheerfully went into her dairy-kitchen, singing:

"Oh, my Prince
Who canst do all these things,
Bless, O God,
My kitchen with Thy right hand.

"My kitchen
The kitchen of the white God,
A kitchen which my King hath blessed,
A kitchen that hath butter.

When the maid, Bridget, a free woman, returned to her father's house, she was so singularly graceful and beautiful, that the fame of her spread far and near. Ardent wooers, in the person of champions, chieftains, young princes in numbers, came to woo her for wife. But she refused them all—for she had resolved to be the bride of Christ. This her father did not like—much less her stepmother who became intensely jealous of her. But her father's objections increased, and her stepmother's dislike for Bridget multiplied many times, when they discovered that the luxurious excess for which their house had been famed, was melting away, by reason of Bridget's bestowing their substance upon the poor who crowded to her.

At the instigation of his wife, Dubtach, for peace sake had to decide to put Bridget away, just as he had once put away her mother. So he took her with him in his chariot to the Palace of Dunlaing MacEnda, King of Leinster. "It is not for honour or reverence to thee thou art carried in a chariot," he said to her, as they went, "but to take thee to sell thee to grind the quern for Dunlaing MacEnda."

When he reached Dunlaing's residence he left Bridget in the chariot while he went to see the King. But, so notorious had she become for her unstinted giving that he left with her in the chariot nothing which she might in his absence bestow on the poor—nothing but his sword. As, however, a leper, coming down the way, begged charity of her, and that she had nothing else to give him, she gave him her father's sword.

When her father returned with Dunlaing MacEnda, and discovered what she had done, he was mightily provoked. He appealed to the King saying: "Thou seest for thyself why I am forced to sell this daughter of mine."

And Dunlaing said to her: "Neither can I take you into my house, for since it is thine own father's wealth that thou takest and givest away, much more wilt thou take my wealth, and my cattle, and give them to the poor."

"Mary's Son, my Friend, cometh
To bless my kitchen.
The Prince of the world to the border,
May we have abundance with Him."

In and out she went chanting, and in and out continuously bearing with her from the kitchen, each time, the butter of half a churning till a large hamper was filled. And says the tale in the Book of Lismore, "If the hampers which the men of Munster possessed had been given her, she would fill them all."

Astonished at the miracle and the miracle-worker, the Druid exclaimed: "Both the butter and the kine are thine. Thou shouldst be serving not me but the Lord." "Take the kine," said Bridget, "and give me my mother's freedom." The Druid thereupon gave her both the kine and her mother's freedom. She gave the kine to the poor. The Druid and his wife were baptised, and were full of faith henceforward.

To which Bridget replied: "The Son of the Virgin knoweth that if I had thy might with all Leinster and all wealth, I would give them to the Lord of the elements."

Then Dunlaing said to Dubtach: "It is not meet for us to deal with this maiden. Her merit before the Lord is higher than ours."

And so was Bridget saved from a second slavery.

She was veiled[4] with seven other virgins by Bishop Macaille whose church was in that part now called Kings County. And the inevitable legends that grew up around all of Ireland's beloved record that, when she was taking her vows, in the wooden pillar of the altar-rail on which she rested her hand the sap circulated and the pillar became green, and bloomed again.

She went into Connaught—where her piety and charity, her faith and her work, were such that she quickly became the most famous personage there. Her Leinster people, learning of her fame, sent to her, besought her to come home to them, and offered a habitation at Kildare to her and the great number of followers she had now gathered around her. Bridget accepted—and there then, she founded the Church of the Oak, and founded the Monastery of Kildare which was to be famous for all time. She founded also the little less famous school of Kildare. This was in the latter years of the fifth century. Her home in Kildare became a centre of religion and of learning, of piety and of lore, whose fame almost rivalled the fame of Patrick's See itself, at Armagh. Great were the crowds that resorted here, not only from all Leinster, but from every corner of Ireland. Crowds of poor came seeking material relief; crowds of the pious to satisfy their souls; crowds of students who thirsted for knowledge—all classes came—those in wealth and those in want; the humble and the haughty; learned and illiterate; chieftain and bondman, layman and ecclesiastic—all attracted by the piety and wisdom, the goodness and greatness, of the foremost woman of the Gael.

Yet the humility of this noble woman remained such that oftentimes when the very greatest sought her, they found her not in the hall nor the church, but, though it might be blowing or snowing, off in the fields

[4] The Tripartite life of St. Patrick implies that in his day he consecrated nuns—that they even thronged to him from abroad. Nine daughters of the King of the Lombards, it says, came to Patrick, over the sea, and a daughter of the King of Britain. It is also said that he veiled the daughters of Laoghaire, the two princesses, Ethni of the Golden Hair, and Fedelm the Ruddy. "Patrick put a white veil upon their heads, and having received the Body and Blood, they fell asleep in death. Patrick laid them side by side on the one mantle, and in the same bed."

herding the cattle that gave milk to the monastery, or the sheep that gave them wool.[5]

Once when Bishop Conlaeth (whom she had selected for the See of Kildare) preached to the sisterhood upon the Beatitudes she proposed to the nuns that each sister should take one of the Beatitudes as her special object of devotion, she herself characteristically choosing Mercy.

In those days many Bishops were skilled in trades—which were then considered noble and ennobling. Her bishop Conlaeth was a fine artificer, skilled in doing beautiful work in metal. He is supposed to have taught decorative metal art in the school of Kildare, which was a centre of that art. Here they turned out chalices, bells, patens and shrines, beautifully ornamented. The art of working in metal was particularly prized in Ireland then: many devoted themselves to it and much tasteful work was produced. Of the multitude of presents that were given to Bridget and her monastery and her church by those who were constantly thronging there, it is recorded that the queen of Crimthann, the son of Enna Ceannselach, gave to Bridget a silver chain of which the Book of Lismore says: "The semblance of a human shape was on one of the ends thereof, and an apple of silver at the other end."

Bridget made many journeys through the south and west of Ireland, consulting, counselling and directing the spiritual leaders, spreading the faith wheresoever she went, and inspiring great numbers to devote themselves to the service of Christ. And wheresoever she was, at home or abroad, crowds of people were constantly thronging to this wonderful woman. The rich came with gifts, the poor came for help; the sick came for healing. She is recorded to have worked many miracles by the power of her surpassing faith—a faith so powerful that it is related that a woman consumptive who touched her shadow was instantly healed. The belief of the people in

---

[5] It was herding thus she was, when occurred the little incident that is related of Ninnid and herself.

Ninnid from Loch Erne whose name as a saint was afterwards to be famed was then a little lad studying at the school of Kildare. On a morning when she sat herding her sheep on the currach, enveloped in a cloak that hid her identity, the little Ninnid came running past—probably in fear of being late for his class. The cloaked nun called out, asking him why he ran. "O nun," the ready-witted boy replied, "I am going to Heaven." "Well," said the nun, "won't you pause and make prayer with me that it may be easy for me to go?" "O nun," replied the hurrying boy, "I cannot, for the gates of Heaven open now, and if I delay they may be shut against me." But she insisted, "Pray to the Lord with me that it may be easy for me to go, and I'll pray to the Lord with you that it may be easy for you to go—and to bring thousands."

Ninnid, thus persuaded, knelt down with Bridget and prayed. And it was ordained that this lad would help to smooth her way to Heaven—he was to give her, at her passing away, the last rites.

And it was this praying of Bridget's on the currach with the little scholar, Ninnid, that constituted her the patron of students.

her power begot many legends—one of these telling us that she was once seen to hang her wet cloak, for drying, on a ray of sunshine.[6]

Cogitosus, a monk of Kildare, who in the eighth century wrote the life of Bridget says, "Uncountable were the numbers who flocked to her: the sick for healing; and the rich with gifts."

This was not by any means the first life of Bridget written. Bishop Ultan of Ardbreccain, who is frequently styled a brother of Bridget's, collected the virtues and miracles of Bridget, and commanded his disciple Brogan to put them into poetry.[7]

A wonderful description of Bridget's Church at Kildare is given by Cogitosus which is evidently imaginary of that day, but which Dr. Petrie (in his "Round Towers") affirms was real for Cogitosus' own day. Cogitosus says that in that church in Kildare "repose the bodies of Bishop Conlaeth and his holy virgin, Bridget, on the right and left of the decorated altar, deposited in monuments adorned with various embellishments of gold and silver gems and precious stones, with crowns of gold and silver depending from above, elevated to a menacing height and adorned with painted

---

[6] Of an old blind sister, Dara, whose sight she had restored, it is told that she begged to be darkened again—

Yet she said, my sister,
Blind me once again,
Lest His presence in me
Groweth less plain.
Stars and dawn and sunset
Keep till Paradise,
Here His face sufficeth
For my sightless eyes.

Oh, she said, my sister,
Night is beautiful
Where His face is showing
Who was mocked as fool.
More than star or meteor,
More than moon or sun,
Is the thorn-crowned forehead
Of the Holy One.

—Katherine Tynan Hinkson.

[7] Ultan, however, could not have been her kin-brother, for his death is recorded only in the year 656, when he died of the great plague—during which he had been father to the flocks of orphans which that plague, the *buidhe-Chonaill,* made in Eirinn. O'Clery's Martyrology says "Ultan of Ardbreccain used to feed with his own hands every child who had no support in Eirinn—so that he often had fifty and thrice fifty with him together."

pictures . . . one partition decorated and painted with figures and covered with linen hangings."

Bridget, it is said, took the Blessed Mother, Mary, as her model. "She was following the manners and the life," says one account, "which the Holy Mother of Jesus had." "It was this Bridget, too," says O'Clery's Martyrology, "that did not take her mind or her attention from the Lord for the space of one hour at any time, but was constantly mentioning Him, and ever constantly thinking of Him. She was hospitable and charitable, and humble, and attended to herding sheep and early rising."

Bridget made Kildare truly great. The old annalists who made a point of recording the names of abbots of monasteries, but not abbesses, always, however made exception to their rule in the case of the abbesses of Kildare. And because of the priority that Bridget's greatness gave it, Kildare's abbess came to be looked up to by all the nuns of Ireland, just as the Primate of Armagh was looked up to by all the clerics.

In her day, because of her power, she ruled the monks of Kildare as well as the nuns. Before she died it was said that as many as thirty religious houses were under her obedience. It is recorded that for nearly a thousand years her name was honoured, and her feast was celebrated, in every Cathedral Church from Grisons to the German Sea. As many as thirty Continental cities are quoted for their devotion, in the middle ages, to Irish Bridget.

Four years after the birth of Colm Cille, Bridget died—in 525—leaving Ireland in mourning. And they mourned for Bridget as they had never mourned for any, high or low, simple or gentle—with the possible exception of Patrick. And in the one tomb with Patrick at Down, was interred Ireland's greatest woman, Ireland's Bridget, the Mary of the Gael.

> "It was she who never turned her attention from the Lord for one hour, but was constantly meditating and thinking of Him in her heart and mind, as is evident in her own life and in that of St. Brendan, Bishop of Cluain-Ferta. She spent her time diligently serving the Lord, performing wonders and miracles, healing every disease and malady, until she resigned her spirit to heaven on the first day of the month of February, and her body was interred at Dun, in the same tomb with St. Patrick, with honour and veneration."

And the Book of Lismore:

> "For, everything Bridget asked, the Lord granted at once. For this was her desire: to satisfy the poor; to expel every hardship; to relieve

every misery. Now never hath there been any one more bashful, modest, gentle, humble, more sage, more harmonious than Bridget. She was abstinent, innocent, prayerful, patient, glad in God's commandments, firm, humble, forgiving, loving. She was a consecrated casket for holding Christ's Body and Blood. She was a temple of God. She was simple toward God; compassionate toward the wretched; she was splendid in miracles and marvels; wherefore her name among created things is like unto a dove among the birds, a vine among trees, the sun among stars.

"She is the prophetess of Christ: She is the Queen of the South. She is the Mary of the Gael."

Stokes, Whitley, D.C.L., LL.D.: Lives of the Saints from the Book of Lismore.

Healy, The Most Rev. Jno., D.D., LL.D., Archbishop of Tuam: Ireland's Ancient Schools and Scholars.

Lannigan, Rev. John, D.D.: Ecclesiastical History of Ireland.

Joyce, P. W.: Social History of Ancient Ireland.

Reeves, The Rev. Wm., D.D.: The Martyrology of Donegal ("O'Clery's Col."), a Calendar of the Saints of Erin. (Edited by Dr. Reeves and Dr. Todd conjointly.)

O'Hanlon, The Rev. Jno., Canon: Lives of the Irish Saints.

CHAPTER XXII

Women in Ancient Ireland

The fact that in such remote time as the fifth century a woman could command the respect, the reverence, and moral obedience which were so fully and freely rendered to Bridget will naturally surprise the many who reflect that in most countries it is only a few centuries since women came out of semi-bondage.

But, in Ireland, from the remotest time of which we have any record, historical or legendary, woman stood emancipated, and was oftentimes eligible for the professions, and for rank and fame. In the dimmest, most ancient legends, casual references to druidesses, poetesses, women physicians and women sages, prove that in the very remote days in which these legends were created, there was nothing uncommon or surprising in women filling these positions. In one of the oldest, if not the oldest, of all invocations in Irish legendary lore, the invocation of Amergin, son of Milesius, praying to the gods for the safe landing of their company against which the Tuatha De Danann were raising magic storms, he says: "Let the learned wives of Breas and Buaigne pray that we may reach the noble woman, great Eirinn."

The ancient Irish had a goddess, Bridget, who represented poetry and wisdom—and, as before mentioned, they had a mortal Bridget who was a famous lawgiver—whose laws and sayings were instanced, and her decisions followed as precedents, by her learned successors, well down into historical times. She was either wife or daughter of Senchan, the Ollam of Ulster, at Conor MacNessa's court.

Woman was then nearly on an equality with man. Particularly great women compelled the admission of this equality, and sometimes of superiority, too. Still, the man-made laws took care to throw the weight of authority in the scale with the so-called lord of Creation. Although the Crith Gablach, in discussing the privileges of a man of the noble classes, lays down the dictum, "To his wife belongs the right to be consulted on every subject," and although before a Brehon's court the husband and wife stood on equal terms, still the law held that the man had headship in the marriage union. Then, however, it proceeds to safeguard the rights of the wife. For it says that though he had headship of the two, he did not own her. "It is only contract that is between them," says the law.

Again, insisting on the man's superior privileges the old commentator on the Senchus Mor, while admitting that the laws therein were equally for the women as well as for the men, goes on to explain why it is entitled the Senchus of the *Men* of Eirinn. "It is proper, indeed," he says, "that it should be so called, so as to give superiority to the noble sex, that is to the male, for the man is the head of the woman. Man is more noble than the woman."

This is the hard, dry lawyer of it. The poet of that day was very far from agreeing with the lawyer on this point, though it must be admitted that while the poet proved the fair sex nobler than the other, he generously did so in spite of the fact that in common with the less visionary part of mankind, he still believed her to be the sole cause of man's downfall—as witnesseth this ancient Irish poem, Eve's Lament.[1]

---

[1] From Kuno Meyer's "Ancient Irish Poetry."

"I am Eve, great Adam's wife,
'Tis I that outraged Jesus of old;
'Tis I that robbed my children of Heaven,
By right 'tis I that should have gone upon the cross.

"I had a kingly house to please,
Grievous the evil choice that disgraced me,
Grievous the wicked advice that withered me!
Alas! my hand is not pure.

"'Tis I that plucked the apple,
Which went across my gullet:
So long as they endure in the light of day,
So long women will not cease from folly.

"There would be no ice in any place,
There would be no glistening windy winter,
There would be no hell, there would be no sorrow,
There would be no fear, if it were not for me."

That it was not considered unwise to open the schools to women is shown by a hundred references in the old records. It will be remembered that Patrick, when he came to the palace of Cruachan found there the two princesses, Fedelm and Eithne, King Laoghaire's daughters, under the tuition of Mal and Coplait. We hear of the delg-graif, the writing style, of the mother of King Brandubh, in the sixth century. When, in the sixth century also, St. Brendan the Navigator, after he had mastered the canons of the old law and the New Testament was about to set out to the school of Jarlath at Tuam to add to his store of lore that of the rules of the saints of Ireland, his foster-mother Ita, the Book of Lismore tells us, warned him: "Study not with women, nor with virgins, lest some one revile thee." And St. Ita herself was a teacher of girls. When St. Mugint went over and founded a school in Scotland in the seventh century, we are given to understand that girls studied there as well as boys. At the school of St. Finian at Clonard, in the sixth century, women attended. For we learn incidentally that when the daughter of the King of Cualann came to it, to learn to read her psalms, Finian put the girl in the companionship of his favourite pupil, Ciaran, with whom she read them. As it was in the Latin that the Bible was read at those schools it follows that some women even studied the classics then.

Under date A.D. 932, the Annals of the Four Masters chronicle the death of Uallach, the daughter of Muinnechan, the chief poetess of Ireland—one of many Irish poetesses. Famous female rulers and famous mothers and wives of male rulers, such as Taillte and Tea and Macha—and fine warriors, too, like Medb—are enshrined in the accounts of the ancient seanachies.

Of course it is not for a moment to be understood that in early Ireland the education of woman was of the same importance as that of man—very far from it. The instances are given only for purpose of showing that women were not excluded from the privileges of education, nor was there any prejudice against their acquiring the learning of the schools. In the various centuries and in the various generations some of the more ambitious of them sought and obtained such an education, at least from the days of Patrick downward. And through all the centuries some of them acquired fame in this, just as they did in other lines of what is considered man's endeavour. There is, in the old Book of Ballymote a sort of history in prose and verse of Eirinn's famous women down to the time of the English Invasion.

By reason of their equality or near equality with man in other realms, women warriors frequently felt it their duty to take up arms and march into battle with their brothers or husbands. It was only in 697 that they were exempted from warfare—by the influence of St. Adamnan at the Synod of Tara in that year. The law that exempted them is known as the Cáin Adamnan. The Feilire of Aongus describes how Adamnan was moved by his mother to fight for this exemption, "It came to pass that Adamnan once travelling in Magh Breagh with his mother on his back saw two battalions smiting each other. It happened, moreover, that Ronait (his mother) saw a woman with an iron sickle," so barbarously tearing to pieces one of her own sex that she, Ronait, laid it on Adamnan to rest not until he had obtained the passing of a law that would prevent such savagery among women forever after.

In Ireland, after marriage, the woman did not become a chattel—thus radically differing from the usual custom in the other countries of Europe. Before marriage she was wooed and courted like the superior being which, later, she was acknowledged to be in all countries. In the exercise of the acknowledged privileges of a superior being she could scorn and frown down the attentions of chieftains and kings—and scholars, too—send them home with hanging heads, and choose whomsoever her heart went out to. And after marriage she was not—as unfortunately was too generally the case elsewhere—the property of her husband. "It was contract that was between them." In the eyes of the law, they were partners in a matrimonial venture—with the husband, however, the leading partner. And so very far in the lead was the Irish law that under it the wife could remain sole owner of property that had been her own before marriage. Also, such property as was jointly owned by them could not be sold or signed away by the husband. Their rights in the joint property were equal; and the voluntary consent of both was necessary for its disposal. This is a remarkable acknowledgment of the equality of the women of Ireland with the men in the remotest days—above all, an equality persisting after marriage, when, down to very recent days, even in highly advanced countries, all such rights were insured to the husband.

A married woman retained the right, too, in her own person to pursue a case at law, and in her own person to recover for debt. In this connection it may be mentioned that when a woman levied upon the goods of a debtor, she distrained such things as were appropriate for women; such animals, for instance, as lap-dogs or sheep; such articles as spindles, mirrors, or comb-bags.

Because of the primary importance of military duty, and the necessity of having men liable therefor—in ancient Ireland, as in all ancient countries, the man had the preference over the woman in the inheriting of land.

If there was a son he inherited the land in preference to a daughter—who, however, got *coibche,* marriage portion, out of the general estate. The daughter, however, inherited the land if there was no son. But by virtue of her getting the land she had to provide and pay a warrior when a military levy was made. It is said that it was the famous law-wise Brigid Brethra, Brigid of the Judgments, who, about the time of Christ, gave the legal decision which granted this right to women.

A woman's coibche, tinnscra, or tochra,[2] as the marriage portion was variously called, took the form of gold or silver, animals, clothes or household articles. But the term coibche, although oftentimes used for dowry, was more properly the price which the bridegroom paid to the father of the bride, or to the bride herself—after the marriage had been consummated. The very old laws laid it down that the coibche should be paid in yearly instalments, the whole of the first year's instalment going to the bride's father, two-thirds of the second year's to him, one-half of the third year's, and on decreasingly. To the wife went the remainder.

There was another payment at marriage, called tinol, a collective gift made by the friends to the *lanamain* (young couple). In this tinol the man had two-thirds right and the woman one-third.

Whether she did or did not bring anything else, however, the wife practically always brought into the marriage contract her own articles of industry, her distaff, spinning wheel, spindle, loom, etc. In the few cases in which she did not bring these, she had a considerably lower legal standing in the partnership.

There were certain cases of legal separation—for legal separation for good cause then existed—in which it was adjudged the right of the wife to take with her all of the marriage portion and the marriage gifts, and an amount over and above that for damages.

The old laws as well as the old stories everywhere testify that Irish women of ancient days devoted much attention to dress, toilet and the general care and adornment of the person. The finger-nails received much attention; and well-kept finger-nails signified that their possessor was a person of taste. The nails of the women of leisure were dyed crimson. The eye-brows also were dyed, usually black—with berry juice. A vegetable dye was sometimes used to tint the face. But the care of the hair was the most elaborate of all—and this applied to men (who then wore their hair long) as well as to women. Much time and attention were bestowed upon the

[2] Hence the Scottish "tocher."

hair's combing and dressing. The oldest illuminated manuscripts reflect this. It was beautifully curled in spiral curls, both in front and hanging down to either side. It was braided down the back, and confined at the end with golden rings, or with light, hollow, golden balls. Women's hair was sometimes, however, bound up, and held in position by golden rings. There were beautiful combs of bone or horn, which were carried in *ciorbolgs* (comb-bags). The bath was regularly indulged in—by the men as well as the women. The Fenians bathed every evening before they took their great meal. It was considered a shameful breach of hospitality if a bath was not at once prepared for the traveller and the stranger in the house that he honoured by his presence.

Gloves and veils were worn by the fine ladies. Maidens went with their heads uncovered; but married women wore on their heads either a hood, or a roll of linen, folded around several times. Their dress of woollen, linen, silk or satin, was oftentimes a single garment falling to the ankles, and consisting sometimes of as much as thirty yards of stuff, tastefully gathered in many and deep folds. And over this dress was worn out of doors a long cloak.

Many of their ancient ornaments and their beautiful toilet articles are still preserved. Very beautifully wrought brooches of silver, and gold, and bronze; great pins for the hair and pins for the cloak; leathern handbags, with embossed patterns for carrying their personal ornaments; veils and gloves; beautiful combs; mirrors, too, called *scadarcs;* may be seen in the museum of the Royal Irish Academy and in the National Museum. They had scented oils for toilet use. They had furs also—skins of the otter, seal and badger.

Chivalrous respect for women, both the married and the unmarried, was a characteristic feature of Irish life in all ages. And the natural chivalry of true men it was that was shown to them, not at all the artificial thing which in later days and in other countries was the base counterfeit substituted for the real thing. True courtesy, respect and honour were accorded the women, every time and everywhere. Most ancient accounts of the most ancient revels show that the women were seldom permitted to be present. They had their own part of the house, where they talked and worked, played and sang, while the men revelled. The account of the Fair of Carmen shows that the women there had a place apart, where they could meet and commingle, and which the law of the Fair forbade men to enter. In the chief residences and palaces, always, the women had their own special wing of the house exclusively reserved for them. It was known as the *Grianan,* signifying the sunny part.

An apparent exception to the rule that women were excused from the revel, occurs in the well-known very ancient account of the feast of Bricriu, where the women are made to play a part which is popularly supposed to be characteristic of woman's nature—and which shows that womanly rivalry in those far-away days was the same human quality that it is in the world today.

Bricriu's feast was not a common revel. It was a great feast of almost national importance, the preparations for which occupied a whole year and which was attended by all the great ones of Ulster. The satirist and cynic, Bricriu of the Poison Tongue, who was the host of this wonderful feast, seeking to indulge his malevolence by creating dissension among the bright heroes of the province, attained his end by artfully playing upon the natural vanity of their beautiful wives. Cuchullain's wife, Emer the Discreet, Conal Cearnach's wife, Lendabair the Fair, and Laoghaire Buadach's wife, Fedelm the Ever-blooming, he made his unwitting tools.

For this feast there was specially built by Bricriu a magnificent house which "excelled in material and art, beauty and gracefulness, in pillars and walls, and variety, and in porticoes and doors, all the houses of the time."

Fergus MacRiogh, knowing well the evil Bricriu, wisely tried to dissuade the Ulster champions from going to this feast—"Because," he said, "if we should go, our dead would be more numerous than our living."

But they went—to their black sorrow. When they were assembled Bricriu took well-planned opportunity to speak privately in the ear of each of these beautiful ladies, impressing on her with all the insinuating power of a poet, that she was by far the most beautiful, lustrous, the greatest and first, of the women of Ulster, just as her husband was the greatest and noblest man and champion.

> "Well done this night, thou wife of Laoghaire Buadach. It is no nick-name to call thee Fedelm the Ever-blooming, because of the excellence of thy shape, and because of thy intelligence, and because of thy family. Conchobar, the king of the chief province of Eirinn, is thy father, and Laoghaire Buadach thy husband. Now I would not think it too much for thee that none of the women of Ulster should come before thee into the banqueting house; but that it should be after thy heels that the whole band the women of Ulster should come (and I say to thee that) if it be thou that shalt be the first to enter the house this night, thou shalt be queen over all the other women of Ulster."

In like manner did he whisper to each of them. "When the serpent, Bricriu, whispered in the pleased ear of these fair ladies, each of them, accompanied by her fifty attendants, was strolling out to take the air, upon the lawn of Bricriu's magnificent house. And as he had told each of them that when they were returning the first woman to enter the hall of the festivities should be queen of the whole province, we can easily conjecture that the return was exciting—

> "The three women moved on then till they reached the same place, that is, three ridges from the house; and none of them knew that the other had been spoken to by Bricrind. They returned to the house then. They passed over the first ridge with a quiet, graceful, dignified carriage; hardly did any one of them put one foot beyond another. In the second ridge their steps were closer and quicker. On the ridge nearest to the house each woman sought to forcibly take the lead of her companions; and they even took up their dresses to the calves of their legs, vieing with each other who should enter the house first; because what Bricrind said to each, unknown to the others, was that she who should first enter the house should be queen of the whole province. And such was the noise they made in their contest to enter the kingly house, that it was like the rush of fifty chariots arriving there; so that they shook the whole kingly house, and the champions started up for their arms, each striking his face against the other throughout the house."

The fine virtues and accomplishments which went to the making of a perfect woman in ancient Ireland, were well exemplified in this Emer, wife of Cuchullain, one of the most famed women in ancient Irish story. "The six maidenly gifts of Emer" faithfully reflect for us what was the popular conception then of a desirable maiden. They were: "Beauty of person, beauty of voice, the gift of music, knowledge of embroidery, knowledge of needle-work, and the gift of wisdom and virtuous chastity."

And when we are first introduced to Emer, we find her at needlework in the midst of a group of maidens likewise engaged, outside the Dún of her father Forgaill. It is when Cuchullain arrives to pay her court. She is shown shy, demure, and self-denying, hesitant about permitting herself to be wooed, and endeavouring to pass the coveted honour to her elder sister. Such is the poet's reflection of the popular conception of maidenly modesty, and maidenly excellence, in the far-away time.

Yet for all their maidenly modesty and true womanliness, the women of ancient Ireland were sensible of the fact that they were man's equal, and where necessary could insist upon equal treatment. A very fine instance of this is the case related in the Book of Lismore of Canair the Pious. She was a holy maiden of the Benntraighe who lived the life of a holy hermit there, in the days when Saint Senan, having his monastery and school on Inis-Cathaig, forbade any woman to come upon the island. The Book says that Canair, praying after nocturne one night, saw as in a vision all the churches of Ireland sending up towers of fire to Heaven. But the greatest of the great fire towers went up from Inis-Cathaig. "Fair is yon cell!" exclaimed Canair. "Thither will I go that my resurrection may be near it." But Senan, meeting her on her arrival on his shore, commanded her: "Go to thy sister on yon island east, for guesting. No woman shall enter here." To which the indignant Canair, fired for her sex and their rights, answered: "How canst thou say that? Christ is no worse than thou. Christ came to redeem women, no less than men. No less did He suffer for sake of women. Women have given service and tendance unto Christ and His apostles. No less than men do women enter the heavenly kingdom. Why then shouldst thou not take women to thee in thine island?"

And this able pleader won over the Saint, and for once shattered his rigid rule.

It was this respect for women, permeating society in every age in Ireland, that gave such moral fibre to the Irish race as enabled it not only to persist through later long and fearful centuries of oppression unparalleled, under which other races would have disappeared—not only to persist through these terrors, but to come out of them still morally stronger than almost any other of the most favoured peoples of Europe. God and Bridget blessed the race that blessed the name of Woman.

Sullivan, W. K., Ph.D.: Introduction to O'Curry's Manners and Customs.
Joyce, P. W.: Social History of Ancient Ireland.
Henderson, Geo., M.A., Ph.D.: Fled Bricrend, the Feast of Bricriu.
O'Curry, Eugene: Manners and Customs of the Ancient Irish.
——— Manuscript Materials of Irish History.
Brehon Laws: the Ancient Laws of Ireland.

CHAPTER XXIII

Colm Cille

Among native Irish saints Colm Cille (Columba) divides the honours with Bridget in the affections of the Irish people—divides the honours for greatness also, some say. But when we consider the works he performed, the monasteries he founded, the power he wielded over princes and provinces, the veneration he compelled from three countries, and the Christian reclamation of which he was the direct cause, added to the powerful personality of the man, which holds him as a living presence in Ireland and Scotland more than thirteen centuries after the green sod of Hy was drawn over him, we recognise that he was without a peer among native Irish saints—and had only one peer—which is to say, Patrick—among all the saints of Western Europe. And in Northern Ireland and Western Scotland he has outranked Patrick himself in the power he has wielded over the imagination of the people. With Patrick and Bridget, Colm Cille also is one of the great personages of the universal Church.

Colm Cille was of Irish royal stock, very close in the line of succession to the kingship of Tir-Conaill, and the high-kingship of Ireland. Indeed one of his historians says: "He had the natural right to the kingship of Ireland, and it would have been offered him had he not put it from him for God's sake." He was a descendant in the third degree from Conal Gulban, the founder of the principality of Tir-Conaill, and consequently in the fourth degree from Niall of the Nine Hostages. He was born a nephew of the then reigning High-king, Muircertach MacErca. And a High-king who reigned later in Colm's career, Ainmire, was his cousin. His father, Feidlimid, was chieftain of the particular territory of Tir-Conaill, in which he was born. And his mother, Eithne, was daughter of a Munster chief, of the line of Cathair Mor. It was only in a time when, as then, the fires of Christianity glowed at white heat, that a man of such, and so many, royal entanglements could turn his back upon wealth, rank and power, and give himself to God.

Colm is said to have been baptised Crimthann, when he was born at Gartan (Donegal) in the year 521. Some think it was in his days of study under St. Finian of Moville (in Down) that, from this gentle boy's haunting the church in the hours between study-times his fellow-pupils gave him the name of Colm Cille, Dove of the Church.

He was fostered and tutored in his earlier days by a priest named Cruithnechan, at the place which is now called Temple Douglas—only a few miles from his birthplace. He went to three or four other schools later, for his higher education—to the school of St. Finian of Moville, as mentioned, where he is said to have been made deacon; later to the other and greater St. Finian, of Clonard, to study divine wisdom. There he was a fellow-pupil to a band of youths who were to be, with him, among Ireland's greatest. He was one of that band of Finian's pupils who came to be known as the Twelve Apostles of Eirinn.

For Colm, Finian had a great liking—took that liking the first day that the youth from Tir-Conaill appeared at his school. For he asked the lad to erect his hut at the door of the church. Finian had a mystic dream later regarding Colm and his other favourite, Ciaran of Clonmacnois. It appeared to him that there arose in the sky a moon of gold from the horizon in the northeast, and a moon of silver over the midlands. The latter lighted the whole centre of Ireland; but the former, the golden moon, lit up all Erin and Alba, and the whole western world, with its brilliance and radiance.[1]

Colm returned home to Tir-Conaill in 544 because of the *Buidhe Chonaill,* the dreadful pestilence that swept Ireland several times in those centuries—and which at this particular time, broke up and scattered the great schools, sending the pupils in drifts to homes oversea, as well as to homes in Eirinn—and which now carried off several of the leading teachers, and some of the leading saints of Ireland, including the famous saint and scholar, Ciaran, the founder of Clonmacnois.

It is generally agreed[2] that Calm was ordained to the priesthood while at Clonard. It throws an interesting light on the character of the ecclesiastics

---

[1] Either before or after his career at Clonard he attended in Leinster the bardic school of one Garman, where he is supposed to have had his well-known poetic talents developed, and his poetic training perfected. Finally, he is believed by some to have been studying at St. Mobi's school at Glasnevin with Comgall and Cainnech as his companions. Lanigan, however, denies that he was at St. Mobi's school. And indeed the only proof on which it rests is the tradition of himself and his fellow-pupils, on the night of a storm, on which the River Tolka was swollen, swimming the river rather than miss vespers at the church on the opposite bank.

[2] Lannigan denies this also.

in early Christian Ireland, several of whom we know, by authentic record, to have been artisans, to learn that when the boy sought out Bishop Etchen for his ordination, he found him ploughing his field.

He was about twenty-four or twenty-five years of age when he returned home from school. His close kinsman, the Prince of Tir-Conaill, gave him a grant of land, a hill of oaks near where the river Foyle debouches into the Loch of the same name—where he founded his famous monastery of Derry. As a love for all of God's living things was a marked characteristic of almost all the early Irish saints, we find Colm, when erecting his monastery here, breaking a precedent, that was not only honoured but blest, by refusing to build his church with its chancel towards the east—because he was thereby able to spare the life of many oak-trees.[3]

His next foundation, after Derry, was the monastery of Durrow (in the present Kings County)—founded seven or eight years later. His missionary activity now became extraordinary. He was travelling east and west, preaching, exhorting, organising communities, founding monasteries. He founded Kells, Swords, Drumcolum, Drumcliff, Screen, Kilglass and Drumhome, and many, many more. In all he is said to have founded thirty monasteries in Northern Ireland—before yet he was exiled, which event occurred in 562, when he was forty-two years of age.

His exile, the greatest, saddest event of his life, for which calamity through all his years after he never ceased to grieve, was yet fraught with seeds of happy blessing for the neighbouring countries to which he and his disciples were to bear the tidings of Christ. The reason of Colm's exile, the terriblest sentence that could be pronounced against one of the most passionate

---

[3] After he left Derry and left Ireland we find him in his beautifully pathetic lament for exile telling how the angels crowded every leaf of the oaks of Derry, listening to the monks chanting the psalms, both at midnight and at morn. For, through the beautiful years that he spent there building up the community, and making the monastery a temple of the living God, the holy man's heart sent down its roots deep into Derry hill. His soul was sorely pained at parting from his many monasteries, but it got a most woful wrench when he had to tear his heart's roots from among the roots of the oak wherewith they had mingled on his beloved Derry hill.

> "The reason that I love Derry is,
> For its peace, for its purity,
> And for its crowds of white angels,
> From one end to the other.
>
> "O Derry, my own little grove,
> My dwelling, my dear little cell!
> O Eternal God in Heaven above,
> Woe be to him who violates it!"

patriots that Eirinn ever produced, is alleged to have been a penance for causing the great battle of Cuildremne (in Sligo) where a host of lives were lost. And the causes of his instigating this battle are popularly supposed to be two: because the Ard-Righ, Diarmuid O'Carroll, in the first place adjudged a case against him—unfairly, as Colm believed; and because, furthermore, Diarmuid violated monastic sanctuary and carried away and punished with death a homicide who had taken sanctuary with the saint.

The case adjudged against him affected a copy of the Psalms which he, Colm, had made surreptitiously from the book of his master, Finian of Moville. When Finian discovered that his pupil had made and carried off a copy he claimed its return as stolen property. The case was laid before the High King, Diarmuid, who, after hearing argument on both sides, delivered the sententious judgment which was popularised ever after in Ireland, "Le gach boin a boinín"—to every cow her calf—a verdict which, as it would make the copy Finian's, Colm hotly resented and rejected.[4]

After this Cuildremne slaughter (in 561) the impetuous Colm gave way to remorse that bit into his soul. His biographer, Adamnan, says there was a synod held at Taillte shortly after, where a motion was made to excommunicate Colm, for his crime—which would have been carried but that his bosom friend, Brendan of Birr, held out against the other members and saved Colm. But his own soul was punishing him. He finally went to St. Molaise—of Devenish, as some say, or St. Molaise of Inishmurry, others say—humbly confessed his crime and asked to be penanced.

For such a great crime the penance must be great. Knowing the intense love that possessed Colm for his native land, Molaise ordered that he should go forth from his country and behold it never more. Also he should bring to Christ as many souls as there had been lives lost at Cuildremne. Sad-hearted for the sore sentence that had been meted out to him—but

---

[4] The violation of sanctuary occurred when Curan, son of King Aed of Connaught, a hostage at Tara, had, at a game of caman, struck and killed the son of the High-King's steward, and had then taken refuge with Colm. King Diarmuid commanded that the young prince should be taken forcibly from Colm and put to death—which was done. For this unforgiveable outrage against traditional sanctuary, Colm, eluding a guard that had been put over him, quitted Diarmuid's domain, and made his way over the mountains to his home in Tir-Conaill. His kinsmen, the princes of Tir-Conaill and Tir-Eogain, took up his quarrel, and joining their army to that of Aed, King of Connaught, father of the prince who had been put to death, met Diarmuid and his forces at Cuildremne, fought and defeated him, with terrible slaughter—three thousand dead, some say, being left on the field.

The battle of Cuildremne was not the only one for which the impetuous Colm was responsible. Other contentions of his had caused the battles of Coleraine wherein his people fought the Dal Araide, and the battle of Culfeda in which they fought Coleman, the son of Diarmuid.

resolute—Colm, taking with him twelve companions, among whom were his uncle, Ernaan, and his cousin, Baoithin, sailed away from the land which his heart loved so fondly, and which now must nevermore be his.

"Alas for the voyage, O High King of Heaven,
Enjoined upon me,
For that I on the red plain of bloody Cooldrevin
Have sinned against Thee.

. . . .

"Three things I am leaving behind me, the very
Most dear that I know,
Tir-Leidach I'm leaving, and Durrow and Derry.
Alas, I must go!

"Yet my visit and feasting with Comgall have eased me
At Cainnech's right hand:
And all but thy government, Eire, had pleased me,
Thou waterfall land!"[5]

---

[5] It was a grievously sorrowful leave-taking of Ireland was Colm's, as, looking back from his boat, his moistened sight embraced the beloved hills that, afar, were sinking forever from view. In his Lament for Erin, one of the several beautiful poems credited to the poet Colm, he says:

"There is a grey eye
That will look back upon Erin:
Which shall never see again
The men of Erin nor her women.

"I stretch my glance across the brine
From the firm oaken planks;
Many are the tears of my bright soft grey eye
As I look back upon Erin.

"My mind is upon Erin,
Upon Loch Lene, upon Linny,
Upon the land where Ulstermen are,
Upon gentle Munster and upon Meath.

"Melodious are Erin's clerics, melodious her birds,
Gentle her youths, wise her elders,
Illustrious her men, famous to behold,
Illustrious her women for fond espousal.

"Carry my blessing with thee to the West,
My heart is broken in my breast:
Should sudden death overtake me,
It is for my great love of the Gael.

"Were all Alba mine
From its centre to its border,
I would rather have the site of a house
In the middle of fair Derry.

"Beloved are Durrow and Derry
Beloved is Raphoe with purity,
Beloved Drumhome with its sweet acorns,
Beloved are Swords and Kells!"

Into a bay on the island of Oronsay in the southern Hebrides they ran their boat, on an evening. Next morning Colm, climbing a high hill to look toward the land where he had left his heart, beheld, on the horizon's verge, low and dim, that land for which his soul so sorely grieved. Here he must not stay!

"To oars again, we can not stay,
For ah, on ocean's rim, I see
Where sunbeams pierce the cloudy day,
From these rude hills of Oronsay,
The Isle so dear to me!"

The sad company had to take to their boat again, and spread their sail to catch a wind that would drive them farther from Eirinn.

Their next landing was their final one. It was on Iona.[6] And on that quiet evening on which the keel of their boat grated on the pebbled shore of this quiet isle, to the world unknown till now, Fame with its thousand wings encircled it and marked it for its own.

Iona was part of the Scotic Dal Riada, colonised and ruled by the Scots (Irish). King Conal, who now reigned there, was of the Tir-Chonaill family, Colm's own kinsman. And to the exile he made a grant of land whereon the holy man founded a home for his monks, where he was to found his monastery, and where he was to build his school, and from whence he and his disciples were to carry Christ, first to the untutored Picts, and later to the Britons and the Saxons of the south.

Starting here with a small number of brothers, and small and poor shelter, they drew to them from Ireland recruits in great numbers, whom the fame of Colm, his power and his piety, perennially attracted. Their buildings grew, their farms spread, their flocks increased. They bore the Gospel tidings to King Brude and to his Pictish hordes in the uttermost corners of Scotland. Their school, too, attained great fame, and attracted students from all these island countries.[7]

---

[6] Called also Hy, and I-Colmcille.

[7] From time to time also to Iona came to visit Colm his brother-saints from Ireland, famous men of that day—the two Brendans, the two Finans, Flannan, Ronan, Comgall, Finbar, all are said to have visited the exile, bringing dearly loved Eirinn to him who to Eirinn could not return. Many others, too, abbots of various Irish monasteries came there, like these, to seek the counsel and advice of one whose counsel was prized beyond that of any other Irishman of that day. Among them, the wandering abbot Cormac Ua Liathain, who, forced from Colm's monastery of Durrow, because he was a

Yet, despite the penance which seemed to forbid it, was he destined to tread Eirinn's hallowed soil again. The romantic, dramatic return to his land of him who had been solemnly forbidden ever to see that land again, is one of the outstanding incidents of a life filled with big incidents. He was to return to Eirinn to the famous Convention of Drimceatt—return, too, without literally transgressing against the penitential ordinance. And this was the reason of his return.

The poets of Eirinn—of which brotherhood Colm was a proud member—had now not only multiplied so largely, but also had become so satirical, so overbearing, and so exacting, that the nobles of the land loudly murmured, because of the burden these people had become. Wandering over the island as they did, surrounded by their hungry bands of attendants, seating themselves down in what court they pleased, commanding whatever their erratic minds fancied, remaining as long as they pleased, exacting what they wished, and leaving when they would, it was little wonder that people began to groan under the intolerable burden. But this state of evil came to a head when at length one of them went so far as to demand, in tribute to his poetic powers, the royal brooch, a rarely beautiful heirloom, of the Ard-Righ—who was now Aedh, the son of Aimmire. The restraint which even a High King had imposed upon himself in deference

---

Munsterman presiding over Northerns who nagged him, was seeking a deserted isle where he might end his days alone with God. And for leaving that land which of all earth's lands was the most delightful, most joyous, from which no man in his sanity could voluntarily exile himself, the home-sick Colm, with affectionate upbraiding, upbraids the errant Cormac. "For," Colm tells him, "I pledge thee my uneering word, which may not be impugned, that better is death in reproachless Eirinn than life forever in Alba."

And his pining heart which dwells forever upon happy memories of his native land, paints for the hapless wanderer such alluring picture of that pleasant Durrow which he madly quitted as should swiftly bring him back to reason, and draw him there again: "How happy the son of Dimma (i.e., Cormac) of the devout church, when he hears in Durrow the desire of his mind—the fingers of the wind playing upon the elm-trees, the black-birds' joyous note when he claps his wings; the lowing of the cattle at early dawn in Ros Grencha; the cooing of the cuckoo from the tree, on the brink of summer."

Even to a sea-gull visitor which comes flying toward Iona from Eirinn, in the west, he addresses a poetic appeal full of affectionate envy for that it saw Ireland so recently, and can see it when it will again. For, this passionate love and longing for the country of his nativity, the intense love and longing which endowed the cold flag of Gartan, that had been his bed, with the virtue of averting home-sickness, persisted in the saint's soul through all his days in Hebridean exile.

On Colm's flag (his stone bed) at Gartan, down to most recent days, poor Donegal boys on the eve of their starting for America, Australia, or other far exile, would pass a night—to obtain the great Exile's blessing, which should avert from them the home-sickness which had racked his heart.

to poetic genius and sacred tradition, was burst by such brazenness. He swore that the island should be cleared of the poet tribe. To pass a decree for this purpose which should be legal, he called a convention of the princes and nobles, scholars and ecclesiastics of the land, to meet at Drimceatt—near the present town of Limavada in Derry.

When the sad news reached him on Iona, Colm, alarmed for his soul-brethren, the poets, knew that some extraordinary measure was immediately necessary to save Ireland from a shame which in the eyes of all noble ones, should stain its honour down the ages. His heart was alarmed and his soul was fired for the injustice about to be done his brethren, the poets. Well he knew that they had grown arrogant and unjust: but no crime whatsoever on the part of a class so justly privileged should draw upon Ireland the sacrilege of their driving out. Despite his penance, he resolved that he should appear in person at Drimceatt to avert from Ireland a dire disaster.

As the words of his penance had been that he should never again see Ireland, he, blind-folded, sailed for Ireland, attended by several bishops, fifty priests, fifty deacons and thirty clerics.

"O Son of my God, what a pride, what a pleasure
To plough the blue sea!
The waves of the fountain of deluge to measure,
Dear Erin, to thee.

"We are rounding Moy-n-Olurg, we sweep by its head, and
We plunge through Lough Foyle,
Whose swans could enchant with their music the dead, and
Make pleasure of toil."

What a dramatic sensation must there have been when in among the assembled nobles and scholars and kings of the nation, was led at the head of his company, this blinded man whose name was a name of wonder in every household in Eirinn, extraordinarily cherished in most, extraordinarily feared in some. What commotion must have been there; what craning of necks; what straining of eyes; what stamping of feet; what rattling of spears! What a fierce hurrah must have torn from the throat of the Conallach and the Eoganach, and from the men of many a sympathetic clan! And what troubled thought must have shown in the curled brow, what burning resentment looked out of the eye, what dour silence sat upon the lips, and what burning memories consumed the breasts of a hostile minority there![8]

And when this blinded man began to speak, beseeching the men of Eirinn to save their famed and loved land from the indelible stain of sacrilegiously violating the most sacred, most ancient tradition, the sanctity of the poet's person, to save it from banishing forever from Eirinn those great and noble, learned and gifted ones, whose tongues, touched with divine fire, had in their slightest word the fearful power of making the name of Eirinn famous or infamous—how he must have swayed and shook his audience as the hurricane from the north shakes the fir-trees of the forest—made them tower with pride, and cower with shame, lashed them and soothed them, roused them and melted them, elevated and prostrated them, now to the highest heavens, and now to earth's dust—how he must have lifted them beyond themselves, and how made them the abject creatures of his will and slightest word—till he had only to say go and they would go; do this and it was done! Colm completely routed all hostility, carried the Convention, and saved the great order of his brother-bards from extinction in Eirinn.[9]

---

[8] For there were some who as fiercely resented Colm's presence at Drimceatt as others ardently rejoiced in it. The wife of Ard-Righ Aed, a bitter opponent of this strong man, had commanded her two sons, Conal the elder, and Donal the younger, on no account to take part in the welcome which the Convention would surely extend to Colm, and to refrain from showing him any respect whatsoever. Conal not only obeyed his mother, but some say went so far as to insult, if not assault, Colm and his companions. The younger lad, Donal, however, moved by instinctive respect and love for such a great and holy man, arose up on Colm's entrance, went forward and embraced him, and kissed him on either cheek—in reward for which generous impulse he was blessed by, as his elder brother was deprived of, the succession to the throne.

[9] The Convention decided that they should not expel the bards, but it was at the same time agreed that the order should be completely reformed. A new set of laws and rules for the order was then drawn up. The High King of Eirinn was to maintain his own special Ollam of poetry; and each petty king and each chieftain to maintain a *filé* also; but the numbers of their pupils and of their attendants were reduced so that they would be less of an imposition to those who extended to them hospitality. Fees for their compositions were fixed, beyond which they could not exact in future. A tract of land was to be set apart for each Ollam, free of all payments. Every member of the order was entitled to universal freedom and sanctuary from the men of Ireland, in their land, person, and worldly goods. To make them useful to the state and to give employment and the means of living to that large portion of them which would otherwise go idle, it was arranged that public schools should be opened wherein they would become instructors and where, in the words of Keating, "any of the men of Ireland could get free instruction in the sciences."

"The educational establishments now endowed," says O'Curry, "were national, literary colleges, quite distinct from the great literary and ecclesiastical schools and colleges, that had formed themselves around individual celebrities, and were then in operation."

Another most important matter with which the Convention of Drimceatt concerned itself was the dispute between Aidan, the King of the Irish colony in Alba, that is the Scottish Dal Riada, and Ireland's Ard-Righ, as to where the allegiance of the Irish Dal Riada (the northeast of Antrim) was due. As the people of the two Dal Riadas were of the same clan, Aidan claimed kingship over both. But Aed, High King of Ireland, held that the tribute and the military support of the Irish Dal Riada were due to Tara.[10]

The convention agreed to leave the decision of this case to Colm, who was equally concerned on both sides. Colm, however, declined to be judge in the matter, and referred it to St. Colman, the son of Comgallen, who decided that the Irish Dal Riada should be directly and entirely subject to the Ard-Righ of Ireland, paying him tribute and supplying him with military levies, but they should be allies of their brethren over the Channel, the Scottish Dal Riada, and in case of a war of theirs against the Picts, or the Britons, should supply them with a fleet.

The Convention of Drimceatt is said to have remained in session for a year, making laws, redressing grievances, adjusting disputes. Colm, however, quitted it when that in which he was interested was finished with. He spent some months in Ireland, however, visiting several of his foundations, sojourning

---

The carrying out of the new order of things was put in the hands of the celebrated blind poet, Eochaid Righ Eigeas, better known as Dallan Forgaill, the Ard-Ollam and King-Poet of Ireland—whose dust now mingles with the earth of the Island of Inis Caoil, in the west of Donegal. This was the poet who composed the poem (still extant), the Arma Colm Cille, by way of reward to the Saint for saving the bards.

In a eulogy written upon this Dallan, after his death, by his great successor Senchan Torpeist, is said:

"The ocean's caverns, which armies dare not,—
The mighty cataract of the great Eas Ruadh;—
The rolling wave of a spring-tide's flow,—
Were the meet images of Dallan's intellect.

Until the shining sun is surmounted,
Which God has created above all creation,
No poet from north to south shall surpass
Eochaidh, the serene royal poet.

He was sage, O God of Heaven!
He was a noble and a chief poet;
Until the wave of death swept placidly over him,
Uch! he was beautiful, he was beloved."

[10] There are different versions of this dispute, but this is Lanigan's view of it.

for some time with one and another of them, settling their affairs, counselling and directing, and leaving them treading the path that he wished them to go. After which he returned to his beloved charge in the Western Islands again, and resumed his arduous duties, working, teaching, preaching, writing, travelling and baptising the heathen into the faith. He wrote much, chiefly copying the Scriptures. And on occasion he set down a poem or a hymn of his own composing. Several such, still existing, are attributed to Colm.[11]

As one of Colm's characteristic qualities was his indomitable, never-tiring energy, he believed in all around him being energetic—and insisted on it. One of the rules which he established in his monasteries, and a rule that became proverbially associated with Iona was that the day should be divided into three parts, one part for good works, one part for prayer, and one part for reading—the good works to be either for a brother's own benefit, for the benefit of his brethren, or for the benefit of his neighbours. His dictum was, "Let not a single hour pass in which you do not devote yourself to prayer, reading, writing or some other useful work." The copying of the Scriptures occupied much of the writing time of the brothers; and the copying of the classics for the use of their schools occupied a marked portion of their time. For, the classical education of their students was in this, as in all Irish schools at that time, an important part of the school's curriculum. And by practical example Colm firmly instilled his favourite precept about work, just as by practical example also he instilled all other of the good monastic precepts.

---

[11] In the Liber Hymnorum, an ancient Irish Book of Hymns saved from oblivion, there are three Latin poems which the general body of authorities believe to be truly Colm's. The most noted of them is the Altus Prosator, a Latin poem of the Abecedaria class; that is the twenty-two first letters of the twenty-two stanzas form the alphabet—following in this case the order of the Hebrew letters. Colm is said to have written it in Derry. He sent it to Pope Gregory the Great in return for valuable presents brought to him by messengers from that Pope.

The celebrated Book of Kells, one of the most beautiful of all ancient books in the world, was said by some authorities to have been written by him. An entry in it asks for "a remembrance of the scribe, Columba, who wrote this evangel, in the space of twelve days." And those who say that the Book of Kells is our Colm's conclude that this evangel was the stolen copy from Finian's book which changed the current of Colm's life. But most authorities deny to Colm the transcription of the Book of Kells. The fact that it was written by a Columba does not advance the proof in the great Colm's favour, for there were innumerable holy men and saints of that name. Archbishop Healy holding that the Book of Kells is a genuine work of Colm Cille, also says that the Book of Durrow is his. However, the proofs advanced by the upholders of Colm's authorship of these books is far from being conclusive.

Original matters attributed to him include the Lament for Erin, his Farewell to Aran, the Dialogue of Colm with Cormac in Hy, and the poem he is alleged to have written as he took his lonely way homeward over the mountain, when fleeing from the court of Diarmuid MacCarroll.

He prayed and he worked wholeheartedly. He went out in the fields with the brothers, and in storm or shine toiled as one of themselves. He devoted much indoor time to copying of the Scriptures and other writings. He chastened himself by marvellous fasting. His bed was on the bare ground, with a stone for his pillow; sparing himself not, and spending himself ever, as well for his own benefit as for his followers' encouragement.

The spiritual humility of this impetuous, fierce, strong, dominant man is well shown in the anecdote recorded in O'Clery's Martyrology, under the anniversary of Baithen (Colm's cousin):

> "It was this Baithen who was permitted to see three grand chairs in Heaven, empty, awaiting some of the saints of Eirinn: namely, a chair of gold, a chair of silver, and a chair of glass. And he told Colm of the vision. And Colm answered him: 'The gold chair is prepared for Ciaran, the son of the carpenter, in reward for his sanctity, hospitality, and charity. The silver chair is thine own, Baithen, for the brightness and the fervency of thy piety. The glass chair is mine, for I am brittle and fragile, in consequence of the battles which I have provoked.' It was after this that he resolved on abstinence from food, except nettle pottage, without dripping or fat, so that soon the impression of his ribs through the woollen tunic that he wore, was to be seen on the sandy beach where for penance he used to lie at night."

Yet like other great men he had not only clear vision of the great work which he was accomplishing, but also a child-like pride and child-like frankness in telling of it—beautifully expressed when in the course of another talk—this time upon the day of General Judgment—with his cousin and soul-friend, Baithen, he said: "Great also shall be my following on that day, Baithen, for its forefront shall be in Clonmacnois, and its rear in Dun Cuillinn in Alba."[12]

[12] The genial humour, which emphasised the Irish character of this Irishman is well exemplified in a story of him and his friend, St. Mochua, set down by Keating. Mochua lived a hermit in the wilderness devoting himself to the service of God—his sole worldly wealth a cock, a mouse and a fly. The cock called him to prayers at a certain hour in the night. The mouse was to scratch his ear if sleep deafened him to the call of the cock. The fly made itself a pointer for him upon his psalter. It crept along the page under each line and each word of the line that he chanted. And when he ceased chanting, to attend to other business, the fly paused upon the word on which he had stopped, thus pointing the place for him when he returned again. The cock and the mouse and the fly at length died on him. He wrote to Colm, in Iona, lamenting his loss. And Colm replied to him: "Brother thou must accept in the right spirit the affliction that has been sent upon thee. Thou shouldst have known that worry always follows in the wake of wealth."

Adamnan's personal description of him has preserved for us a physical picture of the man:

> "Colm was a man of well-formed and powerful frame, his face broad and fair and valiant, lit by large grey luminous eyes; he had a large and well-shaped head crowned with close and curling hair—except where he wore his frontal tonsure. His voice was clear and resonant, so that it could be heard a distance of fifteen hundred paces, yet was sweet with more than the sweetness of the bards."

Colm was by no means a young man when he appeared at the Convention of Drimceatt, in 575. But he lived and worked, inspired countless other workers, and was a big power in two countries for almost quarter of a century after.

In was in 597 that death came to him. In May of that year he visited the farm where the brothers toiled, in the west of the Island. He went among the brothers, spoke affectionately with them and consolingly, told the sorely grieved ones that his days were now numbered, and he should depart from them within a month. He blessed them, blessed their work and blessed the island.

When saying Mass, some time after, an angel appeared to him to warn him that the days were now few till his passing. On Saturday of that week he visited the great barn in which was stored the community's stock of food, and rejoiced in the great store he found there, which would insure plenty for his beloved ones for that year. With exceeding earnestness he blessed the barn, that it should ever hold and give in plenty to the ardent servants of God. Then he said to those who stood around him: "This day in the Holy Scriptures is called Sabbath, which means rest. And this day is indeed Sabbath to me, for it is the last day of my laborious life, and on it I rest. And this night at midnight I shall go the way of my fathers."

As he wended his way slowly back from the barn, he talked consolingly to his faithful attendant, Diarmuid, who was weeping. Half way to the monastery he had to sit to rest by the wayside. And when he had thus sat down an old white horse which for long years had been used to carry the milk from the milking ground to the monastery, approached, thrust his grey face into the saint's bosom, while tears, as if from a human being, rolled from his eyes. The saint would not let the horse be driven away. He was deeply moved by the affection of the prescient animal, which he caressed and soothed.

The hill called Cnoc-na-Carnan, which arose above the monastery, he then ascended and took a last long look over land and sea—and we may be sure a fond, fond look toward the western horizon below which lay the land of his heart. From this hilltop he blessed all that his soul cherished. And uplifting his hands, he blessed his monastery saying: "Small and mean though this place is, yet it shall be held in great honour, not only by Scotic kings and people, but also by the rulers of foreign and barbarous nations, and by their subjects; the saints also even of other churches shall regard it with no common reverence."

It is characteristic of this man who so firmly believed in work and preached work, that when, now within a few hours of his death, he returned to the monastery, he sat him down in his cell, and continued the transcription of the Psalter which he had been copying. At the end of the day, when it came time for the Sabbath vigils, having reached the end of a page, he laid down his pen, saying: "Let Baithen write the rest." And his last written words were those of the thirty-third psalm—"They that seek the Lord shall want no manner of thing that is good."

So that the first words which his successor in the abbacy, Baithen, was to write were: "Come, ye children, and harken unto me. I will teach you the fear of the Lord."

Colm's last hours could not be more finely described than in the words of his biographer and kinsman, his tenth successor in the abbacy, Adamnan: [13]

---

[13] Colm's life was also written by a distinguished one of his own clan, Manus O'Donnell, chieftain of Tir-Conaill in the sixteenth century. But his most distinguished biographer and most successful was St. Adamnan, who was born in Tir-Hugh, in Southwestern Donegal a quarter of a century after Colm's death. Adamnan became abbot of Iona in the last quarter of the seventh century. His "Life of Colm," one of several works written by this able writer, is described by the Scottish historian, Pinkerton, as "the most complete piece of biography which all Europe can boast of, not only at so early a period, but even through the middle ages." And Montalembert says of it, "It forms one of the most living, authentic and vital relics of Christian history."

Of this Adamnan, O'Clery, in his Martyrology, relates the legend how once when he was three days and three nights in the church alone, praying to God, and that messengers from the monks were sent to find what kept their abbot from them, they, peering into the church, saw "a little Boy with brilliance and bright radiance in the bosom of Adamnan. Adamnan was thanking and caressing the Infant. And they were not able to look at Him any longer, by reason of the divine rays around the Boy."

Adamnan was once sent as an ambassador from Iona to England to request the return of Irish captives who had been carried away in one of many raids which the Britons and Saxons made into Ireland in these centuries. Keating says, "The Northern Saxons gave Adamnan great honor, and everything he wanted."

"He was a vessel of wisdom," says the Martyrology, of Adamnan, "and a man full of the grace of God, and with the knowledge of the Holy Scriptures, and of every other wisdom; a burning lamp to illumine and enlighten the West of Europe"

"Having written the aforementioned verse at the end of the page, the saint went to the church, to the nocturnal vigils of the Lord's Day; and so soon as this was over, he returned to his chamber and spent the remainder of the night on his bed, where he had a bare flag for his couch, and for his pillow a stone, which stands to this day as a kind of monument beside his grave. While then he was reclining there, he gave his last instructions to the brethren, saying: 'These, O my children, are the last words I address to you—that ye be at peace, and have unfeigned charity among yourselves: and if you thus follow the example of the holy fathers, God the comforter of the good, will be your Helper, and I, abiding with Him, shall intercede for you; and He will not only give you sufficient to supply the wants of this present life, but will also bestow on you the good and eternal rewards which are laid up for those that keep His commandments.' Thus far have the last words of our venerable patron, as he was about to leave this weary pilgrimage for his Heavenly country, been preserved for recital in our brief narrative. After these words, as the happy hour of his departure gradually approached, the saint became silent. Then as soon as the bell tolled at midnight, he rose hastily, and went to the church; and running more quickly than the rest, he entered it alone, and knelt down in prayer beside the altar. At the same moment his attendant, Diarmuid, who more slowly followed him, saw from a distance that the whole interior of the church was filled with a heavenly light in the direction of the saint. And as he drew near to the door, the same light he had seen and which was also seen by a few more of the brethren standing at a distance, quickly disappeared. Diarmuid, therefore, entering the church, cried out in a mournful voice, 'Where art thou, father?' and feeling his way in the darkness, as the brethren had not yet brought in the lights, he found the saint lying before the altar; and raising him up a little, he sat down beside him, and laid his holy head on his bosom. Meanwhile the rest of the monks ran in hastily in a body with their lights, and beholding their dying father, burst into lamentations. And the saint, as we have been told by some who were present, even before his soul departed, opened his eyes and looked around him from side to side, with a countenance full of wonderful joy and gladness, no doubt seeing holy angels coming to meet him. Diarmuid then raised the holy right hand of the saint that he might bless his assembled monks. And the venerable father himself moved his hand at the same time,

> as well as he was able—that as he could not in words, while his soul was departing, he might at least, by the motion of his hand, be seen to bless his brethren. And having given them his holy benediction in this way, he immediately breathed his last. After his soul had left the tabernacle of the body, his face still continued ruddy, and brightened in a wonderful way by his vision of the angels, and that to such a degree that he had the appearance not so much of one dead, as of one alive and sleeping. Meanwhile the whole church resounded with loud lamentations of grief."

After matins the bereft monks bore the body of their beloved father back to the monastery, chanting psalms. And mourned not only by his monks but by a great multitude of sorrowing Islanders and their chiefs, this singularly great man was laid under the earth, in the humble little cemetery of Iona.

Little wonder it is that signs on the earth and in the heavens should accompany the passing of one so great, whose greatness impressed many lands.[14] "And this unusual favour hath been conferred by God on this same man of blessed memory; that though he lived in this small and remote island of the British sea, his name hath not only become illustrious throughout the whole of our own Scotia (Ireland), and Britain the largest island of the whole world, but hath reached even unto triangular Spain, and into Gaul, and to Italy which lieth beyond the Pennine Alps; and also to the city of Rome itself, the head of all cities. This great and honourable celebrity, amongst other marks of divine favour, is known to have been conferred on this same saint by God who loveth those who love Him, and

---

[14] As might be expected, in his own beloved Ireland at the time of his passing strange signs were seen in the skies. Various holy men were witnesses of symbolic phenomena. Ernan of Drumhome—which it will be remembered was one of Colm's foundations—fishing in the River Finn, beheld the white vault of heaven lit up. He looked to the east and saw an immense clear fire, which seemed to illumine the whole earth, like the sun at noon. A pillar of fire ascended from earth to heaven and then disappeared. The strange sight was also witnessed by many other fishers who were fishing in the Finn with Ernan.

Lugaid, the son of Tailchann, had a beautiful vision at Rosnarca at the same time.

"In the middle of this last night," says Lugaid, "Columba, the pillar of many churches, passed to the Lord; and at the moment of his blessed departure, I saw in the spirit the whole Ionian Island, where I never was in the body, resplendent with the brightness of the angels; and the whole heavens above it, up to the very zenith, were illumined with the brilliant light of the same heavenly messengers, who descended in countless numbers to bear away his holy soul. At the same moment, also, I heard the loud hymns and entrancingly sweet canticles of the angel host, as his soul was borne aloft amidst the ascending choirs of angels."

raiseth them to immense honour by glorifying more and more those that magnify and truly praise Him, who is blessed forever more. Amen."

Lannigan, Rev. John, D.D.: Ecclesiastical History of Ireland.
Reeves, The Rev. Wm., D.D.: Adamnan's Life of St. Columba.
Healy, The Most Rev. Jno., D.D., LL.D., Archbishop of Tuam: Ireland's Ancient Schools and Scholars.
Keating's History of Ireland.
Montalembert: Monks of the West.
O'Hanlon, The Rev. Jno., Canon: Lives of the Irish Saints.
Stokes, The Rev. Dr. Geo. T.: Ireland and the Celtic Church.

CHAPTER XXIV

The Poets

Ireland was the poets' land in earliest days as well as in latest.

In very early times Greece and Rome, only, excelled Ireland as nurturers of poets and nursing grounds of poetry.

From the most remote antiquity of which we have legendary record, the poet was one of the greatest, most honoured, in the land. In social rank he held next place to the king—and at table he was entitled to the king's joint, the haunch. But in sacredness of person, the king usually held next place to the poet. The lives of kings were frequently taken, but seldom occurred the sacrilegious killing of a poet.

When Fachtna Finn (who was Chief Poet of Ulster away before the Christian Era) learned that the Ulster chiefs plotted to slay at a feast their two kings, Congal Clairnach and Fergus Mac-Leide, he saved both their lives by seating each between poets. The assassins then had to stay their murderous hands lest the poets should be accidentally slain or injured. In the very rare instances in which such disaster befell the land, the whole nation mourned the calamity, and the sacrilegious scoundrel, who had been guilty of the appalling crime, was shunned by man, cursed by God and punished, moreover, with immortal obloquy.

When Cuain O'Lochain, chief poet of Erin, was, in 1024, put to death by the people of Teffia, the Annals of Clonmacnois records—"after committing of which there grew an evil scent and odour off the party that killed him, that he was easily known among the rest of the land." And the Annals of Loch Cé, continuing the after history of the sacrilegious ones who had hand in the poet's death, says: "God manifestly wrought a poet's power upon the parties who killed him, for they were put to a cruel death, and their bodies putrefied, until worms and vultures had devoured them."

The poet's *dire* fine[1] was the same as the king's—and his honour-price usually the same. And because of the sacredness of his position he was, like the king, subject to degradation for any sin that besmirched the whiteness of his office. And for sins more venial he was, like king and commoner, amenable to the law—which prescribed, for instance, that he should pay fine for the unfairness of satirising a man, in his absence; and for satirising by proxy—having his satire recited by a substitute, while he protected himself in the cowardly safety of distance. And he had to answer for crimes committed by any paying foreigners among his pupils.[2]

From very ancient times in Ireland almost all things worth recording were put into verse for their more easy remembering, pleasanter reciting and more welcome hearing. The most ancient Lives of the Saints are in verse—or where they have come down in mixed verse and prose, the prose is only a later paraphrasing of verse whose language was becoming obsolete. Ancient history and genealogy were in verse—and likewise the ancient laws. When Patrick had the laws codified it will be remembered that a filé was asked "to put a thread of poetry round them." Such old standard records as the Book of Rights, and the Calendar of Aengus, are in rhyme. Even there have come down to us ancient school text-books, on various subjects, completely in verse.

Some noted Continental scholars such as Zeuss and Nigra, agree with leading Irish authorities that it was the ancient Irish who invented rhyme—and introduced it, through the Latin, to the countries of Europe.

Constantine Nigra (quoted by Hyde) says:

> "The idea that rhyme originated among the Arabs must be absolutely rejected as fabulous. . . . Rhyme, too, could not in any possible way, have evolved itself from the natural progress of the Latin language. Amongst the Latins, neither the thing nor the name existed. The first certain examples of rhyme, then, are found on Celtic soil and among Celtic nations . . . we conclude that final assonance or rhyme can have been derived only from laws of Celtic phonology."

---

[1] His honour-price was seven cumals (twenty-one cows).

[2] A passage from the Brehon Laws:

"The poet (or tutor) commands his pupils. The man from whom education is received is free from the crimes of his pupils, though he feeds and clothes them, and that they pay him for their learning. He is free, even though it be a stranger he instructs, feeds, and clothes, provided it is not for pay but for God that he does it. If he feeds and instructs a stranger for pay, it is then he is accountable for his crimes."

And Zeuss:

> "The form of Celtic poetry, to judge both from the older and the more recent examples adduced, appears to be more ornate than the poetic form of any other nation, and even more ornate in the older poems than in the modern ones; from the fact of which greater ornateness had undoubtedly come to pass that at the very time the Roman Empire was hastening to ruin, the Celtic forms—at first entire, afterwards in part—passed over not only into the songs of the Latins, but also into those of other nations and remain in them."

Dr. Atkinson thinks it was as far away as two thousand years ago that the Irish began to grace their then ancient poetic art with their new invention of rhyme. From the Latin verses of Colm and other earliest Irish saints, we have positive proof that, anyhow, rhyme was in use in Ireland in the very earliest Christian times—both vowel rhyme (assonance) and consonantal rhyme called *comharda*.

The first English poet to use rhyme—in his Latin verse—was Aldhelm, in the eighth century, who, it will be noted, was a pupil of the Irish monk, Mael-dubh, whose school was on the site of the present English city of Malmesbury. And a century later, as Professor Zimmer points out, the poet Otfried, who first introduced rhyme to the German people, received his education at the Irish monastery of St. Gall in Switzerland. Even the first poets to sing in the Icelandic language had the Irish names Kormack and Sighvat, and were from an Irish ancestress—and we are warranted in concluding that their poetic education was Irish. Long centuries before that, the immortal Welsh poet, Caedmon, was educated by an Irishman, surrounded by Irish literary influences, and fed upon Irish literature.

Douglas Hyde says:

> "Already, in the seventh century, the Irish not only rhymed but made intricate rhyming metres, when for many centuries after this, the Germanic nations could only alliterate. . . . And down to the first half of the sixteenth century the English poets for the most part exhibited a disregard for the fineness of execution and technique of which not the meanest Irish bard attached to the pettiest chief could have been guilty."

As is only to be expected, the Irish, the inventors of rhyme, carried it to a wonderful perfection, never approached by any other people—a fact acknowledged even by those who still withhold from them the credit of having originated it.

"After the seventh century," says Dr. Hyde, in his "Literary History of Ireland," "the Irish brought the rhyming system to a perfection undreamt of even to this day, by other nations. Perhaps by no people on the globe at any period of the world's history was poetry so cultivated, and better still, so remunerated, as in Ireland." And Dr. Atkinson pronounces Irish verse "the most perfectly harmonious combination of sounds that the world has ever known." Dr. Joyce says, "No poetry of any European language, ancient or modern, can compare with the Irish poetry for richness of melody."

It was lavish in beautiful metres, in alliteration, in assonantal rhyme, in consonantal harmony. The rhymes were usually not at the end of the line only but were often repeated, again and again, within the line, which spilled over with richness of melody.

The technique of Irish poetry was far and away more elaborate, complex, intricate and subtle than that of any other nation, ancient or modern. It had an amazingly complicated prosody—"astounding" is the term that Dr. Hyde applies to it.

It is proof of the originality of Irish versification that the many technical terms used in this intricate prosody are purely Irish—showing no trace of Latin or other foreign influence. And Latin Christian influence would inevitably have left its impress on the system if that system had not been brought to complete perfection before the coming of Patrick, and the introduction of the general knowledge and use of Latin among the scholars and the clergy.

It is difficult for us to realise that in the ancient Irish Schools of Poets the students were trained in not less than three hundred and fifty different kinds of metre. Twelve years was the minimum period[3] of study in the schools. There were four grades of poet—each requiring three years of concentrated study. Each grade was sub-divided again many times. Of the lowest grade, the bard, there were sixteen divisions distinguished by the metres they had mastered. As instance of the prosodial subtilty and complexity of the metres, let us instance that of one kind alone, the nath metre which was mastered by the king-bard, there were six different kinds, and these six again divided, some of them into as many as six sub-divisions. Therefore, it was an arduous task which arose before the Irish poetic

[3] The English Campion in his "History of Ireland" recorded that in his day (16th century) the length of the course sometimes extended to 20 years.

aspirant—and wonderful and powerful was the mental training through which the Irish poet passed.

The poet's course in literature embraced seven times fifty of the great bardic epics—all of which he must not only have memorised, but have mastered in every detail—and with each of which, when called upon, must be able to hold spellbound every gathering. Furthermore, when he should go for his final degree he must be able to compose an impromptu short poem on any subject suggested. The poet-ollam, the poet of the highest rank, must be a master of Irish history, Irish antiquities and genealogies of all the leading Irish families—and always able and ready at a moment's notice, to recite anything called for in any of these subjects. Few and far between are the twentieth century scholars who are as thoroughly steeped in their subjects as were the poet-ollams of fifteen hundred years ago.

Although poets were attached to certain courts of king or chief, where they received regular stipend together with a residence, land and animals (the ollam twenty-one cows and their grass, two hounds and six horses), they frequently made circuit of their province or of the country—accompanied by their retinue—honouring with their visits various princes and notables whose praises they chanted in such measure as their merits demanded. All courts and all residences were of course thrown wide to the touring poet and his company. Twenty-four was the number of attendants prescribed by law for the ollam poet when he bestowed for only one night, upon each host, the honour of his entertaining. When he intended a longer stay, or went to a feast (to which of course other companies were likewise coming), the law fixed ten for his following. But oftentimes the very famous poets, considering themselves greater than the law, travelled amid three or four times the prescribed number of attendants, and imposed themselves and their tribe for days and weeks, months even, upon courts that they favoured. The sixth century national poet, Senchan Torpeist (Dallan Forgaill's successor), visiting the court of the Connaught king, Guaire the Hospitable, with attendant poets, students, servants, wives, dogs and horses, treated his overpowered host to a year and a day of his party's joyous company! And, since under no conceivable circumstances could any host, much less a royal one, ask a poet to move on, this visitation might only have ended when Guaire was eaten into poverty, had not the king's brother, the holy hermit, Marban, been blessed with the inspiration of commissioning Senchan and his company to go eastward upon a literary mission (in search of the lost Táin Bo Cuailgne, which, tradition said, had been "carried east over the sea with the Cuilmen") which promised to take years, if not eternity, for its fulfilment.

Senchan's parting ode to Guaire must have sounded in that king's ears one of the sweetest by poet ever spoken—if we except the alarming last stanza:

"We depart from thee, O stainless Guaire!
We leave with thee our blessing;
A year, a quarter, and a month,
Have we sojourned with thee, O high-king!

"Three times fifty poets,—good and smooth,—
Three times fifty students in the poetic art,
Each with his servant and dog;
They were all fed in the one great house.

"Each man had his separate meal;
Each man had his separate bed;
We never arose at early morning,
With contentions without calming.

"I declare to thee, O God!
Who canst the promise verify,
That should we return to our own land,
We shall visit thee again, O Guaire, though now we depart."

Since in a land of poetry and of hospitality this privileged class had the strongest incentive to increase and multiply, it is no wonder their numbers and presumption grew to such proportion that they more than once became an unbearable burden upon the land. And three times in the early centuries, one of these being a time when they and their uncountable followers are said to have constituted a third of the population of the Island—the suffering people, goaded even to the point of outraging sacred tradition, purposed banishing from the land the poets and their bands. One of the last of these popular anti-poet outbreaks was that which was allayed by Colm at the Convention of Drimceatt. Though, twice within the half century following, Kings of Ulad (Ulster) had to harbour the bards and save them from extinction.

Of course it was the riotous and disreputable ones—from which the poet-tribe was never free, in modern, any more than in ancient days—who dragged the whole body into these periodic spells of disrepute. The unworthy ones severely hurt the whole body, not only by outrageous imposition on the people's hospitality, but likewise by the exactions which they drew from a too-willing people. The law of custom provided that a poet should be paid for his composition a price that was commensurate with his standing and the worth of his work. But sometimes the reckless ones came to exact what they pleased. No one of any character would refuse a poet's demand. And indeed if any one was either unworthy enough to deny a worthy poet his price or foolhardy enough to refuse an exaction, he did so at the risk of being satirised with a biting poetic satire, which would make him the laughing-stock of the land, and his children's children's children the laughing-stock of generations yet unborn. And so gifted in this malicious art were some that it was legended their satires could not only blight the crops of the satirised, but actually raise blisters on his face.[4]

The greedy ones carried with them a *Coir Sáinnte,* Pot of Avarice, for inviting donations. It was a small pot made of silver and hung by nine chains of *findruine* (white bronze) from golden hooks on the points of the spears of nine men of the poet's company. The *Coir Sáinnte* preceded the greedy poet into a chieftain's presence as he came chanting his poem of praise, chorused by his students. The chieftain and his friends were expected to make the pot-bearers feel the weight of their appreciation.

The celebrated Ulster satirist, of the first century, Athairne, was one of the bitterest and most brazen as well as greediest of his tribe. On a time when he was going on circuit through Leinster, one king, fearful of his tongue, met him at the border of his territory, with great presents of money and cattle, in hope to buy off the threatened visitation. He went so far as, when he was visiting a king who had but one eye, to ask—and accept—that eye in payment for a poem. This account of his request is, we may judge, figurative—and a satire upon the satirist. That famous Leinster circuit of Athairne's was only ended by an Ulster-Leinster war, which his greed provoked.

---

[4] Once, when Dallon Forgaill stopped with Mongan, King of Meath, "Every night the poet would recite a story to Mongan. So great was his lore that they were thus from Halloweye till May-Day. He had gifts of food from Mongan. One day Mongan asked his poet what was the death of Fothad Airgdech. Forgaill said he was slain at Dufery in Leinster. Mongan said it was false. The poet (on hearing that) said that he would satirise him with his lampoons, and he would sing (spells) upon their waters, so that fish should not be caught in their river mouths. He would sing upon their woods so that they should not give fruit, upon their plains so that they should be barren forever of any produce.

"Mongan (thereupon) promised him his fill of precious things, so far as (the value) of seven bondmaids, or twice seven bondmaids, or three times seven. At last he offers him one-third, or one-half of his land, or his whole land; at last (everything) save only his own liberty with that of his wife Breathigrend."

The time of Athairne was one of the several times in which the poet order got out of hand, and produced and prided itself upon such biting, bitter, malevolent and grasping ones as were he and his imitators. One of the latter, named Redg, got from Cuchullain meet reward for his impudent presumption. He had appeared before Cuchullain and recited a poem in his praise—and then demanded for fee Cuchullain's remarkable spear, supernaturally gifted, called the *gae-buaid,* or spear of victory. It was one of Cuchullain's enemies who had instigated the treacherous demand. The champion offered him instead many rich gifts, one after another, all of which were steadily refused by the poet, who at length threatened to satirise Cuchullain, and disparage his honour. "Then, take your gift!" cried the champion, flinging the spear with all his force at the miscreant, whom he transfixed through the skull across. And the satirist, exclaiming, "This indeed is an overpowering gift!" dropped dead.

There were some notable instances of praiseworthy exactions imposed by high-minded poets on people who deserved punishment—exactions heartily approved of by a delighted country. Such was that of the eighth century Meath poet, Ruman (who died in 742), the "Virgil of the Gael," who, when he visited Dublin, then a stronghold of the Danish Galls, composed a poem to these Galls and named as his reward a penny to be paid him from every mean Gall and two pennies from every noble Gall. It is needless to add that he carried away from this city of foreign marauders a very weighty bag of money, indeed—every piece of it a two-penny. He bore his booty to the noted School of Rathain, near Kilbeggan; and there to the crowd of foreign scholars (who occupied seven streets) he distributed one-third of his wealth; he gave another third to the school and kept a third to himself.

The poet of repute in ancient time had no need to be exacting; for so high was the regard for him and for his work that the voluntary fees were handsome. And they were consequently wealthy. The old proverb tells that "Three coffers whose depths are not known are those of the chieftain, the church and a privileged poet." Fees fixed by law were graduated according to a poet's rank. A filé-poet, one of the highest order, was to be paid three milch-cows for a poem; and a bard of the lowest order, to be paid one calf. Naturally it was the latter class who usually sinned by their imposition, impudence and unmerited satirising.

The generous and the pleased paid the lawful fee and as much more as generosity prompted. A chieftain of the O'Donnells of Tir-Conaill who was a worthy patron of literature, once paid to a poet, who made a poem in his praise, a mare for every *rann* (four-line stanza). The patronage of the people of Tir-Conaill for the poet, is well exemplified in a poem by the great Flann MacLonain (tenth century). It relates how Flann and his suite arrived at the court of Eignachan, prince of Tir-Conaill, just when the chieftain had finished dividing among his nobles and his churches great spoil of gold taken from the Danes. Eignachan blushed for shame at being empty-handed on a poet's advent—and his people, seeing their chief's confusion, came forward and put into his hands again the gold he had given them; whereupon, the overjoyed Eignachan, from the restored store, bestowed lavishly on the poet—and divided the remainder among his people.

The same MacLonain in another corner of Ireland was the recipient of another remarkable tribute to poetry—as related in a poem of his equally famous contemporary, MacLiag, the poet-ollam of Brian Boru. MacLiag tells how, one time that MacLonain was travelling in Galway, he met a labouring man of the Dal Cas of Clare returning to his own country with the wages of twelve months' service in Galway, a cow and a cloak. When the poor Dalcassian learnt that it was the noble poet, MacLonain whom he encountered, he begged a poem of him:

"He said to me in prudent words,
Sing to me the history of my country;
It is sweet to my soul to hear it."

MacLonain stirred his auditor with a poem in praise of the Dalcassians and was immediately rewarded with the twelve months' wages of the gratified one. But, for his pride of race, and generosity to a poet, the man was repaid tenfold by his equally proud and patriotic fellow Dalcassians, who, when they learnt what he had done, received him with honour in their assembly, and bestowed on him ten cows for every quarter of his own cow.

But, it was the most illustrious of all Dalcassians, Brian Boru, the warrior king and patron munificent of poets and scholars, who once gave to MacLiag the richest gift probably ever bestowed upon one of the bardic race. On a day when Brian with his court stood upon the battlements of Kincora, gratefully gazing upon the vast tribute of cows[5] from Ulster and from Leinster, that were arriving at the Castle, the poet at his side paid a word of praise upon the great flocks and herds that came to Brian—whereupon the monarch turning to the poet said: "They are all thine, O noble poet!"

---

[5] It was this which gave to Brian his title Boru (of the Cow Tribute).

To this MacLiag is credited a classical piece of satire, one of the rarest ever originated in any language. Moreover, he skilfully combined, in one little off-hand remark, the most withering sarcasm with the dizziest praise.

Once when he and his attendants had returned from circuit and he was entertaining Brian's court with accounts of his travels, the king inquired which of all the visited chieftains had rewarded him most generously. To everybody's amazement, the poet named one who was notorious for niggardliness. "Donal MacDubh O'Daveren," he said, "was the most generous of all." "What did he give you?" asked Brian. "A leathern girdle and clasp," answered MacLiag. "Did you visit Cian, the son of Malloy, chief of the Eugenians of Cashel, and his wife, Sabia, my daughter?" "Yes. They advanced to meet me when they heard I was coming. They had myself and fifty of my train borne on men's shoulders. We were brought to their Dun, and each man was given handsome garments, a chain shirt and a cloak. To me Cian gave his own habiliments, his horse, his armour, his chess-tables and nine score of his best kine. He gave fifty steeds to my train—and lavished gold and fifty rings on my bards." Said the astonished Brian, "Strange it is that you are more grateful to Donal MacDubh O'Daveren for his paltry girdle and clasp, than to Cian and Sabia." "Not strange it is," replied MacLiag, "for it was more difficult to O'Daveren to part with that girdle and clasp than to Cian and Sabia to bestow all their noble gifts."

The tenth-century poet, MacCoise, when ending a visit to Mulrooney, King of Connaught (ancestor of the O'Connors), was presented by that king with a chess-board, a valuable sword, fifty milch cows and thirty steeds. And MacLiag in his eulogy on the death of another great Connaught king, Tadg O'Kelly (whose court-poet he had been), tells how, on the day that Tadg won the battle of Loch Riach, he presented to him:

"An hundred cows, an hundred swords, an hundred shields,
An hundred oxen for the ploughing season,
And an hundred halter horses.

"He gave me on the night of Glenn-gerg,
An hundred cloaks and an hundred scarlet frocks,
Thirty spears of blood-stained points,
Thirty tables, and thirty chess-boards."

In the case of the plundering and burning of the poet MacCoise's home by Donal O'Neill's army, the noted scholar Flann of Clanmacnois assessed the damages due a poet for such insult and loss; namely, full restitution and in addition fourteen cumals (forty-two cows), and the breadth of the poet's face of gold. By the learned men present, O'Neill himself, and his chiefs, it was then agreed that such should be the damages ever after payable in all similar cases.[6]

No great wonder it was that a class of men so favoured, indulged, flattered and honoured, should sometimes find among them many who came to think that no consideration should bar them from the gratification of their lightest whim; and that no man's rights were of any importance, if they came in conflict with their rights. This point of view is strikingly exemplified in a quatrain from a poem of Muiredach O'Daly who considered himself grossly and wantonly persecuted because The O'Donnell pursued him from tuath to tuath, and from kingdom to kingdom over Ireland, after he had killed that prince's steward at Lissadill:

"Trifling our quarrel with the man (i.e., O'Donnell)
A clown to be abusing me,
And me to kill the churl—
Dear God, is this a cause for enmity!"

But a poet's moral attainments were expected to be on the same high level with his intellectual. There were demanded of him:

"Purity of hand, bright without wounding,
Purity of mouth without poisonous satire,
Purity of learning without reproach,
Purity of husbandship."

And, despite grave sins of the few sinners among them, the ancient poets of Eirinn proved themselves worthy of their sacred trust.

Much of the work done by the official poet was of a utilitarian nature. The chief duties of his office, as king's filé, were to keep in verse the historical, genealogical and legal records; to prepare for the public special poetic

[6] It was MacCoise himself, by means of a very clever allegorical poem, which he entitled The Plunder of the Castle of Maelmilscothach, who brought O'Neill to realize the enormity of the insult done by his men—and induced him to volunteer full satisfaction.

accounts of particular actions in which the people were engaged; and to sing the feats of the champions, the hospitality of the princes and the charms of the women. Such were the more important subjects from which the poet was expected to derive inspiration. And very many examples of the ancient poet's work preserved down the centuries, are concerned with these matters.

But the unofficial poet showed a wide range of inspiration. Amongst the old poetic pieces, which escaped the destructive hand of alien enemies and blight of time are several which show the ancient poet's marvellously keen observation, and ardent love, of Nature, as well as his wonderfully subtle sense of beauty. Here is a nature-picture (attributed to Oisin) as vivid as ancient:

> "A tale for you: oxen lowing: winter snowing: summer passed away: wind from the north, high and cold: low the sun and short his course: wildly tossing the wave of the sea. The fern burns deep red. Men wrap themselves closely: the wild goose raises her wonted cry: cold seizes the wing of the bird: 'tis the season of ice: sad my tale."

A poem attributed to Fionn is this description of May-day (translated by O'Donovan) which shows that the love of nature, was, in the far-away days of Ireland as truly cultivated, and as delightfully expressed, as it has ever been in modern countries of modern days:

"May day! delightful time! how beautiful the colour;
The blackbirds sing their full lay. Would that Laegh were here
The cuckoos sing in constant strains. Now welcome is the noble
Brilliance of the seasons ever! On the margin of the branchy woods
The summer swallows skim the streams. The swift horses seek the pool.
The heather spreads out her long hair. The weak fair bog-down grows.
Sudden consternation attacks the signs; the planets
In their courses running, exert an influence;
The sea is lulled to rest, flowers cover the earth."

And now that Erin had become a land of schools, and of scribes, we find one of the latter, entranced with his work, charmingly imparting to us the beauty of his feeling.

THE SCRIBE[7]

A hedge of trees surrounds me,
A blackbird's lay sings to me;
Above my lined booklet
The thrilling birds chant to me.

In a grey mantle from the top of bushes
The cuckoo sings:
Verily may the Lord shield me:—
Well do I write under the greenwood.

A couple of hundred years after Patrick, a passionate desire to live alone with God and Nature swept Ireland, and carried to the wilderness and to remote and lonely islands tens of thousands of intellectual and spiritual ones. One of the many hermit-poets puts his soothed soul into a seductive song which in these days of unrest makes us realise that though he is called hermit it is we who are alone.

HERMIT'S SONG

I wish, O Son of the living God, O ancient, eternal King,
For a hidden little hut in the wilderness that it may be my dwelling.

An all-grey lithe little lark to be by its side,
A clear pool to wash away sins through the grace of the Holy Spirit.

Quite near, a beautiful wood around it on every side,
To nurse many-voiced birds, hiding it with its shelter.

A southern aspect for warmth, a little brook across its floor,
A choice land with many gracious gifts such as be good for every plant.

A few men of sense—we will tell their number—
Humble and obedient, to pray to the King:—

Four times three, three times four, fit for every need,
Twice this in the church, both North and South:—

[7] This poem and the one that follows are from Kuno Meyer's "Ancient Irish Poetry."

Six pairs besides myself,
Praying forever to the King who makes the sun shine.

A pleasant church and with the linen altar cloth, a dwelling for God
from Heaven;
Then, shining candles above the pure white scriptures.

One house for all to go to for the care of the body,
Without ribaldry, without boasting, without thought of evil.

This is the husbandry I would take, I would choose, and will not hide it:
Fragrant leek, hens, salmon, trout, bees;

Raiment and food for me from the King of fair fame,
And I to be sitting for a while praying God in every place.

And when the Connaught King, Cellach, from a hollow-tree where, cornered by his enemy Maelcroin and armed band, he had spent his last night on earth—beheld the spears of that dawn which ushered in his death, he could not, still, withhold the expression of his rapture:

> [8] "HAIL to the Morning, that as a flame falls on the ground! hail to Him too, that sends her, the Morning many-virtued, ever-new!
>
> "O Morning fair, so full of pride, O sister of the brilliant sun! hail to the beauteous morning that lightest for me my little book!
>
> "Thou seest the guest in every dwelling, and shinest on every tribe and kin; hail, O thou white-necked beautiful one, here with us now, golden fair, wonderful!"

"My little book of chequered page tells me," continues Cellach, "that my life has not been right." For, Cellach, even in flight for his life had with him one of the books he dearly loved. A student he had been, and should have continued—but, in a foolish moment that he lived to regret in bitterness, he gave up the student's cloister for the court. And in another poem this sixth-century student-king sighs his sharp regret:

"Woe to him who leaveth lore
For the red world's arts or ore;
Who the true God's love would leave
With the false world's Kings to cleave!

[8] Translated by Douglas Hyde.

"Woe who taketh arms in life
And retaineth hand of strife,
Better far books of whiteness
Where psalms are seen in brightness!"
—From a translation by DR. SIGERSON.

The English poet Tennyson dipped into ancient Irish lore and poetry before singing of Arthur. Knowing this, we are led to wonder if he who wrote Crossing the Bar did not stumble upon the beautiful little piece of our ninth-century Cormac MacCuilleanáin:

"Wilt Thou steer my frail black bark
O'er the dark broad ocean's foam?
Wilt Thou come, Lord, to my boat
Where afloat, my will would roam?
Thine the mighty, Thine the small,
Thine to make men fall like rain,
God, wilt Thou grant aid to me
As I come o'er the upheaving main?"[9]

---

[9] There are dozens of different kinds of the poems of ancient Ireland that must be left unsampled. But here is one on the fleetingness of life, translated by O'Donovan, which while far from being as good as a hundred others that might be quoted, is in a style that will please many readers—

Like a damask rose you see,
Or like a blossom on a tree,
Or like a dainty flower in May,
Or like the morning to the day,
Or like the sun, or like the shade,
Or like the gourd which Jonah made;
Even such is man whose thread is spun,
Drawn out and out, and so is done.

The rose withers, the blossom blasteth,
The flower fades, the morning hasteth,
The sun sets, the shadow flies,
The gourd consumes, the man—he dies.

Like the grass that's newly sprung,
Or like the tale that's new begun,
Or like the bird that's here today,
Or like the pearly dew in May,
Or like the hour, or like the span,
Or like the singing of the swan;

Hyde, Douglas, LL.D.: A Literary History of Ireland, from the earliest times to the present day.
—— Irish Poetry: an Essay in Irish, with translation in English.
Sigerson, Dr. Geo.: Bards of the Gael and Gall.
O'Curry, Eugene: Manuscript Materials of Irish History.
—— Manners and Customs of the Ancient Irish.
Joyce, P. W.: Social History of Ancient Ireland.
Meyer, Kuno: Ancient Irish Poetry.
Carmichael, Alexander: Carmina Gadelica: Hymns and Incantations orally collected in the Highlands and Islands of Scotland, and translated into English.

Even such is man who lives by breath,
Is here, now there, in life and death.

The grass withers, the tale is ended,
The bird is flown, the dew's ascended,
The hour is short, the span not long,
The swan's near death, man's life is done.

Like the bubble in the brook,
Or in a glass much like a look,
Or like shuttle in weaver's hand,
Or like the writing on the sand,
Or like a thought, or like a dream,
Or like the gliding of the stream;
Even such is man, who lives in breath,
Is here, now there, in life and death.

The bubble's blown, the look forgot,
The shuttle's flung, the writing's not,
The thought is past, the dream is gone,
The water's run, man's life is done.

Like an arrow from a bow,
Or like a course of water flow,
Or like the time 'twixt flood and ebb,
Or like the spider's tender web,
Or like a race, or like a goal,
Or like the dealing of a dole;
Even such is man whose battle state
Is always subject unto fate.

The arrow shot, the flood soon spent,
The time no time, the web soon rent,
The race soon run, the goal soon won,
The dole soon dealt, man's life soon done.

Like the lightning from the sky,
Or like a post that quick doth hie,
Or like a quaver in a song,
Or like a journey three days' long
Or like the snow when summer's come,
Or like the pear, or like the plum;
Even such is man, who heaps up sorrow,
Lives this day, and dies tomorrow.

The lightning's past, the post must go,
The song is short, the journey so,
The pear doth rot, the plum doth fall,
The snow dissolves, and so must all.

CHAPTER XXV

THE IRISH KINGDOM OF SCOTLAND

Probably there is nothing in Irish history which has caused more confusion than the terms Scotia and Scot, which, at first applied to Ireland and Irishmen, came to be applied later to Ireland's northeastern neighbour, Alba, and its inhabitants. A statement of the cause of this change may aid to untangle a historical tangle which troubles the minds of many who are not students.

It will be remembered that our most ancient poets and seanachies claimed that an early name for Eirinn, Scotia, was derived from Scota, queen-mother of the Milesians. The derivation may, or may not, be imaginary. But, downward from the days of the Emperor Constantine the Great, when the poet Egesippus tells how "Scotia which links itself to no land, trembles at their (the Roman legions') name"—the term Scotia is, by Continental writers, applied to Ireland more often than any other name. And Scot is the term by these writers most constantly applied to a native of Eirinn. Orosius, the third century geographer, uses "Hibernia the nation of the Scoti."

As late as the end of the seventh century we find the Irishman Adamnan, when residing and writing in the country which is now Scotland, using the word Scotia to designate his own home country from which he is an exile. And down in the eleventh century we have an Irish exile on the Continent, the celebrated Marianus Scotus (Marian the Scot) referring to his countrymen as Scots. The foreigner, Hermann, in the same century, is calling them Scots likewise. And still farther on, in the thirteenth century, Cæsar of Heisterbach, talking of Purgatory, requests any one who doubts its existence to go to Scotia to St. Patrick's Purgatory there, and be convinced. The reference is to the then world-famous St. Patrick's Purgatory in Loch

Dearg (Donegal) where penitents enclosed for many days in a cave, had vision of Heaven, Hell and Purgatory.

Isidore of Seville, writing in the seventh century, uses the phrase, "Scotia eadem et Hibernia." And Charlemagne's biographer, the celebrated Notker le Begue of the ninth century who was intimate with the Irishmen of the school of St. Gall in Switzerland, and a pupil of the Irish teacher Mongan, there—uses the phrase "In the Island Hibernia, or Scotia," when talking of Colm Cille. And again in talking of St. Kilian, the martyred bishop of Wurzburg, he says: "He came from Hibernia, the Island of the Scots."

The modern name of Ireland seems to have originated with the Northmen, in about the seventh century—being probably formed from Eire, they called it Ir or Ire, and after that the English called it Ireland, and its natives Irish. For several centuries longer, however, these terms were not adopted by Continental writers, who still continued to speak of Scotia and the Scot, and designated the Irish scholars on the Continent by the term Scotus. The new name Ireland was on the Continent, first used only in the eleventh century (by Adam De Brème).

To Alba (the present Scotland) was transferred the term Scotia, and to its people the term Scot, because the Scoti of Hibernia, having again and again colonised there, built in it a strong kingdom, which gave the Scotic (Irish) people dominance there, and soon made the Scotic kings the kings of the whole country. The first account of Scotic colonising in Alba occurs in the very beginning of the third century when Conaire the Great, a son-in-law of Conn of the Hundred Battles, was King of Munster—to become later High King of Ireland. One of his three sons, the Carbris, Carbri Riada, namely, led a large body of his people from Kerry to the northeast of Antrim, where he settled some of them, and crossing Sruth-na-Moill to the adjacent coast of Scotland, settled a colony there also—in those peninsulas and islands which are now part of Argyle.[1]

This first colony of Scots from Ireland to settle in Alba, from time to time received increase in numbers from the mother country—and military help also whenever they needed it against their neighbours, the Picts.

A hundred years later, namely, in the first part of the fourth century, Lugaid MacConn, another Munsterman and a descendant of Conn of the

[1] It is held by some that Carbri Riada settled his people entirely in Antrim, and that it was Fergus who first brought the people of Dal Riada over the water, and established the Scotic kingdom of Alba. The former, however, is the popular belief, and is attested by the Venerable Bede as well as others. O'Flaherty and Usher differ with Bede, though.

Hundred Battles, who had to flee from Ireland, brought some accessions of strength to them, when he came there about two centuries later, and made himself a power in the Scotic colony. From his son, Fothaid Canan, whom he left in power there when he returned to Ireland, to wrest the High Kingship from Art the Lonely, sprang the ancestors of the lords of Argyle, variously named MacAllen, Campbell and MacCallum Mor.

About a hundred years after Carbri Riada had established the Scotic Dal Riada in Alba, as well as the Dal Riada in Antrim, there also came to the Scotic colony a considerable accession of strength—a body of their kinsmen from Kerry led by one of their chieftains, Fergus.

The Picts, naturally jealous of these usurpers on their soil, continued exerting the utmost pressure upon them, in the hope of crushing them out, till Niall of the Nine Hostages, going to their assistance with an army, overcame and drove back the Picts, established the Scotic kingdom in Alba on a solid foundation, and, it is said, got the submission of the Picts and the tribute of all Alba.

When the colony had added another hundred years to its age—at the beginning of the sixth century that is—it got its greatest and strongest accession by the coming of a Niallan host, headed by the three grandsons of Erc, Lorne, Aongus and Fergus Mor their leader—who gave new blood, strength and leadership to the Dal Riada of Alba, and made it an island power to be reckoned with. For before the century's end it was strong and plucky enough to demand its complete independence from the mother country—a claim which, in 576, King Aedh, accompanying Colm, carried to the Convention of Drimceatt—and which was settled to the young kingdom's complete satisfaction. While united to Ireland by the closest bonds of blood, friendship, education and military intercourse, it was now a separate and independent kingdom[2]—with the Antrim Dal Riada, some hold, as an appanage.

The Scots' kingdom of Argyle and the islands held its own and more, for a long time. But at the end of the eighth century, in the reign of Don Coirce, the Northmen pushed them eastward from their original seat, and they in turn pushed the Picts east and northeast, and against these Picts conducted a campaign of conquest which lasted half a century, till, in the year 850, their king, Cinead (Kenneth) MacAlpin, completely overthrew the Picts and was the first Gaelic king of (the chief part of) Scotland. Some

---

[2] MacNeill holds that the Alban Dal Riada had got its independence from the mother-country before Drimceatt—and that Aedh's claim at Drimceatt was for sovereignty over his kinsmen of the Antrim Dal Riada.

claim that he got dominion over the Britons, who occupied the southwest of the country and the Anglo-Danish population of the southeast. Now that the Scotic people got complete dominion over all or the main part of the country, it began to be called Scotia—at first Scotia Minor, in contradistinction to Eire, which was Scotia Major—but gradually the title Scotia fell away from Eire, and solely came to signify Alba.

In the eleventh century, when all of the present country of Scotland—with exception of the Western Islands and headlands, and northern islands, which were held by the Danes—had been brought under Scotic sway, the dominant Gaelic power began to wane. A number of leading English families who fled or were driven from the south, in consequence of the Norman invasion, flocked into southeastern Scotland and came into favour at court (in Edinburgh). Then also Malcolm married Margaret, daughter of Edmund, King of the Saxon peoples (afterwards St. Margaret). The new influences began to affect king, court and government from this time forward. And the king began to find it easy to lean upon the newcomers, the southerners, as well as their kinsmen, the old Anglo-Danish colony of the southeast, in the differences that were constantly arising between him and the semi-independent (Gaelic) chieftains of the Highlands. When, at the end of the eleventh century, Malcolm's son, Edgar, English both by name and nature, was crowned king—the Gaelicism of royalty and of the court waned more rapidly, till in the thirteenth century it went out altogether; and the last of the Irish royal line became extinct with Alexander the Third, who died without heir in 1287. Then began the Wars of Succession among the Lowland old-English families, the Bruces and the Balliols.

So, though the greater portion of the country was, and still is, Gaelic—with Gaelic manners, customs, dress and language, still holding in the Highlands and the Islands—the end of the thirteenth century saw the end of Scotic (Irish) rule in Alba.

Keating's History of Ireland.
Joyce, P. W.: Social History of Ancient Ireland.
O'Curry, Eugene: Manners and Customs of the Ancient Irish.
—— Manuscript Materials of Irish History.
MacNeill, Eoin: Some Phases of Irish History.
Skene, W. F.: Celtic Scotland.

CHAPTER XXVI

The Centuries of the Saints

The new impetus and aim that Patrick gave to the Irish nation, turning it from war-love to ideals much higher, wrought in the island a phenomenal transformation. While foreign warring and raiding ceased, and internal warring became more rare, tens of thousands of every rank and class in the nation vied with one another, not, as formerly, for skill in handling war weapons, but for ease in conning the Scriptures; not for gaining fame in fighting, but for gathering favour in the sight of God. The religious development and spiritual revolution were extraordinary. A consuming thirst for knowledge, and burning ardour for spreading the Gospel, swept the eager land, as a Lammas fire would sweep the powder-dry mountainside. Old and young, men and women, teacher and fighter, king and kerne, all were caught up in the Christ-fire that glowed in every vale and leaped on every hill in Erin. The true history of several centuries succeeding Patrick's coming, consists not of the chronicle of Erin's wars, and the roll of her kings, but the record of the thousands of the saints,[1] and the tens of thousands of the teachers of Erin. And let us keep in mind that this period of the spiritual rejuvenation of the island on the verge of the world synchronised with that dark and fearful period in Europe when Christianity and culture were being mercilessly overwhelmed by the onward-rolling, irresistible wave of barbarism that left naught but wild desolation in its wake.

Fortunate for Europe and for the world it was that in this dread hour the Lord called the eager labourers of Eire to His island vineyard; and from it sent the saving vintage far and wide for the reviving of a perishing world.

[1] All men who signally devoted themselves to the religious life then were termed saints.

> "For once, at any rate, Ireland drew on herself the eyes of the whole world," says Kuno Meyer, in the Preface to his Ancient Irish Poetry . . . "as the one haven of rest in a turbulent world overrun by hordes of barbarians, as the great seminary of Christianity and classic learning. Her sons, carrying Christianity and a new humanism over Great Britain and the Continent, became teachers of whole nations, the councillors of Kings and Emperors. . . . The Celtic spirit dominated a large part of the Western world and its Christian ideals imparted new life to a decadent civilisation."

Christianity and learning went hand in hand in Ireland. Almost every one of her multitude of holy men became scholars, and every holy scholar became a teacher. Each holy man's fame went wide over the land, attracting to him crowds who desired to sit at his feet and emulate him. And unexpectedly would he then find himself the head of a school—for, both for their sake and for sake of those with whom they should afterwards work, it was necessary to educate the colony of disciples, whose little huts and bothies arose so thickly around his own modest habitation. Hence, ecclesiastical schools, side by side with their secular forerunners, and soon far overshadowing them, sprang up in every corner of the country, till the land was thickly dotted with them.

Of what is known of the holy men of this period many volumes have been written. It would take infinitely more volumes to record all that has been lost or forgotten regarding them. Here we can only suggest the men and the time, by sketching some shadowy outlines of a few of the more prominent figures—chiefly saints of the second order—with a few scraps of the characteristic folk-lore that has grown entwiningly around their memory.

For, those centuries had three orders of saints, namely: the Patrician or secular clergy, missionaries who travelled and preached Christ to all the land during the hundred years succeeding the coming of Patrick; the monastic saints, who, during the next hundred years, cultivated Christianity in, and radiated it from, their monastic establishments and monastic schools; and the anchorites, the hermit saints, who, succeeding the great ones of the second order, cultivated Christ in solitude, on lonely islands, on wild mountain-tops, and in the impenetrable wilderness. These last, like Fechin, Senach, Coleman, Ernaan, are described as "holy and shone as aurora; the second class, more holy, lighted the land as does the moon; and the first, most holy, were like the sun that warms the land by the fervour of its brightness."

Under the second order such communities sprang up as that of St. Nessan,[2] of Mungret (near Limerick) of which Keating states, "The following was the number of its members, to wit, five hundred monks who were men of learning, whose office it was to preach to the people, six hundred choristers who sang in the choir, and four hundred seniors who were devoted to the meditation of divine things."

One of the most honoured and most beloved of the second order of Irish saints was Finian of Clonard, a child of the Clan Rory—"a doctor of wisdom and tutor of the saints of Erin, in his time," as O'Clery in his Martyrology styles him. For, from his famous school at Cluain-erard—Clonard, on the River Boyne—went forth the twelve saints who were styled the Twelve Apostles of Eirinn: the two Ciarans, the two Brendans, the two Colms,[3] Mobi,[4] Ruadan, Lasserian, Ciannech, Senach and Ninnid of Loch Erne. Strange to say, Finian got his education in Britain—in that part which is now called Wales. There he studied chiefly under Cadoc, who was himself part Irish and had been trained by two Irish teachers. He also studied under the Welshman Gildas, who had conducted some of his own studies in Ireland. After Finian had returned to Ireland, and had established himself, about A.D. 520, on the Boyne, his fame for piety and for wisdom spread so fast that in short time a community was established there. "Abbots left their monasteries and bishops their sees, to come to learn Divine Wisdom from his lips." "His school," says O'Clery, "was in quality a holy city full of wisdom and virtue. And he came to be called Finian the Wise."

The growth of his community, and of his power, are well illustrated in a little incident recorded of Colm Cille's first coming there. Having told the little stranger, to whom he took a liking, to build his hut at the door of the church and finding, later, that he had, instead, in his modesty, gone far off to build, Finian affectionately chided him for not doing what he had been told—to which the princeling from Tir-Conaill prophetically replied, "But here, before long, the door of thy church will be."

[2] "Never came forth from his mouth what was false or deceitful."

[3] Of course this refers to the two most famed Colms—Colm of Iona and Colm of Tir-da-glass. There were scores of St. Colms. O'Halloran reckons of Irish Saints whose names were common: 4 named Colga, 10 named Gobhan, 12 Dicuil, 12 Maidoc, 12 Adran, 13 Caman, 13 Dimian, 14 Brendan, 14 Finian, 14 Ronan, 15 Conall, 15 Dermod, 15 Lugad, 16 Lassaran, 18 Comin, 19 Foilla, 20 Ciaran, 20 Ultan, 22 Cillian, 23 Aidan, 30 Cronan, 37 Moluan, 43 Lasrian, 34 Mochuma, 58 Mochua, 55 Fintan, 60 Cormac, 200 Colman.

[4] Mobi, who had a school at Glasnevin, sent to Colm Cille on Iona, the present of a certain sacred girdle. "Good was the man who had this girdle, for it never opened on feasting nor closed on falsehood."

His school grew so enormously that it is recorded he had at length three thousand pupils, native and foreign.

That Finian's pupils advanced in sanctity as they did in knowledge we learn from a quaint bit of lore recorded in the old Book of Lismore, which tells how Finian, otherwise occupied himself, once sent the student Senach to observe and bring him word how the other pupils were engaged—"Different in sooth was that at which each of them was found, yet all were good. Colm the son of Crimthann was with hands stretched forth, and mind contemplative of God, the wild birds resting on his hands and on his head.[5]

With this Finian is sometimes confounded his contemporary, Finian of Moville[6] in Down, who, Colgan says, is the Irish Frigidius, who became bishop of Lucca in Italy—at whose school the great Colm chiefly studied, and from whose book of the Scriptures he took the surreptitious copy that indirectly caused his exile.

The Senach just referred to—the saintly Senach, on whom attended many miracles, and who was one of the twelve apostles of Erin, is the same who afterwards failed in attempt to turn away from his Island of Iniscathy (at the mouth of the Shannon) the holy woman Canaire. He conducted on this Island of Iniscathy a noted school. It was when (before that) he conducted an establishment at Iniscara, that there is said to have landed in Cork a ship's company of Romans, hither attracted by Erin's fame for holiness and wisdom. Ten of these Romans are said to have joined Senach's Iniscara community. That he should be a worthy and inspiring teacher is not to be wondered at, for as a lad he had an unquenchable thirst for knowledge, which forced him to become that which in later days was termed a "poor scholar." He had read and profited by the verse of Matthew which says: "Whosoever will be great among you, let him be your servant." And for his teaching he paid with service. He herded cows and calves for

[5] Once, says a legend, Kevin of Glendalough prayed so intently that a bird built its nest between his extended palms, laid its eggs, and reared its young.

[6] Of this Finian of Moville is related one of the heavenly bird legends—which, however, for chronological reasons, must have been first related of some other of the many St. Finians. Once when he was in the woods gathering wattles for building a monastery, a beautiful bird sang three enchanting songs to him—which held him spell-bound for, he thought, several minutes. But when the songs were finished and that he went home with his burden of wattles,—which were still green—he was astounded to see a great monastery built—and occupied by a community of men all strange to him. When he and they had got over mutual astonishment and bewilderment, and that the records were searched it was found that a Finian had gone into the woods to gather wattles 150 years ago—and never returned!

Notal of Kell Manach, with whom he read. Senach carried a book with him to the fields, when he went herding.[7]

Like Senach, Ciaran the Wright, he of Clonmacnois, herded in his youth, and carried to the herding his hunger for knowledge. He was herding in Magh Ai for his foster-father, Justus, who was also his tutor when, attracted by the saintliness of Ciaran, a fox out of the woods made itself his servant, it is said.[8]

Ciaran was a beautiful character, who was cut off in the flowering of his manhood.[9] After Colm, he had been the favourite of his master, Finian, at Clonard. To Finian's eyes he was the moon, who was to cheer and enlighten the centre of Ireland, while Colm was the sun which should enlighten Erin and Alba, and all of Western Europe.

His liberality, and love of helping others, made him noted—and won for him a nick-name, when he studied under the loving eye of his spiritual father, Finian. It was on the first day when that little Ninnid the slant-eyed, of Loch Erne, seeking the knowledge for which his soul yearned, came to the big school. When the great-hearted Finian had spoken with, and accepted, and enrolled the shy little fellow from Loch Erne, he told him to go among the scholars and borrow a book. But all whom the timid boy visited were so deep in their studies that they could not spare him what he

---

[7] So that he might not be distracted in his reading, he would, when he went to the pasture, separate the calves from the cows—drawing a line across the field between them, over which neither had the power to go to the other. And when in the grinding season, he had to take his turn sitting up in the mill at night, he also brought a book for study. On one occasion, when they knew that he was there alone, robbers came, but on arriving saw to their dismay two men, one reading and one grinding. And their evil scheme was thus miraculously thwarted.

Of pupils in his school is told a beautiful incident. Two of them, little boys, having gone with another bigger boy, Donnan, the son of Liach, to cut sea-weed for the master, were drowned. To assuage the frantic grief of their parents, Senach recalled their souls to their discovered bodies. Then the re-living lads protested to their mother: "O Mother, though the power of the whole world was given us and its delightfulness and joyance, we would deem it the same as if we were in prison, compared with being in the life and the land we reached."

[8] The fox, we are told, used to carry back and forth between pupil and tutor the psalter wherein Ciaran read. The animal would sit by Ciaran in the field, harkening to the boy reading his lesson to the end, and would watch while Ciaran, with his style, copied the lesson upon the waxen tablets. Then the wise animal, taking the tablets in his mouth, carried them, with the psalter, home to Justus, and brought them back corrected. But, once, tempted by the tastiness of the wax, the fox succumbed to the devil's prompting—and went aside from the straight path to enjoy the lesson under a bush. Aongus, the son of Crimthann came upon him with his hounds and men at that critical moment, and gave chase to Reynard, who, with the tablets, fled for his life. He ran to Ciaran and came under his cowl. And Ciaran saved the fox from the hounds, and the tablets from the fox.

[9] He died A.D. 548, aged only 33. "He never uttered a word that was false."

wanted. He returned to Finian and told him he had made the rounds of the school, but could get no book from the scholars. "Hast thou gone," said Finian, "to yon tender youth who is on the north of the green?" Ninnid, replying that he had not done so, was directed to go there now. The tender youth was Ciaran, the son of the Carpenter. When the slant-eyed one asked Ciaran if he might have his book to read from, the reader was studying that verse of Matthew: "Omnia quæcumque ultis ut faciant homini," etc.—and turning to the timid lad, answered him: "This I read, that I should do unto others what I would desire them to do unto me. So, though I am only half through Matthew, you may have it." And he gave his book to the little fellow with whom no one else would bother. His playful fellow-students hereupon nicknamed him "Ciaran half-Matthew"—and when the story came to the ears of Finian, he proudly said to these students: "Not Ciaran half-Matthew will he be, but Ciaran half-Ireland."

Shortly before his birth, Ciaran's mother came to visit a holy bishop, who, when he heard the roll of her approaching chariot said: "It is the noise of a chariot under a king. And he shall be a mighty king. As the sun shineth among the stars of heaven, so shall he shed on earth miracles and marvels that can not be told."[10]

When he was at Clonard, and would go out to study in the silence of the woods, tradition says that a stag used to come and lie down in front of him, presenting its horns for a reading stand on which he laid his book whilst he read.

After Clonard he went to Aran to study under St. Enda. While studying there he used to thrash the corn for the community; but they had to take this office from him, because he gave of the corn so lavishly to the poor that he often left the students and the community hungering. When he was leaving Aran he had vision of a tree which grew up in the middle of Erin and sheltered all the land. Its branches bent with load of fruit, wherefrom all the birds of the air came to eat. Enda read the vision for him: "That tree is thyself. All Erin shall be filled with thy name, and sheltered by the grace that will be in thee. And many from all parts will be fed by thy prayers and fastings. Go, in God's name, and found thy church on the Shannon's banks."

---

[10] On a certain day Ciaran was sowing seed at Iseal-Chiarain. A poor man asked him for alms. Ciaran threw a handful of grain into his breast, and it turned immediately into gold. King Angus, son of Crimthann, sent two horses and chariots to Ciaran, and Ciaran gave them to the poor man for the gold, and the gold turned into grain immediately, and the field was sown with it after, so that not in the whole territory was there corn better.

Before Ciaran put his foot in his boat to sail away from Enda and Aran, he knelt him down upon the strand to get his teacher's parting blessing. And the grieving Enda, as he would give it, broke down and wept—and was gently chided therefor by his brethren. "Oh, my brothers," said Enda, "why should I not weep; this day our Island has lost its rarest flower."

He went to the place where he had been directed by Enda. He first stopped at Ard Mantain, a beautiful and fertile spot, on the river banks, which attracted him much. But on consideration he said: "No, not here may I found my church. Here indeed are the world's riches in plenty, but from such a place the souls going to heaven would be few." He next stopped at Ard Tiprait, a place unattractive and with soil unyielding. "Here let us remain," he said to his companions, "for many souls will ascend to Heaven from this spot." That was Saturday, January 23rd, 540. In that place and on that day he blessed and drove the first post. When he was making his preparations for this there appeared upon the scene an outlaw—Diarmuid, the son of Fergus Kerbeoll, who was hiding from the High King's armies that sought him. This Diarmuid enthusiastically aided the young cleric in fixing the first post of his church. Turning to the faithful one who was hunted, Ciaran then said: "Though today thy followers are few, tomorrow thou wilt be High King of Eirinn." And his words were fulfilled, for the powerful Ard-Righ of later days, Diarmuid O'Carroll, was no other than the outlaw friend of Ciaran. Ciaran had his church finished on May 9th, of the same year; and then his community and school began to grow. He lived for a very short time to enjoy and to foster both. But even in this short time new lustre was added to a name whose brightness had before been notable.

In his very short life—for he died at the age of thirty-three—he had lifted many thousands toward God. He had evoked wonderful veneration throughout the land, and been a beacon on a mountaintop to the men and women of Eirinn. And the monastery and school which he had started, which he blessed with his name, and inspired with his spirit, was to be among the greatest of the great monasteries and schools of Eirinn; and down the ages the fame of his school was to exceed the fame of all other schools that Eirinn ever knew, and its scholars were to be noted for their wisdom and their learning, both at home in Ireland, and abroad on the Continent.

The last moments of the holy Ciaran are told with simple beauty in the Book of Lismore:

> "When the time of his decease drew nigh to holy Ciaran, in the little Church, in the thirty-third year of his age, on the fifth of the

> Ides of September, as regards the day of the solar month, on Saturday as regards the day of the week: on the eighteenth as regards the day of the moon, he said, 'Let me be carried to the little height above the church.' And when that was done he looked to the sky and the lofty air above his head. And saith he, 'Awful is this way above.' 'Not for thee is it awful,' say the monks. 'I know not indeed,' saith he, 'aught of God's commandments I have transgressed, and yet even David, son of Jesse, and Paul the Apostle dreaded this way.' Then the stone pillow was taken from under him for his comfort. 'Nay,' saith he, 'put it under my shoulder.' . . . Then angels filled all between heaven and earth to meet his soul. Then he was carried into the little church and he raised his hands and blessed his people"—and closed his eyes in Christ.[11]

This Ciaran the Wright is not to be confounded with the other famous Ciaran, Ciaran of Saighir. Ciaran the Wright (the son of the Carpenter), with whom we have dealt, was of Ulster origin; Ciaran of Saighir was of Munster. He was born in Cork. It is he who, some contend, first introduced Christianity in the South of Ireland—before the coming of Patrick. Southern tradition is stubbornly strong on this point, but there are many pieces of circumstantial evidence that tend to prove him of the sixth century. Very great he was though, to judge from tradition—which after all, is one of the most certain proofs of true greatness. So great was he in the popular esteem that one legend has him as conceived of Heaven. A star fell into the mouth of his mother, Liadain, when sleeping: "thereof was born the wondrous birth, Ciaran of Saighir. And after his birth the angels of the Lord tended him, and the ranks of Heaven baptised him. And it is in Corcu

---

[11] Ciaran died of the great plague, the Buidhe Conaill, a kind of yellow jaundice which again and again ravaged Ireland (as well as the neighbouring countries in the sixth and seventh centuries). About the time of Ciaran's death it played havoc with the monastic communities. The schools were broken up, and the pupils sent home. In that visitation during which Ciaran died St. Ultan signalised himself by becoming father and mother to hundreds of children who were orphaned by the pestilence. Apropos of this is a truly quaint legend (recorded by Aongus) how that an invading fleet arrived at this time off the coast of Ireland. Diarmuid, who was then Ard-Righ, sent a messenger, with the alarming news, to Ultan, urging his intercession with God to avert this second calamity coming upon the suffering country. When the message was delivered to Ultan he was busy feeding his children. But he raised against the fleet his unoccupied left hand, whereupon a storm arose and completely wrecked the fleet. And when they would thank Ultan for this he reproached them, "Shame it was not to have left me till my right hand was free. For, against the raising of my right, no foreign foe could ever after invade Eirinn."

Luidaich first that in Ireland the cross was believed in—thirty years before the coming of Patrick."

He was a worker of miracles, was this great Ciaran. And in his love of the poor, the southern Ciaran rivalled his humbler namesake. The Feilire of Aongus tells us, "Many cattle had Ciaran of Saighir, for there were ten doors to the shed for his kine, ten stalls for each door, ten cows for each stall, ten calves for each cow. . . . So long as he was alive, Ciaran consumed not any kine, small or great, of their relish nor of their great produce; but distributed to the poor and needy of the Lord. Moreover, Ciaran had fifty horses for ploughing and tilling the earth, but it seems that of what they tilled he ate not a single cake so long as he was alive. The following was his dinner every night: a little bit of barley bread and spring water as a drink with it, and two roots of sea-fern as relish for it. Skins of fawns was the raiment he wore. A bolster of stone was at his head when he used to sleep."

This Ciaran was of the first order of Saints—a missionary, who did great work in bringing the people of Munster to Christ. And winning them for Christ, he won them also for himself. For his fame in Munster is imperishable.[12]

One of the thousand traditions, which display the Irish sympathy with the animal world and show so many of the saints in intimate intercourse with the dumb living things around them, says that when Ciaran lived in the woods, worshipping God, a furious wild boar came to keep him company. And after that came a fox, and then a wolf, and a badger, and a fawn. And this curious community lived together in loving harmony always. At least except for one little slip when the fox, getting inordinately hungry, stole the saint's sandals, and carried them off to make him a meal. But the badger, discovering the crime, indignantly followed, took the sandals from the thief, and returned them to their owner.[13]

---

[12] A legend, proving—if proof be needed—that the Lord would not suffer His beloved Munstermen to be put to shame before outlanders from less favored provinces, tells how on a fast-day, Brendan of Birr, and Ciaran of Cluain, once unexpectedly dropped in upon Ciaran of Saighair. Finding him with nothing eatable in the house, but a piece of meat, Ciaran, taking the meat, blessed it, and lo he had fish, honey and oil in plenty to put before these outlanders.

[13] Many of the saints were noted for their love of animals, and for the animals' love of them. A flock of wild ducks followed St. Coleman, wherever he went. Brendan, the Navigator, had a pet crow: Colm Cille, a pet crane. When Molua MacOchae died all the birds and all the animals in Erin mourned. One bird whom St. Maelanfaid questioned as to the cause of its sad lamenting, told him that St. Molua had never harmed bird or beast in all his life—"So, not more do human beings grieve for him than the other animals, and the little birds that thou seest."

Another famous southern saint of the early Church was the Kerryman, Brendan—known as the Voyager, or Brendan of Clonfert—to distinguish him from his contemporary Brendan of Birr. Throughout the Middle Ages Brendan was known and famed in all corners of Europe, through the romantic account, then translated into every written tongue, of the wonderful voyage, extending over seven years, which he is said to have gone upon—a voyage, in the course of which, say some, he landed upon the Continent that is now America.

Brendan was born in the last quarter of the fifth century, and lived nearly a hundred years. He studied his theology in one of the very early schools, St. Jarlath's famous school near Tuam. But before that he had been tutored by Bishop Eirc—the same who, tradition says, on the night of the birth of this Brendan, beheld the woods by the home where the child was born, wrapt in one vast flame, which reached up to the skies, and the like of which he never saw before; and a manifold service of angels, in bright white garments, all around the land. And during his childhood it is said, a hind from Sliabh Luachra used to come daily, with her fawn, to give milk for the heaven-favoured child.

It was this Brendan who, when going forth to his studies, was admonished by St. Ita[14] (his foster-mother), "Study not with women nor with virgins lest some should make mock of thee."

But Brendan hardly needed the admonition, for his strenuous objection to feminine company is famed through the incident that happened when his foster-father, Bishop Eirc, took the little lad Brendan, with him, when he went to visit the King and Queen of the territory. He left the lad in the chariot while he called upon the royal pair; and a pretty little yellow-haired princess entered the chariot to play with the boy, but was ignominiously ejected by him. Bishop Eirc penanced him severely for his conduct—condemning him to spend the night in the cave of Fenit. The penitent chanted psalms during the night which were heard for a thousand paces on every side. And, says the legend, about the cave troops of angels were seen up to heaven and down to earth, from night-falling to day dawn.

It was in the middle of the sixth century (556) that he began his school of Clonfert—on an island in Lough Dearg, in the River Shannon—which was to be one of the famous schools of Ireland, and which in

[14] St. Ita, born about 480, founded the first monastery in Munster, at the foot of Sliabh Luachra. She was a great miracle worker. Died 570.

future generations was to boast for Abbot, one of Ireland's famous scholars, St. Cummian Fada.[15]

His famous voyage, accounts of which, in many languages, are still to be found in a dozen old libraries of Europe, was undertaken for purpose of finding the Land of Peace which the Lord had promised to all who did His will. "For Brendan had read in the Gospel, 'Every one that hath forsaken father and mother, sister and land for My namesake, will receive an hundredfold in the present and shall possess everlasting life.' And then the love of the Lord grew exceeding in Brendan's heart, and he desired to leave his land, his country, his parents, his fatherland. And he urgently besought the Lord to give him a land, secret, hidden, secure, a delightful land, separated from men."

In answer to his persistent prayer, an angel of the Lord at length directed him: "Arise, O Brendan, for God hath given thee what thou soughtest, even the Land of Promise." Then he built his ship, and chose his company, and in the name of the Lord, set out upon the trackless ocean. It is noteworthy that the last man to join the boat's company, a buffoon and a notoriously sinful man, was the first to go to heaven.

And Brendan's voyage, if it gave him not the Land of Promise, still gave to the world a wonderful romance, which through a long count of centuries never lost its fascination for the millions of the people of Brendan's land—not to mention other millions in other lands.[16]

Of the ship's company of Romans who, as was said, landed in Cork when Senach was at Iniscara a number probably went to the school of Enda in Aran. In the ancient graveyard there, was discovered a head-stone, commemorating "VII Romani" for the fame of Enda and his school travelled far. It is said that when Colm Cille visited Aran, he saw there the grave of an abbot of Jerusalem, who had made pilgrimage to Enda.

---

[15] It was in his church of Clonfert that Brendan had his vision of the heavenly bird, which coming to him after Mass one morning, perched upon the altar, and so dazzled him with its sun-like radiance that he had to look away from it. Putting its bill behind its wing the bird sang for him. And, sweeter than any music ever heard in the world before, was the music that it made. He hearkened, entranced for twenty-four hours—which passed like a moment of time. And after that Brendan would not any more permit worldly music to be played in his presence; for he did not want to lose from his hearing the music of the people of Heaven.

[16] It was a time of wonderful voyages: Only a few years before Brendan's voyage is fixed the time of the penitential voyage of the sons of O'Corra, who had been foster-children of the devil, and consecrated to him, and had been his faithful servitors. Other two beautiful voyages of romance—of much earlier time—are the Voyage of Bran, and the Voyage of Maelduin.

Under this great Enda—who stood in the front rank of the saints of the second order—the Island home which he selected for his activities, his monastery and school, very properly earned the title of Aran na Naoim (Aran of the Saints). Tradition has it that in the graveyard, at the old church of Killeany there, lies the dust of an hundred and twenty-seven saints. Says the Feilire of Aengus: "It will never be known till the Day of Judgment the countless hosts of Saints whose relics mingle with the sacred soil of Aran na Naoim.[17]

Enda was from near Loch Erne. He was of princely family. He passed a thoughtless youth, gay and sportive in the extreme. He never took heed for the morrow, much less thought he of the world to come. His conversion came as sudden as Paul's. It was wrought through his sister, Fanchea, a girl notably devout. She had a beautiful girl friend, with whom Enda fell in love—and whom he asked to marry him. He asked her on a morning when he was going off with other gay companions to the chase—and insisted that she should have made up her mind to consent by the time of his return. Upon his return Fanchea took him to her room, to see the maiden. From a couch there she drew aside a white coverlet, disclosing to him the girl's corpse. The maiden, who was like Fanchea very pious, and who feared for Enda in the thoughtless life he led, had prayed to God for guidance, and God had called her to Himself. "She chose Christ for her spouse," Fanchea said.

Enda was stunned—and sobered. That instant was born in him a new man. He cast off his former companions, forsook his former ways, and gave himself to study and prayer. He appears to have studied under Manchan the Master, a noted Irish teacher then in charge of the school of Candida Casa in Galloway. He founded his own monastery, and opened his own school on the wild island of Aran, in Galway Bay, in the late fifth century. So, it was one of the earliest of the noted monasteries and schools.

Enda, here, came to have one hundred and fifty personal disciples. The traditional accounts bring to this school a great many of the leading saints of the second order, many of those who had also gone to the school of Finian at Clonard. Healy says that they went to Enda's school after Clonard—when it came time to prepare for the novitiate of their religious life. So great were the numbers that flocked to Aran, from all parts, that

[17] And in his Litany, after invoking the principal of Aran's Saints, Aongus adds: "And all the other saints here deceased whose numbers are so great as to be known to the living God only."

Enda divided the Island into ten sections, each with its own religious house and its own superior—all, of course, under him. The remains of four of the different groups of churches still show on the island.[18]

The great monastery and school of Bangor took, in later days, that leading place which Enda's establishment on Aran had for so long held. The Bangor institution was the work in the mid sixth century, of the great saint of the men of Ulad, St. Comgall—who himself had studied under St. Finian at Cluain-Enach, in the Midlands, and also at the school of Clonmacnois. His Bangor school sent out teachers and missionaries, saints and scholars, in great numbers to Ireland, and to the countries of the Continent. As the Continental St. Bernard says, in his Life of Malachi (a tenth century successor of Comgall): "There stood a most noble monastery, under the first father Comgelius, inhabited by many thousand monks, and the head of many monasteries. The place was truly sanctified, abounding in saints, abundantly fruitful to God; so that one of the sons of this holy congregation, Luanus or Evanus, was said to be the founder of an hundred monasteries. Its disciples not only filled Ireland and Scotia, but swarms poured like a torrent into foreign countries."

Comgall was upwards of forty years director of this hive of sanctity and learning, which arose on the shores of what we now call Belfast Loch, and where we are told three thousand students were at one time. He died about the year 600. Under May 10th, O'Clery in his Martyrology sets down the anniversary of Comgall abbot of Bennchor Ulad (Bangor of Ulster): "A man full of the grace of God and of His love was this man; a man who fostered and educated very many other saints, as he kindled and lighted up an unquenchable fire of the love of God in their hearts, and in their minds, as is evidenced in the old Books of Eirinn."

The Three Sorrows of the Saints of Ireland were—the sending of Colm into exile; the cutting short of the life of Ciaran; the driving out of Mochuda from Rathain.

Rathain was a monastery and school in the midlands, to which it will be remembered Ruman, the Virgil of the Gael, gave a third of the wealth he had, for his poem, extracted from the Galls of Dublin. It was founded by Mochuda—which name was a pet name for St. Carthach, a native of Kerry. As a lad herding swine in his native mountains, Carthach was turned to a

---

[18] Colm Cille is said to have visited Enda there. Some say that he studied under Enda for a while. Anyhow Enda and Aran were in high esteem with the great saint of Iona. To him is attributed the touching Farewell to Aran, written when, with regret, he was quitting its holy ground.

religious life by hearing the monks of a monastery near his home, chanting the psalms—and which so entranced him that he remained spellbound on the spot all night. Having come to Rathain on a pilgrimage, accompanied by a body of his Kerrymen, he fell in love with the place and there settled, and founded his monastery and school which flourished and became famous. There gathered around him a large body of disciples from his own Munster. And the holiness of the life they led was such that the angels are said to have come down and conversed with them. "It was Mochuda that had the famous congregation, consisting of seven hundred and ten persons at Rathain. And an angel used to address every third man of them."

So great was the holiness of Rathain that powerful clerics of the Ui Neill race, in whose territory it was, grew jealous of it; and in the reign of Donal (mac Aoda), they got that Ard-Righ's command sent to Mochuda that he and his people should leave Rathain and return to their own province. The pathetic answer which Mochuda returned to this order was: "Since I have served God for many years in this place, and that now my death is nigh, I desire to end my days here. I shall not depart out of this place unless I am compelled to, lest men should think me inconstant of purpose. And I would be ashamed to become a wanderer in my old age."

Since he would not go of his own free will, two princes of the royal line of the Ui Neill, Blathmac and Diarmuid, were sent, with a body of men, to expel him and his monks. Three times in three successive years the expedition against Mochuda set out, but each of the first two times there was a parley, and a year's respite was granted. The third time it was resolved that nothing should turn the drivers from their object. When they reached Rathain, Diarmuid was deputed to head a body of men into the church, and there arrest Mochuda and lead him forth. But, filled with veneration for this holy man, Diarmuid approached him with the utmost respect, expressed his sorrow for being there, and refused to act against him. Mochuda blessed him, prayed that the kingship of all Ireland might come to him—which it eventually did—and told him that for failing to act on his orders, he should be nick-named by his companions Diarmuid Ruadnaid, Diarmuid the Ruthful—"But that title shall yet become a glory to thee, and thy progeny after thee." And as Diarmuid the Ruthful he is known to Irish history ever since.

After scoffing at and reproaching Diarmuid, his brother Blathmac headed a body of men into the church, forced out Mochuda and his monks and drove them forth.

When the mournful band, after weary wandering, reached the country of the Deisii (now Waterford) the King of the Deisii, with his attendants, came to meet the holy Mochuda, received him with reverence and honour, knelt for his blessing, placed himself under the saint's protection and besought him to choose where he would in this territory to build his church and fix his community.

And the aged saint, strong in God's faith, and supported by God's strength, began his lifework anew at beautiful Lismore—on the banks of that river which is now called the Black Water. Here he erected a new monastery and school, with whose fame not Ireland alone but likewise far foreign lands were destined yet to ring. For it was to give famed teachers and holy evangelisers to distant countries wherein the name of Scotia was yet but seldom heard.

Tradition says it was in these days of the great saints—and by the action of some of the greatest—that ancient Tara of the Kings went down forever. It was Ruadan, one of the Twelve Apostles of Erin, who chiefly brought about that calamity. And it was Diarmuid, the son of Fergus (the friend of Ciaran the Wright) who, then reigning, provoked the calamity.

King Diarmuid was striving against the position of independence which the provincial and territorial kings assumed. He had issued an order commanding that all chiefs should widen their doors so that his spear, carried horizontally, could pass through. It is assumed that the chiefs had narrowed their doors for greater security against assault by the Ard-Righ's forces. Anyhow Diarmuid sent forth his sergeant to see if his order had been obeyed. When the sergeant reached the residence of Aed Guaire of Connaught, he interrupted Aed's wedding feast, in the process of carrying out the Ard-Righ's command—and Aed, drawing his sword, struck off the man's head. Then he sought sanctuary with St. Ruadan of Lorra. Diarmuid, who was almost as much enraged with the ecclesiastics, as he was with the chiefs, for their independence, violated the Saint's privilege of sanctuary, and took Aed Guaire from him for his punishment. St. Ruadan then journeyed to Tara, to curse Diarmuid, and it is said, was joined by many other leading saints of the time, who made common cause with him. The saints first fasted against Diarmuid, and Diarmuid answered them with his fast. Every day the fasting ones gathered on the green before Tara, sang their psalms, and rang their bells against the king—till at length Diarmuid was broken in his fast, and gave in. Then he came forth from his hall in the morning, and joined the saints in their praying and singing. After that he reasoned with them, showed them unwisdom of their course, and at length, carried away by his indignation, cursed Ruadan. Ruadan in return cursed Diarmuid, and Diarmuid's dynasty that it might come to an end—which it did; and he cursed Tara that it might never more be the residence of a king.

So tradition has it that after the year 563, through the cursing of Ruadan, the wild birds roosted in the hall of Tara and the beasts of the field trampled on its hearth and made it their home.[19]

Stokes, Whitley: Lives of the Saints from the Book of Lismore.
O'Hanlon, The Rev. Jno., Canon: Lives of the Irish Saints.
Reeves, The Rev. Wm., D.D.: The Martyrology of Donegal.
Healy, The Most Rev. Jno.: Ireland's Ancient Schools and Scholars.
MacGeoghegan, Abbe: History of Ireland.
Keating's History of Ireland.
Montalembert: Monks of the West.
Colgan: Acta Sanctorum.
Usher's Works.
O'Curry, Eugene: Manuscript Materials of Irish History.
—— Manners and Customs of the Ancient Irish.
Ware's Works (Edited by Harris).
Four Masters, Annals of.
Stokes, Whitley: The Feilire (Calendar) of Oengus the Culdee: Trans. Roy. Ir. Acad., 1880.
D'Alton, Jno.: Prize Essay on Irish History (Proc. R. I. A.).
Stokes, Rev. Dr. Geo. T.: Ireland and the Celtic Church.

---

[19] Some (like MacNeill) hold that the Kings of Meath still made Tara their home for some centuries after that date—and also that Ruadan never cursed it.

CHAPTER XXVII

Learning in Ancient Ireland

When long ago the English poet Spenser, in his "State of Ireland" set down: "For it is certain that Ireland hath had the use of letters very auntiently and long before England; that they had letters auntiently is nothing doubtful, for the Saxons of England are said to have their letters and learning, and learned men, from the Irish"—he was possibly not aware that even for centuries before the English began to value learning, and in shiploads flocked to Ireland to obtain it, Ireland's valleys were dotted with schools, and her hillsides hummed with studying scholars. Babington in his Fallacies of Race Theories says that in the sixth century, "the old culture lands had to turn for some little light and leading to that remote and lately barbarous land" (Ireland).

Says the mediævalist, Arséne Darmesteter: "The classic tradition, to all appearance dead in Europe, burst into full flower in the Island of Saints. The renaissance began in Ireland seven hundred years before it was known in Italy. And Armagh, the ecclesiastical capital of Ireland, was at one time the metropolis of civilisation."

And our own Doheny puts it as gracefully as truthfully (in his Memoir of Keating): "The early literary history of Ireland stands out distinct from that of any other country of Europe. While the revel of the Goth profaned the Roman forum and he stabled his steeds in the Coliseum, the pilgrims of learning from every darkened land found shelter, sustainment, and inexhaustible sources of information, in Ireland."

The late Professor Zimmer, most eminent of Celtologists, states in his remarkable little work, The Irish Element in Mediæval Culture:

> "Ireland can indeed lay claim to a great past; she can not only boast of having been the birthplace and abode of high culture in the

fifth and sixth centuries, at a time when the Roman Empire was being undermined by the alliances and inroads of German tribes, which threatened to sink the whole Continent into barbarism, but also of having made strenuous efforts in the seventh and up to the tenth century to spread her learning among the German and Romance peoples, thus forming the actual fountain of our present continental civilisation."

It is interesting to speculate upon the certain antiquity and activity of that learning as far away as the sixth century, when it would give fruitful soil for the planting of such abiding tradition as that of the fall of the book-satchels[1] at the death of Longarad, "master of study and jurisprudence, history and poetry."

"This is said," says Aongus in the Feilire, "that on the night of Longarad's death Ireland's book satchels and her Gospels, and books of instruction fell from their shelves, as if they understood that never again would there come any one like Longarad.

"Lon is dead (Lon is dead);
To Cill Garad it is a great misfortune;
To Eirinn with its countless tribes;
It is a destruction of learning and of schools.

"Lon has died (Lon has died);
In Cill Garad great the misfortune;
It is a destruction of learning and of schools,
To the Island of Eirinn beyond her boundaries."

One tradition even has the book satchels of Iona falling on this grievous night. They fell in the cell of Colm Cille, who, with the vision of the saint, exclaimed, "Longarad, master of every art in Ossory, is dead." "Long may it be till that comes true," exclaimed the shocked Baithin. To which the impetuous Colm answered: "Misbelief be in thy successor."

Most of the Irish scholars and Continental students of Celtic lore, like Zimmer, agree that when Patrick came, in the early part of the fifth century, he found there such a plenitude of learning and learned men as necessitated a background of previous centuries of educational progress.

[1] The polaires or leathern cases in which the volumes of those days were kept—hung upon the walls.

When the reputation has descended to us of at least two most notable pre-Patrician Irish scholars on the Continent, it is a practical conclusion that there were dozens of others abroad also, whose memories have been submerged in the sweep of the ages. And, interchange of the cream of foreign learning with native Irish learning on Irish soil must have occurred with frequency, in the ages immediately succeeding Patrick, if we accept the learned Petrie's conclusion (in his Inquiry into the Origin and Uses of the Round Towers of Ireland) that "Crowds of foreign ecclesiastics, Egyptian, Roman, Italian, British and Saxon, flocked to Ireland, as a place of refuge, in the fifth and sixth centuries. Of such emigration there can not possibly exist a doubt."

And then there was the exchange of Irish with Continental learning which occurred as a result of the many and great pilgrimages that in Ireland's earliest Christian days were constantly being made to Rome and to the Holy Land by crowds of Erin's faithful. These pilgrimages sometimes extended over years,[2] the pilgrim frequently making wide detours for purpose of visiting temples of the famous living, and shrines of the hallowed dead—and often sojourning for months and seasons in the neighbourhood of a famous preacher and teacher, or at institutional centres of piety and learning.

Besides the dozens of incidental references to such with which the ancient records teem, Petrie cites the testimony in the famous Litany of Aongus Ceile Dé: "The three times fifty canoes full of Roman pilgrims who settled in Ui Mele, along with Notal Nemshenchaid and Cornutan, *invoco in auxilium meum per Jesum Christum,* etc. The other thrice fifty pilgrims of the men of Rome and Latium who went into Scotia, *invoco in auxilium meum per Jesum Christum.* The thrice fifty Gaedhils of Eirinn, in holy orders, each of them a man of strict rule, who went in one body into pilgrimage, under Abban, the son of Ua Cormaic, *invoco in auxilium meum per Jesum Christum,"* etc.

Within two centuries after Patrick, George Stokes (Knowledge of Greek in Ireland) shows that in the very centre of the bog of Allen, in Durrow, there was "a wide range of deep learning, chronological, astronomical, and philosophical." And Joyce says that the earliest of the seventh or eighth century glosses, published by Zeuss, testify to the fact that "the written language of the Irish was then fully developed and cultivated,

[2] An embassy sent from the Irish ecclesiastics to Rome, in 631, was three year absent—and such embassy, naturally, did not journey with the same leisure as did pilgrims.

with a polished phraseology and an elaborate system of grammar, and having fixed and well established written forms for all its words, and for all the rich inflections."

It was Zimmer's opinion that at least the classical learning for which Ireland in those very early centuries became noted, Latin and Greek, were brought there by the many learned people from Gaul who fled to Ireland, the haven of refuge from the overwhelming tide of barbarism, which was sweeping Europe in the fifth century. But the fact that these learned ones should flock to Ireland is in itself partial proof that the fame of Ireland then as a home of learning must have been fairly well established. The brilliance of her beacon must have beckoned these affrighted ones, and the repute of her schools and scholars been ringing in their ears. Whether or not it was those very early scholar refugees, in those early ages, who brought some knowledge of Greek into Ireland, in addition to Latin, M. Darmesteter expresses his astonishment at finding, a couple of centuries later, Greek taught in Ireland when it had become forgotten elsewhere, and when even such a noted scholar as Pope Gregory the Great was ignorant of it. But Zimmer acknowledges that in Ireland, "the standard of learning was much higher than with Gregory and his followers. It was derived without interruption from the learning of the fourth century, from men such as Ambrose and Jerome. Here also were to be found such specimens of classical literature as Virgil's works among the ecclesiastical writings, an acquaintance with Greek authors as well, besides the opportunity of free access to the very first sources of Christianity." "The knowledge of Greek," says Professor Sandys in his History of Classical Scholarship, "which had almost vanished in the west was so widely dispersed in the schools of Ireland that if any one knew Greek it was assumed he must have come from that country."

And the eminent Celtologist, De Jubainville, talking of the Irishman, Columbanus, who, in the sixth century, was evangelising and teaching in Burgundy and Lombardy, says: "We only need to glance at his writings to be at once convinced of his wonderful superiority over Gregory and the Gallo-Roman scholars of his time."

As early as the fifth century, scholars from Wales, Cornwall, Brittany were coming to Ireland for schooling; or were, at home, receiving tuition from the Irish schoolmaster who had even then begun to travel as an educational missionary. Lannigan (in his Ecclesiastical History of Ireland) tells us that the Welsh historian, Gildas, came to Ireland, probably in the middle or end of the fifth century, "to perfect himself in philosophy and theology." He attended several schools there, and finally, according to his countryman, Caradoc, became a teacher at the school of Armagh. He returned to Wales when he heard of his brother being killed by King Arthur. Gildas' Welsh contemporary, St. Caradoc (who was Irish on his mother's side), attended as a boy the celebrated school of Caer, in Monmouth, taught by the Irishman, St. Tathæus. Petrocus from Cornwall was studying the Scriptures in Ireland for twenty years. The Breton St. Paternus was some time in Ireland; and his father Petranus retired to lead a holy life in Ireland—in the beginning of the sixth century.

Then we have the testimony of the Venerable Bede, the Saxon ecclesiastical historian, who, writing in the very shadow of the time of which he spoke, and describing the great plague of 664, says: "This pestilence did no less harm in the neighbouring Island of Ireland. Many of the nobility, and of the lower ranks of the English nation were there at that time, who in the days of Bishops Finan and Colman, forsaking their native land, retired thither, either for the sake of divine studies, or of a more continent life; and some of them presently devoted themselves to the monastical life; others chose rather to apply themselves to study, going about from one master's cell to another. The Scots (Irish) willingly received them all, and took care to supply them with food, as also to furnish them with books to read, and their teaching, gratis."

Patrick and his followers founded Christian schools to supersede those of the Druids. Patrick's school of Armagh became one of Ireland's greatest—attended at a later time by (says Keating) as many as seven thousand students. This school was a favourite resort of the Saxons, who had in the city their own quarter, called *Trian Saxon.* Ibar of Beg-Eire and Ailbe of Emly, Patrick's contemporaries, and his convert Mochae the swineherd of Oendrum, St. Fiach of Sletty, Olcan of Dercan, St. Mochta of Louth amongst others, had each his school in Patrick's day.

Together with crowds of lesser ones, then followed the noted schools of Colman at Dromore, Enda at Aran, Jarlath near Tuam, Finian at Moville, the greater Finian at Clonard, Comgall at Bangor, Ciaran at Clonmacnois, of Kevin at Glendalough, of Senan at Inniscathy, of Brendan at Clonfert, of Mobi at Glasneven, of Finbar at Cork, of Fachtna at Ross, of Finan at Innisfallen, of Colm at Iniscaltra, of Carthach at Lismore—and numberless others—at Roscrea, Slane, Cashel, Inisbofin, Kildare, Limerick, Fore, etc., all of such importance that their fame has come down to the present day. And again and again the records and traditions intimate that several of these schools had thousands of scholars in attendance. We are told that there were two thousand students at Kevin's school at Glendalough, three thousand at Finian's school at Clonard; three thousand at the school of

Comgall at Bangor—and that Clonmacnois at the height of its fame was attended by between six thousand and seven thousand students.

So famous and great did the school of Clonmacnois become that many of the leading families of Ireland had there each its own cathedral, or church, mortuary chapel, round tower, or burial place. And there the dust of students representing every clan in Ireland, and many a people oversea, mingle underneath the green sod of the old cemetery.

There is a fine poem by an Irish bard, O'Gillan, finely translated by Rolleston, on:

THE DEAD AT CLONMACNOIS

In a quiet watered land, a land of roses,
Stands Saint Kieran's city fair:
And the warriors of Erin in their famous generations
Slumber there.

There beneath the dewy hillside sleep the noblest
Of the clan of Conn,
Each below his stone with name in branching Ogham
And the sacred knot thereon.

There they laid to rest the seven Kings of Tara,
There the sons of Cairbre sleep—
Battle-banners of the Gael, that in Kieran's plain of crosses,
Now their final hosting keep.

And in Clonmacnois they laid the men of Teffia,
And right many a lord of Breagh;
Deep the sod above Clan Credé and Clan Conaill,
Kind in hall and fierce in fray.

Many and many a son of Conn, the Hundred-Fighter,
In the red earth lies at rest;
Many a blue eye of Clan Colman the turf covers,
Many a swan-white breast.

Ireland had now truly become, as described by one of the ancients, "a hive of learning": the hum of the scholars in this land of lore was as the hum of the bees on the flowery hillsides in June. There was no corner of the Island, convenient or remote, and even off to the scattered islets of the ocean, but had its centre of learning, to which came alike youth and age, noble and simple—and to which thronged not Irish only, but flocks of foreigners also—from Britain and from the Continent of Europe, all thirsting to drink at the fountains that so lavishly gushed, and the streams that so plentifully flowed, in the Island of the West.

One of the early writers records that when, in neighbouring countries, a man of studious habits, was for a time missed from his usual haunts, it was concluded that he had gone to Ireland to seek education. All of the great schools had their groups of foreign students, who for the most part, were not only educated gratis but lived on the hospitality of the people. We may of course assume that this refers to the bulk of foreign students who, not lavishly endowed with wealth, sought learning for learning's sake. We may conclude that such of the foreign nobility as came to Ireland seeking learning just as an added grace and accomplishment, paid their way—like Dagobert the Second of France, who in 656 was brought (by the Bishop of Poitiers) to be educated at Clonard. And indeed the Brehon law, which, touching upon almost every condition and circumstance of life in Ireland, lays down the rule for teachers and pupils incidentally confirms this—as already shown in the Brehon Law chapter.

Almost all of the greatest, most notable schools of the olden days in Erin grew up incidentally, around the residence of a great teacher. Wherever such a noted man settled thither came students, who seemed to have been continually wandering over the land, seeking masters. First came a few who erected their little huts or bothies close to the hut or the residence of him, the scholar, from whom they expected to absorb knowledge. Soon came a few more, and still others followed. If the master's qualities, his knowledge, his ability, his aptness in imparting instruction, held those who first came, that fact was quickly known throughout the land, and quickly crowds were flocking there. Sometimes the instruction was given in the open; sometimes under cover. Largely the youths read for themselves—under direction of the master, who laid down the general scheme for them, and to whom they resorted for enlightenment when they met with a problem impossible of solution by themselves or their more advanced fellows. Oftentimes students accompanied a teacher upon a journey, harkening to his words, observing his actions, an absorbing knowledge from him as they went.

A pupil who was instructed gratis, was entitled to work for his tutor. Likewise it was the law that to his tutor should go the first fee earned by such student, when he had graduated into a profession.

In the eyes of the law, any one who insulted or assaulted a student was guilty of insult or assault to the teacher. It was to the teacher that the fine was paid for such misdemeanour.

Naturally a powerful bond of affection sprang up between master and pupil—a bond that throughout life was never broken. When old age incapacitated him, the master, if he did not belong to a community, which naturally would care for him, was looked after and provided for by his former pupils. Not only was this a matter of love, but it was a matter of law, also. In the Brehon laws it is laid down that pupils are responsible for the comfort and well-being of their master, in his need and in his age. In the ancient Contest of the Two Sages (Acallam na da Suach) Neide, in enumerating the dire woes that will come over Erin as the end of the world nears, says that pupils will neglect to provide for their tutors in their old age.[3]

Of course it is to be understood that in Ireland any more than in other learned countries of the early ages, the mass of the people was not educated. All who desired it could get an education, and naturally the students came chiefly from the leisured class and the professional class. Among the body of the people, it was only the exceptionally bright and ambitious, who, shaking them free from the fetters of tradition, bade good-bye both physically and intellectually to their kith, and set out as a *Scolaire bocht* (poor scholar) to seek education. Yet then, as now, some of the most noted scholars sprang from the soil.

The learned scholar and noted abbot, St. Adamnan (of Tir-Conaill and Iona) is an interesting illustration of this. From an ancient manuscript account of the reign of Finachta the Festive who was Ard-Righ in the last quarter of the seventh century, O'Curry tells the story of the origin of the famous friendship which existed between the Ard-Righ and the saint. When Adamnan was a poor scholar at Ciaran's school of Clonard, he was one day carrying home on his back, a jar of milk, when a cavalcade, coming up behind, made him jump to one side, strike his toe, fall and smash the jar. Weeping and grieving, and with a bit of the broken jar still hanging over his shoulder he ran alongside the cavalcade, till a great man who was the centre of the group saw and pitied the grieving lad, and stopped the cavalcade to question and console him. Tenderly he spoke to the grieving youth. "We will make thee happy again, for we have sympathy with the unfortunate and the powerless. Thou shalt receive, O student, satisfaction from me." "Oh, good

---

[3] "Instruction without reservation, correctness without harshness, are due from the master to the pupil, and to feed and clothe him during the time he is learning," says the Brehon laws. "To help him against poverty and to support him in old age; these are due from the pupil to the tutor."

man," said Adamnan, "I have cause to be grieved, for there are three noble students in one house, and there are three lads of us who wait upon them, and what we do is, each one in turn goes around the neighbourhood to collect support for the other five, and it is my turn to do so this day; but what I had obtained has been lost, and what is more unfortunate the borrowed vessel has been broken, while I have not the means of paying for it." The simple youth won the heart of the great man, who turned out to be the Ard-Righ, Finachta, who became his friend and patron from that day forward.

While most of the noted schools whose fame has come down to us from those early ages, were ecclesiastical, there certainly were, side by side with them in Ireland, a host of lay schools also, which had been founded and painstakingly built up by great lay scholars. And sometimes lay scholars were employed as teachers in the ecclesiastical schools. The famous Colcu MacUa Dunechda, to whom the Emperor Charlemagne sent presents was a lay fer-leginn or chief professor in the school of Clonmacnois. And in later centuries MacCosse was the chief teacher in the monastic school of Ros Ailithir, in Cork; and the celebrated annalist Flan, chief professor in the school of Monasterboice.

For one who desired to graduate in the highest rank of his profession, twelve years was the course of study—during which the diligent student, if he were successful, passed, step by step through the Seven Degrees of Wisdom—the details and particulars of which, and the course of study for them, are contained in the tract known as the Book of the Ollams preserved in the old Book of Ballymote and in the Books of the Brehon Laws.[4]

The Book of Ballymote tract gives the requirements, year by year, for the twelve years of the scholar's course—from a course of the elementaries up to the mastery of the six-score great orations, and the four arts of poetry—"from the study of the smallest book called The Ten Words, up to the mastery of the greatest book, The Cuilmen." Also the requirements are set down for each of the Seven Degrees of Wisdom, from the first degree called *Fochluc* through the others, *MacFuirmid, Dos, Canna, Cli* and *Anruth* to the final degree of *Ollam*—or in a monastic school, *Rosai* or Great Professor.

O'Curry enumerates and particularises six grades of professors in the ecclesiastical school, with the acquirements of each—from the lowest grade, the Caogdach, up to the highest, the Drumcli (ridgepole), a master who knew the whole course of learning. When the latter ambitioned being

[4] A sequel to the Crith Gablach, in Volume IV of the Brehon Laws, and a law tract called the Small Primer, in Volume V, interestingly deal with these details.

fer-leginn, or chief professor in a college, he "had to be master of the whole course of Gælic literature, in prose and verse, besides the Scriptures and likewise the learned languages."

In the bardic or lay schools a prominent place on the program of studies is given to the tales and the poems of the seanachies and poets, of that day and of the previous ages. Each year was added to the course the memorising and the minute study and expounding of a certain number of historic and romantic tales and epic poems. In the monastic schools, the Scriptures, theology and the Classics very largely took the place of the study of the tales and poems. The other usual subjects of study in both schools were, grammar, geography, history, hagiography, law, mathematics, astronomy, philosophy, logic, rhetoric, music, art and metal work.

The common languages of the schools were Irish and Latin. Archbishop Usher, who says that he himself saw in St. Caimin's (seventh century) Psalter positive proof of Hebrew knowledge, was under the belief that Hebrew was taught in the schools. George Stokes (supported by some other scholars) holds that Greek was well known to the Irish teachers. And such noted Irish scholars as Cummian the Tall, Aileran the Wise, Columbanus, and others, again and again show familiarity with the writings of the Greeks. Greek prayers, Greek glosses and Greek quotations are found in connection with various ancient Irish manuscripts, both at home and in the old libraries on the Continent of Europe.

But with the Latin language all the Irish scholars of those early days show almost a like familiarity that they do with their own Gaelic. They were experts in Latin literature. The Latin classics, sacred and profane, they had at their finger-tips. They wrote in that language with a masterful ease and read in it voraciously.

A single illustration, out of numberless ones available, is the famous letter of St. Cummian (seventh century) written to Segenius, abbot of Iona, in the Easter date controversy that then nearly rent the church.[5] In this letter

---

[5] Cummian, who is combating the Irish Easter, shows that an Irish embassy at Rome in 631, found the Romans celebrating on March 24th the Easter which would not be celebrated in Ireland until April 21st. The Irish continued celebrating the old Roman Easter long after the Romans, by direction of Pope Hilary, had adopted the present (Alexandrian) method of fixing the date of the festival. This was the cause of the great paschal controversy, which, both in Irish communities on the Continent of Europe (as Columbanus' community) and at home in Ireland, and with the Irish in Alba, was waged for a century. It was only in 716 that Iona, the last citadel of the Roman method, capitulated. It may be mentioned that within two years after this capitulation, the Irish tonsure likewise, which required the shaving of the whole front of the head, from ear to ear—yielded to the Continental tonsure, the shaving of the crown of the head.

(preserved for us in Usher's *Sylloge Epistolarum Hibernicarum*) there is displayed a wealth of classic learning, and an intimate familiarity with things Latin, Grecian, Egyptian, Hebrew, that justly amazes the scholars of today—"a marvellous compilation," says Professor Stokes, "because of the vastness of its learning." Beginning with the institution of the Paschal Feast in Exodus (as Stokes points out) Cummian quotes commentators as Jerome and Origen, and many Fathers of the Church; discusses the calendars of the Macedonians, Egyptians and Hebrews; quotes the opinions of Augustine, Cyprian, Pachomius (founder of Egyptian monasticism), Gregory the Great, etc.; refers to the views of the Irish saints; and balances the decrees of the Councils of Nice and Arles. He gives the Hebrew, Greek and Egyptian names of the first lunar month and (says Healy) "refers to almost every cycle and emendation of a cycle that we know of—the Paschal cycle, and those of Anatolius, Theophilius, Dionysius, Cyril, Morinus, Augustine, Victorius, etc."

D'Arbois de Jubainville in the introduction to his Study of Celtic Literature, speaking on the subject of Irish classical knowledge, says of the early Irish missionaries and scholars in Europe:

> "What surprises us most about these Irish emigrants was that they knew Greek, and were probably the only people in Western Europe, then, who knew it. They have Græco-Latin glossaries, grammars, the books of the Bible in Greek. . . . It was considered good taste among the Irish then, to mingle Greek words throughout the Latin text which they composed."

In the library of Laon, France, there is a manuscript written by an Irish scribe in the last half of the ninth century, containing two glossaries of the Greek and Latin languages, some passages in Irish, and a Greek grammar.

Dr. Healy, arguing from the evidence of the Lord's Prayer in Greek, found upon an Irish manuscript (which he says was probably written in Iona), expresses himself as convinced that Greek was taught by the Irish monks in Iona, twelve hundred years ago. The Colophon, in which the scribe in those days often asked the readers' prayers, reads: "Pray to the Lord for me, Dorbenum." And Dorbene was an abbot of Iona, second in succession after Adamnan, who died in 713.

The astronomy was taught in Ireland in the early centuries of Christianity is evident from many of the old writings. And when we reach the eighth and ninth centuries, we find Ireland producing eminent astronomical thinkers, such as Fergal of Aghaboe, and Dungall of Bangor, of whose accomplishments we shall talk in the next chapter. In the commentary on the Senchus Mor is set down a good general description of the universe. From the Saltair na Rann, a collection of poems made about the year 1000, but many of which were then hundreds of years old, Joyce extracts a short description of the universe which gives us a good rough idea of the state of astronomical knowledge then:

> "The earth is stated to be like an apple, goodly, truly round. The names of the seven planets are given ('Saturn, Joib, Mercuir, Mars, Sol, Uenir, Luna'); the distances are given of the moon, and the sun, and the firmament, from the earth: the firmament is round the earth as the shell is round the egg: the signs of the zodiac with their names in order, and the correct month and day when the sun enters each: the sun is 30 days 10½ hours in each sign: the five zones—north and south frigid, and two temperate, with the torrid zone between."

Medicine was taught by physicians, in their own homes, from very early times, and physicians were, as we know from the ancient legends, in great esteem from far beyond the dawn of history. And in this, as in every other phase of Irish life, the old Brehons dealt with the physicians' privileges and obligations. With nice wisdom, they specified cases in which a fee was due from the physician to the patient—as when, either through want of skill, or neglect, he failed to cure a wound—in which case the doctor paid to the patient the same fine as would a man who inflicted the wound.[6]

Ancient traditions indicate that the Cæsarian operation, and also trepanning, were performed by Irish surgeons in olden times.

While ancient stories, poems, and traditions bristle with references to medical men, the Annals, beginning with a record, under date A.D. 860, of

---

[6] A particularly wise provision of the laws affecting the sick, was that the patient must be shielded "from dogs, fools, and female scolds"—an injunction from which many a poor sufferer might be made to profit even today.

He who unjustly wounded another had to pay sick maintenance for that other until he was cured: and he was responsible for the wounded one's being cared for, according to the provisions of the law.

The ancient poems and stories show that the common bath was a matter of daily routine, in the lives of many of the old Irish. The so-called Turkish Bath was at the same time commonly used for the ailing. It is only in comparatively recent times that, in some parts of Ireland, the ancient Sweating Houses, which were once quite common, went out of use. Some of these old Sweating Houses are still to be seen, in various parts of the country. And Joyce points out that at Prague, and in Nuremberg and other parts of the Germanic countries, this kind of bath was denominated Romische-Irische Bader.

the death of O'Tinnri, "the best physician in Ireland," give place to many prominent physicians,[7] henceforward.

Musical tuition received great attention in ancient Ireland. Even as late as the ninth century, we find the Irishman Marcellus, after he had consented to remain at the old Irish foundation of St. Gall, making that school illustrious for its musical teaching, and for the world famous musicians which it turned out. Of the Irish music more will be said in a subsequent chapter.

The big place that learning occupied in those days in the country's life and in the people's esteem, is evidenced not merely by the lavish wealth of traditions of the schools, which have survived both the lapse of ages and the ruthless rule of the destroying conqueror,[8] but also by the frequent

---

[7] As in the case of the other professions, that of medicine usually descended in the same families. Joyce mentions how that the O'Callanans were physicians to the McCarthys of Desmond; the O'Cassidys to the MacGuires of Fermanagh; the O'Lees to the O'Flahertys of Connaught; the O'Hickeys to the O'Briens of Thomond, to the O'Kennedys of Ormond, and to the MacNamaras of Clare. The O'Shiels were the physicians of the MacMahons of Oriel, and of the MacCoghlans of Delvin. Five hundred acres of land was the usual allowance to the physician of the chief,—and perquisites besides. He says "the surviving collection of old Irish medical manuscripts preserved in the libraries of London, Dublin, and Oxford, present probably the largest such collection in existence, in any one tongue."

An estimate of Irish physicians in comparatively modern days, is quoted by Joyce, from the Confessio Authoris of Van Helmont of Brussels, who wrote nearly three hundred years ago: "The Irish nobility have in every family a domestic physician, who has a tract of land free for his remuneration, and who is appointed, not on account of the amount of learning he brings away in his head from colleges, but because he can cure disorders. These doctors obtain their medical knowledge chiefly from books belonging to particular families left them by their ancestors, in which are laid down the symptoms of the several diseases, with the remedies annexed: which remedies are vernacula—the production of their own country. Accordingly the Irish are better managed in sickness than the Italians, who have a physician in every village."

And the following piece, quoted by Joyce, from the preface of an Irish medical manuscript of 1352, beautifully illustrates the singularly lofty spirit which actuated Irish physicians in all the ages: "May the merciful God have mercy on us all. I have here collected practical rules from several works, for the honour of God, for the benefit of the Irish people, for the instruction of my pupils, and for the love of my friends and of my kindred. I have translated them from Latin into Gaelic from the authority of Galen in the last Book of his Practical Pantheon, and from the Book of the Prognostics of Hippocrates. These are things gentle, sweet, profitable, and of little evil, things which have been often tested by us and by our own instructors. I pray God to bless those doctors who will use this book; and I lay it on their souls as an injunction, that they extract not sparingly from it; that they fail not on account of neglecting the practical rules (herein contained); and more especially that they do their duty devotedly in cases where they receive no pay (on account of the poverty of the patients). Moreover let him not be in mortal sin, and let him implore the patient to be also free from grievous sin. Let him offer up a secret prayer for the sick person, and implore the Heavenly Father, the physician and balmgiver for all mankind, to prosper the work he is entering upon and to save him from the shame and discredit of failure."

[8] That learned antiquary, the Rt. Rev. Dr. Reeves (Protestant Bishop of Down), says: "We must deplore the merciless rule of barbarism in this country, whence was swept away all domestic

references of the annalists to the death of men of learning—even to the scribes, who, for their skill in perpetuating the monuments of wisdom, commanded huge respect. In the sixth and seventh centuries the annalists begin to praise as scribes certain men whose passing they record. As, under date 587, we are told of the death of Dagæus of Inniscaltra: "Scriptor librorum peritissimus." And under date 655 the passing of Ultan: "Scriptor et pictor." They begin then, also, to refer to the scholars and the schools.

And when we come down to the days of the ravaging Dane, the books, because of their frequent destruction, begin to get notice from the annalist. During the Danish period the annals record nine different burnings of the great library of Armagh School, the Teach-Screptra (House of Writings). One such characteristic record of burning—though this time evidently by accidental fire—is the following, from the Four Masters:

> "Ard-Macha was burned without saving of any house in it, except the House of Writings only. And many houses burned in the Trians, and the great church burned, and the belfry with its bell. The other stone churches were also burned; and the old preaching chair, and chariot of the abbott; and their books in the houses of the students; with much gold, silver, and other precious things."

The fame of many of the Irish scholars of those early centuries still survives—and, of some of them who have become world figures, always will survive. Bangor gave the world the great Columbanus, scholar extraordinary, preacher, teacher, evangeliser—Columbanus, courted of good (Continental) kings, and fearless denouncer of bad—and remonstrant, too, with one of the greatest of Popes—the learned Columbanus, for whom, on his approaching the Eternal City "all the bells of Rome rang out." He, as we know from his biographer and friend Jonas, carried with him from Bangor, in addition to his great Scriptural and classical learning, a remarkable knowledge of grammar, rhetoric, geometry, divinity, and we may add poetry.

Of this famous sixth century scholar we shall later speak at further length—as also we shall do of another alumnus of Bangor who won Continental fame, the astronomer Dungall, whose intellectual ability won

evidences of advanced learning, leaving scarcely anything at home but legendary lore, and which has compelled us to draw from foreign depositories the materials on which to rest the proof that Ireland of old was really entitled to that literary eminence which the national feeling lays claim to."

him the favour and esteem of the Emperor Charlemagne; and who was by that King's grandson, Lothaire, appointed in charge of the educational system in the city of Pavia. And from the study-halls of holy Bangor, too, emerged in later centuries, another world figure, Marianus Scotus, who, when he had established himself in Germany wrote his Chronicle of the World. Bangor, of which the Saxon Jocelyn said, "It is a fruitful vine, breathing the odour of salvation, whose offshoots extend not only into the ends of Erin, but far over seas into many foreign lands, filling them with abounding fruitfulness." Bangor, the beautiful, whose praise is well sung in the ancient Latin hymn, the Antiphonary of Bangor—property, most probably of Columbanus or Dungall, and discovered in Columbanus' monastery of Bobbio in Italy:

"O BENCHUIR BONA REGULA

> "Holy is the rule of Bangor: it is noble, just and admirable. Blessed is its community, founded on unerring faith, graced with the hope of salvation, perfect in charity—a ship that is never submerged tho' beaten by the waves. A house full of delights, founded upon a rock. Truly an enduring city, strong and fortified. The ark shaded by the cherubim, on all sides, overlaid with gold. A princess mete for Christ, clad in the sun's light. A truly royal hall adorned with various gems."

Noted scholar of those very early days was Aileran the Wise, head of the school of Clonard, and who, along with other works, left to us the scholarly production, "The Mystical Interpretation of the Ancestry of Our Divine Lord." The Benedictine editors who republished it a couple of centuries ago (after finding the manuscript in the old Swiss-Irish monastery of St. Gall) say, "He unfolded the Sacred Scripture with so much learning and ingenuity that every student of the sacred volume, and especially preachers of the Divine Word, should find it most acceptable." To the scholarliness of this work and its author, Dr. Healy bears this remarkable testimony: "Whether we consider the style of the Latinity, the learning or the ingenuity of the writer, this work is marvellous. He cites not only Jerome and Augustine, but what is more wonderful still quotes Origen repeatedly, as well as Philo, the Alexandrian Jew. It shows, too, that a century after the death of the holy founder, Scripture study of the most profound character was still cultivated in the great school of Clonard."

It seems to have been at the time that learned Aileran ruled the school of Clonard that Adamnan of Tir-Conaill, destined to be famed for his literary work, studied there—and as we have already seen, in the capacity of a poor scholar. Besides his Life of St. Colm Cille, which, from foreign scholars as well as Irish, has received a chorus of praise, as one of the best and most remarkable of ancient biographies, Adamnan left us also a book on the Holy Land, De Locis Sanctis.

But probably a more remarkable man than any of the foregoing was the brilliant genius Ceannfaelad. "Undoubtedly one of the most eminent men of his age," O'Curry with good warrant says of him. He had been a warrior in his early days, and only turned scholar when, by a serious wound in the head, got in the battle of Magh Rath (Down) in 634, he was incapacitated for fighting. He was borne unconscious from the battlefield to Armagh, where he seems to have undergone a surgical operation—trepanning, some conclude—which not only restored his mentality but, it is concluded, made that mentality infinitely more vigorous than ever it had been. "His brain of forgetfulness," says the old writer, "was removed."

To convalesce he came to Tuaim Bricin in Cavan—where there were three schools—of Classics, Law and Poetry. The tradition tells that while he was convalescing he interested himself and occupied his mind by frequently sitting in the schools and listening to the lectures and lessons. The memory of this man was so phenomenal that everything he heard he retained. And from this strange beginning and discovery of his ability, Ceannfaelad went onward till he came to be regarded as illustrious amongst the bright scholars of Ireland; esteemed a master by his contemporaries and reverenced as a master by the scholars of Ireland down till today. There are preserved three works which are attributed to Ceannfaelad, a very ancient grammar of the Gaelic language, a book of the laws, and primer of poetry.

Colcu, fer-leiginn, or chief professor at Clonmacnois, author of the Besom of Devotion, must have been a scholar of much distinction, when he won the affection and devotion of Alcuin, the chief scholar at Charlemagne's court, and won tribute from that scholar, and from his master, Charlemagne. Usher, in his *Sylloge Epistolarum Hibernicarum* gives in full the letter of Alcuin to Colcu—which, by a reference in it, is shown to be only part of an irregular correspondence kept up between the court scholar abroad and the scholars in Ireland. This letter addressed by Alcuin to "My dearly loved father and master, Colcu," complains that the writer has not for a long time been gratified by receiving any of Colcu's coveted letters—gives gossip of the Court, news of European politics, and states that the bearer of the letter is likewise taking to Colcu, for the school of

Clonmacnois, a present of fifty shekels of silver from Alcuin and fifty from the Emperor."[9]

Though he was of very much later date than the period we have been dealing with, we can not help referring to another distinguished Clonmacnois man, the famous Tighernach, scholar, linguist and historian. O'Curry says of the Annals of Tighernach, "It is a composition of a very remarkable character, whether we take into account the early period at which they were written, the amount of historical research, or the judicious care which distinguishes the compiler." These valuable Annals of Tighernach cover Ireland's history from 305 B.C. to the year of his own death, 1088. "Tighernach," says O'Curry (in MSS. Material), "was undoubtedly one of the most remarkable of all the scholars of Clonmacnois. His learning appears to have been very varied and extensive. He quotes Eusebius, Orosius, Africanus, Bede, Josephus, Saint Jerome and many other historic writers, and sometimes compares their statements and points in which they exhibit discrepancies, and afterwards endeavours to reconcile their conflicting testimony, and to correct the chronological errors of one writer by comparison with the dates given by others. He also collates the Hebrew text with the Septuagint version of the Scriptures."

Since the subject of Clonmacnois induced us to leap to such a late date as the eleventh century, we may justifiably make passing reference to another remarkable scholar of late date also—but about two centuries earlier than Tighernach—the learned Cormac MacCullinan of Cashel, scholar, warrior, ecclesiastic and king—the most famous man of his time in Eirinn—and one, too, whose fame must have sounded on the Continent of Europe. Cormac was not only a profound Gaelic scholar and commentator on the

[9] Here is George Stokes' summary of this letter: "He begins his letter with telling Colcu the news of the day; tells him how Charlemagne had converted the Saxons and the Frisians, some (as he naïvely expressed it) by rewards, and others by threats. He narrates how, during the previous year the Slavs, Greeks, Huns, and Saracens had been defeated by the master's forces. He describes a quarrel between Charlemagne and the Mercian King, Offa. He laments that he has not received any Irish letters for a considerable time, and continues: 'I have sent to thee some oil, which is now a scarce article in Britain, that you may divide it among the bishops, for man's assistance and God's honor. I have also sent fifty shekels to my brethren from the King's bounty; I beseech you pray for him; and from myself fifty shekels. For the brethren in the South I have sent thirty from the king and thirty from myself, and for the anchorites three shekels of pure silver; that they all may pray for me and King Charles, that God may preserve him to the protection of his Holy Church, and the praise and glory of His holy name.'"

Aengus, in his Feilire praises as "a saint, a priest, and a scribe of the saints of Eirinn, Colcu, Lector of Cluainmacnois." It records of Colcu: "It was to him Paul the Apostle came to converse. He took his satchel of books at Moin-tire-an-air, and it was he that pleaded for him to the school of Cluain."

ancient obsolete language of the Gael, but was also a Hebrew, Greek, Latin, Saxon and Danish scholar. This truly great statesman, churchman, writer and ruler, was cut off in the year 903, on the bloody field of Bellach Mughna—on which disastrous day, by the way, fell many noted scholars. Such respect did the learned Cormac command that even the enemy whom he fought on that fatal day, the monarch Flann Sinna, when the head of Cormac was carried to him that he might exult over it, "kissed it, and turned round three times therewith."

The wisdom of this scholarly king was a heavenly boon to his kingdom of Munster.

> "Great was the prosperity of Ireland," says Keating, "during his reign, for the land became filled with the divine grace, and with worldly prosperity, and with public peace in his days, so that the cattle needed no cowherd, and the flocks no shepherd, as long as he was king. The shrines of the saints were then protected, and many temples and monasteries were built; public schools were established for the purpose of giving instruction in letters, law, and history; many were the tilled fields, numerous were the bees, and plenteous the beehives under his rule; frequent was fasting and prayer, and every other work of piety; many houses of public hospitality were built, and many books written, at his command. And, moreover, whenever he exacted the performance of any good work from others, he was wont to set them the example himself by being the first to practise it, whether it was a deed of alms, or benevolence, or prayer, or attending mass, or any other virtuous deed. It was the good fortune of Ireland during that epoch, that, whilst he was reigning over Munster, the country was abandoned by whatever of the Lochlannaigh (Danes) had previously infested it for the purposes of plunder."[10]

[10] The Will of Cormac, in verse, is of high interest as giving us a glimpse of what were some of the prize possessions of a man of his standing in those days—

> 'Tis time my testament were made,
> For danger's hour approacheth fast;
> My days shall henceforth be but few,
> My life has almost reached the goal.
>
> My golden cup of sacrifice,
> Wherewith I holy offerings make,
> I will to Senan's brotherhood,
> At Inis Cathaigh's sacred fane.

Unfortunately, during the Danish period of destruction great literary treasures of the very early days, and many of the works of the early scholars, perished—and some were carried off to Scandinavia. Vast numbers of books, too, were carried far and wide over the Continent of Europe by the travelling Irish scholars and missionaries in the centuries when they were spreading the light in Europe.

After the Viking tyranny had been broken by Brian Boru, that monarch found it necessary to do all in his power to provide the country with fresh literature, getting the old books rewritten or copied, and sending emissaries abroad for new ones. It is in the century succeeding the Battle of Clontarf, fought on Good Friday, 1014, that were made the great collections of Irish literature which we now have: the Book of the Dun Cow

---

The bell that calleth me to prayer,
Whilst on the green-robed earth I stay;
Forget not with my friend to leave
At Conall's shrine, where Forgas flows.

My silken robe of graceful flow,
O'erlaid with gems and golden braid,
To Ros-cré, Paul and Peter's fane,
And Cronan's guardianship, I leave.

My silver chessboard, of bright sheen,
I will to Uladh's royal chief;
My well-wrought chain of faultless gold,
To thee, Mochuda, I bequeath.

Take then my amice and my stole,
And take my manuple likewise;
To Lenin's son, who lies at Cluain,
To Colman, who has found his bliss.

My psalter of illumined leaves,
Whose light no darkness e'er can hide—
To Caisel I forever leave
This potent gift without recall.

And my wealth, I bequeath to the poor,
And my sins to the children of curses;
And my dust to the earth, whence it rose,
And my spirit to Him, who has sent it.

[11] Such as those other famous ancient books—"The Lebar Brecc" (The Speckled Book), "The Yellow Book of Lecan," "The Book of Ballymote," "The Book of Lismore," etc., etc.—preserved in the Royal Irish Academy, and in Trinity College, Dublin.

about 1100, and the Book of Leinster about 50 years later. It is these books and others like them[11] that contain (mostly in the language of the period, but often shot through with the old Irish forms which the scribes forgot to change) these ancient poems and sagas that date substantially from pagan times, and give us such a wondrous insight into the past of the Celtic race in Ireland, and no doubt of the Celtic race upon the Continent also.

Healy: Irish Schools and Scholars.
Stokes, The Rev. Dr. Geo. T.: The Knowledge of Greek in Ireland Between A.D. 500 and 900. Proc. R. I. A., 1892.
Zimmer: The Influence of Ireland on Mediæval Culture.
Jubainville, H. D'Arbois de: Le Cycle Mythologique Irlandais et la Mythologie Celtique.
O'Curry's Works.

CHAPTER XXVIII

The Irish Missionaries Abroad

And, during these several fruitful centuries succeeding St. Patrick, the story of the Race must concern itself not merely with the saints and the scholars who towered tallest in the nation in those days, and whose acts make the nation's most memorable history, but also with those other commanding Irish figures who, throughout this time, swarming forth from the Irish monasteries and schools, like bees from a hive, bore with them to distant shores the faith and the lore with which Ireland overflowed, and with knowledge, secular and divine, blessed many peoples and brought them out of barbarism.

Says Dr. Wattenbach in his Congregations of the Irish Monks in Germany: "It was thus, when the whole world seemed irrecoverably sunk in barbarism . . . the Irish went forth into every part of the world," to spread Christianity and knowledge.

Says Kuno Meyer (in his Introduction to "Ancient Irish Poetry"):

> "Ireland had become the heiress to the classical and theological learning of the western empire of the fourth and fifth centuries, and a period of humanism was thus ushered in which reached its culmination during the sixth and the following centuries. For once, at any rate, Ireland drew upon herself the eyes of the world, as the one haven of rest in a turbulent world over-run by hordes of barbarians, as the great seminary of Christian and classical learning. Her sons, carrying Christianity and a new humanism over Great Britain and the Continent, became the teachers of whole nations, the counsellors of kings and emperors."

What these loyal bearers of the lamp of knowledge and eager carriers of the cross of Christ did in the neighbouring nation of Britain, we shall glance at first—and then outline what was accomplished by a typical few of the countless many who swarmed for centuries far and wide over Europe.

Mainly from three reservoirs the faith and its accompaniment of learning was borne to the Britons—direct from Ireland—from Aidan's Irish monastery of Lindisfarne on Britain's northeastern coast—and from Augustine's Roman mission in Britain's southeastern corner.

The latter, though last named, was the first to go with the blessing of faith to the Britons, but the two former succeeded in carrying the blessing over by far the greater portion of the field. That the work of the Roman missionary was circumscribed in its area, and its success limited, as compared with the work and the success of the Irish missionaries, and of Saxon missionaries who were pupils and disciples of the Irish, is acknowledged by the authorities who have written upon the subject. The English ecclesiastical writer, Dr. Lightfoot, Bishop of Durham, speaks thus on the subject:

> "Though nearly forty years had elapsed since Augustine's first landing in England, the church was still confined to its first conquest, the southeast corner of the island, the kingdom of Kent. . . . Then commenced those thirty years of earnest, energetic labour, carried on by those Celtic missionaries and their disciples, from Lindisfarne as their spiritual citadel, which ended in the submission of England to the gentle yoke of Christ."

Montalembert (in his Monks of the West) says:

> "The Italians, Augustine and his monks, had made the first step, and the Irish now appeared to resume the uncompleted work. But what the sons of St. Benedict could only begin was completed by the sons of St. Columba."

And Dr. Reeves says:

> "St. Augustine arrived in England in 597 . . . but Christianity made little headway in the provinces until Aidan began his labors in Lindisfarne in 634."

To the work done and the foundations laid by this Irishman, Aidan, the spread of Christianity to the bounds of Britain are chiefly owing. As

Dr. Lightfoot says: "Aidan holds the first place in the evangelisation of our race. Augustine was the apostle of Kent, but Aidan was the apostle of England."

Aidan came into England from Colm Cille's monastery of Iona—by request of Oswald of Northumbria, who had got his faith and his education in Ireland. Bede records, "Many of the Scots came daily into Britain, and with great devotion preached the Word to those provinces of the English over which King Oswald reigned."

In 634 Aidan founded the monastic community in Lindisfarne, or Holy Isle, off the Northumberland coast, which became a bountiful flowing fountain of faith for England. And Irishman after Irishman came there in succession to tend the fount. Aidan was succeeded by Finan, and Finan by Colman. And during three fruitful decades the propagation of the faith to England was directed by these men. They travelled and taught and preached, themselves. And their disciples and their pupils spread themselves out over vast areas doing likewise. We are told that the pious Oswald himself humbly interpreted for them oftentimes, ere yet the missionaries were well enough acquainted with the Saxon tongue to express themselves clearly in it.

> "It can be affirmed," says McGeoghegan, "that the Saxons of the Northern provinces were indebted to those three for the knowledge of the true God. Finan it was who converted Sigebert, King of East Anglia, and Panda, King of the interior provinces, with their courts. And he set his priests instructing and baptising their subjects."

Besides the monastery at Lindisfarne, Aidan founded many monasteries and many churches in other places in northern England. Preaching, teaching, converting, baptising, he tirelessly occupied himself among these Saxons to whom he brought Christ. He won the veneration, the admiration, and the earnest love of all of them, noble and simple. The rich loaded him with gifts—which gifts he promptly distributed among the poor who needed them.

Then many of those Saxons themselves who were going, as Aldhelm said, "in fleet loads to Ireland," to the schools and monasteries there, brought back with them to their native land and propagated among their fellow countrymen the knowledge of the Scriptures, and the secular knowledge which they had absorbed under their holy masters in Eirinn.

Leland tells us of St. Petrocus, renouncing the kingdom of Cumberland, and for twenty years at Irish schools studying the Holy Scriptures and literature.

Camden in his Brittania says:

> "Our Anglo-Saxons went at those times to Ireland as if to a fair to purchase goods. Hence, it is frequently read in our historians of holy men, 'He was sent to Ireland to school,' or 'He went to the Irish renowned for their philosophy.'"

The royal court of Northumbria, in particular, where always were to be found Irish preachers and Irish teachers, and where, we are even told, Irish came to be at one time the court language, acted as the great conduit, through which flowed both the religion and learning of Eire for blessing the English people. The Northumbrian kings, Egbert and Oswald and Aldfrid[1] (whose mother was Irish) spent a long time, all of them, at the Irish schools.

"Edilvinus," says Bede, "was well instructed in Ireland and came back and was appointed bishop of the province of Lindisse." Agilberct, who was

[1] This Aldfrid is said to be the author of the famous ancient poem in Irish, "Aldfrid's Itinerary" which is now best known in Mangan's translation—

> I found in Innisfail the fair,
> In Ireland, while in exile there,
> Women of worth, both grave and gay men,
> Many clerics and many laymen.
>
> I travelled its fruitful provinces round,
> And in every one of the five I found,
> Alike in church and in palace hall,
> Abundant apparel, and food for all.
>
> Gold and silver I found in money;
> Plenty of wheat and plenty of honey;
> I found God's people rich in pity,
> Found many a feast, and many a city.
>
> I also found in Armagh the splendid,
> Meekness, wisdom, and prudence blended,
> Fasting as Christ hath recommended,
> And noble counsellors untranscended.
>
> I found in each great church moreo'er,
> Whether on island or on shore,
> Piety, learning, fond affection,
> Holy welcome and kind protection, &c.

probably a Saxon, though some call him a Frank, studied theology in Ireland for several years, and became bishop of Paris. St. Chad, one of the Fathers of the Anglo-Saxon church, got his education in Ireland. And the English Willibrord, educated in Ireland, became the apostle of Saxony.

The Irish bishop, Diuma, was the apostle of the Mercians, and after him the Irish bishop Cellach accomplished arduous work in the Mercian kingdom. The Irishman, Dicuil, was the apostle of the South Saxons. He founded the monastery of Bosanham. The Irish bishops, St. Sampson and St. Magloire, occupied in succession the See of York, Usher tells us. St. Ciaran, called by the Cornish Piran, was the apostle of Cornwall. St. Cuthbert, a native of Leinster, was the patron of Durham. St. Fursa at Burgh Castle, in Suffolk, founded a monastery, from which centre the faith was radiated over that part of England. The Irish St. Moninna is patron of Burton-on-Trent. The Irish St. Bega established herself in Cumberland, at that place which is now called after her St. Bee's. Maeldubh founded the famous monastery and school at that place which is called after him Malmesbury—in 676—an institution that not only gave the faith but also for long ages, through its teachers, gave the higher learning of those days to nobles from many parts of England, including Aldhelm (who made the complaint about Saxon youths continually streaming from the British shores to Ireland of the schools). Glastonbury in the southwest of England was for a long time known as Glastonbury of the Gaels, because of the great Irish school that flourished there, a centre of evangelisation as well as education. At that school the Saxon, St. Dunstan, studied (says William of Malmesbury) "arithmetic, geometry, astronomy and music, under Irish teachers."

But during this time those eager Irish missionaries were, with ever-burning flames in their hearts, swarming north and south, east and west, over the Continent of Europe, preaching and teaching, baptising and building. From the monastic schools of Ireland thickly they poured forth, resigning forever family and friends, and associates and country—resigning crowns and kingdoms, sometimes—for the purpose of carrying the glad tidings of God's Word to all lands. And to all lands they went, from Arctic Iceland to tropic Africa, and from the Pyrenees to Palestine.

If record had been kept of even a tithe of those who then left Ireland forever, to attend to their Master's work, we should have a roll of missionary heroes whose length would alike amaze and fill us with pride. But so common was their crowding forth, and so natural to them the undertaking, that the incident seemed too common and ordinary to waste good parchment and ink upon its setting down. Were it not that occasionally some Continental writer preserved to us the fact that the evangeliser of his country, his province, or city, was from Ireland, we, depending upon our own records, would be in almost complete ignorance of the proud fact (which fortunately every Continental scholar can now tell us) that from the end of the sixth to the beginning of the tenth century the little isle in the western ocean was the means of giving the Gospel of Christ to the vast tract of barbarian-swept Europe. Indeed, since for one such missionary the memory of whose Irish nationality has accidentally escaped the oblivion of the ages, the natal record of twenty must have been lost, we can only conjecture how truly dazzling would be the list of Irish missionaries and martyrs on the Continent of Europe, if the records of all or even one-half had been spared to us.

> "At that time," says the French historian Allemand, "it was sufficient to be an Irishman to be considered holy and become the immediate founder of an abbey."

In the brief account permitted us here, of early Irish missionary activities in Europe, we can only afford to glance at a few of the more prominent, therefrom to obtain a slight general idea of the whole. If we were to take one to represent them all, that one would undoubtedly be the earliest of all the notable ones, the deservedly famous Columbanus—of whom the Benedictines, in their Literary History of France say:

> "The light which Columbanus disseminated wherever he went caused a contemporary writer to compare him to the sun in its course from East to West."

And Odericus Vitali, in his Church History:

> "This father of wonderful sanctity laboured amongst the most zealous, he shone gloriously among worldlings by his miracles, and taught by the Holy Spirit, he established monastic regulations, and was the first to deliver them to the Gauls."

Of course the memory of several Irish Christians on the Continent before Columbanus came, is accidentally preserved to us—such as the elder St. Sedulius, already referred to, who was teaching in Achaia. And Florentinus, of whom Usher tells us, whose festival is on the calends of December, who was imprisoned in Rome, and who preached and converted many.

St. Eliphius, Bishop of Toul, in the end of the fourth century was, says Abbot Rupert of Duitz (writer of Eliphius Acts) a native of Scotia.[2]

Also St. Renan in the forest of Nevit in Brittany, in the latter part of the fifth century, and St. Sezin in Brittany, in the beginning of the sixth century (both referred to by Lannigan), were Irish. While at about the same time that Rome rang all its bells to welcome our Columbanus, we have an Irishman, Augustine, labouring for God in Carthage. Augustine left us, in the Wonders of the Sacred Scriptures, a remarkable attempt, at so early a time, to reconcile science and revelation.[3]

But Columbanus was certainly the first typically Irish missionary on the Continent, of whose career we have pretty full and accurate details. Fortunately, only ten years after he passed away, his life was written by his follower, friend, and fellow-countryman, Jonas, abbot of Luxeuil in Burgundy. Columbanus was a Leinsterman, born in the year 543, and schooled first with St. Sinnell on Loch Erne—and next under Comgall at Bangor, on whose monastic rule he modelled the rule that he gave to his own monasteries on the Continent. At Bangor he made himself master of grammar, rhetoric, geometry, poetry, the Sacred Scriptures, Latin—and, some believe, Greek and Hebrew also.

When, following the example of hundreds of other holy ones who had gone before him, Columbanus gave up all in order to carry Christ's Gospels to the heathen, he took with him twelve disciples (as was then the common practice of many masters who went forth) and set out through Britain, to the Continent of Europe.

Columbanus' first signal success on the Continent was the conversion of Sigebert, king of Austrasia, whose heart the Irishman won as well as his soul—for Sigebert tried to induce the missionary to settle down close to his court (which was at Metz) offering him generous endowments if he did so. But not for Columbanus was the easy life. He came not to seek worldly

---

[2] Usher says: "St. Eliphius, son of a king of Scotia, abandoned vast possession; was delighted to serve Christ the Lord God, in poverty. In the city of Toul together with thirty-three of his faithhful companions he was betrayed, thrown into prison, but by the goodness of God, was miraculously delivered in the night. After this he preached with constancy and fervour, and made a great harvest in the vineyard of the Lord. He converted and baptised in a short time four hundred persons. But the Emperor Julian, the apostate, being incensed against them, because they boldly proclaimed the glory of Christ of whom he was envious, caused Eliphius to be arrested and had him beheaded."

[3] In the course of this work Augustine correctly details all the animals that are to be found in his native Ireland. He also mentions the recent death of a famous man, Mancheas the Wise, in Central Ireland. An interesting paper upon Augustine's work, written by Dr. Reeves, is contained in Volume VII of the proceedings of the Royal Irish Academy.

favours but to toil for Christ. In the Vosges Mountains he settled, at a wild and barren spot called Anagrai. Here he and his companions lived upon herbs and roots, and sometimes, in their stress, ate the barks of the trees. By timely relief that seems miraculous, they were twice saved from dying of starvation. But the news of the piety, and beauty of the lives, of the wonderful men from Eirinn who had established themselves in this bleak spot, was carried far and wide, and mightily impressed the people of those regions, who began thronging to them, bringing also crowds of the sick and the infirm. And so completely won were they to their holy ways of life that many wanted to join their community—so that after a little time Columbanus and his companions had to quit their rude and cramped quarters at Anagrai and go further down the valley to Luxeuil, where they built a monastery that gave them more spacious quarters, and much better facilities for dealing with the streams of pilgrims which were constantly flowing to them from all sides.

Here also they were in far better position to provide for the teaching of the students who had been pressing upon them, even before they had left Anagrai. A school grew up at the Luxeuil monastery, where the sons of the nobles of that country vied with each other for the privilege of becoming students, and becoming monks.

So marvellously did their fame continue to spread, and their monastery and school to grow, that in a short time again they had to build still another—at Fontaines. And around these three Irish establishments, in the heart of the Vosges mountains, now centred both the intellectual and the religious life of all the eastern part of that country which is now France. "The fame of Columbanus' power," says Lannigan, "brought crowds." To that great school many prominent ecclesiastics of France owed their education.

Yet life at Luxeuil was not one uninterrupted dream of peace. Two notable quarrels disturbed its serenity, and one of them finally resulted in driving Columbanus forth from the great institution which with infinite patience and thought, he had founded, and with infinite solicitude fostered.

The neighbouring ecclesiastics assailed him and denounced him as a disobedient child of the church because his Vosges community celebrated the old Roman Easter—after the custom of the Irish—instead of the new, or Alexandrian Easter, which was now universally observed on the Continent. Columbanus would not bow to the will of his antagonists. He held his own, and wrote some remarkable letters to the bishops, to Pope Gregory the Great, and later to Pope Boniface, defending himself. Pathetic, but at the same time noble, is that beautiful plea, to the Gallic bishops, of this man representing a little band who had exiled themselves for Christ's sake—"Let us live here in Gaul in a like peace in which we hope to live eternally in heaven. But if it be God's will that you should drive me from this wilderness, whither I have come so far for the sake of Jesus Christ, I shall say, with the prophet: 'If for my sake this tempest is upon you, take me up and cast me forth into the sea.'" All he asked was to be left in peace to observe the festivals of the church as all his life he had been used to observe them, as all his countrymen had always observed them—as they had got them from St. Patrick. "Better comfort us poor strangers, than go on disturbing us," he writes to the bishops, when vexed by their continued annoyances—for they had now summoned him to a Council to answer for his crime of continuing to observe the Irish Easter. And as he knows that these bishops, who persecute him for his lack of a letter observance, have been themselves eminently lax in observing the spirit of many church ordinances, and that they have been more than lax in neglecting to hold Councils, when matters of far graver moment than his persecution calls for them, his Irish sarcasm comes into play. So he answers, congratulating them on the fact that they are going to hold a Council—and wishes that they would comply with the Canons and hold them oftener. The saint is all his life a typical Irishman, again and again displaying the Irish qualities. He is frank and fearless; he never shrinks from a fight; he can be fierce as a lion, and gentle as the white dove that gave him his name. By his loving persuasiveness he could win alike the highest and the humblest. And by his terrible denunciation he made the tyrant tremble on his throne. He was possessed of infinite sweetness, and of infinite sarcasm; and to complete his Irishism he was undoubtedly gifted with that insinuating Irish quality which in recent days is dubbed blarney. For we find him when writing to Pope Gregory to defend himself against the bishops, taking occasion to compliment Gregory upon a recent pastoral, and begging from him a copy of his commentary on Ezechiel—compliments which, coming from a notable scholar, admittedly more able than Gregory himself or any of the scholars of that day, must have left His Holiness in that pleasant frame of mind which premises a sympathetic consideration of the complimenter's case. Perhaps Gregory had not forgotten that Columbanus was a man of eminently good literary judgment when, on the Saint's going to visit him, in 599, he ordered the bells of Rome to ring for him, and he and his clergy did all the honours to the exiled Irishman.

Columbanus' other quarrel was with the notorious Queen Brunehilde, who then ruled that kingdom for her young grandson, Theodoric, still in his minority. That wicked queen's love of ruling and of power, induced her to indulge and encourage the young king in all vicious pleasures, which should weaken and keep him subservient to her, and wean him from desire to take his rightful place. Now the young king, for all his weakness, loved and admired the Irish apostle, and would do anything to serve him. To the chagrin of Brunehilde, Columbanus endeavoured to reform him—and indeed succeeded several times in drawing him from his vicious courses, and setting him in the straight path. But the wily old queen-mother could always craftily undo whatever the saint did. Openly and unfearingly Columbanus, when he saw the absolute necessity for it, publicly thundered at the wicked king and at the still more wicked queen, his grand-mother. And her before whom some of the boldest trembled, this Irish wanderer threatened, rebuked, and denounced. And no royal threats in return could silence him.

Once, when Theodoric had relapsed, Columbanus followed him to Epoisses, to reprimand him before his unworthy associates there. The Irishman stood without the castle gate, and demanded that the king should come to him. He indignantly rejected the invitation of Theodoric to enter and enjoy the castle's hospitality. And when then a rich feast was carried out to him Columbanus scattered the feast, and smashed the plates upon the gates of the castle.

He finally succeeded in bringing the wicked pair, the old and the young, to repentance—or apparent repentance—and apology for their wicked conduct.

But after a time they lapsed again and Columbanus now thrust them from the church—excommunicated both. Then they turned upon him. They forced him from under the roof of his monastery, and banished him to Besançon. The prison at Besançon was filled, and overflowed, with condemned criminals, most of them the vilest of the nation. To these Columbanus preached, and converted the most hardened, confessed them, bathed their feet, and freed them. And soon the city which he had entered as an outcast bowed to him as its master, and hailed him as its saviour.

But his heart was torn for his poor fatherless community at Luxeuil. And at length, one morning, with Dogmael, one of his Irish disciples, he stole out of Besançon, and made his way again to Luxeuil. And, oh, the unbounded joy with which he was there greeted! by the long-time grieving monks, his afflicted children. And his joy to be once more with the community he loved—in the hallowed structure whose walls, cemented by sweat and blood, he had reared—outdid the joy of his fellows!

But not long was he left to his enjoyment, for when Brunehilde and Theodoric heard of his return they were enraged, and ordered him to be seized and sent back to his native country. Accordingly, he was taken away forcibly and carried to Nantes, where he was put aboard a ship that was sailing for Ireland. The hand of God, however, intervened. The ship, after reaching the ocean, was driven back upon the land, and he and his companions were disembarked by the sailors who considered that the mishap to the ship was caused by their carrying these holy ones away. He returned to Nantes, where he stayed for a short time, quickly becoming a hero to the people, who came to admire and to venerate him. Then he journeyed into Clothair's kingdom, but turned a deaf ear to Clothair's entreaty that he should settle down there under his patronage. He passed on to the kingdom of Theodobert, where again he was joyfully received, and where Theodobert's nobles begged him to remain and to make their kingdom holy, learned, and famous. But he passed on, and went up the Rhine to Switzerland, where, after journeying and sojourning and preaching for some time, and founding a monastery, he left behind him his disciple Gall, and went into Italy.

Arriving at Milan, the welcoming king, Agiluilph (whom he converted) of the Lombards, was proud and joyous to have this man honour his kingdom. He entreated Columbanus to settle in his dominion, and to choose where he would for his monastery.

In Milan, Columbanus engaged in the Arian controversy that was then threatening to split the church. He preached against Arianism and wrote against it—hurled at it both oratorical and literary thunders. He now wrote a daring letter to Pope Boniface the Fourth, who was accused of harbouring Nestorians; and civilly but firmly upbraided His Holiness for the religious apathy he found among Italian Christians, contrasting it most unfavourably with the religious fervour that held his own people, the Irish. Furthermore, in this letter he says: "We Irish, though dwelling at the far ends of the earth, are all disciples of St. Peter and St. Paul . . . neither heretic nor Jew nor schismatic has ever been among us; but the Catholic faith just as it was first delivered to us by yourselves as successors to the apostles, is held by us unchanged."

In that same year he settled down in Bobbio, and there erected his monastery, which became a centre of holiness and learning and a Gospel-fount which should bestow the knowledge of God on the heathen and the ignorant, and was to be far famed through long centuries to come.

Clothair the Second, who in common with the other Gallic kings hungered to have the honour and the profit of this great saint settling under him, now sent a mission to Columbanus inviting him back to Gaul, and offering gold to pay the expenses of his journey, and promising lavish gifts and endowments for his undertakings, should he return. Although Columbanus had to reject the offer, thanking Clothair and asking him to bestow all favours he had upon his loved monks at Luxeuil, it was a joy to him to receive the ambassador, who was no other than Eustatius, a friend and disciple, and now abbot of Luxeuil. It rejoiced him to get long-wished-for news of the monastery and the community he loved, of the monks and of the students and of the people.

Here in Bobbio, in his very advanced years, Columbanus ended a fruitful and a notable life.[4]

Even before his death, disciples and followers and students of Columbanus had gone forth to many parts, founding monasteries of his rule. They spread rapidly and became very numerous; in northern France, eastern France, southwestern France, in Austrasia, along the Rhine, in Germany, in Switzerland, and in the northern part of Italy—so that for centuries after his death, in many lands and in many tongues, memorial prayers for this saint were, as a perpetual incense, ever mounting up to heaven.[5]

As abbots, as bishops, as evangelisers and saints, many of Columbanus' Irish disciples and followers became famous on their own account. As St. Magnus (Magnoald) who founded two famous abbeys in Germany, that were richly endowed by King Pepin. And St. Deicol (Desle) who, patronised and endowed by King Clothair,[6] founded a celebrated monastery at Lure, not far from Luxeuil, where his memory is honoured on the fifteenth of February—"who was renowned," says the Gallican Martyrology of Laussoius, "for his many virtues, and the splendour of his miracles." At Lure Miss Margaret Stokes saw St. Desle's cup reverently preserved, and found his memory still ardently venerated. And above all, St. Gall, who

---

[4] Bobbio was suppressed by the French in 1803. There are still St. Columbanus' chapel, and his cave, and the holy well of Columbanus, to which the faithful resort for cures.

It may be mentioned as a striking coincidence that, as in the case of so many of the Irish saints at home, Columbanus is said by the foreign legends to have been on the most intimate terms with all living things around him. Birds nestled in the palm of his hand; doves came to shelter in his cowl—and squirrels, too. When he sang his psalms, the wild birds joyously sang with him. And beasts of prey turned harmless in his presence.

[5] Works of Columbanus still extant are the Monastic Rule, a Book of daily penances for monks, seventeen sermons, a book on the eight vices, Latin verses, and epistles, two to Boniface, two to Gregory, and one to the members of the Gallican Synod, and one to the monks of Luxeuil.

Lannigan says of him: "He was a superior and very elegant genius, deeply versed not only in every branch of ecclesiastical learning, but likewise in classical studies, both Latin and Greek."

[6] While Deicol had only a little cell in a marsh, when afterwards he erected a great monastery, he was sitting at his door one day, when a wild boar hunted by King Clothair rushed up and took refuge with him, while he turned away the bloodthirsty hounds and saved the animal's life. Clothair granted him the lands for his monastery, and endowed it by granting to him also the town of Bredana.

with Columbanus' parting words in his ear, "May the almighty God, for whose sake we left our native land, grant that we meet before his face in heaven"—settled on Lake Constance, and built his monastery there, around which sprang the city still known by the name of St. Gall. This saint did great things for the evangelising of that part of Switzerland. He refused the bishopric of Constance, putting forward in his stead his deacon and disciple, John (most probably an Irishman, also) who was elected. He also refused the Abbacy of Luxeuil, though a deputation of six Irish monks travelled to Constance to entreat him. In the year 635, at the age of ninety-five he died, renowned. King Sigebert the Second richly endowed his monastery, and the abbot of St. Gall was raised to the rank of a prince of the Empire. For many centuries after his death this abbey was noted as a centre of Irish activities.

Though St. Gall did much for his part of Switzerland, of course the apostle of Switzerland was that other Irishman, St. Fridolin, who brought the faith there almost in the lifetime of St. Patrick—and who was buried in the Island of Secking in the Rhine in 514—Fridolinus the Wanderer, as he is called by Possevin and other Continental writers. They say he was a son of royalty in Ireland. He wandered much over both Germany and France at the time of Clovis, preaching wherever he went. He founded monasteries in Upper Saxony, in Alsace, Strasburg, and on the frontiers of Switzerland. Colgan in his Acta Sanctorum names eight of his foundations. Baltherus, a monk and canon of Secking the most ancient author of St. Fridolin's life, expressly states that he was an Irishman.

Peter Canisius in his Life of St. Fridolin says: "Old historians are agreed upon this, that Fridolin was of royal descent—that he was born in Lower Scotia, called Ireland." And Guillimanus, in his work on Swiss affairs, says: "Under Clovis, first Christian king of the Franks, Fridolinus, an Irishman by birth, and of royal lineage, spent a long time in Switzerland, and planted in it the name and faith of Christ, where he likewise performed many miracles." Possevin says he died in 595; some others say 574. It is recorded that Fridolin was a councillor at one time to King Clovis. He rebuilt the great basilica of St. Hilary, at Poitiers. His portrait is in the Blason of the Canton of Glarus, Switzerland.

After Columbanus the most famous of Irish saints who laboured to spread the faith in France was Fursey, or Fursa, whom Bede styled "the Sublime"—who was a nephew of Brendan the Navigator, and educated under him. He came to France about forty years later than Columbanus. He had laboured in the conversion of Picts and Saxons after he left Ireland and before he came to France. He was a favourite of Sigebert, King of the

East Saxons, whom he induced to resign the throne for a monk's cell, and under whose patronage he founded the abbey of Cnobersburg, now called Burghcastle in Suffolk. In France, Clovis the Second gave Fursa a place at Lagny on the Marne, where he founded his famous monastery, and drew to him many disciples from his beloved Galway. Erchinwald, Mayor of the Palace, Fursa's first Gallic patron, had tried in vain to hold him at Peronne; but Clovis' wife, Bathilde, it was who succeeded in making him accept Clovis' offer to settle at Lagny. Memory of Fursa's marvellous miracles still survive in that part of France—as also the miracles of his Irish disciples and followers who spread themselves over the country, bringing the people to Christ—especially Saints Algeis, Eto and Gobin (the latter endowed by Clothair II), who are the respective patron saints of the towns of St. Algia, St. Avesnes and St. Gobin. To the holy well of St. Gobin still come the French pilgrims. Even of Fursa's servant, St. Maguille, the memory is honoured at St. Riquier, where is his holy well, and where, more than four centuries after, and again four centuries after that, his body was enshrined in a very precious shrine, and re-enshrined with ecclesiastical honours.

Lamented through the breadth and length, of northern France, St. Fursa passed away in 648. And the city of Peronne which had contended for him in life, contended for him again in death—this time successfully. His body lay in state for thirty days, under a tent of precious tapestry, in their unfinished church. And the legend persists in Peronne that for generations afterward, the pious who flocked to the hallowed spot where his embalmed body had lain, were sensible of the sweet odour of spices, lingering there. His church in Peronne grew very rich, from the wealth bestowed on it by the crowds of pilgrims who for centuries thronged to the shrine of the famous Irishman. Fursa is the patron of Peronne and his figure is in the city banner.

After returning from the first crusade, St. Louis of France went to Peronne in 1256, to be present at the translation of the body of Fursa, to a new shrine—a most beautiful one specially prepared for the body by St. Eloi.

He was called Fursa of the Visions. He had wonderful visions of the other world—which were printed and reprinted in all languages throughout the continent of Europe—and which are said by many to have been the original source from which Dante first got the ideas for his Divine Comedy. Sir Francis Palgrave, for instance, in his History of Normandy and England says: "We have no difficulty in deducing the poetic genealogy of Dante's Inferno from the Milesian Fursaeus."

St. Foilan and St. Ultan (said to be brothers of Fursa) were brought from Ireland by St. Gertrude, the Abbess of Neville in Brabant. Both of them worked for Christ, in the Netherlands. The original cause of her bringing them—along with other Irish teachers—from Ireland, was to expound the Holy Scriptures, and instruct her nuns, as well as to preach the Word of God to the people. The Breviary of Paris thus refers to the fact:

> "Rome at that time took care to have the relics of the saints and holy books brought to her [Gertrude]; she sent to Ireland for learned men to expound to herself and to her people the canticles of the holy law, which the Irish had almost by heart. The monastery of Vossuensis was built on the banks of the Sambre for receiving the saints Fullanus and Ultanus, brothers of St. Furseus."[7]

In France also still another of the many Irish saints who preached and taught the heathen there, is honoured in the vehicle the *fiacre*—called after the Irishman, St. Fiacre, who was Bishop of Meaux and who flourished in the early seventh century and had his cell in the forest of Meaux. He was of noble birth in Ireland, and went abroad with his train of disciples. His austere life and many miracles made him an object of much veneration. After his death an office of nine lessons in his honour was inserted in most of the breviaries in France, the first of which reads:

> "Ireland is dignified by the lustre of a new lamp: that island glitters, to the Meldi, by the presence of so great a light. The former sent Fiacrius; Meaux received the ray which was sent. The joy of both is in common; the latter possesses a father, the former a son."

Such was the recourse of pilgrims to his grave for centuries after, that the special kind of conveyance in use in that part of the country, which

---

[7] In November 1920, Cardinal Mercier and his Belgian Bishops, in the course of their reply to the cry of the Irish bishops against the terrible atrocities then being wrought in Ireland by the English soldiery, say:

"Does not Belgium herself owe the signal grace of belonging to Christ largely to the first pioneers of Christian civilisation from Ireland? The names of the Irish missionaries who in the Merovingian period evangelised the north of Gaul—Saints Columban, Foillan, Ultan, Livianus and many others—are familiar to us. More than 30 Belgian churches have been dedicated to saints who were natives of Ireland.

"Ireland, won to the faith in the fifth century, seems to have received from Divine Providence a special mission for the Apostolate.

"What, then, is your history but a long Calvary of a people incessantly betrayed, despoiled, starved, but ever unfailing in its faith and its passion for liberty?"

used to carry the pilgrims to the grave, came to be called *fiacre*—and retains that name today.

St. Gibrien, after whom is named the village of Gibrien near Chalons-sur-Mer, was, "one of seven brothers and three sisters from Ireland on pilgrimage for the love of Christ." They dwelt on the Marne, and there lived a life of labour united with wonderful holiness, and constant prayer, which won for them great love among the natives of the country. And another ancient French writer says that "they instructed the people and formed in them the habits of faith, piety and morality." St. Gibrien's relics were enshrined in the church of St. Remi in Rheims.

June third is the festival of two other Irish saints, Caidoc and Fricor, who, with twelve companions, landing at the mouth of the Somme in the latter part of the sixth century, there preached and taught. They converted the heathen noble who was to become St. Riquier. They afterwards spread the Gospel in Picardy. Their relics were enshrined with those of Maguille by St. Jervinus in 1070.

The Irishman, St. Rumald—whose church in Malines (of which city he is patron) is now the metropolitan church of the Low Countries, and holds his relics in a beautiful silver shrine—came from Leinster. He was bishop of Malines in Brabant, where Count Ado induced him to settle. Another Leinsterman, Livinus, who was a Latin poet, was martyred in Flanders in 663, after he had preached the Gospel there, and converted many. His relics are preserved in the church of St. Babo in Ghent.

John D'Alton refers to the fact that Vernutaeus in his work on the spread of the Christian faith in Belgium, by the Irish saints, tells how, even at the time that the Danes were ravaging their own country, they were successfully spreading Christianity from Mechlin, Brabant, Flanders, Artois, Namur, Leyden, Gilderland, Holland, Friesland and Luxemburg.

Authberte, bishop of Cambrai, an Irish missionary who converted Hannonia, is styled the apostle of Flanders. The old church of St. Dympna, a king's daughter from Monaghan (in the seventh century), is still to be seen at Gheel. She is honoured as the patron of the insane. Fedegond converted the people of Antwerp, where his name is still revered. St. Briccus, from whom is named the town of Brieux in Brittany, is said to have been a native of Cork.

These are but a few of the hundreds of Irish saints, to whom, in those early ages, France and civilisation owe a debt which they can never repay.

Italy owes to Ireland a St. Bridget and her brother St. Andrew, St. Donatus, St. Cummian and St. Cathaldus—and many unrecorded missionaries.

Philip, a Florentine, who was an ambassador of Pope Boniface in 1390, wrote the life of Andrew who is patron of San Martino a Mensola—"a holy man from the Island of Ireland," says Philip, "more generally called Scotia"—and of Bridget, patroness of San Martino a Lobaca. The tomb of the eighth century St. Cummian who, a bishop in Ireland, became a humble monk at Bobbio, is still to be seen at the latter place. St. Ursus founded a church in the Val d'Osta, in the first half of the sixth century. Pellegrinus, from Ireland, in the time of Columbanus settled down in the Apennines at Garfagnana. The tomb of the Irish St. Siloa is to be seen at Lucca, where he died in the sixth century.

St. Donatus settled in Tuscany in the beginning of the ninth century. He became bishop of Fiesole. He was a poet and author of several works. Colgan quotes a few lines from a Latin poem of his in which he describes his native Ireland. Donatus was much celebrated for his virtues as well as for his intellectual ability.

Donatus is said to have been a brother of the most famous Italian Irish saint Cathaldus (Cathal)—after whom is named the city of San Cataldo in southern Italy. Cathaldus is the patron saint of Tarentum, and his festival is celebrated there with much pomp, on March eighth. He became bishop of Tarentum and rescued all that country from the paganism into which it had relapsed after the Gospel had been given to it by the Apostles Peter and Mark.

In this connection, Usher quotes from Joannes Juvenis:

> "The Tarentines returning to the worship of idols, as a dog to his vomit, the holy Cathaldus born in Ireland brought them back to the ancient faith."

That was in all probability in the sixth century, though his Italian biographers, the brothers Moron, claim that he came there some centuries before that. Bonaventura Moron's poem on St. Cathaldus' life begins:

> "The icy Ierne bewails that so great an ornament of the West, second to none in piety, celebrated in the ancient laws of Phalantus, should be sent to foreign nations."

And from the office sung in honour of Cathaldus at the Church of Tarentum is the following, quoted by Usher:

> "Rejoice, O happy Ireland, for being the country of so fair an offspring! But thou, Tarentum, rejoice still more, which enclosest (within a tomb) so great a treasure!"

This office says that when Cathaldus taught in Ireland (probably at Lismore), Gauls, Angles, Scots and pupils from other countries studied under him.

In 1150 Archbishop Giraldus had Cathaldus' relics shrined in a silver shrine decorated with gold and jewels. The ancient marble tomb which had held the body is by the high altar in the church. There also is a large silver statue of the saint.

With the possible exception of France, there is no country on the Continent, that owes so much to the Irish missionaries as Germany. For at least six hundred years, from the sixth to the twelfth century, the holy men from Ireland were to be met with in almost every part of the Germanic countries; and their establishments became the centres of enlightenment for the vast populations which they so materially helped to lead out of the night of barbarism.

> "Near the end of the seventh century and the beginning of the eighth," says Zimmer, "a long series of these (Irish) missionary establishments extended from the mouths of the Meuse and Rhine to the Rhone and the Alps, and many others founded by the Germans are the offsprings of Irish monks. And throughout the chronicles and Lives of the Saints the purely Irish are constantly found."

But, for long centuries after, their activities in Germany decreased not.

The following words are from a tribute paid to Ireland and her missionaries in an address which the heads of German colleges presented to Daniel O'Connell in 1844:

> "We never can forget to look upon your beloved country as our mother in religion, that already, at the remotest periods of the Christian era, commiserated our people, and readily sent forth her spiritual sons to rescue our pagan ancestors from idolatry and to entail upon them the blessings of the Christian faith."

Dr. Ferdinand Keller of Zurich, in his Illuminations and Facsimiles from Irish manuscripts in the Libraries of Switzerland, says: "The eleventh and twelfth centuries were the greatest for the Irish monks on the Continent. Communities of Scotic monks were formed in almost every large city in southern Germany." And it was only the results of the Norman invasion of Ireland which even then put practical end to their Continental activities.

And of the latter part of the period indicated we may quote the testimony of Dr. Wattenbach in his Congregations of the Monasteries of the Scotic:

> "The most prosperous time of Irish monks was in the twelfth century. They were examples of rigid abstemiousness, and filled with ardent faith that incited them to go afar. Even in Bulgaria the Emperor Barbarossa, going on crusade, fell in with an Irish abbot at the castle of Scribentium. His monastery probably served as a hospice for pilgrims to Jerusalem."

A few of the Irish saints in the Germanic countries are here set down.

St. Gunifort, descended of noble parents in Ireland, preached in Germany at a very early time—some think before St. Patrick's era. His festival is kept at Pavia in Italy on the 22nd of August. The festival of his sister, St. Dardaluch, who went to Germany with him, is observed at Fressing in Bavaria. Usher records these two Irish saints.

St. Arbogast, who converted large numbers in Alsace, became bishop of Strasburg in 646—appointed thereto by King Dagobert. By his dying request Arbogast was interred in the place of public execution called Mont Michel, where a monastery dedicated to his name was founded long afterward.

The honoured apostle of Franconia is St. Kilian. He had gone on a pilgrimage to Rome, and so favourably did he impress Pope Conan for his wisdom and sacred learning, that he sent him to evangelise Franconia. There he converted Duke Gosbert and many of his subjects. But because, following the bold example of most of these remarkable Irish missionaries, whose fearlessness in attacking both ecclesiastics and kings is noted by Dr. Wattenbach he persisted in commanding Gosbert to put away an unlawful wife, that woman, incensed, had him martyred on 8th of July, 689. Kilian's bible is still preserved, and on his feast-day it is exposed on the high-altar in the Cathedral church of Wurtzburg.

St. Tuban, an Irish bishop, founded a monastery on an island in the Rhine at Honau in 720, which was patronised by King Pepin and Charlemagne. There is still extant the confirmation grant "ad pauperis et peregreno gentis Scotorum" attested by the signatures of the abbot, the bishop and one presbyter of this monastery—all of them Irish names.

Disenberg, formerly Mont Disibod, in the Lower Palatinate takes its name from Disibod "an Irish noble of profound erudition," who preached the Gospel for seven years, in different parts of Germany, and founded a monastery on Mont Disibod.

In 742 Albuin (better known to the Germans as Wittan) went to Thuringia, where he converted great numbers, and was made bishop of Tritzlar by the Pope—and by Arnold Wion is styled apostle of the Thuringians.

St. Virgilius (Fergal) who did good missionary work in Germany, and was famous for his scholarship, was made bishop of Salsburg, in the late seventh or early eighth century. More will be said of him in a succeeding chapter.

St. Willibrord who was apostle of the Batavians and the Frieslanders, although of Saxon descent, was educated in Ireland. Alcuin, who wrote his life, says: "Because he heard that scholastic erudition flourished in Ireland, and was roused by his intercourse with holy men who had been taught there, he studied during twelve years among Ireland's most pious and religious masters that he might become a preacher to many people."

St. Finan "of the Celestial Visions" founded the monastery of Richenau, at the end of the eighth or beginning of the ninth century. He was son of a Leinster prince and had been captive of the Danes in Ireland before leaving it to go to Rome—and thence went into Germany, where he preached for many years.

St. Colman, who is the patron saint of Lower Austria and whose festival is on October thirteenth, was martyred between two robbers, in the year 1012. The Martyrology of Donegal says that he was the son of Malachi Mor, Ard-Righ of Ireland. This is uncorroborated by any other testimony.

The martyr, John, who came to Germany in 1057 accompanying Marianus Scotus, worked among the Slavonians at the request of Prince Gothescale—and was martyred by them. Five years after reaching Germany from Ireland he became bishop of Mecklenburg.

Marianus Scotus, the author of The Chronicles of the World, lived a life of wonderful holiness—first at Fulda and later at Mayence, and won great fame and esteem among the German people. He produced several works, but his Chronicle of the World is that by which he is immortalised.

In a book entitled Bavaria Sancta there is listed, by the Bavarian author, a bishop, the names of Irish saints who contributed to the evangelisation of that one country. He gives them as: Agilus, Marinus, Anianas, Magnus, Columbanus, Erhardus, Alto, Virgilius, Marinus the Younger, Theclanus, Fridolinus, Kilian, Colman, Salust, Amor, Arno (who was brother to Alcuin, the great scholar), Murcherel (or, as some call him, Muricherodachus), Vimius, Zimius and Martinus.

In many respects one of the most remarkable of Irish workers for the faith in Germany was the Holy Marianus Scotus of Donegal—whose correct name was Muiredach MacRorty, a native of Tyrhugh in Donegal—who arrived in Germany only eleven years after Marianus the Chronicler, and who in 1076 founded a monastery which was to become famous, at Ratisbon—from which his Irish followers (who for ages after continued thronging there from Ireland) branched out and built many other notable monasteries in Germany and Austria—all of them under the jurisdiction of the Irish Monastery at Ratisbon. Some of these Irish sister monasteries were the monastery of Wurtzburg, Nuremberg, Constance, St. George in Vienna, St. Mary in Vienna and Eichstadt.

The Bavarian annalist, Aventinus, talking of Marianus and his companions and successors, says:

> "By their devotion to the strictest religious exercises, and self-denial, by their writing and teaching, they earned unbounded respect, and became well approved patterns of piety. They were favourites of everybody. And with one mouth the whole people spoke loudly in their praise; kings and nobles built monasteries for them, and invited them east and west."

Strange to say, the Irish monastery at Ratisbon came to have jurisdiction over not only the many other Irish monasteries of Germany, but also over many priories in Ireland, as is proved by two briefs on the subject by Innocent the Second. No less than twelve Irish monasteries in Germany were formally placed under the authority of the St. James' Monastery of Ratisbon by the Lateran Council of 1215.

The monastery of St. Mary of Vienna was founded by Henry, Duke of Austria in 1161. In the charter of this monastery he makes only Scots (Irish) eligible for admission "because of their long and acknowledged piety."

"Well trained in all human and divine knowledge was Marianus, when he came from Ireland," says the monk of St. James who was his biographer. "He was a poet as well as a theologian." One of his prized works is his Commentaries on the Psalms; his most valued one is his Commentary on St. Paul's Epistles. This, written in the form of marginal and interlineary notes is still preserved in the Imperial Library of Vienna. In it his wide reading is shown by the fact that he quotes Jerome, Augustine, Gregory, Origen, Alcuin, Cassian, and many such. Before he established his own monastery at Ratisbon, and while he still occupied a cell there, under the patronage of Abbess Emma, he employed himself constantly, without cease, writing and giving away books; these being chiefly copies of the Scriptures, and of various religious works. His biographer pictures him at this work all day long, while the two companions who had journeyed with him from Ireland, John and Candidus, prepared for him as fast as they could, parchment, and pens, and ink. And as fast as he turned off his books he gave them out gratis to the abbess, to her nuns, to monks, to poor widows, to everybody! This Irishman wanderer who, for sake of religion and learning, had exiled himself to far, strange lands, a man of brilliant parts, of vast reading, and deep learning, toiled, thus, day and night with his pen, to bestow the products of it upon the hundreds of these people who so hungered for what he had to give! What wonder that when this man decided finally to settle down in Ratisbon, "his determination was hailed with joy, by the whole population." And the abbess gave him the church of St. Peter, with an adjacent plot.

> "This holy man wrote from beginning to end, with his own hand, the Old and New Testament, with explanatory comments on the same; and that not once or twice, but over and over again, with a view to the eternal reward—all the while clad in sorry garb, living on slender diet, attended and aided by his brethren both in the upper and lower monasteries, who prepared the parchments for his use; besides, he also wrote many smaller books and manuals, psalters for distressed widows and poor clerics of the same city, towards the health of his soul without any prospect of earthly gain. Furthermore, through the grace of God, many congregations of the monastic order, which in faith and charity and imitation of the blessed Marianus, are derived from the aforesaid Ireland, and inhabit Bavaria and Franconia, are sustained by the writings of the blessed Marianus."

He died on the ninth of February, 1088. Marianus' immediate successors in the abbacy built, and afterwards enlarged and beautified, the new monastery of St. James (first founded in 1090, two years after Marianus' death). It was done almost entirely with money obtained from Irish royalties, especially from Conor O'Brien, King of Munster, and again from King Murtach O'Brien. The old chronicle of Ratisbon says:

> "Now be it known, that neither before nor since was there a more noble monastery, such magnificent towers, walls, pillars, and roofs, so rapidly erected, so perfectly finished, as in this monastery, because of the wealth and money sent by the kings and princes of Ireland."

Yet the monks sought and got aid for their monastery from many quarters. One of these Irishmen penetrated even to Kiev, and from thence brought back a load of furs, contributed by the King of Russia.

And some of these Irish monks were signally honoured by royalty. Gregory and Carus, from St. Peter's, became chaplains for the Emperor Conrad, and the Empress Gertrude, who bestowed on them the church of St. Aegedius at Nuremberg. And Declan, who succeeded them there, was made chaplain to the Emperor Frederick.

The abbot of the Irish monastery of St. James was granted, by King Henry in 1225 the right of bearing in his coat of arms one-half of the eagle—which meant that he was elevated to the rank of one of the princes of the realm.

Dr. Wattenbach in his Congregation of the Monasteries of the Scots, describes for us how the bands of Irish missionaries travelled wide over Europe, seeking the fresh fields to which God urged them. "In this way we find them always wandering in large and small companies. Their outward appearance was most striking, the more so as they were still in the habit of painting their eyelids. Their whole outfit consisted of a pilgrim's staff, a leathern water-bottle, a wallet, and a case of some relics. In this guise they appeared before the people, addressing themselves to them everywhere with the whole power of their native eloquence—some (as Gallus) in the language of the country—the rest employing an interpreter before the people, but to ecclesiastics speaking in the common language of the Latin Church.

It was probably because of their Continental reputation for fearlessness and fight that the Abbot Sampson of St. Edmund's, in journeying to Pope Alexander in 1161—when Italy was excited by schism—being attacked and mobbed by a populace who were against Alexander, acted in the way he picturesquely describes: "I pretended to be a Scot, and having adopted the Scottish dress and behaviour, I shook my staff at those who scoffed at me, crying aloud at them, after the manner of the Scots." In this account it is also interesting to note that he says, "I carried my old shoes on my shoulders after the manner of the Scots"—a custom which still exists among the mountains of Ireland. The Abbot's account of his strange experience is quoted by Wattenbach, from *Cronica Johannes de Brakelonda*.

Of all the hundreds of holy men who in those centuries exiled themselves from Ireland for the purpose of carrying Christ to the still darkened nations and peoples of Europe, we, joining with the Irish monk of Ratisbon who wrote the life of Marianus, may well say:

> "And now my brothers if you ask me what will be the reward of Marianus and the pilgrims like him who left the sweet soil of their native land, free from obnoxious beast and worm, with its mountains and hills, its valleys and groves, so well suited for the chase, the picturesque expanses of its rivers, its green fields and its streams

swelling up from purest fountains, and like children of Abraham the Patriarch came without hesitation unto the land God pointed out to them, this is my answer: They will dwell in the house of the Lord with the Angels and Archangels forever: they will behold in Sion the God of Gods, to whom be honour and glory for endless ages."

Concannon, Helen: Columbanus.

Keller, Dr. Ferdinand: Essay on "Illuminations and Facsimiles from Ancient Irish MSS. in the Libraries of Switzerland." Translated from German with Introductory Remarks by the Rev. Wm. Reeves, D.D., in Ulster Journ. of Archæol. VIII.

Wattenbach: "Die Kongregation der Schottenkloster in Deutschland." Translated by Dr. Reeves, with notes, in the Ulster Journal of Archæology, vol. VII.

Stokes, Miss Margaret: Three Months in the Forests of France: A Pilgrimage in Search of Vestiges of Irish Saints in France.

—— Six Months in the Apennines: A Pilgrimage in Search of Vestiges of Irish Saints in Italy.

Lightfoot, Dr. J. B., Bishop of Durham: Leaders in the Northern Church.

CHAPTER XXIX

Irish Scholars Abroad

Learning, like religion, had its hosts of Irish missionaries, who spread themselves afar, eager to lead to the light benighted peoples over the Continent, as well as in the neighbouring isles. When the Saxon, Aldhelm, who, it will be remembered, was a pupil of the Irishman Maeldubh, founder of the school of Malmesbury, wrote to his fellow-countryman, Eadfride ("who had given six years to philosophy in Ireland, and enriched his mind with the treasures of the Scotic hive")—"Ireland is a fertile and blooming nursery of letters: one might as soon reckon the stars of heaven, as enumerate her students and literature"—many of these Irish literary men were then eagerly pursuing their task of love among Aldhelm's fellow countrymen in all corners of Britain. But many others, too, were working in Continental fields, dispelling the darkness of distant lands with the bright torch which they bore from the beacon-fires of learning that glowed on every hill in Eirinn.

"These Irish torch-bearers founded," says John D'Alton in his R. I. A. Essay on Irish History, "the most flourishing schools of Christian Europe. And to them the world is indebted for the introduction of scholastic divinity and the application of philosophical reasoning to illustrate the doctrines of theology."

And Zimmer testifies: "They laid the corner-stone of western culture on the Continent, the rich result of which Germany shares and enjoys today, in common with all other civilised nations."

O'Halloran, illustrating their feeling of superiority over the Continentals, quotes from the life of the Irish Kilian, apostle of Franconia, how when his fellow countryman, St. Fiacre, encountered him in Gaul, he asked Kilian: "Quid te charissime frater, ad has barbaras, gentes deduxit?" ("What has brought you, dearest brother, to these barbarous people?")

And Columbanus in one of his epistles tells the Continental scholars that the Irish schoolmen regarded some of their boasted Continental philosphers with indulgent tolerance.

Of Irish scholars on the Continent we have already referred to the brilliant genius, Celestius, who is claimed for Ireland. But the claims of another very early and very brilliant genius, Coelius Sedulius, who, as was mentioned, flourished in the time of Theodosius, and dedicated a book to him, are better substantiated. Archbishop Usher quotes from Trithemius:

> "Sedulius, a presbyter, a native of Scotia (Ireland), was a disciple from his earliest youth of Heidelbertus, Archbishop of the Scots. He was conversant in divine learning, and very skilled in profane literature. He excelled in poetry and prose, and leaving Scotia, for the sake of informing himself, came to France. After this he traversed Italy, Asia, Achaia, from thence he proceeded to Rome, where he became illustrious for his erudition."

Corroborative proof of Sedulius being an Irishman is adduced from the fact that the celebrated eighth century Irish geographer, Dicuil, refers to him as "noster Sedulius."

And a very ancient copy of Sedulius' Pauline commentaries, published by John Sichard, which was preserved in the abbey of Fulda, shows on the title page, "Sedulii Scoti Hiberniensis." This occurs also in another edition of his works published at Basle.

Sedulius' works were many and varied. Usher enumerates them thus—fourteen books on the epistles of Paul, two books on the miracles of Christ, a book on Priscianus, a book on Donatus, a book of epistles to various people, four volumes dedicated to the abbot of Macedonia, a volume dedicated to the Emperor Theodosius, many hymns, and his famous poem, Carmen Paschale. Sedulius composed some of the most beautiful hymns in the Catholic service, such as *A Solis Otis Cardine.* In the twelfth century, seven hundred years after his death, a council of seventy bishops in Rome recommended to the faithful his paschal poem, which had won him the title of the Christian Virgil.

Another very remarkable Irishman, who, in distant time, and distant field, had the identity of his nationality almost lost, was Augustine, a monk in Carthage—already referred to—who, in the seventh century, was the author of the remarkable work The Difficulties of Scripture. This is a book in which, with extraordinary ingenuity he tried to reconcile science and Scripture, upon such knotty points as the falling of the walls of Jericho, the standing of the sun at Joshua's command, the speaking of Balaam's ass, the turning of Lot's wife into a pillar of salt and so forth. He essays in each case with astonishing cleverness to demonstrate that the apparent miracles were, in reality, developments of some pre-existing natural law. Stokes says that the work discloses a scholar deeply versed in books, and widely experienced in travel.

And Reeves, in an article on Augustine (in Proc. R. I. A. 1862) says of this work that it is a most creditable monument of learning and religious feeling, at a period when the Irish church was notable for its learning.

Augustine mentions the death in Ireland of an Irishman of some note, Manicheas the Wise, in 652. And in this he is borne out by the evidence of the Annals of Tighernach and the Annals of Ulster, which record at that time the death of St. Manchan of Lemanchan. In the book he enumerates the animals of Ireland, as wolves, deer, wild boars, foxes, badgers, bears, rabbits, and offers sound geological reason for their existence on this island, which he shows had been an integral part of Europe, in a remote age, but was cut off from it by a cataclysm.

The period of most marked activity of Irish scholars on the Continent of Europe was probably during the Carlovingian dynasty—when, it has been said, almost every school in Europe was taught by an Irishman—and furthermore that every scholar who knew Greek was either an Irishman or the pupil of an Irishman. In the preceding period, that is during the Merovingian time, Columbanus, with whom we have dealt, was the most noted example of Irish scholarship in Europe. The great Charlemagne and his successors, ardent patrons of learning, drew to them the choicest flowers of Irish scholarship, and then bestowed their fragrance as a blessing upon many lands.

Usher says: "From Ireland Charles transferred the wisdom of Greece and of Latium. And from her he obtained the doctors and instructors of the uninstructed youth."

"In schools and monasteries all over France," says Zimmer, "the Carlovingian king employed Irish monks as teachers of writing, grammar, logic, rhetoric, astronomy, and arithmetic." And in another place the same authority refers to "the long list of Irish scholars who laboured under Charlemagne, his son, and grandson, on French and German soil. A knowledge of Christianity and secular science emanated at that time from Ireland alone of the whole western world, and established itself at many different points: Clement, Dicuil, Johannes, and Scotus Erigina, at the court school, Dungall at Pavia, Sedulius Scotus at Liege, Virgil at Salsburg, and Moengal at St. Gall." And he quotes from Hieric, in his Biography of St.

Germanus, where in his dedication of the book to the Emperor Charles the Bald this ancient writer (who was himself probably a product of Irish teaching) says: "Need I remind Ireland that she sent troops of philosophers over land and sea, to our distant shores, and that her most learned sons offered their gifts of wisdom of their own free will in the service of our learned king, our Solomon."

A quarter of a century earlier, in 849, we have in the writings of Walahfred Strabo a striking illustration of the fact that these Irish wanderers over the Continent, were everywhere looked up to as the exponents of higher learning. Talking of Errebald, a German abbot of noble birth, who recently died, Strabo says, "After being instructed in theology at Reichenau (St. Finian's monastery) he was afterwards sent in the company of some learned men, to an Irish instructor to enjoy the privilege of his training in secular branches of science and the arts." And this bears out the fact, mentioned by O'Halloran and many others, that it became a sort of proverb on the Continent to say of any ambitious one who was for a time missed from his regular haunts, *Amandatus est ad disciplinam in Hibernia.*

About the year 800 Cambrai was a celebrated rallying ground of the Irish. "Not only Cambrai but also Rheims, Poissons, Laon, and Liege, had at one and the same period colonies of Irishmen," says M. Gougand (Les chretiennes Celtiques). "If we consult the evidence given by their contemporaries concerning the learned men that had come amongst them out of Ireland, we must acknowledge that they all show they are conscious of being greatly in their debt for the progress realised in their studies. Irish knowledge is in their eyes *something apart from all else,* and worthy of their most pompous encomiums."

At this same time, Zimmer tells us, Ratgar, abbot of Fulda, was sending scholarly monks to the Irish Clement, to complete their higher secular education. This Clement is, in the official roster of Charlemagne's household, set down as "Instructor to the Imperial Court."

The first coming of Clement and of another noted Irish scholar of the time, Albinus, and their strange introduction to the Continental world, and to Charlemagne, are thus set down by Notker le Begue himself:

> "When Charles began to reign alone in the West, and that learning had almost everywhere become extinct, it happened that two Scots from Ireland arrived on the shores of Gaul, with some British merchants; these two men were incomparably skilled in sacred and profane learning. While they displayed nothing for sale, they cried out to those who came to purchase, 'If any one be desirous of

> wisdom, let him come to receive it.' They were invited to the presence of Charles, who questioned them, and was overjoyed after they were examined: he kept them for some time with him. Charles, soon after this, being obliged to go to war, ordered the one named Clement to reside in Gaul. He recommended to them some very noble youths, some of the middle classes, and several of the lowest ranks; it was also ordered by the king, that everything necessary for their support should be supplied to them, and convenient houses for their accommodation were provided. The other, named Albinus, was sent to Italy, where the monastery of St. Augustin, near the city of Ticinus, was given him, that all who wished to be instructed might come to learn."

The brilliancy of Clement and the work accomplished by him, caused a fourteenth century writer, Luopoldus Bebenburgius, to say, "The French may be compared to the Romans and the Athenians on account of the works of Clement, an Irishman."

There are several authorities cited by Colgan, including Luopoldus and Vincent Daubais, who hold that Clement, not Alcuin, founded the royal school of Paris.

Clement died at Wurtzburg in 826 on a pilgrimage to the tomb of his fellow-countryman, Kilian. His old companion Albinus died in Pavia—where Charlemagne had sent him to conduct the important school there.

Shortly after the death of Albinus, another illustrious Irishman was appointed to succeed him, by Lothaire, the grandson of Charlemagne. This was the astronomer Dungall who is believed to have studied at Bangor. According to Mosheim he was teaching philosophy and astronomy in a French monastery when, in 811, he first came into prominence by preparing for Charlemagne a scientific explanation of two eclipses of the sun, which had occurred the previous year, and which had terrified Charlemagne's subjects. This document, still in existence, betrays the hand and the mind of a master. Zimmer tells us that in Pavia pupils came to Dungall from Milan, Brescia, Lodi, Bergamo, Versalli, Genoa, and Como. While there Dungall won for himself lasting fame by a noted controversy on Iconoclasm in which he engaged, and, it is said, defeated, the Spanish Claudius. It was a controversy that drew world-wide attention. And Zimmer says it was remarkable also as being the meeting on foreign soil of two learned representatives of the only two countries which had maintained and fostered Greco-Roman culture during the barbaric cataclysm. Dungall was not only distinguished as astronomer and theologian, but also as a deep classical scholar. To end his days Dungall retired to the Irish foundation of Bobbio, among the Apennines, to the Library of which monastery he presented forty of his books. The handwriting of that distinguished man is still to be seen upon some of these volumes—now preserved in the Ambrosian Library at Milan.[1]

Another of the many distinguished Irish whom Charlemagne had gathered around him was Dicuil—a grammarian, geometrician, astronomer, and geographer. In the year 816 he published a treatise on astronomy, and in 825 his most famous work, *De Mensura Provinciarum Orbis Terrae.*[2]

This remarkable work, which was evidently a standard Continental geographical work in those days, was discovered by M. Letronne, the Egyptologist, in the French National Library, in 1812, and was then published in Paris. It proved Dicuil to be the earliest geographer giving account of the Faroe Islands, and Iceland—of which latter it mentioned that during a great portion of the year its sun never set.

Letronne was delighted to find in this ancient work "a description of the pyramids, and measurements of them which exactly tallied with his own." Dicuil told, moreover, of a canal connecting the Nile with the Red Sea—which was at first believed to be a grievous slip on the part of the geographer—until the discovery of the fact that a canal long since filled up, and lost to memory, had actually been constructed from the Nile to the Red Sea, by Hadrian.

In his work Dicuil quotes Pomponius Mela, Orosius, Isadore of Seville, and Priscian the grammarian. And Professor Stokes, comparing the Irishman's geography with that of John Malalas of Antioch, says: "Antioch about A.D. 600 was a centre of Greek culture and erudition, and the chronicle of Malalas a mine of information on many questions, but compared with the Irish work of Dicuil, its mistakes are laughable."

This geography of Dicuil's incidentally affords one of the many evidences of the far wanderings of the Irish in those days, inasmuch as he states that he got his information about Iceland on the one hand, and the Hadrian canal on the other, from Irish monks who witnessed what they told him. His Egyptian information he got from a Brother Fidelis, who Dicuil says "told in my presence to my master Siubhne (Sweeney) that he, Fidelis, was one of an

---

[1] Many manuscripts of the Irish monks of Bobbio are now scattered among the libraries of Italy. The Ambrosian library in Milan, the University library of Turin, and the Real Bibliotica Borbonica in Naples, are all enriched by some of these treasures.

[2] For much information about Dicuil see Reeve's paper in the *Ulster Journal of Archaeology*, volume seven.

Irish company who sailed up the Nile and through the canal into the Red Sea"—after they had completed a Jerusalem pilgrimage.

Under Charles the Bald, Sedulius Scotus another famous Irishman—who is not to be confounded with the older (Coelius) Sedulius—taught the school at Liege. He was a Scripturian, theologian, grammarian, poet, political writer, and classical scholar. He seems to have been deeply versed in Greek, and even Hebrew. The French Thurot, writing about the works of Sedulius which are still extant (in manuscript, in French libraries) says, "he makes a parade of his Greek knowledge." In 1825 a work of his upon the Gospels showing his Greek and Hebrew scholarship, was published by Cardinal Mai—from the manuscript in the Vatican Library. There is a Greek psalter of his in one of the libraries at Paris—and also a compilation on the Gospel of St. Matthew. One of his poems indicates that there were at Liege at the same time as himself, other Irishmen who were learned grammarians—one of whom, Cruinmel, left a grammatical treatise of importance.

Usher, in discussing Sedulius' Scripture commentaries says:

> "As for the edition of the Scriptures used in Ireland at those times, the Latin translation was so received into common use by the learned that the principal authority was still reserved to the original fountain. The efforts of Sedulius in the Old Testament commend to us the Hebrew verity, and in the New, correct oftentimes the vulgar Latin according to the truth of the Greek copies"

—a remarkable compliment both to the learning of the man, and the learning of the Irish schools of that age.

In poetry Sedulius was versatile as well as prolific—ranging from humorous verse, through idyllic, up to stately odes. Of one of his poems, the Contest of the Rose and the Lily, Dr. Sigerson says: "It might, for conception and treatment, be one of Moore's, it is so light, graceful, and harmonious. It leads the way to the lighter poetic literature of Europe. Mingled with the measured thread of its hexameters, one hears the musical Irish chimes."

Virgilius (Fergal), celebrated as a pioneer geometer of his day and who was noted for his learning before he left Ireland, was a protégé of King Pepin, through whom he was, in 772, appointed Bishop of Salsburg—while his Irish companion Dobda became a teacher there. In that city he rebuilt, in splendid manner, the monastery of St. Peter. For Chetimar the Duke of Carinthia, he penetrated the forest wilds of that country, preaching and converting, and ordaining priests—as far as the junction of the Drave and the Danube.

He is described by Gaspard Bruschius as a man of extraordinary piety and learning, and again by another writer, as a subtle philosopher and able mathematician. He astonished the scholars by teaching that the earth instead of being flat was a globe, and that human beings like those around them probably lived on the opposite side of it. The Saxon Boniface, who was then converting Germany and who quarrelled with Fergal and other Irish missionaries, brought complaint to Rome against him, accusing him of heresy—evidently misunderstanding or misinterpreting Virgilius' doctrine. Virgilius had previously had a noted theological controversy over infant baptism with Boniface, which when it had been referred to Pope Zachary, was decided in Virgilius' favour. On this new dispute, however, Pope Zachary replied to Boniface: "If Virgilius maintains that there is another world, and other men, another sun and another moon, he must be suspended from the council, the church, and the priesthood."

It is significant, however, that he was neither excommunicated nor suspended—from which it may be inferred that he explained his doctrine in its true light to Zachary. In 1233 Virgilius was canonised by Gregory the Ninth.

In the middle of the ninth century it was that Moengal, returning from Rome with the Irish Bishop Marcus, his uncle, settled at the Irish foundation of St. Gall on Lake Constance—to which monastery his uncle bequeathed his books. Moengal by his learning was destined to make still more famous this monastery to which many of his countrymen before him had brought fame. It had become, it is said, the most venerated monastery in the interior of Europe, and for three hundred years was looked upon as a chief nursery of lore. Dr. Ferdinand Keller says that it was the Irish teachers there who "by their instructions in Greek, rhetoric, and other subjects contributed not a little to the formation of the scientific character which distinguished this monastery."

Moengal here taught theology and sacred science. Zimmer says he excelled in these subjects, "as well as in every other branch of knowledge." He furthermore made St. Gall famous for its musical teaching, to which Moengal seems to have devoted special attention. Three famous pupils of his were Notker le Begue, Rappert, and Tuotillo, men who held foremost places in their century—famous as musicians, and famous along other lines. The versatile Tuotillo was an orator, sculptor, painter, architect, goldsmith, composer and player on all kinds of instruments.

Of this man Moengal, Zimmer says: "In my opinion there were few men, who, in the middle of the ninth century, exerted a more beneficent influence on the German mind, in the cultivation of the higher arts and sciences, than Moengal and his followers." And Wattenbach says of Moengal and the other Irish teachers here: "We may judge of their industry by the study of Greek, the love of music, and the skill in various arts, which distinguishes the monastery of St. Gall above all others."

It is practically agreed by all authorities that the most remarkable scholar known to Europe in the ninth century, whom worshipping Continental scholars called "the Master," was John Scotus Erigina (John the Scot, from Eirinn), philosopher, theologian, linguist, logician, mathematician, and poet, whom King Charles the Bald made head of the Royal school in Paris. He was a genius of such brilliancy as dawns upon the world only once in any century. Zimmer says of him: "He was the greatest thinker of his age, and his philosophic works mark an epoch in the world's literature." And Archbishop Healy, talking of his five books, *De Divisione Naturae,* which he pronounces "profound, original and learned," says: "No other scholar of western Europe, in any age, was so filled with the spirit of the philosophy and theology of the Greeks, and his mind was closely akin to the mind of Greece."

He was a distinguished controversialist. And on the two great problems which were agitating and dividing the theological world at that time, Predestination and the Real Presence, he jumped into the forefront of the fight, and laid about him with true Irish vim and skill. His book on Predestination caused a sensation which could hardly be said to be allayed for generations. The doctrine which he expounded on the Real Presence, which he held to be both a memorial and a reality, almost brought him under a cloud: for enemies stressed the memorial side of his argument, and gave to the world the impression that he taught it was a memorial only.

The cloud darkened his career later, when, without getting the usual apostolic sanction required in such cases, he translated from the Greek, and published, the writings of the pseudo Dionysius, who was alleged to have preached and died in France. The Pope reprimanded his patron, King Charles the Bald, and ordered him to send John away. He must have recovered his standing though, for, only some years later, Anastasius, the Papal librarian—who had declared himself amazed by the brilliancy with which John had translated Dionysius—says in a letter to Charles the Bald, written in March, 875, that John was a man eminent for his sanctity, holy, learned, and humble. And he says he must have been influenced by the spirit of God in making his wonderful translation.

D'Arbois de Jubainville says of John:

> "He was a disciple of Plato, whose Timaeus he appears to have read in the original. And he has founded on the doctrines of that

celebrated Greek writer, a system of philosophy as astonishing for its time, as it is dangerous for its temerity."[3]

Of him and his patron Charles, it is told that once, at the royal dinner-table, when the king felt prompted to dazzle his courtiers by a sharpening of his wit upon the Scot, he asked John, across the table, what was the difference between a Scot and a sot—to which Scotus replied: "Only the table, sire."

The Cathedral school in Wurtzburg late in the eleventh century was taught by the Irish savant, David, who became chaplain and historian to the Emperor Henry V and accompanied the emperor to Rome in 1100.

The scholarship of holy Marianus Scotus of Donegal has already been referred to. There was another Irish Marianus, tutor of Pope Adrian, who taught in the royal school in Paris, about the same time that Marianus Scotus was doing his good work in Ratisbon. And this latter Marianus only accidentally escapes the oblivion to which hundreds and thousands of his exiled learned countrymen were consigned. He seems to have retired in his old age to the monastery of his namesake at Ratisbon. And when Abbot Gregory, who was a successor of Holy Marianus, visited Adrian in Rome, that Pope paid a wonderful tribute to Marianus the Master. The incident is set down in the Chronicles of Ratisbon, which says: "A distinguished Irish ecclesiastic, Marianus, entered St. James's, who had long taught the seven liberal and other arts in Paris. When Gregory was at Rome, Pope Adrian inquired about his old preceptor, and Gregory answered, 'He is well, and with us at Ratisbon.' Said Adrian: 'God be praised! I know not in the Catholic Church another abbot [than you, Gregory] who has under him a man so excellent in wisdom, discretion, genius, eloquence, than this same Marianus.'"

These we have touched on are but a few of the galaxy of Irish scholars whose brilliancy dispelled the darkness, which, in those centuries had threatened to overwhelm Europe.

Same books as for preceding two chapters, and:

Reeves, The Rev. Wm., D.D.: On Augustin, an Irish Writer of the Seventh Century. Proc. R. I. A., 1861.

[3]Usher says that Erigina translated the ethics of Aristotle into Chaldaic, Arabic and Latin—but the Continental writers who have written upon Erigina do not corroborate him in recording this remarkable feat.

CHAPTER XXX

The Vikings in Ireland

The history of the Viking period, which began in the eighth century and lasted for about four hundred years, reads like a fairy tale. There were two impelling motives which led to the emigration of the Vikings, or "men of the bays," for such is the meaning of the name by which they have made themselves famous. These were the inadequate economic resources of their country, due to over-population, and a desire to seek warmer and more fruitful lands. Coupled with this was a spirit of adventure.

At first the Vikings confined themselves to their native fiords whence, in their long open boats, they would dart out and pounce upon some passing vessel. But they soon extended the field of their operations and undertook expeditions to more remote and less known regions, which they laid waste and plundered. Piracy in those days was not regarded as an ignoble profession. About the year 850, they made their way over the stormy north sea to Iceland, where, intrepid sailors as they were, they learned that Irish monks had been there before them. Thence they sailed to Greenland, to Vinland the Good and even reached the coasts of North America. In the east and south, they were no less enterprising and successful.

In the tenth century we find these adventurous sea-rovers making permanent settlements on the continent of Europe. Bands of them sailed down the coast and forced the king of France to yield to them the fair province ever afterwards known by their name, the Duchy of Normandy. More of them went up the Rhine, the Loire, and the Gironde, and fought the Moors on the banks of the Guadalquivir. Others of them pushed on past the Pillars of Hercules into the Mediterranean and built a powerful kingdom in Italy. Still others even found their way to Greece and the Black Sea.

They planted colonies on the coast of Prussia, rounded the North Cape and discovered a route by water to the White Sea. By way of the Dnieper, the Dniester, the Volga and the northern stretches of the Dvina, their enterprising hucksters and freebooters penetrated into the interior of Russia, and in the year 862 laid the foundations, at Novgorod, of the kingdom out of which has grown the modern Russia. Still more of them sailed down the Volga to the Caspian and, by the Dnieper, entered the Bosphorus and nearly succeeded in capturing the capital of the Sultan.

At the other extreme end of Europe more than half of Britain was already in their power. The kingdom of Alfred the Great was threatened and shaken to its foundation, and the outlying islands were entirely occupied by them. They placed a Danish sovereign on the throne of England. Indeed at one time, that is about the middle of the ninth century, it looked as if the Vikings were on the point of becoming masters of the greater part of northern and western Europe. But their victorious career was stopped for all time and the western world saved from becoming Norse by the final defeat which they met with in Ireland.

Intercourse between the northern lands and Ireland must have begun at a very early date. It was only a few days' journey, and, as the Viking vessels were galleys propelled by oars as well as by sails, they were independent of the weather. The Irish traded and married with them a century before the invasion. Even in the old Irish epic of the heroic period, there is mention of warriors from Norway, "the Northern Way," and of Irish chieftains who were levying tribute on the Shetlands, the Orkneys, and the Faroes. The first acceptedly correct information of the Norsemen in "the Isles of the Foreigners," as the western islands were called, dates from the early part of the seventh century. In the year 617 they burned the cloister of Eig, slew the Abbot Donnan and fifty-two of his companions, and, using the western islands as stepping stones, they robbed and ravaged their way down as far as the Isle of Man. It was perhaps in the same year that they laid waste Tory Island off the coast of Donegal. These attacks lasted some four or five years, and were followed by more than a century and a half of peace, during which the Norse and Irish mingled and settled down on friendly terms.

In the year 794 occurred the first powerful Norse attacks in Irish waters, when the sea-robbers landed on Rechru, now Lambay, off Howth, which they devastated, and some other small islands north of Dublin, and simultaneously they launched attacks at such distant points as the Isle of Skye and Glamorganshire in South Wales. These Vikings had no difficulty in landing, plundering, and getting away to their ships, but they brought away what was still more valuable to those who followed them in their profession, namely, tales of bright green fields, of rich fertile soil, in a word, of a land that was well worth fighting for. Such reports brought Vikings in more frequent bands and in greater and greater numbers to Ireland. As yet, however, they were only reconnoitring parties who confined themselves to the islands and forelands and did not interfere with the internal affairs of the country. Sometimes they showed poor judgment in choosing their points of attack, as in the year 823 when they scaled the almost inaccessible Scelic Michil (the Skelligs), far out in the Atlantic, and carried off the hermit Etgal, perhaps in spite at finding no treasure on that barren, wind-swept rock. During the next two or three years, among other misdeeds, they burned Bangor, an easy prey because of its proximity to the sea, murdered its monks and scholars and violated the sanctuary.

At the confluence of the Liffey and a small stream called the Poddle, was a village which the Irish had founded at least two centuries earlier and which they called, and still call, Ath Cliath, "the Ford of the Hurdles." It was also named Dubhlinn, "Blackpool," from the dark colour of the water under the bog. The Norsemen were struck by the excellent location of the village and, consequently, about the year 837, they threw up a strong earthen fort on the hill where now stands the Castle, and for nearly two hundred years Dublin remained an exclusively Norwegian or Danish city and the capital and headquarters of the Vikings in western Europe. The Irish, however, still regarded Armagh as their national capital.

When, about the year 832, the Norse felt ready to make their first great attack on Ireland in force, they had the advantage of having as their leader one of the most extraordinary and capable figures in Nordic history. This was the famous Norwegian warrior Tuirgeis. Tuirgeis, like most of his race who came after him, was filled with ambition to establish a great pagan empire and to make himself lord of Ireland, as his countrymen had made themselves masters of England and Normandy. He came with a great fleet of 120 ships, which held some ten thousand or twelve thousand picked men, and which he divided into two divisions. One squadron of sixty ships entered the Liffey, while Turgeis himself with the other sailed up the Boyne. From these points small bands of invaders entered into the interior of the country, carrying their boats overland with them when necessary, spread here and there and made the first permanent Norse settlements in Ireland. Turgeis confined his operations to the north. He pitched his headquarters at the southern extremity of Lough Ree, near where Athlone now stands, and threw up earthworks along the upper courses of the Shannon and a line of forts across the country from Carlingford Bay to Connacht. He even got some support from the

Irish and for a time it looked as if the whole northern portion of the island might speedily fall under his sway.

His design included the supplanting of Christianity by the heathenism of his own country. With that end in view he took possession, some years previously, of Armagh, Ireland's Holy City, which contained the staff which Christ himself was said to have given to St. Patrick, and where the Abbot, who was regarded as the spiritual head of Ireland, resided. Turgeis drove away "the Follower of St. Patrick," converted the church into a pagan temple and made himself high priest of the new religion. As if that sacrilege was not sufficient to arouse the special anger of the Irish, he is said to have enthroned his wife Otta upon the high altar of the principal church at Clonmacnois, the next most holy place in Ireland, situated on the eastern bank of the Shannon in the midst of the meadows. From that sacred seat Otta, who seems to have been a sibyl as well as a priestess, delivered oracles in magic strains to the people.

These things took place in or about the year 845, and for some years all the foreigners in Ireland recognised Turgeis as their sovereign, though it could hardly be said that he had founded a kingdom. His ablest opponent among the native chieftains was Niall, provincial king of Ulster. Shortly afterwards, or about the year 845, he was, somehow, taken prisoner by Maelsechlainn (Malachy) king of Meath, and drowned in Loch Owel, either as a criminal or by the miracles of the saints, or, according to the legends, through a stratagem of Maelsechlainn's daughter who, accompanied by fifteen young Irish warriors disguised as maidens, kept tryst with him, and fifteen of his captains. After his death, the Norsemen abandoned their settlements on Lough Ree, moved up the Shannon and fought their way along the rivers and lakes to the Sligo coast where a fleet had assembled to carry them home.

Thereafter the tide of victory turned for a while in favour of the Irish, and a new epoch began in the history of the Scandinavian invasion of Ireland. Hitherto the Vikings, like their great leader Turgeis, were all of Norwegian stock, but with a few Danes and Swedes among them. During the tenth and eleventh centuries, however, the Danes, a people of distinct origin, who at that time were ravaging the southern and western coast of England, took the lead in Viking activities. They were better organised than the Norse and had a more centralised government, and they could always fall back on their kingdom in Northumbria, with its capital at York. They were jealous of the successes which the Norwegians had met with in Ireland and they soon proceeded to deprive them of the fruits of their victories, so that it was not primarily owing to a desire to attack the Irish but purely by accident that the Danes came to Ireland and made it the battleground on which to settle their differences with their cousins from Norway. In the words of the annalist (847), "they disturbed Ireland between them." At first the Irish called all these northern raiders indiscriminately *Genti,* "the heathen," or *Gaill* "the strangers," or *Lochlannaigh.* Later, however, when Irish writers felt the need of making a clear distinction between the two waves of invasion, they either limited the name *Lochlannaigh* to the Norwegians and applied the name *Danair* to the Danes, or, more commonly, they called the Vikings of Norwegian descent white heathens, while those of Danish descent they called black heathens.[1]

The year 847 marks the first sudden descent of the Danes, "in seven score ships," upon the eastern shores of Ireland. They at once proceeded to attack the Norwegians and to contest the possession of the coast settlements with them. In that year the Norwegian chieftain Earl Tomar was slain in the battle of Sciath-Nechtin. In 850 the "Blacks" seized and plundered Dublin and in the following year they defeated the "Whites" decisively at Carlingford Lough. The battle was a fierce one and is said to have continued three days and three nights. At first the Norwegians were successful, but finally the Danes, it is said, by calling upon St. Patrick for help, were victorious. After the battle they remembered their promise and sent a huge vat filled with silver and gold to the shrine of the Apostle. Maélsechlainn (Malachy) I, who was king of Ireland at that time, dispatched an embassy to the victors. Five thousand Norwegians with their kings lay dead on the field. The messengers arrived just as the Danes were preparing their evening meal. They had their kettles set up on stakes driven into the

[1] This was not due to the colour of the hair or complexion, for the overwhelming mass of the foreigners, whether Norwegians or Danes, must have been all fair and ruddy. It is to be found only in the fact that the Danes were clad in body armour. The Irish themselves fought in their ordinary dress and mantles, except in combats of special danger when they donned breastplates and aprons of leather. They used light javelins for throwing and longer and stouter spears for thrusting, and swords, and carried a shield of wicker work to defend the body. The first comers among the Norwegians likewise wore only a tunic of leather, but the Danes wore dark metal coats of mail, helmets and vizors, and were partial to the battle-axe. As they were the first mail-clad warriors the Irish had ever seen, it is no wonder if they seemed to them to be "dark blue" or "blue-green," as they called them. There are many references in the old Irish chronicles and sagas to the mail-clad armour and battle-axes of the foreigners and to the black ships in which they came to Ireland. "For the bodies and skins and hearts of the bright champions of Munster were quickly pierced through the fine linen garments, and their very sharp blades took no effect." This advantage which the Danes possessed helps to explain the successes which they met with in the early years of their invasions. But the Irish soon learned in the hard school of experience how to imitate the superior weapons, armour and science of warfare of the enemy.

bodies of the slain and the corpses crackled with the heat. The Irish envoys expressed their horror at the awful sight and reproached the Danes for their barbarity, but the Danes replied that the Norwegians would have treated them in the same manner had they won the battle.

The next year (852), the Norwegians rallied, and a new warlord arrived to take command over them. This was Oláfr enn hvíti, "Olaf the White," as he is known in Icelandic history, or Amhlaobh, in the Irish records, a man of royal descent and belonging to the same race as the famous Turgeis. In the following year (853) he and his countryman Ivar assumed joint kingship over the foreigners in Ireland and set up their capital at Dublin. From there the Norwegians gradually gained ground and established vassal states and a string of trading posts and stations for their fleets along the coast. Many of these settlements bear Scandinavian names from fiords, Strangford and Carlingford, in the north and Wexford and Waterford in the south, for example. The last of these towns was originally called Port Láirge (Portlaw), by the Irish, but the foreigners renamed it Vedrafiordhr, "Weatherhaven."

The most important artery reaching into the heart of Ireland is the River Shannon. On its banks the Vikings, who were most probably Danes, founded and fortified, in the second half of the ninth century, a city which they called Limerick, "Limerick of the mighty ships," as one of the old chroniclers calls it. The city flourished and exerted an influence over all Munster. There was close connection between it and the distant Hebrides, and it was not long before it became a dangerous rival even of the Norwegian kingdom at Dublin, and for a long time there was enmity between them. The two parties engaged in raidings and hostings, just like the native clansmen. Now one side and now the other invited the Irish to help them, and Irish chieftains in turn, in their internecine wars, sought the aid of the foreigners. The first Irish king who is said to have made such an alliance was Aed Finnliath, father of Niall Glúndubh, king of Ulster in the middle of the ninth century. But, indeed, from the time of the first coming of the Northmen to their final defeat, there probably never was a war in which they and the Irish were not, to some degree, banded together.

Irish literature of a thousand years ago is obsessed with the spectre of the Norse occupation of Ireland, and, if we are to believe the native annalists, a night of misery had really settled down on the country with the coming of the Vikings. On the occasion of a raid, villages were burned and sacked and there was wholesale slaughter and enslavement of men, women and children. The foreign soldiers were billeted on the Irish farmers and a heavy tax was laid upon all the people. In default of paying the tax, "nose-money" (a custom which they had brought from their own country), that is, the loss of the nose, was exacted. In the words of one of the old chroniclers, "even though a man had but one cow, he might not milk it for a child one night old, nor for a sick person, but he had to keep it for the tax collector and the foreign soldiers."

There were no walled towns in those days in Ireland and but few and scattered villages. The population of the country was comparatively sparse. Life, except at the courts of chiefs, was simple and primitive. The people were mostly engaged in cattle raising, and their wealth consisted chiefly of flocks and herds and wearing apparel. The nation was broken up into numerous clans, which of course stood in the way of national union.

By the end of the ninth century there were frequent alliances by marriage between the two peoples. According to legendary history, such marriages had taken place as early as the second century. Naturally the annalists tell of such marriages only in the case of Irish ladies of high degree and Viking chieftains but they must have been even more common among the people. The first historical instance of such marriages was that of Iarnkné to Muirgel, daughter of Maélsechlainn (Malachy) I, Emperor of Ireland about the middle of the ninth century. About the same time Amhlaobh, son of the king of Norway, married the daughter of Aed mac Néill. It scarcely ever appears that the wishes of the ladies most concerned were consulted and, as an old Irish poet remarks, "by no means was it happy for them." Some of these women settled down with their husbands in Ireland. Others followed them to Norway or Iceland, and many other Irish women, even of the highest class of society, were carried away as slaves. Thus, inter-marriage and the adoption of Christianity by the majority of the Norsemen, were strong helps towards the assimilation of the invader.

Another help was the custom of fosterage, in vogue among both peoples, according to which Irish children were sometimes adopted even into families of their country's enemies. Some of these children, who had been adopted at the most impressionable age, forsook the nationality and religion of their parents and embraced that of their fosterers. These apostate Irish, together with companies of mixed Irish and foreigners and Gaelic speaking Norsemen from the Hebrides and other western islands, became bandits, scourged the country and plundered the Irish and Norse indiscriminately. The Chronicles call them Gaill-Gaedhel, "the foreign Irish," but the people knew them as "the sons of death," because of their ferociousness. They were especially numerous and active about the middle of the ninth century and their most conspicuous leader was Caitill Finn, "Ketil the White," a man of Norse descent. Finally the Irish chieftains and the Norwegian kings of Dublin joined forces to destroy them and, in the year 857, Ketil was killed by King Amhlaobh of Dublin, who commanded a troop of independent Norsemen in the south of Ireland.

As in some other countries, France, for example, up to the ninth century, the warrior-churchman was a conspicuous figure in Ireland in the ninth-tenth centuries. The most celebrated of all the priest-warriors was the Abbot-Archbishop Cormac mac Cuilennáin, who reigned as king of Munster from 901 to 908. He was also an accomplished scribe and scholar. Besides his native Gaelic he knew Latin, Welsh, Anglo-Saxon, Old Norse, and some Greek and Hebrew, and he compiled the Psalter of Cashel and the *Sanas Cormaic,* "Cormac's Glossary," the very first comparative vernacular dictionary in any language in modern Europe. In the words of an old annalist, "he was the most learned of all who came or shall come of the men of Erin forever." Cormac was a man of peace and would, no doubt, have preferred to devote himself to the quiet pursuits of the student, but, unfortunately for himself, he followed the advice of his turbulent and warlike counsellor, Flaithbhertach (Flaherty), Abbot of Scattery island in the Shannon, who instigated the king to go to war with the men of Leinster. A pitched battle was fought in the year 908 at Belach Mugna (Ballaghmoon), in Kildare, a couple of miles north of Carlow. It was a hopeless attack for the men of Munster and ended in their complete rout and destruction. Clergy and laity were slaughtered without distinction. Cormac himself was thrown from his horse which slipped on the blood soaked ground and his neck broken. The enemy thrust spears into his body and cut off his head. And thus, in the words of the Four Masters, fell "the bishop, the father confessor, the renowned illustrious doctor, King of Cashel, King of Iarmumha; O God! Alas for Cormac!"

A son of the romantic Gormlaith—who had been betrothed to Cormac before he became a religious—was Muirchertach (Murtogh), a soldier of the first rank and heir to the throne of Ireland. He seems to have sworn to avenge his father's death, and from 918 to 943 he carried on the war victoriously against the Danes of Dublin and attacked their oversea settlements in the Hebrides and on the north coast of Scotland. In the depth of the winter of 941, when he was least expected by his enemies, he made a hostage-levying circuit of Ireland at the head of a thousand picked men whom he had clad in leather cloaks, whence he is known as "Muirchertach of the Leather Cloaks." He, too, was finally defeated by the foreigners.

During the first half of the tenth century the Danes gained possession of large parts of the interior of the country. In 914 strong reinforcements arrived at Waterford. They again sailed up the Shannon in a great fleet and into Lough Ree where they plundered the islands and burned Clonmacnois. Their leader this time was Tomrair, king, or son of the king, of Denmark, who, in the words of the annalist, under the year 922, is reported to have gone "to hell with his pains, as he deserved." By the middle of the century, however, fortune again turned in favour of the Irish. They had learned how to build warships and to employ naval tactics after the manner of the Northmen. The most celebrated of the naval battles in which they engaged is connected with the name of Cellachan of Cashel, who began to reign in 934 and who won back Cashel and most of Munster from the Danes. He was afterwards taken prisoner but was rescued in the course of the famous sea fight, which took place in 950–951 in the bay of Dundalk, the foreigners being under the command of Sitric, who was drowned in the battle. After the fight, Cellachan entered Dublin, collected great stores of cattle, gold, silver and other treasures, burned the town and departed.

The most famous hero of the Danish period in Ireland and one of the most famous in all Irish history was the celebrated Brían mac Cennéidigh, son of Kennedy, chief of Thomond, including the eastern portion of the present county of Clare, and hereditary ruler of North Munster. He was born probably about the year 941 and is known to history as Brian Boru, which he took from the name of the town of Bórime, near Killaloe, on the right bank of the Shannon. He was the youngest of twelve brothers, all of whom fell in battle, except Marcán who was a religious and head of the clergy of Munster, and Anlúan who died of a severe illness.

Brian's eldest brother was Mathghamhain (Mahon) who succeeded his father, and in 968 became king of Munster. Mahon was engaged almost constantly in war with the Danes and with the Leinstermen who, as a rule, were in alliance with them, "for there were many Gael who stood by him (Sitric of Limerick), not so much through love of him as through hatred of the Dál Cais (the Dalcassians, the family to which Kennedy belonged)." In 959 Mahon and the Munstermen plundered Clonmacnois. In 965 they destroyed Limerick, and in 968 they fought a decisive battle with the Irish-Norse at Sulchóid, about two and a half miles northwest of Tipperary. The battle lasted from sunrise till midday and ended in the complete rout of the allies. The prisoners were then collected on the hill of Saingel, near Limerick, and "every one that was fit for war was put to death and every one that was fit for a slave was enslaved." In 976 Mahon was betrayed, some say by an Irish prince, and treacherously put to death by his Norse and Irish enemies. Brian, then thirty-five years of age, became king of Munster and took quick vengeance on the assassins. In three years' time he was the undisputed king of the southern half of Ireland.

In 980 Maélsechlainn (Malachy) II, surnamed Mór, "the Great," king of Meath, became emperor of Ireland, and in the same year he won a victory over the Danes at the battle of Tara. Somewhere about that time Brian became the bitter rival of Malachy and made up his mind to dispute the throne with him. In 985, with a great fleet, he sailed up the Shannon to Lough Ree, raided Meath, and did great damage to Connacht. For a few years there was show of friendship between the two kings, and in 998 they came to an understanding, and made a truce according to which, on certain conditions, Malachy was limited as sole sovereign of the northern, and Brian, of the southern half, of Ireland. Thereupon the Leinstermen allied themselves with the Dublin Danes and revolted. Brian and Malachy united their forces, "to the great joy of the Irish," as the Four Masters say, and, in 999, defeated them "with red slaughter" at Glenmáma, near Dunlavin, County Wicklow. Seven thousand Danes are said to have fallen in the battle. The Irish then marched to Dublin which they sacked of its accumulated treasures, ravaged Leinster and expelled King Sitric, with whom Brian himself was afterwards to make peace and alliance.

The two Irish kings soon quarrelled again, and in the year 1002, Malachy, finding that there was defection in his ranks, was compelled to resign his supremacy to the superior force of Brian and to step down to the position of a provincial king. The fact is Brian violated the treaty. As Tighernach, the annalist, says this was the first "treacherous turning of Brian against Malachy."

Both Malachy and Brian were extraordinary men and it would seem as if Ireland was not big enough for both of them. Of the two, Malachy played the nobler part. He was generous, wholehearted, and loyal to his promises, and Brian's superior in unselfish patriotism and in readiness to sacrifice personal pride and personal rights to the welfare and interests of his country. On the other hand, Brian was the more forceful, energetic and capable. He was clearly a usurper and filled with ambition. Yet had he not done what he did, which, after all, is condoned by modern statecraft and was no more treacherous than what has happened hundreds of times in the history of other countries, Malachy or some other rival would undoubtedly have attempted to over-reach him. Had he begun his career at an earlier age and had he not had to contend with foreign invasion, he would no doubt have succeeded in welding the Irish clans into a strongly centralised and compact empire. That design probably never entered into his calculations. As it was, he did achieve that result to a certain extent and his reign was remarkably successful, prosperous and happy.

He had his royal seat at Kincora, a well situated place near Killaloe, on the Shannon, where he ruled with a steady hand, established his power and authority on a firm basis, enforced law and order, imparted rigid and impartial justice, and dispensed a royal hospitality. Though much of his time was given to preparation for war, in which, whenever occasion offered, he always proved himself to be a good soldier, a brave warrior and a skilful strategist, he still found time to build forts, roads and churches. He founded schools and encouraged learning, dispatched agents abroad to buy books, and during his reign the bardic schools began to rise again. He had difficulties with his own people, and indeed his title as emperor was never admitted by the north. Nor were the Leinstermen any too friendly and he had to maintain permanent garrisons in parts of Munster.

On one of several royal progresses which he made through the country, about the year 1004, he invaded Ulster and visited Armagh where he gave alms of a golden ring in which were twenty ounces of gold and where his official secretary and counsellor, and former instructor Maelsuthain O Cearbhaill (O'Carroll), of Loch Léin, reputed to be the best scholar in Ireland, inscribed in the Book of Armagh these words in Latin: "I, Maelsuthain, write this in the presence of Brian, Emperor of the Irish."

Brian even attempted to extend his power beyond the limits of Ireland. In the year 1005 he fitted out a fleet manned by Norsemen from Dublin, Waterford, and Wexford and Irish and pillaged the shores and levied tribute on the inhabitants of northern and western Britain. He did not extirpate the Danes who were domiciled in Ireland or banish them from the kingdom, but treated them with the utmost leniency, and recognised the element of strength they would add to promote commerce and develop the resources of the country. In return for the Dublin Danes binding themselves to follow him in his wars, he was obliged to guarantee them and the other foreigners possession of their territory in Ireland.

In furtherance of this policy or of his personal ambition, he found it to his interest to bind this peace by ties of marriage even with those who so lately were his bitterest enemies. A few months after Glenmáma he gave his own daughter by his first wife in marriage to Sigtryggr (Sitric), his former opponent and king of Dublin, while he himself, Brian, married, as his second wife, Sitric's mother, Gormlaith, a beautiful, powerful and intriguing Irish woman. Like her namesake, the gentle and unfortunate poet-Queen who lived sixty years before her, Gormlaith had a stormy life and her marriage to Brian was her third matrimonial venture. She was first married to Malachy the Great, then to Oláfr kvaran (Amhlaobh "the Shoe"), Danish king of Dublin (celebrated in the history of England), by whom she had a son, the Sitric mentioned above; and finally she was married to Brian Boru, and was prepared to marry, if one can speak of these connections as legal matrimony, for the fourth time, as we shall see later. In the words of the sagaman, "Gormlaith was the fairest of all women, and best gifted in everything that was not in her own power, but it was the talk of men that she did all things ill over which she had any power."

It was through Gormlaith's machinations and deadly hatred that Brian lost his life, and the last act in the long Dano-Irish drama was effected. A series of petty family quarrels precipitated the dénouement. One day, it was in the year 1013, the Leinster prince Maolmórdha (Molloy), who was Gormlaith's brother and consequently Brian's brother-in-law, and in alliance with the Dublin Danes, was bringing three large pine masts for shipping, probably as a tribute, to Brian at Kincora. As his men were climbing a boggy hill near Roscrea quarrel broke out between them and other clansmen, and Maolmórdha, giving a hand to support one of the masts, tore a silver button from a tunic which Brian had given him. On arriving at Kincora he asked his sister to mend the tunic for him, but instead she threw it into the fire, saying he ought to be ashamed to accept any gift from Brian and thus admit his subjection to him, an indignity, she said, which neither his father nor grandfather would ever have suffered. The taunt left a rankling wound in the heart of Maolmórdha. On another day Maolmórdha, looking on while Brian's eldest son, Murchadh (Morrough) and his cousin Conang were playing chess at Kincora, suggested a move which lost Murchadh the game. Then Murchadh angrily exclaimed, "That was like the advice you gave the Danes which lost them the battle of Glenmáma"—to which Maolmórdha replied, "Yes, and I will give them advice again, and this time they will not be defeated."

One word led to another, and the men parted in anger. When Brian heard of the altercation, he sent a man post-haste after Maolmórdha with gifts to appease him and to invite him back to Kincora. The messenger overtook him on the bridge of Killaloe, but Maolmórdha broke the man's head and kept on his way till he reached home where he made known to his people the great insult he had received from Brian's son. He then joined forces with O'Neill, O'Ruarc, Sitric of Dublin and others and attacked Brian's ally, Malachy, near Sord (Swords) a few miles north of Dublin, and defeated him. Malachy appealed to Brian to come to his aid, but Brian was short of supplies and could furnish no assistance.

In the meantime Brian had put away Gormlaith, who was then free to vent all her spleen on him. She was especially anxious to win the help of Sigurd, Earl of the Orkneys. Sigurd, who was Irish on his mother's side, promised to come, provided, in case of success, he should be king of Ireland and have the hand of Gormlaith. For he had ambition to establish a Danish dynasty similar to the one which his countrymen, Svein, and his son, Cnut, had shortly before founded in England. Though his mother wove for him a "raven banner" with mighty spells which was to bring victory to the host before whom it was flown but death to the man who bore it, it was against his own forebodings and those of his men that Sigurd was induced to take part in the expedition.

Sitric next sought help from two Viking brothers who lived on the west coast of the Isle of Man. Ospak was a heathen and Brodar had been a Christian but apostatised, and was regarded as a kind of magician. He was a very tall man with long black hair which he wore tucked in under his belt, and he was clad in a coat of mail "which no steel could bite." He too stipulated that he would come with twenty ships provided he should wed Gormlaith and become king of Ireland. As Sitric was under instructions to get help at any price, he made no scruple to accept the terms on condition that the agreement was to be kept secret. Ospak, who was dissatisfied with the arrangement, escaped from his brother during the night with his ten ships, sailed round Ireland and up the Shannon where he joined Brian and became his ally.

By Palm Sunday in the year 1014, a great host of the massed forces of the Norselands assembled on the shore of Clontarf, a few miles north of Dublin. It consisted of 1,000 mail-clad Norsemen under Brodar, Vikings from Normandy, Flanders, England and Cornwall, and, above all, fierce fighting men from the Orkneys, Shetlands, Hebrides, and other islands off the west coast of Scotland, all picked men and most conspicuous for valour of the men of their time. With them also were the men of their race who had settled in and around Dublin, and the Ui Cinnselaigh (Kinsellas) from Wexford and the men of Leinster. These latter were under the command of their king Maolmórdha. On the side of Brian and Ireland were, besides his own people from Munster, the men of Connacht and Meath and the Christianised Norsemen. He also had an auxiliary force from Scotland under Domhnall, Great Steward of Mar, but he got no help from Ulster.

In spite of his seventy-three years of age, Brian wished to lead his army in person, but his advisers persuaded him to retire to a tent not far from the field and there to await the issue. The real commander of the Irish forces was Brian's son, Murchadh, a captain of outstanding ability, who stationed himself with a select corps of troops from Desmond and Thomond facing Brodar's mail-clad warriors.

On the night before the battle, the Norse said, their old god of war, Woden himself, rode up through the dusk on a dapple-grey horse, halberd in hand, to take counsel with his champions; and there were other portents. Brian was unwilling to fight on Good Friday, but it had been prophesied to the Danes that if the battle was fought on that day Brian would certainly be slain, but, if they fought on any other day, all would fall who were against him. So they forced the battle on Good Friday, which fell that year on April 23. The combat began at sunrise when the tide was at full, and raged till sunset. This celebrated battle is known as the Battle of Brian, or the Battle of the Weir of Clontarf. But, as a matter of fact, the scene of the battle was not at Clontarf at all, but near Clonliffe, between the Liffey and the Tolka, in what are now the outlying districts of Dublin north of the Liffey. In those days the tide flowed over the plain now occupied by Merrion Square, College Green and up to the very walls of the Castle. The Norse battle-line extended roughly from the Four Courts, Rutland Square and Montjoy Square. It was a faulty position, for all retreat was cut off by Tomar's Wood, a part of which is the Phoenix Park, stretching from Drumcondra towards the Liffey. The Irish lay to the north, their right flank at Drumcondra and their left in Clontarf. Both armies are estimated at about 20,000 men, but the Danes were the better armed, many of them being clad in shirts of mail, while most of the Irish fought in tunics. Before the battle, Brian is said to have mounted his charger and, with a golden-hilted sword in one hand and a crucifix in the other, urged on his men to meet the enemy.

Sitric does not appear to have taken part in the battle, but to have held the garrison in reserve behind the walls on the hill of the city, where the Danish women, among them Brian's daughter, looked on from the battlements; and it appeared to them "that not more numerous would be the sheaves floating over a great company reaping a field of oats, even though two or three battalions were working at it, than the hair flying with the wind from them, cut away by heavy gleaming axes and by bright flaming swords."

At the first onset, Brian's men came in contact with the mail-clad men in the Danish centre and were cut to pieces. But the enemy's success was not lasting, and towards evening the efforts of the Irish were crowned with success and the day was saved by the arrival of Malachy's men who were fresh and unwearied.

Part of the enemy fled to their ships at Clontarf, but the returning tide had carried away the boats and prevented the escape of most of them. Great numbers were drowned in the sea and heaps of them lay dead on the ground. Four thousand of them are said to have fallen on Brian's side and

7,000 on his opponent's. Both parties lost most of their leaders, including the brave Earl Sigurd.

During the battle Brian was guarded in his tent at Magduma, near Tomar's wood, by a "fence of shields," or "skjaldborg," as the Danes called it, composed of chosen warriors who surrounded him with their shields locked together. The king is said to have knelt on a cushion with his psalm-book open before him. News was falsely brought to him that his son had fallen. Then a spy or traitor in the Irish camp, said to be Tadhg O Ceallaigh (O'Kelly), king of Ui Maine (Hy-many, counties Galway and Roscommon), who afterwards fell in the battle, pointed out Brian's position to Brodar. The guard was overcome and, according to one account, Brian took his sword, slew the Norse invader and then killed himself; but the Norse account is that Brian was slain by a blow from Brodar who was slain in turn by an unknown hand.

It was a costly victory for the Irish; the king himself, the heir-apparent (his brave son Murchadh), and the heir apparent's heir (Turlough), all fell in the battle. The bodies of the two former were brought to Armagh and interred honourably in a tomb nearby the sanctuary of Saint Patrick. On the conclusion of the battle the troops disbanded, each clan going to its own territory, and Donchadh, Brian's son, who had been away on a foraging expedition and had taken no part in the battle, took command.

But the days of Ireland's glory were departed. In the words of his eulogist, "Brian was the last man in Erin who was a match for a hundred. He was the last man who killed a hundred in one day. His was the last step that true valour ever took in Erin!" He was a sovereign of whom any nation might justly be proud and one of the world's greatest monarchs. Had he or his family lived, the chance is that with the prestige of his name and the great victory at Clontarf, they would have founded an hereditary monarchy which would have put an end to disunion and demoralisation and provided one of the strongest bulwarks against the Norman invasion which was soon to fall upon the country.

But his death and that of his eldest son brought about the displacement of the Dalcassians and the restoration of Malachy to the throne. In the year after Clontarf, 1015, Malachy led an army against Dublin and suppressed the last attempts of the foreigners. He reigned eight years and died in 1022. Brave, magnanimous, and inspired by a lofty patriotism and chivalry, he was the last Irish king to reign without opposition.

After him, as a consequence of Brian's unfortunate violation of the law of the realm, there were few Irish kings who had not to fight for the throne instead of being chosen to it according to custom. Frequently two or more claimants assumed the title at the same time and desolated and distracted the country. These men, who are known for the most part as "kings with opposition," because they were unable to secure general obedience to their administration of affairs, were weaker than their predecessors and their worthless and futile careers only emphasise the greatness of Brian and Malachy. For twenty years after Malachy's death, the chief government was vested in the hands of two men neither of whom was a king, one being Cúán O Lóchán, the king's chief poet, and the other a religious of Lismore named Corcrán.

The battle of the Weir of Clontarf was one of the decisive battles of history, for it not only warded off Danish rule from Ireland but it probably even altered the whole subsequent history of Europe. Had the Danes been victorious and gotten possession of Ireland, they would doubtless have founded there a kingdom which would have been the greatest step towards the formation of a far-flung northern empire, with its centre at London. For three centuries they strove desperately for possession of the prize, but they were unable to accomplish in those three hundred years in Ireland as much as they had accomplished in one year in northern France and in England.

After Clontarf the Danes who were left in Ireland settled down and became as Irish as the Irish themselves, but nearly 100 years after the battle the foreigners made a final attempt to get control of Ireland. In the year 1098 the famous Norwegian king Magnus Barelegs, so called because he dressed in the Irish fashion, who fills a large place in the romantic history of the period, came to Ireland with a mighty force. He had conquered the Hebrides and Man and had already made many visits to Ireland, and was more than half Irish in feeling and culture. He used Irish in his poems and was in love, as he says, with "the Irish girl whom I love better than myself." According to the Manx Chronicle, he sent his shoes to Muirchertach, Emperor of Ireland, and ordered him to wear them on his shoulders on Christmas day in the presence of his ambassador, as a token of submission, and Muirchertach obeyed the command. Other old chronicles say that Magnus married Muirchertach's daughter and that afterwards he sent her back to her father. When he was killed in battle in Ulster, in the year 1103, he left a son, afterwards King Harald Gille, who was born, either in Ireland or the Hebrides, of an Irish mother.

The Viking age was by no means a starless night in Ireland, nor was society so horribly disorganised as is generally believed. It was a period marked by the lives of Irish chiefs of outstanding ability, of some of the greatest figures in Nordic history, and of women of unusual personality.

Even in those days of terror and danger from foreign invasion, when an enemy fleet stood in every port and soldiers were encamped in many parts of the country, Ireland was still in the full current of European life. Though internecine feuds and battles with the Danes took up much of the chieftains' time, other things besides spears and swords were exchanged between the Irish and the invader. In no other land in which these two peoples of such different culture came together did each learn so much from the other as in Ireland. In matters of agriculture and cattle raising the Irish were the teachers of the Norsemen, but in other purely material pursuits the civilisation of the Norse was superior to that of the Irish. Though by the middle of the seventh century, in the pre-Viking period, Ireland had made considerable progress in the art of ship construction, it was above all from the hardy sailors of the north that they learned to build and sail great ships and to organise fleets, to use iron armour, to fight on horseback and no longer from chariots or on foot, to build stone forts and bridges, and to live in fortified cities surrounded by walls. By the middle of the tenth century, Dublin, Limerick, Cork, Waterford, all Viking establishments, were strong walled places.

Nor were the Vikings mere sea robbers; they were merchants as well. Since they controlled the seas, for a long time all trade and shipping between Limerick and other Irish ports and the west of France and Spain was in their hands. They exported Ireland's products and imported all that Ireland wanted, as wheat, wine, costly silks, and fine leather, and they helped to introduce foreign fashions into Ireland. The first Irish coins that were struck in Ireland were minted by Norse kings who held court in Dublin; they have been found in Norway and elsewhere, and point to the trade carried on between the two countries. The Irish probably also adopted the northern system of weights and measures.

How much Irish society and domestic life were influenced by Norse occupation is seen in the Irish language itself, in which there is scarcely a word meaning a large ship or its parts or markets or trade that is not borrowed from the Norse, if it is not from the Latin. Even the name by which, in English, we call Erin, is from the Old Norse Iraland, and the English names of three of the present-day provinces, Munster, Leinster and Ulster, have a Norse termination, *stadr,* "place," added to the Gaelic stem. Donegal (Dun na Gall), "the Fort of the Foreigners," got its name from a fort built by the Vikings. But these are the exceptions. There are scarcely more than a dozen Norse place names on the whole map of Ireland and these are mostly on or near the sea coast, while there are over a thousand in middle and northern England. This is one of the surest signs that there was no real conquest or occupation of the country. The Norse and the Irish had to understand each other to some appreciable extent, and it was the language of the invader that gave way to that of the invaded.

As a result of intermarriage, there was an exchange of Irish and Scandinavian personal names, and such typical Irish names as Cormac, Patrick, Dubthach (Duffy), are found in Norse sagas. The children of these marriages were called Mael-Muire, Gilla Pátraic, and other Christian names. On the other hand, some Norse personal names such as Somhairle (MacSorley), Rághnall (MacRanald), Amhlaobh (MacAuliffe), Dubhghall (Doyle), Mághnus (MacManus), Iomhar (MacIvors), have become popular and important surnames.

Though the Viking invasions checked the normal development of Irish civilisation, undid what the efforts of successive centuries had realised, and gave Ireland such a shock that learning scarcely ever fully recovered from it, a brilliant intellectual life prevailed during that period and, in all the things that pertained to the mind, the Irish were far superior to their invaders and Irish genius made itself felt upon them. The names of Norse students are found among those who attended Ireland's most celebrated university, Clonmacnois, in the first half of the eleventh century. Streams of professors, students and missionaries continued to flow to the continent, some of them no doubt fleeing from the Vikings.

Irish sculpture, building, metal work, art, and ornament, flourished and influenced the art of the Scandinavians. The most important and most beautifully illuminated manuscripts, both in Latin and Irish, date from that period, and some of the greatest poets in Irish literature, such as Flann MacLonáin, "the Vergil of the Gael," Cináed ua Hartacáin, Eochaid O Flinn, Cormacán Eces, MacLiag, the court bard of Brian Boru, and many others flourished in it. It was Irish scholars who introduced the literature of Greece and Rome to the men of the north. At the Norwegian court of "Dublin of the Festal Drinking Horns," Icelandic skalds and Irish bards composed and sang their poems, and Irish and Icelandic sagamen, the best story tellers in the world, told their stories. The Irish influence on the early literature of Iceland is unmistakable. Indeed, the Norse were the imitators of the Irish, and certain northern types, motives and forms of style are clearly of Irish origin or have been developed through Irish influence. The Irish were also of considerable influence in softening the wild manners of the Norsemen with whom they came in contact, and, above all, it is to the Irish that they owe their Christianity. For at least two generations before Clontarf, Christianity had taken deep root among the Norse in Ireland, and, by the end of the tenth or beginning of the eleventh century,

Dublin was a complete Christian city with churches and cloisters and was known as Ath Clíath na cloc, "Dublin, rich in bells," Ath Clíath na land's na lecht, "Dublin the city of churches and graveyards."

Besides the general histories of Ireland and works in German and the Scandinavian languages (which give the best account of the period), the following books are recommended:

C. F. Keary: The Vikings in Western Christendom, London, 1891.
George Henderson: The Norse Influence on Celtic Scotland, Glasgow, 1910.
Eleanor Hull: Irish Episodes of Icelandic History, Saga Book of the Viking Club, Vol. III, 1908.
Alice Stopford Green: Irish Nationality, Chap. IV, New York, 1911.
Eoin MacNeill: Phases of Irish History, Chap. IX, Dublin, 1919.
Alexander Bugge: Contributions to the History of the Norsemen in Ireland, Christiania, 1900.
Charles Haliday: The Scandinavian Kingdom of Dublin, Dublin, 1884.
James H. Todd: Edit., The War of the Gaedhil and the Gaill, or the Invasions of Ireland by the Danes and other Norsemen, London, Rolls Series, 1867.
The New Ireland Review, Vols. XXIII, XXIV, XXXIII.
The Ivernian Journal, Vol. IV, pp. 73–87.

CHAPTER XXXI

Hospitality in Ancient Ireland

A characteristic of the Irish race for which it has been noted through the ages is its hospitality. In pre-Christian days this quality shone as much as it did in later time. But in later time the virtue was given a sublimely Christian turn. "Christ is in the person of every guest," and "every stranger is Christ," were the sentiments that came to consecrate hospitality. The attitude of the Irish people on the subject is well expressed in one of their ancient poems (translated by Kuno Meyer):

Oh King of stars!
Whether my house be dark or bright,
Never shall it be closed against any one,
Lest Christ close His house against me.

If there be a guest in your house
And you conceal aught from him,
'Tis not the guest that will be without it,
But Jesus, Mary's Son.

As with the Arab, so with the Irish, any one who had partaken of food in one's house, was thereby sacred against harm or hurt from all members of the family. A person of rank had to entertain any stranger without enquiring who or what he was or the wherefore of his coming. Against the coming of unknown guests his door must be open,[1] and his fire must always have on it the *coire ainsec,* undry cauldron.

---

[1] When, in comparatively recent days, the Connaught princess Grainne O'Malley was returning from the state visit which she paid Elizabeth of England, she landed at Howth, and finding Lord Howth's

A guest came when he liked, stayed while he would, and left when he wished. No matter how many the guests that thronged one's house, or how lengthy their sojourn, under no conceivable circumstances could it be intimated to them that they should depart. And, furthermore, under no circumstances, in those times, could or would a guest, departing from any house howsoever poor, so far forget the respect due his host, as to offer any kind of compensation. There is a Munster story of a rude, wild mountaineer, who visited England, four or five centuries ago, and who, among the many wonderful tales of Saxonland which, on his return, he had to tell, had none more extraordinary, more unbelievable, than that the English people actually charged for the food, liquor, and bed, which they provided for a stranger!

The Irishman, who, on the arrival of travellers, discovered that he had not food and drink in the house with which instantly to regale them, suffered keen disgrace. This applied to all ranks, including royalty itself. If the disgrace was incurred, not through wilful negligence on the part of the host, but by the defection of one who had contracted to supply him with provisions, the latter was, then, rendered liable by law to pay to the disgraced one a blush fine, *enech-ruice.*

In the old Irish poets and writers we find a man reckoned wealthy not by what he has but by what he gives. And the right hand of the generous man was often said to have grown longer than his left.

It will be remembered that in the time of the Tuatha De Danann, their king, Breas, was deposed because he lacked the first essential, hospitality: "Breas did not grease their knives. In vain they came to visit Breas. Their breath did not smell of ale at the banquet."

In the early days, because in many districts people might be too poor, or travellers too many, for satisfactory private hospitality, there were, at various points throughout the land, public houses of hospitality called

---

castle-gate closed—as the family and household were at dinner—she, incensed by such Saxon churlishness picked up from a nurse outside the gates and carried off with her to Connaught Lord Howth's child. The Howth family had to pay a goodly ransom for their child—and thereby taught a proper lesson in Irish hospitality. Ever after, when they went to dinner their gates and doors were thrown wide open.

A century or so ago the MacSweeneys of Cork had a stone erected on the highway near their home to notify all travellers that they were expected to call at the MacSweeney home for entertainment.

In the last century the famous Dick Martin of Connemara (who, by the way, was the first man to promote a law against cruelty to animals) used to have a servant awaiting the coming of the long-car to the village some miles off (which was the end of the public conveyance route) whose duty it was to extend the hospitality of his master's house to strangers who arrived on the car.

bruideans (breens). And the honoured officials who were entrusted with these houses were called brughaids (brewys). A bruidean was always set at the junction of several roads, frequently the junction of six. It had open doors facing every road—and a man stationed on each road to make sure that no one passed unentertained. It had a light burning on the lawn all night. A full cauldron was always boiling on the fire. It was stocked with provisions of all kinds in plenty.

The esteem in which was held the virtue of hospitality is exemplified by the fact that the public brughaid was, by law, permitted the same number of attendants, and given the same protection, as the king of a territory. His hospice was endowed with land, and with other allowances. The brughaid had a magistrate's jurisdiction for arbitration of agrarian cases. His house, too, was the house of assembly for election of officers of the territory.

As the brughaid was required to welcome, at all times, every company and every face, his bruidean must always be stocked with three boiled fleshes, three red fleshes (i.e., uncooked) and three living fleshes. The three fleshes were those of an ox, a wether, and a hog. The three living fleshes must be at hand, fattened, and ready for immediate killing; the three red fleshes dressing in the kitchen; the three boiled fleshes in the boilers, ready for instant serving.

Every brughaid was required to have at least a hundred of each kind of animal grazing on his fields—and a hundred servants in his house. He was called a brughaid ceadach, meaning a hundred brughaid. There was a brughaid leitech, two hundred brughaid, who had two hundred of each kind of cattle, and a hundred beds for guests. The good brughaid was expected to have in his house the three miachs (sacks)—a miach of malt to make refreshment for wayfarers, a miach of wheat to give them food, and a miach of salt, to improve the food's taste. Also the three cheers, the cheer of the strainers straining ale, the cheer of the servitors over the cauldron, and the cheer of the young men over the chess-board, winning games from one another.

The six chief bruideans of Ireland were asylums of refuge for homicides—like the six Jewish cities of refuge. Keating estimated the total number of such houses of hospitality in Ireland, as being over four hundred. He says there were ninety in Connaught, ninety in Ulster, ninety-three in Leinster, and a hundred and thirty in Munster.

The Small Primer (Brehon Laws) says:

> "He is no brughaid who is not possessed of hundreds. He warns off no individual of whatever shape. He refuses not any company. He

> keeps no account against a person, though often he come. Such is the brughaid who has *dire* with the king of a territory."

The Irish monks and missionaries on the Continent carried with them to Europe the Irish idea of the House of Hospitality—and established regular lines of these in France, and through Germany, for entertaining the crowds of pilgrims who journeyed to Rome on the one hand, and to Jerusalem on the other[2] including, of course, the crusaders.

The same idea of providing for those who needed it materialised in other directions—as in the case of the very old and dependent. In each territory was an officer called uaithne (signifying pillar), whose duty it was to provide for such as had not any of their own kin to do so. The law provided the uaithne with power to levy a rate for the maintenance of these dependent ones. He was called uaithne because the law tract describes him as "a pillar of endurance and attendance."

If the dependent did have kin but did not choose to live as one of them, the uaithne was to see that a house was provided for him that must be at least seventeen feet long, have two doors, a chest at one side, a bed at the other, and a kitchen or storehouse. Also that he was supplied with a prescribed amount of food, of milk, and of attendance. His head was to be washed every Saturday, and his body every twentieth night. There is displayed a true knowledge of human nature, and a praiseworthy indulgence of the crankiness and abusiveness of the old and dependent, in the wise provision of this law which rules that, contrary to universal custom, the uaithne can suffer the reddening of his face without disgrace to himself or to his kin.

The stories told of a certain seventh century king of Connaught, Guaire the Hospitable, illustrate the very high regard in which hospitality and generosity were held. Once, being beaten in battle by one of the kings Diarmuid, Guaire, in token of submission, had to kneel in front of Diarmuid and take in his teeth the point of the victor's sword. When he was in this humiliating position, Diarmuid, to test whether his famed generosity was sincere or ostentatious, had, first, one of his Druids ask of Guaire a gift in honour of learning—to which request the humiliated Guaire paid no heed: and then a leper ask an alms for God's sake, to whom Guaire, with teeth still closed upon the sword point, gave the gold brooch from his mantle. At the secret

[2] Throughout early Irish history and story, the several references to pilgrims to Jerusalem are made so casually as to suggest the confident inference that great numbers were constantly going. The pilgrimage to Rome seems to have been very common.

instigation of the king, one of his people forced the brooch from the leper, who at once complained of his loss to the kneeling one. Guaire immediately unlinked the golden girdle that bound his waist, and reached it to the leper. This gift was instantly also taken from the poor man, when, with sore complaint the leper came a third time to Guaire. Realising the poor man's distress, and knowing that he had nothing more to give, Guaire's tears ran from his eyes in a stream.

"Arise, Guaire," said Diarmuid, "and do homage only to God!"

Diarmuid then brought his late foe with him to the great fair of Taillte. As was usual with him, Guaire brought to the gathering a sack of silver to make presents to the men of Ireland. Diarmuid, however, had secretly ordered that none should ask or accept a gift from his royal guest. When he had been two days at the fair, he sent for a bishop to give him the last rites of the church. Diarmuid and his friends, alarmed, asked why he sought the last rites. "Because," answered Guaire, "I have seen the men of Ireland for two days assembled together in one spot, without any of them asking me for a bounty. Surely it is the end."

Then Diarmuid lifted the ban, and Guaire was happy once more. In the presence of the men of Ireland, the peace was ratified between the two kings, who kept it ever after.

If Guaire was generous, his enemy, Diarmuid, was considerate. For when the latter, marching to give battle, was met by a messenger with the request that as Guaire was not yet fully prepared to give him battle, he should not cross the river for another twenty-four hours—"I gladly grant his request," said Diarmuid, "and would have granted him a much greater, had he asked it."[3]

---

[3] The ancient historical and poetic accounts are full of instances of this kind of battle chivalry—showing that usually a leader considered it disgraceful to attack an unprepared foe.

It will be recalled that Gol MacMorna could not be induced to surprise an enemy by attacking before daybreak.

We have a fine sample of this chivalry in the Agallam na Seanorach. When Caoilte, with the lute player and the man of beauty, was visiting Bo-bind of the Tuatha de Danann at Assaroe, to get cured of a spear-thrust in the calf of his leg, on a night of revelry there, the alarm was raised that a fleet of maraudimg foreigners (Famorians) had sailed into the harbour. Caoilte was appealed to for his advice in the face of impending disaster, and answered: Let them be asked for a truce till the Tuatha de Danann make a gathering and a muster. "And thus it was done," adds the poet narrator, with naïve simplicity.

The most notable historical instance of this kind of chivalry occurred in the year 1001 or 1002 when Brian Boru demanded from the then Ard Righ, Malachi, submission and hostages—"The latter replied to Brian's ambassadors," says Keating, "by saying that if Brian would grant him a respite of one month in order that he might have time to summon around him the army of Leth-Cuin, he would, at the end of the period, either give battle or send hostages to the king of Leth-Mogha." But

Furthermore, Guaire's messenger, having thoroughly viewed Diarmuid's army, disparaged it to the king for the smallness of their numbers and the poorness of their appearance—to which Diarmuid answered: "Knowest thou not that neither by numbers nor by brave apparel is a battle won, but by the will of God, and a truthful cause. And though thou sayest our host is mean to look upon it is not fair forms but hardy hearts that win a fight."[4]

Joyce, P. W.: Social History of Ancient Ireland.
O'Curry, Eugene: Manuscript Materials of Irish History.
—— Manners and Customs of the Ancient Irish.
Hyde, Douglas, LL.D.: A Literary History of Ireland, from the earliest times to the present day.
Keating's History of Ireland.

---

when Aod O'Neill, king of Ailech, refused to support him, Malachi, at the end of the month journeyed to Brian, and told him frankly that he was not able to get the backing he wished, and consequently regretted he would have to give hostages and submit. Brian, however, instead of at once accepting, entreated Malachi to take a respite of one year to see if in that time he might not do better. In the meantime he himself would ask the submission of Aod O'Neill—and also of the King of Ulidia—"that I may learn what kind of answer they make to me; and then, should they give me battle, thou mayest help them against me if thou wilt." But Malachi refused, declaring that he would not fight against him after any such manner.

Let us imagine, if we can, some of our noble kings and generals in this twentieth century civilisation emulating in chivalry the old Irish "barbarians."

[4] While considering signal virtues of men in those days, it is not inappropriate to set down here a sample of the chivalry and the great boldness of another king of Connaught, Ailill. Ailill was a wanton and a sinful king, who often and recklessly warred upon his enemies. But there came at length a battle in which he was overwhelmingly defeated. As he fled afar from the bloody field, he called upon his charioteer:

"Look behind and see whether the slaying is great, and are the slayers near us."

The charioteer looked behind him, and what he said was: "The slaying with which your people are slain is unendurable."

"Not then their own guilt falls on them, but the guilt of my pride and untruthfulness," said the king. "Turn thou the chariot toward the enemy, for my slaying will be the saving of a multitude."

And he faced the pursuers and gave his life to stay the slaughter. And King Ailill, a monster of wickedness living, in dying won the peace of God.

CHAPTER XXXII

The Tribe

There were nearly two hundred tuaths or territories, in Ireland, each occupied by a tribe, under its chief who was oftentimes designated king of a tuath.

The subdivisions of a tuath were *ballybetaighs* of which there were usually thirty to each tuath. The ballybetaigh was again subdivided into twelve *seasreachs,* each of one ploughland or about one hundred and twenty acres. The ballybetaigh was supposed to be of extent to supply grazing for four herds of seventy-five cows each, "without one cow touching another."

In general, the whole of the lands of the territory belonged to all the tribe. But there was a limited circle, including the king, the nobles, and a few of the leading professional men, each of whom had private rights in a certain portion of the land—the right to use those lands for the benefit of himself and family, but not to transfer them to any person outside the tribe.

The foregoing refers only to special portions of the tribal land. The greater part of the tribal land was free for the use of all the people of the tribe.

These privileged ones who had exclusive rights to the use of certain lands, usually rented large portion in parcels to the *céiles* (tenants)—who formed the *féine,* or general body of the people.

The privileged person usually also rented to the céile cattle for stocking the land. The céile who owned his own stock, or who had to borrow but little, was of much higher standing than the céile who had to borrow or rent all his stock. The former was called a free céile, and the latter an unfree because he was bound to those above him by so many obligations.

The stock borrowed from a noble (or from a certain class between the noble and the céile called *bo-aire,* who had stock to rent) was returned, it or its equivalent, at the end of seven years.

Below the céiles—the féine, or general body of the people of the tribe—were two classes usually rated as non-free. One of them was the *bothach* and *sencleithe,* who were labourers, horse-boys, herdsmen, and hangers-on, supported by particular families to which they were attached, and who were considered members of the tribe, but had neither property rights nor any voice in the tribal council. The other, the *fuidir,* were strangers, fugitives, war captives, condemned criminals or people who had to give up their freedom in order to work out a debt or fine that they could not pay. These latter, were not of the tribe, only belonged to it, and were serfs, pure and simple. Only, they had the right of renting a little land and gradually acquiring property—till, in the course of a certain number of years, having accumulated some substance, and having proved to the tribe that they were people of character, they could, by the general voice of the tribe, be received into the fold, and become of the *féine.* Of course the *bothach* and *sencleithe* were privileged to raise themselves even more easily than the *fuidir.* The very humblest might, by inherent worth, work his way up to be eventually among the noblest. So, the class system in Ireland was not a caste system.

It was only the *fuidir,* the mere flotsam and jetsam of the nation, who were in the state of semi-servitude. The feudal system, the system of the lord and the serf, which was the rule throughout almost all the countries of Europe then, was never known in Ireland—at least not until the English, after they had established footing there, endeavoured to introduce from their own country a form of it. The system in Ireland was something more like the patriarchal system of the east. The tribe resolved itself into family groups called *derb-fine*[1] centring around one leading family from whom the chief was always chosen.

The law of inheritance in ancient Ireland was not that of primogeniture, but of gavel-kind—that is, instead of the eldest son inheriting all the father's property, it was divided, cattle and land, among all the sons. But the eldest son got, with his share, the house and offices and household effects. Special responsibilities fell to him as guardian of his sisters, and of his brothers under age, and as the representative of the family in all cases of stress or need.

The laws protected every one, including the base fuidir. They were especially framed to protect the weak against the strong. "No person," says

[1] Four generations sprung from one man usually went to each derb-fine—so that in each succeeding generation the groups had to be re-arranged.

the law, "shall be oppressed in his difficulty." And the law forbade the rent-payer to give service or rent to one who would exact unjustly. The greedy oppressor had to repent and pay a fine before his céile should resume giving him either rent or service.

The céile contributed to the head of the tribe a certain amount of labour, a portion of the household needs, and a certain number of days military service, which was demanded when the need arose.

But the chief, or king of the territory—as well as the provincial king and the Ard-Righ—kept about him a number of paid permanent troops—his household troops composed of his own people, and a small standing army usually composed of mercenaries. And the strongest, most powerful man was chosen as the king's *airechta*, champion or avenger.

The king of the tuath paid tribute to the provincial king, who in turn paid tribute to the Ard-Righ. And on the other hand, each of the higher kings paid back to his tributary a small courtesy tribute called *tuarastal*. The Book of Rights specifies in full, and curious detail, the *cis*, or amounts of the tribute in cattle, in cloaks, in swords, etc., due from each inferior king to his superior—and likewise the tuarastal from the superior to his inferior.

The headship (whether chief or king) was hereditary only to the extent that the ruler was always chosen by the people, from within one family. From the *righ-damna* (king material) that is, the royal uncles, brothers, sons, nephews, grand-sons and grand-nephews, the people chose whatever male member of the family would make the wisest, bravest, and best ruler. In later centuries, in order to avoid the evils of disputed succession, the king's successor was always chosen during the king's lifetime—and this king-elect was called *tanaiste*. He had to be without physical blemish or deformity. When elected he had to swear to observe the law, and to govern in accordance with the law and the ancient customs. At the inauguration the ollam, in presence of the people, read to him the laws that he must swear to observe, and the ancient customs that he must swear to maintain. And for non-observance of these, he was liable to be, at any time, deposed.

Same books as for preceding chapter, together with:

Sullivan, W. K., Ph.D.: Introduction to O'Curry's Manners and Customs of the Ancient Irish.

CHAPTER XXXIII

Manner of Living in Ancient Ireland

In very early Ireland practically all residences were of wood or of wicker-work, and most of them were in circular form. They were usually thatched with straw, rushes, or sedge. Stone was very seldom used in building residences before the eighth century. The wooden and wicker-work houses were washed with lime on the outside—lime in its natural white state, or coloured with pigments. The older stories and poems show that houses of the better kind had windows that were shuttered. These early residences were seldom divided into apartments—though the stories show that compartments for sleepers were often made along the walls of a large building.

Linen sheets and ornamented coverlets were in use. Small low tables for serving meals were supplied with knives (no forks), with cups, jugs, drinking horns, methers, sometimes with goblets of glass (a precious rarity, however), goblets of silver, flagons of bronze or copper—and occasionally napkins. Cooks wore flat white caps and linen aprons. Wheat meal, oat-meal, eggs, meat, milk and honey, with some vegetables and a very few fruits, supplied the table. Light was furnished by candles of tallow or of beeswax, rushlights, spails of bog fir, and sometimes oil lamps. The lights were stuck on the walls, stood on the tables, were held by attendants, or hung from above.

The residence of one of the higher ranks was either on a lios (a raised mound of earth), or a rath (a lios protected by a surrounding wall, usually of earth), or, in case of a chief or king, a dun, which was a fortified rath having a couple of surrounding walls with a water-filled ditch between.

All of the better class houses had basins for bathing. And the select few had scented oil and fragrant herbs, as accompaniments of the bath. After their day's exertion, and before taking their evening meal, hunters and warriors treated themselves to a bath. And a bath was always a common courtesy to which to treat a newly arrived guest.

The women had mirrors made of highly polished metal. They used cosmetics, and had combs which were often beautifully wrought, and embossed cior-bolgs (comb bags) in which they carried comb, veil, and personal ornaments. Both sexes devoted the greatest attention to the care of their hair, which was often elaborately curled, and often also plaited in several long plaits the ends of which were fastened by little golden balls—one or two large ones on the heads of the men, and six or seven small ones on women's heads. Both women and men (of noble rank) wore beautifully wrought brooches, for fastening their mantle, and beautifully wrought girdles, also. Other ornaments were bracelets, rings, neck torques, diadems, crescents, of gold and silver—beautiful specimens of all which may be seen in the National Museum in Dublin and in the British Museum. Veils and gloves were in use—and sandals likewise.

The chief articles of dress were, in the case of the women, one long robe that reached to the ankles, and of the men a short jacket combined with a sort of kilt. Over these both sexes frequently wore a cloak or mantle. The substance of the dress was usually either of linen or wool. But sometimes it was of silk or satin, imported.

The cloak or mantle was a distinctive and prized article of dress, the one to which most thought was given, and on which most value was expended. In details of gifts and tributes told of in the old stories, and in accounts of beautiful cavalcades, the mantle gets prominent place. For instance, the Book of Rights detailing the tuarastal payable from the king to subordinate kings says:

"Seven mantles with wreaths of gold,
  And seven cups for social drinking,
  Seven steeds not accustomed to falter,
  To the king of Kerry of the combats.

"The prosperous king of Rathlenn is entitled
  To the stipend of a brave great man;
  Ten swords, and ten drinking horns,
  Ten red cloaks, ten blue cloaks.

"The king of Ara of beauty is entitled
  From the king of Eire of the comely face,

To six swords, six praised shields,
And six mantles of deep crimson."

In the poem of the Bruidean da Derga, the Saxon chief Ingcel, in describing King Conaire Mor as he saw him in the Bruidean, gives a glorified description of a king's dress in the early days:

"I saw his many-hued red cloak of lustrous silk,
With its gorgeous ornamentation of precious gold bespangled upon its surface,
With its flowing capes dexterously embroidered.

"I saw in it a great large brooch,
The long pin was of pure gold;
Bright shining like a full-moon
Was its ring, all around—a crimson gemmed circlet
Of round sparkling pebbles—
Filling the fine front of his noble breast
Atwixt his well proportioned fair shoulders.

"I saw his splendid linen kilt,
With its striped silken borders,—
A face-reflecting mirror of various hues,
The coveted of the eyes of many,—
Embracing his noble neck—enriching its beauty.
An embroidery of gold upon the lustrous silk—
(Extended) from his bosom to his noble knees."

The law prescribed that sons of kings in fosterage were to have satin mantles, of scarlet, purple, or blue; scabbards for their little swords, ornamented with silver. Sons of the higher kings were to have their mantles fastened with a brooch ornamented with gold. A son of a king of a tuath, a brooch ornamented with silver.

Mantles and capes were sometimes trimmed with furs of native animals, seals, badgers, otters and foxes.

In welcoming a guest the usual courtesy was for the household to arise to their feet. Sometimes also the host greeted him with a kiss on each cheek. At larger assemblies, as for instance at the king's court, the visitor was sometimes received "with clapping of hands." The custom of the handshake was not used or known.

The guest was feasted with the best that could be had, and he was entertained with story and with poem, with music of the harp, the pipe, or the tympan. Chess was the game always provided—the great and universal game, in which the Irish were highly skilled.

Another entertainment, which however was peculiar to Courts, was that provided by professional jesters and jugglers, buffoons and druiths. The same Ingcel whom we just quoted describes Conari Mar's three court jesters:

> "I saw there," said he, "three jesters at the fire. They wore three dark grey cloaks; and if all the men of Eirinn were in one place, and though the body of the father or the mother of each man was lying dead before him, not one could refrain from laughing at them."

And of Tultinne, the king's juggler, Ingcel says:

> "He had ear-clasps of gold in his ears; and a speckled white cloak upon him. He had nine swords in his hand, and nine silvery shields, and nine balls of gold. He throws every one of them up (into the air), and none of them falls to the ground, and there is but one of them at a time upon his palm; and like the buzzing of bees on a beautiful day, was the motion of each passing the other."

The druith is often interpreted to be a buffoon—but he must have been of an entirely different and indeed far superior order, when we recall the druith Ua Maighlinne (who belonged to the court, at Ailech, of Fergal the son of Maelduin, in the beginning of the eighth century). On the eve of the great battle of Almain (Allen) he entertained the northern warriors by narrating the battles and triumphs of these northmen, and also of their enemies the Leinstermen, from the earliest time down to the time that was then present. And this Ua Maighlinne, taken prisoner in the battle and about to be beheaded, was asked to give the *Geim Druath*, or druith's cry, before he died. And so loud, beautiful, and melodious was this peculiar cry that for three days and three nights after his death the enchanting soft echoes of it were still reverberating about the spot.

The description given of that other wonderful and versatile entertainer, Donnbo, who went on the same expedition, and lost his life in the same battle, may well describe the druith. And, because of its dramatic beauty, we shall make room for it here:

> "And there was not in all Eirinn one more comely, or of better shape or face, or more graceful symmetry, than he; he was the best at singing amusing verses and telling of royal stories in the world; he was the best to equip horses, and to mount spears, and to plait hair; and his was the best mind in acuteness of intellect and in honour."

So famed and so popular was the clever and witty Donnbo that when Fergal summoned the men of Leth Cuinn to go with him upon this expedition, what each of them answered was: "If Donnbo go upon the expedition, I will."

And on the night that was the eve of the battle, on the hill of Allen, when Ua Maighlinne told them the stories, it was Donnbo who had been asked to amuse them, but had refused because his heart was weighted with sad prescience of the morrow's disaster. But he promised that if Ua Maighlinne amused them tonight he would make amusement for his royal master, wheresoever he should be, on the next night. On the next night his royal master and thousands of his devoted ones, not only warriors, but pipers and trumpeters, and harpers, were dead upon the field of carnage. And Donnbo, like his royal master, had had his head severed from his body. A warrior of Murchad, the victorious King of Leinster, who, on a dare from his king came alone to the battlefield at dead of night to bear from it a trophy, heard a voice in the air above the battlefield, calling upon Donnbo, in the name of the King of the Seven Heavens to make amusement tonight, as he had promised, for Fergal the son of Maelduin. And in answer the warrior first heard the dead singers and trumpeters and harpers make music the like of which he never heard before or after. And next, from a cluster of rushes, he heard the head of Donnbo raise the *dord-fiansa*, the sweetest of all the world's music: for Donnbo was keeping his promise to amuse the king. The warrior wished to take back the head of Donnbo to amuse the Leinster king, but Donnbo's head said: "I prefer that nothing whatever should carry me away unless Christ, the son of God, should take me. And thou must give the guarantee of Christ that thou wilt bring me back to my body again." The warrior, giving the guarantee, carried to his king's camp the head of Donnbo.

> "Pity thy fate, O Donnbo," said Murchad and his company, "comely was thy face. Make amusement for us, this night, the same as thou didst for thy lord, yesterday." That it should be the darker for him Donnbo turned his face to the wall, and raised the *dord-fiansa* on high. "And it was the sweetest of all music ever heard on all the

surface of the earth! So that the host were all crying and lamenting with the plaintiveness and softness of the melody."

Same books as for preceding chapter, together with:
Carbery, Ethna: In the Celtic Past.

CHAPTER XXXIV

Structural Antiquities

The structural antiquities which we can still observe in Ireland arrange themselves under five heads: cromlechs, tumuli, the great duns of the west, ancient churches, and round towers.

The cromlechs, sometimes called dolmen, are each composed of three great standing stones, ten or twelve feet high with a great flat slab resting on top of them, and always inclined toward the east. Sometimes these are surrounded by a wide circle of standing stones. The cromlechs are of such very remote antiquity—ancient, at the beginning of the Christian era—that all legends of them are lost. The invariable inclination to the east of the covering slab suggests altars dedicated to sun-worship. The name cromlech may mean either bent slab or the slab of the god Crom. And this latter derivation suggests to some that they were sacrificial altars used in the very ancient worship of that god.

But some of the best authorities have concluded that they were tomb-stones—because beneath every one of them under which excavations were made, were found the bones, or the urns and dust, of the dead. From this, however, we cannot necessarily conclude that they were erected as tomb-stones—any more than we should conclude that the various Christian temples and altars under which honoured ones have been interred were only intended as monuments to the dead beneath them.

Excavations made beneath many cromlechs have turned up, besides urns and bones of the dead, tools of flint and stone, axes, hammers, chisels, spear-heads, knives, and also rings of shale and jet—thus showing that the cromlechs were erected in the far-away Stone Age. And, as Miss Margaret Stokes points out, an advanced religious condition for such age is evidenced by the fact that they then celebrated funeral rights in tombs of imposing grandeur, with cremation, and sometimes urn burial.

The tumuli or enormous burial mounds found in the Boyne section of eastern Ireland show the race in a much more advanced stage of civilisation. These tumuli, as proved by the decorative designs carved upon their walls, were erected at least before the Christian era—and maybe many centuries before it. They are great stone roofed royal sepulchres, buried under vast regularly shaped, artificial mounds. Every one of the tumuli so far explored has shown urn burial. These urns of the tumuli are a marked advance upon those of the cromlechs. Some of them are beautifully formed, and delicately ornamented. Many urns may be found in the same tumulus. Sometimes they are set with one large one in the centre and other small ones circling around it. The walls of the sepulchral chamber, in the interior of these mounds, are oftentimes decorated with carvings, made with chisel or punch, and scraper. The patterns are the circle, semi-circle, half-moon, concentric circle, spiral, zig-zag, stars, and leaves. The double divergent spiral or trumpet pattern, which was introduced into Celtic ornament just prior to the Christian era, has not yet appeared in the tumuli.

The greatest, most beautiful, of these wonderful royal tombs are those at Knowth, Dowth, and New Grange, on the Boyne.

After the tumuli, the next structures in order of time are the great duns of the west coast, such as Dun Angus, and Dun Conor, on the Aran islands in Galway Bay. The great duns were erected sometime during the first three centuries of the Christian era. They consist of enormously thick walls, of stone, which, though built before the discovery of any kind of cement, are of marvellously fine, firm, and impregnable construction. These great walls, in the interior of which are sometimes chambers and passages, surround an amphitheatre of about a thousand feet in diameter. In the amphitheatre are stone huts, the residences of the dun—some of them of bee-hive shape, some of them of the shape of an upturned boat. Tradition says that these great duns were erected by the Firbolgs who maintained themselves along the western fringe for long centuries after the Milesians possessed themselves of the land. Moreover, in the second century of the Christian era a new colony of Firbolgs is said to have arrived in Aran; a tribe led by Angus, who, in that century, coming from the western islands of Scotland (to which they had been driven long centuries before) first settled in Meath, but, fleeing from an exacting king there, went westward, and finally settled in Aran and on adjoining portions of the mainland.

About the round towers, their origin and use, a more bitter controversy has waged than about any other ancient Irish remains. It had been the opinion of many, sustained by the researches of some noted antiquarians, that the round towers were of oriental origin, that they were temples of the sun-worship of ancient Ireland, and that they were erected long before the introduction of Christianity. But the antiquarians now are pretty generally agreed that they are of Christian origin always built as adjuncts to churches, and erected after the marauding Danes had shown the harassed ecclesiastics the need of some immediate, strong, and easily defended, place of refuge for themselves, and of safety for the sacred objects, and the rich objects of church art which the Northmen constantly sought. The round towers of Ireland range in height from about a hundred to a hundred and twenty feet; they are from twelve to twenty feet in external diameter at the base, and a little narrower at the top. They are of six or seven storeys high; with one window usually to each story—except in the uppermost story which has four. The lowermost of these openings is always about ten feet or more from the ground—giving good advantage over attackers. The walls are usually three and a half to four feet thick.

There are still eighty round towers in Ireland, twenty of them perfect. They are always found in connection with churches—and almost invariably situated about twenty feet from the northwest corner of the church—and with the door or lowermost window facing the church entrance.

The antiquarians today conclude that round towers began to be erected at the end of the ninth and beginning of the tenth century—in the period of peace that followed the death of the Danish king Turgesius, and the temporary loss of the Danish grip upon Ireland. The first reference in the annals to a round tower is in the year 950. It is upon the inference to be derived from this fact, taken in connection with the activities of the Danes—and that to be derived from the relation of the round towers to the churches—that is built the now accepted theory of the Danish-time origin of the round towers, as places of ecclesiastical refuge.

Almost all of the earliest Irish churches were of wood. The Venerable Bede talks of the Irishman, St. Finan, erecting on the English island of Lindisfarne, "a church entirely of wood, after the manner of the Scots." Rarely indeed in the first few centuries of Christianity in Ireland was any such building erected of stone—the exceptions being the cases of small oratories or chapels, which, like the oratory of Gallerus (in Kerry) were built of uncemented stone with side walls gradually converging till they were joined by a single stone at the top. It is in the seventh and eighth centuries that the use of mortar and of dressed or partly dressed stone shows in the erection of the occasional small chapels for which stone was yet used.

It was practically in the tenth century that the use of stone for building the large churches began. And it was only in the eleventh and twelfth centuries that it became general. In these last-named centuries the Romanesque style was introduced, and some beautiful churches erected, like that of St. Caimin at Inniscaltra by Brian Boru, and Cormac's chapel at Cashel.

In the Life of St. Malachy, written by his friend, the continental St. Bernard, we incidentally learn how rare, in some parts of the island, were stone churches even then, in the twelfth century. After Malachy had taken charge of Bangor—the old foundation of St. Comgall—he first built a chapel "made indeed of planed timber," says St. Bernard, "but well-jointed and compactly put together, and for a Scottish work elegant enough." And later, more ambitious, he astounded the territory by starting to build a stone church. The ubiquitous pessimist was there to help Malachy along. St. Bernard describes the rude country-fellow turning up to laugh to scorn the idea of building a church of stone! "What has come over you," says the fellow, "to undertake such a novelty in this country? We are Scots, not Gauls. How are you, a poor man, to finish it? Who will live to see it perfected?" And so on, in the usual strain of the helpful hurler on the fence.

The handsome stone churches which began to be erected in the early eleventh century—as soon as the country had been freed from the scourging Danes—and which engrafted the Roman arched style upon the Irish horizontal form, with the primitive Irish inclined jambs, was well established when the Anglo-Normans invaded the country in the late twelfth century. And from that time forward, for some centuries (till the Reformation began to make itself felt in Ireland) the Anglo-Norman barons and the Irish chieftains vied with each other in the erection of many magnificent churches and abbeys, the ruins of which are impressive.

In the decorating of doorways and windows, sculpture began to show in the churches of the tenth century. But Irish sculpture is best exemplified probably on the high crosses of the tenth, eleventh, twelfth and thirteenth centuries. There are some forty-five of these high crosses still remaining, most of them very beautiful. There was an Irish cross, now called the Celtic cross, developed about the tenth century, a compromise between the Latin cross and the Greek cross, having the circle of the Greek cross placed upon the shafts of the Latin. The sculpture on the high crosses included carvings of the saints, scriptural scenes, judgment scenes, royal processions, hunting scenes, stags at bay, horsemen, chariots, etc.

The sculpture of the Irish at this period was infinitely superior to that produced by their neighbours, the Welsh, the Anglo-Saxons, and the Scottish. With these sculpture was a mere harsh, mechanical imitation. But the soul of the artist breathed through the work of the Irish sculptor. Miss Margaret Stokes well defines the difference:

> "So total a dissimilarity of spirit and feeling for Art exists in the works of these different countries, that it becomes impossible to conceive their productions as belonging to the same school. It would be difficult to find two works of Art more different in character than the simple form of the Cross of Ualla in Clonmacnois, and the barbarous extravagance of the Scotch slab at Halkirk in Caithness. Something more than archæology is required to perceive this, and to perceive the qualities which form the essential elements of the individuality of Irish Art. It is not in the quantity, it is not even in the nature of ornamental detail, that true merit lies; it is in its use, and in that indefinable quality which, for want of better word, we term feeling. It is unreasonable to call sculpture, however perfect, which is merely encrusted on any object, ornament. Decoration is beautiful only when found in its right place, when adding to the effect of the fundamental form to be adorned; and when held in subordination and subjection to the primary idea, a noble reserve of power is felt to exist, which comes forth at the right time, and in the right place, to aid in the expression of the essential elements of the subject, emphasising its important points, and adding clearness to the beauty of its outline.
>
> "It is in such qualities that the Manx, Welsh, and some of the Scottish stones are so deficient, as compared with the work upon the sepulchral slabs of Clonmacnois, and Durrow, and other Christian cemeteries in Ireland; and the conclusion our experience would point to is that such Art out of Ireland belongs to much the same date as that seen in this country, but is in no essential element Irish, and merely belongs to a style which overspread the three countries in the ninth and tenth centuries, and which attained a more beautiful result in Ireland, because in the hands of a people possessed of a fine artistic instinct."

Petrie, Geo., LL.D.: The Origin and Uses of the Round Towers of Ireland.
—— Ecclesiastical Arch. of Ireland.
Stokes, Miss Margt.: Early Christian Art in Ireland.

—— Early Christian Architecture in Ireland.
Joyce, P. W.: Social History of Ancient Ireland.
O'Curry, Eugene: Manuscript Materials of Irish History.
—— Manners and Customs of the Ancient Irish.
Wakeman, Wm. F.: Handbook of Irish Antiquities, Pagan and Christian.
Ware's Works.

CHAPTER XXXV

VARIOUS ARTS OF ANCIENT IRELAND

Save that of the scribe, there was no other art in ancient Ireland carried to such beautiful perfection as that of the metal worker. And we have, still remaining, hundreds of beautiful pieces of this work.

Those remaining are in gold, silver, copper, bronze, findruine (a kind of white bronze) and brass. Of Irish gold-wrought objects alone, there are in the National Museum of Dublin twelve times the weight of all the ancient gold objects from England, Scotland and Wales, collected in the British Museum.

These ancient objects are of various kinds; articles of personal adornment, bell-shrines, cumdachs or shrines for books, croziers, etc.

Among the personal ornaments we have brooches, bracelets, rings, necklaces, torques (twisted ribbons of gold or silver) for wearing around the neck, minns or diadems, crowns, amulets, earrings, beads, balls, crescents, gorgets, the niam-lann (a flexible plate of burnished gold, silver, or findruine worn around the forehead), et cetera—a lavish wealth of beautiful ornaments exquisitely wrought, which, after a long count of centuries, in some cases thirteen, fifteen and twenty, tell us the story of the rarely skilled, noble artificers of Ireland, whose genius in metal was not only unsurpassed, but even unequalled, in western Europe. Of a bronze ornament two thousand years old and of which there are some fragments in the Petrie Museum, Kemble (in Horae Ferales) says: "For beauty of design and execution they may challenge comparison with any specimen of cast bronze work that it has ever been my fortune to see." We have many beautiful bronzes of the pre-Christian period, which, in their way, rival the beauty of the gold and silver work of several centuries later.

And of the very ancient gorgets wrought in gold, Dr. Joyce says: "They are so astonishingly fine, and show such extraordinary skill of manipulation, that it is difficult to understand how they could have been produced by mere handwork, by moulds, hammers, and punches. Yet they must have been done in that way." He quotes Sir William Wilde as pronouncing of them:

> "It may safely be asserted that for both design and execution, they are undoubtedly the most gorgeous and magnificent specimens of gold work discovered in any part of the world."

In a country in which, in faraway pre-Christian times, such rarely beautiful ornaments were wrought, surely it needed little poetic license for the old filé, when describing Maine, the son of Ailill and Medb, setting out to seek the hand of the beautiful Ferb of Ulster, thus to picture it:

> "There were seven greyhounds attending his (Prince Maine's) chariot, in chains of silver, with balls of gold upon each chain, so that the tingling of the balls against the chains would be music sufficient (for the march). There was no known colour that was not to be seen upon these greyhounds. There were seven Cornaire (trumpeters), with corna (horns) of gold and of silver, wearing clothes of many colours, and all having fair-yellow hair. Three druids also went in front of them, who wore minda (diadems) of silver upon their heads and speckled cloaks over their dresses, and who carried shields of bronze ornamented with red copper. Three Cruitire (harpers) accompanied them; each of kingly aspect, and arrayed in a crimson cloak. It was so they arrived on the green of Cruachan."

Or for the ancient seanachie, telling us that in Tara there were "one hundred and fifty drinking vessels, ornamented with gold, silver, and carmogal" (possibly enamel).

After studying the wonderful specimens of the ancient metal-work which we possess, we can well understand why it was that nobles and saints oftentimes devoted themselves to the profession of metal-working, and also why it was that the laws rank all followers of the profession with nobles. And, it is worth noting in this connection, that it was from Irish ideas, springing from Irish minds, and by Irish hands in Ireland, that the rare articles in gold and silver were rarely wrought. In corroboration of their native conception and origin, Dr. Joyce in his Social History of Ireland quotes the decision of a Continental expert, M. Solomon Reinach, who had studied the Irish gold ornaments in the National Museum: "Of objects of gold, attesting imitation of Greek and Roman models, there is no trace."

The objects that are of pre-Christian origin are in general easily distinguished from those of Christian Ireland by the difference in pattern. The ornamentation in pagan days consisted chiefly of the circle, spiral, lozenge, and parallels. Under the hand of the Christian artist there developed new patterns the most characteristic being the divergent spiral or trumpet pattern, knotting and interlacing.

Of all the many beautiful articles of personal adornment that remain to us from those ancient times in Ireland, probably the most luxurious, and very frequently the most beautiful (though far from being the most ancient) are the delgs, or brooches—the size and costliness of some of which may be judged from the Dal Riada brooch, which, accidentally dug up in an Antrim field in the middle of the last century, contained two and one-third ounces of pure gold, was five inches long, and two and an eighth inches in diameter.

But for beauty, none of them all equals the Tara brooch. This brooch, found by a child on the strand near Drogheda, is of white bronze. Both the face of the brooch and the back are overlaid with beautiful patterns, wrought in an Irish filigree or formed by amber, glass and enamel. These patterns of which there are no less than seventy-six different kinds in this single article are wrought in such minute perfection that a powerful lens is needed to perceive and appreciate the wonderful perfection of detail. All of the many designs are in perfect harmony; and the beauty of the whole can only be realised by actual sight and study of the remarkable object itself. There are many other handsome ancient brooches, such as the Ardagh brooch, the Roscrea brooch, et cetera—each with peculiar beauties of its own, showing some point or points of superiority to the Tara brooch, but none of them equalling it in total effect.

Only by a very different kind of object, the celebrated Ardagh chalice, is the Tara brooch surpassed in richness and beauty of workmanship. A partial description of this celebrated chalice is here extracted from Miss Stokes' detailed description in her "Early Christian Art in Ireland":

> "This Irish chalice combines classic beauty of form with the most exquisite examples of almost every variety of Celtic ornamentation. The cup is composed of the following metals: gold, silver,

bronze, brass, copper, and lead. The ornaments cut on the silver bowl consist of an inscription, interlaced patterns terminating in dogs' heads, and at the bottom a circular band of the Greek pattern. The mode of ornamentation is peculiar to this cup, being done with a chisel and hammer, as indicated by the lines being raised at each side, which could only be produced in the manner decribed. Round the cup runs a band composed of two semi-cylindrical rings of silver, ornamented with small annular dots punched out with a hollow punch. The space between the rings is filled by twelve plaques of gold repoussé work, with a very beautiful ornamentation of fine filigree wire-work wrought on the front of the repoussé ground, and carrying out, in its most delicate execution, the interlaced pattern associated with the art of this country. Between the plaques are twelve round enamelled beads.

"The handles of this chalice are composed of enamels (similar to those in the borders) and plaques of gold filigree work of the same style, but different in design. Each handle has four circular pieces of blue glass, underneath which the rivets are secured which fasten the handles to the bowl. Round the enamels was a circle of amber, divided into eight spaces by pieces of bronze, which has been eaten away. One of the enamels has a circle of gold grains at the top, which has been pressed in while the glass was in fusion. The two circular ornaments on the side of the bowl are of gold filigree work of the very finest kind, with an enamelled boss in the centre; the frames which hold them are of silver. There are four settings at equal distances, which are receivers of the rivets that secure it to the bowl. In the settings were two pieces of blue glass (the same as in the handles), and two pieces of amber, which have fallen out.

"The stem and supports of the bowl are of bronze metal, gilt, beautifully carved in interlaced and knotted patterns. They are attached to the bowl by a bronze gilt ball, with a strong square tang, and most ingeniously fastened by an iron bolt, which secures all together.

"The foot is of silver, circular, with a framework on the outer rim, having eight spaces, which are filled alternately with gold and bronze gilt plaques of open work; behind them pieces of mica are inserted, which throw out more clearly the very beautiful pierced designs with which these plaques are ornamented. The intermediate spaces contain enamels (inferior to those in the upper part of the bowl), set in bronze.

"In the inside of the foot of the bowl is a circular crystal, round which there has been a circle of amber, divided into twelve tablets, with a bronze division between each tablet; surrounding this is a circle in gold filigree of the same style and workmanship as those already described. The next circle had tablets of amber, but they have all fallen out. In the space between this and the silver is a circular bronze plate, highly carved and gilt, in which are fine enamels in green.

"The extreme outer edge, like the reverse side, is divided into eight spaces, in which are pieces somewhat similar to the gold plaques on the opposite side, with this difference, that six are in silver and two in copper; two of the silver pieces are of the most beautiful plated wire-work I have ever met with. Between those spaces are square pieces of blue glass, underneath which are ornamented pieces of wrought silver, which give them a brilliant appearance when in strong light. Between the circles which form the upper and under surfaces of the rim of the foot are plates of lead to secure and give weight to the whole. The enamels on the foot of the cup are of a coarse kind, the pattern being impressed in the glass, and the enamel melted into it. The number of pieces of which the cup is composed amounts to 354, including 20 rivets.

"The ornamental designs upon this cup belong to the Celtic School of Art, which, according to Dr. Petrie, reached its highest perfection as regards metal-work in this country in the tenth and eleventh centuries. Of these designs there are about forty different varieties, all showing a freedom of inventive power and play of fancy only to be equalled by the work upon the so-called Tara brooch.

"There are two varieties of birds, with heads, necks, and legs elongated, and interlaced; and also animal forms interlaced. There are four dragons' heads, with sharp teeth which bear a strong resemblance to drawings of similar objects in the 'Book of Armagh': also dogs, whose long protruding tongues form a knot above their heads.

"Besides these ornamental designs there are two pieces of plaited silver wire, bearing a strong resemblance to Trichinopoli work."

In the remains of beautiful metal work which we have, representative of various parts of the early ages, there seems to be, strange to say, a gap, when we come to the early Christian centuries of Irish history. We have the magnificent bronzes of the various pre-Christian ages, and again the truly extraordinary work, the brooches, et cetera, of the gold and silver smiths of the tenth to the twelfth centuries—but little or nothing between. Dr. Petrie, in considering the absence of ecclesiastical shrines, representative of those early Christian centuries, concludes—and other authorities agree with him—that the raiding of the Danes may account for this. Before the coming of the raiders he thinks there were few of the churches without beautiful shrines. Both directly and indirectly the Danish raiding might also account for the lack of profane objects of art, representative of those centuries—the transition period between that which is distinctively of the pagan time and that which is distinctively of the Christian. During the Danish time the annals are filled with such suggestive references as, for instance, they "devastated Clonmacnois and took therefrom great spoil of gold and silver, and many precious ornaments." (Annals of Ulster.)

Of the latter span there are in existence many wonderful bell shrines, like that of St. Patrick's bell, St. Cualanus' bell—and shrines like the shrine of St. Mogue, the cross of Cong, the crozier of St. Dympna, the crozier of Liosmor, the crozier of Clonmacnois, et cetera, all of them exquisitely displaying the extraordinarily beautiful work of the artists of those days. The shrine of the bell of St. Patrick, studded with gems, has silver plates ornamented with scrolls, and has handsome golden filigree knot-work. Animal forms on the sides are drawn out fantastically and doubled and twisted into interlaced scrolls.

The making of beautiful shrines called cumdachs, for prized books, rarely occurred in any part of the world except Ireland, where it was comparatively common.

These book shrines, made for particularly prized and valuable books which had sacred association, were tastefully wrought, and richly ornamented—usually by saintly artificers. In the Martyrology of Donegal, for instance, it is said of St. Ernin whose festival is on August 18th: "Ernin, i.e., Mernog, of Fotharta of Leinster, a celebrated artificer. It was he who made 150 bells, 100 croziers, and cumdachs for 60 gospels."

The cumdachs were being made from the eighth century to the late twelfth, and even later. Some of the finest and most celebrated cumdachs are those of the Book of Kells, the Book of Armagh, the Book of Durrow, the Domnach Airgid (containing St. Patrick's Gospels), the Cathach or Battlebook of the O'Donnells (containing St. Colm Cille's Psalter), Dimma's book, the Book of St. Moling, the Stowe Missal, and of St. Malaise's Gospels.

Ordinarily the books of those days were carefully kept in leathern satchels upon the embossing of which, in rare patterns, the plentiful artists of those days bestowed much thought and time and skill.

But the first of the artists and probably the rarest of them, the man who blazed the way for both the leather worker and the metal artificer, was the scribe, who, in copying the sacred books was in the habit of ornamenting their pages and decorating their margins with the Irish knotted and interlaced patterns, and also of beginning the chapters with an initial of elaborate and intricate design, frequently illuminated in colours that time does not fade. In decorating and illuminating the old manuscript books of Ireland he exhibited skill and genius unparalleled in the world elsewhere.

The work of these artist scribes was such as to compel Giraldus Cambrensis—who would rather libel Ireland than laud her—to write of an Irish manuscript volume which he saw in Kildare, that it seemed to him more like the work of angels than of men. He says:

> "If you look closely with all acuteness of sight you can command, and examine the inmost secrets of that wondrous art, you discover such subtle, such fine and closely wrought lines, twisted and interwoven in such intricate knots, and adorned with such fresh and brilliant colours, that you will readily acknowledge the whole to be result of angelic rather than human skill. The more frequently I behold it, the more diligently I examine it, the more numerous are the beauties I discover in it, the more I am lost in renewed admiration of it. Neither could Apelles himself execute the like: and indeed they rather seem formed and painted by a hand not mortal."

The Irish scribes in the sixth, the seventh, and the eighth centuries carried their art to a perfection which today surprises, and sometimes amazes, artists, scholars and critics of all nations. An eminent German authority upon such work, Dr. Waagen, Conservator of the Royal Museum of Berlin, speaking of the old seventh century Irish Book of Kells says:

> "The ornamental pages, borders, and initial letters exhibit such a rich variety of beautiful and peculiar designs, so admirable a taste in the arrangement of the colours, and such an uncommon perfection of detail, that one feels absolutely struck with amazement."

And the English authority, Westwood, in his Palaeographia Sacra Pictoria says of this Irish art:

> "At a period when the pictorial art may be said to have been almost extinct in Italy and Greece, and indeed scarcely to have

existed in other parts of Europe—namely, from the fifth to the end of the eighth century—a style of art had been originated, cultivated, and brought to a marvellous state of perfection, in these islands, absolutely distinct from that of any other part of the civilised world—and which having been carried abroad by numerous Irish and Anglo-Saxon missionaries—was adopted and imitated in the schools founded by Charlemagne and in the monasteries established or visited by the former, many of which in after ages were the most famous seats of learning."

Furthermore, Westwood quotes on the same subject the words of Digby Watt (whom he styles "one of the most accomplished living artists"):

> "In delicacy of handling and minute but faultless execution the whole range of palæography offers nothing comparable to these early Irish manuscripts and those produced in the same style in England—the latter being the work of Irish monks, or Saxon pupils of those monks."

The Irish manuscript books of the early ages—both those in Ireland and the many treasured in a score of the great libraries of Europe—eloquently tell to these late ages not merely the marvellous skill of the Irish scribes, at home in Ireland and wandering everywhere over the Continent, but likewise tell of the highly advanced state of culture (of which this was the flowering) that obtained in Ireland fourteen hundred years ago. And they, furthermore, prove the certainty of preceding centuries of culture needful to account for such perfect efflorescence.

Great were the numbers of learned and pious men who devoted their lives then to the making of beautiful books, copying them in that penmanship whose perfection was, not merely unequalled, but even unapproached, by any other people—and which throughout foreign countries made Ireland, already remarkable, for her learning, pre-eminently so for her caligraphy. For several centuries it was the Irish style of caligraphy, introduced by the Irish teachers, which obtained throughout the European countries.

Ferdinand Keller says that the high degree of cultivation attained in Irish penmanship was not the result of mere individual excellence, but of the emulation of numerous schools of writing, backed by the improvements of many generations.

The activity in copying books then, and the number of scribes engaged in the work, must have been enormous. When we find recorded in the

Four Masters' chronicle of one century (the eighth) the deaths of no less than forty scribes so pre-eminent as to find place in a nation's annals nine hundred years later, we may in some measure imagine how vast must have been the ranks of ordinary workers. And as a corollary from that we may, to some extent, conceive of the multitude of the books of ancient Eirinn.

Miss Stokes accounts for the style of ornamentation and illumination of these books by an art wave which she says originally came out of the southeast of Europe, and swept over the Continent northwestward, finally breaking upon the shores of Ireland—and remaining with Ireland when all traces of it had vanished in the countries over which it had passed. And in the Carlovingian period, when Irish monks and teachers were thronging abroad, the wave, reversing itself, rolled backward over its former course. Traces of this peculiar Irish art, knotwork, and interlaced patterns, most suggestive of the Irish designs, may be found in the very oldest churches in Lombardy, she says, and in the second and third century churches of Syria and Georgia. She acknowledges, however, that if her theory be correct, Ireland so modified the character of this eastern wave of art, as to evolve from it something distinctively Irish.

Dr. Ferdinand Keller as a result of his study of the subject came to the conclusion that because of striking similarity of technique and peculiarities of colouring, Egypt was the cradle of Irish art. We know that early Irish holy men were in Egypt, and some of the old records show that Egyptian monks came to Ireland; the Irish monasteries, Keller says, were framed precisely after the model of the Egyptian ones, even the habit of the hermits dwelling in caves was brought therefrom. The productions of Alexandrian artists, he says, found their way to Irish monasteries. And the serpentine band found in this Irish art work appears in the very oldest Egyptian and Ethiopian manuscripts, "with similarity of colour and combination, truly astonishing." He finds, moreover, that the spirit of the Irish work is not the spirit of the west: "In all these ornaments there breathes a peculiar spirit foreign to the people of the west: in them is something mysterious which imparts to the eye a certain feeling of uneasiness and suspense which must have originated in the east and could not possibly have been the creation of a fancy which derived its nourishment and stimulus from natural objects so devoid of colour and form as present themselves in northern Ireland and the rocky isles of western Scotland.

Romilly Allen's opinion (in his work on Celtic Art) would sustain Miss Stokes and Dr. Keller in their theory that Irish Art, so called, did not originate in Ireland. He holds that the Celt never originated his art ideas, but had a genius for attaching the ideas of others, and giving them such a strong Celtic tinge as entirely changed the outward character and produced something apparently original.

Though many of the ancient Irish manuscripts are lit up with truly wonderful examples of the illuminating art, there is not in all of them, anything finer or more wonderful, nor is there to be found in any of the ancient books of the world anything more beautiful, than the famous monogram of Christ in the Book of Kells.

That monogram, which occupies a full page, is preceded by five illuminated pages, introducing the Gospel of St. Matthew, every one of which is in itself of much beauty. The series is crowned by this one expressing the name of Christ. Miss Stokes puts it:

> "In these six pages there is a gradual increase of splendour, the culminating point of which is reached in this monogram of Christ, and upon it is lavished, with all the fervent devotion of the Irish scribe every variety of design to be found in Celtic art, so that the name which is the epitome of his (the artist's) faith is also the epitome of his country's art."

In examining this remarkable monogram a powerful microscope is needed to bring out all the beauties that are difficult of discovery to the naked eye, and to follow the magic pen of the artist, through all his minute, intricate, elaborate windings, twistings and knottings. This will be appreciated when it is mentioned that on one piece of a ribbon pattern of this work, in a space three quarters of an inch by half an inch, Westwood counted no less than one hundred and fifty-eight interlacings!

Of the superiority of early Irish music, something has already been said in these pages. Giraldus Cambrensis who was acquainted with the music of various nations, said, as a result of his study of the Irish music, "Its melody is filled up, and its harmony is produced by a rapidity so sweet, by so unequalled a parity of sound, and by so discordant a concord." And of the Irish musicians:

> "They are incomparably skilful beyond all other nations I have ever seen. For their manner of playing on these instruments, unlike that of the Britons (Welsh) to which I am accustomed, is not slow and harsh, but lively and rapid, while the melody is both sweet and sprightly. It is astonishing that in so complex and rapid a movement of the fingers the musical proportions (as to time) can be preserved; and that throughout the difficult modulations on their various

instruments, the harmony is completed with such a sweet rapidity. They enter into a movement and conclude it in so delicate a manner, and tinkle the little strings so sportively under the deeper tones of the bass strings—they delight so delicately, and soothe with such gentleness, that the perfection of their art appears in the concealment of art." The Welshman, Powell, tells us that in 1078 Gryffith ap Conan, king of Wales, "brought over with him from Ireland divers cunning musicians into Wales, who devised in a manner the instrumental music now used there."

The Danes borrowed their harp music from Ireland. Ireland was, in the earliest ages, the school of music for Scotland. It continued to be down till a recent period. The Scotchman, Jamieson, writing in the last century, says:

> "Within the memory of persons still living, the school for higher poetry and music was Ireland. And thither professional men were sent to be accomplished in these arts."

Walker in his Irish Bards quotes Vincentio Gallilei as stating that Dante said the harp was first introduced to Italy from Ireland. A Continental writer on the Crusades is quoted as testifying: "We may well think that all the concert of Christendom in these wars would have been as discord, had the Irish harp been absent."

And from Bacon, Walker quotes: "No harp hath a sound so melting, and so prolonged as the Irish harp." It is quite probable that Moengal, at St. Gall, had the Irish harp taught to Tuotilo and others, when he was making that school famous for its music.

Geminiami, says D'Alton, found no music as original as the Irish "on this side of the Alps." And Handel who called our bard Carolan the Irish Orpheus, said he would rather be the author of *Eiblin a run (Eileen aroon)* than all the music he ever composed.

The high esteem in which music was held in very early Ireland is shown in a thousand legends: among others, in that one which has already been told of how St. Patrick, after Cas Corach the son of Bobd Derg had enchanted him on his Cran Ciuil, promised that the professors of his art should be at all times the bedfellows of kings.

The musical instruments were only a less esteemed and a little less adoringly cared for than the musicians. In the story of the Táin, when Fraech goes to court Findabar, daughter of Medb, the three harpers that went with him were the three sons of the famous Uaithne, harper of the Tuatha De Danann.

> "This was the condition of their harp. There were harpbags of the skins of otters about them, ornamented with coral, with an ornamentation of gold and of silver over that, lined inside with snow-white roebuck skins; and these again overlaid with black-grey strips (of skin); and linen cloths, as white as the swan's coat, wrapped around the strings. Harps of gold, silver, and findruine, with figures of serpents, and birds, and greyhounds upon them. These figures were made of gold and silver. According as the strings vibrated (these figures) ran around the men."

Stokes, Miss Margt.: Early Christian Art in Ireland.
Joyce, P. W.: Social History of Ireland.
O'Curry, Eugene: Manners and Customs of Ancient Ireland.
—— Manuscript Materials of Irish History.
D'Alton, Jno.: Prize Essay on Irish History (Proc. R. I. A.).
Irish Caligraphy (Ulster Jnl. of Arch.).
Gilbert, Sir Jno.: Facsimiles of the Natl. MSS. of Ireland.
Keller, Dr. Ferdinand: Illumination and Facsimiles from Ancient Irish MSS. in the Libraries of Switzerland.
Wattenbach: "Die Kongregation der Schottenkloster in Deutschland." Translated by Dr. Reeves, with notes, in the Ulster Journal of Archæol., vol. VII.
Westwood: Palaeographia Sacra Pictoria.
Petrie, Geo.: The Ancient Music of Ireland.
Walker's Irish Bards.

CHAPTER XXXVI

The English Invasion

It was in 1171 that Henry the Second invaded Ireland.

Seventeen years earlier he projected an invasion. And from the newly elected English Pope, Nicholas Breakspeare, Adrian the Fourth, he had then received an approving Bull. He had represented to Adrian that in Ireland morals had become corrupt, and religion almost extinct, and his purpose was to bring the barbarous nation within the fold of the faith and under church discipline.[1]

But first the opposition of his mother, and then political complications, caused Henry to postpone his project.

---

[1] To which Pope Adrian replied:

"Adrian, bishop and servant of the servants of God, to the most dear son in Christ, the illustrious king of England, greeting, health, and apostolical benediction.

"Thy greatness, as is becoming a Catholic prince, is laudably and successfully employed in thought and intention, to propagate a glorious name upon earth, and lay up in heaven the rewards of a happy eternity, by extending the boundaries of the church, and making known to nations which are uninstructed, and still ignorant of the Christian faith, its truths and doctrine, by rooting up the seeds of vice from the land of the Lord and to perform this more efficaciously, thou seekest the counsel and protection of the Apostolical See, in which undertaking, the more exalted thy design will be, united with prudence, the more propitious, we trust, will be thy progress under a benign Providence, since a happy issue and end are always the result of what has been undertaken from an ardour of faith, and a love of religion.

"It is not, indeed, to be doubted, that the kingdom of Ireland, and every island upon which Christ the sun of justice hath shone, and which has received the principles of the Christian faith, belong of right to St. Peter and to the holy Roman church (which thy majesty likewise admits), from whence we the more fully implant in them the seed of faith, that seed which is acceptable to God, and to which we, after a minute investigation, consider that a conformity should be required by us the more rigidly. Thou, dearest son in Christ, hast likewise signified to us, that for the purpose of subjecting the people of Ireland to laws, and eradicating vice from among them, thou art desirous of entering that island; and also of paying for each house an annual tribute of one penny to St. Peter;

For centuries now, dispute unending has raged around the two questions whether Ireland had lapsed into irreligion as represented, and whether the Papal Bull was genuine. Undoubtedly, the centuries of the Danish terror had had disastrous effect upon religion in the island—and the question arises how far had religious Ireland recovered itself in the century and a half since the Danish power was broken. Those whose duty it was to sustain Henry's claim paint a discouraging picture. But Irish defenders say their picture is purposely false. In reply they point to the wonderful work done during this period for the rehabilitation of religion, by the great Primates Cellach, Malachi, and Gelasius; and also the holy St. Lawrence O'Toole; to the synods that were held; to the many beautiful churches and abbeys that were being erected; and to the number of Irish kings, who, resigning their thrones entered monasteries and devoted themselves to God. Many were the princes who went on pilgrimage then. Holy men devoted to the religious life were also flocking abroad to join the noted Irish communities in Germany, that were propagating the faith over Central Europe.

That the standard of learning in the schools was held high is evident from the fact that Primate Gelasius and twenty-six bishops, at the Synod of Clonard a few years before the English invasion, decreed that only graduates of the University of Armagh (which was directly under Gelasius) should be appointed professors of theology in the schools of Ireland. And it will be recalled how that Adrian the Fourth himself heaped eulogy upon his Irish tutor in the University of Paris, the holy and learned Irishman, Marianus, Professor of the Liberal Arts there. And any one who impartially studies the subject can hardly avoid the conclusion that religion in Ireland in the twelfth century, though very far from occupying

---

and of preserving the privileges of its churches pure and undefiled. We, therefore, with approving and favourable views commend thy pious and laudable desire, and to aid thy undertaking, we give to thy petition our grateful and willing consent, that for the extending the boundaries of the church, and restraining the prevalence of vice, the improvement of morals, the implanting of virtue, and propagation of the Christian religion, thou enter that island, and pursue those things which shall tend to the honour of God, and salvation of his people; and that they may receive thee with honour, and revere thee as their lord; the privilege of their churches continuing pure and unrestrained, and the annual tribute of one penny from each house remaining secure to St. Peter and the holy Roman Church. If thou therefore deem what thou hast projected in mind, possible to be completed, study to instil good morals into that people, and act so that thou thyself, and such persons as thou wilt judge competent from their faith, words, and actions, to be instrumental in advancing the honour of the Irish church, propagate and promote religion, and the faith of Christ, to advance thereby the honour of God, and salvation of souls, that thou mayest merit an everlasting reward of happiness hereafter, and establish on earth a name of glory, which shall last for ages to come."

the shining place that it did before the coming of the Danes, must again have become a living issue.

A most convincing piece of evidence in point is the admission of Giraldus Cambrensis, tutor or secretary of Prince John, a man not only in the employ of the conquerors, but notoriously possessed of much anti-Irish prejudice, a man too who travelled over a third of Ireland and must have known whereof he spoke. Cambrensis says: "The clergy of that country are highly to be praised for their religion and among other virtues with which they are endowed, their chastity forms a peculiar feature. Those who are entrusted with the divine service do not leave the church but apply themselves wholly to the reciting of psalms, prayers and readings. They are extremely temperate in their food, and never eat till towards evening when their Office is ended." When the clergy of a country draw from an invading enemy such remarkable testimony to their religious ardour, it is difficult to believe that the people from whom these clergy were drawn, wallowed in the mire of irreligion.[2]

But if we supposed Ireland to be irreligious then, strange indeed would be the choice of an apostle in Henry, a man of vicious life, a supporter of anti-Popes, and reasonably suspected of, and all but excommunicated for, instigating the murder of the holy Thomas à Becket.

Those who contend that the Bull was an English fabrication for impressing the irreligious Irish and making easy their conquest point to the fact (among other assumed proofs) that the most ancient copies of the document discovered lack both date and signature. They say that both Adrian's "Bull" and the later confirmatory letter ascribed to Pope Alexander the Third,[3] exhibit evidence of being fabricated by the same hand—just as they were published at the same time, namely, at the Synod, in 1173, convoked by order of Henry. But the arguments of those who contend that these were

---

[2] A while later, after the island had been wasted by wars, the British Stanihurst bears this testimony: "The majority of the Irish are very religious. Their priests are dignified, and by their wholesome admonition, the consciences of the people who are docile and respectful are very easily worked upon."

[3] "Alexander, bishop, servant of the servants of God, to his most dear son in Christ, the illustrious king of England, health and apostolic benediction.

"Forasmuch as those things which are known to have been reasonably granted by our predecessors, deserve to be confirmed in lasting stability, we, adhering to the footsteps of Pope Adrian, and regarding the result of our gift to you (the annual tax of one penny from each house being secured to St. Peter and the holy Roman church), confirm and ratify the same, considering that its impurities being cleansed, that barbarous nation which bears the name of Christian, may by your grace, assume the comeliness of morality, and that a system of discipline being introduced into her heretofore unregulated church, she may, through you, effectually attain with the name the benefits of Christianity."

forgeries seem to crumble when met by the fact that they were published in the lifetime of Alexander, and were not then disowned or contradicted.

On Dervorgilla, the wife of Tighernan O'Rourke, prince of Breffni, is placed the indirect, and on Diarmuid MacMurrough, king of Leinster, the direct, odium of bringing in the English. Dervorgilla eloped with MacMurrough—when both were of ages not usual to the principals in such escapade, for she was over forty and he over sixty at the time. The tradition is that Dervorgilla invited MacMurrough to carry her off, on occasion when her husband had gone on pilgrimage to St. Patrick's Purgatory in Loch Dearg (Tir-Conaill), and MacMurrough quickly complied.[4]

---

[4] Moore imbeds the tradition, in one of his songs:

> The valley lay smiling before me,
>   Where lately I left her behind;
> Yet I trembled and something hung o'er me
>   That sadden'd the joy of mind.
> I look'd for the lamp which, she told me,
>   Should shine when her pilgrim return'd;
> But, though darkness began to enfold me,
>   No lamp from the battlements burn'd.
>
> I flew to her chamber—'twas lonely,
>   As if the loved tenant lay dead;—
> Ah, would it were death, and death only!
>   But no, the young false one had fled.
> And there hung the lute that could soften
>   My very worst pains into bliss,
> While the hand that had waked it so often
>   Now throbb'd to a proud rival's kiss.
>
> There *was* a time, falsest of women!
>   When Breffni's good sword would have sought
> That man, through a million of foemen,
>   Who dared but to wrong thee *in thought!*
> While now—O degenerate daughter
>   Of Erin, how fallen is thy fame!
> And through ages of bondage and slaughter
>   Our country shall bleed for thy shame.
>
> Already the curse is upon her,
>   And strangers her valleys profane;
> They come to divide—to dishonour,
>   And tyrants they long will remain.
> But onward!—the green banner rearing,
>   Go, flesh every sword to the hilt;
> On *our* side is Virtue and Erin,
>   On *theirs* is the Saxon and Guilt.

Some however say that MacMurrough forced her off against her will. Anyhow, when being carried off she cried out and screamed, either in seeming or real protest. It was in 1152 that this abduction occurred. In the following year O'Rourke was able to move the Ard-Righ, Roderick O'Connor of Connaught, to go against MacMurrough, which he did, punishing his province, and bringing away from him Dervorgilla.[5]

Again, thirteen years later, when MacMurrough's strong northern ally O'Loughlin of Tir-Eoghan died, the injured O'Rourke with Ard-Righ Roderick, the king of the Danes of Dublin, and many Leinster chiefs who hated MacMurrough for his tyranny, went once more against MacMurrough, overcame, and banished him. He fled oversea to Britain, and rested not till he reached Henry II of England who was then fighting in Aquitaine. This king he entreated to aid him in Ireland. The English king, who could not then comply, gave Diarmuid letters authorising any of Henry's subjects who so wished to go to Ireland to aid him. MacMurrough had these letters publicly read in the market-place in Bristol. Richard de Clare the Norman-Welsh Earl of Pembroke popularly known as Strongbow, a bold and daring warrior, but also a spendthrift now nursing broken fortunes, was interested in the prospect of repairing his fortunes in Ireland. MacMurrough tempted him with the offer of his beautiful daughter Aoife in marriage, and the heirship of the Leinster kingdom. Strongbow, however, being then in disfavour with Henry, feared to go until he had got express permission and approval from his monarch. But in the meantime he recommended that some of his close relatives should help MacMurrough. And de Clare's half-brothers, the knights Robert Fitz Stephen and Maurice Fitz Gerald, undertaking to go to his aid in the spring, MacMurrough now quietly returned and spent the winter in the Monastery of St. Madog at Ferns.

In May, 1169, with a small but efficient body of thirty knights in full armour, sixty horsemen in half armour, and three hundred archers, Fitz Stephen (and his Uncle Herve de Mont Maurice) landed at Bannow, Wexford—and another Knight Maurice de Prendergast with a company of about three hundred. The main body of the common fighters were Flemings. On receiving the news of their landing, MacMurrough raised a body of five hundred from among his Leinster subjects and joined them. And together they marched against the Danish city of Wexford, which, after repulsing two assaults, capitulated to the strange army with its

[5] She afterwards entered the Convent at Mellefont and devoted the remainder of a long life to the service of God.

armoured horses and horsemen and its wonderfully skilled and disciplined soldiers. MacMurrough bestowed the city upon Fitz Stephen, and settled near-by lands upon de Prendergast and de Mont Maurice.

Surrounding princes heard with dismay the news of the new kind of fighters that MacMurrough had brought in, and the wonderful skill and discipline which made three of them as good as a hundred. To make matters worse MacMurrough added to his army some two thousand soldiers who were in the capitulated city. Yet this did not deter his enemy MacGiolla Padraic, king of Ossory, against whom MacMurrough now marched, putting up a struggle from which MacMurrough and the Norman-Welsh and their Flemings had much difficulty winning out. But the Chiefs of Diarmuid's own Leinster met him with submission—excepting only O'Toole and O'Faelan, whom he went against and wasted and spoiled—before he again rested at Ferns.

The Ard-Righ and princes of the other provinces looked on inactive. The Four Masters say, "And they set nothing by the Flemings." In almost every century of Ireland's history mercenaries had been brought in from abroad by one prince or another to help in his battles against a neighbouring Irish enemy. And now every prince, occupied as usual with his own problems, was not much concerned about what did not immediately affect his own territory.

Diarmuid went against the Danish city of Dublin, but had to content him with getting hostages and lavish presents of gold and silver.

Roderick O'Connor at length took alarm, gathered an army and marched against MacMurrough, and his mercenaries. MacMurrough and Fitz Stephen, however, met him with offer of negotiation instead of battle. Roderick commanded that MacMurrough should make submission and that the foreigners should at once depart for Britain. MacMurrough readily accepted the first condition, giving his own son as hostage—but only secretly agreed (or rather pretended to agree) that he would manage to get the foreigners out of the country quietly and leisurely. Then Roderick acknowledged MacMurrough as King of Leinster.

MacMurrough having got needed peace, pursued his own plan. He was now fired with ambition to be High-King. He got a fresh accession of strength in the arrival of Maurice Fitz Gerald and another body of troops from Wales. He instigated to rebel against Roderick his son-in-law, O'Brien of Desmond—who, with the help of Fitz Stephen defeated the High-King. Diarmuid sent again to Strongbow pleading with him to come over. But the latter, having not yet received Henry's permission, sent over a small body of men under Raymond le Gros, who on landing, being joined by

Mont Maurice, won (by clever strategy) a signal victory over an attacking army composed of the Waterford men, the men of Ossory, and O'Faelan's men, at Dundonald, near Waterford. Of forty prisoners whom they took, they broke the limbs and flung them from the cliffs into the sea—giving Ireland the first taste of the conqueror's savagery that was henceforth to fill the centuries.

Strongbow followed, in a few months, with two hundred knights and a thousand men, and joining le Gros and Mont Maurice, twice attacked the important city of Waterford, and was twice repulsed. Then, when it seemed unlikely they could succeed, le Gros had the good luck to discover that one of the city houses projecting through an angle of the wall, had its projecting corner supported by timbers. Cutting away the supports, the house fell, giving a breach in the wall through which the attackers poured, overcame the surprised garrison, slaughtered the inhabitants, and put the two Danish rulers of this Danish city to death, and held Waterford for their own.

On hearing of Strongbow's landing, Diarmuid, with the fair Aoife hurried south to join him. And the marriage of himself and Aoife was celebrated amid the still bloody scenes in Waterford.

Then, to punish O'Rourke they marched into Meath and Breffni, laying everything waste as they went. Roderick, weakling that he was, and not able to command the support of his subordinate princes, sent warning to MacMurrough to desist—and got insulting reply that when O'Rourke was finished with, Roderick and his own province of Connaught would receive their attention. Diarmuid's death, that winter, put an end to an inglorious career.

Then Strongbow would assert his right to the throne of Leinster, much of whose lands he divided amongst his followers. But the Leinster chiefs refused to have him. Moreover, Henry, hearing of his successes in Ireland, had grown jealous, and fearful of Strongbow establishing his independence. He now peremptorily summoned Strongbow and all his subjects to return to England, forthwith.

Strongbow readily found reasons for refusal and delay. By a brilliant feat of arms he saved Dublin from capture by the combined forces of Roderick and his princes with thirty thousand men on land, and Godred, Danish king of Man, with thirty ships in the bay—not only saved the city but completely broke and scattered the army of Roderick, and captured great booty and provisions. Then he wasted Meath and Breffni, and afterward hurried south to Wexford, where Fitz Stephen was besieged by the Irish—but arrived too late to save the city. Then in response to another summons from his royal master, he hastened to Henry, very humbly laid his conquests, cities and territories, at his angry monarch's feet—only begging that he might be made Henry's tributary from Leinster.[6]

Strongbow's report upon the goodliness of the prize beyond the Channel, stimulated Henry now to go to the winning of it. And he went—with five hundred knights and four thousand horse and foot soldiers, in four hundred ships—landing at Waterford, October, 1171. His conquest of the southeast of the island was little more than a triumphal march; for the Irish princes and chiefs of the south and east thronged in to do homage to the great man. Without question the extraordinary skill of the Normans in the art of war, their effective system and wonderful discipline, their eminently superior equipment, their armour against which the weapons of the Irish were of little use—all had telling effect upon the minds of the chiefs. Besides, they knew that there was not, and had not been, the cohesion amongst them that would enable them to maintain a united front against an invader with such powerful army. Of course they only considered it in the light of minor kings giving a kind of formal acknowledgment to the might of a greater—a thing which they had always been used doing toward the greater one of their own. The acknowledgment of a greater, the giving of hostages, and even paying of tribute to him, had never affected and had never been meant to affect, their own independence, and the independence of their own territory. Yet well they must have known the vast difference between submission to one of their own, and to a foreign invader. It shows lamentable demoralisation, and stamps their memory with lasting shame.

MacCarthy of Desmond first came in and made submission at Waterford. He was followed by O'Brien of Thomond, at Lismore, then O'Faelan of the Deisi, MacGillapatrick of Ossory, and other Leinster chiefs as Henry marched to Dublin. In Dublin came to meet him and pay homage, O'Rourke of Breffni, O'Carroll of Oriel, and O'Mellaghlin of Meath.

None of the northern chiefs came in, nor of the western. Nor did Roderick, the Ard-Righ—but he contemplated, with growing alarm, the successive submissions of the various princes, and finally sent messengers to Dublin inviting a parley at the Shannon. To the rendezvous came Henry's envoys—with the result that Roderick O'Connor, through these

[6] While Strongbow was absent Dublin was again attacked, this time by its Danish king Hasculf MacTurkell, who had escaped to Norway when the city was first taken, and now returned with ships and armies from Scandinavia, Denmark, the Western Isles of Scotland and the Isle of Man—ten thousand men under John the Dane. Again, the clever strategy of the Normans, now under Miles and Richard de Cogan, defeated and destroyed the great attacking army.

envoys, made peace and friendship with Henry, as one king with another, and also an act of submission to one whom he acknowledged to be greater than he.

During that winter Henry made still more progress in winning and securing to himself the fealty of the princes. In a Dublin palace which he had constructed of osiers he kept court and entertained lavishly all the winter long. With the choicest repasts, prepared by the best Norman cooks, he won through their stomachs to the hearts of the chiefs—this supplemented by his own gracious suavity, in contrast to the bluntness, sometimes brutality, of the Norman-Welsh who had preceded him. The adroit Henry's affability and politeness, and apparently real friendship and affection, had far more compelling force in winning fealty than would have had the shock of his army.

Then he won Rome, too. He had a synod of the Irish ecclesiastics—all but the Primate Gelasius, and the other northerns—called at Cashel, where, following the example of their chiefs, the Bishops acknowledged Henry as lord supreme in Ireland. At this synod they passed decrees for the bettering of church discipline, which, being sent to Rome, confirmed the fact that Henry was carrying out his undertaking, and reforming morals in the land, and evoked from Alexander the Third the letter confirmatory of Adrian's Bull.

At Easter Henry had to return in haste to England, carrying with him the undisputed lordship of Leinster, Meath and the cities of Dublin, Wexford and Waterford. Meath he gave in trust to De Lacey—who had the governorship of Dublin also. The city of Dublin was given to the occupation of the merchants and people of Bristol. Strongbow was left in possession of Leinster.

The strange mesmerism which the presence of Henry seemed to have wrought on the Irish princes was dissipated on his going. They awoke to the rude reality that they had welcomed an invader and meekly accepted him. From the various quarters they began to rise up against the enemy, harass him, and endeavour to drive him out. Now more familiar with, and therefore less daunted by, Norman discipline and equipment, the Irish princes set strategy against skill, and discovered that the Normans were not omnipotent. O'Brien of Thomond inflicted a big defeat upon them at Thurles—not the only big defeat that he was to give them. Strongbow the mighty was beaten back in the south and bottled up in Waterford in imminent danger of capture. And, only that the redoubtable le Gros hurried back from Wales to release him he would have been overthrown. Roderick O'Connor with the help of O'Neill, O'Mellaghlin,

O'Carroll, MacDunleavy of Uladh, and an army of twenty thousand overran Meath, and set out for Dublin which he might easily have captured but for his vacillation. He soon after thought it to be to his advantage to make treaty with Henry. He sent to England for that purpose Concord, Abbot of Clonfert, Catholicus, Archbishop of Tuam, and Archbishop Lawrence O'Toole of Dublin. This treaty, known as the Treaty of Windsor, acknowledged Henry's right to the lordship of Leinster, Meath, and the other few places and cities then occupied by him. He was also acknowledged as the overlord to whom Roderick should pay formal tribute. On the other hand it acknowledged Roderick's right to the high-kingship of five-sixths of Ireland.

But such pacts had little effect either in securing peace or insuring the rights of either party. Every Norman chief warred on his own account, for purpose of extending his power and possessions. And of course every Irish chief and prince, when opportunity offered, warred against the invader.

But such demoralisation set in, that in short time not only was Irish chief warring upon Norman baron, but Irish chief was warring with Irish chief, Norman baron warring with Norman baron, and a Norman-Irish alliance would be warring against Normans, or against Irish, or against another combination of both.

The Normans not only marked their progress by much slaughter and many barbarities, but signalised themselves by robbing and burning churches and monasteries, and oftentimes slaughtering the inmates.[7]

They harried, robbed, ravished, and destroyed wheresoever they went. And against one another, in their own feuds, they oftentimes exercised as much barbarity as against the Irish. Fearfully true is the Four Masters' word that MacMurrough's treacherous act "made of Ireland a trembling sod."

After a time Milo de Cogan and Robert Fitz Stephen won territory for themselves in Munster. John de Courcy won the ancient territory of Ulster—Down and Antrim—and established himself at Downpatrick. Cardinal Vivian, the Pope's legate, saw de Courcy, on his entrance thereto, slaughtering the people on the street. Connaught (despite the Treaty of Windsor) was granted to De Burgho (Burke). But it was a long time after it was granted to him before he was enabled—with the help of some of Connaught's own—to find a foothold there.

---

[7] Giraldus complains to John, "The poor clergy are reduced to beggary, the Cathedral churches which were rich, endowed with broad lands by the piety of the faithful in olden times, now echo with lamentations for the loss of their possessions of which they have been robbed by these men and others who came over with, and after them; so that to uphold the Church is turned into spoiling and robbing it."

Prince John, whom Henry had appointed Lord of Ireland, came over in 1185, when he was nineteen years of age, and made himself most beneficial to the country by reason that he, with the crowd of young libertines who formed his court, made mock of and insulted such Irish chieftains as hastened to pay him homage. His attitude and actions during the short time he was permitted to remain in the country were proving splendidly disastrous to English prospects there and magnificently helpful to Irish.

Only a few years later John de Courcy, the conqueror of Ulster, and the very strongest figure among those Normans, was overwhelmingly defeated in an attempt to conquer Connaught, and his army almost annihilated. And the Irish princes had recovered enough proper pride and national spirit to form a compact, under Connor of Maenmagh, son of Roderick, for driving out the English—which might now have been easily accomplished. But before their plans were perfected Connor was slain, and the growing compact dissolved. Indeed had they at any time after Henry's leaving been able to combine and strike together, the English, despite the great advantage of discipline, skill, and equipment, could have been driven into the sea. The key of the arch, however, which should have been the strongest stone was the weakest—ever ready to crumble. This was Ard-Righ Roderick, who not only lost Ireland but eventually lost Connaught. His own sons warred against him and warred against one another as well. He was deposed, exiled, recalled, travelled—a kind of royal beggar—to princes who had been tributary to him, entreating them to put him on the throne again. With an Ard-Righ thus disobeyed and disrespected by his own, and his kingdom, which should have been the dominant one, warring within itself, the fates were with the foreigner, and they precariously held their own in the east, occasionally making effective plunges into the independent provinces that surrounded them, and occasionally too having their own insecure possessions lunged into by the Irish enemy.

The English royal house was in worse condition even than the Irish royal house. Henry died cursing his sons, and his sons may be said to have lived and died cursing one another. John, who had essayed to oust his worthier brother Richard—while the latter was on the Crusade—and also while he was languishing in a German prison—began to reign over England in the last year of the twelfth century, very shortly after Donal MacCarthy of Desmond defeated the English of Munster and drove them out of Limerick. The great northern prince, Flaherty O'Muldory of Tir-Conaill, had just then passed away. And also just then had passed unfortunate Roderick O'Connor—who died where he had spent his last days, in the Abbey of Cong in Mayo—and was buried in the ancient cemetery of Clonmacnois.

CHAPTER XXXVII

Norman and Gael

The Norman Kings used the Church for all purposes of statecraft, its higher officers were checks and spies upon popular movements, while its ablest bishops, neglecting their spiritual offices, were wholly absorbed in temporal administration. The episcopate was thoroughly secularised and the character of the bishops became very bad. The pious chroniclers in England have left us lurid pictures of the moral degradation of their greater Churchmen of these ages. Their passage to Ireland brought no access of sanctity. They acted as viceroys for the King of England. The Irish Church was treated with great cruelty and the direst oppression. Its bishops were driven from their sees, the canons from their cathedrals, the priests from their parishes. A Gaelic monk could not be harboured in a monastery, or an Irish nun in a convent, in any district where their writ ran. From the pulpits they thundered: "It is no offence against God to kill any Irish human being." They displayed real ability and amazing zeal in leading their troops in the field and in building mighty castles at all strategical points, throughout the land. The sword of Mars, God of War, was their sceptre, not the Cross of the Prince of Peace. They extended the long arm of excommunication against our race; rarely did they uplift the hand of benediction. In their complaint to Pope John XXII, Donald O'Neill, King of Ulster, and the other princes of the Gael (1318) declared: "As it very constantly happens, whenever any Englishman, by perfidy or craft, kills an Irishman, however noble, or however innocent, be he clergyman or layman . . . nay, even if an Irish prelate were to be slain, there is no penalty or correction enforced against the person who may be guilty of such wicked murder, but rather the more eminent the person killed, and the higher the rank which he holds among his own people, so much the more is the murderer honoured and rewarded by the English, and not merely by the people at large, but also by the religious and bishops, of the English race, and, above all, by those on whom devolves officially the duty of inflicting on such malefactors a just reward and equitable correction for their evil deeds."

Henry of London was typical of his race and class. At once King John's Viceroy of Ireland and Archbishop of Dublin, he spent more time in hunting the red deer than in seeking out lost souls. He had a passion for other people's money. He flayed the humbler English, as well as the Irish, under his jurisdiction. To build the notorious Dublin castle, he pulled down several churches. By wiping out the Gaelic See of Glendalough, in Wicklow, hallowed by the sanctity, and famed for the Greek, Latin, and Irish learning, of Saint Kevin and his successors, he erected St. Patrick's Church into a cathedral. He gave the people their first experience of foreign landlordism in Irish history and received the title of *Scorch-Villain* or *Burn-Bill* in return. On being installed Archbishop he summoned his tenant farmers to arrange their rents, telling them to bring their title deeds with them. "Mistrusting nothing," they placed their parchments in his hands, which, before their faces, he cast into the fire. Before they recovered from the shock and amazement their title deeds were turned to ashes. It was then the turn of the men of Glendalough to blaze and burn: "*Thou*, an archbishop! Nay, thou art a *Burn-Bill*, a *Scorch Villain*." Another drew his weapon and cried: "As good for me to kill him as to be killed, for when my title deeds are burned and my living taken away, I am killed." The prelate, thoroughly frightened, escaped by a back door, but his officials and bailiffs were well beaten, and some of them "left for dead." The outraged tenants even threatened to burn the palace, and would have done so if their just wrath had not been appeased by "fair promises that all should be to their content."

The process of reducing Ireland by incastellation—or castle-building—was pursued with restless enthusiasm; and so successful was it that in less than seventy years three-fourths of the country was under Anglo-Norman sway. The contemporary Gaelic historian lamented that the Irish, who wore no armour, were no match for their foes "in one mass of iron." The Normans were well supplied with the most efficient and the most deadly war weapons of the Europe of that day, and were much better organised than the Irish.

Yet the remarkable fact remains that the Gaels were not driven back upon any one part of the kingdom, but remained scattered, yet unconquered, among the foreigners. The Normans in great strength occupied the present Counties of Antrim and Down in Ulster; in Leinster, Louth, Meath, Dublin and Kildare, with the greater part of Westmeath, were densely held by Normans, and by their allies, Flemings, Welsh and Saxons. They had a firm hold of Limerick and the adjoining districts; their stone fortresses stretched to the very mouth of the Shannon. In Connaught the rule of De Burgo extended from Galway northward and eastward over the western plain and communicated through Athlone with their allies in Leinster. On the other hand, the remainder of Ulster and the adjoining districts were stoutly maintained by the O'Neills, O'Donnells, O'Farrells, O'Reillys, and O'Rourkes. In the Central Plain of Leinster, the O'Conors of Offaly, the O'Mores of Leix, and the O'Carrols of Ely, sat tight on their ancestral lands, in spite of the foreigners' efforts to dislodge them. In the mountainous parts of Wicklow, along the uplands of Carlow and Kilkenny, the Gaels kept undisputed rule. In Munster, MacCarthy More reigned in Muskerry and preserved the title of King of Desmond; Thomond, in great part, retained the royal sway of the O'Briens. Along the western coast, beyond Lough Corrib, the fierce O'Flahertys continued to live free men, and the north-east of Connacht still elected its own sovereign as The O'Conor. The Normans recognised the O'Conors as Kings of Connacht.

Surveying with not a little pride and much vainglory the results achieved by the invaders, Giraldus Cambrensis gave to his Latin story of the events the title "Hibernia Expugnata"—"Ireland fought to a finish." But he did not understand, nor did his successors down the ages understand, the amazing vitality of the Gaels' power of recuperation, mental and physical. Beaten they have been, time and again, but never conquered. The spirit of exaltation of our manhood, the intense prayerfulness of our spiritual-minded, white-souled, indomitable womankind, have mocked at Despair, laughed in the face of Misfortune itself. And when the race was thought to have been prostrated forever it arose and rang out its triumphant battle-cry!

Neither then, nor ever after, did the foreign invader come to understand Ireland's soul. Spenser, in Elizabeth's days, vainly tried to solve the problem of the resurgent spirit of Irish nationality. Why did not the Gaels acknowledge defeat? "Yet surely," he allows, "they are very valiant and hardy, for the most part great endurers of cold, labour and all hardiness, very active and strong of hand, very swift of foot, very vigilant and circumspect in their enterprises, very present in perils, very great scorners of death." The resurrection of thirteenth century Ireland, and its subtle conquering of the conqueror, has been a source of wonder to English-Irish historians who have tried to explain it in many futile ways. The truth is that the free-hearted, culture-loving, gracious comity of the Gaels and of

Gaelic civilisation irresistibly insinuated itself into the mind and soul of the Norman French—and won from them eager capitulation.

In their darkest hour of affliction the princes of the three greatest Gaelic clans—almost all that possibly could assemble—met at Caol Uisage near the Belleck on the river Erne (in 1258) to knit the country into one body to withstand the foreigner. The men of Connacht, under Felim O'Conor and the warriors of Thomond under O'Brien, cheerfully elected Brian O'Neill of Tir-Owen King of Ireland. This menace was met by the treacherous capture and the poisoning of O'Neill by De Courcy, who defeated the combined forces at the battle of Downpatrick (1260). The lesson of this disaster by which "Eire was left an orphan" was most fruitful. The Irish were "clad in fine linen garments, the foreigners in one mass of iron": as the contemporary Gael narrates. Hence was seen the need of better means of defence against the common foe. The epochal advent of the *gall-oglach* (gallowglass) into Ireland's armies resulted.

From the Western Isles of Scotland were invited the heavy-armed, mail-clad, battle-axe-bearing *gall-oglach* to aid in the cause. These stalwarts were the descendants of the Ulster Gaels who had migrated there and inter-married with the Norse. Like their forebears they, too, were "very great scorners of death." Later, the princes throughout Ireland raised and similarly equipped regular field troops. In fact, Eire saw the form and spirit of her ancient Fianna or national militia, come to life again. By this new factor the tide of foreign conquest was turned. No longer did the Norman cavaliers "in one mass of iron" inspire terror, no more were their castles regarded as impregnable fortresses. O'More of Leix levelled eight such strongholds in one day. Sir Henry Savage, the Norman, expressed his views pithily on this altered condition of warfare. "Never shall I, by the grace of God," he declared, "cumber myself with dead walls: my fort shall be where young bloods are stirring and where I have room to fight. Better is a castle of bones than a castle of stones." The Norman policy of conquest by incastellation was defeated by the *gall-oglach* enterprise, so quickly adopted now by all the leading Irish chiefs.

To quicken the tide of liberation Donal O'Neill and the other Gaelic lords invited Edward Bruce, brother of the King of Scotland, to the throne of Ireland. The winning, in rapid succesion, of eighteen victories, made the gallant Bruce reckless, so engaging a vastly superior force at Faughart, near Dundalk (1318), he was slain. His Connacht allies, the O'Conors, were routed at Athenry. But after a temporary ebb success after success again followed the banners of the intrepid Irish. Even the English rulers in Dublin were brought under subjection. MacMurrough Kavanagh, King of

Leinster, became virtually King of Dublin, and received from the city an annual tribute. When Murrough O'Brien, King of Munster, burst upon the English assembled at Castle Dermot in Kildare they were so terrified that they would not fight; they gave him vast sums of money, war-horses, and other equipment to buy peace. As the fourteenth century approached its end the English everywhere trembled.

To remedy this state of affairs, Richard II, of England, landed in Ireland with an immense army and swore a mighty oath that he would not leave the country until he had taken Art MacMurrough alive or dead.

Art was a true Irish King. The chroniclers record that "he held in his fair hand the sovereignty and the charters of the province of Leinster. At his approach the whole (of the English of) Leinster trembled." Again, "he was replete with hospitality, knowledge and chivalry; the prosperous and kingly enricher of churches and monasteries, with his alms and offerings," Art barred Richard's way. Even his 30,000 men were no match for the Irish. The French author who has left us a record of this invasion declares that the Gaels were utterly fearless, were "as bold as lions." In contest after contest the English were shattered. In this Frenchman's opinion the Irish could not be conquered "while the leaves were on the trees." So with a heavy heart Richard hied him back home a sad, broken man, to be deprived of his crown and kingdom by the Duke of Lancaster. He was the last English monarch until the seventeenth century who tried the impossible task of conquering Ireland. MacMurrough was poisoned by an agent of the English Government. The final result of the Irish rally was that English rule was cooped within the Pale—a palisaded district stretching some thirty miles around Dublin—and it held shadowy sway in a few of the walled towns, which were, in reality, little Republics. Almost all Ireland was independent early in the fifteenth century.

Irishwomen have been famed, and wooed, in all ages and in many lands for their chastity, wit, vivacity, tenderness, intelligence, and beauty. Intermarriages with the British, or Welsh, princes went on from the twilight of history. Many Saxon lords, too, sought wives in Ireland. Even before the Invasion the Norman Earl of Shrewsbury (1100) sent an ambassador to crave a princess of the House of O'Brien in wedlock: but Magnus, King of Denmark, secured her for his own son, Sitric, King of Man. On the day when the victorious Richard, Earl of Pembroke, surnamed Strongbow, married Eva, daughter of Dermot MacMurrough, King of Leinster, on the blood-soaked battlefield of Waterford (1170), the Irish conquest of the Norman conquerors was begun. For marrying the Lady Rose O'Conor, daughter of Rury, King of Connacht, the elder Hugh de Lacy roused the ire of Henry II, and won dismissal from his post as chief Governor of Ireland. The second Hugh de Lacy took unto wife the daughter of Alan, Lord of Galloway, grandson of King Baliol of Scotland. The renowned Richard de Burgh, the mighty "Red Earl" of Ulster, espoused Una, daughter of Prince Hugh O'Conor. Their daughter married into the Royal house of Scotland. Hence the Bruces, through the female line, were descended from MacMurrough, King of Leinster, and Robert's wife, Ellen, Queen of Scots, daughter of the "Red Earl," came of the royal lineage of the O'Conors of Connacht. William Marshall, Earl of Pembroke, the ablest soldier of his day, wedded Isabella, daughter of Eva and Strongbow. Their eldest son, William, was the husband of Eleanor Plantagenet, sister of Henry III of England. On his death, she became the wife of the famous Simon de Montfort, Earl of Leicester. The King of Scotland took another of her sisters to wife. The daughter of the last Earl of Ulster married Lionel, Duke of Clarence, brother to Edward III of England. The seed of MacCarthy More, King of Cork, and of Petronilla de Bloët, passed into the House of Stuart and fructified in the person of the Sixth James of Scotland (First James of England). As generation succeeded generation all the Irish clans, in the five-fifths of Eirinn, were united in ties of blood with, and helped to conquer to Gaeldom, all the Norman families.

With Scotland, north of the Grampians, Gaelic Scotland, there was no break in relationship adown the ages. It is no exaggeration to say that intermarriage and community of language, customs and interests, made the north and west of Ireland and Argyll and the western Scottish Isles one family estate. Inverness was the capital of Gaeldom in the Middle Ages. The Scottish Kings made commercial treaties and social compacts in favour of the Irish of Ireland and to the detriment of the English of Ireland.

The result of the blending of the two races, Irish and Anglo-Norman-French—Gaels and Sean Ghalls—was an enriching and deepening of national life in every department—paralleling like happenings in England and Scotland. The absorption of the invaders occurred earlier in the Green Isle.

"If the speech is Irish the heart is also Irish," as an English official bitterly declared. So long as the Irish retained their native culture and language, their power of assimilating what was best in other resident races was marvellous. The Sean Ghalls (old foreigners) became "more Irish than the Irish themselves." They donned the Irish national dress, used the Irish tongue, fostered Irish literature and music, ruled their subjects by the Brehon laws, and because they thus became essentially Irish they won the devotion and fidelity of the people. They even discarded their own Norman names in favour of Irish names. Sir John Davies, in the reign of James I of England, deplored their conduct: "As they did not only forget the English language and scorned the use thereof, but grew to be ashamed of their very English names, though they were noble and of great antiquity, and took Irish surnames and nicknames." The De Burghs were transformed, first into Burkes, then into MacWilliams. The De Birminghams became MacYoris; the Dexecesters, MacJordans; the De Angulo family was henceforth known as MacCostello. "In Munster, of the great families of the Geraldines planted there, one was called MacMorice, chief of the House of Lixnaw; and another MacGibbon, who was also called the White Knight." . . . "And they did this in contempt and hatred of the English name and nation whereof these degenerate families became more mortal enemies" to England than the Gaels.

Because they fell under the spell of the wide culture of the Gaels, with its deep humanities, its kindly, genial atmosphere, there was "utter ruin" to English interests. Perhaps in no other race was the doctrine of the equality of man so well understood as among the Gaels. The meanest clansman of an O'Neill or a MacDonnell stood on an equal footing with his chieftain. When Art MacMurrough and three other Irish kings visited Richard II in Dublin the English were horrified to see the royal guests sitting down to table with their minstrels and whole retinue. "They told me this was a praiseworthy custom of their country," records the official scribe, but such democratic conduct would not be allowed by this feudal master of ceremonies. So they were separated—the kings were sequestered at one table, the retinue at another. "The Kings looked at each other and refused to eat, saying I had deprived them of their old custom in which they had been brought up." But the boorish "allotted tutor in manners" informed them that it was not decent or suitable to their rank, "for now they must conform to the manners of the English." "With the dignity of courteous guests" they yielded. When Sir John Harington visited O'Neill he found him seated in the open surrounded by his clansmen. In such a position he averred he would rather be "The O'Neill than the King of Spain." Harington marvelled at the love and admiration the Gaels exhibited toward their lord. "With what charm such a master makes them love him I know not: but if he bid come they come; if go, they do go; if he say do this, they do it."

The habit of the Normans fostering their children with mothers of the Gael and having them to act as sponsors in baptism for their children, was hateful to the English Government. "Both of which," adds Davies, "have ever been of greater estimation among this people than with any other nation in the Christian world. . . . Fostering hath always been a stronger alliance than blood, and foster-children do love and are beloved of their foster fathers and their sept more than of their natural parents and kindred, and do participate of their means more frankly, and do adhere unto them in all fortunes with more affection and constancy."

England bitterly bewailed the "degenerate" fate in Ireland of its own original conquerors—the Norman-French. On the other hand, the Gaels, with truer insight, declared that these Sean Ghalls (Old Foreigners) "gave up their foreignness for a pure mind, their surliness for good manners, their stubbornness for sweet mildness, and their perverseness for hospitality."

Drastic steps were taken to prevent the amalgamation of the races, to blight the bloom of Gaelic-Anglo-Norman civilisation. The notorious Statute of Kilkenny (1367) was but one of a long series of legislative acts designed for this purpose. It begins thus: "Many of the English of Ireland discarding the English tongue, manners, style of riding, laws and usages, lived and governed themselves according to the mode, fashion and language of the 'Irish enemies,' and also made divers marriages between themselves and the Irish, whereby the said lands and the liege people thereof, the English language, the allegiance due to their lord the King of England, and the English laws, were put in subjection and decayed, and the *Irish enemies exalted and raised up, contrary to reason.*" So it declared any such alliance high treason.[1] It declared war on gossipred, on fostering, on the Irish language, on Irish culture, on Irish music and its professors, on Irish law and its judges, on Irish games and pastimes, on the Irish clergy, on Irish manners and customs, on Irish trade and commerce. The English born in England were no longer to be dubbed "English churls or clowns," nor were the English born in Ireland to be called "Irish dogs." To crown all, the English Archbishops and Bishops pronounced sentence of excommunication against all who disobeyed the statute.

Love mocked at such penal laws. The wedding bells continued to ring down the corridor of the centuries. The prospect of being hanged, drawn, disembowelled, and quartered—the legal penalty—had no terrors for the

[1] The godfathers and godmothers of the same child were gossips. The children nursed by the same mother were fosters. Two boys nursed on the same milk were foster-brothers.

Irish, New or Old, Sean Ghalls or Gaels.[2] Every avenue of tyranny and of terror was explored to find means of arresting the irresistible tide of Gaelicism. If a wayfarer was seen either riding in the Irish fashion, or dressed in Gaelic costume, or not wearing "a civil English cap," it was "advisable and lawful" to murder the offender. Even the sporting of a moustache after the Irish fashion (the fashion on the Continent then also) and not having a shaven upper lip like the English, was denounced by Act of Parliament (25 Henry VI, 1447) as deserving of death, and the delinquent's estate was to be forfeited to the Crown.

---

[2] "I would not give my Irish wife for all the dames of the Saxon land;
I would not give my Irish wife for the Queen of France's hand;
For she to me is dearer than castles strong, or lands, or life—
An outlaw—so I'm near her, to love till death my Irish wife.

"I knew the law forbade the banns—I knew my king abhorred her race—
Who never bent before their clans must bow before their ladies' grace.
Take all my forfeited domain, I cannot wage with kinsmen strife—
Take knightly gear and noble name, and I will keep my Irish wife."

CHAPTER XXXVIII

Trade in Mediæval Ireland

The risen waters of a common Irish life flooded even the walled towns. At the first Invasion the King of England had banished all the Irish, who were not granted "English liberty," from these urban communities, and replaced them with his own subjects, allowing, however, the numerous Portuguese, Spanish, French-Norse and Flemish merchants and traders to abide therein. From that time onward it had been an accepted principle that no Irishman should be allowed to engage in trade or commerce, or accepted as an apprentice to any handicraft where English power was felt. Then, with delicious irony, their writers derided our people as "idlers, hating honest business." By letters of denization, by peaceful penetration, by intermarriage, the Gaelic clansmen, by the fifteenth century, formed the bulk of the Craft Gilds, even in Dublin, and made not a little headway in obtaining a foothold in the Merchant Gilds. The town merchants, from the very beginning, had to journey into the country to buy the far-famed Irish woollens, rugs, mantles, and linens, to bargain for hides and beautiful peltries, flax, beef, and corn. So in time, partnerships were formed with the Clans, and Irish law in the Irish tongue was pleaded in the town courts. The merchants, like the Norman lords, dressed themselves in the banned national costume, spoke, even in Dublin and Waterford, the Irish tongue, and took part in all the inhibited festivities of the Gael. If proof were needed that these merchants were not, as is so often stated, English, it will be found in the fact, attested by the records in Continental archives, that whilst English traders and factors in Spain, Portugal, Oporto, Italy, the Hansa Towns, Flanders, Russia and elsewhere, used their own, or the French language, in commercial transactions, the Irish and the Scots employed Latin only. Latin was spoken by all educated people throughout Gaeldom.

Moreover, in nearly all commercial treaties the foreign potentates describe our merchants as of "the Irish Nation." In Spain and Portugal, "the noble Irish," as they were there known, obtained more valuable privileges than the English. So great was the commercial intercourse with the Peninsula, of the O'Sullivans, MacCarthys, Desmonds, O'Driscolls, O'Flahertys, O'Malleys, and of the merchants from the seaports from Waterford to Sligo, that the waters which lapped the southern and western coasts of Ireland were designated by map-makers "The Spanish Seas." "Portingal" became a proper name in Southern Ireland. Men of that race were elected as Mayors of our towns. "Spain" yet survives as a surname in our land. The great Italian financial houses, the bankers of Lucca, the Ricardi, the Friscobaldi, the Mozzi and the Bardi of Florence, were active agents in Mediæval Ireland. The wine trade, as shown by the Pipe Roll accounts, and other sources, was of great dimensions, with Clan and Town. Bordeaux, Dordogne, Libourne, St. Emilian, besides Spain, Portugal and Oporto, traded direct with the Irish ports.

With France the records of our trade go back to the days of St. Patrick. Rouen was the chief port of Normandy and obtained from Henry II the "monopoly of Irish trade." Bordeaux had a colony of Irish merchants—as had St. Omer, Marseilles, Bayonne, St. Malo, La Rochelle, Nantes and other ports—who were importers of Irish wool, skins, hides, fish, woollen cloth, fine linen, leather and corn, and they sent to Ireland their own manufactures and products.

The enterprising Flemings were stationed in many of the Irish ports. Their influence on maritime and inland trade was as beneficent here as it was in England. In Kilkenny, Youghal, Cork, Waterford and New Ross they were most numerous. On the other hand, Irish merchants had their own settlements in all the leading ports of Flanders. In the old records of Bruges, Ireland, as distinct from England, is mentioned as one of the seventeen nations whose corporations added to the fame of that port. It had its own commercial houses there—two bore the proud name, "Ireland," and the third "St. Patrick," "a lofty and beautiful edifice." This last was a sixteenth century foundation. In 1399 Philippe le Hardi made Ecluse (Sluys) a staple town for Irish mantles and cloths. This duke's safe-conducts to Irish merchants in 1387 and in other years have been printed. In all trading charters to Englishmen, Irishmen are specifically mentioned likewise. With a view to encourage the home manufacture of wool the Duke of Flanders (1496–7) forbade the importation of foreign cloths. Thereupon a clamour arose from the populace to be allowed still to buy the cheaper Irish cloth and linens, Irish cloaks and Scottish kerseys;

and Archduke Philippe gave orders that such goods from Ireland and Scotland should continue to be imported and sold "according to the old custom." A Flemish writer of the sixteenth century, lamenting the decay of Bruges, its rival Antwerp, obtaining all its commerce, tells us that the Irish merchants in his own time held two fairs a year at Bruges where they exposed for sale their friezes, mantles, serges, and great quantities of furs and skins. He laments their loss because the Irish friezes and serges were of such stout material and so cheap that they were largely used by the working men and the poorer classes. Irish leather goods were renowned throughout Europe, so it is not a matter of surprise that Irish names should figure on the Tanners' Gild of Liège, then the most extensive and famous body of this craft on the Continent. At Brabant fairs Irishmen were busy also. Their corporation retailing, not merely all varieties of furs, skins, "beautiful leather goods," but also rough cloth and high class serges. Antwerp, too, had its Irish trade, linen being mentioned, amongst other items. Lubeck had commercial intercourse with Ireland, and Irish woollens were carried down the Rhine: Cologne being one of the marts. Through the Hansa Towns Irish commerce flowed on to Russia.

The Irish had a hospital at Genoa, before the Norman Invasion, *circa* 1160. In 1398, there is record of Patrick Galway, a member of an opulent mercantile family in Cork, trading there in copper, tin, linen cloth, and "innumerable other things," "wools and merchandise." As yet little concerning the commerce between mediæval England, Ireland and Italy is known. Bonifazio del Uberti, in his poem, *Dittamondi,* tells us that "Ireland is worthy of fame for the woollen stuffs she sends us." Irish serge was used in Naples as trimmings for the robes of the king and queen. Its presence in Florence, Genoa, Como, and Bologna, is known to all students of Commerce in the Middle Ages. Irish mantles were heirlooms in the families of many wealthy Italian merchants. It was worn by the fashionable ladies of that luxurious town, Florence. Machiavel declares that woollen manufacture was the principal industry in this city, and maintained the majority of its operative classes. In that opulent emporium of European and Asiatic trade, the Florence of 1350, the "noble stuffs" of Ireland were eagerly sought for by the haughty dames of the princes of Commerce and Finance. In 1382 the Pope's envoy obtained the privilege of bringing with him to Italy, duty free, a number of articles in which figure "Five mantles of Irish cloth—one lined with green. One russet garment lined with Irish cloth."

Irish silk is mentioned in the wardrobe accounts of Queen Clemence of Hungary. She had two robes of this material, the one violet and the other without indication of colour. The dearer must have been a most expensive article, for it is priced twenty Parisian pounds (probably £400 of our money). Our "silk" is mentioned in many French accounts during the Middle Ages. Its fame attracted the cupidity of the London mercers, evidently, for in a sixteenth century lawsuit, there is a claim for some London silk stolen "called Irish silk." Whether this was a superfine linen or the *srol* mentioned in the ancient Irish MS. I cannot decide.

Irish cloth, mantles, rugs and serges were highly esteemed in Spain and Portugal, likewise. "At this time," writes Macpherson, "there were some considerable manufactures in Ireland. The stuffs called *sayes* (serges) made in that country were in such request, that they were imitated by the manufacturers of Catalonia, who were in the practice of making the finest woollen goods of every kind." The Irish merchants traded with the Canaries and pushed their way into the Land of the Moors. Prince Henry the Navigator had his own agent in Galway, to whom he sent an African lion, one of the earliest seen in Europe, knowing that "never before had such a beast been seen in that part."

One of the most famous legends in the Middle Ages was the "Voyages of St. Brendan." This saintly old mariner of Ardfert, Co. Kerry, was said to have been the first discoverer of "Great Ireland," as the Icelanders of the tenth and eleventh centuries called North and Central America. Washington Irving in his "Life of Columbus" narrates that "during the time that Columbus was making his proposition to the Court of Portugal, an inhabitant of the Canaries applied to King John II for a vessel to go in search of the island. The name of St. Brendan was from time immemorial given to this imaginary island, for when the rumour circulated of such a place being seen from the Canaries, which always eluded the search, the legends of St. Brendan were revived, and applied to this unapproachable land." "It is a well known fact," avers the Rev. D. O'Donoghue in his learned work, "St. Brendan the Voyager," that Columbus while maturing his plans for his great expedition, visited Ireland as well as Iceland in quest of information bearing on his theories. He was assisted in his researches by an Irish gentleman named Patrick Maguire, who accompanied him also on his great voyage of discovery. There are other Irish names on the roster of the ship's crew, preserved in the archives of Madrid; but by Father Tornitori, an Italian priest, in the seventeenth century it is specially recorded that Patrick Maguire was the first to set foot on American soil. He says that on the eventful morning of the landing the boats bearing Columbus and some of his crew were launched; but approaching the land, the water shallowed, and Patrick Maguire jumped out to lighten the boat, and then waded ashore.

Space forbids the recital of the interesting history of the commercial fame of Irish horses, hawks, and of the great wolf hounds which were eagerly sought for by the crowned heads of the Continent of mediæval Europe.

Only a brief reference can be made to the widespread commercial intercourse with England. The records of trade with Bristol and the Welsh ports go back to the fringe of mythological times. Irish weavers emigrated in large numbers to Bristol, where they acquired great power. They were represented on that town's Corporation. Its Coopers' Gild had many Gaels among its members. From Ireland came more than seventy per cent of its trade. Irish commercial activity aroused the jealousy of the merchants of Canterbury against such "alien Irishmen." Gloucester, Chester, Runcorn, Cambridge, Coventry, Oxford, Preston, Winchester, London, Hereford, Southampton, and St. Albans are some of the towns where Irish manufactures were sold and Irish merchants busy. There was bitter contention and long strife between Gloucester and Bristol, Bristol and Chester, Chester and Runcorn, over the monopoly of Irish trade. In 1481, Edward IV issued a proclamation that every Irish ship charged with goods for Runcorn, or any other place in Cheshire, should first discharge at Chester. Yet, in this very year, one Edward Walshe obtained a license to sail his ship direct from Runcorn to Ireland. In 1439 an ordinance was made that no Irishman born "shall henceforth be elected on the Council of Bristol by the Mayor under a penalty of £20 each from the Mayor and from the Irishman." The Coopers' Gild shut down its doors "from henceforeard" against Irishmen, "rebels against our liege lord the king." "These strangers and aliens not born under the king's obedience . . . but rebellious . . . were put in occupation of the craft of weavers; . . . and have so greatly multiplied and increased within the town of Bristol that the king's liege people within the town and other parts were vagrant and unoccupied, and may not have their labour for their living." Withal these enactments would seem to have become a dead letter, for in Tudor days Irish was spoken there, and its Irish residents numerous.

There is unimpeachable evidence that agriculture was skilfully and extensively pursued from the thirteenth to the sixteenth century. The exportation of enormous quantities of wheat, oats, barley, rye and of other cereals, and of flax (besides what was used for the big home consumption of linen), of beef, mutton, and other food stuffs, as well as of wool, point to intensive land cultivation and stock raising. To a modern Irishman the quantities of these products exported to France, Scotland, Flanders and England, as recorded in official and other documents, seem incredible. This was when England was ruled by the first three Edwards (1272–1377). The Editor of the Calendar of Documents, Scotland, is of opinion that Ireland must have been a veritable Land of Goshen then, and truly adds that no merchants would go there to seek corn today. In the fifteenth century London Corn Market Irish wheat was sold. English agents reported that "Ireland fed Spain and Portugal with corn."

CHAPTER XXXIX

Learning in Mediæval Ireland

After the crushing defeat of the Norsemen by King Brian at the Battle of Clontarf (1014) there was a flowering of the National Mind in literature. So the political freedom of the fourteenth and fifteenth centuries saw a re-birth of intellectual, as well as of agricultural and commercial activity in Ireland. It was a Golden Age of Gaelic Literature.

As the wider gates of Ireland's commerce opened on the South and West coasts, so her scholars, pilgrims, clerics and craftsmen followed in the wake of her merchants, through the Gaulish seas into France and Italy, and "over the brief ocean" into Spain and Portugal, to drink at the fountains of knowledge there. The universities of these Romance lands knew a long succession of our brilliant scholars. The congregation of Irish and Scottish students at the University of Paris (1300–1600) was greater than even the number who enriched their minds at Oxford. "The Latin education of Ireland," observes the erudite Scotch Professor Ker, "began earlier, and was better maintained there than elsewhere" in Europe. The reason whereof may be found in the truth that the culture and refinement of these Romance or Latin lands made a more lively appeal to the Gaelic mind and soul than did the civilisation of England. The restless ebb and flow of the Irish of the Middle Ages from Eirinn to the Continent, carried with it much that was noblest in literature, in civility, and in manners. It is interesting to note the most popular Irish translations made by these scholars of the Greek and Latin classics. For the delectation of their readers and auditors they gave admirable adaptations, amongst others, of the Tale of Troy, the Saga of Alexander the Great and Philip of Macedon, The Wanderings of Ulysses, The Theban War, and the Æneid. Some of the Greek stories were rendered through the Latin versions. It would be idle to conjecture, at the present stage of our enlightenment, how far the famed knowledge of Greek of eighth and ninth century Ireland was maintained and carried to and through the fifteenth century. Such of these translations as have been brought to light indicate how expert and how original was Gaelic scholarship. The Irish used their authorities as Shakespeare used his, transforming them into virtually new works. They gave us transmutations rather than translations. The infinite tenderness of the Gaelic heart, the loving minuteness of observation of the Irish eye, is evidenced by the exquisite Nature touches in their verse and prose—for they were enamoured of the blue sky, the rhythm of the rustling leaves, the subtle magical lure of Spring's annual awakening. The exquisite song of the stars, the haunting music of running waters, the mysterious tongue of boughs shaken by the wind, were wine to their veins. They talked to the joyous birds, to the frisking rabbits, and even to the shy fishes, as though they were their brothers, sisters and lovers. Strangely enough, these literary men eliminated all references to supernatural agencies, found in the classical texts. The tales became Irish sagas, in spirit and in truth, with the foreign names alone standing for their national heroes. Like all peoples who have passed through seas of sorrow, through "the seven waves of tribulation!" they abounded in mercy. Tenderness and Chivalry, quite unknown to the classical originals, are commingled, with the texture of the tales whenever possible. But the most remarkable fact lies in the emergence of the Love Story, pure and simple. This form of narrative is one of the glories of early Irish literature, wherein feminine influence sheds a glow of sweetness and dignity, of benignity, chastity and refinement. From English literature the Irish made many notable translations. Thus Fingin O'Mahony, "a wise man skilled in Latin, English and Irish," gave us a fine interpretation of Sir John Maundeville's "Travels" (1475). "Guy of Warwick," "Bevis of Hampton," and Turpin's "Chronicles" are among the present known translations, which have escaped the ravages of time. As might be expected, Spanish and French romances were turned into Irish for the entertainment of the people. The extent of the learning of these days is known, in small part only, to archivists. It awaits generations of Irish and Scottish scholars to glean, garner and elucidate, so that the ordinary student may realise its depth, comprehensiveness and grandeur.

In the knowledge of Astronomy mediæval Ireland was in advance of most European lands. All the greater Lords of the Gaels and Sean Ghalls had their official astronomers. It was but natural that a nation of rovers and travellers should have maintained a sound standard of geographical learning in their schools. In medicine, Europe could teach the Gaels but little.

The King of England had not better pharmaceutical lore or more adept surgical skill at his command than the O'Briens in Munster or The MacCailim Mor in the Western Isles of Scotland. Only a very tiny portion of a world of medical Gaelic MSS. has been edited and translated by experts. An O'Shiel, clan doctor to O'Neill, banished from Ulster into the Low Countries by the cruel hand of persecution, becomes at the Court of Brussels European-famed, thereby justifying the *Four Masters'* epithet, "The Eagle of Physicians." The contemporary Spaniards and Portuguese praised the skill and acquirements of the medical Doctors of Gaeldom. It is worthy of remembrance that Lionel, Duke of Clarence, brother to Edward III, King of England, and promulgator of the Statute of Kilkenny, employed none but Irish physicians for himself and his court. In science, in architecture, in the changing fashions of the goldsmiths' art, we see how the Irish were influenced by the skill and the refinement of the European Continent.

The Irish Brehon Law Code goes back to a much earlier epoch than the days of St. Patrick. Its interpreters were deeply reverenced by the Irish people because of their even-handed justice. There is not a single instance in recorded history of a brehon (a Gaelic judge) accepting a bribe, or being deflected a hair's breadth from the dictates of equity through personal bias or family interests. The refined attention of Gaelic law to the minutiæ of the rights of property has won praise from its bitterest foes. Every chieftain had his own Brehon "to decide the causes of that country." "Three doors," declared the Irish, "through which truth is recognised: a patient answer, a firm pleading, appealing to witnesses. Three glories of a gathering: a judge without perturbation, a decision without reviling, terms agreed upon without fraud." English officials exhausted the vocabulary of abuse in condemnation of the Brehon Law, "hateful alike to God and Man," as they said. Yet they were amazed how cheerfully, how uprightly, the Gaels obeyed its decisions. Even their traducer, Sir John Davies, was fain to pay this tribute: "There is no people under the sun that doth love equal and indifferent (impartial) justice better than the Irish, or will rest better satisfied with the execution thereof, although it be against themselves, as they may have the protection and benefit of the law upon which just cause they do desire it." Chief Baron Finglas has left the valuable testimony that his countrymen, who were loudest in jibing at the Irish law, did not obey their own laws. "Yet divers Irishmen doth observe and keep such laws which they make upon hills in their country, firm and stable, without breaking them for any fear of favour." Let another English official give just judgment. Payne says Gaelic government was "done with such wisdom, equity, and justice as to be worthy of all praise." "For I myself," he continues, "have seen in several places within their jurisdiction well nearly twenty cases decided at one sitting, with such indifference (impartiality) that for the most part both plaintiff and defendant hath departed contented." This balanced justice displeased such of his countrymen as "live by blood," hence "they utterly mislike this or any other good thing that the poor Irish man doth." "The Irish keep their promise faithfully and are more desirous of peace than the English; nothing is more pleasing to them than good justice."

The Irish brehons were men of deep learning, of wide influence and of riches. Three signs marked their abodes, so said the people, "wisdom, information, intellect." In the Annals we read of many of them being professors of new and old laws, Civil and Canon law.

If the English hated Brehon laws, the Irish had comedies, which were played in the open air, burlesquing English law and its judges.

A contemporary author (1351) gives a vivid and joyous picture of the intellectual gatherings in mediæval Ireland, wherein clan feuds and distinctions were forgotten and the spirit of a common nationality supplanted the passion of war by the nobler craving for peace. Liam O'Kelly, Lord of Hy-Many in Connacht, in that year invited all that was best in the mind and the hand of Gaeldom, as well as the professors of fun and merriment, to his castle. For it was the lofty privilege of lords, chieftains and of the wealthy, to foster such assemblies. "The company that read all books, they of the Church and of the poets both: such of these as shall be perfect in knowledge, forsake not thou their intimacy ever"—such was the admonition given to their rulers by the people. "The chroniclers of comely Ireland," says our authority, "it is a gathering of a mighty host, the company is in the town; where is the street of the chroniclers?"

O'Kelly, chief poet, in a fine description of the gathering, compared the streets of tents that lodged the learned to the letters in a manuscript, and his princess' banner-decked castle to the illuminated capital letter.[1]

---

[1] "The fair, generous-hearted host provides another spacious avenue of white houses for the bardic companies and the jugglers. Such is the arrangement of them, ample avenues between; even as letters in their lines. Each thread, bare, smooth, straight, firm, is contained within two threads of smooth, conical-roofed houses. The ridge of the bright furrowed slope is a plain lined with houses.

"O'Kelly's castle, as it were, a capital letter, a star-like mass of stone, its outer smoothness like vellum—a castle which was the standard of a mighty chieftain; bright is the stone thereof, ruddy its colour. The work is a triumph of art. There is much artistic iron-work upon the shining timber. On the smooth part of each brown oaken beam workmen are carving animal figures.

"The bardic companies of pheasant-meadowed Fola (Ireland) and those of Scotland—a distant journey—will be acquainted with one another after arriving in O'Kelly's lofty stone castle.

Nearly a century later the lofty-souled Mairgret O'Carroll, princess of Offaly, presided over another such gathering. "She was the only woman," narrate the Annalists, "that made the most of repairing the highways and creating bridges, churches and Mass books, and of all manner of things profitable to serve God and her soul, and, while the world stands, her many gifts to the Irish and Scottish nations shall never be numbered."

> "It is she," runs the ancient account, "that twice in one year proclaimed to and commonly invited (i.e., in the dark days of the year, to wit on the feast day of Da Sinchell—26th March—in Killachy) all persons, both Irish and Scottish, to two general feasts of bestowing both meat and moneys, with all manner of gifts, whereunto gathered to receive the gifts the matter of 2,700 persons, besides gamesters and poor men, as it was recorded in a Roll to that purpose, and that accompt was made thus, *ut vidimus*—viz., the chief *kins* of each family of the learned Irish was by Gilla-na-naemh MacEgan's hand, the chief judge to O'Conor, written in the roll, and his adherents and kinsmen, so that the aforesaid number of 2,700 was listed in that Roll with the Arts of *Dán*, or poetry, Music and Antiquity. And Maelin O'Maelconry, one of the chief learned of Connacht, was the first written in that Roll, and first paid and dieted, or set to supper, and those of his name after him and so forth, every one as he was paid he was written in that Roll, for fear of mistake, and set down to eat afterwards. And Margaret, on the steps of the great church of Da Sinchell, clad in cloth of gold, her dearest friends about her, her clergy and Judges too. Calvagh (her husband) himself on horseback by the Church's outward side, to the end that all things might be done orderly, and each one served successively. And first of all she gave two chalices of gold as offerings that day on the Altar to God Almighty, and she also caused to nurse or foster two young orphans. But so it was, we never saw nor heard neither the like of that day nor comparable to its glory and solace. And she gave the second inviting

---

"Herein will come the seven grades who form the shape of genuine poetry; the seven true orders of poets. . . .

"Men coming to the son of Donnchadh from the north no less from the south, an assembly of scholars: a billeting from west and east. . . .

"There will be jurists of weighty decisions, wizards; the writers of Ireland, those who compose the battle rolls, will be in his dwelling.

"The musicians of Ireland—vast the flock—the followers of every craft in general, the flood of companies side by side—the tryst of all is to one house."

(1443) proclamation (to every one that came not that day) on the feast day of the Assumption of our Blessed Lady Mary in harvest, at or in the Rath-Imayn, and so we have been informed that that second day in Rath-Imayn was nothing inferior to the first day."

In state-craft and in peace-making she was equally distinguished. Her sanctity became proverbial. Like all Irish women of noble repute she led the men folk with the subtle liens of purity and of prayer—led them so surely and so unobtrusively that they believed they went forward of their own free will. She announced her intention of visiting the shrine of St. James of Campostella in fair Spain and forthwith a big gathering of warriors, hardened war-dogs in holy Ireland's cause, led by MacGeoghagan, wished to accompany her (1445). They went together. The flood of Irish pilgrims to their own Saints' shrines as well as to the Holy Land, to Rome, to St. James of Campostella, to the tomb of Thomas à Becket at Canterbury, went on unceasingly through the Middle Ages. These pilgrimages need a modern historian—the material is by no means scanty. When Mairgret paid the debt of mortality (1451) the Annalists wrote: "A gracious year this year was, though the glory and solace of the Irish was set but the glory of heaven was amplified and extolled therein." "The best woman of her time in Ireland"—such was the Irish verdict on this lofty and magnanimous soul. "God's blessing, the blessing of all saints and every other blessing from Jerusalem to Inis Gluair be on her going to Heaven, and blessed be he that will read and hear this for blessing her soul."

Her daughter Finola—"the most beautiful and stately, the most renowned and illustrious of her time, her own mother alone excepted," blessed with "the blessing of guests and strangers, of poets and philosophers"—married O'Donnell, Lord of Tir-Chonnail. When O'Neill, aided by MacDonnell and his *gall-oglach,* invaded her territory, she "after the fashion of the strong-hearted and independent women of Ireland," met them at Inishowen, and "made peace without leave from O'Donnell." Finola, "the fairest and most famous woman in Ireland beside her own mother," after the death of O'Donnell in an English prison, married the golden-haired Hugh O'Neill, "who was thought to be King of Ireland," "the most renowned, hospitable and valorous of the princes of his time, and who had planted more of the English in despite of them than any other man of his day." He died on Spy-Wednesday (1444) "and we never heard since Christ was betrayed on such a day, of a better man." Three years later Finola, "renouncing all worldly vanity, betook herself into the austere devout life in the monastery of Killeigh; and the blessing of guests and strangers, and poor and rich, and both of poet-philosophers and archi-poet-philosophers be on her in that life."

In history Ireland's fame stands high. She was justly styled a "Nation of Annalists." Each sept, each province, had its own genealogist and chronicler whose business it was to record the deeds of the clan and its princes, and the deaths of its leading personages, lay and ecclesiastical. Truth and accuracy were regarded as of paramount importance. "To conceal the Truth of History," ran one saying, "is the blackest of infamies." The scribes travelled throughout the whole country to verify their references and their facts. The Philosophy of History was unknown in these ages. Many of the entries in the Annals are aggravatingly brief and bald. But as the poets celebrated in ample verse the fame and exploits of the popular heroes and heroines, the chronicler must have believed that brevity was the soul of discretion. The course of study the aspiring recorders underwent was long, arduous and specialised. They were trained in the bardic schools or under some well-known tutor. They handed on from age to age the traditions of their sept. The office of scribe and genealogist was usually continued in certain families, the son succeeding his father, as a matter of course. The Annalists were held in the highest esteem, ranking next to the head of the clan; they fed at his table and were supported by his bounty. No important public business was conducted without their presence and their directing influence. The greater portion of the existing annals have been the resultant of the Revival of the fourteenth and fifteenth centuries.

CHAPTER XL

The Geraldines

The history of the Gaelicised Fitzgeralds (the Geraldines) is in a sense, the history of the fortunes of Southern Ireland for an extensive period. The poet says, "They channelled deep old Ireland's heart by constancy and worth."[1] In Desmond, South Munster, and the lands adjoining, they ruled as absolute monarchs over a hundred miles of territory.

[1] While our scholarly contributor, "Sean Ghall," is permitted to chaunt the pæan of the very brave Geraldines in these pages, it is at the same time proper to remind readers that though they were with fair thoroughness Gaelicised (both in manners and in blood) these usurpers always retained, in their subconsciousness, memory of the fact that it was England who had placed them in the seat of the displaced Gael. And so long as England properly respected their sovereign rights in their dominion—which should not be theirs—they were in turn willing to respect England's suzerainty over Ireland in general—and even act as her Deputies. It is true that, openly or secretly, they hated England with a holy hate—England and the later English. And they hated English tryanny to the extent of becoming chronic rebels against England—even when they were nominally serving her. It was their hatred of England, and resentment of English interference, rather than the higher principle of Ireland's nationality, that kept them in rebellion.

True, the real Irish chieftains had, at times, diplomatically pretended to resign the principle of Irish nationality; but with them it was always pretence—shameful pretence to be sure. The principle, for all that, was kept warm in their hearts—and as soon as occasion presented itself, blossomed vigorously forth again.

The Geraldines were the cream of the *sean-Ghall*. They were as good as could be expected. But no better. When O'Neill was marching to Kinsale he asked who owned a castle that took his attention in passing—and when told that the owner's name was Barry, he heartily cursed him. "But," interrupted his informant, "he's a Catholic whose family has been here four hundred years." "No matter," retorted O'Neill, "I hate the robber as though he came yesterday." And indeed till O'Neill's day (and later) there was far more than a grain of reason behind the exasperation of the Gael. It was not till newer usurpers robbed them of that which they themselves had usurped that the *sean-Ghall* became flawlessly Irish.—S. M.

"They made barons and knights," records Sir John Davies, "did exercise high justice on all points within their territories; erected courts for criminal and civil cases, and for their revenues, in the same form as the King's courts were established at Dublin; made their own judges, seneschals, sheriffs, coroners and escheators; so the King's writ did not run in those counties. . . . These great undertakers were not tied to any form of planatation, but all was left to their discretion and pleasure, and although they builded castles and made freeholders, yet there were no tenures or services reserved to the Crown, but the lords drew all respect and dependency of the common people unto themselves."

The Geraldines of Kildare held the entire county of Kildare, with parts of Meath, Dublin, and Carlow, while their castles stretched beyond Strangford Lough on the coast of Down, to Adare, a few miles from the town of Limerick. They had their own fleet to patrol the seas. Intermarriages with the great houses in England and with Norman and Gaelic families in Ireland were, at first, a settled part of Geraldine policy.

When they tasted of the pure milk of Gaelicism they never forgot its savour, so they became kindly Irish of the Irish, root and branch. Irish culture refined the Normans. There were no scholars, no poets or authors, among the first invaders. Yet when Jenico Savage, the descendant of the warrior who preferred "a castle of bones to a castle of stones" died (1374), the Annalists lamented that the learned of Ireland "were left an orphan by his death." The higher refinement of native civilisation altered the Normans' very nature. Mrs. J. R. Green says:

"There remains a token of how the lords of Athenry had thrown themselves into Irish life, in the shrine made by Thomas de Birmingham (1374) for St. Patrick's tooth, the most venerated relic in Connacht—a shrine of silver, decorated with raised figures in silver and settings of crystals, coloured glass, and amber with spiral and interlaced work of Celtic art. Nugents and Cusacks and Englishes, and other foreign names, were entered on the roll of Irish poets. In the ardour of Irish studies a Fitzgerald, even a Butler, was not behind a MacCarthy or an O'Sullivan. But it is to the Geraldines we must look for the highest union of the culture of (Norman) England and Ireland. By a fine custom the Irish chiefs, 'heroes who reject not men of learning,' were in their own houses 'the sheltering tree of the learned,' and of the whole countryside.

> When a noble made a set feast or 'ushering' there flocked to it all the retainers and many a visitor, the mighty and the needy—a gay and free democracy of hearers and critics, with 'a welcome for every first-rate and free-hearted man that is refined and intelligent, affable and hilarious.'"

The Geraldines afford the most numerous instances of mere men of blood, apostles of the sword, turning, under the influence of Gaeldom, into gentle sages and wise scholars. Thus, "Gerald the Rhymer," as his subjects named him, fourth Earl of Desmond (1359–98), was known as "the Poet." His learning was so deep and his acquirements so wide, that he was regarded as a magician. His son, James, was fostered and reared by the O'Briens of Thomond, the Statute of Kilkenny notwithstanding. This Fitzgerald is described as a nobleman of wonderful bounty, mirth, cheerfulness in conversation, charitable in his deeds, easy of access, a witty and ingenious composer of Irish poetry, a learned and profound chronicler. He excelled all the English and many of the Irish in the knowledge of the Irish language, poetry and history, and other learning. This Earl lived long in Irish legendary lore. Once in every seven years he is said to revisit his Castle of Gur, near Limerick.

The eighth Earl of Desmond was the flower of the Southern Geraldine stock. The Irish people have taken this Thomas Fitzgerald to their hearts, and enshrined him there as a "Martyr of Christ." He was the first of a long and fine line of Sean Ghalls to be martyred in the cause of Irish freedom. He was an affable, eloquent, hospitable man; kind and munificent to the poets and antiquaries of the Irish race. "Educate that you may be free." Acting on this maxim Earl Thomas founded the famous College of St. Mary at Youghal (1464). The foreigners had destroyed the glorious University of Armagh (1133–1202) with its 3,000 scholars and its famed tutors, presided over by Florence O'Gorman, who spent over a generation in acquiring knowledge in the universities of France and England. Armagh had been regarded as the National University for all the "Irish and Scots," and Rury O'Conor, the High King of Ireland, had given to it the first (1169) annual grant to maintain professors for the whole of the Irish race—in Scotland as well as Ireland. Thomas of Desmond tried to re-establish a National University, and for that purpose had an Act of Parliament passed at Drogheda (1466). By precept and by practice he had endeavoured to unify the two races in Ireland. He was a promoter and a patron of trade and commerce between Ireland and the Continent. The English hated him for such fruitful and healing activities—"Enormities" they called them.

His marriage with an Irish lady, in despite of the Statute of Kilkenny, was a crowning infamy. "Who dare say to Geraldine, 'Thy Irish wife discard'?" For Thomas Desmond, when he was murdered in Drogheda by the Earl of Worcester, afterwards known as "The Butcher," all Ireland went into the deepest mourning.[2]

Gerald, the eighth Earl of Kildare (1477–1513), was named by Ireland "Gerait Mor"—Gerald the Great. He had the fine stature, the manly beauty and goodly presence of his race; his liberality and his merciful deeds passed current as household words. He was a man of strict piety. His mild just government drew the hearts of his people to him in passionate devotedness. During the fifty years which preceded the Reformation, the office of Lord Deputy of Ireland, was filled, with a few broken intervals, by this Fitzgerald and by his son. They pursued a National policy and so incurred the hatred of the permanent English officials.

By liens of blood-relationship he obtained great influence amongst the great Irish houses, Old and New. So powerful had he become that he retained the deputy-governorship of Ireland in despite of King Edward IV and his nominee.

He ruled it wisely and justly. A knight he was in valour—princely and religious in his word and judgments. His daughters, Eleanor and Margaret, were unquestionably two of the most remarkable women of their age and country. In vain endeavour to join in amity the rival houses of Kildare and Ormond (Geraldine and Butler) the Earl married Margaret to Piers Butler, Earl of Ormond. She founded the famous school of Kilkenny. Ormond was ably seconded by her in his efforts to promote more advanced methods of agriculture. Whilst Sir Piers is forgotten, "Magheen" or "Little Margaret" Fitzgerald's deeds are recounted beside the fire of many a peasant's cot in the Kilkenny of today.

Gerait Og, "Gerald the Younger," ninth Earl of Kildare (1487–1534), although educated in England was even more Irish than his father. He continued the policy of intermarriage with the Irish, and so consolidated the power of his house. Maynooth under him, was one of the richest earls' houses of that time. "His whole policy was union in his county, and Ireland for the Irish." He was first appointed Lord Deputy by his cousin, Henry VIII, in 1513. After seven years' rule he was removed, charged by the English with "seditious practices, conspiracies, and subtle drifts." The people were gladdened when a few years later he re-assumed the post.

---

[2]For his cultured daughter Katherine, wife of MacCarthy Reagh (1450–1500), the famous Book of Lismore was made from the now lost Book of Monasterboice.

His cousin, the Earl of Desmond, had entered into a solemn league and covenant with Francis I, King of France (1523), to drive the English out of Ireland, whilst Scotland was to render assistance to the cause by invading England. But the heart of the leader of the Scottish army, the Duke of Albany, failed him at the last moment and the gallant Scots dejectedly turned homewards (20th May, 1525). All Ireland's hopes were again shattered. Kildare was summoned (1526) to England by Cardinal Wolsey to answer the charge of complicity in the plot. His brilliant wit, subtle brain and eloquent tongue alone saved his head from the block. Wolsey denounced Kildare as a traitor. In his six years' detention in the Tower of London, Kildare's Irish friends convinced Henry VIII that Gerald's release was the most politic course, for the moment. So he was re-instated (1532). Henry's plans for the pulling down of the House of Kildare and the extermination of the Desmonds were not yet ripe. So, until his final imprisonment and death, Gerald Og continued to rule as a God-fearing, just, wise man. When he took the ordnance from the royal castles and placed them in his own it was a portent to the country that he had secretly thrown in his lot with Desmond, who had not given up the hope of obtaining French, Scottish and Spanish aid. He was of a deep piety. His confidence in the goodness and mercy of God was unbounded. As a patron of learning he endowed a college on the lands assigned by his father for that purpose. This building was erected in 1518 "in a most beautiful form," it was called "The College of the Blessed Virgin Mary of Maynooth." It was razed with the ground when the beneficent Geraldine's rule was ended (1538). O'Mulconry was his ollav, "man full of the grace of God and of learning." Gerald had "The Red Book of Kildare," now in the British Museum, compiled for him. Philip Flattesbury, his secretary, likewise drew up "divers chronicles of Ireland." He possessed an excellent library of Latin, Irish, French and English books—122 in all. Almost all the classics were included in this collection, which would compare favourably with the finest private library in any English nobleman's castle. Kildare was a man of culture, and was well read not only in the ancients but also in the literature of his day. His fame was European. "His hospitality is to this day rather of each man commended, than of any man followed."

Such a man's doom was certain. The Dublin Castle officials soon made up a bill of charges against his Irish rule, and Kildare found himself back in the Tower of London for the last time (1534).

Before his departure from Dublin he appointed as vice-Deputy his son, a boy of twenty, the famous Silken Thomas. Disregarding his father's advice to be guided by his elders, young Thomas fell an easy prey to the veteran

English intriguers of Dublin Castle, who had been secretly mining the foundations of the House of Kildare for generations. A forged letter was shown round in official circles in Dublin alleging that the Earl's neck "was already cut shorter" in the Tower of London, "as his issue presently should be." Lord Thomas, "rash and headlong and assuming himself that the knot of all Ireland was twisted under his girdle," having consulted with the young bloods, inopportunely raised the standard of revolt—against the entreaties of all the wisest heads. His enemies rejoiced; his well-wishers were in despair. On 11th June, 1534, he rode through Dublin, attended by a guard of 140 horsemen in coats of mail, with silken fringes on their helmets, on which account he became known as "Silken Thomas." On reaching St. Mary's Abbey where the Council of State was assembled, his bard chaunting the ancient glories of the Geraldines adding fuel to his ardour, Thomas flung the Sword of State "the English churls among." "This sword," he declared, "was already bathed in Geraldine blood and now newly whetted in hope of a further destruction. I am none of Henry's Deputy. I am his foe. I have more mind to conquer than to govern, to meet him in the field than to serve him in office."

At first Lord Thomas swept all before him. Then England poured troops lavishly into Ireland—accompanied by the new invention, the cannon, which proved the young leader's undoing.

The impetuous valour of Geraldine and his skilful leadership won many battles. The fall of Maynooth Castle, the mightiest stronghold in the land, after ten days' battering with "great guns," was heard throughout Ireland. "Fooboon on the foreign grey gun" cursed the Irish. It was a portent that Silken Thomas's victories would avail him nothing. The eagerly awaited French army arrived not. After several reverses the iron tongue of the cannon told him further resistance was useless. He submitted and was sent to the Tower of London—where his father had already died of a broken heart, on learning of Thomas's insurrection. Here the young "rebel" was treated with the utmost cruelty. Finally, he was hanged, drawn and quartered at Tyburn (1537). With him perished his five uncles, the half-brothers of his father, and the near kinsmen of Henry VIII. Three of these nobles, gentle, scholarly men, had failed to aid the rebellion. The other two having actually helped to suppress it, were, in requital of their service to England's crown, seized at a banquet to which they had been invited by the English Lord Deputy. But the troublesome house of Kildare must be wiped out for good. Two children, however, escaped from the butchery. The blotting out of the very name, the uprooting of the seed of the Leinster Geraldines, became the policy of the subsequent three years. Whilst Gerald, a boy of 12 years, remained free, the "extirpation" of the race was incomplete.

Lady Eleanor Fitzgerald, widow of MacCarthy Reagh, and aunt of the orphan Gerald, had learnt with grief and horror of the six outraged corpses of her kinsmen at Tyburn. She had seen the deeds of the English soldiers and officials in the Geraldine country who came to wean the people, so they said, "from the inordinate tyranny of their Irish lords" and "to teach them the sweets of civil English order." She had heard the wail of the ravished maidens, of the erstwhile gentlefolk lamenting beside heaps of ruins, once stately dwellinghouses; she saw the charred harvest fields, the "slaughter heaps" of youth and age. The churches and the schools, the abodes of the men of culture and refinement, had gone the way of the cot of the peasant. Such "sweets" were gall and wormwood to her compassionate soul. The Act of Parliament (1537) decreed all the Geraldine countries to be forfeited to the Crown. Her nephew Gerald was being nursed in illness by his sister, Lady Mary O'Conor, wife of the chieftain of Offaly, whilst the English people held the confident belief that the House of Kildare had ceased to be. Through this Lady Eleanor's amazing energy, dauntless courage, and exquisite tact, all the great families were united in a vast confederacy against the English government. Everywhere local feuds and personal enmities were sacrificed on the altar of Nationality. All Ireland, Old and New, Gael and Sean Ghall, took the boy under its protection. In spite of all political divisions and tribal distrusts, Ireland was essentially a nation to the seventeenth century: one in soul and mind, though not in body—one in language and in literature, one in manners and customs, one in religion and in spiritual feeling, one in the nobler and more gentle arts of human fellowship, rooted in the soil of sufferings, kindred, fosterage, marriage and death.[3]

[3]The only family of the "Old Foreigners" the Anglo-French-Norman, to be artificially kept outside the influence of Gaelicism, was the Butlers of the House of Ormond. The Butlers had not become Gaelicised, because for nearly two hundred years its wards were minors, and so reared and trained by the Kings of England as Englishmen. Their policy and outlook was anti-Irish. But James Butler, the ninth Earl, broke away from the traditional family policy. He, the son of "Magheen" Fitzgerald, the renowned Countess of Ormond, could not but regard Ireland as his first love. The pervading spirit of a common Irish life pervaded him as it had filled all the land outside official Dublin. Though the destruction of the rival House of Kildare added enormously to the Ormond estates, yet Butler was horrified at the Tyburn butchery. Hardened soldier though he was, Ormond played the woman openly, "tears pouring down his cheeks" when he pictured the six stark Geraldine corpses. Intermarriage with the Powers, the O'Briens, and the MacGillapatricks, established the Butlers' power. By an alliance with a daughter of James, eleventh Earl of Desmond, James Butler united the southern

Through her marriage with the scholarly author, wise politician and stout warrior, Manus O'Donnell, Lady Eleanor healed an age-long animosity between Tir-Eoghan and Tir-Chonaill. The news caused consternation at Dublin Castle and so in England. "Never was I in despair of Ireland until now," exclaimed the Lord Deputy; another official added that their trust was "by the aid of the North of Ireland and of Scotland" to make war. O'Neill and O'Donnell "by the procurement of the said Eleanor" had taken a solemn oath to take one part with the said Gerald against the Englishry (1538). For security the boy was conveyed to France, via the territory of O'Donnell. And, savage at being robbed of his precious prey, Henry VIII sent Lord Leonard Grey, his Deputy of Ireland, to the scaffold, for not having effected Gerald's capture.

Lady Eleanor unified the whole country. The French king and the Emperor Charles V promised their aid, once again, and Scotland's weight was to turn the balance in Ireland's favour. O'Neill was to be proclaimed High King at Tara. Once again foreign aid was illusory. The Earl of Desmond began by the invasion of the English districts of Tipperary; and the Northern chieftains "invaded the Pale" (1539). Against the field of the new English artillery, "the great grey guns," they had no adequate defence, so Irish hopes were once more futile.

But hope never yet died in the Irish breast. The name of the exiled young Gerald Fitzgerald became a source of inspiration and of hope to his countrymen at home. He had had a royal reception in France, in the Lowlands, in Italy and was acclaimed "King of Ireland" by the people who denounced Henry VIII as a mere usurper. He was followed by cheering crowds whenever he appeared in public. Kings and princes, the Emperor Charles, and the Pope vied with one another in honouring and aiding him. In Italy the Bishop of Verona and of Mantua provided him with the best education the Peninsula afforded. The Duke of Milan pensioned him. Cosmo de Medici pensioned him. In the service of the Knights of Malta he fought the Turks. He afterwards became Master of the Horse to the Grand Duke of Tuscany.

Geraldines to his interests. This brought down upon him the vengeance of England whose policy was to divide and conquer. On the death of Desmond, Ormond claimed the Earldom. The union of the two families would have made Butler ruler of almost the whole of Southern Ireland. Henry VIII took up Ormond's challenge. At a supper given at Limehouse, London, the whole of Lord Butler's retinue, fifty, sickened, seventeen dying of the poison. The Earl himself was carried to Ely House, Holborn, where he succumbed after some days' suffering. Irish writers blame Henry and his Deputy for this atrocity. Others accuse the Earl of Northumberland, "a rare poisoner" (1550).

France concluded to use Gerald in uniting Scotland and Ireland. Lady Eleanor Fitzgerald had guaranteed the support of the MacCarthys' land of Carbery; the O'Neills and O'Donnells "who had the whole North hanging on their sleeves," would give the French a glad welcome. Irish ambassadors were passing to and fro from the lands of the Gael and Sean Ghall to the French King. The English believed that there would be a universal rising as soon as the French and Gerald made their appearance. Irish monks and friars carried the fiery cross of revolt from Malin Head to Cape Clear—from North to South. A large French fleet had assembled at Brest, and 15,000 veteran soldiers were ready to embark.

But, at the last moment, the patching up of the quarrel between France and the Empire led to a change of plans. The French went direct to Scotland, from thence intending to invade Ireland. The English, wishing the beautiful and fascinating child, afterwards the world-famed Mary Queen of Scots, as a wife for Edward VI, to unite the two countries, sent an army to enforce their demand. The armies of Scotland and England met at Pinkie (10th Sept., 1547). The defeat of the Scots and their French and Irish allies was the result of the contest.

In Ireland, however, the O'Donnells and 15,000 Scots kept the flame alight in the North. The Geraldines and the O'Conors were ravaging the English Pale. The Earl of Desmond had all ready to join the oft-expected French. It was at this juncture that French opinion favoured the marriage of Gerald Fitzgerald with Mary of Scots. English agents in Scotland reported that when the Geraldine landed at Dumbarton "Gerald of Kildare should marry the Scottish queen and array all Ireland in their party against England." But the death of Francis I and the accession of Henry II, who wished Mary for his own son, altered all these plans. Scotland and Ireland found themselves but pawns on the Continental chess-board. Realising that all hope of freeing Ireland by the help of foreign princes was but as idle wind, Gerald, at the instance of his aunt, Lady Eleanor, made his submission to the English Queen and was restored to a portion of his lands and his title "legitimatised" (1554).

Though, even "legitimatised" he settled down to become the willing centre of endless,—and alas! fruitless—"rebellious" intrigue. The Irish chieftains, the Scots, the French, and the Spanish, plotted for Ireland's freeing—ever with the young Geraldine as the hero around whom the hosts should rally.

CHAPTER XLI

Henry VIII's Policies

From the beginning of his reign (1515) Henry VIII undertook to destroy the basis of Irish resistance. With this object in view he issued "most secret" instructions to his officials to capture our trade and commerce, by every subtle device. All the laws against Irish civilisation, against marriage, fosterage and gossipred, against the use of native literature and its language, against every phase and aspect of National life, were re-enacted. By a Parliament (May 1536) composed of English colonists only, and convened by fraud, corruption, and terror, Henry was acknowledged as Head of Church and State; and the Catholic religion, with its ritual and teachings, declared null and void, "corrupt for ever." Five years later the same body proclaimed Henry "King of Ireland."

"Irishmen," wrote one of the would-be exterminators in the light of sad later experience, "will never be conquered by war. They can suffer so much hardness to lie in the field, to live on roots and water continually, and be so light, ever at their advantage to flee or fight; so that a great army were but a charge in vain and would make victuals dear.... The Irishmen have pregnant subtle wits, eloquent and marvellous natural in comynaunce. They must be instructed that the King intendeth not to exile, banish, or destroy them, but would be content that every one of them should enjoy his possessions taking the same of the king . . . and become his true subjects, obedient to his laws, forsaking their Irish laws, habits and customs, setting their children to learn English" (Cowley's Plan for the Reformation of Ireland, 1541 *STATE PAPERS*).

The Lord Deputy, St. Leger, preached and acted on this Gospel. The unfortunate result was the submission of O'Neill, O'Donnell, O'Brien, the MacCarthy, the Burkes, and all the rules of the Irish, Old and New.

They went through the form of acknowledging Henry as King of Ireland, as Head of Church and State in Ireland, and promised to substitute English for Brehon law, and English manners, and customs for Irish. "They have turned, and sad is the deed, their back to the inheritance of their fathers." Yet in spite of "doing knee-homage, they would not get from the King of England for Ireland a respite from misery. There is not one of them in the shape of a man in Ireland at this time. O misguided, withered host, say henceforth nothing but Fooboon!" The people, faithful to Ireland in woe as in weal, resented, lamented, and even cursed their "diplomatic" chiefs.

The fate and fortunes of any one of the compromisers is typical of all. Take O'Neill for example. When Con O'Neill, Lord of Tir-Eoghan, submitted to Henry VIII at Greenwich (24th Sept., 1542), he renounced the title "The O'Neill," and was created Earl of Tyrone instead. A sturdy adventurer "called an O'Neill," Mathew Kelly, the son of a Dundalk blacksmith, selected by the English Government to disintegrate Tir-Eoghan, received the title of Baron of Dungannon, and so Con's successor by feudal law. O'Neill then acknowledged Henry as Head of Church and State, and undertook to substitute English for Irish civilisation. All the legal incidents of feudalism were to replace those of the Brehon law. The number of his soldiers was to be determined by the Lord Deputy, whom he was to accompany in all warlike expeditions against "rebels." A mansion and lands in the Pale were to be bestowed upon him, when he attended the English Parliament in Dublin. Though "he received the mocks of all men" for his conversion to Anglicisation he tried to fulfil his side of the shameful bargain. When Henry II of France and the Sovereign of Scotland sent letters and ambassadors to O'Neill inviting him to join the Catholic League against England, he forwarded the letters to London as a proof of his loyalty. Yet England had no intention of allowing any Irish lord to rule his people as his peers in England ruled theirs. Slowly it dawned on the victimised Con that her real aim was the seizure of his lands and the extermination of his people. Nicholas Bagenal, who had fled from justice for man-killing in England, was appointed Marshal of the North. He began an indiscriminate slaughter of O'Neill's subjects, burning even the very grass, killing every living thing on four legs, destroying habitations and churches. The recreant Con's letters of protest against such barbarity to England's King and the Privy Council, were returned unopened or disregarded. The "Baron of Dungannon" was maintained against him—"borne up by the chin" by the English Government. Daring to arrest one of the ravishers of his country, he was imprisoned in Dublin by the Governor till he was enforced to deliver the plunderer (1550). When he performed his duty of visiting the Deputy in the Pale he was told by that humane dignitary were it not that he was old he would have off his head and see his blood poured in a basin. After a victory to which O'Neill's troops contributed, he provided a banquet for his companion in arms, the Lord Deputy, the latter, "leaving the banquet unconsumed for haste," at Armagh "did imprison the said Earl O'Neill and took him prisoner to Dublin, and sent a garrison to Armagh and to Dungannon, his chief manor, since which time the country was impoverished" (1552). Vainly did he try to obtain a reason for this treatment. Con's letters describing the horrors his people endured by the acts of English soldiery, whilst he was "a true and faithful subject to the King's Majesty" make bitter reading.

After seventeen years as an English Earl Con lay on his dying bed, a broken, dispirited man, despised by his subjects. He called his people to him and pronounced malediction on all his descendants who should trust in English faith or give credence to English promises. He cursed those who would speak the English tongue, "for language bred confusion"; who built houses after the English fashion, "to be beaten out by the hawk"; who grew corn in the open, unfortified country, "to nourish the ravishers and destroyers."

Yet he suffered no more than any other of the confiding chieftains who had put their trust in English faith, in its policy of "Conciliation."

Throughout disillusioned Ireland the fighting men deserted the English-made lords. They flocked to the standards of the chieftains selected in the way their forebears had elected them for more than a thousand years. The Penal Laws against Irish Civilisation made the people love it the more passionately.

Another of Henry's devices for the conquest of Ireland was the kidnapping of noblemen's sons and having them reared and educated in England, hostile to every tradition and instinct of their nationality. "Politic practices," said Henry, "would serve till such time as the strength of the Irish should be diminished, their leaders taken away from them, and division put among themselves so that they join not together." A modern historian thus passes judgment on Tudor policy: "If there had been any truth or consideration for Ireland in the royal compact some hope of compromise and conciliation might have opened. But the whole scheme was rooted and grounded in falsehood, and Ireland had yet to learn how far sufferings by the quibble and devices of law might exceed the disasters of open war. Chiefs could be ensnared one by one in misleading contracts, practically void. A false claimant could be put on a territory and supported by English soldiers in a civil war, till the actual chief was exiled or yielded the land to the King's ownership. No chief, true or false, had power to give away the people's land, and the king was face to face with an indignant people, who refused to admit an illegal bargain. Then came a march of soldiers over the district, hanging, burning, shooting, 'the rebels,' casting the peasants out on the hillsides. There was also the way of 'conquest.' The whole of the inhabitants were to be exiled, and the countries made vacant and waste for English peopling: the sovereign's rule would be immediate and peremptory over those whom he had thus planted by his sole will, and Ireland would be kept in a way unknown in England; then 'the King might say Ireland was clearly won, and after he would be at little cost and receive great profits, and men and money at pleasure.' . . . Henceforth it became a fixed policy to 'exterminate and exile the country people of the Irishry.' Whether they submitted or not the king was 'to inhabit their country' with English blood."

Henry hoped to have a royal army of Ireland as "a sword and a flay" to his subjects in England and to his enemies abroad. His dream seemed to be realised when Earl Con O'Neill and other Irish lords, in the full flush of faith and confidence in English justice, sent an army to aid Henry's troops against Francis I, King of France—Ireland's best Continental friend—at the siege of Boulogne (1544). The false, disillusioned Irish did not repeat this experiment.

Also, Henry believed he could raise a big revenue out of Ireland's pockets for his sensualities and his political objects. But this likewise failed, because his "cormorants and caterpillars" (as one of their number happily described his fellow officials in Dublin Castle) were too busy amassing wealth for themselves.

The introduction of the Protestant Reformation principles added sources of fresh outrages, new oppressions. In Ireland Protestantism was not given a chance to appeal to the people by any ethical, religious, or political ideals. The licentious unpaid English soldiery who had to maintain themselves by plunder and rapine, were accompanied by incendiaries who left not a homestead, not a blade of corn, standing; these apostles were followed by ministers of the Gospel, with hangmen and escheators in their train. So, amidst an orgy of slaughters and executions, in which neither age nor sex, neither the infirm nor the strong were spared, and of burnings, the true teachings of the Prince of Peace were supposed to be inculcated. The soul of Ireland, resurrected through the crucifixion of her body, became the most devoted daughter of the Catholic Church. The destruction of monasteries, churches and schools, became a passion. Even the possession of a manuscript on any subject whatever incurred the death penalty. Poets and historians were put to the sword, and their books and genealogies burned, so that no man "might know his own grandfather." All Irishmen, Old and New, were to be confounded in the same ignorance and abasement, all glories gone and all rights lost. The great object of the English Government was to purge the land of Ireland of its rightful sons, to destroy the National tradition, to wipe out Gaelic memories, and to begin a new English life.

Henry's well-defined policies were religiously pursued by his successors, Edward and Mary.

The ministers of his son, Edward VI, intensified the vigour of his religious crusade. Religion was to be made sweet to the heretical Irish—"with the Bible in one hand, in the other the Sword." The English Liturgy in English was to be "rammed down the rebels' throats." Edward's sister, "Bloody Mary," who at Smithfield set alight the pyre, to burn those who dared to worship the God of Truth, the God of Mercy, in a way different from hers, in Ireland, amid great rejoicings, restored the Catholic religion. Religious bigotry has not—to the credit of the Irish Catholics be it proclaimed—ever found favour in Eirinn. Hence it is not surprising to find history record that the Reformers were nowhere persecuted when the long-suffering Irish Church was now restored to its own.

Mary's political policy did not differ from that of her father. Her Irish rule was no less merciless than that of her two predecessors. Catholic England, Protestant England—both were, to Ireland, as one in savage tyranny.

The O'Conors of Offaly and the O'Mores of Leix having dared to defend their lands against the English invaders were outlawed and their countries forfeited to the Crown. A long and bloody warfare, conducted with terrible ferocity, was the result. "Civil" English people and licentious soldiery were "planted" on the O'Conors' and O'Mores' lands; their owners being "rooted up by the sword" and burnt out by the torch. This "godly reformation" being achieved, these clan districts were named King's and Queen's County in honour of Mary and her Spanish husband, King Philip. The remnants of the broken clans were to be allowed to inhabit the boglands provided they became English in every sense of the word. Even in Ireland there is nothing so heroic, so persistent, so indefatigable as the efforts made by these two gallant clans to recover their homes and altars. The struggle was maintained for generations. Like storm-beaten birds in crannied nooks they emerged at every lull in the National storm and carried fire and sword among the "planters." Even to this day O'More and O'Conor are the principal families in the district, where their forefathers ruled as just, munificent princes.

FOR THE NORMAN PERIOD IN IRISH HISTORY READ IN ADDITION TO USUAL IRISH HISTORIES:

Davies: The Reason Why Ireland was Never Entirely Subdued.
Richey: Lectures on Irish History.
Green, Mrs. A. S.: The Making of Ireland and Its Undoing.
Hull, Eleanor: History of Irish Literature (vol. ii).
Hyde, Douglas: A Literary History of Ireland.
Gilbert: History of the Irish Viceroys.
MacNeill, Eoin: Phases of Irish History.

CHAPTER XLII

Shane the Proud[1]

Dublin Castle, the seat of English power in Ireland, stands on the site of the fortress of Haskulf the Dane. Before its first stone root struck into the ground, while the newly arrived Norman adventurers held Dublin, Haskulf came sailing back with fifty ships manned by men in ringed hauberks, with red painted shields, of iron hearts, of iron hands, says the chronicler, to win back his home. He was defeated, his men put to the sword, and he, for a brave defiant word, had his old bald head shorn from his shoulders.

---

[1] SHANE O'NEILL

On thy wild and windy upland, Tornamona,
High above the tossing Moyle,
Lies in slumber, deep and dreamless now, a warrior
Weary-worn with battle-toil.
On his mighty breast the little canna blossoms,
And the scented bog-bines trail;
While the winds from Lurigaiden whisper hush-songs
Round the bed of Shane O'Neill.

Time was once, O haughty Warrior, when you slept not
To the crooning of the wind;
There was once a Shane whom daisies could not smother,
And whom bog-weeds could not bind—
Once a Shane with death-shafts from his fierce eye flashing,
With dismay in fist of mail—
Shane, whose throbbing pulses sang with singing lightning—
Shane, our Shane, proud Shane O'Neill!

Him the hungry Scot knew, and the thieving Saxon,
Traitorous Eireannach as well;

Thus on the site of feasting was now a tradition of blood. The new justiciary carried up the walls; and by the time the story of Ireland reached the sixteenth century the castle was a large quadrangular building with towers, high walls, and strong defences. It was fortress, a Parliament House, a Council Chamber, a Prison. It was the very heart of English rule in Ireland. That heart had been beating there four hundred years and, if an old prophecy is true, it had yet to beat three hundred more. Then it would cease.

In 1567 a gift was brought to a group of gentlemen in the Castle's Council Chamber. The bearer was handsomely rewarded from the public Treasury, and the gift put in its place. Tarred, stuck on a pole thrust horizontally from the north-west gateway, it was left there for all Dublin to see. The Lord Deputy hastened to write to Elizabeth of England to tell her the good news. For that gift had brought her statesmen a step further in the conquest of Ireland.

It was the head of Shane O'Neill, captain and chief of Northwest Ulster. Shane was a bad man in private life, but a born soldier, a sagacious ruler, and a believer in his rights. When Conn, the Lame, his father, accepted an English title, and became Baron of Dungannon, Shane went into rebellion. On his father's death, he slew his half brother, the next baron, and was inaugurated the O'Neill. Shane the Proud, Ulster called him. He stood across England's advance into the province. Wherever he set up his tent, the great King-Candle before it, thicker than a man's body, shining there in the night, his battle-axe guard at the door, the trained soldiers of his territory, the hired Scottish *gall-oglach* around, victory generally fell to his side. Elizabeth and her Lord Deputies tried to cajole him, to deceive him, to

---

For their mailed throats often gurgled in his grasping,
    As he hurled their souls to hell.
Sassenach, now, and flouting Scot, and Irish traitor,
    Breathe his name and turn not pale,
Set their heel upon the warrior's breast, nor tremble—
    God! the breast of Shane O'Neill!

Will you never, O our Chieftain, snap the sleep-cords?
    Never rise in thunderous wrath—
Through the knaves and slaves that bring a blight on Uladh,
    Sweeping far a dread red swath?
O'er the surges shout, O you on Tornamona,
    Hark, the soul-shout of the Gael!
"Rise, O Chief, and lead us from our bitter bondage—
    Rise, in God's name, Shane O'Neill."

—Seumas MacManus.

defeat him, to capture him, to murder him. Then when his soldiers had pierced to the Pale, they recognised him as the O'Neill.

Once Sussex, the Lord Deputy, sent a force into his territory. The English general seized Armagh, left men there, gathered spoil, and set homeward.

O'Neill heard, followed, slew the spoilers, and recaptured the booty. The Lord Deputy wished to make terms. O'Neill answered that he would make no terms till the English soldiers were withdrawn from Armagh. The Deputy temporised, applied to England for soldiers, got them, and marched a great army into Northeast Ulster. But he struck at the air; O'Neill withdrew his men into the forests and mountains, and sent an envoy to France to ask for six thousand men.

Then Elizabeth bade her Deputy win him over with promises, with offers of friendship. He was won, or appeared to be. She invited him to London. So he went, taking his retinue with him, being not only chief of Tyrone, but a prince with far descended rights.

London stared. He brought a company of *gall-oglach.* They were picked and selected men "of great and mighty bodies, men choosing rather to die than to yield." They wore shirts of mail, iron caps, bright coloured trews to the knees, leggings of leather. Their arms were swords by their sides, battle-axes in their hands. The company being on an embassy of peace, in courtesy to a queen, marched with bare heads. An English writer saw them, wondered, marvelled with London and the court at their uncivilised mode of wearing their hair. Long on their necks it hung; close-cut in front above the eyes. And such eyes as must have looked out from under the combed unparted glib, proud, wondering, thinking of the spoil, no doubt, that the big foreign city could give. And Elizabeth, favourable to all well made men, received their Chief in honour, bestowing her friendship and gifts upon him; for which friendship and gifts, and the recognition of his Chieftainship, he paid her allegiance and promised to drive brave Sorley Boy McDonnell and his Scottish soldiers out of Antrim. So they parted, Lady paramount, and semi-independent prince.

But it was not her policy nor the policy of her statesmen to let such a man live. He was dangerous as an O'Neill who might try to recover full independence, a man also who remembered his direct descent from the High Kings of Ireland. He went home, the Proud, with what thoughts in his mind who shall say? But he had passed his word; remembered his honour; made war on Sorley Boy and his Scots, defeated them and captured McDonnell. For two years he lived in state, ruling justly. Every day he put aside the first dish from his table for the poor. "We serve Christ first," he said. Sinner, soldier, chieftain, he was a strong figure in the century.

These great dynastic houses maintained large retinues. Many, since the Invasion, had lived and ruled as if no England existed. They sent embassies and heralds to one another, proclaimed war or peace; collected their tribute. The point of England's sword had entered the nation's body, but the wound was scorned or forgotten. Each House had its hereditary officials: a marshal of forces; a master of the horse; chief doorkeeper; chief butler; superintendent of banquets; an immediate guard; keeper of treasure and chess-board; keeper of arms and dresses; answerer of challenges from outside territories; avengers of insult; chief steward; keeper of hounds; inaugurator and deposer; rearer of horses; carriers of wine from harbour to the court; builders and erectors of buildings; stewards of rent and tribute; hereditary historians and poets, men highly trained in the schools.

Shane's territory was now supposed to be safe from English interference or invasion. He and England's queen were friends. Sussex, the Lord Deputy, wrote offering him his sister in marriage with a safe conduct to Dublin. His intention was to capture Shane. Later he sent him a present of wine. Elizabeth knew of the gift; knew what was in it.

Shane and his household drank of the wine—and just escaped death. The poisoner was unskilled. But Shane knew now forever with whom he had to deal. It was the second attempt that English statesmen had secretly made to assassinate him. There is a State paper, a letter from Sussex to Elizabeth in which he tells of his efforts to get Shane murdered.

Shane flung off his allegiance. Allegiance sat on these Irish nobles like a red saddle loosely girt. After that draught of wine he thought his sword his best security. He won a victory notable for its name. Strange poppies lay among the harvest of the slain reaped by his *gall-oglach.* They were three hundred English soldiers, not in buff but in scarlet coats. The clansmen counted and wondered at the new uniform of their foes. So that battle was called the battle of the red coats.

But hard were the strokes of his enemies—"Queen's" O'Donnels, "Queen's" O'Neills, Elizabeth's forces—and the Proud was left the choice of submission or an appeal to the Scots mercenaries. He chose the latter, freed Sorley Boy McDonnell, and went to a banquet they gave. To that banquet also went a man whom the Lord Deputy had maintained privately in Tyrone when he and Shane were in friendship and peace. The spy waited till the wine had made men drunk and think of their wrongs. Then O'Neill was slain. The spy hastened to Dublin Castle and received from Sir Henry Sidney a thousand marks from the public treasury. So Shane's head went upon the north-west gate of Dublin.[2]

[2] Our Irish poet, John Savage, wrote a fine poem entitled "Shane's Head"—in which a clansman of Shane standing outside the wall of Dublin Castle is apostrophising the head—from which poem are taken the following stanzas:

> Is it thus, O Shane the haughty! Shane the valiant! that we meet—
> Have my eyes been lit by Heaven but to guide me to defeat?
> Have *I* no chief, or *you* no clan, to give us both defence?
> Or must I, too, be statued here with thy cold eloquence?
> Thy ghastly head grins scorn upon old Dublin's Castle-tower,
> Thy shaggy hair is wind-tossed, and thy brow seems rough with power;
> Thy wrathful lips, like sentinels, by foulest treachery stung,
> Look rage upon the world of wrong, but chain thy fiery tongue.
>
> That tongue, whose Ulster accent woke the ghost of Colm Cille,
> Whose warrior words fenced round with spears the oaks of Derry Hill;
> Whose reckless tones gave life and death to vassals and to knaves,
> And hunted hordes of Saxons into holy Irish graves.
> The Scotch marauders whitened when his war-cry met their ears,
> And the death-bird, like a vengeance, poised above his stormy spears;
> Ay, Shane, across the thundering sea, out-chanting it, your tongue
> Flung wild un-Saxon war-whoopings the Saxon Court among.
>
> Just think, O Shane! the same moon shines on Liffey as on Foyle,
> And lights the ruthless knaves on both, our kinsmen to despoil;
> And you the hope, voice, battle-axe, the shield of us and ours,
> A murdered, trunkless, blinding sight above these Dublin towers!
> Thy face is paler than the moon; my heart is paler still—
> *My* heart? I had no heart—*'twas* yours, 'twas yours! to keep or kill.
> And you kept it safe for Ireland, Chief—your life, your soul, your pride;
> But they sought it in thy bosom, Shane—with proud O'Neill it died.
>
> . . . .

CHAPTER XLIII

Elizabeth Continues the Conquest

The conquest of Ireland had been going on for four centuries. The rock against which every attempt to complete it had broken was the immemorial laws of Ireland, the Brehon Laws. These bound Irishmen within the four seas to one social and legal rule. All attempts to plant the feudal system in Ireland by England went down before them.

Their land system was the chief evil in the eyes of the invaders. The clan owned the land as well as the chief. He had a life interest in the chief's portion; but he could not sell the clan-lands or eject free owners. This was a hindrance to confiscation. Now, the Irish laws were declared barbarous. During four centuries the ambulatory Parliament of the Pale passed laws against it. These laws reached just as far as English swords could carry them. The Parliament had now not to discuss, but to pass, the commands of Her Highness. They were two, to be carried out by all methods. Ireland was to be brought completely under her authority, each chief's territory admitting English law: and the Protestant religion was to be firmly established. These two cardinal commands each Lord Deputy was to enforce upon Ireland.

The time had arrived when the two civilisations stood at last fully face to face. The one represented by feudalism—feudalism unshackling itself—and the one represented by the Brehon Laws.[1] The first had long denounced the other as barbarous. Irish dress, Irish customs, were the dress and customs

[1] Dr. Sigerson says of the early Brehon Laws, "I assert, that, speaking biologically, such laws could not emanate from any race whose brains have not been subject to the quickening influence of education for many generations."

of savages.[2] England's wish, often expressed in the four hundred years, was to civilise Ireland. If that were impossible, then extermination.

The other objective, besides the Irish laws, was now the religion of the people. The Reformation had rolled back from the shores of Ireland. To the devout soul of the race it was blasphemy to call Henry VIII, or Elizabeth, the Head of the Church. Strong measures were now used. Abbeys were suppressed and destroyed; churches seized; Protestant ministers supplanted the priests. But no real headway was made. The Irish-Norman nobles, the Desmonds and others, held to the Catholic Faith; the clans and their chiefs did the same. Fiercer measures followed. The Dublin Parliament enacted that the lives of priests were forfeited. They were to be hanged, cut down when half dead, disembowelled and burnt, and their heads impaled in some public place. Any one sheltering a priest was to be hanged, and his lands confiscated. The Act only ran where England's arm reached. In free Tirconnel, in free Tyrone, in the Desmond country, in the O'Rourke's of Breffiny, in hundreds of places in Ireland it had no effect. Priests ministered to their flocks openly; learned monks wrote in their monasteries. But here and there the hands reached, struck, and captured. It captured the Archbishop of Cashel, played with him for a while, as a cat with a mouse, then finding him inflexible tortured him and put him to death. Other priests were seized and tortured and hanged.

The strongest Norman house in Irish history was the Geraldines. They must be suppressed. The Ormonds were Castle men, guardians of English authority. The Black Earl of Ormond seized Gerald, Earl of Desmond, and sent him to London, and Elizabeth sent him to the Tower. A little later his brother was seized and sent there too. Their cousin, James Fitzmaurice,

---

[2] In the first century of the Invasion the vehement Norman-Welsh Archdeacon, Giraldus Cambrensis, exclaims, "Verily a wild and inhospitable race! Yet Nature fails not to rear and mould them through infancy and childhood, until in the fulness of time she leads each to man's estate conspicuous for a tall and handsome form, regular features, and a fresh complexion. But though adorned to the full with such natural gifts as these, still the barbarous fashion of their garments, and their ignorance, reveal the utter savage. They apparel themselves in small closely fitting hoods extending over the shoulders and down to the elbow, generally made of parti-colour scraps sewn together. Under this instead of a coat they wear a gown. Woolen trews complete that attire, being breeches and hose in one, usually dyed some tint. The "barbarians" honoured learning. The Leinster prince who invited the Normans to Ireland could write, and not only write but quote Ovid. Most of the Norman chivalry had to employ clerics to read and write their letters. We read of banquets and tournaments in other countries where young knights showed their prowess in the saddle, their skill with the lance: but we do not read of banquets and tournaments given to learned men where the contest was not steel against steel, but epic against epic, song against song, harp against harp—such as those arranged by Liam O'Kelly and the Lady Mairgret of Offaly.

drew his sword to protest against the seizures. "Spirited youths" joined him, and held the Desmond country. They won victories; they routed a queen's army. Then Elizabeth made peace with Fitzmaurice. And she then directed a plot for the treacherous murder of himself, his brothers and cousins—which, by discovering in time, he escaped. After a time the new Earl had to fly to Spain for safety and succour.

He visited Rome, too, got Italian mercenaries, fourscore Spaniards, a promise of more, and returned to Ireland, where he vanished out of life in a skirmish. Spain remembered her promise. Eight hundred Spaniards landed on the coast of Kerry. They fortified themselves on the Golden Island, a rock connected with the land by a narrow neck. The Lord Deputy, Gray, hastened to attack them, and invested the rock by sea and land. But no breech was made; the Golden fort was impregnable; winter was approaching. Gray sent in a flag of truce and offered honourable terms if the Spaniards would surrender. The Spanish commander accepted the terms, and his men laid down their arms. Then Gray sent in his soldiers and massacred seven hundred men. The massacre, note well, was directed by Sir Walter Raleigh and an officer named Wingfield.

The Earl and his kinsmen, fighting now for their religion and their homes, joined hands with the MacCarthys, the O'Sullivans and other Munster chiefs. Carew, a Devonshire knight, claimed Desmond territory, and brought an army to seize it and "pacify" the province. The Desmond war lasted three more years, altogether five. When it terminated the "pacification" was continued. The Earl, finally defeated, after wandering through woods and bogs and in the ravines of the mountains, was at last captùred and beheaded. At Elizabeth's request his head was sent to London and impaled in an iron cage on the Tower. English adventurers flung themselves on the confiscated lands. Sir Walter Raleigh raided over the thousands of acres assigned to him, and smoked the "Virginia weed" in Youghal after work that would discredit a savage chief.

There is a gigantic preternatural Figure in Irish Myth; the Red Swineherd. Where it passes, where it lays its foot, smoke and flames and blood and death and destruction are there. It comes out of some antique past, some dread forgotten ritual. The Figure of the Myth was upon Munster. Beneath it the little figures of men move; the mail-clad *gall-oglach,* the swift running Kerne, the red-coated, iron-plated soldiers; Irish nobles and chiefs, the marshals of England's forces. Away from all these, from Irish and Norman chiefs, the MacCarthys, the Desmonds, the O'Sullivans, all the princelings, away from the English Deputies, marshals and adventurers thirsting for Munster soil, away from all those that storm across this page of Irish history—glance at the unnamed people. Munster was the fairest province in Ireland. It had fifteen hundred schools. When the Munster wars were ended, when Elizabeth sent her thanks to Sir George Perrin.[3] For the "pacification" of the province, the schools had been wiped out. The storm of battles and skirmishes, of sieges, of intrigues, of massacres is the shifting blood-red veil above the homes of thousands. That was no barbarous land where scholars filled the schools, where science and the classics were taught; where the pride of youth was stimulated, the imagination fired by the Hero-Tales of Ireland. It is a psychological fact that the Elizabethan Englishmen, many of them brave, gallant and chivalrous, became barbarians in their contact with Ireland. The old Greeks explain the reason for the fall. It is Pride and Injustice; these things bring moral death. In their attempt to conquer Ireland the avenging Furies fell upon them.

Carew in his Pacata Hibernia writes that English soldiers entered an Irish camp, "found none but hurt and sick men, whose pains and lives they soon determined." And again that he having burnt all the houses and corn and taken great prey diverted his forces into another place, "and harrowing the country, killed all mankind that were found therein for a terror to those who would give relief to runagate traitors." He passed into Arleagh woods "where we did the like, not leaving behind us man or beast, corne or cattle." The slaughter continued after the war had ended. "Those whom the sword could not reach were deliberately given a prey to famine."

"The English nation," says Froude, "was shuddering over the atrocities of the Duke of Alva. Yet Alva's bloody sword never touched the young, the defenceless. . . . Sir Peter Carew has been seen murdering women and children and babies that had scarcely left the breast."

Spenser, the English poet, to whom Raleigh had given a few acres of the forty thousand he had seized, saw still living creatures "creeping out of every corner of the woods and glens on their hands, for their legs would not bear them. They did eat the dead carrion where they could find them, yea, and one another soon after." He thinks English rule can never be secure till the Irish race is exterminated. The gentle English idyllist suggests a way. The people are not to be allowed to till their land or pasture their cattle next season, then "they will quickly consume themselves and devour one another."

---

[3] Perrin reported that he had "left neither corn, nor horn, nor house unburnt," between the two ends of Munster.

English Law had made a breach in Connacht. A Lord President was appointed, and a court held. From Sligo to Limerick men were to be netted and brought before it. The head of the Burkes, Clanrickard, a "queen's" man, was seized and sent to Dublin. Then all the Burkes loosened their swords in their scabbards and sprang into rebellion. The rebellion grew and strengthened, before the "strong measures" of the Lord President. The Lord Deputy, Fitzwilliam, an old man, afflicted by ills of the body, crafty, cautious, treacherous, freed Clanrickard, and sent him down to make terms. The bloody hand was stayed; for a moment there was peace in Connacht. Soon, the disarmed Catholics were taken and hanged. Surrendered garrisons were put to the sword; a search for "rebels" in West Connacht saw women, and boys and old men, and all who came in Bingham's way, slain.

Into Leinster, too, English Law had driven a wedge. Mary of England's Deputies had seized Offaly and Leix, the territories of the O'Conors and the O'Mores. They had planted English settlers there; abolished the ancient territorial names and in Irish blood rechristened them King's and Queen's counties. The dispossessed chiefs and their clansmen bided their time. A noble boy grew up among them, and in manhood became an avenging sword. This was Ruari Og O'More. He attacked the homes of the English settlers; burnt their towns; took the governor of Leix and a Privy Councillor prisoners; made truces and kept them. After six years of successful guerilla warfare he fell when reconnoitring a force brought against him. His soldiers avenged his death and put the army to flight. His name remained an inspiration to oppressed Irish, down to the present day. "God, and Our Lady, and Rory O'More!"

The English troops were commanded in Leix and Offaly by a Sir Francis Cosby. This man gave a banquet in the Rath of Mullaghmast in Kildare. And he stretched out friendly hands to the O'Conors and O'Mores and their followers. He invited them to the banquet. He gave it in the Queen's name; he promised her protection. They went. One gentleman, arriving late, suspected something, and paused. Guests went in, he saw, but none came out. Advancing, he reconnoitred, beheld slaughtered bodies, and being now attacked himself, cut his way through and escaped. Of the O'Mores alone, one hundred and eighty were murdered. Cosby lived at Straballly. A tall tree with spreading branches grew before his door, upon which he hanged men and women and children. If he hanged a mother and an infant he hanged the child in the mother's long hair.[4]

---

[4] *Ireland under Elizabeth*. O'Sullivan Beare. 1621.

But a day of reckoning came. In the battle of Glenmalure Cosby fell in the rout when the soldiers of Feach O'Byrne cut down the flying forces of Lord Gray. O'Byrne, there, in the Wicklow mountains, had held his country against all attempts of the English to seize it. Gray, newly arrived in Dublin, thought at one stroke to break O'Byrne's power. He gathered a great army and marched into Wicklow. He believed he had trapped O'Byrne. The glen was deep; its sides dark wooded heights and rocks; a shallow stream with a rugged bed flowed through. He raised an earthwork across the mouth that the flying Irish might be trapped and cut down there. To see that flight and slaughter he went up on a height, he and his courtiers and staff. His soldiers entered the glen, moving up it in silence, a long array in mail and buff and scarlet, gunsmen and horse. No sight of the foe; silence save for the tramp of their marching feet. The watchers on the height began to laugh. "The game had broken away," they jested. "The old fox had run to earth." Then as the ranks of the column loosened on the broken course, the silence of the wood was shattered and the bullets of the Irish swept the line. O'Byrne's men sprang from the tree-clad slopes, leapt over the rocks, and threw themselves upon the flanks of the foe. Gray and his jesters fled. Of the great force with which he had marched out of Dublin, but a few broken companies returned.

CHAPTER XLIV

Red Hugh

In the North the smouldering fire had flamed forth again. Two things rekindled it. One: The predestined boy had come whose advent a Tir-Conaill seer had long ago foretold. Young Hugh O'Donnell, Aod Ruad, the golden-haired, minatory, deadly foe to England; who was to stride through the history of the last years of the sixteenth century—the boy whose fame and renown was noised through the five provinces of Eirinn even before he reached the age of manhood, as being conspicuous for wisdom, understanding, personal beauty, and noble deeds.

The fame and renown of him had reached the ears of Lord Deputy Perrot, illegitimate son of Henry VIII. Where a strong and ruthless hand, or treachery, was necessary to advance his Queen's interests in Ireland Perrot used either, as suited the occasion. He would have the boy.

The dreaded lad was being fostered by MacSwiney, Lord of Fanat on the Northern sea's verge. When the boy was fourteen an innocent looking merchant ship once sailed into Loch Swilly, and anchored under the white stone castle of MacSwiney. The courteous captain had wine for sale. The courteous captain invited visitors aboard the ship. The courteous captain would like MacSwiney and his retinue and friends to do him the honour of a visit aboard, and to partake of some rare wine. They came—and with them the noble boy, erect and eagle-eyed, bright, proud and confident, "of a countenance so alluring that none could look at him without loving him." When the guests sat them down to wine in the captain's state cabin, they suddenly found themselves entrapped and captured by fifty soldiers who were conjured out of the ship's bowels. MacSwiney and the others were released, and given hostages, but the boy's release could not be purchased. It was for him the ship had come. Red Hugh was carried away to

Dublin and placed, a prisoner, in the Birmingham tower of the castle. In Fanat, throughout all Tir-Conaill, and indeed through Eirinn there was weeping, wrath, shame and anger. In Donegal Castle the boy's mother, the dauntless Inghín Dubh, "Dark Daughter" of MacDonnell of the Isles, now devoted her life to keep Tir-Conaill for the boy. She negotiated and plotted for his release—in vain.

After three years the boy made a wonderful and daring escape on a December night—but alas! was retaken. After another year, this time spent in irons, in company with Henry and Art, the sons of Shane O'Neill, both in irons also, he made another daring attempt—and this time succeeded in freeing all three.

A file had been passed in to him. It was Christmas Eve, 1591, a dark snowy evening. Christmas cheer was flowing among the jailers and guards. Now, the boys thought! Outside the Castle, in a friend's stable, four horses bitted and saddled have stood for three nights. The faithful horse-boy is waiting. While the feast was being celebrated with wine and jollity by the Elizabethan soldiers in the Castle, the boy industriously worked the file. "Link after link yielded to the fierce attrition and the hungry gnawings of the sharp toothed steel, and Red Hugh stood forth free! Free, and the guard giving no sign! Henry O'Neill stretched out his hands, while Art held the lamp. Swiftly the good file did its work, and Henry, unfettered, snatched the lamp from his brother's hands. Art was the last freed, and Hugh, youngest of the three, did all the filing with his own sinewy untiring hands." (Standish O'Grady.)

Free now, unshackled, swift hands tore down the hangings of the bed, knotted them together, and the rope was ready. The hangings secured, Henry went first, then Red Hugh, and last of all Art, who in his descent loosened a stone which fell and struck him. They flung their cloaks from them when they reached the open air, stole to the moat, and entered the icy water. The snow was still falling; waiting on the bank, whitened, listening for the strokes of the swimmers, the horse-boy stood. He carried three pairs of strong shoes; their horses had unfortunately been taken away. Swiftly their guide led them through the dark streets and alleys to the outer rampart. And there Henry O'Neill was missing, having fallen behind and lost his way. There was no time to return; to look for him. The Castle and death were behind.[1]

[1] Henry O'Neill succeeded in getting to Ulster and was imprisoned by the Earl of Tyrone, who considered him a rival as the son of Shane who had slain the Earl's father.

They were over it; out into the deeper darkness; past the outskirts of the city; into the open country, on towards Slieve Ruadh, the Three Rock Mountain; snow everywhere. They passed over bogs glimmering white, through ravines; up among the snow drifts on the slope, the hardy tireless horse-boy leading, Red Hugh's pace "vigorous and swift." But Art—his strength and wind had given way—dropped behind. The swift-paced Red Hugh fell back to his side, supported and cheered him; kept slow step with his slow step. Soon Art could only limp, and moved haltingly along, with an arm on Red Hugh's shoulder and another on the horse-boy's. Dawn came; Christmas Day; in the city bells were heralding the Birth; in the Castle there was wrath and fear—and hot pursuit. Then Art could walk no longer. Red Hugh and the horse-boy carried him, Red Hugh himself with blistered feet and his own strength failing. All day they were on the white mountains, lingering, resting, advancing, till at last Red Hugh could go no further, and the horse-boy left them, hastening if he might to save them and bring help from Feach O'Byrne. Between the two loughs, Dan and Glendalough, under a rock, or in an open cave, it is thought, the boys waited. They slept heavily that night, and awoke in the morning to a second day of cold and hunger. For forty hours they had eaten no food. Their cloaks were gone, shed by the Castle moat; they had only their doublets and hose.

The day passed, the helpless boys waiting in the snow, and the furious foe engirdling the white mountains. When the morning of the third day came Art was dying. Red Hugh ate leaves, and brought some to Art. "Eat something, no matter what," he said. "See the brute animals, Art, they feed on leaves and grass. True, we are rational, yet also we are animals."

But Art was beyond such food, beyond any food indeed. White death there by the rock was numbing body and brain. The snow began to fall again. Evening came. Red Hugh lay down by Art's side; the boys clasped their arms about each other. The snow covered them.

In the closing twilight Feach's soldiers found them in that embrace. Not at once, so hidden were they under the snow. By the light of their lanthorns the four soldiers groped about, finding the search not easy. "So overlaid were they with the snow as if with blanket which had congealed around them, and frozen to them their skirts of fine linen, and their moistened shoes and leather covering of their feet, and they themselves were completely covered with snow and there was also no life in their members, but they were as dead."

Their arms were disentwined, their bodies chafed, spirits put between their lips, "the men deeply grieving as they uncovered the white faces, and the limp motionless limbs of the noblest born youths in all the land, the heir of Tir-Conaill and the son of Shane." Art passed away. Red Hugh revived, spoke, asked for his dying friend. Passionately he wept when, all saving efforts failing, Art died. He refused to eat or drink; he himself, famishing, cold, just snatched from Death. For a time the men respected his grief, then removed Art's body from his sight, persuaded him with kindly insistence to eat and drink a little. They wrapped him in their cloaks, made a litter of their spears, and bore him "within the rim of the broad shield extended over that region"—the shield of Feach—his feet swollen within the horse-boy's shoes, and brought him to Feach's house; Feach, of whom Spenser wrote that he "overcrowded high mountains and dictated terms of peace to mighty potentates."

Red Hugh's escape sent a thrill through Ireland. Messengers rode north and south and east and west with the joyous word.

After hairbreadth escapes the boy eventually reached the North. On a grey of speed and endurance Red Hugh rode with yellow-haired Turlough Boy O'Hagan into Dungannon—to Hugh O'Neill, "Earl" of Tir-Owen. An alliance was made between him and the earl, he, the boy of eighteen, who had been so deeply injured, and the grave sagacious man, who foresaw that the English State was working secretly for his overthrow; to whom the time must come when he would have to defend his life, his territory, his people. That alliance buried forever clan-diplomacies and feuds between the two great houses.

O'Neill sent him on to the Lord of Fermanagh, Hugh Maguire, a very tall, handsome, gay-spirited young man, valiant in arms, who when a lord Deputy proposed to send a sheriff into Fermanagh, suggested to the Viceroy that he had better let him know the price of the sheriff's head first. Accompanied by a fleet of boats, Red Hugh was carried in Maguire's state barge in triumphal processsion down the Erne to a point on the western shore. There gentlemen of Tir-Conaill met him, and he went to his own castle of Ballyshannon. There was joy in its hall; feasting, the music of war-pipes; vows to follow him; men's courage renewed. He was laid on a "bed of healing," with swollen feet—one permanently lamed by those nights in the snow. But not long did he lie there. Bingham's captain was besieging Donegal castle. Within it his brave mother, Inghín Dubh,[2] waited for succour. The captain had gathered much spoil, intending, the castle taken, to bring those beeves to Connacht and Bingham. Red Hugh rose, laughed at

[2] Literally Dark Daughter.

his surgeons, called out his men, and marched to Donegal. He recovered the spoil, freed the castle and the Dark Daughter, and drove the captain and his soldiers out of Tir-Conaill. What a meeting then between him and his dauntless mother. For the four years of his captivity, aided faithfully by MacSwiney of the Battle Axes, she had never ceased to try to obtain his release and keep the chieftaincy for him.

On a May day the lad was made The O'Donnell. Sir Hugh, his father, gladly gave place to a son so fit to rule. A weak, hesitating man, he had let his wife, the Dark Daughter, strike the blows for her stolen son. Now a mild old man, tired of a vexatious world where treachery and dark ways prevailed, he was about to seek the goal of old war-worn Irish princes, the rest and shelter of a monastery.

Therefore on that May day, young, valiant, beautiful, but lame in one foot—the mark of his captivity—the boy with gifts of mind and body that had made men look to him as the hope of Ireland, stood on the Rock of Doone, the immemorial throne of the O'Donnells, the white wand in his hand, symbol of Authority and of what his rule must be, white and straight; and turning thrice from left to right, and thrice from right to left, in honour of the Holy Trinity, he viewed from every point his territory. Then as he stood still, erect and kingly, the inaugurator called "O'Donnell!" giving him a title higher than any the foreigners could give, the ancient title of his ancestors, the princes of Tir-Conaill. And each man among the high officials, according to rank, cried out "O'Donnell!" and the voices of hundreds of clansmen carried "O'Donnell!" far into the distance. Thus Red Hugh's star rose and shone high in the north over Ireland; and still shines in the dark sky of her history.

The Nine Years' War had begun. A spear darted through Tir-Conaill. The invader was driven out; chiefs who had given their allegiance to the foreigner were taught that the O'Donnell was their chief and prince. He swept through Ulster, and drove out the English sheriffs. He entered Connacht and hurled Bingham's forces before him. Hugh O'Neill watched events; waited, held his hand, still uncertain; could he and those like him live under English rule or not? He visited London, answered to the queen the charges made against him and won her favour for the time. But his destruction was decided upon. He was to be inveigled to Dublin to explain certain fresh charges, a safe conduct being given him. Then, by Elizabeth's order, he was to be seized. It was feared he might not come. But he came, walking into the Council Chamber as a man who had nothing to dread. He would have been arrested had not the Black Earl of Ormond declared that he "would not use treachery to any man." Later he warned O'Neill to leave

Dublin that night as the Deputy was preparing to prevent his getting away from the city.

So the issue of an independent Ireland or a conquered country was now to be put to the sword. Almost for the first time since the invasion Ireland had a statesman who saw the root of her weakness, and who placed the politics of the nation before the politics of the clan.

CHAPTER XLV

THE NINE YEARS' WAR

The war was not only one of independence but a religious war as well. Men looked to Spain, the great Catholic country; would she help? Messengers crossed and re-crossed the seas. On one side was the entire power of England aided by her Irish auxiliaries. That fact, the Irish auxiliaries, had kept the English forces from being driven out of Ireland. Another, the Irish during the centuries had not realised (maintaining as so many of them did their own independence) that the invasion, and the subsequent colonies, were calculated and unswerving attempts to shatter the whole fabric of Irish civilisation, and supplant it by an alien one. In the sixteenth century the mass of the people had not fully realised it yet. They were but beginning to do so.

And those auxiliaries—Irishmen ranked with Henry's or Elizabeth's troops, winning victories over their countrymen, let the fact explain itself. I think it explains itself primarily by clan-politics, which had so often guided the actions of the chiefs. The policy of centralisation, attempted by one or two of the Irish kings, had never developed. "Despotism tends to centralisation, freedom of the people to decentralise," says Eoin MacNeill. And he says, "among the Celts as among the Greeks of antiquity and the Italians of the Middle Ages, the instinct of local freedom usually prevailed over the policy of centralisation, and what we may call neighbourhoods, in which the people knew all about each other, so to speak, formed themselves into states for the regulation of their own affairs. The principle was the same as that which measures the areas of local district councils in our time, but the district council of antiquity had all but sovereign powers."

The instinct of local freedom had gathered round the Norman houses in Ireland during the centuries. Thus Irish soldiers, always true to their leaders, marched with the Earl of Ormond, or the Earl of Kildare, or other Norman lord who paid allegiance to England; or followed the "queen's" O'Reilly, or "queen's" MacMahon, or other chief, as affection, or the love of warfare, or the pay of the mercenary, induced them. But local freedom was only the skin of the nation. The heart was true to nationality. The bards voiced its beat. They wrote not only in praise of their own *tuath* and chief, of Offaly, or Thomond, or Tir-Owen, or other portions of Ireland, but of Ireland as a whole, as a national unit.[1]

O'Neill cast off the title of Earl, and was proclaimed The O'Neill. Ulster was already organised; a Northern Confederacy was formed. His weapon was ready. Those companies whom he had trained were keen steel fit for use. Seven miles from his castle a fortress was held by the English. It stood by the Abhainn-Mor. The great river, Ulster called it; the Blackwater, the English. Men said they gave it that name, not because of its turgid waters but because they had so often met disaster and defeat on its banks. O'Neill's men stormed the fortress, drove out the English garrison, levelled the fort, and burnt the bridge. The queen's forces held Monaghan. He marched thither; gave battle to Norris, the English general, who was advancing to its relief, and defeated him. Hugh Maguire, finest horseman in Ireland, twice rode down with his cavalry on the English musketeers, and twice broke them. Monaghan fell; the English commander was allowed to go free.

England proclaimed O'Neill an enemy and a traitor. Armies were sent against him. He evaded or defeated the armies. He showed generalship of a high order. She recalled her best soldiers from the Spanish war in Belgium, and flung them into Ireland. She sent skilful commanders against him, Norris and Russell and Bagenal. Generals and soldiers failed to break his power. Then Elizabeth opened negotiations, offering fair and honourable terms. O'Neill knew how to meet them; how much to trust. A message came from Spain: Fight on! Spanish soldiers are coming. O'Neill broke off the negotiations and the war was renewed. Sligo had fallen, taken by Red Hugh; Bingham's army was in retreat followed by O'Donnell who "harried it with missiles." Norris and his veterans marched out of Athlone to meet and crush Red Hugh.

---

[1] "The names of Erin, Banba, Fodhla, the Land of Conn, are in their mouths every moment, and to the last they persisted in their efforts to combine the Gael against the Gall." *Literary History of Ireland.* Hyde.

For this reason Spenser hated them. "They are tending for the most part to hurt the English, for the maintenance of their own lewde libertie," he says.

Here are moving pictures, snatched out of the Nine Years' War. A river in Mayo, a village; on the south bank an army of ten thousand horse and foot; men in scarlet or buff, tunics, with puffed sleeves, and iron breastplates and backs; forests of weapons; bright pennants, and the banner of Saint George. A great and well ordered army. The general in shining steel, wide ruff, and plumed helmet; officers in shining steel and feathered caps. The general is Sir John Norris, who in France and Belgium had earned a great name, come out of those countries to clear Ulster and Connacht of the rebels, his laurels now a little draggled by his late encounters with O'Neill. On the other bank are the Irish horse and foot, about five thousand men. The boy who had broken England's gyves from his wrists is there; the army is his; everywhere he has led it to victory. His cavalry are armed with head pieces, shirts of mail, a sword, a skian, a spear. Very skilful horsemen, who ride upon saddles without stirrups, and who carry the lances not under the arm when riding to the charge, but by the middle, above the arm. And his infantry—those picked and selected men of mighty bodies, the "greatest force of the battle"—they are the gall-oglach (gallowglasses), "great scorners of death," men choosing to die rather than yield, "so that when it came to handy blows they are quickly slain or win the field." And his light infantry, the *ceitherne* (Kernes), with targets of wood, barbed darts and muskets: and the horse-boys, "not less serviceable in the meating and dressing of horses, than hurtful to the enemy with their darts." The Robe flows between; along its banks there is fighting for a day and a night. A pause; Norris's drums beat a parley; the boy and the veteran meet. There is a truce all day; every day; but fierce fighting at night, attacks on each other's camps; captures of out-posts and scouts; hand to hand encounters. And each day till sun-down the truce lasts; and Red Hugh and his chiefs and his friend, "the ever valiant Maguire," the gay young Lord of Fermanagh who is heart and soul in the war, discuss terms of peace with Norris. Did ever boy commander and experienced general meet thus as equal peers in war before? A month passes, and the terms come to nothing. A messenger gallops into the Irish camp; he brings news; a Spanish ship is in Rathmullan Bay; Spain has promised help. Norris raises his camp and retires, rear and wing harassed by the swift-following *ceitherne*. But to neither wing nor rear does he send help. Behold that high hedge in front; he will entrap the pursuers across, then turn and cut them down. Young falcon eye sees the danger. That is Red Hugh on that galloping horse. He holds in the men; he bids none cross. So Norris, baulked of his plan, continues his retreat in wrath, uttering terrible imprecations against fate which had condemned him "to lose in Ireland, the smallest speck of the wide world, that fame which his valour and military skill had earned for him in France and Belgium."

Red Hugh went like a flame through the west. He scattered his enemies, and drove Bingham before him. He re-captured Sligo castle; defeated Clifford, the English governor of Connacht, in the Curlew pass; brought the Burkes—the turbulent haughty Norman clan—to his standard and to accept his right to choose and inaugurate their chief; and for every day of his captivity he paid by the stroke of his sword.

The war spread to Leinster; for young Eoiny O'More, son of Rory O'More, had returned to Leix, a boy men thought "not yet of an age for war." Faithful friends had brought him when a little child to Feach O'Byrne who had guarded him in his Wicklow fortress. But Feach could no longer protect him for Feach was dead, killed in an ambush, and his sons, Felim and Raymond, gallant young men fighting the enemy, could not take care of a boy considered too young for arms. So he was sent back to Leix. There he declared he was a man and would lead men. His father's clan gathered round him, rejoiced, and made him their chief. The English governor of Leix sent a force to seize him. They were beaten with the loss of fifty men. "A stirring youth who hath lately taken weapon," wrote old Fitzwilliam to London, "the O'Mores look to him to be their captain." Before he was of age Eoiny had won a name for skill and daring. He recognised O'Neill's authority; visited the north, and received his consent to strike a blow at the English forces in Munster. With eight hundred foot and a handful of horse the boy darted into the province. Ormond, in command of the queen's troops, was too late to oppose him. Eoiny and his men shot past. There was alarm; rapid musterings. The Lord President Thomas collected soldiers in haste and waited at Mallow to beat the audacious Leinster lad. The lad came up very readily. A herald rode to the gate and handed in a letter. Eoiny O'More challenged the Lord President to bring out his army and give battle. He wrote several "bold letters." Norris took counsel; left a small garrison in Mallow and retreated to Cork followed by Eoiny whose light-armed men skirmished with his rear. That retreat rang through Munster. Men enrolled; leaders and captains were found; messages were sent to O'Neill. The boy's dart-like stroke had re-kindled the war in the province.

In the North a beautiful woman flits into the war scene—an English girl, a beauty of nineteen. Her name was Mabel Bagenal. Her father, one Nicholas Bagenal, having killed a man of position in England, had sought refuge in Ireland. The earl's grandfather, Conn the Lame, had befriended him, and had obtained his pardon from Henry VIII. Bagenal got large grants of forfeited lands, became a foe of O'Neill's and died Marshal of Elizabeth's forces in Ireland.

In the summer of 1591, Hugh O'Neill, still in friendship with the queen and her Deputy, met the beauty, and they fell in love with each other. Her friends approved. The marriage was a great one for the girl. Up there in Tyrone she would be a countess and something more. But she had a brother, Sir Henry Bagenal, Marshal of Ireland, O'Neill's secret enemy. When the earl asked for her hand, not directly refusing, he raised difficulties about the "incivilities" of the earl's country. By "incivilities" he meant barbarism, the word so frequently used by the English when the two civilisations met. He sent her to her sister, living near Dublin, who encouraged the lovers. Their betrothal took place, and O'Neill gave the girl a gold necklace of great value. A month later O'Neill went to a dinner at this sister's house with a retinue of English friends. People dined at noon. In the long August afternoon when the feast was over, the guests wandered on the lawns and played at games. But the girl slipped out of the house to where a pillioned horse and a gentleman of O'Neill's suite were waiting. There was a swift ride to a friend's house. O'Neill followed. The Bishop of Meath, the "queen's" bishop married them, and the earl took his bride north, built a fine house for her, and "furnished it out of London."

Bagenal was now his mortal enemy. The beautiful girl lived to see her husband throw off his English title and unfurl the banner with the Red Hand of O'Neill. A little change of fate—and she might have been a queen. She became a Catholic, and died in 1596.

Two years later O'Neill and Bagenal met. Not alone. To that encounter each brought an army. Bagenal at the head of the queen's forces had been sent to crush a prince who aimed at an independent Ireland. So far O'Neill had been the victor in Ulster. So victorious had he been that several attempts at negotiation had been made by the English. He had refused to meet the queen's commissioners except at the head of his army. Once he had dictated terms; the Catholic Church was to be left undisturbed; no sheriff admitted into Irish territories; and payment made to him of his wife's dowry which Bagenal had kept. While he was moving thus triumphantly through Ulster "every blow he dealt was re-echoed by Red Hugh in Connacht."

It was 1598, the sixth year of the war; the month August. Bagenal was to relieve Portmore, held by a queen's garrison, now starving, and wipe "the rebels" out of existence. He had already made successful stroke. He had got provisions into Armagh, occupied by queen's troops, and had surprised O'Neill's camp. From the latter he had been quickly dislodged, and fell back on Armagh.

Before sunrise he marched out of that city to attack O'Neill. His English soldiers were veterans who had fought in France, or had been picked from Belgian garrisons. His Irish auxiliaries were mercenaries who had given proof of their valour. The son of the "queen's" O'Reilly was with them; a young man so extremely handsome, of splendid figure, called the "Fair." This battle, the biggest of the war in the North, is called the Battle of the Yellow Ford.

Bagenal went out, his horse and foot sheathed in mail, heavily armed. It was an army gleaming with crested plumes, silken sashes, military ornaments. Brass cannon it had, mounted on wheels, drawn by horses. These made the army formidable.

In the Irish camp a council of war was held. The stars had not waned when the leaders met. Before the tent a guard was drawn; around it were gathered high-born faces, "the youth of the nobility of Ulster," and "young Connachtmen of by no means ignoble birth." The lines of the camp, covering the field, stretched far in the dim dawn; men standing to their horses; close-knit ranks of gall-oglach; light armed foot; all waiting for the command; to accept battle or to retire.

For patrols had brought O'Neill information of the heavy muskets carried by Bagenal soldiers; of the veterans trained on the continent; of the disciplined Irish mercenaries; of the brass cannon. Was it right to risk a battle? Red Hugh was with him. He had marched up from Connacht with three thousand men, one thousand Connacians, two thousand Ultonians. And there was Angus MacDonnell, Red Hugh's cousin, son of the famous Sorley Boy whom Shane the Proud had once taken prisoner. And Hugh Maguire, lord of Fermanagh, first cavalry officer in Ireland. As O'Neill hesitated a man stood up. He was a high official, Feareasa O'Clery, hereditary historian of Tir-Conaill. He held a vellum in his hand, centuries old. Why did the great O'Neill doubt, the descendant of many kings, he asked; why the noble O'Donnell, his prince, son, too, of kings; why the Maguire, the high-born and generous; why MacDonnell of the Isles; why the captains, sons of heroes, gathered at that council? Listen to the words of Berchan, one of the four prophets of Ireland. And the men listened. To Berchan, nine centuries before had been given a vision flung far in time. He had caught the sounds of a battle as he walked by the Yellow Ford; strange thunderings; battle-shouts of men; the clash of arms; the charge of horse. And on him had come the spirit of prophecy; whereupon he wrote down that there far in the future the men of Erin would meet and defeat their foes.

This decided O'Neill. The prophecy was read to the men; none doubted its fulfilment that day. O'Neill made them a speech—one sentence golden:

"Victory lies not in senseless armour, nor in the vain din of cannon, but in living and courageous souls."

He awaited battle on the ground on which the army stood. Across the plain that lay before the camp a deep trench had been dug and an embankment four feet high made. Bogs lay on each side of the plain, and a muddy yellow stream flowed into the trench. Beyond the plain was a scattered wood of hawthorns and junipers. Beyond this again pits had been dug and covered with hay and brambles. A body of light armed troops were stationed in the wood, "beardless youths," about five hundred, armed with muskets. Bagenal had to pass through the wood. The August morning was bright and fine. By seven his vanguard, musketeers and horse, was seen marching up the road. In the main body—pikemen in three columns formed the centre; cavalry and a second division of musketeers the rear. The "beardless youths," posted among the trees, fired on the van. Then they darted from tree to tree firing repeatedly from snaphance or matchlock. The van could not charge; could not dislodge them. Bagenal galloped up; tried to keep his men steady; tried to clear the wood. But the smooth bold young faces mocked his efforts. "Very angry," says the historian, "were Bagenal and his veterans at being attacked and harassed by such boyish and silly sort of men."

In time he extricated his troops, and got on the plain. The beardless ones held the ground in front. Bagenal ordered his cavalry to charge. Men and horses fell into the pits, and the boys fired on those who came to their rescue. There were skirmishes, retirements, charges, advances of fresh battalions, but it was not till eleven o'clock, four hours after he had entered the wood, that Bagenal's army found itself in front of O'Neill's camp.

There was the ditch. It was lined by O'Neill's men. The battle raged here. The brass cannon soon made a breach; three of Bagenal's divisions got over. The Irish pikemen who had retired in disorder before the cannon re-formed and rushed upon the musketeers. Bagenal, oppressed by the weight of his armour and the heat of the fight, raised his visor. A bullet, then entering, ended his career. The Irish horse charged; the queen's musketeers broke and fled; their cavalry joined in the flight. A number were cut down as they tried to re-cross the ditch. The three divisions were panic-stricken, broken and flying. Nothing could stop the helter-skelter. The Yellow Ford was fought and won. Portmore and Armagh surrendered to O'Neill.

The brilliant victory freed Ulster. It made an immense sensation in England. It was talked of on the continent. "The general voice," says the English contemporary historian, Moryson, "was of Tyrone after the defeat of the Blackwater, as of Hannibal among the Romans after the defeat at Cannae."

O'Neill's authority was recognised over the greater part of Ireland. He strengthened his defences, appointed or dismissed officials, nominated chiefs, acted with justice and wisdom. No English forces could stand before him. The confederation of the chiefs seemed firmly knit. Ireland appeared about to achieve her freedom.

For a time the question was alone put to the sword. Elizabeth, an old woman now, with the levity of youth among her courtiers, an ungovernable temper when roused, sent Essex, her favourite, to re-conquer Ireland. He came with the largest army yet sent to the country. O'Neill outwitted him at every move; beat his troops; reduced him to impotency. Once they had an interview on the banks of the Lagan. O'Neill learnt his ambitions, mastered his thoughts; turned his mind practically inside out. He dictated terms; Essex accepted them as far as he could without royal authority. When the enraged Elizabeth heard of them she recalled Essex, whose head went to the block.

Then O'Neill made something like a royal progress from the north to the south. The southern noblemen and gentlemen visited him on the banks of the Lee. He issued a proclamation styling himself Defender of the Faith. He showed himself a statesman and soldier. When he returned to the North his power was confirmed.

If the sword failed there were other methods for England to use. Mountjoy and George Carew were sent to Ireland. These men were to break up the confederation. Craft, treachery, offers of friendship (not to be kept), gold, bribes, were their weapons. Letters of betrayal were forged purporting to come from a member of the confederation. In time these methods succeeded. The confederation was weakened. There were serious defections, and O'Neill and O'Donnell were eventually left to carry on the fight in Ulster. This they did heroically. O'Donnell held the coast lines on the north against an English force that had landed there; O'Neill the southern frontier. "They fought as it were back to back against the opposite lines of attack." Through the spring and summer of 1601 that fight went on. By September little had been gained by the English except in Munster. Then came the long promised aid from Spain; three thousand men were landed at Kinsale—instead of the five thousand which O'Neill had warned must be the minimum, if landing was made in the south. The English troops were at once concentrated in the south, and Kinsale invested by an English fleet. The general in command of the Spaniards was unfit for the work; an ill-tempered, impatient man with no grasp of generalship. He was dismayed and angry at finding himself besieged instead of meeting friends. Sorely against their will he forced the Northern Chiefs to march and fight their way south to him. And then, again contrary to O'Neill's expert advice, forced them to attack his besiegers (under Carew) when it were wiser to besiege them. A series of fatal mistakes, aggravating d'Aquila's bad generalship, lost them a battle that they could have won—and which, being won, would, in all probability, have left Ireland an independent kingdom.

By error and accident it was lost. A council was held that night. Though O'Neill wished to continue the war in Munster, as some of the northern chiefs for private reasons decided to return to their own territories, Hugh O'Neill was forced to fall back on Ulster. O'Donnell sailed for Spain to see the king, and ask for further help. After bright promises, delays, disappointments he fell ill on his way to see the King again, died, and was buried with princely honours in the Cathedral of St. Francis, Valladolid.

For three hundred years his death was supposed to be from natural cause. Then, by chance, it was discovered in an English State paper that Carew with Mountjoy's approval had sent an agent to Spain to poison Red Hugh. He was twenty-eight when he died. His captivity when a boy, his escape, his brilliancy as a commander, his many victories, his unalterable hatred of the invader, his loyalty to O'Neill, the whole romance of his story has attracted Irish hearts to him through the centuries since his death. "He was the sword, as O'Neill was the brain, of the Ulster confederation." His voice was sweet and musical. He loved justice and was faithful to his promises. He showed courage and resource in the presence of difficulties; was quick to seize opportunities; maintained rigid discipline in his army; was patient in hardships; courteous and affable in manner; absolutely open and sincere. He never married; his private life was without a stain. One who knew him said "he was a great despiser of the world." Noble, generous, with tireless activity, daring, with his handsome person, his splendid spirit, as one of the last of Ireland's princes, his name has been a star in the nation's memory.

Three strongholds remained for the Irish in Munster after d'Aquila had capitulated, getting off safe with his men. They held out, hoping for new aid from Spain. Each was isolated. In time they fell. The defence of Dunboy castle by Donal O'Sullivan and his captain, MacGeoghegan, and, when it fell, of O'Sullivan's march with one thousand persons including women and children from Kerry to O'Rourke's castle in Leitrim, is a great epic, unknown outside Ireland. It has all the elements of the great Tragedies; indomitable souled men; defiance of fate; encounters with foes; encounters with the elements, with storm and frost and snow; men with dying bodies and unquenchable spirit, battling, marching, praying. Of the company scarce one hundred reached O'Rourke's country.

O'Neill fought his way up to Ulster, fought there, held his own for months. When news came of O'Donnell's death and he knew the cause was lost, he accepted terms offered him by the Lord Deputy. His territories were to be restored to him; the Catholic religion given free exercise within them; a fresh patent of earldom drawn out. Red Hugh's younger brother, Ruari O'Donnell, had already submitted, obtained terms, and was made Earl of Tir-Conaill.

Before the treaty was signed Elizabeth died—a maniac. James of Scotland, who succeeded her, formed a plan for planting Ulster with Scotch and English settlers. But the two Earls were in the way. It was necessary to destroy them. The method was the old one. They were to be charged with a plot. An anonymous letter found by the Council Chamber in Dublin Castle revealed the plot. According to it O'Neill intended to seize the Castle, slay the Deputy, and start another rebellion.

The letter really emanated from London. It was devised by Cecil, the Secretary of State; St. Lawrence, Lord Howth, was to carry out the plot and to inveigle O'Neill and O'Donnell to a meeting in his house. It was sufficient. They were cited to appear in London to answer the charge. With his perfect knowledge of the English Government's craft, and aware that the planters were waiting for the word to fall upon O'Donnell's and his own territories, O'Neill knew that their destruction had been decided upon. Their case was desperate. Safety alone was in flight. Yet the thought filled them with bitter sorrow.

Into exile they must go. There were those who would welcome them on the continent; the Archdukes in Brussels; the King of Spain; the Pope in Rome. And there were Irish swordsmen in the continental armies. A chance might arise. If O'Neill was old, he was yet unbroken; and there were his sons, Hugh and Shane and Brian, and his nephew Art; to them, or to one of them, might be given the task to take up that sword that he had laid down, when he accepted Mountjoy's terms.

A French ship entered, anchored in, Lough Swilly. O'Neill journeying northward at the news, stayed at a friend's house on the way "wept abundantly when he took his leave, giving every child and every servant in the house a solemn farewell, which made them all marvel, because in general it was not his manner to use such compliments." He remained two nights in his own home, Dungannon castle. There must have been anguish in his soul. Statesman, soldier, victorious general he had been; now all was over. On the border of old age, beset with cruel enemies, what fate might await him? And Ireland—Tyrone? The wolves were out, the bitter planters, the greedy adventurers; who could resist them?

It was 1607. He journeyed to Lough Swilly with his wife Catherine, daughter of MacGuiness, Lord of Iveagh, his three sons, other relations and attendants. Ruari O'Donnell was already there with his two brothers, his sister Nuala, his hereditary bard and attendants. And there was Conor Maguire, brother of Hugh now dead; fifty persons in all in the flight. The Flight of the Earls it is called in Irish history. It stirred darkly the hearts of the Irish. The ominous news went from province to province. The bards dirged it. Men knew that the last bulwark against the Saxon sheriff and the Saxon Law had fallen. "It is certain that the sea has not borne, and the wind has not wafted in modern times," wrote the Four Masters nearly thirty years later, "a number of persons in one ship more eminent, illustrious, noble in point of genealogy, heroic deeds, valour, feats of arms, and brave achievements than they. Would God had permitted them to remain in their inheritance."[2]

---

[2] THE PRINCES OF THE NORTH

BY ETHNA CARBERY

Summer and winter the long years have flown
Since you looked your last for ever on the hills of Tyrone;
On the vales of Tyrconnell, on the faces strained that night
To watch you, Hugh and Rory, over waves in your flight.

Not in Uladh of your kindred your beds hath been made,
Where the holy earth laps them and the quicken-tree gives shade;
But your dust lies afar, where Rome hath given space
To the tanist of O'Donnell, and the Prince of Nial's race.

O, sad in green Tyrone when you left us, Hugh O'Neill,
In our grief and bitter need, to the spoiler's cruel steel!
And sad in Donegal when you went, O! Rory *Ban*,
From your father's rugged towers and the wailing of your clan!

Our hearts had bled to hear of that dastard deed in Spain;
We wept our Eaglet, in his pride by Saxon vileness slain;
And, girded for revenge, we waited but the call of war
To bring us like a headlong wave from heathery height and scaur.

Ochon and *ochon!* when the tidings travelled forth
That our chiefs had sailed in sorrow from the glens of the North;
Ochon and *ochon!* how our souls grew sore afraid,
And our love followed after in the track your keel had made!

And yet in green Tyrone they keep your memory still,
And tell you never fled afar, but sleep in Aileach Hill—

After a fearfully perilous voyage they landed in France. They visited different courts, in time settling in Rome where the Pope gave them a handsome pension. O'Donnell died within a year; O'Neill in 1616. English spies surrounded him till his death. Their reports mention that in the evenings, after dining, O'Neill had but one topic: "his face would glow, he would strike the table, he would say that they would yet have a good day in Ireland." On his death every honour paid to royalty was paid to him. He was buried in the Franciscan Church of San Pietro di Montorio, on the Janiculum hill. One of his sons had died before him; and another, Brian, page to the Archdukes in Brussels, was murdered by agents of the English Government.

The Nine Years' War was the last stand that Ireland as a nation under her own laws made against England and English laws. After the battle of Kinsale the new rule rushed in. Not every thing native went down at first; the schools for a time continued. Wherever breathing space was found they arose and flourished. They kept the learning and the traditions of the past. They produced a generation of scholars who saved from utter destruction the records of Irish civilisation and Irish history. "During the first half of the seventeenth century, the Irish, heavily handicapped as they were, and deprived of the power of printing, nevertheless made tremendous efforts to keep abreast of the rest of Europe in science and literature. It was indeed an age of national scholarship which has never since been equalled. It was this century that produced in rapid succession Geoffrey Keating, the Four Masters, and Duald MacFirbis, men of whom any age or country might be proud, men who amid the war, the rapine, and conflagration that rolled through the country with the English soldiers, still strove to save from the general wreck those records of their country which today make the name of Ireland honourable for her antiquities, traditions, and history, in the eyes of the scholars of Europe." [3]

In stony sleep, with sword in hand and stony steed beside,
Until the Call shall waken you—the rock gate open wide.

Will you come again, O Hugh, in all your olden power,
In all the strength and skill we knew, with Rory, in that hour
When the Sword leaps from its scabbard, and the Night hath passed away,
And Banba's battle-cry rings loud at Dawning of the Day?
—From "The Four Winds of Eirinn."

[3] Douglas Hyde, "Literary History of Ireland."

Not till the end of the seventeenth century were these schools finally crushed. The hedge-schools were their shadowy children. While the Irish language was the language of the mass of the people the history and traditions of the country were familiar to them. To the 18th century belong the majority of those manuscripts written in beautiful script, on coarse paper stained brown by turf-smoke, bound in untanned sheep-skin covers, which re-tell the Heroic Tales and folklore of Ireland. And so vivid and strong was oral tradition enshrined in the language that a poor blind wandering poet in the early years of the 19th century can relate in verse after verse the history of his country from the mythic invasions to the Tithe-war of his own day.

At the end of the Elizabethan wars the conquest of Ireland appeared completed. The beginning of the 17th century saw the overthrow of the clan and communal system, the destruction of the great Gaelic Houses, and the establishment of centralisation by a despotic power. The centralisation, carried out rigorously, placed the government, patronage, power, and the ownership of the land in the hands of the English colonists. The standing fact, however, is that the conquest was not completed. It was surface deep, no more. On that surface the English Law ran, and her armed forces moved. But the soul of Ireland was unconquered. For two centuries after the conclusion of the Elizabethan wars the great bulwark of Irish nationality was the Irish language. England recognised this; she made every effort to destroy it. The memory of the Brehon Laws survived to the 19th century, and showed itself in the Land League and the people's claims. Ireland's body was in chains, but her soul and mind were free.

FOR THE ELIZABETHAN PERIOD:

Carew's Manuscripts.
Dymmok's Treatise.
Hyde's Literary History of Ireland.
Sir John Davies' Letters.
Mountjoy's Report to English Privy Council.
Rev. C. P. Meehan, M. R. I. A., Irish Franciscan Monasteries.
O'Clery's Life of O'Donnell.
Edmund Spenser's View of the State of Ireland.
Don Philip O'Sullivan's History of the Catholic War in Ireland.
Pacata Hibernia.
Fynes Morryson.
Sir William Stanley's Letters.

CHAPTER XLVI

Suppressing the Race

Through these many dread centuries England's energies were concentrated upon an effort, seemingly, to annihilate the Irish race.

Says Edmund Burke (Letter to Sir Hercules Langrishe): "All the penal laws of that unparalleled code of oppression were manifestly the effects of national hatred and scorn towards a conquered people whom the victors delighted to trample upon and were not at all afraid to provoke. They were not the effect of their fears, but of their security . . . whilst that temper prevailed, and it prevailed in all its force to a time within our memory, every measure was pleasing and popular just in proportion as it tended to harass and ruin a set of people who were looked upon as enemies to God and man; indeed, as a race of savages who were a disgrace to human nature itself."

Yet with that sublime disregard of humour which is the privilege of an elect people, one old English historian and champion piously exclaims anent "how much Ireland is beholden to God for suffering them to be conquered, whereby many of their enmities were cured—and more might be, were themselves only pliable."

Differing from most other conquered peoples the Irish have been made to suffer through the centuries not only from the conqueror's dreadful sword but perhaps even more from the conqueror's far more dreadful "justice." The laws imposed upon Ireland from the Norman's first coming, down till today or yesterday, far surpassed in ferocity any of the repressive systems temporarily imposed upon any other of the sorest suffering conquered ones of the world.

For many cruel centuries British law in Ireland only took notice of the native as a subject on which to exercise its repressive or exterminating power. We have record of a trial in Waterford as early as 1310—when the British law was still new to the nation—in which Robert le Waleys, a Briton, was charged with the murder of John, the son of Ivor MacGillemory. The defence taken was that while admitting the prisoner had killed John, yet it was no murder, since the slain one was only an Irishman! To meet this effective line of defence the public prosecutor contended that the man killed was not Irish but Ostman (Dane). In the same era we find Donal O'Neill, in his remonstrance addressed to Pope John XX, stating that the murder of an Irishman was not a felony, and "it is no more sin say even some of their religious to kill an Irishman than to kill a dog." "They were out of the protection of the law," says Sir John Davies, "so that every Englishman might oppresse, spoile, and kill them without controulement."[1]

And Sir Richard Cox, himself one of the elect, records: "If an Englishman be damnified by an Irishman not amenable to law, he may reprise himself on the whole tribe or nation."

Says the English historian Leland: "Every inconsiderable party, who, under pretence of loyalty, received the king's commission to repel the adversary in some particular district, became pestilent enemies to the inhabitants. Their properties, their lives, the chastity of their families, were all exposed to barbarians, who sought only to glut their brutal passions, and by their horrible excesses, saith the annalist, purchased the curse of God and man."

The solemn and well considered statutes of the realm were likewise well designed to make smooth the lot of English exiles among the wild Irishrie. "It shall be lawful," says one of these statutes (5 Ed. IV) "to all manner of men that find any thieves robbing by day or by night, or going or coming to rob or steal, having no faithful man of good name in their company, in English apparel, upon any of the liege people of the king, to take and kill them, and to cut off their heads, without any impeachment of our sovereign lord the king, his heirs, officers, or ministers, or of any others." In plain language this empowered any of the British in Ireland to kill at sight any Irishman whom he wished to kill.

---

[1] Davies, in his "Discoverie," said that the plagues of Egypt were short, but the plagues of Ireland lasted four hundred years. It was three hundred years ago that Davies wrote this when the said plagues were only beginning to get the stride which carried them through centuries after with ever-increasing impetus. Davies, then, had just aided in imposing on the stricken country one of the worst of the plagues—the British Undertaker on whom was bestowed the lands of which his master, James the First, robbed the Ulstermen.

In the reign of the third Edward was passed the famous Statute of Kilkenny for reclaiming or preserving the English in Ireland from Irish witchery. Although the beneficent laws had branded Irishmen outlaws in their own country, and the rulers had proclaimed them savages, barbarians, it was noticed that their manners, their customs, their dress, their ways, their language, had uncanny attraction for the Anglo-Norman settlers who quickly became Irish in all these things; so the Statute of Kilkenny was in 1367 considered necessary. This Statute made it high treason to adopt the Irish dress, speak the Irish language, practise the Irish customs, avail of the Irish laws (which were "wicked and damnable"), follow Irish fosterage or gossipred, or intermarry with the Irish. Yet, despite this Statute, and many others to the same purport passed again and again in later generations, the ways—and the women—of the outlawed "barbarian" still bewitched and won the hearts of the Anglo-Normans, till at length they became—in the historic phrase used in the English complaint "ipsis Hibernicis Hiberniores"—more Irish than the Irish themselves. They had become savage of the savage, adopting all the "savage" manners, customs, dress, language.

Languages it should be said, for the Irish "savages" spoke Irish and Latin indifferently. Sir Richard Cox complained that "every cowboy in Ireland" tried his tongue at Latin. Sir John Perrott (1585) reported of one of "the degenerate English"—the term applied to those who had voluntarily resigned their English heritage, and assimilated with the Irish—"I found MacWilliam verie sensible, and though wanting the English tongue yet understanding the Latin."

When the De Burghos renounced England to become Irish in all things (under the name of MacWilliam) they came before the English Castle at Athenry, and in sight of the garrison there, threw off their English dress, and donned the Irish costume.

In 1569 one of the Galway English, Dominick Linche, makes complaint to the English Privy Council that "the brothers of the erle of clan-Rickerde, yea, and one of his uncles, and he a byeshop (bishop) can neither speak nor understand anything of the English language." Their languages, like that of the Irish of their class, were Irish and Latin. In 1535 a Welsh officer marching in the South with Lord Butler, wrote in surprise of the type of "degenerate English" which he met. One of them, a brother-in-law of Lord Butler, whose name, had he not fallen away, would have been FitzGerald, but who now wore the Irish name of MacShean, could speak never a word of English, "but he made the troops good cheer in the gentlest fashion that could be." Refinement and gentility, in a man who scorned the English language, were amazing to find!

And in 1589, after Munster had been successively devastated by first ruthless war, then famine, and then planted with English undertakers, one of the latter, Robert Paine, writing from Limerick to his partners in England, says that "English is being taught to Irish pupils there through the medium of Latin." (Paine's "Brief Description of Ireland in 1589.")

"The verie English of birth," complains Campion, "conversant with the brutish sort of that people [the Irish] become degenerate in short space, and quite altered into the first ranke of Irish rogues." Yet, elsewhere we discover from Campion regarding these brutish Irish: "They speake Latine like a vulgar tongue, learned in their common schools of leachcraft and law, whereat they begin children, and hold on sixteene or twentie years conning by roate the aphorisms of Hypocrates, and the Civill Institutions."[2]

After the new religion had been introduced to Ireland new doors were open for the persecution of the Irish Race, and fresh inspiration for the work was supplied. By virtue of Henry's warrant, the churches and monasteries were robbed of their riches, shrines were defiled, sacred relics were burned or scattered, beautiful statues were smashed, orders of religious were expelled from hundreds of their houses—which went to enrich his minions—and beautiful churches were wrested from the people.

And as the Reformation progressed in age, its ingenious methods for bringing the knowledge of the true God to the people progressed likewise. Some of the subjects chosen for inducting of religion into, "were burned before a slow fire; some were put on the rack and tortured to death; whilst others, like Ambrose Cahill and James O'Reilly, were not only slain with the greatest cruelty, but their inanimate bodies were torn into fragments, and scattered before the wind." The fate of the gentle and saintly Archbishop Plunkett is only too well known: "His speech ended and the cap drawn over his eyes, Oliver Plunkett again recommended his happy soul, with raptures of devotion into the hands of Jesus, his Saviour, for whose sake he died—till the cart was drawn from under him. Thus then he hung betwixt Heaven and earth, an open sacrifice to God for innocence and religion; and as soon as he expired the executioner ripped his body open and

[2] And the prejudiced Campion admits of these savages: "The people are thus inclined; religious, franke, amorous, irefull, sufferable of paines infinite, very glorious, great givers, passing in hospitalitie; the lewder sort are sensual, but reformed, are such mirrours of holinesse and austeritie, that other nations retain but a shewe or shadow of devotion in comparison of them. Abstinence and fasting is to them a familiar kind of chastisement. They are sharp-witted, lovers of learning, capable of any studie whereunto they bend themselves, constant in travaile, adventurous, intractable, kinde-hearted, secret in displeasure."

pulled out his heart and bowels, and threw them in the fire already kindled near the gallows for that purpose."[3]

Under Elizabeth it was enacted that every Romish priest found in Ireland after a certain date should be deemed guilty of rebellion, that he should be hanged till dead, then his head taken off, his bowels taken out and burned, and his head fixed on a pole in some public place.

Keating tells us how Bishop Patrick O'Healy and Cornelius O'Rourke were put to the rack, had their hands and feet broken by hammers, needles thrust under their nails, and were finally hanged and quartered.

It was under Elizabeth that the price fixed on the head of a priest was made uniform with that on the head of a wolf.[4] And under her was passed the law of Recusancy fixing heavy penalties upon all delinquents who refused to attend Sabbath services in the church of the new religion.

It was not alone the religion of the Irish people that was then sought to be wiped out, but their very life. Her armies with torch and sword, converted a smiling fruitful country into a fearful desert. Edmund Spenser in his "View of the State of Ireland" thus graphically pictures a little of what Elizabeth accomplished: "Notwithstanding that the same was a most rich and plentiful country, full of corne and cattel, yet, ere one yeare and a half, they were brought to such wretchedness as that any stony heart would rue the same. Out of every corner of the woods and glenns, they came creeping forth upon their hands, for their legs could not bear them; they looked like anatomies of death; they spake like ghosts crying out of their graves; they did eate the dead carrions, happy where they could finde them; yea, and one another soone after; insomuch as the very carcasses

[3] The following are a few samples of the tens of thousands of such efforts for the reforming of the Irish.—Two Franciscans were taken and thrown into the sea, and another was trampled to death by horses. Three laymen, at Smerwick, had their legs and arms broken with hammers, and then were hanged, and similar torture was inflicted on the abbot of Boyle. Three Franciscans, at Abbeyleix, were first beaten with sticks, then scourged with whips until the blood came, and finally were hanged. One Roche was taken to London and flogged publicly through the streets, and then tortured in prison until he died; another being flogged, had salt and vinegar rubbed into his wounds, and then was placed on the rack and tortured to death. And Collins, a priest at Cork, was first tortured, then hanged, and whilst he yet breathed, his heart was cut out and held up, soldiers around crying out in exultation, Long live the Queen.—From "Our Martyrs," quoted by E. A. D'Aiton in his "History of Ireland."

[4] Five pounds was the usual price for both—but Burton's Parliamentary Diary of June 10th, 1567, records the words of Major Morgan, M.P. for Wicklow—who was protesting in Parliament against striking more taxes on Ireland—"We have three beasts to destroy that lay burdens upon us; the first is a wolf upon whom we lay five pounds; the second beast is a priest on whom we lay ten pounds—if he be eminent, more; the third beast is a Tory," etc.

they spared not to scrape out of their graves, and, if they found a plot of water-cresses or shamrocks, there they flocked as to a feast for the time; yet, not able to continue there withal; that in shorte space, there was none almost left, and a most populous and plentiful countrey suddainlie left voyde of man and beast."

Lecky in the preface to his History of Ireland in the Eighteenth Century says: "The slaughter of Irishmen was looked upon as literally the slaughter of wild beasts. Not only men, but even women and children who fell into the hands of the English, were deliberately and systematically butchered. Bands of soldiers traversed great tracts of country, slaying every living thing they met." And he also says: "The suppression of the native race was carried on with a ferocity which surpassed that of Alva in the Netherlands, and which has seldom been exceeded in the pages of history."

The honest Scottish Protestant Dr. Smiles sums up the Elizabethan work in Ireland, "Men, women and children wherever found were put indiscriminately to death. The soldiery was mad for blood. Priests were murdered at the altar, children at their mother's breast. The beauty of woman, the venerableness of age, the innocence of youth was no protection against these sanguinary demons in human form."

The Protestant Rev. Dr. Taylor, in his History of the Civil War in Ireland, bears testimony to the fact that these Irish barbarians, when opportunity offered for avenging themselves on their persecutors, took their revenge in a manner that would have done credit to a civilised people—say, to the gentle English. He tells how, when in the reign of Queen Mary the persecutors of the Catholics found their occupation gone, "The restoration of the old religion was effected without violence: no persecution of the Protestants was attempted; and several of the English, who fled from the furious zeal of Mary's inquisitors, found a safe retreat among the Catholics of Ireland. It is but justice to this maligned body to add that they never injured a single person in life or limb for professing a religion different from their own. They had suffered persecution and learned mercy, as they showed in the reign of Mary, and in the wars from 1641 to 1648."[5]

---

[5]For more light upon the subject of this Chapter see the later Chapter on Cromwell.

CHAPTER XLVII

The Ulster Plantation

Within a decade after the "Flight of the Earls" came the Ulster Plantation—a scheme of fatal and far-reaching consequence for the Island ever since.

It was the Sixth James of Scotland who, after he became James I of England, perpetrated this crime. The land-greedy and gain-greedy among his Scotic fellow-countrymen, and among the English, were the instigators. Upon Ireland the covetous eyes of such people were ever turned. The flight of the Earls proved a welcome excuse for the wholesale robbing of the clans. It was a very simple matter to find that all the Northern chiefs had been conspiring to rebel—against England. Hence they were "traitors"—to England! And naturally their estates were forfeit and for distribution among James' hungry followers.

That the clan-lands did not then, or ever at any time, belong to the chieftain, but to the whole clan community, was a matter of no consequence. According to English law and custom it should belong to the people's lords (chiefs). And if "civilised" law did not obtain in Ireland, it must be imposed wheresoever British profit could be reaped from such imposition.

The English Lord Lieutenant, Sir Arthur Chichester, and the Attorney General, Sir John Davies, were the instruments, under James, for giving effect to the great Plantation. The lands of the six counties of Donegal, Derry (then called Coleraine), Tyrone, Fermanagh, Cavan and Armagh—four million acres—were confiscated. (The lands of the three remaining Ulster counties, Antrim, Down and Monaghan were bestowed upon Britons at other times.) The true owners, the natives, were driven like wild fowl or beasts, from the rich and fertile valleys of Ulster, which had been theirs from time immemorial, to the bogs and the moors and the barren crags—where it was hoped that they might starve and perish. English and

Scotch Undertakers (as they were called), and Servitors of the Crown, scrambled for the fertile lands which were given to them in parcels of one thousand, one thousand five hundred, and two thousand acres. The County of Coleraine (Derry) was divided up among the London trade Guilds, the drapers, fishmongers, vintners, haberdashers, etc.—who had financed the Plantation scheme. The Church termon lands were bestowed upon the Protestant bishops. And thus a new nation was planted upon the fair face of Ireland's proudest quarter.

The new nation was meant to be the permanent nation there. The written conditions upon which the new people got their lands specifically bound them to repress and abhor the Irish natives—conditions which through hundreds of years since the new people have faithfully endeavoured to carry out. They were bound never to alien the lands to Irish, to admit no Irish customs, not to intermarry with the Irish, not to permit any Irish other than menials to exist on or near their lands. And they were bound to build castles and bawns, and keep many armed British retainers—thus constituting a permanent British garrison which would help to tame if not exterminate the Irish race. Sir John Davies, the Scotic king's very faithful servant, assures us that his master did tame the whole race. In his book, "A Discoverie of the True Causes why Ireland was never Subdued and Brought under Obedience to the Crowne of England until the Beginning of His Majestie's Happie Reign," he says, "The multitude having been brayed as it were in a mortar with sword, pestilence and famine, altogether became admirers of the Crowne of England."

And when they were made true admirers of the Crown of England it was that their fertile possessions were given to the stranger, and they sent to co-habit with the snipe and the badger among the rocks and heather. And the faithful servant, Sir John, a pious Puritan rogue who strained his powers to rob and wrong the natives even far beyond the sweeping robbery powers which the "law" provided to his hand—this Saint, in the traditional British fashion, tells us: "This transplanting of the natives is made by his Majestie like a father, rather than a lord or monarch. . . . So as his Majestie doth in this imitate the skilful husbandman who doth remove his fruit trees, not on purpose to extirpate and destroy, but the rather that they may bring forth better and sweeter fruit!" And when the starving one, from his perch among the rocks, glanced over the smiling valleys from which James had transplanted him for his own betterment, it is easy to conceive the depth of feeling with which he appreciated that kind father's solicitude.

The character of the Planters who were given the lands of the hunted ones is recorded for us by the son of one of them, and also by a later one of their own descendants. Reid in his "History of the Irish Presbyterians" says: "Among those whom divine Providence did send to Ireland . . . the most part were such as either poverty or scandalous lives had forced hither."

And Stewart, the son of a Presbyterian minister who was one of the Planters, writes: "From Scotland came many, and from England not a few, yet all of them generally the scum of both nations, who from debt, or breaking, or fleeing justice, or seeking shelter, came hither hoping to be without fear of man's justice."

Sore indeed was the lot of the poor Irish in the woods, and mountains, and moors. Thousands of them perished of starvation. Other many thousands sailed away under leaders to enlist in the Continental armies. To far Sweden alone went no less than six thousand swordsmen. But the lot of those who lived and remained was sorer far than of those who went either to exile or to death.[1]

Hill's Plantation of Ulster.
Sir John Davies' Irish Tracts.
MacNevin's Ulster Plantation.

---

[1]The great wrong inflicted upon those who were robbed of their all, to enrich James' Scots and English, is well exemplified in an incident related by the Loyalist Duchess of Buckingham (married to the Earl of Antrim), who, when she was taking a thousand men southward, to strengthen the cause of Charles, went aside at Limavady to see the wife of O'Cathain, late chieftain of that country. In the ruined hall of the O'Cathain castle—once the frequent scene of light-hearted revelry, but whose window-casements now were stuffed with straw—was huddled O'Cathain's lady whose beauty and whose bounty had evoked sweet tunes from many harps, and inspired many a minstrel's lay. Wrapt in an old blanket, she was seated on her hams on the hearth, cowering over a miserable fire of brambles which she had laboriously gathered from the woods.

CHAPTER XLVIII

The Rising of 1641

But the Irish were not content to starve and die upon the moors, while they watched the usurper wax fat upon their fathers' fertile plains. As their suffering and starvation were prolonged and increased, their wrath against the foreign robber daily grew greater also; and ere a generation had elapsed, it burst in a fierce red flood that swept the terrorised Undertakers before it—and just narrowly missed sweeping them from Ulster forever.

The Rising of 1641 was the natural outcome of the great wrong of the generation before. And the reader can easily understand the frenzied fury with which this rebellion overswept northern Ireland, and the swift vengeance wreaked by the frenzied ones upon the callous robber and oppressor—a vengeance, however, lacking the calculated savagery, and unspeakable brutality, which, in return the Scottish and English troops visited upon the native population, of both sexes and all ages, during the fearful decade that followed.

To Rory O'Moore,[1] of the Offaly family of the O'Moores, a cultured and travelled gentleman, is chiefly due the credit for that great resurgence of

---

[1] RORY O'MOORE

(An Ulster Ballad of the Rising)

On the green hills of Ulster the white cross waves high,
And the beacon of war throws its flames to the sky;
Now the taunt and the threat let the coward endure,
Our hope is in God and in Rory O'Moore!

Do you ask why the beacon and banner of war
On the mountains of Ulster are seen from afar?

the Irish race. For years he patiently worked both among the leading Irish families at home, Irish Generals in the Continental armies, and other representative Irish exiles and sympathisers in the European countries—to bring about the overthrow of the British power in Ireland. And, plans being all matured, the Rising broke in Ulster on the night of the 21st October, 1641.

The Rising of that memorable night was a wonderfully dramatic *coup.* Leaders of the old Ulster families—Phelim O'Neill, Magennis, O'Hanlon, O'Hagan, MacMahon, McGuire, O'Quinn, O'Farrell, O'Reilly—at the head of their cohorts, staunch, wild-eyed, long repressed, burst from their fastnesses in the hills and the woods with one loud, long, strong, victory shout that might well have been heard by the straining exiles on the Continent—and in a few hours made Ulster their own again. Practically in one night they may be said to have reconquered their province, having sent the Planters scurrying into the few Ulster cities that they still could hold—Enniskillen, Derry, Coleraine, Belfast. Outside these few places Ulster was Ireland's again, as far south as, and including, the city of Dundalk. And in a few days Phelim O'Neill was proclaimed head of a numerous Ulster army of 30,000 men—of whom, however, two-thirds were, for want of arms, ineffective.[2]

'Tis the signal our rights to regain and secure,
Through God and our Lady and Rory O'Moore!

For the merciless Scots, with their creed and their swords,
With war in their bosoms, and peace in their words,
Have sworn the bright light of our faith to obscure,
But our hope is in God and Rory O'Moore.

Oh! lives there a traitor who'd shrink from the strife
Who, to add to the length of a forfeited life,
His country, his kindred, his faith would abjure?
No! we'll strike for our God and for Rory O'Moore!

[2] Joy! joy the day is come at last, the day of hope and pride,
And see! our crackling bonfires light old Banna's joyful tide,
And gladsome bell, and bugle horn, from Inbhar's captured towers,
Hark! how they tell the Saxon swine, this land is ours, is ours!

Glory to God! my eyes have seen the ransomed fields of Down,
My ears have drunk the joyful news, "Stout Phelim hath his own."
Oh! may they see and hear no more, oh! may they rot to clay,
When they forget to triumph in the conquests of today.

Now, now we'll teach the shameless Scot to purge his thievish maw,
Now, now the courts may fall to pray, for justice is the law,

It was Ulster only that had risen that night. The other quarters remained quiescent because of a miscarriage of plans. The seizing of Dublin Castle, which was to be their rising signal, was frustrated—through a traitor, Connelly. MacMahon and McGuire who (with O'Moore) were to have taken the Castle, were themselves taken. But O'Moore fortunately escaped. It was some months before Leinster and Munster took up arms for Ireland. And later still when Connacht joined.

For purpose, now, of inciting the English at home to wipe out the Irish—and thus provide more estates for the covetous in Britain, there was invented a story of a fearful massacre of almost all the Protestants of Ireland, on the night of the Rising. Not only did the eager English readily believe it, but after a while, the parties in Ireland who started the story almost came to believe it themselves. And many thousands of good, sincere Irish Protestants, and many thousands of ardent English, to this day believe the tale of a wild and indiscriminate massacre. So far went this effort to lay unbridled savagery at the doors of the Irish people, and so far succeeded, that many earnest and sincere historians, accepting the carefully prepared "facts" put upon record for the purpose, themselves believed, and through succeeding generations and centuries perpetuated the memory of, "the great Popish Massacre." Many ludicrous estimates of the numbers of thousands and hundreds of thousands of Protestants massacred in Ulster on the night of 21st October, 1641, were, in succeeding decades, given to the world by both innocent and crafty Englishmen and Anglo-Irish. But it was left to the magnifying mind of the

---

Now shall the Undertaker square for once his loose accounts,
We'll strike, brave boys, a fair result from all his fake amounts.

Our standard flies o'er fifty towers, o'er twice ten thousand men;
Down have we plucked the pirate Red, never to rise again;
The Green alone shall stream above our native field and flood—
The spotless Green, save where its folds are gemmed with Saxon blood!

Down from the sacred hills whereon a Saint communed with God,
Up from the vale where Bagnall's blood manured the reeking sod,
Out from the stately woods of Truagh, M'Kenna's plundered home,
Like Malin's waves, as fierce and fast, our faithful clansmen come.

Then, brethren, on!—O'Neill's dear shade would frown to see our pause—
Our banished Hugh, our martyred Hugh, he's watching o'er your cause—
His gen'rous error lost the land—he deem'd the Norman true,
Oh, forward! friends, it must not lose the land again in you!

—Charles Gavan Duffy.

great Milton (when he was Cromwell's secretary) to give to Europe the astounding information that the savage Irish papists had massacred 610,000 Irish Protestants in the great massacre—a prodigious feat surely for the Papists, seeing that in all Ireland at that time, there were, as the English authorities afterwards admitted, less than 200,000 Protestants altogether.

The Rev. Ferdinand Warner, Protestant minister, in his "History of the Irish Rebellion" written shortly after the event, says: "It is easy enough to demonstrate the falsehood of the relation of every English historian of the rebellion"—and he calculates that 4,028 Protestants were killed within the first two years of the war, and 8,000 died of ill-usage. But the Cromwellian commission appointed after the war to investigate all murders and injuries inflicted upon all the British settlers in Ireland, during the whole ten years' war—a commission animated by plenty of healthy prejudice, and eager to accept anything in the shape of evidence against the Irish—found 2,109 murders in the ten years of war. And it has been since shown that in this number the same murder, dressed up in various ways, was counted several times.[3]

After the legend of "the great Popish Massacre" was once started it grew with the rapidity of a rolling snow-ball—till, at the hearings of the Commission ten years later, excited and imaginative witnesses, including Dr. Maxwell the Protestant rector of Tynan, made oath to the fantastic happenings which make those records a source of entertainment to the curious, ever since.[4]

Finally this long cherished and widely advertised great Popish Massacre may be disposed of in the words of the zealous, old-time, Protestant historian,

---

[3] The reports of the Lords Justices to the English Parliament, and other state documents of the end of October and beginning of November, ten to twelve days after "the massacre," make no mention of the tremendous killing—for the good reason that the clever propagandists who originated the idea, had not yet been inspired to its conception as a fine means of spurring English to the extirpation of the Irish—and quieting the conscience of Europe during the extirpation.

In December the Lords Justices issued a commission to the Dean of Kilmore and seven other Protestant clergymen to make diligent inquiry about Protestants who were "robbed and plundered." There is no mention of any of them being murdered.

Six days after the Rising, Lord Lieutenant Chichester wrote to the King: "They took four considerable towns, and have but killed one man." The Scottish settlers, in particular, were, strange to say, spared. One of the Irish proclamations of the time decreed the penalty of death to any native who should molest a Scotsman "in body, goods, or lands." The historian, Leland, says: "In the beginning of the rebellion it was determined by the Irish that the enterprise should be conducted in every quarter with as little bloodshed as possible." The Bishops' Synod at Kells in the following March condemned all acts of private vengeance and all who usurped other men's estates. And the Irish National Synod in May went so far as to issue a decree of excommunication against any such guilty one.

[4] The Rev. Dr. Maxwell, Rector of Tynan (afterwards the Bishop of Kilmore), swore to apparitions, "by day and by night walking upon the river, sometimes brandishing their swords, sometimes

Rev. Dr. Taylor (in his "Civil Wars of Ireland"): "The Irish massacre of 1641 has been a phrase so often repeated even in books of education that one can scarcely conceal his surprise when he learns that the tale is apocryphal as the wildest fiction of romance." He also says: "The stories of massacre and of horrid cruelty were circulated in England because it was to the interest of the patriot party in Parliament to propagate such delusion."

The Scottish troops and Scottish planters are on the other hand accused by the Irish of sallying out from Carrickfergus and driving Irish women and children, variously estimated at 1,000 and at several thousand, to dreadful death over the fearful Gobbins cliffs on the peninsula called Island Magee.[5]

The fearful cruelties perpetrated by Sir Charles Coote, leader of the English army in Leinster, and by St. Leger, English commander in Munster,

---

singing psalms, and at times shrieking in a most fearful and hideous manner. I never heard any man so much as doubt the truth thereof."

Catherine the relict of William Coote, late of County Armagh, a carpenter "being duly sworn and examined, saith: About the twentieth December she saw the vision of a man stand upright in the river, with hands uplifted to heaven, etc., etc." The English army and her husband also saw it. The fervent ghost was standing in that trying position, testifieth said Deposition, "from the 20th December to the end of Lent"!

Elizabeth, wife of Captain Price of Armagh, "deposeth and saith that she and other women went unto the aforesaid bridge at twilight in the evening, and saw a woman standing out of the water, waist high, crying out: 'Revenge! Revenge!' Whereat this deponent and the rest, being touched to a strong amazement and fright, walked from the place." Out of respect for the ghost they showed no indecent haste.

The Rev. Mr. Creighton of Virginia, in Cavan, "deposeth that women brought into his house a young woman almost naked whom the rogues had attempted to kill. She had said: 'You can't kill me unless God gives you leave.' And although one, I think, ran his sword through her three times, she was not hurt—he, being much confounded, went away." If the demonstration had not confounded him, we might well conclude that he was a difficult subject.

[5] The present writer is unable to say how much truth, if any, is in this charge. The *pro* and *con* have been as hotly disputed as those of "the Great Popish Massacre."

The singer of Ireland's woes and Ireland's joys, Ethna Carbery, believing the truth of it, sang a fierce song of it—

BRIAN BOY MAGEE

I am Brian Boy Magee—my father was Eoghan Ban—
I was wakened from happy dreams by the shouts of my startled clan;
And I saw through the leaping glare that marked where our homestead stood,
My mother swing by her hair—and my brothers lie in their blood.

In the creepy cold of the night the pitiless wolves came down—
Scotch troops from that Castle grim guarding Knockfergus Town;
And they hacked and lashed and hewed, with musket and rope and sword,
Till my murdered kin lay thick in pools by the Slaughter Ford.

it was, combined with fear for themselves and their estates, that at length drove the Anglo-Irish Catholic lords of the Pale and their fellows of Munster, leisurely to join in the Rebellion—after the great success in Ulster gave them confidence of a like success elsewhere. Connacht was for a much longer time restrained from casting its lot with the rest of Ireland—mainly through the influence of the leading and loyal Catholic lord there, Clanrickarde (British Deputy), the head of the Burke family.

When the Lords Justices Parson and Borlase sent out Coote to ravage Wicklow he was ordered to spare none above a span high. And it is related by various historians that when his soldiers caught Irish babes upon their spears for sport, he said he "liked such frolics."[6]

I fought by my father's side, and when we were fighting sore
We saw a line of their steel, with our shieking women before.
The red-coats drove them on to the verge of the Gobbins grey,
Hurried them—God! the sight! as the sea foamed up for its prey.

Oh, tall were the Gobbins cliffs, and sharp were the rocks, my woe!
And tender the limbs that met such terrible death below;
Mother and babe and maid they clutched at the empty air,
With eyeballs widened in fright, that hour of despair.

(Sleep soft in your heaving bed, O little fair love of my heart!
The bitter oath I have sworn shall be of my life a part;
And for every piteous prayer you prayed on your way to die,
May I hear an enemy plead while I laugh and deny.)

In the dawn that was gold and red, ay, red as the blood-choked stream,
I crept to the perilous brink—great Christ! was the night a dream?
In all the Island of Gloom I only had life that day—
Death covered the green hill-sides, and tossed in the Bay.

I have vowed by the pride of my sires—by my mother's wandering ghost—
By my kinsfolk's shattered bones hurled on the cruel coast—
By the sweet dead face of my love, and the wound in her gentle breast—
To follow that murderous band, a sleuth-hound that knows no rest.

I shall go to Phelim O'Neill with my sorrowful tale, and crave
A blue-bright blade of Spain, in the ranks of his soldiers brave,
And God grant me the strength to wield that shining avenger well—
When the Gael shall sweep his foe through the yawning gates of Hell.

I am Brian Boy Magee! And my creed is a creed of hate;
Love, Peace, I have cast aside—but Vengeance, *Vengeance* I wait!
Till I pay back the four-fold debt for the horrors I witnessed there,
When my brothers moaned in their blood, and my mother swung by her hair.

[6] From Dublin, under date 25th February, 1642, the Government issued for the guidance of its generals, the very clear and explicit command, "to wound, kill, slay and destroy by all the ways and means

The Irish army of Leinster securely held for Ireland almost all of that province except Dublin and a little radius around it, which Ormond and Coote were enabled to raid. Philip O'Dwyer in the south had taken Cashel. And when the nobility arose there, they easily held the greater part of the province, driving St. Leger, the English Deputy, back into Cork. The greater part of Connacht was, soon after, under control of the Irish rebels.

And when the great and historic Synod met in Kilkenny in May of '42, and nobility, gentry and lay leaders, foregathered with the ecclesiastics of the country, and formed the Confederation of Kilkenny, the Irish practically owned Ireland, English power merely clinging by its teeth to some outer corners of the country.

---

you may all the rebels and adherents and relievers; and burn, spoil, waste, consume and demolish all places, towns and houses, where the said rebels are or have been relieved and harboured, and all hay and corn there, and kill and destroy all the men inhabiting, able to bear arms." (Carte's "Ormond.")

Sir Charles Coote, typical of the English generals in this war, employed rack and dungeon and roasting to death, for appeasing of the turbulent natives. He stopped at nothing—even hanging women with child.

Lord Clarendon, in his narrative of the events of the time, records how, after Coote plundered and burned the town of Clontarf, "he massacred townpeople, men, and women, and three suckling infants." And in that same week, says Clarendon, men, women and children of the village of Bullock frightened of the fate of Clontarf, went to sea to shun the fury of the soldiers who came from Dublin under Colonel Clifford. But being pursued by the soldiers in boats and overtaken, they were all thrown overboard—and drowned."

Coote and Clifford were not better or worse than the average of the pacifiers of Ireland. One could quote here more instances of the blood-freezing kind than would fill a large book. But for our purpose one or two samples are as good as a thousand. Castlehaven sets down an incident characteristic of the humanity of the English troopers. He tells how Sir Arthur Loftus, Governor of Naas, marched out with a party of horse, and being joined by a party sent out by Ormond from Dublin: "They both together killed such of the Irish as they met . . . but the most considerable slaughter occurred in a great strait of furze, situated on a hill, where the people of several villages had fled for shelter." Sir Arthur surrounded the hill, fired the furze, and at the point of the sword drove back into the flames the burning men, women and children who tried to emerge—till the last child was burned to a crisp. Says Castlehaven in his Memoirs, "I saw the bodies—and the furze still burning."

It should be particularly noted that the suckling infant sometimes aroused in the British soldiers the same blood-thirst that did the fighting rebel. The butchering of infants was more diligently attended to during this period than in any previous or subsequent English excursion through Ireland. It is matter of record that in the presence and with the toleration, of their officers—in at least one case with the hearty approval of a leader—the common soldiers engaged in the sport of tossing Irish babes upon their spears. The old English historian, Dr. Nalson, in his history of the Civil Wars (Introduction to his second volume) states—"I have heard a relation of my own, who was a captain in that service (in Ireland) relate that . . . little children were promiscuously sufferers with the guilty, and that when any one who had some grains of compassion reprehended the soldiers for this unchristian inhumanity, they would scoffingly reply, 'Why? nits will be lice!' and so despatch them."

CHAPTER XLIX

The War of the Forties

The Confederation of Kilkenny proved to be perhaps more of a curse than blessing to Ireland. The establishing of the Confederation was the establishing of a Parliament for Ireland. As, to please the Catholic Anglo-Irish (the "New Irish") lords and gentry, the Confederation proclaimed its stand "for faith, country, and *king*"—meaning King Charles of England—so also to please the same party the susceptibilities of their king was supposed to be saved from hurt, by naming it a Confederation instead of a Parliament.

In England Charles and his Parliamentary Government were now at bitter odds—beginning the great civil conflict there. Most of the Anglo-Irish, including all of the Catholic Anglo-Irish, espoused King Charles' cause. And though to appease his Puritan opponents he loudly proclaimed his hostility to popery, and refused to relax the anti-popery laws, the Catholic Anglo-Irish—whose affections for English royalty could seldom be shaken—held, not him, but the minions of the Parliamentary party, responsible for all of Ireland's woes. And they fostered the belief that Charles was a friend of Ireland and of the Catholic faith. It was the same absurd loyalty, which, crossing Ireland's national claims, was, for centuries before, handed down through all generations of this particular portion of the Irish public.

A portion of the Old Irish, the real Irish, now, as always, taking this absurd loyalty by contagion, believed also in a crossed fealty. But the vast majority of these wasted no love and no reverence upon a foreign king who held them by force. Yet for unity's sake they yielded the point to the New Irish, and subscribed to the battle-cry "for faith, for country, and for king."

The Confederation of Kilkenny then, which might have been a great blessing to Ireland, eventually proved to be Ireland's curse—in this, the country's greatest, fiercest struggle. Not entirely because the New Irish in it were given their way from the start; but more because a clique of the most unnational and reactionary of them secured inside control—the control of the Supreme Council of the Confederation's General Assembly.

Ormond, the head of the main branch of the Butler family, who was then the chief power in Ireland standing for King against Parliament, found this clique to be his ready tool—even though he was a bitter hater of popery and opponent of all concessions to popery. He was reared in England, a ward of the British Government—reared Protestant, and imbued with the deepest animus against the religion to which the Butler family had hitherto clung. The President of the Supreme Council, Lord Mountgarrett, was kinsman to Ormond—being head of the Kilkenny family of the Butlers. Consequently, Ormond, while bitterly hating Irishism and Catholicism, was able to work this Irish Catholic Parliament to his own and England's advantage. And through the cruel wars of the 'Forties the protest of the great majority of the Assembly who were truly Irish, and of the great bodies of truly Irish fighting men in the field, could but seldom counteract the prejudicial machinations of the Ormondite faction.

When Father Peter Scarampi, envoy of the Pope, came there with moral and material help for the Irish rebels, the Ormondist, pro-British, faction quickly disgusted him, and put him on the side of the Irish Nationalists. And the same happened, when, in succession to the envoy came the Papal Nuncio, Rinuccini, who eventually had to break openly with the Ormondist faction, leave them in disgust, and denounce them.

As matters got more and more critical for King Charles in Britain and his following there lost power, he was more and more willing to court the Kilkenny Confederation through his representative Ormond. And the Kilkenny Supreme Council was always eager to act the part of the willing coy maiden whenever Ormond whispered—even though his anti-Catholic bias made him presume to tone down each grudging little concession that his master would yield. They were again and again right heartily willing to accept from Charles bare toleration for their religion—without actual repeal of the anti-popery laws—and a mere modicum of their other liberties as Irishmen. As was ever the case with the New Irish, if their property and their religion were left unmolested they were tolerably content to be ruled by England as England wished. Now they were content to let England hold the Irish church lands for use of her foreign church, and hold Ireland in the fetters of Poyning's law.[1]

The Supreme Council wasted the energies of Ireland and dampened the spirits of the fighters by years of futile negotiation with Ormond and his king, and practically threw away in a truce two valuable years of the middle 'Forties. And at times when they were pushed to positive action, they took action that was misguided. They never for an instant forgot that they, the Anglo-Irish, were the elect. Their forefathers had been set over the Old Irish, the mere Irish; and now the mere Irish—who were of course the bulk and backbone of this war—should be content to take a subordinate position in guiding the war. And armies of Old Irish, led by Old Irish generals, must not be permitted to take too much of the glory from their own pet Anglo-Irish commanders.

Altogether their snobbery, their bias, and oftentimes their foolish trustingness—verging on stupidity—in Charles and his minions, combined to make a mess of Ireland's case, and to render fruitless long and sore years of struggle, which, without this Old Man of the Mountain upon the nation's neck, might have been crowned by complete success.

They manacled, and thwarted, the great Irish figure of the 'Forties, him who, but for them, could have been Ireland's saviour—the truly admirable man and signally great military leader, Owen Roe O'Neill. With Owen Roe's coming arose Ireland's bright star of hope—and with his passing, that star set.

Owen Roe was a nephew of Hugh O'Neill, "Earl of Tyrone," who fled at the century's beginning, and had died abroad. Owen Roe was a young man at time of the Flight of the Earls, had fought in that last disastrous fight at Kinsale, and going abroad also, had won signal distinction as a military commander in the Spanish Netherlands—especially in his brilliant defence of Arras where he successfully held three armies at bay. He had never ceased to hope that he would yet be the means of freeing his Fatherland. And through the years in which his sword had been in the service of Spain, his heart was ever with Ireland. He came to his own North, when, close following its first bright burst the clouds of despair had come down, and begun to sit heavy on it again.

For the Ulster army did not maintain its first successes. Its leader, Phelim O'Neill, was only a lawyer, not a military commander. After Ulster had been won for him, he wasted his army sitting long before Drogheda, which,

[1] This famous (or infamous) law established the supremacy of the English Parliament over the Irish Parliament within the four seas of Ireland, forbidding the latter to begin legislating on any Irish subject without first getting permission from the former to do so, and giving the former absolute and unquestioned veto over every enactment of the latter—thus making the Irish "Parliament" an Irish farce.

without siege guns, he could not take. And when eventually he raised the siege, and faced an enemy army that had been forming in the North, his own wasted force was not only defeated, but almost wiped out. Then were the Irish of Ulster overwhelmed with despair, and considering making the best of the bad terms which they could now get from the enemy, when suddenly, from the Boyne to the sea, the province quivered with a magic thrill as from mouth to mouth was passed the word "Owen Roe is come!"[2]

On the 6th July, 1642, with a hundred officers in his company, the long-wished for saviour stepped off a ship at the old castle of MacSwiney, at Doe, in the North of Donegal. At Charlemont he was given command of the Northern army—the little that was left of it. And he proceeded at once to build it up, and train it into fighting form. So potent was the name and fame of Owen Roe that even while his army was still in embryo, Lord Levin, from Scotland, at the head of twenty thousand men refused to meet such a formidable battler and strategist.

---

[2] THE COMING OF OWEN ROE

Ho! Phelim, rouse your sorrowing soul, and raise your head once more!
Glad news, glad news for aching hearts comes from the northern shore!
Magennis and Maguire, come each from out your 'leagured tower,
And spit upon their Saxon laws—defy their Saxon power!
O'Reilly and O'Hanlon come into the light of day!
Come forth, come forth, and chase the gloom that wraps your souls away!
Ho! fling the Sunburst to the winds—sound trumpet loud, and drum!
Ho! ring thy echoes, Ulster, out, Owen Roe, Owen Roe is come!

To North and South, to East and West, speed with the joyous news,
Press Heaven's own winds into your cause the tidings to diffuse;
On, on, o'er mountain, moor, and march—through wood, and brake, and fell—
On, on, as though pursued by all the vengeful powers of hell!
On, on, nor sleep, nor bait, nor pause, till starts from sleep the land,
And hope has gleamed in every heart, and steel in every hand,
And eyes are fired that erst shone meek, and tongues loosed that were dumb—
Till Heaven is rent with thunders of Owen Roe, Owen Roe is come!

Ho! proud and haughty Sassenach, look to your powder now!
Look to your spoils, O robber! for, sore need you have, I trow;
Look to your lives, ye sleuth-hounds false! for naught shall us withstand,
Since Owen Roe, our own beloved, with Vengeance is at hand;
Ho! Saxons, tyrants, spoilers, by Liffey, Foyle, or Maigue,
Where'er you're found, Owen's heavy hand shall scourge ye as a plague!
Oh, hellish memories steel our hearts, our mercy-sense benumb!
Up Gaels! Up Gaels! Revenge! Revenge! Owen Roe, Owen Roe is come!

—SEUMAS MACMANUS.

Though the name of O'Neill helped to keep the enemy at bay while he built up his army and trained them on the plateau of Southern Leitrim—from which he made an occasional sally to whip some body of the enemy, and refresh their respect for him—the Supreme Council at Kilkenny, jealous of the popularity of the great Irishman, sometimes stooped to hamper when they should have helped him, and at length went so far as to slight and curb him by appointing over him as commander in chief, one of their own, Lord Castlehaven. But Owen Roe went steadily forward with the work that lay to his hand. And in June '46 fought and won his great pitched battle, the famous victory of Benburb. Here he met and smashed the Scottish General Monroe, who then held the British command in Ulster.

In this battle, O'Neill had five thousand men and no artillery whatsoever. Monroe had six thousand men and a good field of artillery. Monroe took position in the angle formed by the junction of the River Oonah and the Black Water, adjacent to the village of Benburb. He drew up his army that morning, with five divisions on the front line and four divisions in the second line. O'Neill's seven divisions were placed, four in the first line and three supporting divisions behind. Monroe awaited the attack. His men were fresh, and he had the sun in his favor. O'Neill, who had sent his cavalry northward to intercept assistance coming thence to his enemy, took pains to disappoint Monroe, and to keep his nerves and the nerves of his troops on edge for many mortal hours, while he merely engaged in skirmishing. By these tactics he not only got the accession of his cavalry (after their successful Northern sally) and tired out Monroe's army, but he also got the westering sun in their eyes. Then, everything being favourable, he gave the word, "Sancta Maria!" and in the name of the Trinity launched an impetuous whirlwind attack of such mighty momentum that nothing could withstand it. His cavalry captured the enemy's guns. His infantry overswept and overwhelmed the legions of Monroe, cut most of them down in masses, and hurled the remainder into the river—in one brief hour wiping out a splendid and well-equipped army that had been the hope of the British in Ulster!

Thirty-two standards were taken. Lord Ardes, with thirty-two Scottish officers were captured. Cannon, baggage, two months' provisions, and 1,500 draft horses were bagged; 3,300 of the enemy lay dead on the field. Many more were drowned in the river and killed in the pursuit. While Owen Roe's loss was seventy men killed and a hundred wounded.

All remaining Scottish forces were, by this signal victory, sent scurrying into the two strongholds of Derry and Carrickfergus. The province was Owen Roe's and Ireland's!

So would the whole country soon have been—but unfortunately, the Supreme Council, flinging away the golden opportunity, not only signed a peace with Ormond, acting for King Charles, but went so far as to put under his command all of the Confederate Catholic Army.

It is little wonder that Nuncio Rinuccini and the Bishops rose up against such traitorous peace—and went so far as to excommunicate the traitorous peacemakers. Owen Roe hurried south with his forces to overawe the traitors, and try to counteract the harm they had done. In the south with an army whose numbers had now mounted to 12,000 (including 1500 horse) he was joined by General Preston and his southern Catholic army. Preston, like Owen Roe himself, had served his military apprenticeship, and won well-deserved fame for himself on the Continent. He had landed at Wexford two months after Owen Roe had landed in Donegal—and, as he was of the New Irish, he was given by the Confederacy a southern command. The united forces of these two able commanders might well have counteracted the ill-effect of the unworthy peace proclaimed by the Supreme Council. But the ferment of the Old Irish and New Irish jealousy was at work even in the combined forces. And on top of this, O'Neill discovered that Preston was being tampered with by the Ormond faction. And Ormond was trying to negotiate a peace with him. So he rose up and went north with his army again. And the victory that had seemed almost within Ireland's reach, was snatched away once more.

The progress of events for the ensuing couple of years, to the coming of Cromwell, was puzzlingly kaleidoscopic in effect. And probably never before or since was there such an interminable tangle in the political affairs of any nation. There were half a dozen distinct parties and as many distinct armies rending the National fabric—the Old Irish Nationalists, the New Irish Nationalists, the New Irish Royalists (for Charles), the Anglo-Irish Parliamentarians, the Scoto-Irish Royalists, and the Scoto-Irish Parliamentarians. These many parties were uniting in all sorts of odd combinations, and dividing along the most unlooked for lines. Although the Parliamentarians in Britain steadily treated all sections of Irish as if they were, not humans but beasts,[3] each of the two sections of the Irish at times united with the bitterest of the anti-Irish to fight the other.

[3] Captain Swanley in '44 seized a ship that was carrying loyalist troops from Galway to Bristol, picked out from amongst them seventy whom he considered to be Irish, and threw them overboard. And the *Journal* of the English House of Commons for June of that year records—"Captain Swanley was called into the House of Commons and thanks given to him for his good service, and a chain of gold of two hundred pounds in value."

But, every move made by Owen Roe, and every combination, was wisely directed toward the great end. At one time, in the summer of '48 he was bravely standing against the five armies of five other parties that moved in unison against him. And against all five this magnificent general was able not merely to hold the field, but to march south to Kilkenny with 10,000 men—and from there in safety return to his camp at Belturbet again. From time to time during these years, while he stood like a rock defying the storm, he saw one after another of the Catholic commands disastrously defeated, and almost annihilated. He saw the Nuncio temporarily turn against him, himself declared a rebel, and out of the range of pardon, by the Confederation!

Yet the noble man held steadily to his task, and when eventually Cromwell came like an avenging angel Owen Roe was the one great commanding figure to which the awed and wasted nation instinctively turned.

But, as by God's will it proved, their turning to him was in vain.

In pursuance of the same admirable policy, Napier in his "Life of Montrose" tells us that, in Scotland, in one day, eighty Irish women and children were thrown over a bridge, and drowned.

Clarendon says that when the Earl of Warwick captured Irish frigates he "used to tie the Irish sailors back to back, and fling them into the sea."

CHAPTER L

CROMWELL

For, Owen Roe, the hope of Ireland, was not destined to stay the bloody whirlwind that now entered Ireland for its final devastation. In face of the fearful disaster that threatened in the coming of Cromwell, Owen Roe not only brought himself to league with the abhorrent Ormond, but, with characteristic nobility, he, one of the great military leaders of the era, agreed to subordinate himself and his army to Ormond's supreme command.

But on his way south to join Ormond he fell ill in Cavan, and died—to the heartrending sorrow of a woe-stricken nation. As they poisoned Red Hugh O'Donnell in Spain, a short time before, the English are accused of poisoning this man whose fighting qualities they feared. One of their agents is said to have presented him with a pair of poisoned slippers at a ball which he attended in Derry on the eve of his starting south.[1]

---

[1] LAMENT FOR THE DEATH OF EOGHAN RUADH O'NEILL

"Did they dare, did they dare to slay Eoghan Ruadh O'Neill?"
"Yes, they slew with poison him they feared to meet with steel."
"May God wither up their hearts! May their blood cease to flow!
May they walk in living death, who poisoned Eoghan Ruadh!

"Though it break my heart to hear, say again the bitter words."
"From Derry, against Cromwell, he marched to measure swords;
But the weapon of the Sassanach met him on his way,
And he died at Cloch Uachtar, upon St. Leonard's Day."

"Wail, wail, ye for the Mighty One! Wail, wail ye for the dead;
Quench the hearth, and hold the breath, with ashes strew the head.
How tenderly we loved him! How deeply we deplore!
Holy Saviour! but to think we shall never see him more!

The fine and well-trained army of Owen Roe, of which Ormond is said to have been jealous, was, after the beloved leader's death, broken up, and distributed among various commands.

Several months before Cromwell's coming the Papal Nuncio was declared a rebel by the General Assembly—and, utterly disgusted with the whole horde of Anglo-Irish Catholics whose presence cursed the country, had shaken the dust of the country from his feet, and sailed from Galway. The General Assembly having reaped rich promises—and little else—from King Charles and Ormond, had in return humbly and dutifully laid Ireland at Charles' feet. His cause was henceforth their cause.

It was in August of '40 that Cromwell landed in Dublin, with eight regiments of foot, six of horse, and several troops of dragoons—in all seventeen thousand of the flower of the Puritan army. They were extraordinary men, his Ironsides—Bible-reading, psalm-singing soldiers of God—fearfully daring, fiercely fanatical, papist hating, looking on this land as being assigned to them the chosen people, by their God. And looking on the inhabitants as idol-worshipping Canaanites who were cursed of God, and to be extirpated by the sword. They came with minds inflamed by the lurid accounts of the "great Popish Massacre," which for some years now had been, by the Parliamentarians sedulously circulated among the English people.[2]

"Sagest in the council was he, kindest in the hall;
Sure we never won a battle—'twas Eoghan won them all.
Had he lived—had he lived—our dear country had been free;
But he's dead, but he's dead, and 'tis slaves we'll ever be.

"O'Farrell and Clanrickarde, Preston and Red Hugh,
Audley and McMahon—ye are valiant, wise and true;
But—what, what are ye all to our darling who is gone?
The rudder of our ship was he, our castle's cornerstone!

"Wail, wail him through the Island! Weep, weep for our pride!
Would that on the battlefield, our gallant chief had died!
Weep the Victor of Beann-borb—weep him, young men and old;
Weep for him, ye women, your beautiful lies cold!

"We thought you would not die, we were sure you would not go
And leave us in our utmost need to Cromwell's cruel blow.
Sheep without a shepherd when the snow shuts out the sky—
Oh! why did you leave us, Eoghan? why did you die?"

—Thomas Davis.

[2] A sample of this literature is the pamphlet published in London in 1647 by a noted Puritan preacher (and writer) Nathaniel Ward: "I beg upon my hands and knees that the expedition against them

To keep the men's venom at the boiling point there were chosen to travel with the troops, and also to sail with the fleet, Puritan preachers of the Word distinguished for their almost demoniacal hatred of the papistical Irish. Stephen Jerome, Hugh Peters, and their like, noted for the violence of their invective against all things Irish and Catholic, preached a war of extermination in the most startling and fearful manner—in the pulpit invoking the curse of God upon those who should hold their hands from slaying "while man, woman or child of Belial remains alive." Peters exhorted his hearers to do as did the conquerors of Jericho, "kill all that were, young men and old, children, and maidens."

The great leader of the grim Ironsides, himself, was destined to leave behind him in Ireland for all time a name synonymous with ruthless butchery.[3]

The first rare taste of the qualities of this agent of God the Just, and first Friend of the Irish was given to the people at Drogheda. When he took this city he gave it and its inhabitants to his men for a three days' and three nights' unending orgy of slaughter. Only thirty men out of a garrison of three thousand escaped the sword; and it is impossible to compute what other thousands of non-combatants, men, women, and children, were butchered. They were slain in the streets, in the lanes, in the yards, in the gardens, in the cellars, on their own hearthstone. They were slain in the church tower to which they fled for refuge, in the churches, on the altar steps, in the market-place—till the city's gutters ran with red rivulets of blood. In the vaults underneath the church a great number of the finest women of the city sought refuge. But hardly one, if one, even of these, was left to tell the awful tale of unspeakable outrage and murder.[4]

(the Irish) be undertaken while the hearts and hands of our soldiery are hot; to whome, I will be bold to say, briefly: happy be he that shall reward them as they served us, and cursed be he who shall do the work of the Lord negligently. Cursed be he who holdeth back the sword from blood: yea cursed be he that maketh not the sword stark drunk with Irish blood; who doth not recompense them double for their treachery to the English; but maketh them in heaps on heaps, and their country the dwelling place of dragons—an astonishment for nations. Let not that eye look for pity, nor hand be spared, that pities or spares them; and let him be cursed that curseth them not bitterly."

[3]No more illuminating light could be thrown upon the extraordinary attitude adopted by Britain toward Ireland, through all the centuries, than to quote here the sentiments of the great Englishman Carlyle upon the coldest-blooded butcher of all the many butchers by whom Ireland has been in seven centuries afflicted: "Oliver Cromwell came as a soldier of God the Just, terrible as Death, relentless as Doom doing God's judgments on the enemies of God . . . . It was the first King's face that poor Ireland ever saw, the first Friend's face." Since thus spoke one of the very great and noble of the English people, there is no reason for being astonished at the attitude toward Ireland of the mass of the British people.

[4]Arthur Wood, the Historian of Oxford, gives us a narrative compiled from the account of his brother who was an officer in Cromwell's army, and who had been through the siege and sack of

In his despatch to the Speaker of the House of Commons, after Drogheda, Cromwell says: "It has pleased God to bless our endeavour at Drogheda . . . the enemy were about 3,000 strong in the town. I believe we put to the sword the whole number. . . . This hath been a marvelous great mercy. . . . I wish that all honest hearts may give the glory of this to God alone, to whom indeed the praise of this mercy belongs." And again, "In this very place (St. Peter's Church), a thousand of them were put to the sword, fleeing thither for safety. . . . And now give me leave to say how this work was wrought. It was set upon some of our hearts that a great thing should be done, not by power or might, but by the spirit of God. And is it not so, clearly?"

On October 2, 1649, the English Parliament appointed a national Thanksgiving Day in celebration of the dreadful slaughter—and by unanimous vote placed upon the Parliamentary records—"That the House does approve of the execution done at Drogheda as an act of both justice to them [the butchered ones] and mercy to others who may be warned by it."

After Drogheda, Cromwell, in quick succession reduced the other northern strongholds, then turned and swept southward to Wexford—where he again exhibited to the people the face of the King and Friend. Two thousand were butchered here. He thought it a simple act of justice to "the Saints," his soldiers, to indulge them in the little joy of slaughtering the Canaanites. He writes: "I thought it not right or good to restrain off the soldiers from their right of pillage, or from doing execution on the enemy."

Lingard, in his History of England says: "Wexford was abandoned to the mercy of the assailants. The tragedy recently enacted at Drogheda was renewed. No distinction was made between the defenceless inhabitants and the armed soldiers, nor could the shrieks and prayers of three hundred females who had gathered round the great Cross in the market-place, preserve them from the swords of these ruthless barbarians."[5]

Drogheda—which throws interesting sidelight upon the British methods, and the quaint point of view of the most cultured of them. "Each of the assailants would take up a child and use it as a buckler of defence to keep him from being shot or brained. After they had killed all in the church they went into the vaults underneath, where all the choicest of women had hid themselves. One of these, a most handsome virgin, arrayed in costly and gorgeous apparel, knelt down to Wood, with tears and prayers begging for her life; and being stricken with a profound pity, he did take her under his arm for protection, and went with her out of the church with intention to put her over the works, to shift for herself, but a soldier, perceiving his intention, ran the sword through her, whereupon Mr. Wood, seeing her gasping, took away her money, jewels, etc., and flung her down over the works."

[5] Nicholas French, Bishop of Wexford who escaped from the city, and after terrible suffering and privation, escaped from the country, records: "On that fatal day, October 11th, 1649, I lost everything I had. Wexford, my native town, then abounding in merchandise, ships, and wealth, was taken at the

Cromwell reduced the garrisons of Arklow, Inniscorthy and Ross on the way to Wexford. After Wexford he tried to reduce Waterford, but failing in his first attempt, and not having time to waste besieging it, passed onward—and found the cities of Cork an easy prey. For, as Lord Inchiquin had garrisoned them with English Protestants, these garrisons readily sold the cities—and were later well rewarded with large grants of Irish lands in the North. He rested at Youghal, getting fresh supplies and money from England. In January he took the field again, reduced Fethard, Cashel, Carrick, and eventually got Kilkenny by negotiation.

Against his new and powerful cannon, the ancient and crumbling defences of the Irish cities were of little avail.

Perhaps the pluckiest fight put up against Cromwell was by Hugh O'Neill (nephew to Owen Roe) at Clonmel. With his little garrison of 1500 men he resisted magnificently. He quickly turned to splendid advantage a treacherous trick by which Cromwell was to be given entrance to the city—and quietly turning the tables, entrapped, fought and killed, five hundred of Cromwell's men. So finely did O'Neill defend the place that Cromwell had at length to turn the siege into a blockade. Then O'Neill, being out of provisions, worked a second clever bit of strategy. With the garrison, he secretly slipped away in the night to Waterford, after having arranged that when he and his forces had got twelve miles' start, the Mayor of the town should obtain good terms from the impatient and unwitting Cromwell. And, as anticipated, Cromwell was taken in, and eagerly gave fine terms to a town that, without his knowing it, was completely at his mercy.

The conqueror then—in the end of May—sailed from Youghal for England, after having in eight months, subdued almost all of Ireland, destroyed the effective Irish forces, and left the country prostrate at the feet of the Parliament. Swiftly, terribly, and effectively he had done his fearful work—"a very handsome spell of work," says the great minded Carlyle.[6]

---

sword's point by Cromwell, and sacked by an infuriated soldiery. Before God's altar fell sacred victims, holy priests of the Lord. Of those who were seized outside the church some were scourged, some thrown into chains and imprisoned, while others were hanged or put to death by cruel tortures. The blood of the noblest of our citizens was shed so that it inundated the streets. There was hardly a house that was not defiled with carnage and filled with wailing."

[6] A few sidelights on the "handsome spell of work" (out of thousands which happened):

At Cashel, where two thousand were slain, Cromwell's general, Broghill, took the Bishop of Ross, cut off his hands and feet, and then hanged him. A Dominican friar had his fingers and toes cut off before he was slain. And at Clonmel, a Franciscan was first drawn on the rack and then had his hands and feet burned off, after which he was hung. The parish priest of Arklow was tied to a wild horse's tail and dragged to Gorey, where he was hanged.

He left in command his general, Ireton, who, on his death soon after, was to be succeeded by Cromwell's son, Henry.

It took his successors, however, another two years to finish up the remnant of work that he had left unfinished.

Waterford, Limerick, and Galway still held out. Scattered bands of fighters here and there, and an army of the North, about five thousand foot and a thousand horse, under Heber MacMahon, Bishop of Clogher, kept Ulster resistance still alive.

But MacMahon, very little of a military man, though he swept the enemy before him at Toome, at Dungannon and Dungiven, was disastrously defeated near Letterkenny—when he had persisted in engaging the enemy under disadvantageous circumstances, and against the pleadings of military counsellers. There he lost half his army, and with the remnant of it was overcome at Enniskillen. He was hanged, and his head set above Derry gate, as a warning to "traitors"—the term always applied by Englishmen to such Irish as perversely persist in doing their duty by their own country instead of their country's conqueror.

The few towns—Waterford, Limerick, Galway[7]—and the scattered fighting forces were gradually conquered, or capitulated. Till on the 12th May, '52, Articles of Kilkenny signed by the Parliamentary Commissioners on the one hand and the Earl of West Meath on the other—yet fiercely denounced by the Leinster clergy—practically terminated the longest, the most appallingly dreadful and inhumane, and the most exhausting, war, with which unfortunate Ireland was ever visited.

The attitude adopted by the exterminators towards those whom they were exterminating, is illumined to us when we know that the most wildly grotesque stories told of the latter, were greedily accepted by the former. In Nash's edition of the Hudibras, it was gravely stated that when seven hundred Irish had been put to the sword by Inchiquin, "Among them were found, when stripped divers that had tails nearly a quarter of a yard long. Forty soldiers, eye-witnesses, testified the same on their oaths." A Protestant minister with the troops in Munster wrote home to London that when they had stormed a certain castle, many of the slain defenders were found to have tails several inches long!

[7] One of Galway's gallant defenders, a young man, Geoffrey Baron, condemned to the scaffold by the conquerors—for the same crime for which through the ages since, other thousands of Ireland's young men have made sacred to us the gallows steps—asked and was permitted to dress for his execution. He went to his room, chose from his wardrobe a suit of white taffetie, and, so garbed, joyously climbed the gallows stairs and went to his death for Ireland.

Incidentally, let it be here set down that on the day these lines are being penned I lift the newspaper, read a report of six young men—"rebels"—just hanged in Cork, and of the chaplain, Canon O'Sullivan's announcement, "They went to their death like school-boys going on a holiday."

The centuries roll on, the struggle grows ancient, but the spirit, proud, glad, indomitable, weakens not, nor changes ever.

CHAPTER LI

The Cromwellian Settlement

But Ireland's sufferings, great and terrible as they had been, were yet far from ended. True, she had quaffed her chalice to the last bitter drop, but it was ordained that she must now lap up the poisoned dregs.

Peace had been proclaimed over the torn land. But peace is a bitterly ironical term to apply to the state of things in Ireland now. This may well be realised by reading any description of life in Ireland during these years. Hear this description of a place in time of "peace"—taken from Lynch's "Life of Bishop Kirwan":

> "Along with the three scourges of God, famine, plague, and war, there was another which some called the fourth scourge, to wit, the weekly exaction of the soldiers' pay, which was extorted with incredible atrocity, each Saturday—bugles sounding, and drums beating. On these occasions the soldiers entered the various houses, and pointing their muskets to the breasts of men and women threatened them with instant death if the sum demanded was not immediately given. Should it have so happened that the continual payment of these taxes had exhausted the means of the people, bed, bedding, sheets, table-cloths, dishes, and every description of furniture, nay, the very garments of the women, torn off their persons, were carried to the market-place and sold for a small sum; so much so, that each recurring Saturday bore a resemblance to the Day of Judgment, and the clangour of the trumpet smote the people with terror, almost equal to that of doomsday."

When the wars were ended and "peace" had been established then was the exhausted remnant of the nation condemned to shoulder its bitter burden—slavery worse than death, and a terrible exile, worse than either—

the transplanting of all of the Irish race who were still alive, in Ulster, Leinster and Munster, to the barren bogs of Connacht; so that the smiling fields of the fertile three-quarters of Ireland might be divided among the children of the conqueror. It was the great Cromwellian Settlement.

One of the articles of the peace provided that the Irish soldiers could, if they would, enter the army of any foreign power friendly to England. Thirty-five hundred of them, under Colonel Edmund O'Dwyer, went to the Prince Condé; five thousand under Lord Muskerry, to the King of Poland; smaller numbers to other Continental armies; and about thirty thousand to the King of Spain.

Because by far the greater portion of the Irish who were able to bear arms had been killed off, few young men now remained to Ireland. And of these few remaining young men, and of the young women and boys and girls, numbers were, during the following years shipped into slavery to the American colonies and the West Indies.[1] The numbers thus sent to slavery are variously estimated at between thirty thousand and eighty thousand.[2]

---

[1] There is a tradition that, as a result, on some of the smaller islands of the West Indies up till a little more than a century ago, the negroes still spoke Gaelic.

[2] Prendergast in his "Cromwellian Settlement of Ireland" names four Bristol merchants who were the most active of the slave trading agents. For illustrating the formal legal way in which the horror was commercialised Prendergast quotes "one instance out of many"—the case of Captain John Vernon, who as agent of the English Commissioners (who then governed Ireland) contracted "under his hand, of date 14th September, 1653" with Messrs. Sellick and Leader of Bristol to supply them with two hundred and fifty women of the Irish nation above twelve and under forty-five years of age. Also three hundred men between twelve years and forty-five years of age.

Following the conquest of Jamaica in 1655, after thousands of the Irish had, through years before, been shipped into slavery, the Governor of that island asked for a thousand girls from Ireland to be shipped there—to the most appalling kind of slavery.

Secretary Thurloe's Correspondence, Vol. 4, gives Henry Cromwell's reply to this modest request—in his letter of September 11, 1655:

"Concerninge the younge women, although we must use force in takeinge them up, yet it beinge so much for their owne goode and likely to be of soe great advantage to the publique, it is not in the least doubted you may have such number of them as you thinke fitt to make use upon this account. . . . I desire to express as much zeal in this design as you would wish, and shall be as diligent in prosequution of any directioaes . . . judgeinge it to be business of publique concernment. . . . Blessed be God, I do not finde many discouragements in my worke, and hope I shall not, soe longe as the Lord is pleased to keep my harte uprighte before him."

And under date of September 18, 1655, Henry of the Uprighte Harte, writing from Kilkenny, again to Thurloe, says in the course of his letter, "I shall not neede to repeat anythinge about the girles, not doubtinge but to answer your expectationes to the full in that; and I think it might be of like advantage to your affaires there, and to ours heer, if you should thinke fitt to sende 1500 or 2000 young boys of from twelve to fourteen years of age, to the place aforementioned. We could well spare them, and they would be of use to you; and who knowes but that it may be the meanes to make them Englishmen, I mean rather Christians."

Comment upon this—especially the final pithy sentence—would surely spoil it.

On the Continent, in almost every country, the exiled Irish came in course of time to adorn all ranks and all classes. One historian says, "They became Chancellors of Universities, professors and high officials in every European state. A Kerryman was physician to Sobieski, King of Poland. A Kerryman was confessor to the Queen of Portugal, and was sent by the King on an embassy to Louis the Fourteenth. A Donegal man named O'Glacan was physician and Privy Chancellor to the King of France, and a very famed professor of medicine in the Universities of Tolouse and Bologna."

"There was not a country in Europe, and not an occupation, where Irishmen were not in the first rank—as Fieldmarshals, Admirals, Ambassadors, Prime Ministers, Scholars, Physicians, Merchants, Soldiers, and Founders of mining industry."

Of the fearful condition of Ireland now, Prendergast gives us a terrible picture: "Ireland, in the language of Scripture, lay void as a wilderness. Five-sixths of her people had perished. Women and children were found daily perishing in ditches, starved. The bodies of many wandering orphans, whose fathers had been killed or exiled, and whose mothers had died of famine, were preyed upon by wolves. In the years 1652 and 1653 the plague, following the desolating wars, had swept away whole counties, so that one might travel twenty or thirty miles and not see a living creature. Man, beast and bird were all dead, or had quit those desolate places. The troops would tell stories of the place where they saw a smoke, it was so rare to see either smoke by day, or fire or candle by night. If two or three cabins were met with, there were found none but aged men, with women and children; and they, in the words of the prophet, 'became as a bottle in the smoke,' their skins black like an oven because of the terrible famine."

In September, 1653, was issued by Parliament the order for the great transplanting. Then all the fertile fields of the Irish natives of Ireland were declared to be the property of the British soldiers who had won them by the sword, and of the English Adventurers who had purchased the sword and financed the expedition into Ireland—and, under penalty of death, all the ancient inhabitants were ordered to repair themselves from the ends of Ireland to the wastes of Connacht, where their lot was to be laid henceforth. Under penalty of death, no Irish man, woman, or child, was to let himself, herself, itself, be found east of the River Shannon, after the 1st May, 1654.[3]

[3] Edward Hetherington was hung from a tree near his own house while a placard struck upon his breast, and another upon his back, warned the rest of the Irish world that this was—"For not transplanting."

To the countless thousands of weak, weary, and starving creatures—worn old men and women, and weakling babes—direct sentence of death would have been ten times more welcome and infinitely more merciful. That was a fearful winter of '53–'54; fearful for the tottering old and the crawling young, who, from the four ends of Ireland were dragging their skeleton frames over the hills and the plains, and forcing themselves along every highway that headed to the west, to deeper misery, more painful starvation, and slow and painful death. The Lord and the commoner, the palsied old man and the toddling orphan child, all alike were driven forth from their homes, and goaded over the blood-stained flints to their dread Siberia.[4]

The Barony of Burren in Clare, to which the first batch of these unfortunates were consigned, was such a God-forsaken region that it was

---

Certain artisans and labourers who would be absolutely needed by the British Settlers were excluded from the edict of banishment. There was also a clause—evidently put in more for effect than for anything else—that people who could prove themselves innocent of having been rebels or having aided, harboured, or sympathised with rebels, and who were guiltless of any offences against British soldiers, settlers, or sympathisers, would be excluded from the edict of banishment. This was "a concession of mercy" to the Irish nation. And its value may be estimated by the fact that a fair-minded one of the British Settlers themselves, Vincent Gookin, in his Vindication of the Irish Transplanting, records his protest against "the narrowness and straightness of the Parliament's concessions of mercy to that nation which doth not declare one in five hundred pardonable either for life or estate."

This same Vincent Gookin in endeavouring to show the vital necessity to the new colonists of holding back from banishment the working portion of the Irish people, sheds light for us upon the manual accomplishments of the common Irish worker then. And his testimony is valuable in view of the constant English assertion that the Irish were in a state verging on savagery (which, considering the circumstances, might well have been the case). Gookin says: "There are few of the Irish commonalty but are skilful in husbandry, and more exact than any of the English in the husbandry proper to the country. . . . There are few of the women but are skilful in dressing hemp and flax, and making of linen and woollen cloth. . . . It is believed that to every hundred men there are five or six carpenters at least of that nation, and these more handy and ready in building ordinary houses, and more prudent in supplying the defects of instruments and materials, than English artificers."

[4] From the Government records, Prendergast gives us samples of the official description of the migrating Irish, both the high brought low, and the lowly still lower:

"Sir Nicholas Comyn of Limerick numb on one side of dead palsy, accompanied only by his wife, Catherine, aged thirty-five, flaxen hair, of middle stature, and one maid servant, Honour MacNamara, aged twenty, brown hair, middle stature—having no substance."

"Ignatius Stacpool of Limerick, orphant, eleven years of age, flaxen hair, full face, low of stature; Catherine, his sister, orphant, age eight, flaxen hair, full face—having no substance."

"James, Lord Dun Boyne in County Tipperary, describes himself as likely to be accompanied by twenty-one followers, and as having four cows, ten garans, and two swine."

The grinding of the mills of the gods brought it around that among the multitude of poor creatures who, in pain and suffering, were now driven from Cork into exile was the grandson of the poet Edmund Spenser, who in his time had driven forth the native Irish that he might enjoy the lands of which he robbed them.

popularly said to have not wood enough on which to hang a man, water enough to drown him, nor earth enough to bury him. Beside it Siberia was Eden. And many of those consigned to it returned to face death at the hands of the soldiers.

And it is to be noted that even Connacht was not entirely left to them. For, not satisfied with obtaining the three more fertile quarters of Ireland, the covetous eyes of the British followed these creatures even across the Shannon—and the one fertile county of Connacht, Sligo, was filched from them, as well as many fruitful patches that God had granted to the remainder of Connacht.

Sir William Petty, in his Political Anatomy of Ireland, estimated that the wars had reduced the population of Ireland from 1,466,000 in '41 to 616,000 in '52—so that much more than one-half of the population of the whole country had been at that time exterminated. And they were probably dying more thickly during the terrible transplanting—and in the years immediately after, when they were cooped up in Connacht, without houses, cattle, or implements of tillage, striving as it were to live on manna from heaven.

Petty also tells us that, whereas before 1641 the British in Ireland were to the Irish as two to eleven, when the Cromwellian Settlement was effected, three-fourths of the lands, and five-sixths of the houses belonged to the British Settlers. And when Petty wrote, in '72—after a period of twenty years' rest during which the exiled Irish had got some time to rehabilitate themselves—he records that three-fourths of the population existed upon milk and potatoes, and lived in cabins that had neither chimney, door, stairs, nor window—"So," exclaims Sir William, and we can see the pious and gallant Briton rub his hands for glee, "they will never rebel again."

Now, as ever in Ireland, the gloom is illumined by a radiance behind. While things are at their blackest, the people, like driven animals, agonising most sorely, both learning and religion are still cherished—cherished not only by those cooped up in Connacht, but by the dispossessed who had remained hewers of wood and drawers of water for their dispossessors; and among the thousand who, escaping back from Connacht, were in every corner of the country insinuating themselves into its life once more. Keeping in mind that these creatures, under the terrible conditions pictured, were just clinging to a life of unparalleled hardship, it is something noteworthy and characteristic of the indomitable soul of the race, to find Petty testifying: "The superior learning among them is the philosophies of the schools and the genealogies of their ancestors—both which look like what St. Paul hath condemned!" The superior Briton in Petty makes him set down the priests as having small learning. But he admits in the next breath: "They can often outtalk in Latin those who talk with them."

It was shortly before this time that King James' Commissioners—the learned Protestant Primate, Archbishop Usher, sad to say, being one of them—suppressed the classical school conducted in Galway by John Lynch, the noted author of Cambrensis Eversus—praised it and suppressed it, and bound over Lynch in four hundred pounds "to forbear teaching."

And cooped together in Connacht, or scattered fugitives, haunting the fields that had once been theirs, they clung to their religion too, with a perseverance that was sublime. Just before the Wars the people had been venturing, here and there, to bring their religion into the open. That good Puritan, Sir William Brereton, in the record of his journey in Ireland in 1635, expressed himself shocked at the painful sight that met his eye at Dundalk—"wherein the Papists boldly dare to go to Mass openly." And wherever they were, there also, lurking too, was the hunted priest with price upon his head.[5]

O'Hagan (afterwards Chief Justice) in his Essay on Irish History cites one of the edicts of that time: "If any one shall know where a priest remains concealed, in caves, woods, or caverns, or if by any chance he should meet a priest on the highway, and not immediately take him into custody and present him before the next magistrate, such person is to be considered a traitor and an enemy of the Republic. He is accordingly to be cast into prison, flogged through the public streets and afterwards have his ears cut off. But should it appear that he kept up any correspondence or friendship with a priest, he is to suffer death."

---

[5] Here are a few sample disbursements taken from the Government records for 1657:

"Five pounds to Thomas Gregson, Evan Powell, and Samuel Ally, to be equally divided upon them, for arresting a Popish priest, Donogh Hagerty, taken and now secured in the County jail at Clonmel."

"To Lieutenant Edwin Wood, twenty-five pounds for five priests and three friars apprehended by him—namely, Thomas McGeoghan, Turlough MacGowan, Hugh Goan, Terence Fitzsimmons, and another—who on examination confessed themselves to be priests and friars."

"To Humphrey Gibbs and to Corporal Thomas Hill ten pounds for apprehending two Popish priests, namely, Maurice Prendergast and Edward Fahy."

"To Arthur Spollen, Robert Pierce, and John Bruen, five pounds for their good service performed in apprehending and bringing before the Right Honourable Chief Justice Pepys on the twenty-first January last, one Popish priest, Edwin Duhy."

Both the perseverance of the people in their thirst for learning and religion, and also the hard lot of the hunted priest, then, is well pictured for us by a Jesuit, Father Quinn, who, in the early 'fifties, in a Latin report, from Galway, made to his superiors in Rome (and preserved in St. Isidore's) writes:

"On a spot of ground in the middle of an immense bog, Father James Forde constructed for himself a little hut, whither boys and youths came and still come to be instructed in the rudiments of learning, virtue, and faith. Then they go from house to house and teach parents and neighbours what they learnt in the bogs.

"Our life is therefore daily warfare and living martyrdom. We never venture to approach any houses of Catholics, but live generally in the mountains, forests, and inaccessible bogs—where Cromwellian troopers can not reach us. Thither crowds of poor Catholics flock to us, whom we refresh by the Word of God and consolations of the Sacraments. Here in wild mountain tracts, we preach to them constancy in faith and the mystery of the Cross of Our Lord." In spite of all precaution taken for the secret exercises, Cromwellians often discovered it: then the wild beast was never hunted with more fury, nor tracked with more pertinacity, through mountains, woods, and bogs, than the priest.

"I cannot omit a lamentable incident which occurred here lately," says Father Quinn, "three hundred Catholics bound in chains, were carried to a desolate island—where they were abandoned. All of them starved to death except two who swam away. One sank. One reached land."

After the Puritan fury had expended itself, and the native Irish were everywhere mysteriously springing up again—out of the bowels of the earth as it seemed—we have interesting testimony of the rapid recovery of the race, and revival of its religion, from the French traveller Janvin de Rochefort, who went through Ireland in 1668. He found: "Even in Dublin more than twenty houses where Mass is secretly said, and in about a thousand places, subterranean vaults and retired spots in the woods." Spending a Sunday in Drogheda he was told he could hear Mass two miles outside the city—where he found it being celebrated in a poor chamber in a mean hamlet. He was astonished at the numbers he saw flocking through the woods and across the mountains to attend. And he adds: "Here I saw, before Mass, fifty who confessed and afterwards communicated with devotion truly Catholic."

Like all the many other English attempts of the like kind, the Cromwellian Settlement did not settle—and the Cromwellian extirpation did not extirpate—the perverse race.

For the wars of the 'Forties and Cromwellian Settlement see the following:
Belling's History of the Irish Confederation.
Meehan's Confederation of Kilkenny.
Warner's History of the Rebellion.
Carte's Life of the Duke of Ormond.
Green's Short History of the English People.
Lord Maguire's Narrative.
Murphy's Cromwell in Ireland.
Taylor's Life of Owen Roe.
Leland's History of Ireland.
Lingard's History of England.

CHAPTER LII

The Williamite Wars

When to England's throne and Ireland's governorship came James II (1685), his first act was to suspend the Penal Laws against Catholics and Dissenters—whereby he filled the majority of his English subjects and the Puritan settlers in Ireland with horror. Furthermore, he decided to effect a reform in the government of Ireland.

So, he sent over Richard Talbot, later known in Irish history as the Duke of Tyrconnell. Talbot had been attached to King Charles's suite since the Restoration. He was an Irishman and a Catholic; "a large powerful-looking man, brilliant and handsome in his youth" says Gramont in his "Memoirs," "of nobility, not to say haughtiness in his manners." It was recorded of him that he always paid his debts. He was fifty years of age when the king chose him for the service. A tall cavalry officer of Irish birth, then in England, captain in Hamilton's dragoons by name Patrick Sarsfield, held an opinion later that Tyrconnell lacked decision and boldness.

However, on being appointed to the command of the army in Ireland, and in the following year to the Lord Lieutenancy, he showed no lack of decision. He had been at the sack of Drogheda, a boy of sixteen. That memory, and the king's cause to serve, caused him speedily to make a radical change in the army. The Puritan element was removed from the ranks; regiments were recruited from Irish Catholics; the Cromwellian officers were replaced by Irishmen. "I have put the sword in your hands," he is reported to have said to the Irish Privy Council; and the statement was true.

He went further. The charters of the Corporations, all framed in favour of the foreigner, the English settler, were called in. He appointed Catholics as judges and magistrates, and placed Catholics on his Council. These mere acts of justice appeared crimes to the settlers. To complete his sins Tyrconnell sent three thousand Iris soldiers to England as a reinforcement for James's army. Their arrival was regarded with horror. The English believed them to be bloodthirsty banditti.

From the Hague a man closely connected by birth and marriage with the king was watching in silence the march of events. A man with a high aquiline nose, a pale face, with light brown hair and penetrating eyes, asthmatic, a slender awkward figure, ungraceful, taciturn, fond of hunting. Agents began to pass between him and certain Englishmen. From Versailles Louis XIV watched him in turn. He bade his ambassador in London warn James against William of Orange. The warning was resented. Then, shortly after the birth of the Prince of Wales, the blow fell.

William of Orange landed in England, and James's army melted away. His cause there became hopeless; the country went over to William. Deserted by relations and friends, James ordered his army to be disbanded. He then fled from London, and later to France. Some jokers, dressed as clowns, entered London and said the Irish regiments had seized their arms and were slaughtering all Protestants. The report was believed; a mad panic seized the citizens; alarm bells were rung; beacons kindled in the adjoining counties, and the night was known in England as the "Irish night." It was the 12th of December, 1688. Meanwhile the disbanded Irish soldiers were getting home as best they could.

William knew men. He offered Sarsfield a colonelcy in his army, and his favour generally, if he would desert James and act as William's agent in Ireland. The colonelcy and the favour were spurned. It became evident now that the issue between James and William would be decided in Ireland. To some of the Irish, complete independence, with James for king, seemed a not impossible hope.

As a body the Irish nation declared for him; the English settlers, Elizabethan and Cromwellian, for William. Tyrconnell at once set about strengthening the Irish army. He empowered the Catholic nobility and gentry to raise regiments. Foot and Horse were soon enrolled. Arms were deficient; for this reason many of the new levies were of little practical aid.

Within the space of two months fifty thousand Irishmen enlisted themselves. These men were known as "Tyrconnell's blackguards" by the Williamites. Many were ragged; some half naked. Their fathers had been robbed of all; their oppressors just allowed them to exist. One of their enemies described their appearance. "Some had wisps of hay or straw bands about their heads instead of hats. Others tattered coats or blankets cast over them without any breeches. Stockings and shoes were strange things. As for shirts three proved a miracle. However, they mustered." To the cold, hostile eye they seemed but savages. But there was native learning, and poetry, and wonderful oral tradition, wit, generosity, resource and clever brains among them in spite of the frightful poverty of their lives, and the grinding cruelties of their oppressors. They were the material which, later, drilled and armed, was to form the Irish Brigade in the service of France, and prove the best fighters in Europe.

War, thus declared, Tyrconnell sent to France to invite James to Ireland. He came. By a successful war here, he hoped to recover the crown of England. To him, Ireland was the pawn; England the prize. He brought gifts from Louis, gold, arms, and ammunition. He was accompanied by his illegitimate son, the Duke of Berwick, a boy of nineteen, and by four hundred French officers and gunners; Scotch and English Jacobites; and as Louis's agent and ambassador the Count d'Avaux. A Frenchman, de Rosen, was to command the army that was to advance on Derry held by the settlers; a man of fierce temper, with little ability. Another Frenchman, also of the party, was Boisselaux, who proved his worth at Limerick, and with James came Patrick Sarsfield.

The landing was at Kinsale. It was March 19th, 1689. Tyrconnell met James at Cork. He aroused foolish enthusiasm everywhere. All the way to Dublin he was greeted with acclamations of joy. Speeches were made, songs sung; young girls danced along the road. Men took off their serge coats and laid them in the mud before his horse's hoofs; women kissed him as the deliverer of the country. James bore the kisses for a short time; then ordered that no more kissers were to be allowed to approach him.

Dublin showed the same delight. It was Palm Sunday when he entered the city. Embroidered cloths, silks, tapestries hung from windows; the streets were freshly gravelled; bells rang; royal salutes were fired. Next day he summoned a council. Five proclamations were issued—one, for the summoning of a Parliament.

His next act was to march against Williamite Derry. Negotiations had been opened with Lundy, who was in command of the defenders. Lundy stipulated that while these negotiations were going on the Irish army was to remain a distance of four miles from the city. De Rosen advised James to show himself in force before the walls. The army was set in motion. News reached the city; the 'prentice boys closed the gates in the king's face with shouts of "no surrender!" From that day Derry defended herself gallantly until she was relieved. It was one of the magnificently gallant defences of history.

Disgusted at his reception, the king returned to Dublin. On the 7th of May the Parliament met. He opened it robed and crowned.[1] It was the first Parliament since the Parliament of the Pale had been established in the thirteenth century that represented the Irish nation. It is known as the Patriot Parliament. Its detractors then, as now, point to it as a specimen of what an Irish Government would be. "Unruly, rash, rapacious, and bloody" they call it.

James said he had come to venture his life in defence of Irish liberties and his own right. The nation, he promised, should flourish under his rule. He spoke to fifty-four peers and two hundred and twenty-four members of the Commons. Among the peers were Iveagh, Clare and Mountchashel, whose regiments afterwards, as part of the Irish Brigade in the service of France were to keep the name of Ireland before Europe. Among the seven prelates was Anthony Dopping, Protestant Bishop of Meath, who led the opposition, and who, after the last siege of Limerick, urged in a sermon, the Lord Justices to break the Treaty they had signed.

The Parliament passed in all thirty-five Acts with due deliberation and the advice of counsel. The most memorable are:—The Act that declared the Parliament of England could not bind Ireland, or that writs or errors of appeal, or the removing of judgments, decrees, and sentences given in Ireland could not be brought to England: The Act for the repeal of the Act of Settlement that had confirmed the Cromwellian settlers in their possession of the lands they had seized: The Act for liberty of conscience which repealed "such acts or clauses in any Act of Parliament which was inconsistent with the same"; The Act relating to the army, and the one dealing with the payment of tithes.

The Act of supply for the army is remarkable for its equity in the distribution of the tax. It empowered the king to raise £20,000 pounds a month by land tax distributed over the counties and towns according to their abilities, the two rebellious counties, Derry and Fermanagh, receiving no heavier tax than the others. It provided against the oppression of the tenant, as "in these distracted times," it says, "the tenants might not be able to pay rents, the tax in such cases was to be paid by the landlord or occupier, who, where the land was let at its value, was to pay the whole tax (out of the rent); where the land was let at half its value or less, the tenant was to pay a share." Thomas Davis, commenting on this Act, asks, "Where, in distracted or quiet times, since, has a Parliament of landlords in England or Ireland acted with equal liberality?"

---

[1] The crown was made in Ireland.

The Tithes which had been borne by the Catholics in the Ascendancy Parliaments were adjusted fairly; the Protestants were to pay tithes to their own church, the Catholics to theirs. No Protestant bishop was to be deprived of stipend or honour. They were to hold their incomes; they were to sit in Parliament. The estates, plundered by the Cromwellians thirty-six years before, were restored to the previous owners, but compensation was to be given to all innocent persons. It endeavoured to make a war-navy. It passed Acts for the relief and release of "poor distressed prisoners for debts"; for the settling of intestate estates; for delays in the execution of the laws; the unnecessary arrests of judgments, and the prevention of frauds and perjuries. It prohibited the importation of English, Welsh and Scotch coal. Large sums of money, it declared, were sent out of the kingdom, which hindered the industry of labourers in supplying Dublin and other places with fuel, and gave opportunity to persons importing coal to raise the prices when they pleased. As, however, occasion might arise when it would be necessary to import coal the government could issue a license for its importation then. The Irish coal pits were to be worked. The owners were not to take dishonest advantage of the law to raise their prices.

It further passed an Act for the improvement of shipping and trade. It drew attention to the size and safety of Irish harbours. "They stand very fit and convenient for trade and commerce with most Nations, Kingdoms and Plantations; although this trade and commerce had been hindered by laws, statutes and ordinances that had prohibited and disabled Irish men from importing or exporting direct into or from Ireland, all exports and imports having to pass through England; thus cutting Ireland off from direct communication with Europe, America, Africa, Plantations and Colonies." It provided schools of navigation in Dublin, Belfast, Limerick, Cork and Galway, where youths were to be instructed in Mathematics and Navigation; the instructors to be paid out of the public revenue.

Such was the Patriot Parliament against which its detractors hurled the words "bloody" and "rapacious."

Schomberg, William's Dutch general, arrived in Belfast Lough with twenty thousand men. He took Carrickfergus after a week's siege; the garrison were allowed to march out with the honours of war. Then he formed his camp at Dundalk. It was ill-omened ground. A year before a Mr. Hamilton "a sober rational man" riding towards Dundalk one evening saw several little lights in the air and two large ones. He heard the most dismal groans coming from the plain. The sober and rational man was startled, as were his companions.

The camp soon rang to groans and curses. The autumn rains fell; the lines were flooded. The plague broke out; six thousand men died. The living made ghastly revelry; sang ribald songs, sitting on the dead bodies of their comrades, and drank healths to the devil. As the patrols came to bury the dead they grumbled that their seats should be taken away.

When Schomberg struck his camp, de Rosen would have attacked him. James, again with the army, forbade the attack. Then, leaving his soldiers to take care of themselves, he returned to Dublin, where he amused himself with "disgraceful amours." "There were two frightfully ugly creatures," says the Duchess of Orleans, "with whom he was on the most intimate terms."

He thought little of Sarsfield. "Sarsfield is a brave fellow," he said, "but very scantily supplied with brains." Louis's ambassador, d'Avaux, had another opinion. "Sarsfield has valour," he wrote to Louis's minister, Louvois—"but, above all, honour and probity which is proof against any assault." He had "all the trouble in the world to get him made Brigadier." Tyrconnell had opposed the promotion. Sarsfield was a very brave man, Tyrconnell said, but he had no head. d'Avaux carried his point, and Tyrconnell sent Sarsfield with a handful of men into Connacht. He raised two thousand more men there on his own credit, and held Connacht. d'Avaux wished to send him to France. "He is a man who will always be at the head of his troops," he wrote to the French minister, "and will take great care of them. First class colonels will obey him when they will not obey another." He had asked the king for Sarsfield. But the Connacht campaign had changed James's opinion. He grew very angry. He walked three times around the room; he charged d'Avaux with wishing to take his officers away. "I bore it all meekly," said d'Avaux, "having a good notion of my own how to get Sarsfield to France." This was to offer him the chief command of the Irish troops there.

But Sarsfield did not go. His work, he knew, was in Ireland.

Meanwhile, in spite of asthma and a continual cough, William prepared for his campaign in Ireland. He sent over seven thousand men to the aid of Schomberg. In the same month, March, seven thousand French soldiers under the command of the Duke of Lauzun landed at Kinsale in exchange for five thousand Irishmen that had been sent to France. Lauzun was a mere courtier; a man who made a jest at everything. He did not take the Irish campaign seriously; nor did many of the French officers.

But William made no mistake about its importance. He brought everything to secure a successful issue. Among his arms was the prototype of the machine gun. It had been recently invented; a wheel-engine that discharged 150 musket barrels at once, and on being turned the same number again. The campaign was opened by Schomberg in the spring. But not till William landed in June was the advance made in force. The prince stopped plundering, and hanged the plunderers. He paid for all he took. He struck with his own cane a soldier who was robbing a woman, and had him afterward hanged.

James at once abandoned his advanced post in the north. He then abandoned every pass. He might have annihilated, certainly held back, the enemy at the Pass of Moira. Instead he retreated to the Boyne. He had prepared for his flight. Ships, by his order, lay ready at Waterford to carry him to France. Reluctantly he waited his son-in-law on the bank of the river.

The battle of the Boyne was fought on Tuesday, July 1st, 1690.[2] It was not the cardinal battle of the war. Aughrim was that. James had about twenty-six thousand men, many of them raw levies, and ill armed. He was also short of guns. William had ten thousand more men—a composite army—Danes, English, Dutch and French Huguenots, all highly drilled, and well armed. He had also a strong artillery. By his order his men wore green sprigs in their hats. The Irish, in compliment to the French, wore the white cockade.

James had secured his retreat to Dublin. He commanded Sarsfield to hold a body of horse in the rear. Should the day go against him, he could gallop back to the city. The command kept Sarsfield in enforced inaction during the day. Though warned by his Irish officers that the enemy would probably make a flanking movement to cross the Boyne at Slane, James heeded not the warning. At sunrise Schomberg's men were seen along the height making in that direction. James gave a hasty order. His whole wing, part of the centre, and his six remaining guns were sent to meet the flanking division. It was too late; the enemy had crossed. Other fords remained, were hotly contested. It was low water; the fords at Oldbridge were attempted by William's men. One battalion of infantry held the ford at Oldbridge. "For a half a mile the Boyne was filled with thousands of armed men struggling to gain the opposite bank." "Schomberg remained opposite to us," says the Duke of Berwick in his Memoirs. "He attacked and took Oldbridge in spite of the resistance of the regiment there. Seven battalions went down to the help of the infantry. Two battalions of Irish Guards scattered them; but their cavalry managed to pass at another ford, and proceeded to fall upon our infantry. I brought up our cavalry, and thus enabled our battalions to retire." Berwick and his

---

[2] Old Calendar. In the New Calendar, July 12th, of course, became the Boyne anniversary day.

Horse had a very unequal combat, as the ground was broken and they were outnumbered. "Nevertheless we charged again and again ten different times," he says, "and at length the enemy, confounded by our boldness, halted, and we reformed before them, and marched at a slow pace to rejoin the king."

The unequal battle raged all day. The miserable James began to look toward his body-guard. At five in the evening he left the field. By the end of the day the Irish were forced to retire; the majority doing so in good order. The battle of the Boyne was not a decisive victory for the Prince of Orange; it was in reality a drawn battle.

The king reached Dublin at ten o'clock. He had taken two hundred men from the body-guard, and rode helter-skelter to the city. Lady Tyrconnell met him at the Castle-gate. Upstairs she asked him what he would have for supper. "He then gave her an account of what a breakfast he had got, which made him have little stomach for his supper." It is said, when he declared that the Irish army had run away, she answered, "But your Majesty won the race."

From the aspect of his men, Dublin expected to see but the remnant of a broken army pouring into the city. "It was greatly surprised," says a Person of Quality, "when, an hour or two after, we heard the whole body of the Irish Horse coming in, in very good order, with kettle-drums, hautboys, and trumpets; and early the next morning the French and a great body of the Irish Foot. These being rested a little, marched out again to meet the enemy, which was supposed to draw near."

And while the army went out to meet his foes, James railed at it. He summoned the Lord Mayor and Council. "The Irish had basely fled the field," he told them; henceforth he determined never to lead an Irish army again; "And now he resolved to shift for himself, as they themselves must do." He advised them to submit to the Prince of Orange. Then he hurried to Waterford, took ship to Kinsale, and thence to France.

The army he had deserted and reviled marched west, discomfited but not subdued. Deeper hopes than the restoration of the Stuarts stirred many of the soldiers' hearts. James had gone! Let him go! He was no true king, no leader! They would defend Limerick, Galway, Athlone, the passes of the Shannon!

The generals conferred. James's cause was lost, Lauzun said; the French troops must return to France; favourable terms might be made with William. Tyrconnell now "grown stout and lethargic" was in agreement with Lauzun. But Sarsfield stood firm; all was not lost; the three towns, the Shannon, could and must be defended.

Athlone was held by Colonel Grace. Douglas, William's general, summoned the town to surrender. Grace fired a pistol. "These are my terms," he said, "and before I surrender I'll eat my boots!" So he held Athlone till Sarsfield relieved it. And now, through the three quarters of Ireland an irregular force was moving, waging guerilla war. They were undrilled, armed with half pikes, sgians, scythes, some muskets. Irish history knows them as the Rapparees. One of them, Hogan, scout and hard-rider, gallops across a page.

A council, final in its decision, was held at Limerick. William's army was advancing on the city. Make terms with the Prince of Orange, Lauzun and Tyrconnell said. And Sarsfield, resolved, answered, "No terms!" He was supported by the Irish officers. Lauzun laughed at them. "Why should the English bring cannon against fortifications," he said, "that could be battered down by roasted apples!"

But Sarsfield and his supporters won. An agent was sent to France to let both kings know that the Irish meant to defend their country. A day or two later, the Irish officers, backed by the Irish army, declared that Sarsfield should command in chief next to Tyrconnell. Disapproving of the appointment, Tyrconnell sent Sarsfield off with a handful of men to watch the enemy. He returned on William's approach to find that Tyrconnell and Lauzun had been making every effort to persuade the officers to agree to a capitulation. Some, who had estates to lose, had been won over. But the majority stood by Sarsfield.

Lauzun withdrew to Galway. He took his French soldiers, eight guns, and a quantity of ammunition.

On the 9th of August, William was close to Limerick. Three regiments guarded the fords. Without consulting his generals, Tyrconnell drew them off, and taking them with him retired to Galway. Boisseleaux was appointed Governor of Limerick. The Duke of Berwick, Sarsfield, Dorrington and three Brigadiers had command of the army.

There was truth in Lauzun's taunt. Limerick had no fortifications worth regarding. There was a wall without ramparts, and "some miserable little towers" without ditches. A covered way was built before the great gate, horn shaped, and palisaded. Time was required to strengthen the defences. William was within a few miles of the city. If he brought up his great guns before this was done, men might die, but Limerick must fall.

The prince expected little resistance. He looked for an early capitulation. He knew Tyrconnell's vacillating mind and that Lauzun was anxious to get back to France. There was Sarsfield, unbuyable; but a man of sense would not defend a lost cause. He would offer fair terms; the Irish might practise their religion; to those who joined him he would give rewards.

So, confident, he drew near. He had left his heavy battering train at Cashel. Within two miles of Limerick he was attacked by Irish skirmishers. Retreating from one strong position to another, they drew his men close to the city walls. Then the Irish guns opened fire, and the skirmishers re-entered Limerick.

A trumpeter rode forward. He summoned the town. "Open your gates! Let the King of England in!" "Limerick will not open her gates; will not surrender!" Boisseleaux answered. William had laid out his camp. The city guns were trained upon it and so well served that he had to withdraw both his camp and his light artillery.

Messengers rode to Cashel: send up the battering train! A Captain Pulteny commanded it; heavy guns, mortars; 150 waggons of ammunition for the artillery; tin boats to cross the Shannon; provisions; 500 draught horses. A deserter from the camp stole into Limerick. He brought word of its approach. Sarsfield acted at once. He rode out of Limerick and galloped to the cavalry camp on the Clare side. A swift order; and six hundred men stood to their horses. A guide was found; Galloping Hogan, Rapparee, famous rider and scout, who knew every track and pass.

They rode inland; then wheeled and kept in line with the river. A Williamite force held Killaloe bridge. A ford, unknown to the English, lay below Lough Derg. It was a bright night with a harvest moon. They passed behind the town of Killaloe and the column crossed the river. Then it headed for the Keeper mountain, and lay that night in a fold of its shoulder. The day came. The convoy trailed out from the southern mountains and along the plain. Its guard marched at ease. That night it encamped at Ballyneety. Down from the Keeper rode Sarsfield and his troopers: scouts had brought them the convoy's watchword—"Sarsfield!"—good omen! Moonlight and clouds whitened and darkened the plain in turn. Under the cloak of the clouds the Irish advanced. A sentry challenged. "Advance and give the word!" "Sarsfield!—Sarsfield is the word and Sarsfield is the man!" and the Irish Horse dashed on the convoy. The startled guards ran to their picketted horses; were caught in their flight and cut down; the camp was captured. Each gun was loaded to the muzzle, its head sunk in the ground; the tin boats were smashed; stores, ammunition were heaped together, powder placed round, and a train laid. Then the Irish galloped away; and the roar of the explosion echoed across the Golden Valley to Limerick city and William's camp.

They were met at Banagher Bridge by some Williamite Horse sent to intercept them. An Irish Protestant, "a substantial country gentleman," who had seen the Irish cross at Lough Derg, had gone to the English camp and told what he had seen. But Sarsfield got back to Limerick with scarcely any loss. The capture of the guns had been of the first importance. William's siege operation had to be delayed till a new battering train arrived. This gave Limerick a week in which to strengthen herself.

They made the best of the time. When William's heavy guns were trained on the city and his trenches advanced, Limerick met and bore the shock. Counter mines were laid; her guns answered. By the second week, however, her wharfs were on fire, many houses burnt, parts of her walls levelled. On Tuesday, August 26th, his trenches were within four yards of her counterscarp, and her palisades had been beaten down. All through the night the enemy poured in a discharge of shells and red hot balls, and the breach lay thirty feet wide. But behind that breach a retirade had been made and a battery of guns planted, while others were so placed as to take the stormers on both flanks. The bugles rang at daybreak; drums beat. Men left their trenches as the soldiers fell in; the butchers armed themselves with their cleavers; the blacksmiths with their hammers. Women seized bottle and stones, and followed the men. Limerick was prepared to die rather than yield.

The morning began dull and cloudy; a thick mist lay on the Keeper mountain. As the day advanced the sun broke through the clouds, and the heat became intense. At two o'clock the guns ceased, and the city was again summoned. For an hour there was a pause after the confident demand and the resolute answer. Then three guns were fired from the enemy's camp—a signal! Immediately the attacking column, ten thousand strong, moved forward to the assault. The English grenadiers, in their piebald uniform of red and yellow, leapt out of their trenches, sprang upon the counterscarp, firing and throwing their grenades. Driving the defenders before them, they pressed on, reached the breach, and poured into the city. The masked battery opened upon them, mowed a wide path through their lines; and, cut off from their supports, they were overpowered, few escaping back to their trenches.

The fury of the fight raged at the breach. For three hours the Irish infantry stood there, filling up again and again their bloody gaps as regiment after regiment of the foe was brought up and hurled against them. Slowly, at last, the line was pushed back, and the stormers once more entered the city. A fierce hand to hand fight ensued in the streets. Boisseleaux ordered up the reserves; those who had been driven from the breach rallied. The citizens, women as well as men, rushed again to the attack. The enemy was dislodged and forced back on the gap.

There a deadly struggle followed. William sent forward his reserves. The Irish met and held them in check; an order was sent to the Irish Horse to take the foe in the rear. It had been inactive till then. Now its turn was come.

Galloping across Ball's Bridge, it swept through the streets, and passed out by the sally port at St. John's Gate into the covered way which led to the breach. Two regiments of Danish Horse stood in their path as they emerged. The Irish charged; rode through them; cut them down; swept on. Galloping up to the breach, they took the stormers in the rear, made a path through their ranks, and rode across with crimson sabres and exultant cheers.

As their suddenness and dash staggered the foe, the mine laid by the defenders in the Black Battery blew up, and a number of men of William's Brandenberg regiment were killed. The Irish infantry rushed upon his reserves, forced them from the breach, drove them across the counter-scarp, back to the trenches, and followed them to their camp. The Horse charged the flying foe; sabring their disordered ranks.

The assault had failed; Limerick was saved!

William drew off his army, and returned to England. A French fleet carried Lauzun and his troops back to France. Tyrconnell followed him there. Lauzun reported the king's cause lost. Tyrconnell, encouraged by the defence of Limerick, said that there was a chance of success and asked for money and men. In January of the following year he returned with money but no men. The Irish camp was divided into two parties; those who wished to carry on the war; and those, men with estates, who wished to make peace. Tyrconnell fostered this party. The campaign of 1690 ended with the taking of Cork and Kinsale by an English fleet under the command of Churchill. The Irish army was shut up in Connacht. Sarsfield, resisting the policy of despair, kept the passes of the Shannon. Little was done from the closing of the campaign till the opening of the next one with the arrival of the French general, St. Ruth, in the following year. Only the indomitable Rapparees kept up an unceasing guerilla warfare. They harassed the Dutch general, Ginckel, destroyed his forage, watched for his patrols, captured numbers of horses.

In May, the French general, St. Ruth, landed in Ireland. He brought arms, ammunition, clothing and provisions, but no troops. The man was a real soldier; no jester like Lauzun, but of a haughty and jealous nature. He knew what Irish troops could do. In the Piedmont campaign he had seen enough of Irish valour to know that Irish soldiers were the best missile force in the world. He let Tyrconnell see, Viceroy as he was, that he, St. Ruth, alone was to command the army.

The Irish held Athlone. William's generals, Ginckel and Mackay, with a large and well armed army, marched upon it. St. Ruth encamped within two miles of the town on the Connacht side; occupied the high ground commanding the river, and strengthened the entrenchments along its bank. Mackay, attempting to cross at a place further down the river, was driven back. He then determined to pass by the bridge. The Irish broke the arches. He spanned them with beams. Every bit of his work was hotly contested. The siege was nine days old when the bridge was nearly ready. One link remained for completion. Beams already rested on the broken arch; planks were being laid across; the Irish, driven from their last shelter in the trenches, had little power to prevent it.

But one brave man dared to save the town. His name was Custume, a sergeant of dragoons. He boldly called for ten volunteers, with him to break the bridge. He could have had that number a hundred fold. With breast and back pieces on, the eleven bold ones, rushed upon the bridge, drove back the carpenters, began pulling up the planks, breaking down the beams, flinging them in the river. A tremendous fire from the English wiped out eleven heroes with the job only half done. Another eleven noble ones sprang out upon the bridge. Hatchet and axe were plied like fury. The last beam floated down the Shannon; two men returned alive; twenty wore the martyr's crown.

Ginckel made a covered way to repair the bridge. Three Danes under the sentence of death were offered their lives if they would find a ford. They entered the river at three places and were fired at as if they were deserters. The water was low; they got across easily. An attempt to storm the town was ordered for the next morning. Ginckel's men were to cross at three points, the bridge, the ford, and by a pontoon of boats. St. Ruth heard of the intended assault. He threw reinforcements into the town; brought his army from the camp, and awaited the attack by the river. No attack was made. The Irish burnt the covered way. Ginckel, held back so long, was discouraged. He called a Council of war. He wished to retire. His generals advised him to remain. In the midst of the debate two deserters were brought in. They had important news. St. Ruth, confident that the siege was raised, had marched back to camp, and had left the defence of the town to his rawest levies. This report decided Ginckel; he ordered a fresh attack for six that evening.

Two of the newly enlisted regiments left to defend the town had no bayonets and but a round or two of ammunition. When the attack commenced an urgent message was sent to St. Ruth, who was about to go out shooting, and who made light of it. "It was impossible," he said. Thus, in half an hour Athlone was captured after a stout defence of ten days.

The cardinal battle of the war was now to be fought. That battle decided Ireland's fate. St. Ruth withdrew his army and encamped on the Galway side of the River Suck. The position was admirably chosen. It lay on the side of Kilcommodan Hill, extending for nearly two miles. At the base of the hill, to the east, a small stream flowed through boggy ground. His right wing, spread beyond the hill, rested on firm soil, and faced the river. His left lay near a half ruined castle protected in front by a bog. The centre, formed in two lines, was ranked behind breastworks bordering the boggy land. The camp was entrenched; two raths on the hillside were held. The slope of the hill, lined with hedges and ditches, had openings cut through them for the passage of the cavalry and foot. The reserve, under Sarsfield, who had received strict orders not to move, was stationed on the other side of the hill at a considerable distance from the main body of the army. There were but two points near the bog by which Ginckel could advance—the Pass of Aughrim and that of Urrachee. The latter ran to the right of the Irish camp; the former from Aughrim Castle to a piece of firm ground bordered by two bogs, and joined by a narrow strip of land to the firm ground opposite.

On the 11th day of July Ginckel reached the hills opposite Kilcommodan. Seeing the strength of St. Ruth's position, he hesitated to give battle. He began a cautious advance on the morning of the 12th. In the Irish camp at the same time, Mass was celebrated. A dense fog hung between the two forces. By noon it lifted, and Ginckel saw the Irish massed in strong positions awaiting his advance. The Pass of Urrachee was the weakest point in their front. Yet, there, some guns had been placed. Two outposts had been stationed on Ginckel's side of the river. He sent a small force to drive them in. An hour's fighting followed. The Irish posts were driven back; they recovered their posts. This was but an affair of the advanced guard. At two o'clock Ginckel's army fell into position. At three he held a council of war. Should he attack or not? he asked. For himself, he hesitated. Mackay urged him to accept battle; propounded a plan. This was to advance on St. Ruth's left, assault the castle of Aughrim, cross the bog, and attack the Irish centre. His advice prevailed.

It was near five o'clock. Mackay took command of the division that was to force the Pass of Aughrim. Ginckel was to direct the movement on the Pass of Urrachee; the Duke of Wurtemberg the centre. Ginckel made a feint attack on St. Ruth's right. He hoped he would draw off some regiments from his left to support the threatened wing. The battle commenced with this advance. A Danish regiment spread out as if to out-flank the Irish right. A body of Huguenots advanced on the troops beyond the Pass, attacking the Irish through the hedges. The Irish Horse charged them. After a fierce fight the foe was driven back to the bog. The attack on this point was renewed again. Mackay hoped that St. Ruth would draw off troops from his right wing to support his left. Then the real attack would be made on Aughrim. St. Ruth did as he wished. The officer to whom he gave the order took the first line as well. At once Mackay sent cavalry to force the Pass, while he with the main body commenced the passage of the bog, supported by two batteries of field pieces. The ground had been sounded; found possible for foot. Opposite the Irish centre the ground narrowed, widening out by Aughrim. His troops were in two divisions; one was to cross the bog and attack the Irish centre, seize the first hedge row, and halt till Mackay and his cavalry came to their support.

Protected by the batteries the men reached the base of the hill. When within a few yards of the hedge, the Irish opened fire. Their orders were to draw the enemy up the hill. This they did, then stood their ground, and the Irish cavalry swept down upon both flanks of the enemy and threw them into disorder.

While this was happening Mackay's second division was getting through the bog. At the first ditch the Irish met them, and Mackay's van was broken. His other regiments were hurried up, but the Irish held their ground. Mackay sent to the officer who was to force the Pass of Aughrim, ordering him to come to his help and not attack the castle. But before the order could be obeyed Mackay's men were forced back to the bog. This was the second repulse of the enemy at Aughrim.

Seeing that Mackay could not break his centre, St. Ruth was now certain of victory. "I shall beat them back to the gates of Dublin!" he cried. It was no boast. His troops had successfully resisted every attack. At all points, save one, Ginckel's army had been repulsed.

That point was the Pass of Aughrim. The Pass was an old broken road, narrow, boggy, sixty yards in length. Not more than two horsemen could ride on it abreast. It was commanded by the castle, a crumbling building. Two regiments of Foot, under Colonel Burke, were stationed there. Two guns commanded the way. The men were armed with French fire-locks. There were four barrels of gunpowder and ammunition chests in the castle. When the chests were opened it was found that the bullets were cast for English muskets and that the cannon balls were two big for the guns. The soldiers tore the buttons from their coats and chopped their ramrods into bullets. The enemy came up the Pass protected by their own guns. The Irish fired their pellets with little effect. Their guns had no bayonets. The Irish Horse, posted on the other side of the castle, rode round to the left to check the advance. They found this way blocked, though St. Ruth had ordered it to be kept open. They had to swing round and make a detour before they could charge. A sharp fight followed; the enemy's regiment were driven back to the bog.

St. Ruth had watched the attack on the Pass. Not knowing that Burke's men had no ammunition, he had been astonished that the enemy had got up the way. He sent an aide-camp to the cavalry reserve under Sarsfield. This reserve was stationed on the other side of the hill, out of sight of the battle. He ordered that half of the men were to advance. Sarsfield was not to command it. He was to remain with the other half. By this act Aughrim was lost.

The detachment came up, reformed before St. Ruth, and he placed himself at its head. He rode slowly down the hill. His brilliant uniform glittered in the evening light. "The day is ours, boys!" he cried. "They are broken! Let us beat them to some purpose!"

Then something sped through the air from the enemy's right; struck him and carried his head away. The dead man's horse swung round, the body upright in the saddle for a pace or two before it fell to the ground. A paralysis seized his officers. The battle was all but won; this charge would have completed the victory, yet his second in command, de Tesse, a Frenchman, did not advance. Instead of making that charge for victory, he began to retire. Ginckel's almost beaten army saw the movement, pressed forward. Mackay's Horse turned the left flank of the Irish. In the centre the Irish held the ground till they were caught between Ginckel's and Mackay's men. Then the rout commenced.

And Sarsfield, waiting for orders on the other side of the hill, only knew the day was lost as the Irish regiments broke over the crest. To keep back the foe was now impossible. But cool, great, he kept his head, and organised the retreat in so masterly a way that a document in the French annals says—"He performed miracles, and if he was not killed or taken it was not from any fault of his own." He led his soldiers in order to Limerick.

The Irish army gathered there. On the 25th of August, Ginckel invested the city on three sides. William wanted the war ended; Ginckel was empowered to give favourable terms. A free pardon was offered to all; the Catholic gentry would be restored to their estates. The offer created at once a peace party within the city. It was opposed by Sarsfield. French aid might come; the army could defend Limerick again. He won, and Ginckel's summons was refused. Sixty guns then opened upon the city; an English fleet bombarded it from the river. But Limerick remained untaken. Once more she showed the soul of her army and her citizens. Unable to carry the town by assault, Ginckel turned the siege into a blockade. Then Luttrel, an Anglo-

Irish officer, long suspected, showed him a pass over the Shannon. One morning the Irish beheld the foe on the Clare side of the river. Again Ginckel offered favourable terms.

The peace party said it was folly to refuse. This party, resisted, Sarsfield saw, would attempt to hand over the city to Ginckel.

Yet Limerick made one more fight. It was September 23rd. From dawn the bloody struggle lasted. Then a parley was held; firing ceased. For the third time Ginckel offered his terms. At last, Sarsfield accepted them. When the soldiers and citizens heard that the defence had ended, they uttered loud cries of anger and grief, many ran to the ramparts and broke their weapons there. Limerick had capitulated!

The terms were to be signed in the presence of the Lord Justices. Sarsfield demanded that. They came posting down from Dublin; they put their signatures to the treaty. Irish Catholics were to have the right to exercise their religion; to have the rights of citizens; to be preserved from all disturbances. By the military articles, the garrison was to march out with arms and guns, baggage, colours flying, drums beating. Officers and men, Rapparees and volunteers, who wished to expatriate themselves, were free to do so, and might depart in companies or parties. If plundered on the way, William's government was to make good their loss. Fifty ships were to be provided for their transportation; two men-of-war for the officers.

Ginckel did not want that fine war material to escape. Would the Irish regiments join France or William? On the 5th of October they were to march out of Limerick. That day they were to make their choice. The royal standards of England and France were set up in a field. To one standard or the other each regiment was to turn. Sarsfield, Ginckel and their staffs watched the scene. The Irish Foot Guards came first, the finest of the regiment, fourteen hundred strong. They marched to the Standards. Then, without a pause, the splendid column wheeled to the side of France. That day of the fourteen thousand men of the Irish army, only one thousand and forty-six men turned to William's standard.

A few days later a French fleet came up the Shannon. It brought men, money, arms, ammunition, stores and clothing. The news reached Sarsfield. Stunned, he remained silent for a few moments. Then:—"Too late," he said, "the Treaty is signed. Ireland's and our honour is pledged. Though one hundred thousand Frenchmen offered to aid us now, we must keep our word!"

In his quarters Ginckel heard that the fleet had come. He was alarmed. Would Sarsfield tear up the Treaty? Would the French soldiers land?

Would the Irish regiments listed for France, men with their arms, renew the fight? The cautious Dutchman, an honest brave man, himself, feared.

But his anxiety was soon ended. Sarsfield, the unbuyable—Sarsfield, the man of honour—had forbidden the French to land. Instead, their ships were to transport the Irish regiments to France.

Not a man of these saw Ireland again.

CHAPTER LIII

The Later Penal Laws

When fire and sword had signally failed to suppress the Irish race, new means to that end must be found. So the fertile mind of the conqueror invented the Penal Laws.

Professor Lecky, a Protestant of British blood and ardent British sympathy, says (in his History of Ireland in the 18th Century) that the object of the Penal Laws was threefold:

(1) To deprive the Catholics of all civil life

(2) To reduce them to a condition of most extreme and brutal ignorance

(3) To dissociate them from the soil.

He might, with absolute justice, have substituted *Irish* for *Catholics*—and added, (4) To extirpate the Race.

"There is no instance," says Dr. Samuel Johnson, "even in the Ten Persecutions, of such severity as that which the Protestants of Ireland exercised against the Catholics."[1]

---

[1] Dr. Johnson evidently laboured under delusion that these dreadful persecutions were entirely the fault of the Protestants of Ireland, not of the Government of England. Lecky, however, knew Irish history; and this is what he has to say of the Penal Code (in his "History of Ireland in the 18th Century"): "It was not the persecution of a sect, but the degradation of a nation. It was the instrument employed by a conquering race (the Anglo-Irish) supported by a neighbouring Power, to crush to the dust the people among whom they were planted. And, indeed, when we remember that the greater part of it was in force for nearly a century, that its victims formed at least three-fourths of the nation, that its degrading and dividing influence extended to every field of social, political, professional, intellectual, and even domestic life, and that it was enacted without the provocation of any rebellion, in defiance of a treaty which distinctly guaranteed the Irish Catholics from any further oppression on account of their religion, it may be justly regarded as one of the blackest pages in the history of persecution."

Like good wine the Penal code improved with age. It was only in the 18th century that it attained the marvellous perfection which caused Edmund Burke to describe it as "a machine of wise and elaborate contrivance, as well fitted for the oppression, impoverishment, and degradation of a people, and the debasement in them of human nature itself, as ever proceeded from the perverted ingenuity of man"—and the French jurist Montesquieu to say of it that it was "conceived by demons, written in blood, and registered in Hell."

In the treaty of Limerick the faith and honour of the Crown were pledged not only that the Irish in Ireland should, in their lives, liberties and property be equally protected with the British usurpers in Ireland—but it was especially pledged that they should be "protected in the free and unfettered exercise of their religion." And this solemn pledge of the British crown by which the Irish were induced to lay down their arms marked the beginning of a national robbery and national persecution which for cold-blooded systemisation was hitherto unapproached in the history of Irish persecutions. Just as the flagrant breaking of the solemn Treaty of Limerick is hardly paralleled in history.

When the Lords Justice returned to Dublin after signing the treaty, Dr. Dopping, Protestant Lord Bishop of Meath, preached before them in Christ Church Cathedral upon the sin of keeping faith with Papists. All over the country the persecution and plundering of the papist began again, and was soon in full swing. A million acres of papists' lands were confiscated, and their owners reduced to beggary.[2] The British settlers in Ireland began bombarding Parliament with petitions against the Irish papists. If these people got their liberties it was shown that Ireland would be no place for decent British people.[3]

So it is not to be wondered at that in the early part of the 18th century a foreign observer in Ireland noted that a Catholic could easily be told by his stooped carriage and subdued manner. Even when Thackeray visited Ireland the Catholic priests, he noted, had an abashed look. The innocent man wondered why that was so!

[2] An English gentleman who received the estate in Cork robbed from the McCarthy, was in the twilight of a summer day walking in his easily acquired demesne, when he came on an old man seated under a tree, sobbing heart breakingly. He approached the grieved one, and asked the cause of his grief. "These lands," said the broken old man, "and that castle were mine. This tree under which I sit was planted by my hand. I came here to water it with my tears, before sailing tonight for Spain."

[3] *Exempli gratia*—

"A petition of one Edward Spragg and others in behalf of themselves and other Protestant porters in and about the city of Dublin, complains that one Darby Ryan, a captain under the late King James, and a Papist, buys up whole cargoes of coals and employs porters of his own persuasion to carry the same to customers, by which the petitioners are hindered from their small trade and gains. The petition was referred to the Committee of Grievances to report upon it to the House."—(*Commons Journals*, ii, 699). The impudent villainy of the papist Darby!

And, just three years after the faith and honour of the British crown had been pledged for the protection of the papists, the Parliament passed its "Act for the Better Securing of the Government against Papists." Under this Act, no Catholic could henceforth have "gun, pistol or sword, or any other weapon of offence or defence, under penalty of fine, imprisonment, pillory, or public whipping." It was provided that any magistrate could visit the house of any of the Irish, at any hour of the night or day, and ransack it for concealed weapons. Says John Mitchel of this clause, "It fared ill with any Catholic who fell under the displeasure of his formidable neighbours. No papist was safe from suspicion who had money to pay fines—but woe to the papist who had a handsome daughter!"

Under the pledged faith and honour of the British crown, which promised to secure the Irish from any disturbance on account of their religion, there was passed, next (in the ninth year of William's reign), "An Act for banishing all Papists exercising any ecclesiastical jurisdiction, and regulars of the Popish clergy, out of this kingdom." This Act provided that "All Popish Archbishops, Bishops, Vicars-General, Deans, Jesuits, Monks, Friars, and all other regular Popish clergy shall depart out of this kingdom before the first day of May, 1698"—under penalty of transportation for life if they failed to comply—and under penalty to those who should dare to return, of being hanged, drawn, and quartered.[4]

And by such liberality of the British was the Irish nation repaid for the generosity it had shown them in its short hour of triumph. And the new and improved era of persecution which began under William—whose faith and honour were pledged that the Irish Catholics should be "protected in the free and unfettered exercise of their religion"—marched onward henceforth with marvellous stride.

Before going on to enumerate the new Penal Laws that were enacted, and the old that were confirmed, it is worth while to glance back a couple of

---

[4] Lecky: "In Ireland all Catholic archbishops, bishops, deacons and vicars-general were ordered by a certain day to leave the country. If after that date they were found in it, they were to be first imprisoned and then banished, and if they returned they were pronounced guilty of high treason and were liable to be hanged, disembowelled, and quartered. Nor were these idle words. The law of 1709 offered a reward of fifty pounds to any one who secured the conviction of any Catholic archbishop, bishop, deacon vicar-general."

Every Irish Catholic could be compelled at any time of the day or night to go before two Justices of the Peace and swear where he heard Mass, who officiated, and who was present. He was forbidden to harbour a schoolmaster or a priest under pain of having all his goods confiscated.

The Anglo-Irish House of Commons of 1719 carried a Bill against Papists in which it was provided that a captured priest who had been officiating in secret, should be branded with a red hot iron upon the cheek. The bill was vetoed in England.

years, and note how Irish Catholics, when the rule of their own country came into their hands, treated their long-time persecutors. We have seen, in a previous chapter, the toleration shown by the Irish Catholics to their late persecutors, when Mary of England re-established the Catholic church and Catholic power. When the poor creature, James the Second, came to Ireland in 1689, and that the Irish got complete control of their own country, an Irish Parliament met in Dublin on May 7th of that year. This was a Catholic Irish Parliament, representing a Catholic Irish country. The members of it were men summoned together in the fury of Civil War—men, too, every one of whom was smarting from memory of the vilest wrongs ever wrought by conqueror on conquered. "They were almost all new men animated by resentment of bitterest wrongs," says Lecky—"men most of whom or of whose fathers had been robbed of their estates." Yet though they burned with holy indignation for the persecutions that they and their people and their land had suffered at the hands of the plunderer and murderer—and though in this their hour of triumph they held the power of life and death over their wrongers, Lecky confesses, with evident astonishment, "They established freedom of religion in a moment of excitement and passion." By this Parliament of cruelly wronged and persecuted papists was enacted the golden statute—"We hereby declare that it is the law of this land that not now, or ever again, shall any man be persecuted for his religion."

Four Protestant bishops sat in the Upper House. No Catholic bishop was called to sit there. While fifteen outlawed Catholic peers were recalled, only five new ones were made. Six Protestant members sat in the Lower House—almost all the rest of the Protestant members having espoused the cause of William, or fled to England.

This Parliament established freedom of religion. Says Lecky, "The Protestant clergy were guaranteed full liberty of professing, preaching, and teaching their religion."

It established free schools.

Where Catholic Ireland had before been compelled to support the Protestant Church, this Parliament enacted that Catholics should pay dues to Catholic pastors, and Protestants should pay dues to Protestant pastors.[5]

---

[5] The Catholic Bishop Moloney, in writing to the Parliament, went so far as to recommend that compensation should be provided for all Protestant church beneficiaries who would now lose the state payments that they had been receiving.

The Protestant William Parnell, member of the Anglo-Irish Parliament at the end of the eighteenth century, says (and shows) in his historical treatise upon Ireland: "The Irish Roman Catholics are the only sect that ever resumed power without exercising vengeance."

And thus did these Irish Catholics, in their brief moment of triumph, to the usurpers who had persecuted and plundered them till, as one Protestant historian admits "Protestantism came to be associated in the native mind with spoliation, confiscation, and massacre."

The Penal Laws enacted or re-enacted in the new era succeeding the siege of Limerick, when under the pledged faith and honour of the English crown, the Irish Catholics were to be "protected in the free and unfettered exercise of their religion," provided amongst other things that:

The Irish Catholic was forbidden the exercise of his religion.
He was forbidden to receive education.
He was forbidden to enter a profession.
He was forbidden to hold public office.
He was forbidden to engage in trade or commerce.[6]
He was forbidden to live in a corporate town or within five miles thereof.
He was forbidden to own a horse of greater value than five pounds.[7]
He was forbidden to purchase land.
He was forbidden to lease land.[8]
He was forbidden to accept a mortgage on land in security for a loan.[9]
He was forbidden to vote.
He was forbidden to keep any arms for his protection.
He was forbidden to hold a life annuity.
He was forbidden to buy land from a Protestant.
He was forbidden to receive a gift of land from a Protestant.
He was forbidden to inherit land from a Protestant.

---

[6] "They are not only excluded from all offices in church and state, but are interdicted from the army and the law, in all its branches. . . . Every barrister, clerk, attorney, or solicitor is obliged to take a solemn oath not to employ persons of that persuasion; no, not as hackney clerks, at the miserable salary of seven shillings a week. No tradesman of that persuasion is capable of exercising his trade freely in any town corporate: so that they trade and work in their own native towns as aliens, paying, as such, quarterage, and other charges and impositions. . . ."—Edmund Burke (Laws Against Popery in Ireland).

"Every franchise, every honour, every trust, every place down to the very lowest (besides whole professions) is reserved for the master caste." (Burke's letter to Langrishe.)

[7] Standish O'Grady tells the story of a Catholic gentleman of the County Meath who having driven four blood-horses into the assize town was there held up by a Protestant and tendered twenty pounds for his four valuable horses—whereupon he drew out a pistol, and shot the animals dead. Ever after, he drove into town behind six oxen—his mute protest against "law." "Incidents like this," says O'Grady, "aroused and fed the indignation which eventually compelled the annulment of the law."

[8] So, a man dead and buried is said, in Ireland, to have "a Protestant lease of the soil."

[9] "All persons of that persuasion are disabled from taking or purchasing directly, or by trust, any lease, any mortgage upon land, any rents or profits from land, any lease, interest, or permit of any land; any annuity for life or lives, or years; or any estate whatsoever, chargeable upon, or which may in any manner affect any lease."—Edmund Burke (Laws Against Popery in Ireland).

He was forbidden to inherit anything from a Protestant.

He was forbidden to rent any land that was worth more than thirty shillings a year.

He was forbidden to reap from his land any profit exceeding a third of the rent.[10]

He could not be guardian to a child.

He could not, when dying, leave his infant children under Catholic guardianship.[11]

He could not attend Catholic worship.

He was compelled by the law to attend Protestant worship.

He could not himself educate his child.

He could not send his child to a Catholic teacher.

He could not employ a Catholic teacher to come to his child.

He could not send his child abroad to receive education.[12]

The priest was banned and hunted with bloodhounds. The school master was banned and hunted with bloodhounds.

If he had an unfaithful wife, she, by going through the form of adopting the Protestant religion compelled from a papist the heaviest annuity that might be squeezed out of him—and would inherit all the property at his death. If he had an unnatural child, that child by conforming to the Established religion, could compel from him the highest possible annuity, and

[10] Lecky says: "If a Catholic leaseholder, by his skill or industry so increased his profits that they exceeded this proportion, and did not immediately make a corresponding increase in his rent, his farm passed to the first Protestant who made the discovery. If a Catholic secretly purchased either his own forfeited estate, or any other land in the possession of a Protestant, the first Protestant who informed against him became the proprietor."

To encourage among the Anglo-Irish ardour on behalf of the law, the Anglo-Irish Parliament in 1705 passed a resolution "that the persecuting of and informing against a Papist is an honourable service."

[11] Lecky says: "The influence of the code appeared, indeed, omnipresent. It blasted the prospects of the Catholic in all struggles of active life. It cast its shadows over the inmost recesses of his home. It darkened the very last hour of his existence. No Catholic, as I have said, could be guardian to a child; so the dying person knew that his children must pass under the tutelage of Protestants."

[12] "Popish schoolmasters of every species are proscribed by those acts, and it is made felony to teach even in a private family. Being sent for education to any popish school or college abroad, upon conviction, incurs (if the party sent has any estate or inheritance) a kind of unalterable and perpetual outlawry. He is disabled to sue in law or equity; to be guardian, executor, or administrator; he is rendered incapable of any legacy or deed or gift; he forfeits all his goods and chattels forever; and he forfeits for life all his lands, hereditaments, offices, and estate of freehold, and all trusts, powers, or interests therein. All persons concerned in sending them or maintaining them abroad, by the least assistance of money or otherwise, are involved in the same disabilities, and subjected to the same penalties."—Edmund Burke (Laws Against Popery in Ireland).

inherit all his property at his death—to the total exclusion of all the children who had remained faithful to their father, and their religion.[13]

If he was discovered in the act of having his son educated at home, a ruinous fine and a dungeon awaited him. If he sent his son to be educated abroad, all his property was confiscated—and the child so educated was thereby debarred from all rights and properties in the country, and debarred from inheriting anything.

He was compelled to pay double for the support of the militia. And he was compelled to make good all damages done to the state by the privateers of any Catholic power in which the state was at war.

"After Limerick," says Edmund Burke in his "Tracts"—that is, after the Irish had, by the faith and honour of the British Crown, been pledged protection in their lives, liberties, and property, "there was not a single right of nature or benefit of society which had not been either totally taken away, or considerably impaired."

The law soon came to recognise an Irishman in Ireland only for the purpose of repressing him. Till in the reign of George I, Lord Chancellor Bowes and also Chief Justice Robinson, in their official capacity, pronounced: "The law does not suppose any such person to exist as an Irish Roman Catholic."

Lecky says that it was more through rapacity than fanaticism that the English and Anglo-Irish so ferociously oppressed, repressed, and robbed of both their moral and material rights, the Irish Catholics.[14]

---

[13] Lecky says: "The undutiful wife, the rebellious and unnatural son, had only to add to their other crimes the guilt of a sacrilegiously vain conversion, in order to secure both impunity and reward, and to deprive those whom they had injured of the management and disposal of their property."

[14] One historian says that they were really more anxious to have the soil of Ireland turn Protestant, than the people.

The insignificant number of Irish who embraced the new religion did so in practically every case for purpose of holding their property. There was in Roscommon a celebrated character named Myers who craved for salvation through the Protestant religion when he found that a rapacious Protestant neighbour was about to bring against him a Bill of Discovery—whereby he would be compelled to disclose the value of his property, which on its being found to be more than the few acres that a papist was legally entitled to, would be confiscated to the discoverer. As, before being accepted and baptised, it was necessary to undergo a period of instruction by a minister of the Established Church and an examination by one of the ecclesiastics, Mr. Myers, for his theological study, dined every day for a week with a boon companion, the Protestant rector of Castlerea—after which a social hour's chat with the Archbishop of Dublin secured for him the certificate that guaranteed him to be a fit subject for "Baptism unto the true Faith." On the day on which he was received into the Established Church the Archbishop gave a dinner in Myer's honour. For the edification of the guests, the good prelate at suitable moment requested of the spotless neophyte that he would "state to his fellow-diners his grounds for abjuring the errors of popery." Promptly replied Myers, "Twenty-five hundred acres of the best grounds in the County Roscommon."

But Lecky elsewhere admits that fear of the conquered people ever again taking rank with their conquerors likewise inspired the persecutions. His words are: "It was intended to make them poor and to keep them poor, to crush in them every germ of enterprise and degrade them into a servile race who could never hope to rise to the level of their oppressor." The British traveller, Arthur Young, in the last quarter of the eighteenth century found "an Anglo-Irish aristocracy of half a million joying in the triumph of having two million slaves."

Young tells how he found the gentry for little or no cause, lash with horsewhip or cane, or break the bones of the people, "and kill, without apprehension of judge or jury." "The Punishment Laws," says Young, "are calculated for the meridian of Barbary."[15]

Throughout those dark days the hunted schoolmaster, with price upon his head, was hidden from house to house. And in the summer time he gathered his little class, hungering and thirsting for knowledge, behind a hedge in remote mountain glen—where, while in turn each tattered lad kept watch from the hilltop for the British soldiers, he fed to his eager pupils the forbidden fruit of the tree of knowledge.

Latin and Greek were taught to ragged hunted ones under shelter of the hedges—whence these teachers were known as "hedge schoolmasters." A knowledge of Latin was a frequent enough accomplishment among poor Irish mountaineers in the seventeenth century—and was spoken by many of them on special occasions. And it is authoritatively

---

[15] It is scarce a century since papists were for the first time permitted to reside in some of the walled cities such as Derry in the North, and Bandon in the South.

On the gates of Bandon was written the legend:

"Enter here, Turk, Jew or atheist,
Any man except a Papist."

Underneath these lines a rascally papist, possessed of some wit and some chalk, tried his hand at a little "poetry" of his own:

"The man who wrote this wrote it well;
For the same is writ on the gates of Hell."

On a Government return of 1743 the Provost of Bandon reports, "Neither priest nor papist was, ever since the hated King James his reign, suffered to reside within this town. The inhabitants are all Protestants and by our Corporation Laws no other can live among us."

But the mills of the gods were in motion, all unknown to the pious Provost. Today Bandon is an overwhelmingly Catholic town. And Derry, the very Mecca of Orangeism, has a Catholic majority, a Nationalist Corporation, Nationalist Mayor, and Nationalist representative in the Irish Parliament.

boasted that cows were bought and sold in Greek, in mountain market-places of Kerry.[16]

Throughout these dreadful centuries, too, the hunted priest—who in his youth had been smuggled to the Continent of Europe to receive his training—tended the flame of faith. He lurked like a thief among the hills. On Sundays and feast days he celebrated Mass at a rock, on a remote mountainside, while the congregation knelt on the heather of the hillside, under

---

[16] Dr. Douglas Hyde tells of the famous Munster poet, Owen Roe O'Sullivan, how, while still a common farm-hand, he amazed his master's son (just returned from a Continental college) by construing for the latter a Greek passage that had puzzled him. O'Sullivan was taken from behind the spade then. And after a little while he opened, near Charleville, a school where he taught Latin and Greek.

The present writer had a friend, an old mountaineer in Donegal, who told him how, in the beginning of the nineteenth century, his father, then a youth, used to hear at "the Priest's Dinner" in the mountain station house, the priest, the schoolmaster, and many of the well-to-do mountaineers discourse in Latin.

To these hedge schoolmasters who at the cost of their happiness and risk of their lives fed the little flame of knowledge among the hills and glens of Ireland, throughout Ireland's dread night, Ireland can never repay her debt.

THE HEDGE SCHOOLMASTERS

When the night shall lift from Erin's hills, 'twere shame if we forget
One band of unsung heroes whom Freedom owes a debt.
When we brim high cups to brave ones then, their memory let us pledge
Who gathered their ragged classes behind a friendly hedge.

By stealth they met their pupils in the glen's deep-hidden nook,
And taught them many a lesson was never in English book;
There was more than wordy logic shown to use in wise debate;
Nor *amo* was the only verb they gave to conjugate.

When hunted on the heathery hill and through the shadowy wood,
They climbed the cliff, they dared the marsh, they stemmed the tumbling flood;
Their blanket was the clammy mist, their bed the wind-swept bent;
In fitful sleep they dreamt the bay of blood-hounds on their scent.

Their lore was not the brightest, nor their store, mayhap, the best,
But they fostered love, undying, in each young Irish breast;
And through the dread, dread night, and long, that steeped our island then,
The lamps of hope and fires of faith were fed by these brave men.

The grass waves green above them; soft sleep is theirs for aye;
The hunt is over, and the cold; the hunger passed away.
O hold them high and holy! and their memory proudly pledge,
Who gathered their ragged classes behind a friendly hedge.—SEUMAS MACMANUS.

the open heavens. While he said Mass, faithful sentries watched from all the nearby hilltops, to give timely warning of the approaching priest-hunter and his guard of British soldiers. But sometimes the troops came on them unawares, and the Mass Rock was bespattered with his blood,—and men, women and children caught in the crime of worshipping God among the rocks, were frequently slaughtered on the mountainside.[17]

Then, bishops and archbishops, meanly dressed in rough homespuns, trudged on foot among their people—and often dwelt, ate and slept, in holes in the ground.[18]

Thus, in their miserable lairs, in the bogs and barren mountains, whither they were trailed by wolf-hounds and blood-hounds, were sheltered all

---

[17] To enable the members of their congregation to baffle the inquisition before which they were liable at any time to be compelled to swear when and where they last attended Mass and who was the priest that officiated, an improvised curtain was oftentimes hung between the celebrant and the worshippers—so that they could truthfully swear they did not see the celebrant. With the same object in view, at the ordination of priests not the bishop alone laid on hands, but several others together with him.

[18] Edmund Spenser, in his day observing all this, "did marvel" how these hunted priests, foregoing all the comforts and pleasures of life, and inviting both life and death's fearfulest terrors, pursued their mission "without hope of reward and richesse."

"Reward and richesse!" exclaims the non-Catholic Mitchel, commenting on this. "I know the spots within my own part of Ireland where venerable archbishops hid themselves, as it were, in a hole of the rock. . . . Yet it was with full knowledge of all this, with full resolution to brave all this, that many hundreds of educated Irishmen, fresh from the colleges of Belgium or of Spain, pushed to the Sea Coast at Brest or St. Malo, to find some way of crossing to the land that offered them a life of work and of woe. Imagine a priest ordained at Seville or Salamanca, a gentleman of high old name, a man of eloquence and genius, who has sustained disputations in the college halls on questions of literature or theology, and carried off prizes and crowns—see him on the quays of Brest, bargaining with some skipper to work his passage. He throws himself on board, does his full part of the hardest work, neither feeling the cold spray nor the fiercest tempest. And he knows, too, that the end of it all, for him, may be a row of sugar canes to hoe under the blazing sun of Barbados. Yet he pushes eagerly to meet his fate; for he carries in his hands a sacred deposit, bears in his heart a holy message, and must tell it or die. See him, at last, springing ashore, and hurrying on to seek his bishop in some cave, or under some hedge—but going with caution by reason of the priest catcher and the blood-hounds."

In the middle of the seventeenth century the Primate of Ireland lived in a little farmhouse under the name of "Mr. Ennis." The bishop of Kilmore, who was a good musician, travelled his diocese as a Highland bagpiper. And other ecclesiastics assumed what disguise suited their bent. The Archbishop of Tuam used to address his letters from his (undisclosed) "place of refuge in Connemara."

The learned and saintly Bishop Gallagher (still famed for his sermons), a noble and beautiful character, had many escapes in his unending peregrinations, travelling stick in hand, and homespun clad, among his flock—sleeping sometimes in human habitation, sometimes in a hole in the bank and frequently among the beasts of the field. Once when he had the good fortune to be sheltered under a poor roof in Donegal, he was aroused in the middle of the night by the alarm that the priest-hunters were close upon him. Half-clad, he escaped—but the poor man who had been guilty of housing him was taken out and cruelly done to death. After this Bishop was translated to the midlands, the Palace of this learned and truly noble man was a bothy built against a bank in the Bog of Allen!

that was noble, high, and holy, in Ireland—while rascal and renegade, silk-and-fine-linen-clad, fattening on the fat of an anguished land, languished in the country's high seats of honour![19]

From time to time, to satisfy itself that the Penal Laws were being enforced, the Government called for returns on the subject, which returns, still preserved with the other State records, throw interesting side-light upon the Penal activities. The returns, for instance, of 1714, made by the High Sheriffs of counties and Mayors of cities, show the number of priests and schoolmasters then held in various jails, and in apology for the numbers not being more impressive, explain that the fugitive priest and schoolmaster are "difficult to take." A High Sheriff of Longford reports holding in jail: "Patrick Ferrall and John Lennan, convicted of being popish schoolmasters, and sentenced to

[19] It is good to record that many and many a time during the centuries of Ireland's agony, decent God-fearing, truly Christian Protestants hid the hunted priest when the bloodhounds, and human hounds, were close upon him, saving the hunted one's life at the risk of his own.

And many a time, too, the decent Protestant—sometimes a poor man—accepted legal transfer of the lands of his Catholic neighbour and held them for his Catholic neighbour's benefit—thus saving them from being forfeited to a "Discoverer."

There was a poor Protestant blacksmith in Tipperary in Penal times, who, to save their property to his Catholic neighbours, was in legal possession of thousands of acres of land. Yet the brave fellow, with all those broad acres at his mercy, lived and died in proud poverty.

The late date down to which these persecutions were carried may be judged from the fact that the present Irish Primate's predecessor, Archbishop McGettigan, used to tell how, as a lad, at the Mass Rock in the mountain, he acted as sentry, as acolyte, and as candle-stick (one of the two boys who at either side of the altar-rock held the lighted candle and shielded it from the wind).

On the occasion of a recent lecture tour in California, I met, in a valley of the Sierras, a middle-aged Donegal man, who told me how, when he was a little boy in Donegal, a man with a much disfigured face came one day to his father's house, of whom his father told him how he had escaped with only this disfigurement from a Mass Rock massacre—when the priest-hunters and soldiers had, unawares, surprised the congregation in their crime.

Even in recent days, in some of the remote parts of Ireland, often the local representatives of the governing power, the landlord and magistrate, would not permit the erection of a Catholic Church within the district of which he was over-lord. The Church of the famous Father McFadden of Gweedore, had to be erected on a No-man's land, the dead-line between the possessions of two English landlords—a gulch which had been the bed of a mountain torrent—now diverted. On a fatal stormy Sunday in the eighties the torrent, finding its old way again, swept down upon the little chapel, packed with its mountain congregation, and left sad hearts and lone hearths in bleak Gweedore.

In this writer's own parish of Inver, a relic of the Penal Days was with us till he had reached mature manhood. It was a *scalan*—a three-walled thatched Mass-shed which sheltered the altar and the officiating priest. In front of the open end, every Sunday morning, the congregation, gathered hither from miles of moor and mountain, knelt on the bare hillside under the open heavens—often with miry slush soaking their knees, and pelting rain or driving hail mercilessly lashing their bodies, and whipping their upturned faces. Whether blowing or snowing, shining or showering, every Sabbath saw there the crowd of devotees from remote homes—man and woman, boy and girl, barefoot child and crawling old.

transportation." The High Sheriff of Dublin holds "two popish schoolmasters under sentence of transportation." The Mayors of Galway and Kilkenny have priests awaiting transportation. The High Sheriff of Wicklow reports the dispersal of "a riotous assembly" at St. Kevin's in Glendalough—meaning the ancient pilgrimage in honour of St. Kevin. "We rode all right," he says, "and reached the scene at 4 A.M. on June 3rd. The *rioters* immediately dispersed: and we pulled down their tents, threw down and demolished their superstitious crosses, destroyed their wells, and apprehended and committed one Toole, a popish schoolmaster."

In 1731 the bishops of the Established Church made interesting returns for the "Report of the State of Popery in Ireland." Sample returns for parishes in the diocese of Clogher will give an idea of the whole. In one parish, "The papists have one altar made of earth and stone, uncovered." In another parish, "Mass is celebrated in ye open fields at two distant places." In a third, "No Mass house, but two or three altars." And in still another parish, "No Mass house but ye people meet in ye fields—Owen O'Gallagher, an old Fryer, instructs a great many popish students." In another, "Edward McGrath and one Connelly officiate in several parts of ye parish, in woods near ye mountains." Henry, Bishop of Derry, reports: "We are frequently infested with strolling Fryars and Regulars who say Mass from Parish to Parish as they pass, in ye open fields or ye mountains, and gather great numbers of people about them. Sometimes a straggling schoolmaster sets up in some of ye mountains, but upon being threatened, as they constantly are, with a warrant or a presentment by ye church-wardens, they generally think it proper to withdraw."

In the days when this writer, a light-footed *bouchaillin,* scudded the moors to Mass, there mothered England and step-mothered Ireland, a respectable, homely-minded lady, who had developed a comfortable embonpoint, and fattened a very large brood of children, at the expense of poor, lean, famished, famine-haunted Ireland—a worthy enough old lady who represented the power that robbed us of everything except our hardships, and bestowed on us nothing but our poverty. About the very time that our *scalan* congregation would be kneeling in the mud on the arctic shoulder of Ardaghey Hill this good old lady and her middling well-trained children would probably be bogging their knees in the yielding plush of their *prie-dieux,* in the magnificent Chapel of Buckingham Palace—or before a comforting fire, languidly sinking out of one another's sight in the caressing upholstery of their Palace drawing-room. And the writer can vividly remember the queer questioning that started in his boyish mind one fierce February Sunday when, with the miserable multitude at Mass on that storm-lashed hillside, their knees sunk in the marrow-freezing mire, their few sorry clothes soaked through and plastered to their bones by snow-broth, bared heads battered, and faces whipped and cut by the driving sleet, he heard the *sagart* (a simple saintly soul) lead in supplicating the Lord to grant health and happiness to, and shower His manifold blessings upon, "Her Majesty, the Queen of this Realm, and all the Royal Family"!

And the Bishop of Down and Connor reports: "Dr. Armstrong[20] takes upon him to be bishop, and holds visitations at which there appear great numbers—the Itinerant Preachers, I suppose, making part of them. There were several of those that have great concourse about them."

The marvellous spirit that inspired the young Irishmen who gave their lives for the preserving of their people's faith in these times of terror, could not be more strikingly illustrated than by presenting to the reader—from another Parliamentary return—one of the late date of 1782—the following list of some of the many places, far and wide over the Continent of Europe, to which they penetrated in search of education and ordination. These "registered" priests (only the smaller portion of the priestly body), all of them ordained between 1760–80, were educated in:

> Toledo, Barcelona, Mechlin, Paris, Brussels, Prague, Como, Rome, Viterbo, Treves, Compostella, Cremona, Lisbon, Toul, Bordeaux, Bazas, Sarlate (France), Lombez (France), Antwerp, Liège, Vaison (France), Avignon, Monte Fiascone, Bagnovea, Orvieto, Dol, Spire, Toulouse, Sarni, Arezzo (Tuscany), Nepi (Italy), St. Lizie, St. Papule (France), Pampelona (Spain), Zaragossa, Placence (Italy), Puy, Ypres, Dizd, Seville, Nantes, Rennes, St. Malo, Chalons, Vienna,

[20] The following few lines from The Will of this Dr. Armstrong (who "takes upon him to be Bishop") who died in 1739, is an interesting commentary on the man, his office, his circumstances, and his time. These are some typical extracts from the whole, as printed in Archivium Hibernicum I (It is to be remembered that while the will had to be made in English—in compliance with form—this man, like almost all the learned Irish of his day, probably knew little or nothing of the English language, while in all likelihood, he could freely converse in French, Italian, Latin, and perhaps Greek)—

"I order my horse, and my oats, and my pewter, foure chears, and the furr table, and my six new shirts to be sould in order to defray my funerall expenses and to pay my just and lawfull details.

"I order John Taylor of Ballyverly thirteen pence.

"I order the Convent of Castlewilliam one moydore and the Convent of Dromenecoil one guinea.

"I order Jon. O'Doherty, my servant, my wearing cloathes, and my mare, and both my sadels and bridels, my little oake table and my Dixonary.

"I order Patt O'Doharty my bed and bed cloathes, my oveal table, my two pots, and my gridle, and a grediron.

"I order Neale Armstrong and Mary Donevan my ould lennin and my three chists and two bed steds. I order Neale the green drogged.

"I order Henry Armstrong my big coat.

"I order the Rev. Mr. Patt Byrne and the Rev. Mr. Edward Jennings my books.

"I order Meary Doharty fifteen shillings. I order Anne Killin two shillings and eight pence halfpenny.

"I order the Rev. Mr. Jon. Fitzsimons my vestments, and my hat, and the shute of cloaths that Mrs. Russell gave me, and he to say sixty Masses to her intention.

"I order Oliver Taylor one shilling and one penny, if my substance will afford it."

> Ageu (France), Orte, Azola, Elvas (Portugal), Louvain, Milan, Crema (State of Venice), Montpellier, Perpignan, Santiago (Spain), Macoa, Caizo (Naples), Orleans, Clermont, Caserta, Naples, Besançon, Emesenus, Bayeux, Jaen (Spain), Cordova, Genoa, Nauli (Italy), Segovia, Brabant, Valladolid, St. Ildefaro, Zamora (Spain), Douai (Flanders), Arras, St. Omer, Rheims, Emaus (Treves), Salamanca.[21]

The Penal Laws were enforced with much rigour till the latter part of the 18th century. In 1773 the Anglo-Irish Parliament refused to pass a Bill making it legal for papists to lend money on land mortgage. In 1776 Lord Charlemont threw the House of Lords into a tumult when he brought in a bill to make it lawful for a Catholic to lease a cabin and a potato garden. He was dubbed "papist" and voted out of the chair for such infamous proposal. An uncle of Daniel O'Connell, Arthur O'Leary, was, near the century's end, shot by a soldier for refusing to sell his beautiful horse to a Protestant for five pounds. And O'Connell's father, Morgan, made his first purchase of land through the medium of a Protestant friend—in whose name the land had to be bought, and held. O'Connell's grandfather would not let Smith, when he was writing a history of Kerry, dilate upon the ancient greatness of the clan Conal. "There has been peace in these remote glens," he warned Smith. "Do not draw the attention of the authorities to us."

In 1775 the English traveller, Twiss, was saddened to see crowds of boys learning writing on the roadside—saddened, because, to his well-trained English mind, it was "not judicious to teach the lower orders." In 1776 Arthur Young everywhere met with schools held aback of a hedge: "I might as well say 'ditch' for I have seen many a ditch full of scholars," he adds.[22]

---

[21] There was then (as now) an Irish College at Salamanca. Other Irish Colleges were at Lisbon, St. Omer, Louvain, Douai, Tournay, Antwerp, Lauzanne, etc.

In the above report we find, under various parishes such items as, in one parish, "One popish priest who officiates in different parts of ye parish in open air,"—"One popish priest who officiates in ye open fields,"—"One popish priest who officiates in some open field, or some poor cabin,"—"Several itinerant popish priests and friars do at some times officiate in this parish."

[22] In 1796 the French traveller de Latocnaye tells of seeing the hedge schools. And at the River Shannon he saw Mass being celebrated among the ruins of an ancient abbey—and the priests, sitting upon tombstones in a cemetery, hearing Confession, holding little flags to shield the penitents at their knee. In the first quarter of the 19th century Cæsar Otway describes one of the outlawed schools which he saw (on Cape Clear Island). It was a low hut with no chimney, covered with a network of rope, and hung like a wasp's nest on the side of a cliff. He said he had to bend double in order to enter, as going through a cavern's mouth. Inside was a dark, smoky, smelly cave, where he could not at first discern anything. But when he was able to see he observed twenty children, sitting on stones, humming like hornets preparing to swarm. Every urchin, he said, had a scrap of paper or a leaf of a book in his hand.

In Ireland in these trying times, just as in the more glorious days of Ireland's golden age more than a thousand years before, learning and learners were held in high reverence. And the poor people now (as then) vied with each other in offering share of the little they possessed to the young students who sojourned among them. The Poor Scholar was honoured and loved, and was entertained free of all charge, wherever he went and howsoever long he stayed. Doheny in his introduction to O'Mahony's Keating says, "As late as 1820 there were in many counties classical schools in which the English tongue was never heard." The languages were Irish, Latin and Greek. Furthermore, down to his own day (middle of the 19th century),

> "Literary hospitality continued unimpaired. The ablest masters, classical and scientific, have taught thousands of students who for years were entertained with the most lavish kindness in the houses of the farmers in the districts around the schools, of late a barn or deserted dwelling of mudwall or thatched roof. In Tipperary, Waterford, and Limerick it was usual to have two of these scholars living (free) for four and five consecutive years with a family, and treated with extreme courtesy and tenderness. In the first cycle of this century there was scarcely a farmer of any competency who did not give one son or all of his sons, a classical education, without any reference to intended professions or pursuits."

The Volunteer movement in the 1780's first began to take the edge off Protestant prejudice—which had been so astonishingly narrow and bitter that Burke states in his letter to Langrishe, "There are thousands in Ireland who never conversed with a Roman Catholic in their whole life unless they happened to talk to their gardeners' workmen, or to ask their way when they had lost it in their sports." On all occasions, in conversation or in writing, and in all official documents, including the King's speeches and Acts of Parliament Catholicism was referred to as popery, and Catholics always named either papists or "persons professing the popish religion." In 1793 all good Protestants of both England and Ireland gasped to find the term Catholic employed in a speech from the Throne! Revolution was then in the air, and it was wisdom and statesmanship to begin to rub the papist with the fur. And in that year, of 1793, was passed an Act [23] relieving

[23] In the debate on that Bill of 1793, it is good to find—standing out from among the Protestant bishops, who usually led in hatred of Catholicism—the high-minded Protestant bishop of Killala. In his

the Catholics of many of their disabilities—in theory at least. Another thirty-six years were to elapse before the next step was taken, under compulsion from the O'Connell agitation, and the Act known as Catholic Emancipation made law.

Burke's Tract on the Popery Code.
Burke's Letter to Sir Hercules Langrishe.
McGee's Protestant Reformation in Ireland.
Simon Butler's Digest of the Popery Laws.
Lecky's History of Ireland in 18th Century.
Scully's Penal Laws.

---

speech in the House of Lords he expressed sentiments that did credit to his Christian heart—"I look upon our Catholic brethren as fellow subjects and fellow Christians, believers in the same God, and partners in the same redemption. Speculative differences in some points of faith, with me are of no account: they and I have but one religion—the religion of Christianity. Therefore, as children of the same Father—as travellers on the same road—and seekers of the same salvation, why not love each other as brothers? It is no part of Protestantism to persecute Catholics; and without justice to the Catholics there can be no security of the Protestant establishment. As a friend, therefore, to the permanency of this establishment, to the prosperity of the country, and the justice due to my Catholic brethren, I shall cheerfully give my vote that the Bill be committed."

The Christian character of the papist-hating English appointees who usually filled the chairs of the Irish Protestant bishoprics, may be guessed at from Dean Swift's description of them: "Excellent and moral man had been selected upon every occasion of a vacancy, but it unfortunately happened that as these worthy divines crossed Hounslow Heath, on their way to Ireland, they were set upon by highwaymen, who frequented the Common, robbed and murdered—who seized their robes and patents, came over to Ireland, and were consecrated bishops in their stead."

CHAPTER LIV

"The Wild Geese"

War-battered dogs are we,
Fighters in every clime;
Fillers of trench and of grave,
Mockers bemocked by time.
War-dogs hungry and grey,
Gnawing a naked bone,
Fighters in every clime—
Every cause but our own.
—Emily Lawless, "With the Wild Geese."

"The bright as contrasted with the dark side of the national story," O'Callaghan calls his own record of the *Irish Brigades in the Service of France.* "Ormuzd abroad to compensate for Ahriman at home."[1] Lecky, too, affirms that it is in the continental Catholic countries, where the Irish exiles and their children had risen to posts of the highest dignity and power, and not amid the "outcasts and pariahs" in the motherland, "the real history of Irish Catholics during the first half of the eighteenth century is to be found."

Ireland herself has never taken this view of the question. Again and again she has caught

"echoing down the wind
Blown backwards from the lips of Fame"

the names of her exiled children: Marshals of France like Lord Clare, Prime Ministers of Spain like Don Ricardo Wall, creators of victorious armies like

[1] Ormuzd was in Persian mythology "the good principle" as opposed to Ahriman, "the bad."

Count Peter Lacy in Russia, mighty war lords like Field Marshal Brown, in Austria; founders of empire like Count Lally in India, leaders of European diplomacy like Tyrconnell, O'Mahony, Lawless and de Lacy. So their titles, loud-sounding, came to her, borne on the trumpet music of the world's applause. But Ireland had a name of her own for them. Ransacking all nature for its most desolate image to figure forth her thought of them, its most desolate cry to render the wailing music made in her ears by their last farewell, she called them *na Geana Fiadhaine,* "the Wild Geese."

"She said: 'Not mine, not mine that fame
Far over sea, far over land
They won it yonder, sword in hand.'"

Not hers in truth that fame. Hardly one of them—field-marshal, diplomat, prime minister, empire-builder, was able to do for her the slightest service, or even to win for her the sympathy (much less the active help) of the nations to which they had given their all in life and in death. To Ireland, and to those who look at history through her eyes, the story of the "Wild Geese" is a tragedy—stately and stirring, and noble if you will, in its grandiose setting and majestic movement—but almost unredeemed, and the essence of that tragedy is, like the poignant and vain regret for the life blood of Sarsfield spilled at Landen, "that this was not for Ireland." Only one service the "Wild Geese" did for their own country. Always the hope remained with her that one day they would return, and avenge her wrongs on her iniquitous oppressor. And that hope gave her courage to endure. Eighteenth century Irish poetry is buoyant with it:

"The Wild Geese shall return, and we'll welcome them home
So active, so armed, so flighty,
A flock was ne'er known to this island to come
Since the days of Prince Fionn the mighty.
They will waste and destroy,
Overturn and o'erthrow,
They'll accomplish whate'er may in man be!
  Just heaven they will bring
Devastation and woe
On the hosts of the tyrannous *Seaghan Buidhe.*"

Surely, of all Ireland's sorrows, none was greater than seeing her boys go forth from her, year after year, to serve as cannon-fodder for foreign princes—their departure as fixed a moment in the sorrowful calendar of her seasons, as the annual flight of the wild geese, when even the stubble had withered from her wintry fields.

Mrs. Morgan John O'Connell gives us, in *The Last Colonel of the Irish Brigade,* a lively picture of such a departure from the coast of Kerry about the year 1761. The fleet little smuggling clipper that recently slipped into Derrynane harbour has unloaded its wines, teas, tobaccos, brandies, its velvets and silks for the ladies, its gilt mirrors for their parlours, and has taken on its return cargo, contraband Irish wool. But another portion of its cargo—more precious, equally contraband—remains to be shipped. "Of the productions of Ireland, the wool and the men, rendered equally incapable by law of becoming the great sources of wealth they might have been at home, were in request for the manufactories and the armies in France." The skipper would be ill-satisfied with his run if he were not bearing back with him to France a number of clean-limbed, gallant Irish lads to fill the ranks of The Brigade. Here they come: O'Connells, MacCarthies, O'Sullivans, O'Donoghues, sons of the noblest families of the South; and as their barque weighs anchor, they hear a voice raised in a sorrowful song of farewell that might be the voice of Ireland herself. It is Maire Ni Dhuibh,[2] mother of one of these young "Wild Geese" (of him destined afterwards to make history as Count Daniel O'Connell, "Last Colonel of the Irish Brigade in the French Service," and kins-woman of all the others, who is standing there by the shore singing to a poignant old Gaelic strain, her lament for the passing of all this youth from Irish soil.

The O'Connell correspondence—thanks to Mrs. Morgan John O'Connell—enables us to follow in some detail the further fortunes of the young emigrants. We will suppose that the smuggling craft, built for speed and lightness, has skimmed safely through the rocks and shallows of the Smuggler's Sound, outraced the Revenue Cutter in the open seas, and made in safety its destined port. If she had a recruiting officer of the Brigade[3] on board he would take the more mature of his young recruits straight to his

---

[2] Maire Ni Dhuibh, the grandmother of Dan O'Connell, "The Liberator," was a poetess of exceptional gift. These she transmitted to her children. There is nothing finer in any literature than the wonderful "Lament" composed by her daughter, "dark Eighlin," for her murdered husband, Art O'Leary.

[3] The post was one of much danger. Recruiting for the Brigade was punishable under English law with death. The most famous victim of this law was Morty Og O'Sullivan, the hero of the famous *caoine,* translated by O'Callanan and beginning: "The sun in Iveara no longer shines brightly." Caught after a gallant defence of his castle he was tied to a boat and dragged through the sea from Bearhaven to Cork, where his head was cut off and affixed on the Jail.

regiment. The other little boys, sons of wealthier households, were boarded for a time, at their families' expense, with some retired officer of the Brigade, who made a regular business of keeping a sort of preparatory school for lads of this class, taught them languages, and the rudiments of a military education and saw that they attended classes for the rest. And so the years passed until the boy was old enough to be enrolled as a subaltern in the regiment of his choice.

Some well authenticated figures will give us an idea of the enormous drainage on Irish man power during this period. L'Abbé MacGeoghegan, the historian, himself a chaplain of the Irish Brigade in the French Service, established as a result of researches made at the French War Office, that no less than 450,000 Irishmen *died* for France in the half-century between the Fall of Limerick (1691) and the year of Fontenoy (1745). Cardinal Manning states that another half-million shed their blood for her during the half-century that followed, until the dissolution of the Brigade (1792). Twenty-thousand Irish soldiers followed Sarsfield to France and by the date of the Peace of Utrecht (1713) less than a quarter of them remained alive. The five-and-a-half thousand fighting men, who had been sent to France, before King Louis would consent to despatch a single soldier to Ireland, had been almost wiped out in the famous campaigns against the Vaudois.

Though French Kings in court and in battlefield, and French generals in their despatches, were lavish enough in their praises of the Irish, French historians from Voltaire downward have failed to do our countrymen justice. You might read through a library of them without suspecting all that France owes to Ireland. "Mes braves Irlandais," King Louis called them to Major O'Mahony, when the latter had been chosen to bear to Versailles the news of the Irish defence of Cremona (1702), of which he himself was the hero. After the victory of Marsaglia, Catinat writes enthusiastically of the "surprising things" done by the Irish dragoons, who broke the famous bayonet charge of the Savoyards and drove them from the field. Marshal Vendôme eulogised Irish heroism after many a combat. From the field of Cassano he praised their "exemplary valour and intrepidity," and affirmed that they formed a band "whose zeal and devotion might be relied upon in the most difficult emergencies of war." He had long before appraised Irish valour at Barcelona, and Chevalier de Bellerive, writing in 1710, records the Marshal's "particular esteem for this warlike nation, at whose head he had delivered so many combats and gained so many victories," and his confession of surprise at "the terrible enterprises" the Irish had achieved in his presence.

But on the whole, France has taken her obligations to Ireland lightly enough, and if we would seek a fitting appreciation of what our poor boys did for her we must turn to a rather unexpected quarter—"a letter to the Right Honourable Sir Robert Sutton, for Disbanding the Irish Regiments in the Service of France and Spain," written by the Whig pamphleteer Forman, from Amsterdam in 1727. He speaks of the Irish regiments "as seasoned to dangers, and so perfected in the art of war, that not only the Sergeants and Corporals, but even the private men can make very good officers. *In what part of the army soever they have been placed, they have always met with success, and upon several occasions, won honour, where the French themselves, warlike as they are, have received an affront.* To their valour, in a great measure, France owes not only most of what trophies she gained in the late war, but even her own preservation." He goes on to enumerate the Irish services: the victories won against the Duke of Savoy, the extraordinary affair of Cremona. "They wrested Cremona out of the hands of Eugene, when by surprise, he had made himself master of all the town, except the Irish quarters, and saw the Marshal, Duke de Villeroy, his prisoner, who was taken by Colonel MacDonnell, an Irishman in the Emperor's service. By that action, hardly to be paralleled in history, they saved the whole French army on that side of the Alps. At Spireback, Major-General Nugent's Regiment of Horse, by a brave charge upon two regiments of cuirassiers, brought a complete victory to an army, upon which Fortune was just turning her back. At Ramillies, the Allies lost but one pair of colours,[4] which the Royal Irish in the service of France took from a German regiment. At Toulon, Lieutenant-General Dillon distinguished himself, and chiefly contributed to the preservation of that important place. To the Irish regiments also, under the conduct of that intrepid and experienced officer, Count Medavi himself very generously attributed the victory over the Imperialists in Italy. And the poor Catalans will for ever have reason to remember the name of Mr. Dillon, for the great share he had in the famous Siege of Barcelona, so fatal to their nation. Sir Andrew Lee, Lieutenant-General, showed likewise how

---

[4] This was the celebrated flag long preserved at the Convent of the "Irish Dames of Ypres" referred to by Davis in his "Clare's Dragoons":

"When on Ramillies' bloody field,
The baffled French were forced to yield;
The victor Saxon backward reeled,
Before the charge of Clare's Dragoons.
The flags we conquered in that fray
Look lone in Ypres' choir they say," etc.

consummate a soldier he was, when he defended Lisle, under the Duc de Boufflers, against those thunderbolts of war, the Prince of Savoy, and our own invincible Duke of Marlborough."

To the trophies won for France by Irish bravery previous to the date of this letter (1727) l'Abbé MacGeoghegan, writing in 1758, has a long list to add: Having enumerated Neerwinden, (or Landen), Marsaglia, Barcelona, Cremona, Spires, Castiglione, Almanza, Villa, Viciosa as "witnesses of their (the Irishmen's) immortal valour," he goes on to recall to them the more recent glories of Fontenoy (1745), that great day for ever memorable in the annals of France. "Let me remind you," he says to the Irish troops to whom he dedicates his *History of Ireland,* "of the plains of Fontenoy, so precious to your glory—those plains where, in concert with chosen French troops, the valiant Count of Thomond being at your head you charged with so much valour an enemy so formidable. Animated by the presence of the august sovereign who rules over you, you contributed with so much success to the gaining of a victory which till then appeared doubtful. Laufeld beheld you, two years afterwards, in concert with one of the most illustrious corps of France, force intrenchments which appeared to be impregnable. Menin, Ypres, Tournay saw you crown yourselves with glory under their walls; whilst your countrymen under the Standards of Spain performed prodigies of valour at Campo Sancto and at Velletri. But whilst I am addressing you, a part of your corps (the Regiment of FitzJames) is flying to the defence of the allies of Louis; another (Count Lally and his regiment) is sailing over the seas to seek amidst the waves, in another hemisphere, *the eternal enemies of his empire—the British."*

He did not know, the good Abbé, that the service of Count Lally, after unheard of labours, the display of the greatest ardour, disinterestedness, fidelity and perseverance, in the endeavour to establish a French Empire in India, were to be rewarded by an imprisonment of nearly four years in the Bastille—and death, amidst every species of indignity, at the hands of the common executioner!

It is hard to imagine how the Irish remained in the French service after this atrocious treatment of this, their countryman to whom France owed amongst other victories, the glory of Fontenoy. The wonder becomes all the greater when we read in the correspondence of many of them which has come down to us, how dissatisfied they were with their treatment and prospects. Nevertheless, the Irish Brigade still remained on until its dissolution by the Revolution in 1791.

In 1792 the Count de Provence (afterwards Louis XVIII) presented the remnant of the Brigade with a "farewell banner," bearing the device of an

Irish Harp embroidered with shamrocks and fleurs-de-lis. The gift was accompanied by the following address:—

> "Gentlemen, we acknowledge the inappreciable services that France has received from the Irish Brigade, in the course of the last 100 years; services that we shall never forget, though under an impossibility of requiting them. Receive this Standard, as a pledge of our remembrance, a monument of our admiration, and of our respect, and in future, generous Irishmen, this shall be the motto of your spotless flag:—
>
> 1692—1792
> Semper et ubique Fidelis."

Dr. Sigerson has pointed out the very curious effect which close connection with "the Brigade" had on Munster at the time of the '98 Rising. "The fact that Munster did not join generally in the Insurrection of 1798 has not been understood by writers. Its quiescence was the result, not of loyalty to the Irish Parliament or Government, then in the hands of a cabal, but of its Jacobite and anti-Jacobin principles. Many families had kinsmen in 'La Brigade Irlandaise,' and were Royalists." This observation is quite just, and explains many things: the fact that Daniel O'Connell's uncle, old "Hunting Cap," claimed a reward for conveying to the Government the first news of the appearance of Wolfe Tone and the French in Bantry Bay; his nephew, Dan's Whiggery and the deplorable pronouncement of many of the Irish Bishops (educated in France), after the failure of the Rising.

The Irish Officers who threw in their lot with the Revolution, were mostly Connacht, Ulster and Leinstermen. Among whom may be named: General O'Moran, Charles Jennings, afterwards Baron Kilmaine, and the group of Irish officers so often mentioned in Wolfe Tone's memoirs: Madgett, Clarke, and Shea. The name of the officer who was the hero of the following dramatic incident has not come down to us, but his nationality is sufficiently indicated:—

A certain Irish Capuchin, Father Donovan of Cork, was a chaplain of a noble French family in Paris when the Revolution broke out. His friends fled, and he, as having been concerned with aristocrats, was thrown into prison. One morning, after he had spent the night preparing a number of his fellow-prisoners for death, he was suddenly called out with a batch of condemned and trundeled off to the guillotine. Just as he was about to get his foot on the ladder, an officer of the French guard called out in Irish:

"Are there any Gaels among you?" "Seven," answered Father Donovan, in the same language. "Then let there not be any fear on you," shouted the officer, and the seven were saved. Never since the days of Hugh Roe, himself, had the knowledge of Irish proved such a safeguard.

In truth it was not the "Wild Geese" who forgot the tongue of the Gael or let it perish. We are told that the watchwords and the words of command in the "Brigade" were always in Irish, and that officers who did not know the language before they entered the service found themselves of necessity compelled to learn it. And it was in Irish the famous war cry was composed, to which the exiles charged at Fontenoy:

"Remember Limerick and Saxon Perfidy."

Many other instances we have of these soldier-exiles' love for their old tongue, and the old literature. Captain Sorley MacDonnell, serving in the Low Countries about 1626, had a copy made for himself of the Fenian Tales, and to his passion for Irish hero-lore we owe, as Professor Eoin MacNeill reminds us, "the preservation of Duanaire Finn." John O'Donovan, in the appendix of his edition of the *Four Masters,* has an interesting tale to tell of a young Charles O'Donnell from County Mayo, who in the middle of the 18th century went out to seek his fortune in Austria, where his uncle, Count Henry O'Donnell, the "handsomest man in the Austrian service, and an especial favourite with the Empress" had risen to high rank in the Imperial Army, and won a princess of the royal house of Cantacuzeno for his bride. Poor Charles was on the point of being packed home again because he answered in English when the General addressed him in Irish. The kind Irish Friar to whom the young man related his discomfiture, advised him to go back to the General *and speak nothing but Irish,* and all would be well. The advice was taken, and the reassuring prophecy fulfilled, young Charles in his turn rising to be a Major-General and a Count. His initial *faux-pas* was all the less excusable, because his uncle, writing to his father Manus, had directed him to have whichever of his sons he intended sending to Austria carefully educated in the Irish language, for Count Henry desired to have his nephew's help in instructing his own children in the language of their ancestors. "The tongue being Irish, the heart must needs be Irish, too."[5]

---

[5] A century later we find one of the Austrian O'Donnells affirming that "though reared in Austria their hearts were none the less Irish." And perhaps one of the reasons the Irish in the Austrian service remained so Irish is that, again acting on a Spenserian prescription, wherever possible, they married Irish girls. Count Henry's son Joseph and his cousin Theresa were hero and heroine of a

The great Field-Marshal, Ulrich Maximilian Count Brown—"whose ashes are every day watered with the tears of the soldiers to whom he was so dear" (l'Abbé MacGeoghegan)—was perhaps the greatest of the great soldiers Ireland gave to Austria—and that is saying much. Born in 1705 and educated in Limerick, he had gone out as a boy to his uncle, George Brown, who commanded an Infantry Regiment in Hungary. He was present at the Siege of Belgrade (where his countryman, General O'Dwyer commanded a division), was made Colonel in 1725 (at the age of twenty) and in 1730, with his uncle, invested Corsica. In 1739 he was raised by the Emperor Charles VI. to the dignity of Field-Marshal and Member of the Council of War. On the accession of Maria Theresa, she appointed Brown one of her Privy Councillors, and in 1752 nominated him Generalissimo of all her forces; while the King of Poland, Elector of Saxony, in the following year, invested him with the order of the White Eagle. At the memorable battle of Prague in 1757, this hero received a wound of which he expired in two months.

Field-Marshal Brown was, as we have said, the most famous of the Irish soldiers in the Imperial Service, but there were many other distinguished Irishmen in the Austrian Armies, and the Imperial Rulers showed the highest appreciation of their qualities. In a document written by the Emperor Francis I, and found among his papers after his death, we read:—"The more Irish officers in the Austrian service, the better our troops will always be disciplined; an Irish coward is an uncommon character, and even what the natives of Ireland dislike, they generally perform through a desire of glory." "Such is our established reputation," said Colonel O'Shea, a veteran officer of the Austrian army, "that Arch-Duke Charles said to me that never was

---

very pretty love-story in which the Empress Maria Theresa, herself, played the part of fairy God-mother. The Imperial Lady was fond of doing so, and, what is better, showed herself a real human mother to the Irish girls who went out as brides to Officers in her Majesty's armies. Mrs. Morgan John O'Connell tells a charming story of the homely way the Empress comforted one of the O'Connell girls, the young wife of Major O'Sullivan, whom she found one day sobbing out her poor homesick heart in a dark corner of the Chapel of the Imperial Palace. It may have been the Empress who suggested Father Bonaventure O'Brien, guardian of the Irish Franciscan Convent at Prague, as a suitable matchmaker when "General Brown, son and heir to the late Marshal of that name," thought of seeking a wife among his Irish kinfolk? A letter of Father O'Brien's to "Hunting Cap" O'Connell shows the good will with which Father Bonaventure entered on his mission. It would appear that Lord Kenmare's daughter was suggested, and Father Bonaventure writes to ask Maurice O'Connell "how old she was, her humour and other qualities, *also her fortune.*" The General on his side was a very eligible *parti.* "He has a charming estate in this Kingdom, and his post besides, brings him in a thousand a year."

The match did not come off, perhaps for the reason that the little maid was less than twelve years old when her Austrian cousin sought her hand. She eventually married the Marquis de Syverac, and brought him an immense fortune, according to the standard of those days.

the House of Austria better served than when possessing so many Irish, of whom at one time upwards of 30 were Generals." There have been no less than 14 Irish Field-Marshals in the Austrian Service at various times. On Saint Patrick's Day, in the year 1765, the Spanish Ambassador to the Court of Vienna, gave a grand entertainment in honour of the Apostle of Ireland, to which were invited only persons of Irish descent. The Ambassador himself was an O'Mahony, son of the hero of Cremona, and the illustrious assembly included Count de Lacy, President of the Austrian Council of War, Generals O'Donnell, MacGuire, O'Kelly, Brown, Plunkett and MacEligott, four Chiefs of the Grand Cross, two Governors, several Knights Military, six Staff Officers, four Privy Councillors with the principal Officers of State, who to show their respect for the Irish Nation, wore crosses in honour of the day, as did the whole court.

Many of the Irish Officers in Austria had relatives in the Russian Army, or had served in it themselves. Thus we find in Russia, Nugents, O'Rourkes, Browns, and de Lacys. Count Peter de Lacy, born in Limerick, first entered the French service, passed thence into the Polish, and was presented by the Polish Count de Croy to Peter the Great, who was then in alliance with Poland. "The Czar took him into his own service, in which he obtained a Majority in 1705, and a Lieutenant Colonelcy in the following year. In 1708 he was promoted to the command of the Siberian Regiment of Infantry, and joined the Grand Army. He was wounded at the battle of Pultowa (1709), where he acted as brigadier. In 1710 he distinguished himself in the attack on Riga. In 1737 he was appointed to command an expedition into the Crimea. This was the General who, according to Ferrer, *taught the Russians to beat the army of the King of Sweden, and to become from the worst, some of the best soldiers in Europe.* Before the battle of Pultowa, he advised the Czar to send orders that every soldier should reserve his fire until he came within a few yards of the enemy, in consequence of which Charles the Twelfth was there totally defeated, losing in that single action the advantage of nine campaigns of glory." He died, Governor of Livonia in 1751.

The history of the de Lacys would bring us through every country in Europe. Thus, Count Peter's son, Joseph, died a Marshal of the Austrian Army; his kinsman, Maurice, entered the Russian service we are told, *at ten years old.* He served under Suwarrow in the Italian campaign, in campaigns against the Turks, and also in the Crimea. The Lacys in Spain were numerous and important. The most famous was Count de Lacy, General and Diplomatist. Born in 1731, he commenced his military career as an Ensign in the Irish Brigade of Ultonia Infantry, was named Colonel in 1762, and a Commander of Artillery in 1780, when he was employed at the celebrated Siege of Gibraltar. After the Peace of Versailles in 1783, he was made Minister Plenipotentiary to both Sweden and Russia and died at Barcelona in 1792.

The Irish Legion in Spain has a much longer history than that in the French service, but its records have not been collected into a convenient form. They go back to the days when Irish soldiers, recruited by Sir John Perrott, were sent to the Low Countries under Sir William Stanley, as part of the expeditionary force led by Leicester to help the Dutch then in revolt against Spain (1586). Their leader, Stanley, having become a Catholic, surrendered Deventer, which he held for the Dutch, to the Spaniards, and was joyfully followed over to the side of the Catholic King by all his Irish fighting men.

This was the nucleus of the famous Irish Legion in the Low Countries, which for long years kept the English in continual fear of an invasion of Ireland. Illustrious names illumine the lists of officers: Colonel Henry O'Neill, son of the great Hugh; his younger brother, John; "Don Hugh O'Donnell, Earl of Tyrconnell, page to the Infanta in Flanders," Don Tomaso Preston, and

> "The worthiest warrior of them all
> The princely Owen Roe."

And great deeds of arms illumined its records: at Bois-le-Duc, Dourlen, Amiens, under Pontecarrero and Montenegro, the stupendous defence of Louvain by Preston, the no less stupendous achievements of Owen Roe and his men at Arras.

The misfortunes of Ireland, her inability to provide for her young men at home, kept the ranks of this Legion filled. After the battle of Kinsale, after the confiscation and plantation of Ulster, the dispossessed swordsmen trooped to it in countless numbers. The poignant phrase of the *Four Masters* paints their sad lot—"offering themselves for hire as soldiers to foreigners, so that countless numbers of the freeborn nobles of Ireland were slain in distant countries and *were buried in strange places and unhereditary churches.*" But always the hope remained with them, that one day they would return and strike a blow for Ireland. As they lay one night outside the town of Aire, waiting to storm it on the morrow, their thoughts and feelings were vocal in an Irish sentence which pierced the darkness:—"Tomorrow we are to adventure our lives for the succouring of a scabbéd town of the King of Spain, where we may lose our lives, and we cannot expect any worse if we go into our own country and succour it."

And they did "go into their own country," the brave boys, and "succour it" with Owen Roe O'Neill!

The triumph of Cromwell again drove many thousand trained soldiers to Spain and other countries—in accordance with a definite policy, that of "voiding the swordsmen out of the country." It is estimated that between 1651 and 1654 "40,000 of the most active spirited men, most acquainted with the dangers and discipline of war" went out of Ireland to die for Princes and causes that were none of theirs. Of these Spain received the largest number.

After the fall of Limerick a great number of swordsmen sailed to Spain, and their numbers were subsequently increased by accession of Irish soldiers from France during the War of the Spanish Succession. L'Abbé MacGeoghegan enumerates the names of the most distinguished: "O'Mahony, MacDonnell, Lawless, the Lacys, the Burkes, O'Carrolls, Croftons, Comerford, Gardiners, and O'Connors crowned themselves with laurels on the shores of Tagus."

A very remarkable Irishman in the service of Spain was Don Alexander O'Reilly, "Count Commander of the Spanish Armies, Field-Marshal, Captain-General at the Havannah; Governor and Lieut.-General of Louisiana, which he took possession of in 1761, when surrendered by the French. Born in Ireland 1725, died in Paris 1794. There can scarcely be found anywhere a more romantic or exciting career than that of O'Reilly. He fought in Spain, Italy, Germany, France and America. He saved the King's life, was at the head of his armies and Government, was in disgrace and exile, and everywhere and always showed high spirit, the greatest bravery and the most devoted loyalty to the King."

It is worthy of note that the best officers in the Spanish army during the War of Independence, bore Irish names. At this time there were three Irish Regiments in the service of Spain: Hibernia, Irlanda, and Ultonia. An English historian, Oman, not inclined to be unduly favourable to Ireland, writes:—"An astounding proportion of the officers who rose to some note during the war, bore Irish names, and were hereditary soldiers of fortune, who justified their existence by the unwavering courage which they always showed, in a time when obstinate perseverance was the main military virtue. We need only mention Blake, the two O'Donnells, Lacy, Sarsfield, O'Neill, O'Daly, O'Mahony, O'Donoghue. Their constant readiness to fight contrasts very well the behaviour of a good many of the Spanish Generals. No officer of Irish blood was ever found among the cowards."

It is related of Don Alexander O'Reilly that it was his delight to visit a certain Irish College in Spain and tell the boys there that the dream of his life was to head a Spanish invading force and land in his own country to set her free. How many of the "Wild Geese" cherished that dream? Alas! Alas! It was never realised. Only as disembodied spirits was it granted to them to revisit the land of their hearts' desire. Far, far away from Ireland their bodies have mingled with foreign earth "and the graves in which they are buried are unknown." But a poet (Emily Lawless) had a vision of a company of them "Sailing home together from the last great fight! Home to Clare from Fontenoy in the morning light!"

And surely it was not from Fontenoy alone, but from the thousand European battlefields on which Irish valour asserted itself that such a "singing company" set forth, and reach the shores of Ireland at last:

"Mary Mother shield us! Say what men are ye
Sweeping past so swiftly on this morning sea?
Without sails or rowlocks, merrily we glide,
Home to Corca Bascin on the brimming tide.

"Jesus save you gentry! Why are ye so white
Sitting all so strange and still in the misty light?
Nothing ails us brother, joyous souls are we,
Sailing home together on the morning sea."[6]

O'Callaghan (John Cornelius): History of the Irish Brigades in the Service of France.
O'Conor (Matthew): Military History of the Irish Nation.
O'Connell (Mrs. Morgan John): The Last Colonel of the Irish Brigade.
D'Alton (John): Illustrations, historical and genealogical of King James's Irish Army List.
Mitchel: History of Ireland.

[6] It must not be forgotten that the Irish Brigade in the French service joyously sent its quota to meet the old enemy of the race on American battlefields. The regiments of Dillon and Walsh came with Lafayette to strike for American liberty. And it is recorded that they demanded the right to be the first of the French service to strike Britain on American soil.

CHAPTER LV

The Suppression of Irish Trade

The systematic ruthlessness with which Ireland's trade and industries were wiped out by England, has, like the Irish Penal Laws, no parallel in the history of any other subject land. We shall briefly summarise the extraordinary story.

In the early centuries of the Christian Era the highly civilised Celt was slightly inclined to trade and commerce—probably stimulated thereto by the Phœnicians who carried on a large commercial intercourse with Ireland. The early Irish, the reader will recollect, were famous for their excellence in the arts and crafts—particularly for their wonderful work in metals, bronze, silver and gold. Ten hundred hills and bogs in Ireland constantly yield up testimony to this—even if we discarded the testimony of history, story and poem.

By the beginning of the 14th Century, the trade of Ireland with the Continent of Europe was important—and trading ships were constantly sailing between Ireland and the leading ports of the Continent. Irish merchants were known in the great Continental markets. And Irish money commanded credit.

This condition of things naturally did not suit commercial England. So at an early period she began to stifle Irish industry and trade.

In 1339 England appointed an admiral whose duty was to stop traffic between Ireland and the Continent (34 Edward III, c. 17). He must have been but indifferently successful; for a little more than a century later, Edward the Fourth deplores the prosperity of Ireland's trade, and he orders (in 1465) that since fishing vessels from the Continent helped out the traffic with Ireland, these vessels should not henceforth fish in Irish waters without an English permit (5 Edwd. IV).

And since even this failed to stop the stubborn Irish, in 1494 an English law was enacted prohibiting the Irish from exporting any industrial product, except with English permit, and through an English port, after paying English fees.

This handicap, too, failed. For, we find English merchants in 1548, unofficially taking a hand at trying to end the traffic—by fitting out armed vessels to attack and plunder the trading ships between Ireland and the Continent—commercialised piracy.

But official piracy had to be fallen back upon. Twenty years after, Elizabeth ordered the seizure of the whole Continental commerce of Munster—much more than half of the trade of the Island—and a fleet under Admiral Winter was despatched to do the good work. In 1571 she ordered that no cloth or stuff made in Ireland, should be exported even to England, except by English men in Ireland, or by merchants approved by the Government. (Nearly thirty years before, her much married father, Henry, had forbidden Irish cloths to be exported from Galway.)

And Irish trade was attacked from yet another angle. At the same time that the pirate admiral was appointed by Edward III, Irish coinage was forbidden to be received in England. However, Irish merchants and Irish money had such worthy repute that not only did they still succeed with it on the Continent, but, one hundred years later, Irish coinage had to be prohibited again in England. That was in 1447.

In 1477, after imprisoning some Irish merchants who traded with Irish money in Bristol, the English Government adopted a radical reform by introducing into Ireland an English coinage debased twenty-five per cent below the English standard, and compelled Ireland to accept it as her legal currency.

This accomplished two good objects. English merchants bought in Ireland by the cheap standard and sold these purchases abroad by the dear standard. Also England was enabled to pay her army in Ireland with cheap Irish coin. When Ireland's merchants refused to honour at its face value the debased coinage tendered by the soldiers, an Act was passed (in 1547) making such refusal treason.

By reason of their big Continental trade the shipping industry had in itself become an important one to Irishmen. Hence it was advisable to extinguish it. The Navigation Act of 1637 provided that all ships must clear from English ports for foreign trade. But as this did not sufficiently discourage Ireland, the Act was amended, in 1663 (15 Charles II, c. 7), to prohibit the use of all foreign-going ships, except such as were built in England, mastered and three-fourths manned by English, and cleared from English ports. Their return cargoes too, must be unladen in England.[1]

Ireland's ship-building industry was thus destroyed, and her Continental trade was practically wiped out.

Yet, Ireland, ever persevering, began, even under such heavy restriction, to develop a lucrative trade with the Colonies. This was cured in 1670 by 22 Charles II, c. 26, which forbade Ireland to export to the Colonies anything except horses, servants, and victuals!

Then Ireland fell back upon the little profits to be derived from imports from the Colonies. And England, observing this, put a bush in the gap (7 & 8 Wm. II, c. 22) decreeing that no Colonial products should be landed in Ireland—till they had first been landed in England and paid all English rates and duties. "Thus," says Newenham, "was Ireland deprived of the direct lucrative trade of the whole western world."

But England must get credit for repentance. By 4 Geo. II, c. 15, Ireland was permitted to import directly from the Plantations all goods, etc., of the growth, production or manufacture of the said Plantations, except sugar, tobacco, indigo, cotton, wool, molasses, ginger, pitch, turpentine, tar, rice, and nine or ten other specified items—which, stripped of its facetious verbiage, just means that she was permitted to import West Indian rum—thus aiding the planters and rum makers of the West Indies, at the expense of Irish farmers, distillers, and constitutions.

The foregoing will seem to many readers a good English joke. But from constant reiteration through the centuries these English jokes proved rather wearing on Ireland's health.

The woollen joke was not the least trying.

At a very early period Ireland had been forbidden to export her cattle to England, and then, turning to sheep-raising, was, by 8 Eliz. c. 8, forbidden to export sheep. She next essayed woollen manufactures.

This quickly became a great Irish industry. In the Continental markets, and even in the British, Irish woollens were in brisk demand. Consequently this trade should be stopped. Though, as usual, it took a long time to convince the pig-headed people who inhabited Ireland that it was for their benefit to stop it. The good work was, for the good step-mother, a tedious and thankless task. But with praiseworthy perseverance, she persisted till her good end was accomplished.

[1] "The conveniency of ports and harbours with which nature had blessed Ireland as of no more use than a beautiful prospect to a man shut up in a dungeon."—*Swift*.

The Irish woollen manufacturers began, at an early period, to rival England's. So, in 1571 Elizabeth imposed restriction upon the Irish woollen trade that crippled the large Irish trade with the Netherlands and other parts of the Continent. Yet half a century later Lord Strafford, then Lord Lieutenant of Ireland, begs for a little more discouragement. In 1634, he writes to Charles the First, "That all wisdom advises to keep this (Irish) kingdom as much subordinate and dependent on England as possible; and, holding them from the manufacture of wool (which unless otherwise directed, I shall by all means discourage), and then enforcing them to fetch their cloth from England, how can they depart from us without nakedness and beggary?" (Strafford's Letters.)

But it was not until 1660 that was taken the radical step of forbidding by law the export of woollens from Ireland to England. When this blow fell the Irish resorted to exportation of their raw wool. This was stopped by 12 Charles II, c. 32, and 13 and 14 Charles II, c. 18—which Acts prohibited Ireland from exporting sheep-wool, wool-fells, mortlings, shortlings, yarn made of wool and wool-flocks. The Acts were thorough.

In 1673, Sir William Temple (by request of Viceroy Essex) advised that the Irish would act wisely in giving up altogether the manufacture of wool (even for home use), because "it tended to interfere prejudicially with the English woollen trade!"[2]

Now Ireland was almost completely cured of the bad habit of exporting both woollens and wool—almost. But a trace of the habit still lingered. While the British Colonies (possibly by oversight) had been left open to her, she continued exporting to them. This needed attention. So, in 1697 an act was introduced to prohibit Ireland from sending out any of her woollen manufactures to any place, whatsoever![3]

But it was very soon found that even this Act was incomplete. It inadvertently left the Irish market open to the Irish wool manufacturers—which market must, of course, or ought to be the private property of the English manufacturers. The mistake must be remedied. So on June 9th, 1698, both English Houses of Parliament addressed King William beseeching

---

[2] This is the same English statesman who pithily put the maxim which England has always observed in protecting Ireland, and fostering Irish welfare—"Regard must be had to those points wherein the trade of Ireland comes to interfere with that of England, in which case Irish trade ought to be declined so as to give way to the trade of England."

[3] Swift said: "Ireland is the only kingdom I ever heard or read of either in ancient or modern story, which was denied the liberty of exporting its native manufactures and commodities wherever it pleased."

him to chide his Irish subjects for that—in the language of the Lords—"The growth of the woollen manufactures there hath long been, and ever will be, looked upon with great jealousy by all your subjects of this kingdom, and if not timely remedied may occasion very strict laws totally to prohibit and suppress same." The impending punishment for continued wilfulness on the part of the naughty Irish child was going to give the noble lords more pain than it would the child, which was being punished for its own good.

And the Commons in the course of their address say, "And therefore we cannot without trouble observe that Ireland, which is dependent on, and *protected by, England, in the enjoyment of all they have,* should of late apply itself to the woollen manufacture, to the great prejudice of the trade of this kingdom . . . make it your royal care, and enjoin all those whom you employ in Ireland to make it their care, and to use their utmost diligence, for discouraging the woollen manufacture of Ireland." And in token of their solicitude for the country which was "dependent on, and protected by England in the enjoyment of all they have," it was suggested that Irishmen should turn from woollens to hemp and linen—which England had little means of making—and which, more betoken, Ireland had then less means of making.

King William answered his faithful Lords and Commons, "I shall do all that in my power lies to discourage the manufacture of woollens in Ireland." And the king was this time as good as his word (despite the slanders of Limerick men). In this year of 1698 he signed an Act to the effect that because these manufactures are daily increasing in Ireland (disastrous to relate!), the exports of wool and woollen manufactured articles from Ireland are hereby forbidden under pain of forfeiture of the goods and ships that carried them, and five hundred pounds fine!

It is worth remembering that though the mere Irish in Ireland were the workers, earning a subsistence at the trade, it was almost entirely the Anglo-Irish, the purely British-blooded people of the Island, who were the manufacturers—the only monied people in the country—and traders. They, having had the misfortune to be born and bred in Ireland, were penalised and striven to be crushed out by their own kin beyond the Irish Sea. That they richly deserved, however, to be throttled and robbed, is proven by the fact that they, servile creatures, acting at the behest of William and their kin beyond the water did, in September, 1698, actually pass in their own House of Parliament (from which the real Irish were carefully excluded) an act laying prohibitory duty (four shillings in the pound) on their own woollen manufactures—"the better to enable His Majesty," said they, "to provide for the safety of his own liege people!"[4]

Except for a few little items such as coverlids and waddings which were overlooked in the act of William the Third—but carefully attended to by his successors—the great Irish woollen manufacture was now extinguished forever. But to make assurance doubly sure, by 5 Geo. II, c. 11, three ships of war and eight or more armed vessels were appointed to cruise off the coast of Ireland with orders to seize all vessels venturing to carry woollens from Ireland.

The Irish woollen joke was now, at last, concluded; "So ended," says Lecky, "the fairest promise that Ireland had ever known of becoming a prosperous and a happy country. The ruin was absolute and final."

For a long time after this destruction of one of the country's chief supports, the economic conditions in Ireland were fearful. Swift, who had stated that "since Scripture says oppression makes a wise man mad, therefore, consequently speaking, the reason that some men in Ireland are still not mad is because they are not wise"—Swift thus describes the pass to which the country was now brought—"The old and sick are dying and rotting by cold and famine, and filth and vermin. The younger labourers cannot get work, and pine away for want of nourishment to such a degree that if at any time they are accidentally hired to commence labour, they have not the strength to perform it."

When William took from Ireland its woollen manufactures, he promised to compensate by encouraging in its stead hemp and linen. And his Lords Justice in their address to the Irish Houses of Parliament, Sept. 27, 1698, after suavely requesting the country to commit *felo de se* by resigning the woollen manufacture, said: "Amongst these bills there is one for the encouragement of the linen and hemp manufactures which we recommend to you. The settlement of those manufactures will contribute much to the people of this country, and will be found much more advantageous to this kingdom than the woollen manufacture, which, being the staple trade of England, from whence all foreign markets are supplied, can never be encouraged here for that purpose: whereas, the linen and hempen manufactures will not only be encouraged as consistent with the trade of England, but will render the trade of this kingdom both useful and necessary to England."

---

[4] In this connection it is worth comparing the spinelessness of the Anglo-Irish in 1698 with the spinefulness of their cousins in America, three quarters of a century later.

Now to see how the promises of William and his Lords Justice were kept. First, the Irish linen manufacture.

In 1705 it was enacted that only the coarsest kinds of undyed Irish linen should be admitted to the British Colonies. Checked, striped and dyed Irish linens were excluded. Besides, no Colonial goods could be brought in return. And Irish linens of every kind were forbidden to be exported to all other countries with the exception of Britain. There a thirty per cent duty met it with a laugh, and turned it home again. And, to the British linen manufacturers a bounty was granted on all linen exports!

But English attention followed and sought out the Irish linen trade even within the four seas of Ireland. When Crommelin, the Huguenot, who had helped to build up the linen trade in Ulster, tried to bring the manufacture into Leinster, the fiercest English opposition blazed up.

Edmund Burke excoriated the English Government for its gross breach of faith. And the poor, servile, Anglo-Irish Parliament in 1774, addressing the Lord Lieutenant Harwood on the subject of the linen ruin, said, "The result is the ruin of Ulster and the flight of the Protestant population to America." So, it was the ruin of the linen trade by England who "protected them in the enjoyment of all they have" which helped to give to America her so-called Scotch-Irish population.

Next, the promised help to the hempen manufacture. Although no Act came to their aid, the Irish went ahead with the hemp as well as with the linen, and soon developed a considerable trade in the export of sail-cloth to Britain. Then came the long promised aid. By 23 Geo. II, c. 33, there was a heavy import duty placed upon sail-cloth shipped to Britain. And to pursue the beast to its lair, very soon after British manufacturers were granted a bounty on sail-cloth exported from Britain to Ireland!

The British had given to the Irish the linen and hempen manufactures to play with, while they were carrying off their woollen trade. And when the woollen was safely got away from them, they were politely requested to hand over the linen and hempen manufactures also.

Ireland tried its hand at manufacturing cotton. England met this move with a twenty-five per cent duty upon Irish cotton imported into England. And next (in the reign of Geo. I) forbade the inhabitants of Great Britain to wear any cotton other than of British manufacture. So the cotton comedy was ended before it was well begun.

From an early period, as before mentioned, the Irish had a large trade in the export of cattle to England. This was soon prohibited. But when England felt need for Irish cattle, they were admitted once more. In 1665 Irish cattle were no longer welcome, and an Act of Parliament in that year put a heavy import duty on black cattle and sheep.

The resourceful Irish then began killing their cattle and exporting the dead meat to England. Their equally resourceful protectors countered with a law (18 Chas. II, c. 2) declaring that the importation of cattle, sheep, swine and beef from Ireland was henceforth a common nuisance, and forbidden. And to leave no little hole without a peg—they added pork and bacon for good measure.

But the contrary Irish ferreted out a hole to get through. They developed dairying, and began exporting butter and cheese from Ireland. Their exasperated protectors had to go to the trouble of amending the prohibition laws—adding butter and cheese to the items which the Irish were invited to keep at home.

When both their live cattle, their dead cattle and all the products of cattle were shut out from Britain the Irish again fell back upon curing the killed meat, and exporting it to the Continent. They soon developed a highly profitable trade in this line. "And," says Newenham, "Ireland became the principal country from which butchers' meat was exported." At the instigation of the English contractors, then, the English Parliament began laying embargo on the exportation of Irish provisions, on pretence of preventing the enemies of Britain from being supplied therewith! And the trade in salted provisions was no more.[5]

In the middle of the eighteenth century Ireland, developing an important silk weaving industry, began to disturb the dreams of English silk weavers. So Britain, which imposed a heavy duty on Irish silk imported into England, politely requested the Irish Parliament to admit British manufactured silk into Ireland free! What is more, the despicable Anglo-Irish Parliament complied. Within the next generation the number of silk looms at work in Ireland was reduced from eight hundred to twenty. "And," says Newenham, "three thousand persons were thereby driven to beggary or emigration."

Ireland attempted to develop her tobacco industry. But a law against its growth was passed in the first year of the reign of Charles the Second. And

---

[5] The Irish next killed their cattle and horses for their hides, and began what soon proved to be a prosperous trade in leather—which was in demand not only in England, but on the Continent of Europe. And their vigilant English masters soon came along with another prohibition bill, which put an end to that business. Before quitting the cattle drive, however, it is only fair to say that one of England's most representative commercial writers of the early eighteenth century, Davenant, pleaded that England should permit Ireland to resume the cattle trade—because it would hold the Irish from manufactures!

again, in 1831, under William the Fourth, it was enacted that any person found in possession of Irish-grown tobacco should suffer a heavy penalty. The tobacco trade was tenderly shown out.

In the latter part of the eighteenth century Ireland began not only making her own glass, but also making glass for export: and Irish glass was gaining a name. Then by 4 Geo. II, c. 15, the Irish were forbidden to export glass to any country whatsoever under penalty of forfeiting ship, cargo, and ten shillings per pound weight of cargo. And it was forbidden to import any glass other than that of English manufacture.

Four and five centuries ago and upward, the Irish fisheries were the second in importance in Europe. Under careful English nursing they were, a century and a half ago, brought to the vanishing point. Then the independent Irish Parliament at the end of the eighteenth century saved them. It subsidised and revived the Irish fisheries—till they were rivalling the British. A few years after the Union, in 1819, England withdrew the subsidy from the Irish fisheries—at the same time confirming and augmenting the subsidies and grants to the British fishermen—with the result that, notwithstanding Ireland's possession of the longest coastline of almost any European country, it is now possessed of the most miserable fisheries. Where 150,000 Irish fishermen in 27,000 Irish boats worked and thrived at the time that the English Parliament took away the subsidy in 1819, only 20,000 Irish people get a wretched support from Irish fisheries today. The British fisheries, four centuries ago, about equalled the Irish. The fisheries of Britain today are valued at £9,000,000 annually. The fisheries of Ireland are worth £300,000. The Irish fish were, with typical British solicitude, protected into the British net.

Here have been set down only the principal Acts and devices for the suppression of Irish manufactures and Irish industries, but yet sufficient to show how England protected her beloved Irish subjects in the enjoyment of all they have—how Ireland prospered under English Rule in a material way—and how England, in her own step-motherly way, took each toddling Irish industry by the hand, led its childish footsteps to the brink of the bottomless pit, and gave it a push—thus ending its troubles forever.

And thus is explained in part why Ireland, one of the most favoured by nature, and one of the most fertile countries in Europe,[6] is yet one of the poorest. And why it is that, as recent statistics show, ninety-eight per cent

[6]Hear the testimony, two-edged, of Carew (sixteenth century): "Would you had seen the countries we have seen in this our journey, and then you would say you had not seen the like, and think it were much pity the same were not in subjection."

of the export trade of the three kingdoms is in the hands of Britain and in Ireland's hands two per cent.

Even the bitter anti-Irish Froude, in his English in Ireland, is constrained to confess, "England governed Ireland for what she deemed her own interest, making her calculations on the gross balance of her trade ledgers, and leaving her moral obligations aside, as if right and wrong had been blotted out of the statute book of the Universe."

Says Lecky, "It would be difficult in the whole range of history, to find another instance in which various and powerful agencies agreed to degrade the character, and blast the prosperity of a nation."

And here endeth what may be considered by those who know not England's way with Ireland an amazing chapter—but quite commonplace to those who have a bowing acquaintance with Irish history.

And again: "I never, nor no other man that ever I have communed with, but saith that for all things it is the goodliest land that they have seen, not only for pleasure and pastime of a prince, but as well for profit to his Grace and to the whole realm of England." The final clause is the kernel of the matter.

CHAPTER LVI

The Volunteers

On Lammas Eve of the year 1778, a certain harassed English official sat him down in his room in Dublin Castle to pen a letter to one Mr. Stewart Banks, the Sovereign of Belfast.[1] The letter cannot have been a very pleasant one to write, for it confessed the utter bankruptcy of the system of government under which England had held Ireland since the advent of "civil and religious liberty," with the victory of William III. Such as it is, however, it is an historic document—

> "Dublin Castle, August 14th, 1778.
>
> "Sir:
>
> "My Lord Lieutenant having received information that there is reason to apprehend that three or four privateers in company may in a few days make an attempt on the northern coast of this kingdom, by his Excellency's command I give you the earliest account thereof, in order that there may be a careful watch, and immediate intelligence given to the inhabitants of Belfast, in case any party from such ships should attempt to land. The greatest part of the troops being encamped near Clonmel and Kinsale, his Excellency can at present send no further military aid to Belfast than *a troop or two of horse, or part of a company of invalids,* and his Excellency desires you will acquaint me by express, whether a troop or two of horse can be properly accommodated in Belfast, so long as it may be proper to continue them in that town. Richard Heron."

[1] This office in the smaller town corresponded to that of Mayor in the larger.

The shrewd Belfast man, who received this letter from Chief Secretary, Sir Richard Heron, was well able to read between the lines and interpret the panic confession of impatience it contained. He knew—none better—that all over the world the power of England was at a very low ebb. In America her affairs were desperate. The surrender of General Burgoyne at Saratoga in the previous autumn (1777) had been followed in Spring by the formal adhesion of France to the American cause.

An invasion of England or Ireland by the allies was on the cards—and how easy it would have been, Mr. Stewart Banks and his fellow townsmen had special reason for knowing; for in April, 1778, John Paul Jones in his saucy "Ranger," after a foray marked by the capture of Dublin and Wexford merchantmen, the plunder of Kircudbright, the burning of shipping at Whitehaven, had sailed boldly into Belfast Bay, in broad daylight, and sunk a British man-of-war in sight of them all! Here he was back again, it seems, with new companions "three or four privateers in company"—and all the pauper Irish Government (which had been refused a paltry loan of a few thousand pounds a month or two by its own official bankers) was able to send to oppose him was "a troop or two of horse, or part of a company of invalids."

Thus, moneyless, soldierless, amid the ruins of the industries it had deliberately set itself to wreck, amid the starving remnants of a people it had deliberately set itself to exterminate, the English power in Ireland stood, a shivering and impotent thing, after a century during which it had full scope to work its will, and to apply unopposed its own chosen methods!

What *written* answer the Sovereign of Belfast sent, in the name of his town, to the Chief Secretary's amazing document we do not know. But the real answer of Belfast is a matter of history.

It was the institution of the first corps of volunteers. "England sowed her laws in dragon's teeth, and they had sprung up in armed men!"

The example of Belfast was speedily followed over the country, and within two years the Volunteers numbered 100,000 armed and disciplined men, officered by the greatest personages in Ireland: Lord Charlemont, the Duke of Leinster, the Earl of Clanricarde, Flood, Grattan, Ponsonby, and the élite of the landed aristocracy, the professions, high finance and politics. Though Catholics were not admitted to their ranks at first, they supported the movement from the beginning, and to this circumstance the Volunteers themselves are indebted for the achievement which the after-world recognises as the only lasting one to their credit—their paternity of the "United Irishmen."

Government on the other hand looked askance on the Volunteers. But the position being described, it had no power to oppose them openly—and was finally constrained to help to equip them by turning over to them 16,000 stand of arms intended for the Militia.

The threat of invasion, though apparently increased when Spain joined America and France in 1779, did not materialise. But as the lessons of the American War were pondered by citizen soldiers on their way to the reviews, which soon became a prominent feature in Irish colonial life, or discussed at the banquets which re-united them in good fellowship afterwards, the determination materialised in the movement to secure redress for the intolerable evils under which the British Colonists in Ireland, in common with the native Irish, were suffering. Of these evils none was more keenly felt than the trade restrictions, which with their disastrous consequences, have been discussed in a previous chapter. The ruin of the centuries old Irish woollen trade, completed by the third William, was followed, under the third George, by the destruction of the linen and provision trade, which had, to some extent, taken its place. The cries of the starving unemployed filled the land. In Dublin alone, twenty thousand artisans were out of work, and they and their families were only kept from dying of hunger by the exertions of charitable institutions. In Cork things were equally desperate. Ulster was quiet for the moment—but it was the quiet of exhaustion. Her fair countrysides had been drained of their population by landlord oppressions, and the ruin of the linen industry—and the flower of her manhood in Washington's armies was avenging her quenched hearths and wrecked homes.

The Volunteers therefore needed no special perspicacity to see that the most formidable enemy even of the English Colony in Ireland was the English trade interests, to which their advantages were ruthlessly sacrificed.

The first invasion they set themselves to repel was that of English manufactured goods.

Starting in Galway a "non-importation" movement spread itself rapidly through the country. Meetings organised by the Volunteers, and supported by the press and scientific societies, as well as the most influential people in the colony, high sheriffs, grand jurymen, county magnates, and—more important still—the women of fashion, adopted resolutions pledging themselves to boycott English manufacture, and to "wear and make use of the manufactures of this country only." Shopkeepers and merchants who imported foreign goods, or tried to impose them on their customers as Irish manufacture, were warned of the consequences. The Volunteers were there to see that the boycott was duly observed.

When Parliament met in October, 1779, Grattan moved his celebrated amendment to the Address to the Throne, demanding Free Trade for Ireland—that is the right to import and export what commodities she pleased, unrestrained by foreign legislation. His speech was doubtless very eloquent, as were those of Hussey, Burgh and Flood, who supported him. But it is safe to say that the solid ranks of the placemen and "tied" borough members, who made up the Government's permanent majority in the Irish House of Commons, would have been as little moved by them, were it not that, outside in College Green, bold Napper Tandy had his artillery corps mustered, all in their gallant uniforms of emerald and scarlet, his cannon trained on the Parliament Houses and placarded with the inscription "Free Trade or—."

To the pregnant argument of that unwritten alternative, the prudent placemen yielded. The amended address was carried by a huge majority, and next day it was borne to the Castle, along streets lined by Volunteers in full war kit, and thence dispatched to England marked "urgent."

And as "urgent" the English Prime Minister and the British Legislature treated it. Acts were rushed through the English Houses of Parliament in a few weeks which restored to the Irish the trade rights of which they had been robbed. The embargo was taken off their export of woollens and glass; the colonial trade was thrown open to them; trade between Ireland and the British settlements in America and Africa was placed on an equal footing with that between Great Britain and these settlements. Those Acts were repealed which prohibited the carrying into Ireland of gold and silver. "The Irish were allowed to import foreign hops, and to receive a drawback on the duty on British hops. They were allowed to become members of the Turkey Company, and to carry on a direct trade between Ireland and the Levant Sea."

But the British Parliament from which Free Trade had thus been wrung by the Volunteers—and the vivid fear of Ireland following the example of America—still held the Irish Parliament in bondage. At any moment England might revoke the concessions she had granted under duress. There still remained on the Statute Books of the two countries the Acts which gave her this power—Poyning's Act, and the Sixth of George I.

Poyning's Act was a piece of suicidal legislation imposed on the Parliament of the Pale in 1495, by Lord Deputy Sir Edward Poyning, who was sent over to supersede the Earl of Kildare after the latter had failed in two attempts to set up a rival kingdom in Ireland. It bound the Irish Parliament to legislate only as the British Parliament permitted it. The other provided that all the "causes and considerations" for calling a Parliament in Ireland, and all the Bills which were to be brought in during its Session, must be previously certified to the King by the Chief Governor and Council of Ireland, and affirmed by the King and his Council under the Great Seal of England, and that any proceedings of an Irish Parliament which had not been so certified and affirmed before that Parliament was assembled should be null and void.

The "Sixth of George I" called also "the Declaratory Act," was passed in the English Houses of Parliament in 1719, and "declared that the King, with the advice of the Lords and Commons of England hath had of right, and ought to have, full power and authority to make laws and statutes of sufficient force and validity to bind the people and the Kingdom of Ireland." It further took away from the Irish House of Lords its power of appellate jurisdiction.

In April, 1780, Grattan moved in the Irish House of Commons his "Declaration of Right." There were three resolutions contained in it, and on these was ultimately built the very shaky "Independence" with which his name is associated. They were:—

(1) That His Most Excellent Majesty by and with the consent of the Lords and Commons of Ireland is the only power competent to enact laws to bind Ireland.
(2) That the Crown of Ireland is, and ought to be, inseparably annexed to the Crown of Great Britain.
(3) That Great Britain and Ireland are inseparably united under one Sovereign, by the common and indissoluble ties of interest, loyalty and freedom.

Though the stage had been carefully prepared, though the Volunteers were again mustered in the streets of Dublin, though the ladies thronged the galleries in their most bewitching gowns, and the orators of the Opposition had prepared their most eloquent speeches—it was all in vain. "Mr. Flood, who well knew that the ministerial members were committed to negative the motion if it came to a division, recommended that no question be put, and no appearance of the business entered in the journals, to which Mr. Grattan consented." It was a distinct set-back, not alone for Grattan, and for those politicians who thought with him, but for the Volunteers. Fortunately the latter saw the lesson to be learned from it, so they began not only improving and consolidating their organisation, but giving it a national extension by including the Catholics.

Finally, feeling themselves able to speak at last for the whole Irish nation, they determined to make their voice heard above that of the corrupt Parliament. The expedient they adopted for this end was that of provincial conventions. The most famous of them was the Convention of the Ulster Volunteers, held in Dungannon on the 15th of February, 1782.

It was, however, when all is said and done, the progress of events in America which ultimately won a hearing for Grattan, when, in April, 1782, he moved an address to the King, asserting the principles already embodied in his "Declaration of Right." On the 19th of October, 1781, Cornwallis surrendered at Yorktown, and not only the cause of American Independence, but that which Grattan called Irish "Independence" was won that day.

The Duke of Portland wrote:—"If you delay, or refuse to be liberal, Government cannot exist here in its present form, and the sooner you recall your Lieutenant and renounce all claim to this country, the better. But, on the contrary, if you can bring your minds to concede largely and handsomely, I am persuaded that you may make any use of this people, and of everything they are worth, that you can wish."

Lord Rockingham and his friends took the hint. They brought their minds to concede "largely and liberally"—that is to say all that was asked. A Bill repealing the Sixth of George I was introduced at once in the English Parliament and carried rapidly, and when the Irish Parliament met in May 27th, 1782, the Lord Lieutenant was instructed to announce to it that the King was prepared to give his unconditional assent "to Acts to prevent the suppressing of Bills in the Privy Council of this Kingdom, and the alteration of them anywhere, and to limit the duration of the Mutiny Act to two years."

The following year, 1783, under pressure from the Volunteers and Flood a *"Renunciation Bill"* was carried through the British Parliament. It declared that the "right claim by the people of Ireland to be bound only by laws enacted by His Majesty and the Parliament of that Kingdom in all cases whatever, and to have all actions and suits at law, or in equity, which may be instituted in the Kingdom, decided by His Majesty's courts therein finally, and without appeal from thence, shall be and is hereby declared to be established and ascertained *for ever, and shall at no time hereafter be questioned or questionable."*

How England kept that promise we shall see.

MacNevin: History of the Volunteers of 1782.
Lecky: Leaders of Public Opinion in Ireland.

" History of Ireland in the Eighteenth Century.
Davis: The Patriot Parliament.
Grattan's and Flood's Memoirs.
Sir Jonah Barrington: Rise and Fall of the Irish Nation.

CHAPTER LVII

THEOBALD WOLFE TONE

"I have now seen the Parliament of Ireland, the Parliament of England, the Congress of the United States of America, the *Corps Législatif* of France and the *Convention Batave;* I have likewise seen our shabby Volunteer Convention in 1783, and the General Committee of the Catholics in 1793; so that I have seen, in the way of deliberative bodies as many I believe as most men; and of all those I have mentioned, beyond all comparison the most shamefully profligate and abandoned of all sense of virtue, principle, or even common decency, was the legislature of my own unfortunate country. The scoundrels! I lose my temper every time I think of them!"

The keen-faced young man in uniform of an Adjutant General of the French Army, whom we discover writing these angry words in his Journal on returning to his *auberge* from visiting to the Batavian Convention at the Hague in April, 1797, has every claim to have his opinion of the "Independent" Irish Parliament accepted as the ultimate verdict of the Irish people on that body. For he was the first to lay his fingers on what was really wrong with it—and to show the Irish people the way to remedy it.

This man was registered at his Dutch inn as "J. Smith, Adjutant-General of the Army of the Sambre and the Meuse." His true name, written in letters of undying light across the most memorable page of Irish History, was Theobald Wolfe Tone.

The earlier days, when, though "the untameable desire—to become a soldier," which was the dominant passion of his boyhood and young manhood, yet politics seemed the one career open to him. Young Counsellor Tone used to spend much of his free time (which a slender law practice left him in abundance) in the galleries of the Irish House of Commons. There he speedily made the "Great Discovery," which was to influence not only the whole course of his own life, but the future direction of Irish History. Let us hear him state that discovery in his own words:—

"That the influence of England was the radical vice of our Government, and that Ireland would never be either free, prosperous, or happy, until she was independent, and that independence was unattainable whilst the connection with England existed."

Other people had felt long before this that the so-called "Independence" which Ireland had won from England in 1782, was not the genuine article, and that the "Independent" Irish Parliament was a libel on the name of free institutions. But until Tone presented a true diagnosis, these others, like unskilled physicians, went on applying remedies to the symptoms, and neglecting the root cause of the malady which laid waste the Irish Nation in sight of all men's eyes. And that root cause was *the connection with England.* The defect of the Constitution of 1782 was inherent in the clause that "united Great Britain and Ireland under one Sovereign," and "annexed the crown of Ireland inseparably to the crown of Great Britain."

It is perhaps not to be wondered at that those who had deliberately chosen this constitution were unable to perceive that it was wrong and unworkable from the start, and that its evils were inherent in its very essence. But it was hardly in action when they began to see that there was *something* the matter with it, and to look round for a remedy. They imagined if the machinery were improved it would function satisfactorily.

The two defects that struck everybody were:—

First, that more than three-fourths of the Irish Nation were totally unrepresented in this "Irish" Parliament; for the Catholics, who made up more than three millions of the four, which then constituted the population of Ireland, could neither sit in it, nor vote for a member of it.

Second, that even as the instrument of the Protestant minority of the nation, it was hopelessly corrupt and unrepresentative. Of its 300 members, only 64 were returned by counties. The remaining 236 represented "rotten boroughs" (where there were sometimes as many as *six* voters, sometimes only *one*), and these boroughs were the *property* of certain peers and wealthy commoners who trafficked in them most shamelessly. "The price of a seat in Parliament," said the Belfast Reformers in one of their petitions, "is as well ascertained as that of the cattle in the fields."[1] Of the total number of

---

[1] Lecky gives an idea of the tariff: "Borough seats were commonly sold for £2,000 a parliament; and the permanent patronage of a borough for from £8,000 to £10,000. In his examination before the Select Committee of the House of Commons (August, 1798) Arthur O'Connor quoted as the common talk of the House when he himself was a member: 'How much has such a one given for his seat? From whom did he purchase? Has not such a one sold his borough? Has not such a peer so many

members more than a third were "placemen and pensioners" in the direct pay of the English Government.

The true effect of the so-called "grant of Independence" of 1782 has been admirably summed up by Arthur O'Connor. "What was called the emancipation of the Irish Legislature in 1782 was nothing more than freeing a set of self-constituted individuals from the absolute control of the British legislature, that they might be at liberty to sell themselves to the corrupt control of the British Ministry."

At first Grattan (who, though a brilliant orator and phrasemaker, was no statesman) was so delighted with his new toy, that he could not bear to have it touched or criticised. He accordingly set himself strenuously against the continuance of the Volunteers, who under the leadership of Flood, were pressing for the reform of the Parliament. A great national Convention of the Volunteers summoned to Dublin for December, 1783, was split on the Catholic question, boycotted by Grattan, and so "nobbled" by his friend, Lord Charlemont, that it dispersed *"re infecta"*; and it seemed for a moment that the Volunteers, as an effective force in Irish public life, had absolutely disappeared.

The truth was that they were eclipsed for a time, only to emerge from a temporary obscuring in the form of the United Irishmen.

* * * * * * * * *

Up in his place in the gallery of the "House" in College Green, Theobald Wolfe Tone had at length got his own political theory clear. "To subvert the tyranny of our execrable government to break the connection with England, the never failing source of all our political evils, and to assert the independence of my country, these were my objects. To unite the whole people of Ireland, to abolish the memory of all past dissensions, and to substitute the common name of Irishman in place of the denominations of Protestant, Catholic, and Dissenter—these were my means.[2]

Absolute freedom from England and no absurd theory of "Sister Kingdoms united by the golden circle of the crown," of "colonial" independence—absolute union among Irishmen, and no cutting off of "Pales" or reserved territories—such was the solution of the "Irish Problem" which presented itself to Theobald Wolfe Tone a hundred and thirty years ago.

---

members in this house? Was not such a member with the Lord Lieutenant's Secretary to insist on some greater place or pension?'"

[2] Padraic Pearse considered the whole Gospel of Irish Nationality as contained in these words, which he paraphrases, "I believe in an Irish Nation and that free and indivisible."

Our Theobald had his theory well defined, when on a memorable day he turned from the contemplation of the antics of the "placemen and pensioners" on the floor of the House, to answer an observation addressed to him by another occupant of the gallery. Agreeably attracted by the appearance of his interlocutor (whose name, he presently learned, was Captain Thomas Russell) he entered into a discussion with him, and before those two left the gallery, there was laid the foundations of a friendship which was destined to become one of the supreme motive forces of Irish history.

Let us look at these two as they clasp hands for the first time—conscious that we are assisting at one of the great moments in our country's story. Is there need to describe Tone? Have we not felt him like a living presence in our midst all through these great, if sorrowful, days across which we are passing? A "rapid moving angular man with something of the eagle in nose and eyes, the face sallow and thin under the close-cropped upstanding hair." And Thomas Russell? Does he not live for us in the portrait painted of him by the hand of dear Mary MacCracken, the woman who loved him to the end, and who claimed as the sole reward of her years of unrequited devotion the privilege of building for him the tomb in holy Downpatrick, wherein his martyred body awaits the Resurrection: the tall black-haired young soldier, built and modelled like an Apollo, with the fire and pride of his dark eyes and passionate mouth softened by the sweetness of his soul—with his voice as moving and melodious as that of Red Hugh himself? So we picture them standing together, and we keep the picture in our hearts for all time.

Tone was so taken by his new friend that he lost no time in introducing him to "the little box of a house on the seaside at Irishtown," where Mrs. Tone and her baby girl were that summer, installed for the sea bathing. A charming society soon made that "little box of a house" its *rendezvous*. Tom Russell frequently brought his father and his brother, John. William Tone came for week-ends from his cotton factory at Prosperous, and as often as not was accompanied by his sister, Mary. They lived a delicious, picnicky kind of life, where everybody helped with the cooking and washing-up, and then spent the long care-free hours of the afternoon camped out on the seashore, in endless discussions.

What did they talk of? Of everything under the sun—and then always they came back to the one great subject, Ireland, and how she too might take up her position in the march of liberated nations who, with France at their head, were advancing toward the supreme ideals which the French people in July, 1789, had postulated as the true basis of human society:

"Liberty, Equality, Fraternity." For the French Revolution was in these days in its first generous and soul-stirring phase—in that pure dawn of which the poet has told us

> "Bliss was it in that dawn to be alive,
> But to be young was very heaven."

And all those who gathered round Matilde Tone's board at Irishtown that summer were young—even seventy-year old Captain Russell. Here they were

> "They who had fed their childhood upon dreams."

And behold! their dreams had become true, and there had sprung forth

> "helpers to their heart's desire
> And stuff at hand plastic as they could wish."

* * * * * * * * *

Tone has told us the enormous effect produced on the whole people of Ireland by the French Revolution. "The French Revolution," he writes in his *Autobiography*, "became, in a little time the test of every man's political creed, and the nation was fairly divided into two great parties, the Aristocrats and the Democrats."

The "Ascendancy Party"—the British-blooded ones, who, though only a small fraction of the population, held, "by right of conquest," five-sixths of the landed property of the country, and were in possession of all its place, power and patronage—hated the new manifestations of popular power, which threatened their old monopoly, and were, in their detestation of "French" principles, brought more close even than before to England (who was presently to stand forth as the arch-enemy of these principles, and the champion of reactionary aristocracy all over Europe). The Catholics were divided. The bishops, like Dr. Troy, and aristocrats like Lord Kenmare, as well as the country people of those parts of Ireland which had furnished, for generations, recruits for the "Irish Brigade in France," full of horror at the stories of Jacobin "atrocities" carefully disseminated, and full of loyalty and sympathy for the *Ancien Régime*, were bitterly opposed to the French Revolution. On the other hand, it was greeted with a warm welcome by the new class of educated, enlightened and progressive men among the Catholics: wealthy merchants and manufacturers like John Keogh and John Sweetman of Dublin, or Luke Teeling of Lisburn, and young professional men, trained in foreign universities, like Dr. MacNevin. These recognised that the doctrines of "Liberty, Equality and Fraternity" held in them the salvation of the enslaved, debased, and outcast Catholics of Ireland. The Dissenters of the North, republican both by tradition, and the genius of their religion, were to a man, enthusiastic admirers of the French Revolution from the start.

One of the truths presently discovered by the keen minds which canvassed these things, that summer of 1790 at Irishtown, was that England, through the instrumentality of the "Protestant Ascendancy," had kept her hold on Ireland by the deliberate fostering of religious differences. *Ergo* it followed that if Dissenters and Catholics could be persuaded to make common cause, the "Protestant Ascendancy" would not only suffer a rude shock, but the supremacy of its "owners and inventors," the English Government, would meet with an immediate downfall. The first task, therefore, of anyone who wanted to free Ireland was to *unite* Catholics and Dissenters.

Their similarity of views on the French Revolution was a first step to this *union*—and we shall presently see how skilfully Tone and his friend, Tom Russell, manœuvred from it.

Other things we shall see, likewise: how England, and the servile Irish Parliament, which was the instrument moulded to her hand, set themselves with demoniac fury to break the union of Irishmen, making of it a crime punishable by tortures terrible and fearful death.

CHAPTER LVIII

The United Irishmen

During the leisure of these days, Tone, who had a ready pen and an extraordinary gift of convincing exposition, dashed off a pamphlet addressed to the (Presbyterian) Dissenters, and entitled "An Argument in behalf of the Catholics of Ireland," in which he demonstrated that Dissenters and Catholics had "but one common interest and one common enemy: that the depression and slavery of Ireland was produced and perpetuated by the divisions existing between them, and that consequently, to assert the independence of their country and their own individual liberties, it was necessary to forget all former feuds to consolidate the whole strength of the entire nation, and to form for the future but one people."

The pamphlet had an enormous and immediate success, and though it was signed "A Northern Whig," the identity of its author was no secret. Presently Counsellor Tone found himself quite a personage, and he was assiduously cultivated by the two sections of the people whom it was his object to unite. The leaders of the advanced party among the Catholics—John Keogh, Byrne, Braughall, Sweetman, etc., showed their appreciation of his efforts on their behalf, not only by inviting him to all their splendid social gatherings but, in a still more practical way, by appointing him (at a salary counted liberal in those days) to the post of Assistant Secretary to the Catholic Committee, left vacant by the departure of Richard Burke, son of the great Edmund.

At the same time the Dissenters of the North were eager to do him honour—their eagerness to meet the author of the pamphlet being doubtlessly increased by the encomiums of his friend Captain Russell, who had, since the close of those pleasant days at Irishtown, been stationed at Belfast on regimental duty. The Volunteers of the Northern capital, "of the first or green company" paid him the rare compliment of electing him an honorary member of their corps (a privilege never before extended to any one except Henry Flood) and they invited him to Belfast, in the words of the *Autobiography*, "to assist in forming the first club of United Irishmen."

The idea of the United Irishmen as a political organisation originated with Samuel Neilson (son of a Presbyterian minister), a prosperous woollen merchant in Belfast. Some months before Tone first set foot in the North, he had discussed the matter very fully with Henry Joy MacCracken and Thomas Russell, and won over to his views other enlightened Belfast merchants like the Simmses, MacCabe, Sinclair, MacTier, etc. Tone's services were sought, probably at the suggestion of Russell, to organise the Society, frame its declaration, elaborate its constitution, etc.

The first general meeting of the United Irishmen was held on 18th of October, 1791, and the following resolutions were proposed and carried:

(1) That the weight of English influence in the Government of this country is so great as to require a cordial union among all the people of Ireland, to maintain that balance which is essential to the preservation of our liberties, and the extension of our commerce.

(2) That the sole constitutional mode by which this influence can be opposed is by a complete and radical reform of the representation of the people in Parliament.

(3) That no reform is just which does not include Irishmen of every religious persuasion.

There we have the original programme of the United Irishmen—no other than the reform programme of the Volunteers, strengthened by the frank and free adoption of the principles of religious equality, and united action, among all sections of the Irish people.

Shortly after its establishment in Belfast, a branch of the Society was started by Tone in Dublin—his chief adjutant in the business being that sturdy veteran, Napper Tandy, whose cannon had played a great, if silent, part in the early successes of the Volunteers.

The new Society went ahead by leaps and bounds, and the establishment in Belfast early in 1792 of the famous newspaper, The Northern Star, under the editorship of Samuel Neilson, did much to spread its principles. Neilson and his friends took the greatest possible interest in the Catholic Convention, which the Catholic Committee, and their energetic Assistant Secretary, Tone, were organising at the time; and the union between Dissenters and Catholics was demonstrated in a dramatic and startling way at the end of the Convention. The delegates chosen to go to London to bear to the King of England that assembly's demand for the complete emancipation of the Catholics chose (for reasons we can conjecture) to make the journey via Belfast, and their presence was made the occasion of a unique demonstration. "Upon their departure the populace took their horses from their carriages and dragged them through the streets amid the liveliest shouts of joy and wishes for their success."

England on the point of war with France found it prudent to make the Irish Parliament—whose policy she absolutely controlled—yield to the Catholic demands, at least in part, and the Franchise of 1793 was passed.[1] The concessions were not made without advertence to the fact that Catholics, having got portion of their demands, might be detached from the Dissenters, and the "Union" be broken up.

To break up that "Union"—all the weight of England's power in Ireland was, henceforth, consistently directed. And now begins one of the most extraordinary struggles of which history has record. While Tone, Neilson and their friends were doing everything in their power to "found a brotherhood of affection, a communion of right, and a union of power among Irishmen of every religious persuasion, and thereby to obtain a complete reform of the legislature founded on the principles of civil, political, and religious liberty,"[2] the Clares, Beresfords, Fosters, Duignans, etc., were "exhausting the resources of civilisation" to keep the Irish nation "a heap of un-cementing sand." The servile Parliament passed "Convention Acts" and Irishmen were deprived of the right of public meeting, and magistrates and policemen were given *carte blanche* to search houses by day or night, for arms. The "Black and Tans" of that period smashed up newspaper offices and newspaper plants, wrecked the houses and business premises of men suspected of "United" principles with thorough vigour and zest. The forces of bigotry were invoked in a series of Grand Jury resolutions, and finally, as a supreme effort, the Orange Order was established. And while all this was being done the men who worked for the union of all Irishmen were persecuted in every possible way, their properties destroyed, and they themselves clapped into jail—as often as not a step to the foot of the gallows. Cried the poet, as he stood by the bloody bier of young William Orr:

"Why cut off in palmy youth?
Truth he spoke and acted truth.

---

[1] This gave Catholics the elective franchise, but not the right to sit in Parliament.

[2] Extract from a Manifesto of the *United Irishmen*.

'Countrymen, unite,' he cried,
And died for what our Saviour died."

It became plain to the leaders of the "United Irishmen" that if they wanted to effect their purpose they must do more than pass resolutions. Accordingly, the Society, which had been started as a purely "constitutional" organisation, after about four years of existence was remodelled on a new basis—a military one. Government had turned down their efforts to reform by peaceful methods, and now they were determined to fight for their rights.

With the example of America before them, it is natural that they turned to France for aid. It so happened that France about the same time was thinking much of Ireland. One Jackson, an English clergyman, exiled to France on account of his Jacobin principles, was sent by the revolutionary authorities in Paris to England and Ireland on a secret mission. In London he communicated his plans to an old friend, an English attorney called Cockayne. Cockayne immediately put the information thus obtained in the possession of Pitt, who instructed him to accompany Jackson to Ireland and report all his proceedings. Through the instrumentality of Leonard McNally (then, and for long years afterwards, posing as a patriot barrister, but in reality a Castle spy), some of the United Irishmen, especially Tone, Hamilton Rowan, and Dr. Reynolds, were implicated with Jackson, and when the case against the latter was complete and he was put on trial for high treason, they had to fly the country.

Before Tone left Dublin for America, he promised his friends, Thomas Russell and Thomas Addis Emmet (a prominent Dublin barrister), that he would take the earliest opportunity of interesting the French minister to the United States in the cause of an alliance between France and Ireland, and, furnished if possible with a recommendation from that official, present himself in Paris to seek aid from the French Directory. On his way through Belfast he made a similar engagement with his Republican friends of that city. On a certain June day in 1795, Tone, in company with Russell, Neilson, MacCracken, Simms and some others, climbed to the top of MacArt's Fort on the top of Cave Hill—and there looking down on the quiet little city, they swore "never to desist from their efforts until they had subverted the authority of England over their country, and asserted their independence."

A little more than half a year later, Wolfe Tone was in Paris, in direct touch with the French Directory, and received as the representative of the people of Ireland, on a mission for "the separation of Ireland from England, and her establishment as an independent Republic in alliance with France." By the following June, matters had so far advanced that the republicans in

Ireland sent another mission to France, this time consisting of Lord Edward Fitzgerald and Arthur O'Connor, and those negotiations were concluded which led to the great expedition under Hoche in the winter of 1796—the "Bantry Bay" expedition, whose story we shall presently relate.

During the year 1796, events had moved in Ireland with extraordinary rapidity. On the one hand the Government had let loose on the country a storm of organised terrorism, and on the other the country, as a measure of self-protection, if nothing else—had gone solidly into the ranks of the "United" men.

It was mentioned that among the sinister measures adopted by Government to break the "Union," was the establishment of the Orange Society. Of this association, and its works, it becomes necessary now to speak.

The Orange Society was established in the village of Loughgall, Co. Armagh, on the 21st September, 1795, the evening of the "Battle of the Diamond."[3] Their "test" at that period is said to have been "In the awful presence of Almighty God, I, A. B., do solemnly swear that I will to the utmost of my power support the King and the present government and I do further swear that I will use my utmost exertions to exterminate all the Catholics of the Kingdom of Ireland."

The extermination clause was afterwards repudiated, but, whether the original Orange oath contained it or not, the Orangemen themselves left no doubt that the *raison d'être* of their existence was the extermination of the Catholics of their neighbourhood. "They would no longer permit a Catholic to exist in Co. Armagh." They forced masters to get rid of their Catholic servants and landlords of their Catholic tenants. They posted up on the cabins of the unfortunate Catholic small farmers, and cottiers and weavers, ill-spelt notices threatening dreadful things if the inmates did not clear out at once "to Hell or Connacht." If the persons whose houses were thus "papered" as the phrase went, neglected the warning, large bodies of armed Orangemen, mad with drink and religious fanaticism, assembled at night, destroyed the furniture, broke down the looms, burned the habitations and forced the ruined families to fly elsewhere for shelter. Several Catholic chapels were burned, and the disturbances presently extended to Derry, Down, Antrim and Tyrone. It is estimated that in Co. Armagh alone over 7,000 persons were thus left homeless—and turned out in the dead of

---

[3] The "Battle of the Diamond" was fought between the "Peep o' Day Boys," fanatical Protestants of the lower order who used to raid Catholic houses for arms at the break of day, and the "Defenders," Catholics, who had banded themselves together to resist these outrages. It resulted in the defeat of the "Defenders" who left many of their number dead on the field.

winter to die by the wayside, or find shelter—God only knows where. Those who died were the happiest. As the others wandered from place to place seeking shelter, they were met by the magistrates and their armed followers—and clapped into jail as "vagrants." From the jails the pick of the young men were press-ganged for the English Fleet![4]

What did the Irish Government do to protect the defenceless Catholics, and to punish their Orange aggressors? The atrocities, the murders, the extermination campaign against the Catholics, were all "according to plan," and those who carried them out were sure of Government protection. It happened, however, that some of the zealous "law and order" men were too zealous. Lord Carhampton, for instance, and other magistrates who had ("acting with a vigour beyond the law,") been conscripting hundreds of untried prisoners for the Fleet, had not the slightest sanction of legality for their proceedings. What did it matter? "Let us," said the Irish Parliament, "make their illegalities legal." And accordingly, that Parliament proceeded to pass the "Insurrection" and "Indemnity" Acts. The Attorney General, in introducing the Bills, explained the former as designed for "preventing insurrections, tumults and riots in this kingdom,"[5] and the latter for "indemnifying magistrates, and others, who in their exertions for the preservation of the public tranquillity, might have acted against the forms and rules of law." But Grattan's famous commentary on them explained far more clearly their true *inwardness.* "A bill of indemnity went to secure the offending magistrates against the consequences of their outrages and illegalities; that is to say, in our humble opinion, the poor were stricken out of the protection of law, and the rich out of its penalties, and then another bill was passed to give such lawless proceedings against his Majesty's subjects continuation, namely, a bill to enable magistrates to perpetrate by law those offences which they had before committed against it; a bill to legalise outrage, to barbarise law, and to give the law itself the caste and colour of outrage. By such a bill the magistrates were enabled, without legal process, to send on board a tender, his Majesty's subjects, and the country was divided into two classes—his Majesty's magistrates and his Majesty's subjects; the former without restraint, and the latter without privilege."

---

[4] If the atrocities of the Orangemen had stopped at house-wrecking they would have been bad enough. But there were still worse crimes to their account—and some of these had been collected in a famous pamphlet, praised by Presbyterian Jamie Hope "as containing more truth than anything ever written of the events that led up to the Rising of '98."

[5] This Act gave magistrates the most unlimited powers to arrest and imprison and search houses for arms.

Thus deprived of the protection of the laws, the people were more rapidly driven into the ranks of the "United Irishmen"; and by the end of 1796 the organisation had a membership of half-a-million, and included men of all classes of the nation: Lord Edward Fitzgerald (son of the Duke of Leinster), Arthur O'Connor (nephew of Lord Longueville), Thomas Addis Emmet the successful barrister, Dr. MacNevin the clever physician, John Sweetman the wealthy brewer, and innumerable Catholic priests and Presbyterian clergymen joined the Society in the year. Presently it was reckoned that 100,000 men were drilling secretly—ready to take the field when the French should land.

In order to break up the organisation, Government, in 1796, arrested the best known of the leaders, Samuel Neilson, Thomas Russell, Henry Joy MacCracken, William MacCracken, etc., in Belfast; young Charles Teeling in Lisburn, and numerous others in Dublin. But for every man arrested, ten men sprang forward to fill his place, and when the message came that the French, with Tone on board "were on the sea," there was the proud feeling that the "United Irishmen" were ready to give a good account of themselves.[6]

When the news of the arrest of his "dear friends, Russell and Samuel Neilson," reached Tone, he was on his way to Brest to join General Hoche

---

[6] THE SHAN VAN VOCHT
(A Street Ballad of '98)

Oh! the French are on the sea,
Says the Shan Van Vocht;
The French are on the sea,
Says the Shan Van Vocht;
Oh! the French are in the Bay,
They'll be here without delay,
And the Orange will decay
Says the Shan Van Vocht.

And where will they have their camp?
Says the Shan Van Vocht;
Where will they have their camp?
Says the Shan Van Vocht;
On the Curragh of Kildare
The boys they will be there
With their pikes in good repair
Says the Shan Van Vocht.

Then what will the yeomen do?
Says the Shan Van Vocht;
What will the yeomen do?
Says the Shan Van Vocht;
What should the yeomen do,
But throw off the red and blue,
And swear that they'll be true
To the Shan Van Vocht?

And what colour will they wear?
Says the Shan Van Vocht;
What colour will they wear?
Says the Shan Van Vocht;
What colour should be seen
Where our fathers' homes have been,
But our own immortal Green?
Says the Shan Van Vocht.

And will Ireland then be free?
Says the Shan Van Vocht;
Will Ireland then be free?
Says the Shan Van Vocht;
Yes! Ireland shall be free,
From the centre to the sea;
Then hurrah for Liberty!
Says the Shan Van Vocht.

and the great expedition then preparing for the invasion of Ireland. A fortnight later, he was giving messages for Oliver Bond, Richard MacCormack, etc., to MacSheehy, before the latter embarked in a "safe American" vessel to tell the republicans in Ireland what was forward at Brest.

There is no more dramatic or moving narration in all history, than that set forth in Tone's "Journals" dealing with the Hoche expedition. Those vivid pages make us actually live through all the events they commemorate. We share his exasperation at the unaccountable delays, his exultation when he saw his cherished dreams at length realised, and on board the "Indomptable" he set sail for the land of his heart's desire. The expedition consisted of forty-three sail under Admiral Morand de Galles and Bouvet, with an army of fifteen thousand men under General Hoche, one of the greatest generals in Europe, and General Grouchy. It had on board abundance of stores and artillery, and arms for 45,000 men.

But treachery seems to have been at work from the start, and if Tone knew some of the things we know now, much that puzzled him might have been explained to him. Since French ministers and French generals were tempted by English gold and fell,[7] can we assume that the virtue of French Admirals was altogether temptation proof. A few very suspicious facts are to be recorded. The English fleet (though the English Government through its spies was quite as well informed of the incidents of the expedition as the promoters themselves) never once showed up to bar its passage. Was it because it was understood that there was no need? A mysterious message, the source of which never was traced (but the purport of which was obvious), reached the Irish leaders shortly after MacSheehy's arrival, stating that the expedition was postponed. The French fleet had only been a day at sea when the frigate, the "Fraternité," having General Hoche on board, as well as Admiral Morand de Galles, got separated from its companions—and by some very curious fatality never reached the Irish coast at all—but rejoined its companions, safe and sound, when the remnants of the expedition returned to Brest in January.[8] At daybreak on the

[7] Barthélemy, the French minister in Switzerland, with whom, in the summer of 1796, Lord Edward Fitzgerald and Arthur O'Connor conducted the negotiations which led to the expedition, was a *paid* agent of Pitt. Many of the French Generals like Pichegru were also in the pay of England. When Doctor MacNevin went to Hamburg as an envoy of the United Men all his proceedings were carefully retailed to the English Government and the Memoir he wrote for the French Directory passed straight into the hands of Pitt who submitted it to the Irish Executive.

[8] "I believe," writes Tone, "it is the first instance of an Admiral in a clean frigate, with moderate weather, and moonlight night, parting company with his fleet." But he does not seem to have allowed himself to entertain the suspicion we cannot avoid, viz., that General Hoche was the victim of a trick. Tone blamed him, however, for not embarking on the flagship with his staff.

21st December, Tone was looking once more with emotions one may not describe on the "fair hills of holy Ireland." At eight in the morning of the 22nd his ship was at the mouth of Bantry Bay. "I am now so near the shore," he writes later that day, "that I can see distinctly two old castles, yet I am utterly uncertain whether I shall ever set foot on it." The following day, so desperate was he, that he proposed to head a landing himself and asked General Chérin to give him "the Legion de France," a company of the *artillerie légère* and as many officers as desired to come as Volunteers in the expedition, with what arms and stores remained, and to land them in Sligo Bay. The proposal appealed to the gallantry of the French officers—and on Christmas eve Grouchy determined to land with the force he had.

What a strange Christmas that must have been for Tone—so near the land "that he could in a manner touch the sides of Bantry Bay with his right and left hand," yet conscious how doubtful it was that he should ever tread again the sacred soil of Ireland. What thoughts were his, when, wakened by the wind at two o'clock on Christmas morning, he paced the galley in his great coat "devoured by the most gloomy reflections."

That night, at "half after six, in a heavy gale of wind," orders came to the "Indomptable" from Admiral Bouvet "to cut her cable and put to sea instantly." "Our first idea," writes Tone, "was that it might be an English frigate lurking in the bottom of the bay, which took advantage of the storm and darkness of the night to make her escape, and wished to separate our squadron by this stratagem; for it seemed incredible that an Admiral should cut and run in this manner without any previous signal of any kind to warn the fleet, and that the first notice we should have of its intention should be his hailing us in this extraordinary manner with such unexpected and peremptory orders."

The brave Captain Bedout and officers on board the "Indomptable" refused at first to accept the orders as genuine, and on the 27th December, a council of war was held, at which a plan of Tone's for a landing at the mouth of the Shannon was carefully discussed. But a frightful storm that arose the same night made any further effort impossible and on the morning of the 29th the Commander made the signal to steer for France.

The Bantry Bay expedition was ended. "England had not had such an escape since the Spanish Armada."

Wolfe Tone's Autobiography.
Barrington: Personal Sketches.
MacNevin: Pieces of Irish History.
Lecky: History of Ireland in the Eighteenth Century.

CHAPTER LIX

The Rising of 1798

After the failure of the "Bantry Bay Expedition" there were many who thought the United Irishmen ought to take the field themselves without waiting for foreign aid—and during the course of 1797 this opinion gained ground, especially in the North. But the Dublin men, Thomas Addis Emmet, John Keogh, William Murphy, were opposed to it—and their views prevailed when it was learned that through the efforts of the indomitable Tone, a new expedition was being fitted out. This time it was the Dutch, who claimed for themselves the rôle of chief helper in the drama of Ireland's deliverance.

In the meantime Government was making a desperate attempt to break up the United Irishmen, or, failing that, to goad the people into a premature and unsupported rising. In March, General Lake was sent to Ulster to disarm it. The Lord Lieutenant, Camden, in a letter of instructions, gave Lake to understand that he was not to be too squeamish about the means he used, "if the urgency of the case demanded a conduct beyond that which could be sanctioned by the law, the General was not to suffer the cause of justice to be frustrated by the delicacy which might possibly actuate the magistracy."

The hint not to spare "frightfulness" was not lost on General Lake and the "Yeos,"[1] and "Ancient Britons" and "Essex Fencibles" who formed his army. The burning of peaceful homes, the slaughter of old men, women and children, the torturing of prisoners (picketing and half-hanging were familiar forms), the most shocking outrages on women, this was

[1] The "Yeos" were Orangemen and other British Colonists armed by Government.

what General Lake and his heroes interpreted as comprehended in the "conduct beyond that sanctioned by the law," which Viceregal recommendations favoured. Lecky found in the Government archives a letter from one John Giffard, an officer in the Dublin militia, to Under-Secretary Cooke, describing what happened in one of the raids for arms. As his damaging testimony cannot under the circumstances be doubted I select it in preference to other evidence—even that of Lord Moira in the English House of Lords—to show what was done during the disarming of Ulster in the summer of 1797. The scene is laid near Newry where the "Ancient Britons" had their Headquarters. Giffard tells how the "Britons burned a great number of houses, and the object of emulation between them and the Orange Yeomen seems to be who shall do most mischief." He describes an expedition to the mountains in search of arms. His party returned to the main body of the Ancient Britons, "to which," he says, "I was directed by the smoke and flames of burning houses, and by the dead bodies of boys and old men slain by the Britons, though no opposition whatever had been given them, and, as I shall answer to Almighty God, I believe a single gun was not fired, but by the Britons or Yeomanry. I declare there was nothing to fire at, old men, women, and children excepted. Sixteen prisoners were taken and marched to Newry where their captors were asked *why they made any prisoners at all,* meaning that we should have finished them. . . . Two of the Britons desirous to enter a gentleman's house, the yard gate was opened to them by a lad, whom for his civility *they shot and cut in pieces.*"

The perfect discipline of the "United Men" kept the people quiet, and this effect was the more readily obtained, as it was felt their time would come speedily. The Dutch were fitting out a great expedition at the Texel.

It is a sad story, that of the new disappointment caused by the failure of the Dutch expedition to materialise. In May and June a great mutiny broke out in the English fleet, the Mutiny of the Nore. If the Dutch had been ready then—with the United Irishmen in the full perfection of their organisation to cooperate with them after a landing—the cause of Irish liberty would have been surely won. Unfortunately the chance was missed, and the defeat of the Dutch fleet by the English at Camperdown, on the 11th October, put a definite end to the hopes connected with it.

A few weeks previously a blow even heavier fell on the Irish cause—the death of General Hoche.

The disappointments and the sufferings of the tragic year had a bad effect on many of the United Irishmen of the North, who, by this time, were convinced that the cause was doomed to failure, and that it was the part of wise men to save themselves, and what they could, from the impending catastrophe. Accordingly, we find some of them, to their eternal disgrace, selling themselves as spies and informers to the Government.[2] The most noted of these traitors was one Samuel Turner, of Newry, who had fled to Hamburg in June, 1797. Here he was in touch with Madame Matthiessen, a cousin of Lady Edward Fitzgerald (Pamela), through whom the communications of the United Irishmen with the French minister at Hamburg, Reinhardt, were conducted. As a consequence all the plans of the republicans in Ireland and the efforts of their envoys Levins and MacNevin at Hamburg, were at once communicated to the English Government. In Ireland, too, the "battalion of testimony" was numerous and unsuspected. There was the unspeakable Leonard MacNally, who acted in public the part of a patriot barrister, shared with Curran the task of defending the United Irishmen at the trials—and put the knowledge he thus gained at the service of the Government, whose secret pensioner he had been for years. There was MacGuckin, the legal adviser of the Northern leaders, who acted the same part towards his unfortunate clients. There was Reynolds, a sworn "United man," the friend of Lord Edward, there was Magan, the *immaculate* Catholic barrister—the horrible list is too long to finish!

In consequence of information thus received the English Government, early in 1798, arrested Arthur O'Connor and Father Quigley, on their way to France to make a new effort to secure French aid. O'Connor they kept in prison or internment until 1801, but Fr. Quigley they hanged. On the

[2] As it has been a fashion with English and pro-English people falsely to taunt the Irish that informers could always be procured in any of their movements, it is worth while adducing a bit of valuable testimony to the contrast between Irish staunchness and British, in the "United" movement. Gamble, an eminently just-minded man, and an able writer, of British stock, residing in Strabane in the early part of the eighteenth century, knowing intimately both his own stock and the Irish, and evidently well versed in the local United Irish chronicles, gives in his "Tour in Ireland" (published in 1825) striking testimony on the matter. On page 271 of his book he says: "On these occasions the Protestant was almost always the informer. The fidelity of the Catholic could rarely be shaken." And on page 272: "The Government therefore was probably benefited, rather than injured by the share the Protestant had in the rebellion—hanging, as he often did, a dead-weight about the neck of his Catholic associate, restraining his efforts and discovering his plans. * * * Events of that day (at least as far as present generations are concerned) have placed an everlasting bar between the two—the one has no wish to be trusted; but if he had, no inducement, I daresay, would prevail on the other to trust him." However, the latest Irish movement, in which more than a hundred thousand people have conspired, struggled, fought, without a single individual being purchasable by all the gold of England, is the most striking proof of Irish fidelity.—S. M. M.

12th March 1798, acting on information supplied by Reynolds, the Irish Government swooped upon a meeting of the Leinster Directory at the house of Oliver Bond, arrested all those present, and seized their papers, which put them in possession of all their plans. The same day the authorities arrested Thomas Addis Emmet, John Sweetman, Dr. Nevin, Oliver Bond, and issued warrants against Lord Edward Fitzgerald, Richard MacCormack and Sampson—who immediately went "on the run." The two latter escaped to the continent, but nothing would induce Lord Edward to leave Ireland, though strong hints were given to his family (by Lord Clare himself) that the ports were open to him. He knew that the country would rise now, and he was determined that the Commander-in-Chief should not be proclaimed a deserter.

The vacant places in the Directory were filled by Henry and John Sheares, two successful barristers, and Lord Edward, assisted by his sturdy lieutenant, Sam Neilson, was very active in superintending operations. A new promise came from the French that they would send an expeditionary force in May.

On the 30th March, Martial Law was proclaimed all through the country. The most frightful atrocities were committed by the troops under its shelter, for the purpose avowed by Lord Castlereagh himself "to cause a premature rebellion." To the "frightfulness" associated with General Lake's conduct in Ulster in 1797, new terrors were added by the policy of "free quarters." A savage and undisciplined soldiery, mad with lust and drink, were let loose in the pure homes of the countryside, and the land was filled with the cries of ravished women, the shrieks of the victims of pitch cap and triangle, the lamentations of those who saw their homes go up in flames. So dreadful was the conduct of the troops, that their Commander-in-Chief, Sir Ralph Abercrombie, unable to stomach them any longer, resigned. He had previously declared the "army was in a state of licentiousness, which must render it formidable to everyone but the enemy." "Within these twelve months," he writes, on another occasion, "every crime, every cruelty that could be committed by Cossacks and Calmucks has been transacted here."

Whether the French came or not the people could hold out no longer. The insurrection was fixed for the 23rd May, and the signal was to be the stopping of the mail coaches from Dublin.

Four days before the appointed date Lord Edward was taken at Murphy's house in Thomas Street, on information supplied by Magan; and the following day, while he lay in Newgate prison, wounded to death, the two Sheares were betrayed by Captain Armstrong.

On the day of Lord Edward's death, Napoleon definitely abandoned the Irish cause, and set out on his Egyptian campaign.[3]

The insurrection, long delayed in the hope of the promised aid from France, now broke out under the worst possible conditions for success. Left without leaders, is it astonishing that it should have been confined to only a portion of the country, and that the efforts of the counties that "rose" were speedily suppressed? The astonishing thing is to find what these poorly-armed, leaderless people *could* do when they had capable officers. Between 24th and 27th May there were engagements with the military at Naas, Clane, Prosperous, Kilcullen and Monasterevin in Kildare, at Dunboyne and Tara in Meath, at Baltinglass in Wicklow, at Lucan, Rathfarnham, and Tallaght in Dublin. Though the only definite success on the insurgents' side was at Prosperous, where they were capably led by Lieutenant Esmond, they gave such a good account of themselves that Government was very glad to make terms. How these "terms" were kept will be long remembered. Around Gibbet Rath on the Curragh of Kildare, where the assembled insurgents surrendered their arms, having previously obtained a

---

[3] In St. Helena Napoleon expressed bitter regret for this act. He intimated that if he had chosen Ireland instead of Egypt, the current of history could have been radically changed.

For Lord Edward's death—and the blow it was to Ireland—Ethna Carbery sings the lament of Mairin-Ni-Cullinan:—

MAIRIN-NI-CULLINAN
(Ireland's Lament for Lord Edward)

Underneath the shrouding stone,
Where you lie in Death alone,
Can you hear me calling, calling,
In a wild hot gush of woe?
'Tis for you my tears are falling—
For you, *mo Chraoibhin Cno!*

When you stood up in the Green
As beseemed the Geraldine,
Slender sword a-glancing, glancing,
Over you the tender skies,
How the warrior-joy kept dancing,
In your brave bright eyes.

"*'Stór,*" I said, "*A stór ma chroidhe,*
Hope of Mine and Hope of Me,
Take our honour to your keeping,
Bare your swift blade to the Dawn.
Freedom's voice hath roused from sleeping
Máirín-ní-Cullinán."

So I dreamt the Day had come,
Now your ardent lips are dumb,
And the sword is rusty, rusty,
Through a hundred weary years;
All the winds are blowing gusty
With a storm of tears.

"*'Stór,*" I cry, above your bed,
Where I kneel uncomforted—
"Feel you not the battle-anger
Shake the Nations of the World?
While amid the stress and clangour,
Still my Flag is furled.

"Were you here, O Geraldine,
This oblivion had not been."
Thus I mourn you pining, pining,
For the gallant heart long gone.
Whose love was as a true star shining
To Máirín-ní-Cullinán.

promise of "pardon and liberty," they were set upon by Lord Roden, and his mounted "fencibles" and butchered in cold blood!

In the meantime Wexford had "risen," goaded to the step by the atrocities of the Yeos and British troops these let loose. The story of Father John Murphy might stand for the story of Wexford: its efforts for peace, its disinclination to resort to the arbitration of the sword as long as any other choice was left it—and then its sturdy courage, the extraordinary military ability shown by its improvised leaders: priests like Father John Murphy himself or his namesake, Father Michael, Father Philip Roche, and Father Doyle, young farmers like Edmund Kyan or Myles Byrne. It is in the vivid narrative of the latter that we must follow the events of the Wexford campaign—from that Whit Saturday when Father John Murphy "seeing his chapel and his home, like many others of the parish on fire, and in several of them the inhabitants consumed in the flames . . . betook himself to the next wood, where he was soon surrounded by the unfortunate people who had escaped, all came beseeching his Reverence to tell them what was to become of them and their poor families. He answered them abruptly that they had better die courageously in the field than be butchered in their houses; that for his own part, if he had any brave men to join him, he was resolved to sell his life dearly, and prove to those cruel monsters that they should not continue their murders and devastations with impunity. All answered and cried out that they were determined to follow his advice, and to do whatever he ordered. 'Well, then,' he replied, 'we must, when night comes, get armed the best way we can, with pitchforks and other weapons, and attack the Camolin Yeomen cavalry on their way back to Mountmorris, where they will return to pass the night after satisfying their savage rage on the defenceless country people.'"

Father John's plans succeeded—and by the arms taken in the ambush of the Camolin Yeomen that night, and at Camolin Park the next day, his men reinforced their pitchforks with more effective weapons. The following day, Whit Sunday, he won a great victory with his Pikemen on Oulart Hill and followed it with the capture in quick succession of Camolin, Ferns, Enniscorthy, and Wexford. In a few days that whole southeastern country was in the hands of the insurgents except Duncannon Fort and New Ross.

They had three encampments, one at Three Rocks, one seven miles west of Gorey, and one at Vinegar Hill, just outside Enniscorthy. An attempt was made on New Ross on the 5th June but it failed after desperate fighting and severe losses on both sides. A few days later Gorey and Carnew were captured and the way to Arklow lay open. This town was assaulted on the 9th June, but by this time strong reinforcements had been sent to the military from Dublin. The battle lasted from four in the morning until late at night, but the death of Father Michael Murphy, charging bravely at the head of his column, turned what was on the point of being a success into a defeat.

Government made a huge effort to stamp out the flames, and General Lake, who had succeeded Abercrombie as Commander-in-Chief, took the field in person. On June 21st the insurgents were attacked by overwhelming forces and defeated at their last stronghold in Vinegar Hill.

Even Castlereagh was roused to unwilling admiration of the martial qualities and achievements of the "boys of Wexford." "He could never have believed," he said, "that untrained peasants could have fought so well." Compared with their exploits the Ulstermen, who had been the "backbone" of the United Irish movement, and its most ardent advocates, made a poor showing. It was not until the 7th of June that Ulster made any move. The explanation is that the Ulster leader, Simms, got cowardly and shirked his post. The Rev. Mr. Dickson, who was appointed to take his place, was arrested, and only that the gallant Henry Joy McCracken rose from a bed of illness to step into the gap, Ulster's disgrace would have been complete. Under McCracken an attack was made on Antrim town on 7th June, which was retained by the military after a desperate struggle. A few days later McCracken was taken prisoner, and after a summary trial, was executed in Belfast. He, for one, had faithfully kept the oath made on the bright June day three years earlier when he had stood with Tone on Cave Hill—and swore to sacrifice everything even life itself for Ireland's liberty.

The only other important engagements in Ulster were at Saintfield and Newtownards, where the insurgents were successful, and at Ballinahinch where Monroe and his United Men were defeated by General Nugent.

News of those events came in due time to Tone in France, and made him frantic with anxiety and impatience to be with his comrades in Ireland, sharing their desperate fortunes. The last entry in his Journal, written on the 20th June—his thirty-fifth birthday, and the eve of the Battle of Vinegar Hill—shows him straining every nerve to get the dilatory French authorities to hurry forward the promised aid while the Irish were still in the field. General Grouchy (who had never forgiven himself for not throwing Bouvet overboard in Bantry Bay when the latter, opposing the landing, lost the greatest chance France ever knew) did all he could to second him; but General Kilmaine was more inclined to take the Minister of Marine's point of view and defer the expedition until it could be carried out on "the grand scale," and at a more favourable opportunity. Tone pointed out that it was now or never. An expedition on a "grand scale" was all very well, but "5,000 men that could be sent were better than 50,000 that could not." The time to assist the Irish was when they were still fighting; "in three months it might be too late, and the forces then sent, if the Irish were overpowered in the meantime, find themselves unsupported, and in their turn, be overpowered by the English!"

By the beginning of July these arguments had their way with the the Directory. Tone was called to Paris to consult with the Ministers of War and Marine in the organisation of a new expedition. Tone's son explains clearly which were the proposals now accepted.

The plan adopted was to dispatch small detachments from several ports, in the hope of keeping up the insurrection, until an opportunity should be found for landing the main body under General Kilmaine. General Humbert, with about 1,000 men, was quartered for this purpose at La Rochelle, General Hardy with 3,000 at Brest, and Kilmaine with 9,000 remained in reserve.

But the preparations were very slow, owing to the poverty of the French Government; and Humbert, a gallant soldier of fortune, whose heart was better than his head, fired by the recitals of the Irish refugees (who came to France in large numbers with awful tales of Irish suffering), and urged on by the impetuous old Napper Tandy, determined to act on his own responsibility. Towards the end of August he requisitioned money and stores from the merchants and magistrates of La Rochelle, and "embarking on board a few frigates and transports, with 1,000 men, 1,000 spare muskets, 1,000 guineas, and a few pieces of artillery, he compelled the Captains to set sail for the most desperate attempt which is perhaps, recorded in history." Three Irishmen accompanied him: Matthew Tone, a brother of Theobald, Bartholomew Teeling, and Sullivan. The little expedition landed at Killala on 22nd August. That town, as well as Ballina, was taken without difficulty, and on the 27th of the month the French inflicted a great defeat on the "Red Coats" of General Lake at Castlebar. So swiftly did the English soldiers run from the desperate charge of the French and their Irish allies that the battle is known to this day as "the Races of Castlebar."

In the meantime Cornwallis had landed in Ireland with immense reinforcements. Hastening to Lake's aid, he met Humbert at Ballinamuck (8th September), overpowered him by the mere force of numbers and compelled his surrender. The French soldiers taken were treated as prisoners of war. Their Irish auxiliaries were slaughtered. Matthew Tone and Bartly Teeling were courtmartialed and hanged.

The Directory were naturally thrown into the greatest perplexity by the news of Humbert's proceedings. They determined to hurry up the dispatch of the force under General Hardy. "But such was the state of the

French navy and arsenals that it was not until the 20th September that this small expedition, consisting of one sail of the line, and eight frigates under Commodore Bompard and 3,000 men under General Hardy were ready for sailing. Four Irishmen accompanied the expedition: Wolfe Tone, Corbett, Maguire, and Hamilton.

Tone had absolutely no delusions as to the expedition's chances of success. But he had said that if the French Government sent only a corporal's guard he would go with them. Such was the wretched indiscretion of the Government, that, before his departure, he read in a Paris newspaper, the *Bien Informé,* a detailed account of the whole armament, where his own name was mentioned in full letters, with the circumstance of his being embarked on board the *Hoche.*

The flotilla, which had taken a wide sweep to avoid the English fleet, met with contrary winds and was scattered. After twenty days' cruise the *Hoche,* with two frigates, the *Loire* and the *Résolue,* and one schooner, the *Biche,* arrived off Loch Swilly. An English squadron under Sir John Borlace Warren, consisting of six sail of the line, one *Razee* of sixty guns, and two frigates, instantly bore down on them. The *Hoche,* a large and heavy man-of-war, had no chance of escape, so Bompard signalled the two frigates and schooner to make off through the shallow water and he, himself alone "to honour the flag of his country by a desperate defence." At that moment a boat came from the *Biche* for his last orders. That ship had the best chance to get off. The French officers all supplicated Tone to embark on board of her. "Our contest is hopeless," they observed, "we will be prisoners of war, but what of you?" "Shall it be said," replied he, "that I fled while the French were fighting the battle of my country?"

And so, through the long hours of that desperate engagement wherein the *Hoche* stood up alone to the guns of five heavy British ships, he commanded one of the batteries, fighting with a courage which even these brave Frenchmen had never seen equalled.

"During six hours the *Hoche* sustained the fire of a whole fleet, till her masts and rigging were swept away, her scuppers flowed with blood, her wounded filled the cock-pit, her scattered ribs yawned at each new stroke and let in five feet of water in the hold, her rudder was carried off, and she floated a dismantled wreck on the waters; her sails and cordage hung in shreds, nor could she reply with a single gun from her dismounted batteries to the unabating cannonade of the enemy. At length she struck," and her *personnel* surrendered.

At first, Tone, who had become in language and appearance a regular Frenchman, was not recognised among the French officers. His discovery was the act of a college friend of the old days in Trinity, one Sir George Hill. Narrowly scanning the features of the French officers who sat at breakfast at Letterkenny with the Earl of Cavan, he stopped before one and said, "Mr. Tone, I am very happy to see you." Cool as ever, Tone rose from his seat with a courteous: "Sir George, I am happy to see you, how are Lady Hill and your family?" A moment later he was being put in irons by military in the next room. The indignity roused him to a momentary outburst. Flinging off his uniform, he cried, "These fetters shall never degrade the revered insignia of the free nation which I have served." Then a new thought struck him—and he stretched forth his limbs proudly for their chains: "For the cause which I have embraced, I feel prouder to wear these chains than if I were decorated with the star and garter of England."

For the credit of human nature one would fain believe that even the Earl of Cavan and Sir George Hill and their followers would have been shamed into admiration at his generous and noble act. Alas! no indignity was spared him—and he was compelled to make the big journey from Letterkenny to Dublin, on horseback, with his legs pinioned beneath the horse's belly and his arms manacled! On reaching Dublin he was thrown to the tender mercies of Major Sandys in the Provost's prison—whence he was only taken for his court-martial on the 10th November.

He made a gallant figure as he stood before his judges in the uniform of a French Colonel, making his last profession of faith in the principles to which he had devoted all that was his to give. "From my earliest youth I have regarded the connection between Ireland and Great Britain as the curse of the Irish nation, and felt convinced, that while it lasted, this country would never be free or happy. In consequence, I determined to apply all the powers which my individual efforts could move, in order to separate the two countries. That Ireland was not able, of herself, to throw off the yoke, I knew. I therefore sought for aid wherever it was to be found. . . . Under the flag of the French Republic I originally engaged with a view to save and liberate my own country. For that purpose I have encountered the chances of war amongst strangers: for that purpose I have repeatedly braved the terrors of the ocean, covered as I knew it to be with the triumphant fleets of that Power which it was my glory and my duty to oppose. I have sacrificed all my views in life; I have courted poverty; I have left a beloved wife unprotected, and children whom I adored, fatherless. After such sacrifices, in a cause which I have always considered as the cause of justice and freedom—it is no great effort at this day to add the sacrifice of my life!"

How that final sacrifice was made all the world knows. He had made but one request of his foes, that in deference to the uniform he wore he should be adjudged the death of a soldier. Even this poor favour was denied him. He was condemned to die the death of "a traitor" within forty-eight hours of the promulgation of his sentence. To save himself from that crowning indignity, while in the winter night the soldiers were erecting the gallows for him before his window, he inflicted a deep wound across his own throat with a penknife he had managed to secrete. Of this wound he died in great agony a week later—19th November, 1798.

They buried him at dead of night in the old cemetery at Bodenstown, by the side of his brother, Matthew, who had died for the same glorious cause a few weeks earlier.

And there, side by side, those two mangled bodies—each broken so cruelly in the conqueror's murder machine—await the Resurrection—in the "green grave" which Ireland cherishes as the most precious thing she owns.

Authorities on the 1793–1803 period:
Madden: Lives and Times of the United Irishmen.
Tone: Autobiography of Theobald Wolfe Tone.
Concannon (Mrs. Helena): Women of '98.
Fitzpatrick: Secret Service under Pitt, and The Sham Squire.
Kavanagh: Rebellion of '98.
Rev. Mr. Gordon: History of the Rebellion.
Mitchel: History of Ireland.
Fitzpatrick: Ireland before the Union.

CHAPTER LX

The Union[1]

Although Ireland was officially conquered to Britain centuries before, the Island was alleged to have a Parliament of its own, under the British Crown, up to the year 1800.

It was, of course, a Parliament of, and for, the British in Ireland. The mere Irish had no say in it—except for an insignificantly brief period. Had no right even to vote for a member of it. It was not considered that they whose land this was, and who constituted six-sevenths of the population of the land, could presume to take even the humblest part in governing their own country. The Parliament was for half a million British in Ireland—to hold three million Irish in subjection. Moreover, of the 300 members, only 72 were really elected. Three-fourths of its members were just appointed by the Borough owners, the British Lords who owned Irish towns.

It was only at rare intervals that the Anglo-Irish who owned and ran this Parliament dared assert their right to make it a Parliament in reality, as well as in name. For centuries it was held in the stranglehold of Poyning's Law—a law which forbade it to initiate any legislation—only gave it liberty to legislate under the direction and command of the English Parliament—to pass into law whatever the English Parliament recommended—and to refrain from legislating upon all things that the English Parliament forbade it to legislate upon.

Under this state of things naturally Ireland's woes increased with the years. Just before the Anglo-Irish Parliament, in 1782, took heart to shake

[1] This chapter, with trifling change, is taken from *Ireland's Case,* by Seumas MacManus.

from its shoulders its Old Man of the Sea, the English Parliament which paralysed it, Hely Hutchinson, speaking in the Irish House of Commons (in 1779) said: "Can the history of any other fruitful country on the globe, enjoying peace for eighty years, and not visited by plague or pestilence, produce so many recorded instances of the poverty and the wretchedness, of the reiterated want and misery of the lower order of people? There is no such example in ancient or modern story."

In 1782, as we saw, when Britain's hands were filled with an American problem, Henry Grattan and the great army of Ireland's Volunteers, 100,000 strong, demanded the independence of their Parliament. And as they had in their hands, when making the request, a hundred thousand muskets, their request was graciously granted. During the succeeding years, this Anglo-Irish Parliament, acting independently of the British Parliament, was enabled to do wonderful things for the restoration of Ireland's commerce and manufactures. Many of the disabilities of the Irish Catholics, too, were, under it, removed—and an Irishman was acknowledged to have some citizen rights.

But, it did not suit England's book to have any body of people in Ireland, even their own Anglo-Irish kin, running Ireland with profit to Ireland—and consequently a curtailment of English profit. So, the mistake must be corrected. And the best way to correct it was bodily to remove the cause of the trouble. Parliament, both in reality and in name, must be taken from Ireland altogether. So, Prime Minister Pitt of England conspired with his good instruments, Cornwallis, Lord Lieutenant of Ireland, and Castlereagh, the Irish Secretary, to attain the desired end. For this splendidly corrupt object Pitt fortunately had, in Cornwallis and Castlereagh, a pair of splendidly corrupt tools.

To undermine the prestige of the Irish Parliament and prove its incompetence for governing Ireland, they first goaded the Irish people into a premature rebellion. And they then launched their campaign for giving to the English Parliament the sole right of directly governing this Island.

That the Anglo-Irish inhabitants of the Island would not easily yield their right Pitt and his instruments knew well. But that a large portion of their representatives was purchasable, they divined. So they set themselves enthusiastically to the congenial work of bribing and debasing right and left, and buying men's souls.

Lies, perjury, and fraud were the official stock-in-trade during all of Britain's connection with Ireland. But there was never another period in which so much baseness was crowded into so little time as now, when they were debasing their own kin and robbing them of their "rights." No other scandal of British administration, before or since, ever equalled this one of buying the Union. The immediate chief instruments, Cornwallis and Castlereagh, were probably no worse than any other English administrators in Ireland—only that this large job gave them an exceptional opportunity to distinguish themselves.[2]

Cornwallis, through all the vile business, took the superior stand of the hypocrite who thinks he conceals his hypocrisy beneath the cloak of frankness. He writes to a friend, "My occupation is of the most unpleasant nature, bargaining and jobbing with the most corrupt people under Heaven" (the Anglo-Irish). "I despise and hate myself for ever engaging in such dirty work." In another place he confesses that he is "involved in this dirty business beyond all bearing."

The people were wheedled, coaxed, threatened, and bribed, into signing petitions in favor of Union with England. Barrington tells us that, under promise of pardon, felons in the jails were got to sign the Union petition. Everyone holding a government job in the country had not only to sign the petition himself, but was compelled to make his relatives and the relatives of their relatives sign it likewise.

Not merely those who held positions under the government were required to do this; but to every man who hoped or dreamt of ever standing chance of a position under the government, it was plainly intimated that he and his relatives' relatives must become petitioners. Mixed bribes and threats were scattered over the land like seed corn—falling upon, sticking to, and germinating in thousands upon thousands of every rank from the public hangman all the way up to the Archbishop of the Established Church.

The pro-British historian, Lecky, says, "Obscure men in unknown political places were dismissed because they or some of their relatives declined to support it." He says, "The whole force of Government patronage in all branches was steadily employed. The formal and authoritative announcement was made, that, though defeated Session after Session and Parliament after Parliament—the act of Union would always be reintroduced—and that support of it would hereafter be considered the main test by which all claims to government favor would be determined."—"Everything in the government of the Crown in Ireland," Lecky further states, "in the church, in the army, in the law, in the revenue, was uniformly and steadily

[2] Castlereagh indeed partly redeemed himself by living to cut his throat.

devoted to the single purpose of carrying the Union. From the great noblemen who were bought for marquisates and ribands; from the (Protestant) Archbishop of Cashel who agreed to support the Union on being promised the reversion of the See of Dublin and a seat in the Imperial House of Lords, the virus of corruption extended and descended through every rank and title, and saturated the political system, including even crowds of obscure men who had it in their power to assist or obstruct addresses on the subject."

Men who dared be independent and stand for their rights were hounded and persecuted and dismissed from office. Even the highest in rank, such as the Chancellor of the Exchequer, and a Prime Sergeant and Privy Chancellor, were kicked out for daring to deny England's divine right to do wrong.

Men who refused to be bribed were forced out of their seats in the Irish Parliament by every vile means known to vile men. Their own instruments, their own official aides, even, were put into office and put into Parliament for the openly avowed purpose of voting away Ireland's rights. Englishmen who never before had given any thought to Ireland, were actually imported to sit as Irish members of Parliament—and vote away Ireland's Parliament to England.[3]

They overawed patriotic people who ventured to make any protest against the proposed Union. Barrington relates how, on the occasion of an Anti-Union meeting in King's County, Darley, the High Sheriff, and Major Rogers (acting of course under instructions from Dublin Castle) placed two six pounders, charged with grape shot, opposite the Court-house where the meeting was being held—bringing England's logic to bear on the misguided ones who thought they could better know than England, what was for Ireland's benefit.

The Habeas Corpus Act was suspended.

Martial law was proclaimed.

England stationed in Ireland, 126,000 soldiers.

All constitutional guarantee was annulled.

The use of torture was frequently availed of.

Meetings of the people were dispersed by military force.

---

[3] Some of these latter rascals never saw—sometimes hardly knew—the name of the Irish Borough for which they sat. When one of them, one day, presented himself at the English House of Parliament and requested some privilege that was of courtesy accorded there to members of the Irish Parliament, he was asked for what Irish Borough he sat. "By Heaven," he replied, "the name of the devilish place 'as escaped me.—But if you bring me the Irish Directory I believe I can pick it out."

Offices and commands were trafficked in.

Every foul device that the most ingeniously mean-minded tools could contrive was employed against Irish liberty—or Anglo-Irish liberty.

And by use of all conceivable and inconceivable mean devices they managed, at length, to secure a bare majority in favour of the Union—162 out of 303 members. One hundred and sixteen of these 162 were their own salaried tools—placemen.

They carried their "Union." It has been stated that as much as eight thousand pounds was paid for one vote. Henry Grattan is authority for it that, of those who voted in favour of the Union with England, not more than seven were unbribed. Cornwallis had no illusions about the quality of the men whom he purchased—knew right well that they could be just as faithless to him, despite his gold, as they were to their adopted country, despite their duty. He wrote, "I believe that half of our majority would be as much delighted as any of our opponents, if the measure could be defeated."

Place, title, and gold, were the inducements for sacrificing Ireland at England's bidding. As reward for good work done or to be done—twenty-eight Irish peerages were created. Six Irish peers got English peerages. Twenty Irish peers were elevated in rank. New and lucrative jobs, offices, government appointments, were created—for bestowal on those who rendered "services."

In those days the boroughs in Ireland were "owned" by Lordly proprietors who put in for them such puppet members of Parliament as they pleased. In 1782, out of 300 members, only 72 were really elected—and of course only one-seventh of the people in Ireland (the British portion) got a chance at electing those. This ownership came to be recognised by law! And to compensate eighty titled Borough owners in Ireland (who owned one hundred and sixty members) an act was passed appropriating for them £1,260,000—being at the rate of about £8,000 for each member.

And, crowning joke of all the grim jokes played upon Ireland by England, this million and quarter for greasing the groove down which Ireland's Parliament was to be skidded to England—was added to the Irish National Debt!

Lord Ely, who had at first been opposed to the Union, but came finally to see the light and voted for it, received £45,000 for his Boroughs.

These moneys were paid as "compensation" for "disturbance" caused, or to be caused, or in danger of being caused, by the Union. And not only Anglo-Irishmen but likewise every pocket-picking Englishman and hungry

Scotchman who could get near it, fought and struggled and mauled one another, for the chance of getting a hand in the Compensation bag.[4]

And this wonderful story of Ireland's eager Union with England is a fair illustration of England's clean handedness, clean mindedness, in dealing with the island that was and is "dependent on and protected by England."

The carrying of the Union reflected nearly as much credit upon England's nice honour, as did the Treaty of Limerick upon the pledged faith and honour of the British Crown.

Barrington: The Rise and Fall of the Irish Nation.
" Personal Sketches.
Swift MacNeill: The Irish Parliament.
Lecky: History of Ireland in the Eighteenth Century.

---

[4] Barrington records that even the necessary woman of the English Privy Council asked "compensation" from Ireland for the extra trouble which the influx of Irish Privy Councillors would cause in her department!

And the Lord Lieutenant's official rat catcher insisted on the right to get his paw in the bag as compensation for "decrease of employment." Why the Union with England should affect this gentleman's employment is not stated—but it is easy to suppose that he foresaw the certainty of droves of British rats quitting the sinking ship.

Daniel O'Connell once said, that he could not, under Heaven, apprehend how it was that they forgot to charge against Ireland the price of the razor with which Castlereagh afterwards cut his throat.

CHAPTER LXI

Robert Emmet

When the Insurgents had laid down their arms, the country was given over to further horrors. The idea was to break the spirit so thoroughly, by a calculated campaign of "frightfulness," that Ireland should never dare to dream of liberty again, or offer the slightest resistance to the new chains that were being forged for her in the "Legislative Union" with England.

So all through the bright summer days that followed the day of "Vinegar Hill" the shrieks of tortured men came from the Prevot Prison in the Royal Barracks, Dublin, where Major Sandys had set up his triangles, or from the "riding school" in Marlborough Street, where Mr. John Claudius Beresford carried on his pitch-cappings and picketings, his half hangings and his lacerations. Day after day were court martials, followed immediately by executions. Day after day the most terrible tales reached the Capital of the atrocities committed by the militia, the "Yeos" and the "Hessians" in the districts where they were now supreme. The statistics preserved by Cloney, for Wexford alone, of women violated, and then bayoneted or shot, of unarmed folk slaughtered in the fields and along the roads, of whole families burned alive in their cabins, of wounded men incinerated in the hospital at Enniscorthy (which went ablaze through *a mere accident*—"the bed clothes being set on fire by the wadding of the soldiers' guns, who were shooting the patients in their beds"), represent a degree of human suffering which even at this distance of time makes us sick to read of.

What of those who in their prison cells—the State Prisoners like Thomas Addis Emmet, Thomas Russell, John Sweetman, Arthur O'Connor, Samuel Neilson—were hearing of them from day to day? Does one wonder that when a proposal came from Government that these horrors would be stopped, on certain conditions when men of honour could accept, they felt it their duty to explore the avenues to peace thus indicated? On the initiative of Mr. Dobbs, acting for the Government, seventy-three prisoners in Newgate, Kilmainham and Bridewell, put their names to a paper engaging to give every information in their power as to the whole internal transactions of the United Irishmen, and their negotiations with foreign states, with the proviso that they were not by naming or describing to implicate any person whatever. In return the executions were to be stopped, and the State Prisoners allowed to emigrate to a country to be agreed upon between them and the Government.

This agreement was kept with the most scrupulous exactitude by the State Prisoners. But nobody who knows the Government's record for tearing up "scraps of paper" will be very much surprised to learn that its conditions were grossly violated by the Irish Executive—even though one of its own members, Lord Clare, had thus expressed himself to one among the prisoners, who raised a doubt as to the Executive's good faith: "Gentlemen, it comes to this—a Government that breaks faith with you could not stand, and ought not be allowed to stand."

The ink was hardly dry upon the paper when one of the condemned prisoners, Byrne (to save whose life was the immediate object of the treaty), was, in flagrant violation of its provisions, led forth to execution. The other, Oliver Bond, was murdered in prison.

The State Prisoners, themselves, who signed the agreement were (also in violation of it) kept in prison, or internment in Fort George, Scotland, during the remaining four years of the war then raging with France. Worse still—though the fact will surprise no one acquainted with the records of English propaganda—a garbled account of the whole business, very injurious to the United Irishmen, was sent forth broadcast; and the prisoners' remonstrations were met by a peremptory message from Lord Lieutenant Cornwallis that if they dared to say another word he would annul the agreement, and go forward with wholesale executions.

This breach of faith on the part of Government caused the State Prisoners to consider the contract null and void on their side also; and as may readily be surmised, they looked eagerly around, after their liberation from Fort George in the summer of 1802, for a chance to strike a blow once more for Irish Independence.

Everybody knew that the war between France and England, to which the peace of Amiens had put a temporary cessation, would soon break out again; and it was common belief likewise that when the war did break out, an invasion by Bonaparte either of England or Ireland would be attempted.

The United Irishmen, both on the continent and in Ireland, therefore (and in spite of all that had happened they were still numerous and powerful in the homeland), were prepared to sacrifice their just resentment against France for her failure to keep her engagements with them in '98, and enter into a new alliance with her. They had recruited unexpected allies in Ireland, itself, from among certain statesmen and politicians, who had formerly been their bitterest enemies, but who now saw themselves, to an equal degree, the victims of English intrigue—left high and dry by the "Legislative Union." It is morally certain, indeed, that though these statesmen kept themselves well and safely in the background during the events which make 1803 as tragic a memory as 1798, they took the initiative in the secret negotiations which led to them. Who were they? Shall we ever know more than Robert Emmet (who paid the penalty of their deeds) has chosen to tell us of them as he stood in the dock, making his immortal appeal to the yet unborn tribunal of his liberated country's judgment? "When I came to Ireland I found the business ripe for execution. I was asked to join in it. I took time to consider, and after mature deliberation I became one of the Provisional Government; and there then was my Lords, an agent from the United Irishmen and Provisional Government in Paris, negotiating with the French Government to obtain from them an aid sufficient to accomplish the separation of Ireland from Great Britain; the preliminary to which assistance has been a guarantee to Ireland similar to that which Franklin obtained for America." And again: "I have been charged with that importance in the efforts to emancipate my country as to be considered the keystone of the combination of Irishmen, or as it has been expressed, 'the life and blood of this conspiracy.' You do me honour overmuch; you have given to the subaltern all the credit of the superior. There are men concerned in this conspiracy, who are not only superior to me but even to your own conceptions of yourself, my lord; men before the splendour of whose genius and virtues I should bow with respectful deference, and who would not deign to call you friend—who would not disgrace themselves by shaking your blood-stained hand."

The Agent of the United Irishmen in Paris, referred to above, was Thomas Addis Emmet, who left Brussels for the French Capital early in 1803, to act in that capacity on definite instructions from the Provisional Government in Ireland. We possess in his diary from the 30th of May, 1803, to the 10th of March, 1804, with its detailed account of his transactions with the French Government, then controlled by Bonaparte and Talleyrand, all the evidence required to prove that the Rising of 1803, so far from being, as Lord Castlereagh estimated it, "the wild and contemptible project of a young man of heated and enthusiastic imagination" was the well thought out plan of long-headed men and had *a priori* good reason to promise success.

In the first place there was an absolute promise on the part of France of a large expeditionary force to aid the Rising in Ireland. In the second, there was an understanding with, and guarantees of cooperation from the revolutionary societies in England and Scotland. In the third, there were pledges from men of the highest social, military and political standing in Ireland to aid the movement with money, moral and other backing. If ever an effort for Irish Liberty seemed destined to succeed, it was that to which Robert Emmet found himself committed when he returned to Ireland, after his "Grand Tour" on the continent, in the Autumn of 1802.

His first care, after he became organiser for the Provisional Government (which, as has been already said, had been formed before his return) was to get in touch with surviving fighters of '98, men like Myles Byrne of Wexford, and Jimmie Hope of Belfast. It is to the narratives of these two in particular that we owe our best knowledge of his aims and hopes, and the methods he adopted to attain them.

His primary object was to get the country organised and armed, ready to cooperate with the French landing. The organisation of the counties was left to tried men of local influence, and as early as the Autumn of 1802 Emmet was able to assure John Keogh and John Philpot Curran that "nineteen counties could be relied upon." Very influential promises of help came from the North in particular, and the business of procuring arms went briskly forward. Early in 1803 Thomas Russell, his nephew-in-law, Hamilton, and Quigley, came over from France to help, and the greatest hopes were entertained that Russell's influence in Ulster would keep it straight this time, at least—though it had failed so grievously in '98.

Emmet's own work was mainly confined to Dublin, but he was in close touch with the men of Carlow, Wicklow, Wexford, through his friends Michael Dwyer and Myles Byrne, and with the men of Kildare through one Bernard Duggan and others. Alas, Mr. Bernard Duggan, as we now know, was a paid Castle spy; and all the preparations for the Rising were faithfully retailed to his employer, the Under Secretary Mr. Alexander Marston, who let them go forward, having the comfortable assurance that he could circumvent them the moment it suited his own purpose!

On the 16th July an explosion took place in a house in Patrick Street, which Emmet had taken as a depot for arms and explosives. This event, which made him regard the discovery of his plans as imminent, caused him to fix an early date for the Rising without waiting for the promised French aid.

It may have been that Russell had infected him with his own fears that Bonaparte was only playing with the Irish, and this may have been an additional motive for hurrying him on. Assurances came from all over the country that if Dublin rose the rest of Ireland would speedily follow.

Saturday, the 23rd of July, was the day arranged for the Rising in Dublin, in which the Wicklow, Kildare and Wexford men were to assist. The plans included an attack not only on Dublin Castle, but on the Pigeon House Fort and the Artillery Barracks at Island Bridge. But on the day appointed it was discovered that only a small fraction of the men expected to help had turned up. "I expected," Emmet himself tells us, "two thousand to assemble at Costigan's Mills—the grand place of assembly. The evening before the Wicklow men failed through their officer. The Kildare men, who were to act particularly with me, came in, and at five o'clock went off again, from the canal harbour, on a report from two of their officers that Dublin would not act.

"In Dublin itself it was given out by some treacherous or cowardly person that it (the Rising) was postponed until Wednesday. The time of assembly was from 6 to 9, and at 9 instead of 2,000 there were only 80 men assembled."

The romantic sequel of Robert Emmet's story has given to the occurrences of the 23d of July an importance which the men who organised the conspiracy of which they were only an incident, did not recognise. One part of the plan, the Rising in Dublin, had miscarried, through no fault of Robert Emmet's; but if the French had been true to their plighted word the rest of the country would have risen later, according to plan, and the dream to which the gallant youth sacrificed fortune, life, and love, might yet have come true.

But the French failed their Irish allies once more, and Thomas Addis Emmet, though he still continued for a time his negotiations with the agents of the First Consul, and though he actually saw an Irish Legion embodied, and Irish colours prepared for an expeditionary force, had at length to convince himself that "Bonaparte was the worst enemy Ireland ever had," a man who played with her hopes and utilised them for his own purpose. In 1804 Emmet shook the soil of France from his feet forever, and set sail for the great Western Republic where fame, success and happiness, and in the fulness of time, an honoured tomb were awaiting him.

As for his brother, Robert, when he saw the blood of Lord Kilwarden stain the stones of that Dublin street, he dispersed his followers, and sought out Michael Dwyer in the Wicklow hills. Dwyer and his men (whose failure to be present at the *rendezvous* was due to a gross dereliction of duty on the part of the man charged with the message for them) urged that an attempt should be made on the neighbouring towns, but Emmet determined to do nothing more until the promised French aid had arrived. To expedite its coming he sent Myles Byrne to France with an urgent message to his brother, Thomas Addis.

Before Myles Byrne had arrived in Paris, Robert had been arrested by Major Sirr at Harold's Cross, to whose dangerous neighbourhood he had been drawn by an overpowering desire to see once more his "bright love" the exquisite Sarah Curran. On the 19th of September, two days after Byrne had delivered his message to Thomas Addis, Robert Emmet stood in the dock in Green Street, uttering that immortal oration which no one who loves great poetry or high passion can ever read without all that is best in him flaming up at the contact of its fire. On the 20th of September the sacrifice was consummated. The brave youth was publicly beheaded on a Dublin street.

Authorities:

Madden: Lives of the United Irishmen.
Myles Byrne's Memoirs.
Thomas Addis Emmet: The Emmet Family.
O'Donoghue: Life of Robert Emmet.
Mitchel: History of Ireland.

CHAPTER LXII

Daniel O'Connell

Throughout almost the first half of the nineteenth century Ireland's history is reflected in the life of Daniel O'Connell.

O'Connell was thirty-three years of age when his national career began. That was in 1808, when the Catholic Committee, which sought to get for Catholic citizens their rights, began to be riven between the aristocratic advocates of "dignified silence," led by the aged Keogh, and the revolutionary advocates of agitation, of whom O'Connell assumed the spokesmanship.

The great man was born in Cahirciveen in the southwest of Kerry. Various biographers of O'Connell give us interesting glimpses of what life was like on the western seaboard in the latter part of the eighteenth century. Cut off, as they were, from the rest of the world by wild mountain ranges, the ancient family of the O'Connells had succeeded in retaining a larger share of the world's goods than the laws permitted to Papists, though even for their partial good luck they had to thank strategy as well as the mountain barriers. O'Connell's father held his lands for long years by leaving them in the legal possession of his Protestant friend, Hugh Falvey (who had conformed for emolument sake). From the smuggling trade then common in the whole west of Ireland, the O'Connell family had long derived a steady income. Wines, brandies, velvets, and other taxable commodities, were being constantly imported from the Continent, without getting the gauger's blessing—and circulated inland. The smuggling smacks which constantly ran these goods into the western bays, carried away with them miscellaneous export cargoes—"Wild Geese," young men for the Irish Brigade in France and for other Continental armies; students for the schools of Spain, Italy, Austria, France, Flanders; the flannel homespun of the cottage looms; Irish butter, hides and wool. And the seaweed called *slaucan* (sloke) for which the Spanish appetite craved, was exported by the women to raise spare money for themselves. We are told that in the O'Connell country—as probably happened in many other western regions—the women used to borrow one another's cloaks to go to the Spanish market in the smuggling smacks, and there sell their own *slaucan*.

O'Connell's uncle, Daniel, was one of the many Wild Geese which the smuggling smacks carried away to the great world of war and romance, abroad; and when that man sailed there were no less than seventeen of the O'Connell kinsmen in foreign service. He became Count O'Connell, and was the last Colonel of the Irish Brigade. As he was a royalist, the French Revolution, in time, threw him back upon England—where he became a fine, crusty old Tory—and bitter opponent of his nephew's Repeal idea.

In O'Connell's infancy the splendid Paul Jones was scouring the seas off the Kerry headlands, and giving England many uncomfortable gasps. Then, the banned priest, Father O'Grady (graduate of Louvain) hidden by the great hills from the Government's eyes and spies (though once tried for the crime of being a Papist priest, and freed for want of evidence) was teaching the child Dan his catechism. And the itinerant schoolmaster, David O'Mahony, likewise banned by the paternal government, was instructing the child in the complications and combinations of Cadmus' invention—and while he nursed him and combed his hair "without hurting," the infant protégé, it is recorded, learned the whole alphabet in an hour and a half. And the child saw "Cousin Kane," a landless half-sir who was typical of the times, with his pair of hunters and twelve couples of dogs, circulating among the gentry of Kerry, and honouring and living off each in turn.

The O'Connells were a great, strong, long-lived and prolific family. Though, in those days and in those districts, such was too common to deserve mention. Dan's immediate parents indeed were somewhat exceptional. They had only ten children. Grandfather O'Connell and his celebrated wife (of the O'Donohue family) Maire Ni Duibh, had twenty-two. The ancient Irish system of fosterage was still common in the mountains, and Dan's father and many uncles had all, for the first few years of their lives, been fostered by neighbours, relatives, friends, tenants.

Young Dan himself was fostered by his Uncle Maurice—"Old Hunting Cap" as he was known, because to evade the tax upon gentlemen's beaver hats, Uncle Maurice resolutely lived under a hunting cap. The unceremoniousness of Old Hunting Cap and his household is well illustrated by a characteristic incident recorded of the country carpenter's shoving his tousled head in at the dining-room door when the household with their guests had well begun upon the plentiful pile that always bent their festive board.

"Go away, Buckley," said Mrs. O'Connell. "This is no time to talk business."

"I'm sorry, ma'am, in troth, but I just only wanted a word of his honour, about his coffin."

Old Hunting Cap a few days before had given orders that a coffin should be prepared for him from a loved oak-tree that was being cut down on the lawn.

"Coffin or no coffin, tomorrow will be a long enough day to talk of it."

"No, no, *bean a'tighe,* let us hear what he wants—what's the matter about the coffin, Buckley?" says Old Hunting Cap.

"'Tis to fix about the measurements that will make your honour comfortable."

Then ensues a wrangle between Old Hunting Cap and the carpenter regarding the space that should make a coffined man comfortable—while the diners pause and listen. Old Hunting Cap objects to the generous measurements that the carpenter insists on allowing him. "You know my height is only six foot two."

"But your honour forgets that you'll stretch after you're a corp."

"That's so, to be sure. You're right, Buckley. Then leave me three inches for stretching."

"All right, your honour, I'll make it six foot six to the good, so as to give you no chance of complaint. Good night and excuse me."

"Good night, Buckley, and thank you."

And while knives and forks begin to ply again, Old Hunting Cap bravely resumes the discussion in which he had been interrupted by the coffin-maker's intrusion.

After David O'Mahony's fireside teaching, and then some schooling in Cork, Daniel O'Connell had a short university term at St. Omer, in Flanders, and then at Douay in France—short, because of the French Revolution, which closed Douay in the beginning of 1793—just when he had completed two years of university study.

What he saw and heard of this revolution made him a Tory. It might be more correct to say that it confirmed Toryism in him; for the O'Connell family, taking example from their friends, the well-to-do Anglo-Irish county gentry, were always Tory.

And when the French came into Bantry Bay in '96 to assist the United Irishmen, Uncle Maurice, good loyalist, just missed being the first to get the intelligence to the English Government. The man who was first got a fortune. In his diary Dan then wrote *apropos* of the French visit (probably recalling his experience of one revolution): "Liberty is in my bosom less a principle than a passion. . . . But Ireland is not yet sufficiently enlightened to bear the sun of liberty. Freedom would soon dwindle into licentiousness. They would rob; they would murder. The altar of liberty totters when cemented only with blood, when supported with carcasses. The liberty I look for is that which would increase the happiness of mankind."[1]

But Dan's Toryism almost completely fell away from him when, studying for the Bar at Lincoln's Inn in London in '94—for the ban against Papists entering the outer bar, had just been lifted—he attended the trial of Horne Tooke, and saw and learnt at first hand the astounding tyranny and intolerance practised by the rulers on their own people.

And in Dublin, a few years later, he associated with the United Irishmen and, it is believed, joined them. Anyhow he shared their national sentiments. Yet, when the hour of action came, Daniel O'Connell slipped out of Dublin by sea, and rusticated for a time in the safety of his Kerry home. There evidently reading the official accounts of the barbarity of the wicked rebels, whom the kind Government reluctantly chastised, he grievingly communes with his diary about the outrages that are committed in liberty's name! He thinks he sees in Ireland a repetition of what he knew in France—the unbridled blood-lust of a frenzied and ignorant populace that had suddenly burst its bonds.

And when he returned to Dublin he evidently became a good, pious Tory again. For although he was bitterly anti-Union (like the great body of the Tories in Ireland), when the Emmet alarm burst on the country in 1803, he flew to arms to preserve the Constitution. He was one of the Lawyers' Corps that was then formed for defence of the realm against the assault of French principles. In far later days when it was less objectionable to sympathise with Emmet, O'Connell tried to justify his action by exclaiming: "Poor Emmet, he meant well! But was ever a madder scheme conceived outside of Bedlam than that of facing, with seventy-four men and twelve hundred pounds, King George and one hundred and fifty thousand of the best troops in Europe—with finances unlimited."[2]

---

[1] This is the first indication we have of O'Connell's abject respect for law. It did not press itself upon him that the foreigner in his country was every year indulging in robbery and murder—even of his own kin. The foreigner did it "legally"—prescribed robbing and killing by Parliamentary Statute, and hence it shocked him not.

[2] This is one of the many instances we have of the astonishing nearsightedness of a very great man. Emmet's failure in Dublin was a more permanent more far-reaching success than Wellington's triumph at Waterloo—for, more than a hundred years after, the memory of his heroism, his

It was in 1808, as before mentioned, that O'Connell first got marked prominence in Irish affairs. In that year Fox and Greville, in the British Parliament, had sought to remove a few of the smaller restrictions under which the banned Catholics laboured. It was a belated pretence at redeeming the bribe-promise made them in '99 that after the Union the British Parliament would emancipate them. But even the very sorry bill of Fox and Greville, which only emphasised their slavery by essaying to hack away some of the loose links that dangled from their chains, aroused a no-popery wave which overswept England, engulfed Fox, Greville and their Parliament, and put in power a no-popery party. This dashed the hopes of the Catholic Committee of Ireland—a committee which almost entirely represented the aristocratic Catholics, the bishops and the wealthy merchant and professional class. It was then that the former Catholic leader, Keogh, now an old man, recommended as the best policy for the Catholics "dignified silence." But O'Connell, with the bounding blood of youth, caught the ear and the mind of the country at large, by hotly opposing this servile policy, and urging agitation for their commonest rights. All the more thoroughly did he arouse the country by hammering on the fact that the aristocrats and their fellows were willing to give the English government a veto upon the appointment of Roman Catholic bishops in Ireland in exchange for the few beggarly crumbs with which Fox had tempted them.

When it was now disclosed that in '99 ten bishop trustees of Maynooth College had secretly agreed to the veto, O'Connell so roused the country and evoked such an outburst of wrath as compelled twenty-six bishops in council to repudiate the offer, and swing into the popular camp. And then the nation, which since the cataclysm of 1798–1800 had been pitifully drifting, joyfully hailed a new captain!

But several years were yet to pass before the new captain called up in his people's hearts the extraordinary confidence and the pride that were to make him the mightiest power in the nation. His defence of John Magee in '13 was to put him on a unique pedestal, and, a little later, the tidal wave of enthusiasm created by his victory over D'Esterre was to sweep him into the popular heart and there enthrone him.

But before those golden milestones were reached the people had learnt to know his great qualities as he fought shoulder to shoulder with them in

---

patriotism, and his faith was enthusing, inspiring, stimulating and sustaining one of the world's smallest nations in its unending struggle against earth's most powerful Empire. But Daniel O'Connell throughout his wonderful career was always the lawyer or politician who could only be convinced by immediate results.

the Catholic cause. The demure Catholic Board he turned into a Board of such boldness that the Government suppressed it in 1811. And, beginning the legal and political strategy that was to be, later, his staple manœuvre, he re-formed the association under the name of a General Committee of the Catholics of Ireland. And henceforward, through his career, immediately his organisation under one title was suppressed, he was ready to re-start it next day under a new name.

But, leading his people in the desert now, he had not only to fight the oppressor without but also the aristocratic and reactionary element within. And when in '13 those Protestant champions of Catholic Emancipation, Grattan and Plunkett, had introduced in Parliament a Catholic Relief Bill which had every chance of passing, and which had the approval of the Irish Catholic aristocratic party and the English Catholics, O'Connell aroused Ireland against it because it was saddled with the objectionable veto and also gave to the British the right to supervise all documents passing between Rome and the Roman Catholic hierarchy in these islands.

The British Government got Quarantotti, Secretary and Vice-Prefect of the Sacred College who was then, so to speak, acting Pope—Pius the Seventh being a prisoner of Napoleon—to approve the veto and the supervision right, and issue a rescript to the Irish bishops to that effect. Then was precipitated turmoil in Ireland. From the altar steps of the chapel of the Friars in Clarendon Street, Dublin, O'Connell denounced the rescript to an excited gathering. He threatened the prelates and threatened the secular clergy, that, if they signed themselves over to England, the people, refusing their ministrations, would import poor friars from the continent of Europe, and willingly revert to the deprivations and sufferings of the worst of the penal days.

And a little later, when the Pope had returned to Rome, and there were rumours that he was bargaining with England, Dan boldly rang out his defiance to the Pope himself if he dared to bargain away Ireland's traditional rights and the national rights of the Church. "Though I am a Catholic," he thundered, "I am no Papist! And I deny temporal rights to the Pope in this island."

And prelates who, in synod assembled, had previously sent to Quarantotti a respectful, very firm, remonstrance, not to say threat, now for Pius' behoof and warning, unanimously passed this resolution:

"Though we sincerely venerate the supreme Pontiff as Visible Head of the church we do not conceive that our apprehensions for the safety of the Roman Catholic Church in Ireland can, or ought to be, removed by any determination of His Holiness, adopted or intended to be adopted, not only without our concurrence but in direct opposition to our repeated behest, and so ably supported by our deputy, the most Rev. Dr. Murray, who in that quality was more competent to inform His Holiness of the real state and interests of the Roman Catholic Church in Ireland than any other with whom he is said to have consulted."

The passion of O'Connell, the people, and the prelates had the desired effect. The rights of the Irish church were no longer to be considered a negotiable security at Rome.

CHAPTER LXIII

O'Connell the Idol

In 1813 occurred the John Magee trial which lifted O'Connell on a mighty wave of popular favour. Magee, a Dublin Presbyterian of staunch Irish principle, owned *The Evening Post,* one of the only two or three journals (out of a dozen) in Dublin which the Government could not corrupt. When in May of '13 the Duke of Richmond resigned the Viceroyalty, he and his administration left a bad taste in the public mouth; and *The Evening Post* published a scathing article on the occasion. Of various previous administrations it said, "They insulted, they oppressed, they murdered—the profligate unprincipled Westmoreland, the cold-hearted and cruel Camden, the artful treacherous Cornwallis, left Ireland more depressed and divided than they found her. They increased coercion and corruption, and uniformly employed them against the liberties of the people." But bad as they were, he said, "Richmond out-matched the worst of them."

The Government immediately instituted proceedings against Magee. Attorney General Saurin, a bitter, Irish-hating Orangeman, had charge of the prosecution. Magee engaged O'Connell for his chief counsel, and both sides girded themselves for the battle of the age. But of course Saurin held the cards, and dealt them unscrupulously. In choosing the jury every man who was suspected of the possibility of entertaining the most remote regard for Irish liberties, was set aside. A solidly Orange jury, every man of them a noted bigot, was picked. The Bench was occupied by Lord Chief Justice Downes, who was clay in the hands of the administration, and three other judges of the same quality.

O'Connell, recognising that his clients had as much chance of escape from the Bench of Tory tools and the Box of bigots, as would a sparrow in a field of hawks, resolved to use the opportunity, not to seek justice in a court of manifest injustice, but to fire the already excited nation by pillorying the mockery of justice to which the British Government treated them.

In all his career O'Connell made no more popular speech than his pretended "defence" of Magee—and made few that had more far-reaching effect. Peel who had come to Ireland as Chief Secretary, and who was present in a court that was crammed and surrounded by masses of men who could not get near the door—Peel wrote to the Viceroy that O'Connell's speech was an infinitely more atrocious libel upon the Government and the administration of justice in Ireland than the gross libel which he professed to defend. O'Connell browbeat and insulted the jury in the box, and the judges on the bench, flaying the Chief Justice himself more cruelly than any of them; besides arraigning, denouncing, defying, and scarifying the Government and all its works, its hangers-on and tools, and the whole vulture tribe which formed the British administration in Ireland. "I have unfeigned respect," he said, to the Orange jury, "for the form of Christian faith you profess. Would that its preaching were deeply impressed on your mind—that its substance rather than forms and temporal advantages appealed to you. Then should I not address you in the cheerless and hopeless despondency which now clouds my mind. I respect and venerate your religion—but I despise your prejudices as much as the Attorney General has cultivated them. There are amongst you men of great religious zeal—of much public piety. Are you sincere? Do you believe what you profess? With all this zeal, with all this piety, is there any conscience amongst you? Is there any terror of violating your oaths? Be ye hypocrites, or does genuine religion inspire you? If you be sincere, if you have consciences, if your oaths can control your prejudice—then Mr. Magee confidently expects an acquittal. If amongst you there be cherished one ray of pure religion, if amongst you there glows a single spark of liberty, if I have alarmed the passion of religious liberty, or roused the spirit of political freedom in one breast amongst you, Mr. Magee is safe, his country is served. But if there be none—if you be slaves and hypocrites, he will await your verdict and despise it."

With astounding audacity he taunted, mimicked, scoffed to his face, and whipped, the squirming Lord Chief Justice, cowering on the bench in his scarlet and his ermine before the inspired man who spoke for an outraged people. "At some future period, my lord," he mocked him, "some man may attain the first place on the Bench by the reputation, which is easily acquired, of a certain degree of church-wardening piety, added to a great gravity and maidenly decorum of manners. Such a man may reach the Bench—for I am putting a purely imaginary case. He may be a man without passions, and therefore without vices. He may, my lord, be a man superfluously rich, and therefore not to be bribed with money, but amenable to the smile of the masters on whom he fawns and to whom he is partial by his prejudice. Such a man, inflated by flattery and bloated in his dignity, may hereafter use his character for sanctity which has served to promote him, as a sword to hew down the struggling liberties of his country." And he told the jury not to stand dictation from this man.

Saurin who, above all others, richly deserved it, he excoriated, lashing him till almost he yelped, and to his face branding him an infamous and profligate liar.

A vivid picture of Saurin, under his castigation, was drawn by Dennis Scully, in an introduction which he wrote for O'Connell's speech, published immediately after by *The Post,* and distributed in tens of thousands: "How did you feel when Mr. O'Connell branded you as a libeler before the court, a calumniator in the face of your country, and in your beard a liar? The sweat trickled down Saurin's forehead," continues Scully. "His lips were as white as ashes, his jaws elongated, and his mouth unconsciously open, while the lava of the indignant orator poured around him with unsparing tide, and seemed absolutely to dry up and burn the source of respiration."

O'Connell's speech, by most authorities reckoned his greatest forensic effort, set the country wild with enthusiasm—and no wonder, for he had bearded the lion of injustice in his very lair, and he had lashed him till his roars of rage were heard to the corners of the land. All the vultures attendant upon the Government of Ireland were screeching and screaming in discordant chorus, for the astounding brazenness of a common demagogue attacking and mocking all sacred things which it had hitherto been considered most shocking sacrilege to breathe the faintest whisper against. In their wrath the Government minions went so far as to try to have O'Connell disrobed or driven from the Bar. But for their petty persecutions, which went by him as the wind, O'Connell was repaid a thousandfold by the exuberant gratitude of a prostrate people arising to the knowledge that they had found, if not a deliverer, at least a defender, who feared not to face and defy their oppressor.[1]

---

[1]Magee was of course found guilty. He was sentenced to two years' imprisonment and a heavy fine, besides having to find securities to be of good behaviour for seven years. He was, moreover, given another six months' imprisonment, together with a heavy fine, for a further aggravation of his offence in publishing in *The Evening Post* after the trial a resolution from the Irishmen of Kilkenny, condemnatory of judges and jury, and the whole carriage of the trial.

And if anything was now needed to further endear O'Connell to the people, his duel with D'Esterre supplied it.

D'Esterre was a retired Lieutenant in the English navy, who, by a most audacious bit of bravery, had escaped hanging at the hands of the sailors in the Mutiny of the Nore. He was now a wealthy pork merchant in Dublin, and a member of the Orange Dublin Corporation. O'Connell, having in one of his speeches at the Catholic Association abused the "beggarly Corporation," D'Esterre, then running for High Sheriff, and so coveting popular favour, leapt forward as its defender. He wrote O'Connell a tart letter, demanding to know whether it was true, as reported in the press, that he had applied the opprobrious term to the Corporation. O'Connell made a characteristic reply, wherein refusing to answer yes or no to a demand impertinently made, he at the same time assured D'Esterre that "no terms attributed to me, however reproachful, can exceed the contemptuous feeling I entertain for that body."

O'Connell's reply, evoking from all Dublin another hearty laugh at the ridiculed Corporation, brought from D'Esterre the announcement that he was going to chastise the man publicly. He went about the proceedings elaborately. With horsewhip in hand he set out at an advertised hour from the Mansion House, accompanied by the Lord Mayor and other prominent members and friends of the Corporation, and followed by a crowd that swelled as it went, till the Four Courts was reached.

When O'Connell, who was pleading a case in the courts, heard of the treat that awaited him, he doffed his gown and went out into the hall. But D'Esterre and his friends now considered that the fashionable thoroughfare of Grafton Street, through which the miscreant libeller always passed on his way home, would be a more fitting place to make a public example and point a moral. So they set off again, and took position on the steps of a drapery establishment in the popular street. All Dublin was now agog. Great was the crowd that jammed the thoroughfare. Beauty and Rank at all the windows took advantageous and comfortable positions. And to get satisfactory view of the humiliation of the meddlesome demagogue whose audacity had been getting on their nerves, the noblest and most prominent members of the Administration got the choicest windows and balconies, right above the spot where the victim was to dance to the music of the horsewhip.

When O'Connell heard where he was now expected to present himself for punishment, he took in his fist his good blackthorn, clapped his hat on his head with the slightly rakish tilt that was his wont, and with a trusty friend on either side jauntily set out to overtake his Nemesis. The sublime seriousness with which the gentleman in Grafton Street apprehended the situation did not properly sink into O'Connell's soul; for, as the giant strode along, he lightly twirled his staff, winked at friends who here and there studded the crowds that lined the way, and with his jokes kept his companions in hearty laughter en route.

The crowd that had followed D'Esterre was but a drop in the ocean to the huzzäing multitude that followed "the Counsellor" (as he was affectionately known to the populace). And when the cheers were heard, and the Counsellor himself and the head of his following were seen, at the foot of Grafton Street, D'Esterre rolled up his horsewhip and retired to a back parlour for meditation. Tory window-holders who had come to feast upon the final humiliation of the bad man of Ireland, had, instead, to endure the deep mortification of seeing him on triumphal march through Grafton Street, elevated into a favour before undreamt of.

But of course it did not end there. Whatever might or might not be D'Esterre's qualifications with the horsewhip, his skill with the pistol was famous. After first demanding an apology from O'Connell, and getting instead a hearty laugh, he challenged his man to a pistol duel—which Major MacNamara, O'Connell's friend, arranged to take place at four o'clock on the afternoon of the day of the challenge, over the border in Kildare. Though both sides, with a few friends and surgeons, stole off quietly enough to the place of combat, the news overswept Dublin like wildfire, and horses, coaches, traps, gigs, and carts, every vehicle and every animal of burden that could be secured, flew over the road in O'Connell's wake. And when D'Esterre arrived on the field, half an hour late, he was surprised to find there a goodly gathering indeed of all sorts and conditions of Dublin people, in addition to crowds of Kildare country folk and a throng of citizens from the town of Naas, a few miles distant.

Major MacNamara won the toss for choice of ground. The men were placed, the signal was given—the dropping of a handkerchief—the two fighters, with pistol points lowered, steadily watched each other for half a minute. Then D'Esterre stepped to one side, to confuse his opponent, both pistols came up simultaneously, O'Connell's shot rang out first—and laid D'Esterre upon the ground mortally wounded.

The Dublin Corporation and Tory ascendancy had, in the eyes of the tense crowd, gone down in the person of the seriously wounded D'Esterre—and from the top of the field where the country people were assembled went up a cheer of triumph that, it may be said, ceased not, till, twenty-four hours later, it had reached the four ends of Ireland.

The man who had thrown the Old Man of the Sea, the aristocratic incubus, off the shoulders of the Catholic Association, who had then made the creatures of the administration yelp under his lash, and made the creatures' masters tremble, had compelled the hierarchy to the side of their people and broken the intrigues of Rome, and had finally overthrown hated privilege in the person of the champion of the most bitterly anti-Irish Orange body that Ireland knew, was now truly the people's Dan!

CHAPTER LXIV

Catholic Emancipation

O'Connell now had complete control of the national mind. And his voice was the voice of Ireland. The unquestioning faith of his multitudinous following put in his hands a power which he unsparingly wielded to work out the people's emancipation.

And to that end he spared himself not—either physically or morally, it might be specified. For when George IV of Britain came to visit Ireland in 1821, the popular leader, in anxiety to attain his great end, abased himself and through himself the nation. The abasement was not the less humiliating to Ireland even when we admit that the servile homage which he did George was as much the genuine homage of one who had an almost superstitious reverence for royalty, as it was the blarney of the Prince of Blarney.

The man's ever-amazing veneration and love for the royal representative of that Empire which trod upon his nation's neck, and kept himself and his fellows in servitude, will be treated of later on. Sufficient to say now that to the generations since this has seemed almost an enigma in O'Connell's nature. But the blarney Dan always considered a worthy and legitimate instrument, as it was an effective one, for attaining a good end.

The debauch of debasement in which O'Connell revelled before George was all the more remarkable because nine years before he had held him up to ridicule and opprobrium when, as Prince of Wales, the royal youth had worked maliciously and effectively against Catholic relief. The Catholic Board, under O'Connell's direction of course, passed the celebrated "witchery" resolution, which (between the lines) gave to the scandal-mongering multitude the tid-bit that it was a bigoted anti-Catholic mistress who had compelled the Prince's anti-Irish attitude. The resolution, and O'Connell's flippant treatment of his quasi-secret heart entanglement, had envenomed George against the Irish leader. This well-known fact made all the more strange the leader's effusively enthusiastic humility now. To cap the absurdity, O'Connell was not more delighted at lavishing servile homage upon his royal master than the royal master himself was childishly delighted to receive it.

O'Connell, in organising the reception, so worked upon his faithful people with his lavish eloquence that, arising out to welcome George with wild delight, they seethed with enthusiasm during every day of his stay. All dissensions of Orange and Green were drowned in the great draught of loyalty that both parties now quaffed. Royal blue, the blend of the two parties' colours, was by O'Connell's direction, sported by all. The climax was reached when at Dunleary (whose ancient name was that day dropped in favour of the glorious new one of Kingstown) O'Connell, on bended knee, presented George with a laurel crown, and the pledge of the nation's eternal gratitude and loyalty. George shook the hand of the Great Dan right cordially, and, in the language of *The London Times* correspondent, "noticed Mr. O'Connell in the most marked and condescending manner!" To the cheering crowds the king said in a voice almost broken with emotion, "May God Almighty bless you all until we meet again." And on the deck of his ship, when it started, he waved his white hand to the adoring ones, crying: "Farewell, my beloved Irish subjects!"

O'Connell, in his joy at discovering the extraordinary devotion which flowed between British royalty and Irish subjects, proposed the erection of an Irish royal residence, offering a subscription of twenty guineas a year from himself. And to commemorate the occasion of the discovery, and the man, he asked the select of Dublin, both Green and Orange, to form a Royal Georgian Club, the members of which, sporting rosettes of blue, should dine six times a year, and at the festive board help one another to recall the happy memories of their beloved king's visit.

So touched was George with his reception by his "beloved Irish subjects," that he bestowed on Lord Fingall, the ranking Catholic layman, the Order of St. Patrick. And immediately after his return to England he sent to the Lord Lieutenant of Ireland a message of gratitude, and hope for the bright future of his Irish people—which assured O'Connell and his followers, if assurance were needed, that their fondest hopes for religious freedom would now at length be satisfied.

But they had still a weary way to go to their religious freedom, many an arduous hill to climb, and many a furious battle to fight, before the goal was won. And it was destined that in the agony of the fight the rueful Dan should groan: "I am sorry to say that the greatest enemy of the people of Ireland is his most sacred majesty!"

It is true that in '21 the English House of Commons passed the Catholic Relief Bill which, while proposing to make Catholics eligible for Parliament and for offices under the Crown was again saddled with the impossible veto, and with another equally unacceptable condition, namely, that the Roman Catholic clergy should take oath to elect only bishops who were loyal to the British Crown. O'Connell, who cursed it as worse than all the penal statutes, fought this Bill with all his power—and the priests in a solid body backed him. But, anyhow, the Lords who could not stomach such concession to the Irish, threw it out—and saved Ireland the trouble of rebelling against it.

O'Connell entering into negotiation with Lord Lieutenant Wellesley—specially sent over to soothe Catholic feeling—agreed to a compromise form of veto, whereby the questioned loyalty of any man chosen for a bishopric should be investigated and decided upon by two bishops. But as the Government absolutely refused to entertain this proposition, O'Connell had to start from the beginning again.

He found it a particularly good time for agitation because it was a particularly bad time for the country. The year '22 and again '23 brought with them much want and hardship to the nation. There was a famine; the French Wars had ended, and a period of greatly inflated prices intensely aggravated the other woes under which the people laboured. The secret society of the Ribbonmen, which terrorised profiteers, bad landlords, Government officials, and all enemies of the people, helped to develop and swell the unrest throughout the island. And the Government was embarrassingly trying to cope with a difficult situation. It was the right moment for organising the mass of the people and giving them a lead. Richard Lalor Shiel, orator and Catholic leader, who had differed with and separated from O'Connell, now consented to join forces with him. So O'Connell founded a new Catholic Association and resolving to bring into politics a new great power that had never before been systematically enlisted, namely, the priests, organised the Association by parishes with the priest in each case as natural leader. To provide the sinews for the fight a Catholic rent was established, one penny per month per man—to be lifted at the chapel gate on the first Sunday of each month—which small subscription from a vast number of people soon supplied the Catholic Association with a steady income of more than a thousand pounds a week. So, in a short time the country was more thoroughly organised than it had ever been before. The Association, too, was more virile and determined in its demands.

Strange to say the triumphs of the South American Revolutionaries under Bolivar—to whom Ireland had contributed an Irish brigade, O'Connell's son Morgan one of its officers—and even also the triumphs of the Greeks over their Turkish enslavers, enthused and emboldened the people. And O'Connell, most loyal of men, grew belligerent—in his speeches at least. "If the Irish be driven to desperation," he rang out, "they may wish for a new Bolivar to arise who will call forth the spirit of the South Americans, the spirit, too, of the Greeks, to animate the people of Ireland." And the threat was applauded from sea to sea. So dangerous became the people's attitude that the English Government was forced to take a decisive step. The Catholic Association was suppressed, and an Emancipation Bill brought in.

The speech of one of the very liberal-minded Parliamentarians, Plunkett, on the suppression of the Association, illuminates to us the liberality of the British Constitution as interpreted for Ireland. "An Association assuming to represent the people," said Plunkett, "and in that capacity to bring about a reform of church and state is directly opposed to the British Constitution. . . . We deny that any portion of the subjects of this realm have the right to give up their suffrages to others—the right to select persons to speak their sentiments, debate their grievances and devise methods for their removal, those persons (the committee of the Catholic Association) not being recognised by law. That is the privilege alone of the Commons of the United Kingdom." And the reformer, Channing, endorsed these sentiments!

This Emancipation Bill, of 1825, omitted the veto; but instead there were attached to it two conditions, named the "wings"—that were to carry it through. They were—payment of priests, and the disfranchisement of the forty shilling free-holders. Archbishops were to be paid fifteen hundred pounds per year, bishops a thousand pounds, parish priests two hundred pounds, and curates sixty pounds. This of course was the bribe that would secure their loyalty to the British connection for all time. O'Connell found himself willing to compromise and accept these conditions, but priests and people rebelled—and Mahomet had to come to the mountain.

The Bill passed the House of Commons—and in all probability the House of Lords would have felt compelled to accept it, but that the Duke of York, brother to George IV, came before them, threatened, stormed, implored, entreated, and even wept at the prospect of their becoming traitors to the Established religion, to the crown, and to God, truckling with, bribing, and subsidising iniquity. The Lords, deeply moved, and emboldened by the fierce harangue, threw out the Bill. An anti-Catholic wave again overswept Britain, on the crest of which rode the hero of York, the saviour of his nation and religion. The Parliament dissolved in a tumult. A general election followed, in which, once more, no-popery carried the day. And a bitterly anti-Papist Government took up the reins in England.

O'Connell, nothing daunted, started to build anew. When the Catholic Association was suppressed, he penned a valedictory, wherein, still strong with irrepressible loyalty, he urged upon the people "attachment to the British Constitution, and unqualified loyalty to the king!" But as he always loved to show defiance to illegal laws—in a legal manner, however—he, to replace the suppressed Catholic Association now founded the New Catholic Association, "for the purpose of public and private charity and such other purposes as are not forbidden by the statute of George IV, cap. 4." And by the simple device of the slightest change of name, and the definite statement of purposes not forbidden by the recent Suppression Act, he quickly had his agitation going in as full blast as if the British Imperial Parliament had only winked at it. And the intensity of the anti-popery agitation in England, and the success of the anti-popery party there, instead of dampening the ardour of the people, gave fresh vigour to the fight.

Though the general election in England went very happily for the no-popery party, the new no-popery Government was frightened to discover that the election in Ireland had gone entirely the other way. The mighty power of combined priests and people was taking form, and the Irish nation now realised the solidity of their power more surely and more boldly than ever before.

Lecky says that this election of '26 won Emancipation. It certainly gave the Government pause, and prepared them for a salutary change of mind.

But with far more force, it can be said that Emancipation was won by the epoch-making Clare election. That was the first truly golden milestone met by the Irish people upon their weary march from the century's beginning. The Clare election was to Ireland a joyful surprise, and a fearful one to England.

It will be recalled that Catholics were debarred from sitting in Parliament. Every member taking the oath had to swear to his conviction that "the Sacrifice of the Mass and the invocation of the Virgin Mary and other saints, as now practised in the Church of Rome, are infamous and idolatrous." Now, in 1828 a Parliamentary vacancy was created in County Clare, by reason of the member, Fitzgerald (a supporter of Emancipation), taking office under the Government. Fitzgerald had no doubt whatsoever of his re-election for Clare. It was, like many another, a family seat. It had been his father's before him, and was now his. But since he took office under Government it was decided by the Association that Fitzgerald should be opposed.

O'Connell was trying to pick out a strong, desirable and reliable candidate, when there was made to him the startling suggestion, "Why not stand for Clare, yourself?" The audacity of the idea first took him aback. Then he smiled at it, and finally, seized by bold resolve, electrified his friends by declaring: "I'll do it." The news electrified Dublin within an hour, and Clare and all Ireland, within twenty-four hours. It was the most audacious resolve of the generation.

It was then the middle of the week. O'Connell was pleading in the Dublin Four Courts most important cases with which he could not get through before the week's end. The nomination was to take place in Ennis, the capital of Clare, on the following Monday, and the election began on Tuesday. A party of O'Connell's ablest and most eloquent friends, including Tom Steele (his Head Pacificator), Major MacNamara (his second at the D'Esterre duel), and Father Tom MacGuire, the famous controversialist from County Leitrim, were at once rushed off to the seat of war. O'Connell was to follow when he could.

It was the afternoon of Saturday when O'Connell got through with his cases. He slammed his papers into his bag, threw aside his wig and gown, rushed out of the Four Courts, and sprang into a waiting coach, at which four impatient horses were straining—and amid the huzzas of a throng that had gathered to shower blessings on him, was tearing along the way to Ennis.

Speeding across Ireland during all of that night and of the next day, the champion was cheered by the splendid reception accorded him at every important point; in every town and village masses of men and women waited up to hail the bold chieftain, and to speed him forward with shouts of encouragement. Crowds were gathered at cross-roads, and knots at little cabins, all of whom took up and passed along the tremendous cheer which before his flying carriage and behind it, rolled all the long way in accompaniment. Ahead of him, behind, and alongside, ran swift-footed men and boys with blazing torches, lighting the way for him and for Ireland's triumph. In some places bodies of men on horseback, spur at heel, and crouched in their saddles, lined the way, awaiting to dash out with the flying coach of the champion, as guards of honour; and ere their horses tired down, other waiting ones on horses fresh sprang out to do their part.

It was two o'clock on Monday morning when O'Connell's coach dashed into Ennis, which, blazing with lights, had its streets even at that hour jammed with the wildly joyous, and frantically cheering, multitude.

O'Connell and Fitzgerald were that day nominated. And, on Tuesday morning began the tug of war. The crux of the situation lay in the voting of the forty shilling freeholders. These men had been technically given votes which were really meant as endowment to their landlords. No sane politician ever thought that they would dare exercise choice as to the candidate for whom their vote would be cast. They had always voted in platoons under the landlord's orders. Only, in the recent general election, for the first time in their existence, the Forties as they were called, had showed unmistakable signs of revolt in places where their landlords were supporters of the unpopular candidate.

But in this great Clare election, in which every landlord stood behind Fitzgerald, the Forties finally and completely broke the shackles of tradition and landlord control, and went cheering to the polls for O'Connell. Exciting was the scene when they came into Ennis in bodies, sometimes openly proclaiming their new freedom, sometimes seemingly submissive and demure under leadership of their landlord, and herded by his bailiffs and understrappers. But when the suitable moment arrived these demure ones, breaking away, rent the skies with shouts for O'Connell, and rushed to the poll, for the first time in their lives to vote as their hearts prompted. The priests of Clare played a prominent part. Their sermons on Sunday had been impassioned appeals and heart-reaching exhortations to their congregations to quit their landlords for their God, and vote for O'Connell and Catholic Emancipation. Where they succeeded in driving out of the hearts of their flock the terror of the landlord, they headed their flocks to Ennis. In cases where the landlord, still retaining his hold, led in his platoon of voters, they were met at the town's entrance by priests inspired with holy zeal, who, with crucifix held aloft, barred the way and in torrential eloquence urged the people by the sufferings of Him who died for man not to play traitor to their faith in this supreme hour. And the embittered, deserted, landlord often had to stand aside and curse, as he beheld his tenants burst their bonds, and with great shout follow their priest to the polling booth. The tens of thousands who thronged there that week not only filled the streets and the houses but encamped in the meadows, and along the roadside, for miles around. There was no drinking, there was no fighting; there was no disorder. The people had been put on a vow most sacred to bring no disgrace on the cause, but conduct themselves with the decorum that they would at church. And in the face of opportunity and provocation before unequalled, they amazed friend and enemy by exercising a restraint that was marvellous. The anecdote is told of Sheedy MacNamara, a man who would welcome a fight more warmly than a fortune, being openly and most provokingly insulted in the streets by one of the enemy, and, instead of knocking the fellow down, taking him gently aside and saying to him in the sweetest way: "I have just one little pig at home, and I'll promise you the price of it if you'll repeat them same words to me the day after the election."

At the end of the first day of the polling O'Connell was a little ahead of Fitzgerald. On Wednesday night his lead was larger, and his majority went on progressing, during Thursday and Friday. Till on Saturday night, when the poll closed, he was, by two to one, elected member of Parliament for Clare.

A few months before the Clare election the English Prime Minister, Sir Robert Peel, had emphatically declared in the House of Commons: "I can not consent to widen the door of political power to Roman Catholics. I can not consent to give them the same civil rights and privileges as those possessed by their Protestant fellow-countrymen." But, a few months after the Clare election he prepared to pipe to another tune: "In the course of the last six months England, at peace with the world, has had five-sixths of her infantry force occupied in maintaining peace in Ireland. I consider such a state of things much worse than rebellion." And the king's speech in Parliament in the February following asked his faithful Commons to consider the unrest in Ireland and review the laws causing it. County Clare had conquered England.

Says Lecky: "The population was in ferment, the army itself was affected. The influence of the landed aristocracy gave way. Ministers, feeling further resistance hopeless, brought in the Emancipation Bill confessedly because to withhold it might kindle a rebellion extending over the length and the breadth of the land."

Lord Wellington, in the Lords, excused his promoting the Bill on the ground that it might be less evil than civil war, which, if the bill were refused, would surely be precipitated in Ireland. Fear of the consequences, not the injustice, was the only reason offered by any of its English promoters, for pressing the measure.

The Emancipation Bill was brought in—and passed—but not without fierce opposition. The Lords also felt constrained to allow it—though one can easily imagine the bitter aversion with which they did so. The Duke of Brunswick (brother to King George) and Lord Eldon, the most violent opponents of the measure, then went to the king, to entreat, threaten, and coerce him into refusing his signature. And they succeeded in breaking him down so that when the Government leaders, Peel of the Commons, and Wellington of the Lords, brought him the Bill, he would not sign it. They argued with him for five hours, but with no avail. He alternately stormed and wept. They handed him their resignations. He called them back, kissed them, and cried again. When he found himself unable to form a new ministry, he sent again for Wellington and Peel, signed the bill, and in a fit of rage smashed on the floor the pen with which he had, as he believed, betrayed his trust to God and the English people.[1]

In the House of Lords the Archbishop of Canterbury moved to reject the bill, and was seconded by the Protestant Primate of Ireland, Beresford. Every bishop except one, Dr. Lloyd of Oxford, voted against Catholics getting citizen rights in their own country.

The Emancipation Bill was passed, the commonest citizen rights from which Irish people had hitherto been debarred, because they were heretics and idolaters, were now permitted by law. And civil offices from which they had been, for their crime, shut out, were supposedly thrown open to them. Technically these reforms were instituted by the passing of the Act—"The manacles," said O'Connell, "are riven from our limbs after we had gone near to breaking them on the heads of our enemies." But practically speaking Irish Catholics continued, for many decades after, to labour under their former disability. And in many parts of Ireland, even down to a short generation ago, they were in practice still shut out from all offices except the most menial.

---

[1] Three months after, when King George at one of his levees caught sight of O'Connell, he muttered, "There is O'Connell, G—— d—— the scoundrel!"

O'Connell did not present himself in the House of Commons until the Bill had been passed—though not yet gone into effect. Every member was in his place on the day and at the hour that O'Connell was expected. In the Strangers' Gallery were crowded the nobility of England and the diplomats of many foreign countries. When the objectionable oath was presented to O'Connell he of course refused to take it. He was told by the speakers that under the circumstances he could not take his seat, and he marched out of the House of Commons again—and went back to Clare where he was re-elected without opposition.

When the Emancipation Act went into effect, it of course eliminated the objectionable oath; and the several Catholics who were returned from various parts of Ireland at the next general election, were permitted to seat themselves in the House.

CHAPTER LXV

O'Connell's Power and Popularity

Though it was in his character as political leader that he was greatest to his people, it was undeniably in his capacity as lawyer that Daniel O'Connell—"Dan" as they affectionately called him—got nearest to their hearts. They who had always been condemned before they were heard, were accorded human rights in the courts of law after O'Connell had successfully stormed those citadels of injustice. To the regular Crown prosecutors he made his name a name of fear. And indeed it was not much less a terror to those irregular Crown prosecutors who, on the Bench, masqueraded as judges.

He was one of the most powerful pleaders that the Bar ever knew. His enemy, Peel, once said that if he wanted an efficient and eloquent advocate, he would readily barter all the best of the English Bar for the Irish O'Connell. In conducting an important case he called into play all of his wonderful faculties. He went from grave to gay, from the sublime to the ludicrous. He played with ease upon every human feeling. He carried away the judge, the jury, the witness that he was handling, and the very prisoner himself in the dock. He could in a few minutes' cross-examination tear the ablest witness to shreds, and show the pitying court the paltry stuff he was made of. He might at first play his man, go with him, blarney him, flatter him, convince him that Dan O'Connell had become his most enthusiastic admirer and dearest friend. And when he had thus taken him off his guard, led him by hand into a trap, the Counsellor (another of the people's titles for O'Connell) would come down upon his man with a crash that stunned and shattered him and left him a piteous victim at the great cross-examiner's feet. And to judge and jury and the whole court it was now the witness, not the prisoner in the dock, who was on trial for his life.

He had a most disconcerting way of passing pungent *viva voce* remarks, when the prosecuting lawyer was making his speech or examining his witness, which provoked the prosecutor to wrath, lost him his train of thought, and often spoiled him his case. If the judges' protection was invoked by the enraged prosecutor, the wise potentate on the Bench usually considered discretion the better part of valour. Baron McClellan trying a case in a Kerry court was annoyed to find O'Connell interjecting remarks in a case in which he felt his interest enlisted. "Mr. O'Connell," asked McClellan, cuttingly, "are you engaged in this case?" "I am not, my lord, but I shall be." "When I was at the Bar," said the judge, in his most crushing manner, "it was not my habit to anticipate briefs." "When your lordship was at the Bar," answered O'Connell, "I never chose you for a model. And now that you are on the Bench I shall not submit to your dictation."

Once when O'Connell found himself in possession of absolutely no case, in defending a prisoner who was on trial for his life before a newly-appointed, timid, and scrupulous judge, O'Connell deliberately proceeded with a line of argument which—as he intended—compelled reprimands from the judge again and again; then giving way to an outburst of apparently terrible indignation, he said: "Since your lordship will not permit me to defend this man whose life is in the balance, I withdraw from the case, and throw the prisoner upon the tender mercies of an evidently hostile court. If he is condemned, on your head, my lord, be his blood." Then he slammed down his brief and left the court. The frightened judge, finding himself compelled to act the part of Counsel for the defence, cross-examined for the prisoner, charged for him—and sent him out of the court a free man.

The Doneraile conspiracy case, in October, 1829, memorably exemplified O'Connell's power. The Government, making a grand sweep at Doneraile, gathered in many men charged with conspiracy to murder savage landlords and unjust magistrates. The greatest importance was attached to the case. A Special Commission was sent down to Cork to try the conspirators. "Long John" Doherty, the Solicitor-General, a bitterly anti-popular official, went down himself to prosecute. They were to be tried in batches. The first four were put forward, found guilty, and sentenced to be hanged. At this result the remaining prisoners and their assembled friends were thrown into panic. It was then Saturday afternoon. The next batch would be put on trial on Monday morning. A cry went up for Dan O'Connell. Dan was then resting at Derrynane—ninety Irish miles away. That he could be got to the trial in time, even if he consented to come, was hardly possible. But in desperation the forlorn hope must be chanced. A messenger, William Burke, set out from Cork on a fast horse, on Saturday evening, and, after a marvellous night ride, on Sunday forenoon clattered into Derrynane and threw himself from his horse at O'Connell's door. The Counsellor, when he learnt the circumstances, said: "I'll go."

He rushed Burke off ahead to have fresh horses awaiting him at certain points, and to carry to the distracted ones the news of his coming. O'Connell started in the afternoon, and all that evening and all that night was galloping over the rough, steep, and broken mountain-roads of Kerry, and then over the plains and hills of Cork, without pausing to eat, drink, or sleep. At ten o'clock on Monday morning, one hour after the court-sitting began, the waiting throngs on the streets of Cork were electrified by the cry, "The Counsellor's coming!" The wild exultation which found voice from the waiting ones away beyond the suburbs rolled onward to the city's heart gathering volume as it went, till it rocked the court-house, bringing dismay to the prosecutors there, and genuine displeasure to the judges—all of whom too well knew what that terrific cheer meant. Through the frantically huzzaing lines of people O'Connell tore onward, to the courthouse, where, as he jumped to the ground his horse fell dead!

Attired as he was, and mud-spattered, he tore into the hall where the State trial was staged, and, to the scowling prosecutors and the frowning judges, announcing, "I appear for the prisoners in the dock," sat down at the Counsel's table to a repast of bread and milk, that had been rushed in after him. While he hastily bolted his single meal lawyers for the defence were pouring into his ear the points of the case. He gave one ear to them and one to Prosecutor "Long John" who was then on his feet addressing the court. Now and then, between mouthfuls, he would emit a short sharp comment, objection, or rebuke to the sorely-provoked Doherty—spoiling half-a-dozen of the fellow's finest points, by rapping out on the heels of them, "That's not law!" And every time, the judges had to uphold O'Connell's objection.

"The allegation is made upon false facts," said Doherty, enlightening the Judges upon a particular point. "Never was such a thing as a false fact," snapped O'Connell. "There are false facts and false men too," sneered the enraged Doherty. "Yes, your case and yourself," retorted O'Connell.

When Doherty, with his temper and his arguments shattered, sat down, O'Connell, now both refreshed and informed, got to his feet and began his case. The prosecution pursued in this case the selfsame line of action, produced the selfsame witnesses, and got the selfsame "proofs" against this second batch of prisoners as against the first—but O'Connell's defence made such breaches in the prosecution's structure that the jury disagreed. And when the third batch was tried he had so far progressed as to procure a quick verdict of "Not Guilty." The prosecution was broken. They would go no further with the trial; all remaining prisoners were released; the condemned ones were reprieved—and a host of men who had looked into the noose that awaited their necks, walked home amid cheering crowds, free men.

O'Connell had some good stories to tell of some of the characters whom his genius had freed. There was a robber whom he defended on three different occasions—and for whom he won out every time. On the occasion of the third victory, the fellow gratefully grasped his hand, exclaiming: "May the Lord long spare you to me, Counsellor O'Connell." And a cow-stealer whom he had defended repaid him with a tip on how to extract the maximum of profit from a cow raid. "When your Honour goes to stale cows," the expert confided to him, "always choose the worst night that falls from the heavens, because then there'll be no one about to see you. And, on such a night, too, when you reach the field, you'll aisily know the fat ones. Don't take any of the scrawny bunch, your honour, that shoulder one another in the shelter of the wall. They are the craitures that have nothing on their bones but a hide. Take them that stands out in the open, disregardless of the storm, for they're the fat ones that has nothing to fear from wind, rain, or hail."

For fifteen years before Emancipation, O'Connell was, it seemed, the greatest man in Ireland. When he achieved Emancipation he became one of the greatest men in Europe—in the world. Such was his universal fame then that there was nothing surprising about his getting a letter from America beginning "Awful Sir"—or in the German students' answering the examination question: "Who is Daniel O'Connell?" with the reply: "He is the man who discovered Ireland." In the election of a king for the newly-formed Belgian nation three votes were given for "le Grand O'Connell." And ten years afterward, in the fervour of the Repeal movement, Dan himself said to his friend, O'Neill Daunt, "If the Belgian election had waited till now, I don't doubt but I would have run old Leopold close." In '35 he was flattered to find himself invited to France to defend the Lyons Conspirators—which signal honour he had to refuse for want of fluency in French. His friend Daunt records the pronouncement of a London stockbroker who was no way partial to O'Connell or his principles: "Your Daniel O'Connell is one of the Great Powers of Europe. His movements have a sensible effect on the Funds."

All over the Continent he was now revered as the greatest leader of Catholic democracy that the world ever knew. His wonderful Continental popularity was well pictured by Lord Macaulay speaking (some years later) in the English House of Commons: "The position which Mr. O'Connell holds in the eyes of his fellow-countrymen is a position such as no popular leader in the whole history of mankind ever attained. You are mistaken if you imagine that the interest with which he is regarded is confined only to these islands. Go where you will on the Continent, visit any coffee-house, dine at any public table, embark upon any steam-boat, enter any conveyance—from the moment your accent shows you to be an Englishman, the very first question asked by your companions, be they what they may—physicians, advocates, merchants, manufacturers, or peasants of the class who are like your yeoman in this country—is 'What will be done with O'Connell?'" And his greatness thus inspired Bulwer Lytton's muse:

"Once to my sight the giant thus was given,
Walled by wide air and roofed by boundless heaven;
Beneath his feet the human ocean lay,
And wave on wave flowed into space away.
Methought no clarion could have sent this sound
E'en to the centre of the hosts around,
And, as I thought, rose a sonorous swell,
As from some church tower swings the silvery bell;
Aloft and clear from airy tide to tide,
It glided easy as a bird may glide.
To the last verge of that vast audience sent,
It played with each wild passion as it went:
Now stirred the uproar, now the murmurs stilled,
And sobs or laughter answered as it willed.
Then did I know what spell of infinite choice
To rouse or lull has the sweet human voice.
Then did I learn to seize the sudden clue
To the grand troublous life antique—to view,
Under the rockstand of Demosthenes,
Unstable Athens heave her noisy seas."

After having first viewed the champion at close range—for he helped to fight him—Gladstone, later looking back at him in far perspective, pronounced O'Connell one of the greatest popular leaders the world had ever known.

But it was in the hearts of the Irish people that Dan's greatness was most truly appreciated, and admiration of him grew akin to worship.

In the years when he was in his climax his word was to the Irish people electric, and his power was invincible. With joyous thrill these long-suffering ones felt that when Dan spoke there was fearful trembling in the seats of the mighty. In him the nation that was dumb had found a voice. The despised had found a champion and the cruelly wronged an avenger. He was to them in the ranks of the gods.

And what less exalted position should an oppressed people give to him who for the first time in man's memory, stood up in the court of law, the court of Injustice, and made the most awful of the judges, who dispensed injustice there, cower—faced those judges' Masters too in their own Parliament and made them writhe!

It is not to be wondered at, then, that O'Connell should, more than once, in his speech in defence of a prisoner, get the jury in the box cheering. An Englishman in a party accompanying O'Connell over a mountain-road was shocked to behold the mourners at a funeral which they met, burst out cheering for their uncrowned king. "Arrah, man, dear," O'Connell reassured him, "sure the corpse in the coffin would have joined in the cheer himself, if he could only have found his voice." An old crippled beggar woman when her hand was shaken by the great Dan, threw her crutch in the air and gave a bound and a whoop that would do credit to a mountain goat. O'Neill Daunt tells how, at a reception to O'Connell in Limerick, where a hundred thousand jubilant men were throwing their hats in the air, an enthusiastic poor woman tossed up her child.

So affected even were the English by Dan's greatness that (as told by himself) two maiden ladies who were at one time his hostesses in England insisted every night before retiring, on standing up to sing a hymn in his praise to the air of "God Save the King."

After Emancipation was won O'Connell abandoned his law practice to devote himself entirely to the people's cause. To compensate him, the famous Tribute was then started—a popular nation-wide subscription which gave him an average income of thirteen thousand pounds a year. Though in its first year, in special gratitude to the man who had wrung the Emancipation Act from England, fifty thousand pounds were subscribed.

His law practice had been netting him about eight thousand pounds per year. If, foregoing Ireland's cause, he had given all his time to the law he might have doubled that sum. It was the taking of the Tribute, every penny of which was richly earned, and every penny of which in truth he well spent, that won for him from his unloving English friends the title of the

Big Beggarman. It was sometimes amusing to him to hear the scornful phrase used by some English politician who, if he had had half O'Connell's talent, would not have lent it to any cause, good or bad, for double the sum. A few of their broader-minded ones, however, frankly admitted that it was a noble honorarium, nobly earned, nobly given, and nobly accepted. So large was the scale on which O'Connell had to live, and so great his expenses, that the Tribute together with the income of his estate was seldom sufficient to keep him out of debt.

CHAPTER LXVI

Through the Thirties

When Emancipation was won, Repeal of the false and corruptly-purchased "Union" of Ireland with England was the great issue that the Leader started. It had always been mulling in his mind. Indeed there were times when he would have preferred to accept repeal of the Union in preference to repeal of the Penal Laws. He stated that at the time of the Union, and the wish haunted his heart every year after.

In 1810 the grand jurors of Dublin, all of them of course Tories and British-Irish, tried to start the Repeal movement. But the promises of British politicians who dangled before their eyes the bait of Emancipation, kept the Catholic party from joining their Protestant fellow-countrymen on this occasion. Now that Dan was free to throw himself into the repeal movement, and the Catholics almost to a man were behind him, no support could be got from their Protestant fellow-countrymen. There were two reasons for this—the fierceness of the fight for Emancipation had embittered the Protestants against their Catholic fellows; and besides all the offices and patronage of the country which had been securely theirs in pre-Emancipation days were getting shaky in their grasp now that Catholic disabilities were by law removed. Repeal of the Union would now finally break their monopoly; so the overwhelming body of the Protestant population was henceforth as bitterly anti-Repeal as they had formerly been anti-Union—and more bitterly than they had been anti-Emancipation.

Strange to say, the famous Bishop Doyle of Limerick, dearly loving the people whose fearless champion he was, but curiously lacking the Nationalist instinct, withstood O'Connell on Repeal. Richard Lalor Shiel was against him, too—though this will not seem strange to any one who studies the many shallows of Shiel's nature. And it will surprise some who thought that Tom Moore was not a mere drawing-room patriot to learn that he too bitterly resented O'Connell's new national move, saying that it would divide the upper, and madden the lower, classes. And his indignation inspired him to write his song: "The dream of those days when I first saw thee, is o'er."

The Government, not desiring to see the 'Thirties repeat the *débâcle* of the 'Twenties, took an emphatic grip on Time's forelock, and determinedly set themselves to stamp out his repeal agitation at its inception. When in 1830 he started his anti-Union Association they proclaimed it at once; and from that time forward it was an exciting race between O'Connell and the Government—he restarting his repeal movement under a new name each week, and they, close following, proclaiming it.

He started a weekly Repeal Breakfast, and promised that if it was suppressed, he would have Repeal Lunches, Repeal Dinners, Repeal Suppers in succession. Its next form was a General Association for Ireland. When that was proclaimed, he started A Body of Persons, in the Habit of Meeting Weekly for Breakfast, at a place called Holmes' Hotel. When this was proclaimed he had A Party Meeting for Dinner at Gray's Tavern. When it was proclaimed he proposed to make himself the Repeal Association, with an assisting council of thirty-one people. He said they couldn't disperse an individual by proclamation.

But it was never a question of what the Irish Government could do. Whether they could or could not do a thing they would do it—and did it. He started his Association under the title of the Irish Society for Legal and Legislative Relief; after that, again the Anti-Union Association; then an Association of Irish Volunteers for Repeal of the Union; and, succeeding that, an Association of Subscribers to the Parliamentary Intelligence Office.

It was an exciting game of hide-and-seek in which he so provoked and tired the Government that at length they arrested him. Even then he outwitted them—for he compromised on a plea of guilty for technical offence against a temporary Act (the Act for Suppression of Illegal Societies) and contrived to have sentence postponed until, at the expiration of Parliament, the Act expired, too.

To help the English Whigs in their great fight for Parliamentary Reform, O'Connell, much against the wish of many wise ones, slackened the Repeal fight, while he let the popular fight against tithes forge to the front. And he cast all his weight to the English Whigs in their Reform struggle.

The Established (Protestant) Church was supported in Ireland by the farmers of all religions paying to it tithes, a tenth of their products. In this way the poorer five-sixths of the Irish population was mulcted to support the very rich church of the remaining one-sixth. In the more Catholic parts of Ireland there were thousands of parishes from which the Established clergyman drew an enormous salary for ministering to his own family and the family of his sexton only. Whether his congregation was few or entirely non-existent, both he and his church had to be kept prosperous—by a people of another faith, who oftentimes had not meal for the mouths of their own children. In the year immediately succeeding Emancipation, the smouldering anger against this injustice leaped up in flame tongues, here and there. Little more than a year after the passing of Emancipation the yeomanry killed seventeen people who tried to rescue their seized cattle from the tithe-proctor at Bunclody in Wexford. The Government, after inquiry into the affair, concluded that the arms of the yeomanry were not effective enough for teaching a needed lesson to conscienceless people who could be guilty of hindering a tithe-proctor's purposes. So they granted them new and better equipment.

At Carrickshock in Kilkenny, in November of the same year, the people fell upon an armed force who guarded two tithe process-servers—and killed eighteen or twenty of them. The tithe war was almost getting out of hand. The Government, goaded by the suffering church, must make desperate efforts to suppress it. Twenty-five Carrickshock men were put on trial for murder at the Kilkenny assizes before a Special Commission sent down by Government. O'Connell went down to defend them, and here gave another fine example of his quality, most deftly shattering the Government's case, by breaking, at the first going off, the chief prop on which it rested. At the very outset of the trial they put forward their leading witness, a policeman, who gave direct, clean-cut, and definite testimony, proving home murder against some of the prisoners. His evidence was so definite in the most minute details as to be eminently convincing to an average jury. On cross-examination, he proved to be a rock that O'Connell could not shake. Things looked dark, almost desperate for the defence, when there was a little note passed from the body of the court to Counsellor O'Connell. He glanced at the note in the most casual manner, and learnt from it that the witness' father was a notorious and convicted sheep stealer. Apparently paying little attention to the note, he went on mechanically asking further questions in such an indifferent way as indicated that the witness' evidence was unshakable. Before dismissing him he paid the witness a couple of compliments on his evidence—which put the fellow in mighty good humour with himself and the world. Then as the witness was stepping out of the box, triumphant and elated, O'Connell said: "Just one minute, my friend"—and in a casual way said to him,

"I suppose you're fond of mutton." "Why, yes, Counsellor O'Connell. I wouldn't make strange with a good piece of mutton." "You don't happen to know any really clever sheep-stealers, now?" "No, I can't say that I do." "Did you ever know any sheep-stealers?" "I never had that pleasure." "You, of course, never have had any connection with any such person?" O'Connell spoke in an apologetic way as if he was, under compulsion, asking questions that he was ashamed to ask of a decent man. He led the witness on to swear over and over again, in the most solemn and most definite manner, that he had never known of, associated with, or been related to, any such disreputable person. "Then it was," says Fagan, in his Life of O'Connell, "that O'Connell pounced upon him. The court rang and echoed again with the thunders of his voice. The silent-stricken audience looked on with amaze at the portentous change of voice and manner which had taken place in the advocate, as well as in the witness; and, amid the hush of the multitude, the deep breathings of the prisoners, and the silent, heartfelt expectations of all present, the man was obliged to confess that his father had been the expert sheep-stealer, which, on his oath, he had so solemnly denied knowing but a few minutes before." And that man's evidence went at once to the scrap-heap.

The tithe war spread like wildfire. The people refused to pay the iniquitous imposition. They fought against the seizing of their cattle. All cows liable to be seized were branded "T" so that nowhere a purchaser could be found for them. Any one who paid was ostracised. Thousands of troops were poured into the country to protect the tithe proctors and process-servers. The Protestant clergy, unable to collect the tithes, were now in such real distress that the Government had to provide a Relief Fund for them. Many parts of Ireland were proclaimed; martial law was instituted; there were shootings, hangings, transportings. All meetings were suppressed. The Government assumed the tithe proctor's business, and after many marchings, countermarchings, and bloody conflicts, collected (out of hundreds of thousands of pounds due) twelve thousand pounds at a cost of fifteen thousand!

They finally rested from an impossible task and talked compromise. They suggested the reduction of the tithe by a fourth and shifting it in its reduced form to the landlord's shoulders—who should then increase his tenants' rents in proportion. O'Connell wanted the tithe reduced two-fifths. Neither proposition went into effect, just then. But the Vestry Act and the Church Temporalities Act of '34 made minor reforms and economies in the Establishment—including the suppression of ten ornamental but highly lucrative bishoprics, and a tax upon the fatter livings to help the lean ones. The tithe-war dragged on, in varying intensity, till in '38 was passed the Act which reduced the tithe by a fourth, and shifted it to the landlord. As almost all landlords raised the rent to recoup themselves, the people still had to continue bearing the burden of a foreign church.

In his desire to help the English Whigs in their Reform struggle, O'Connell had put Parliamentary Reform temporarily before Repeal, worked for it with might and main, and with his Irish following finally gave the Whigs the margin of majority that carried the Reform Bill. And when the Whigs came into power in the new Reform Parliament of '34, their first measure was a Coercion Bill for Ireland! The fiercest, too, of the many such boons to Ireland since the century's beginning!

Thus did the Irish leader find himself recompensed for shelving Repeal in the interests of the Whigs. "Six hundred scoundrels" was his designation of the Britishers who sat in the Reform Parliament. And the king's speech, recommending Coercion, he called "a brutal and bloody speech." In his fiery fighting trim, with the forty Repeal members (including eight members of his own family) which the General Election gave him from Ireland, he went to Westminster to try a fall with the "six hundred scoundrels" over the Coercion Bill. "The atrocious attempt to extinguish public liberty makes me young again," he wrote to Edward Dwyer, from London. He was now on the eve of sixty. "I feel the vigour of youth in the elastic spring of my hatred of tyranny." But his Reform friends overwhelmed his opposition, and gave a fresh turn of the screw to his suffering country.

When in '31 he had been warned against abandoning Irish Repeal for British Parliamentary Reform, he said to the people: "Let no one deceive you and say that I have abandoned anti-Unionism. It is false. But I am decidedly of opinion that it is only in a reformed Parliament that the question can properly, truly, and dispassionately, be discussed."

Yet, at the very time he said this, he had put Repeal aside to save his English friends. In a letter to his Whig friend, Lord Duncannon, in December, '31, he says: "On my arrival (in Dublin) I found a formidable anti-Union Association completed, called the Trade Union, headed by a man of popular qualifications, who was capable of success. I took his people out of his hands, and not only turned them, but I can say turned the rest of the country, from the overpowering question of Repeal to the suitable one of Reform."

Notwithstanding the Whigs' betrayal of him he returned them to power again after they had been thrown out, and kept them in power by the dependable bulk of his following.

Throughout the 'Thirties O'Connell seemed to work in complete forgetfulness of the one big fact which the agitation of the 'Twenties should have stamped indelibly on his mind, namely, that an Ireland lulled by the opiate of English friendship always proved to be an Ireland fooled; while an Ireland rebellious was an Ireland successful.

The Whigs, now needing his support, made formal alliance with him, flattered him, promised him, lured him on, gave minor offices to his friends, tried to tempt himself with office—an idea that indeed he pleasantly toyed with, but finally dismissed—and left him in the lurch.

Acting under the opiate, he, in '34, called on the country to try a six year "experiment"—to let Repeal remain in abeyance for that time, and see what Ireland's good friend, the Whigs, would do for her. And such was the faith and the confidence of the people in O'Connell, that, almost without a murmur they spiked their own guns on the battlefield, just to prove their trust in a generous enemy! And the poor fools were, of course, repaid according to their folly.

And during those years, the "experiment" years, Ireland got from the Whig Government the Poor Law Act (which O'Connell considered a curse instead of a cure), the Tithes Act which added three-quarters of that impost to their rent—and on the strength of which complacent Dan called upon the people to cease their tithe agitation—an Act forbidding subletting, and an Act to make ejectments easy. Bishop Doyle approved of the latter two Acts on the ground that they would help to save Ireland from poverty, and he was sorry they were not enacted thirty years before!

It was little wonder that in the late 'Thirties the Whig-befooled Dan found his popularity waning, got down-hearted, depressed, discouraged, and in '39 made retreat in Mt. Melleray to regain his calm. "It mortifies but does not surprise me," he wrote to a friend, "to find that I have exhausted the bounty of the Irish people. God help me! What shall I do?" He talked of retiring permanently into a monastery.

He came out of his Mount Melleray retreat—with a mind much calmed—able collectedly to review his position and make his plans. But only a miracle could rehabilitate him.

CHAPTER LXVII

The Great Repeal Fight

But the miracle happened.

And the blessed word that evoked the miracle was Repeal!

When, by a fortunate inspiration, the great man boldly uttered again the witching word which, for six years forbidden, had been heard not, or only heard in whispers, it resounded from hill to hill to the island's uttermost corner. It seemed whisked on the wings of life, till a million mouths re-echoed it. A land that had been settling into the silence of mild despair, suddenly burst into a great song of hope again; and the hero who was falling from his pedestal, was, by this magic word, now lifted to a pinnacle that he had never reached before.

In 1840 O'Connell founded the National Association of Ireland for repeal. The statements of principle which he wrote were led in by a true O'Connell flourish of superlative loyalty, pledging "most dutiful and ever inviolate loyalty to our gracious and ever-beloved sovereign queen, Victoria, her heirs and successors forever"—and by another characteristically O'Connell flourish of law-worship, spiced with piety: "The total disclaiming of, and absence from, all physical force, violence, or breach of the law, or in short, any violation of the laws of man or the ordinances of the Eternal God whose holy name be ever blessed." The hero was getting his old rhetorical stride again.

And in the intensity of his loyalty to his beloved sovereign the name of the Association was, in '41, improved into the Loyal National Repeal Association.

The Repeal movement was undoubtedly popularised—if such were possible—and materially stimulated by a couple of big happenings in the Dublin Corporation in these years. In '41 was elected, for the first time in history, a Nationalist corporation in Dublin. Under the Municipal Reform

Act, just obtained, the old Dublin Corporation, citadel of ultra-Orangeism, was wiped out and replaced by one that was five-sixths Nationalist. And to the frenzied delight of Dublin, and all Ireland, Dan O'Connell was elected the first Nationalist Lord Mayor.

So profound was the respect for Dan's sincerity and broad-mindedness that the few Orangemen left in the new Corporation stood up, in company with the Nationalist members, to do him honour. And Dan, in accepting the office, then said: "I pledge myself to this, that in my capacity as Lord Mayor no one will be able to discover my politics from my conduct.—In my capacity as a man though," he added, "I am a Repealer to my last breath."

When, in response to the myriad cries of the multitude of citizens who surged outside the City Hall, Dan, coming to a window, showed himself in his robes of office, the dramatic sight of a real Irishman filling the robes of the Lord Mayor of Dublin, set the multitude frantic with joy. In that rare sight they saw concrete token that their fearfully long toil was bearing fruit; and ages of suffering and striving being crowned by heaven with reward. The rags were surely falling from the Mother's shoulders, the fetters from her limbs; she was coming into her own again. With lighter heart and more hopeful, Ireland bent to the fight for Repeal.

The second stimulus was the great Repeal debate in the Dublin Corporation, where the new Lord Mayor made a Repeal speech, which, to the eager people who in every corner of the land devoured the report of it, was one of the most wonderful of his career. By overwhelming majority was carried a resolution to present a Repeal petition to Parliament. The great debate, from its first word to its last reported verbatim in all the papers, and carried to the farthest remote cabin in the most remote valleys of the Island, mightily swelled the enthusiasm with which the nation simmered, and multiplied the people's determination this time to win their goal.

From the day of his election to the Mayoralty it felt fine to the people to address Dan, one of their own, as "Your Lordship" and "My Lord." And it was all the happier for that the rich expression, far from having to be said in a frightened or cowering fashion, could be trolled out in a hail-fellow-well-met tone—to a lordship, who, instead of freezing one with an Arctic token of acknowledgment, answered with a smile that would melt the heart of a millstone. The mob henceforward delighted to run ahead of his lordship, on the street, crying to the waiting crowd, "Hats off, for his lordship!" And woe to the beaver head-covering of any crusty old Tory who was slow to uncover at the cry!

There was a great scene when, in his rich robes of office, Lord Mayor O'Connell rode through the streets attended by the Aldermen in their robes, to the Roman Catholic Cathedral. The very hardihood of making those robes, so long consecrated to Orangeism, ride to a Roman Catholic Cathedral, was refreshing to the populace.

But the great man never forgot method in his madness. As, with truly British ingenuity, the Act which emancipated Catholics decreed a fine of one hundred pounds for the criminal who would attend a Papist place of worship in robes of office, Dan got from under his robes outside the Cathedral door—where the Orange vestments surlily waited on the porch till his lordship returned from his idolatry.

Now the Repeal movement was in full swing. And O'Connell filled the land with the agitation. In wonderful speech after speech bristling with urge, ringing with hope, and thundering with defiance, he fostered the ferment in which the populace found itself.

"What good have we obtained from England in the season of her prosperity?" he thundered in the Association Hall. "She has made us weep tears of blood. *But she may want us yet.* Is there, even now, no hurricane threatening her from the other side of the Atlantic, careering against the sun, advancing with the speed of heaven's lightning? Hear we not the rattling of the hail, the driving of the tempest? Is there no danger that we may be needed to defend the western possessions of Britain? Look next at France—is she so kind, so friendly, as she has been? Does the aspect of the Continent in general promise to England a continuance of Continental friendship? Then, England's eastern territories—are they safe? Let Afghanistan answer! Saw you not the gallant regiment that passed along the quay a few moments ago? Whither go they? To India or to China? What signs are there of peace? From east to west, from north to south, a storm is lowering—through the darkening atmosphere we can hear the boom of the distant thunder—we discern the flashes of the coming lightning." But then, ever mindful of his loyalty, seasoning the defiance with the spice of fealty, he continues: "Yet even in the midst of the tempest may England have safety. She will need the aid of Irishmen. She shall have that aid. But"—his loyalty having testified, the politician speaks, "Irishmen require a bribe. Here am I who want a bribe. I *will* take a bribe. I must get a bribe. And my bribe is Repeal of the Union!"

"Grattan," he told them, again, "sat by the cradle of his country, and followed its hearse. It has been left to me to sound the resurrection trumpet, and show that our country was not dead, but only slept." And by such figures, rung out in the magnificent tones of one of the most rousing orators of the age, did he drive the nation forward in the joyous fight. The leader was in the finest fettle of his life. He had already forgotten the dark days when he lost his grip; his loving people had forgotten them. He rode on the ridge of his world again—lifted infinitely higher than ever before.

The Repeal organisation grew splendidly systematised and marvellously complete in every detail, in all corners of Ireland. Commemorating the three hundred Volunteer representatives in 1782, and the three hundred members of Grattan's Parliament, it had a Central Council of three hundred. As, under the Convention Act of 1793, the people could not elect delegates to represent them, the members of the Council were men from various parts of Ireland chosen to carry to the Repeal Treasury in Dublin a hundred pounds or more from their own neighbours and fellow-workers. Every parish had its branch of the Repeal Association. They appointed their Repeal wardens; they organised Arbitration courts to keep peace among neighbours who must march shoulder to shoulder in the great fight. They had their cavalry for marshalling and leading them at meetings. They had their Repeal Reading rooms. All faction and all crime was by them sternly put down. Their Repeal rent was regularly lifted from ready subscribers—and the whole country, organised and marshalled, was in finer fighting trim than at any time for forty years gone. They were ready for anything—peace or war—just as the fearless leader should direct.

But howsoever much he might indulge in the rhetorical storm, peace was with O'Connell a fetish.

The climax of the great Repeal fight came in '43. That was the year of the Monster meetings, the year of the sublime hope and the undaunted resolve, of the mighty welding of two million men into one solid bulwark of freedom. And yet, alas, it was the sad year of real defeat!

To a nation hanging on his every word and implicitly accepting every dictum, he proclaimed '43 "Repeal year"—and the jubilant nation pushed onward, with redoubled vigour, to the blessed goal. In that great year the fearless leader rode the whirlwind. The Repeal rent, flowing from the pockets of the ready people, multiplied with every succeeding week. His personal tribute that year mounted to the handsome figure of twenty thousand pounds. And the people considered it not half enough—and would have repeated it again and again if they only got the hint.

All Ireland was full of fight as well as jubilation, and full of a new-found confidence in its own power, which all of England's armies could not down.

The people were full of fight in the literal as well as the figurative sense of the word, and hundreds of thousands of them cherished the half-concealed belief that if Prime Minister Peel did not surrender to O'Connell peacefully, their leader, despite his oft-shouted warning that freedom was too dearly purchased at the price of a single drop of blood—would whisper a word which should thrill the nation to its uttermost headland, and conjure up a countless, indomitable, army in a single night.

The fighting spirit which stirred the hearts of the people that year expressed itself at those wonderful gatherings, unique in the history of nations—the Monster meetings. It is somewhat difficult for Irishmen, and almost impossible for outsiders, today, to realize that at each of a series of forty meetings held all over the land, in that memorable year, there gathered one hundred thousand people, two hundred thousand, four hundred thousand, and upwards to numbers uncountable. Yet such was the fact. A quarter of a million people in attendance came to be considered moderate. *The London Times* conceded a million to the gathering on the hill of Tara.

O'Connell, feeling that the hostile English Parliament would not consent to bow to the will of the Irish people, again and again in his speeches, which were swaying the multitude, appealed over the head of Parliament to Royalty. He pointed out that the Queen of England had the right, of her own accord, to summon a Parliament in Dublin. And, influenced by his worship of Victoria, he seems actually to have worked himself into the belief that her love for the Irish people was such that she might resort to this extraordinary step.[1]

The mighty development of the movement in Ireland, the ferment, the astonishing spirit of the people, the organisation, the gatherings, the speeches, deeply alarmed the English Government. Prime Minister Peel felt it necessary, publicly and authoritatively to declare that his Queen's sentiments on the question of Repeal were the very opposite of what O'Connell had attributed to her. Peel also declared that if O'Connell forced the issue of civil war or Repeal, England would without hesitation choose the former.

And, for all his ludicrous loyalty to the crown of England and for all his oft-sworn antipathy to bloodshed, O'Connell, several times during this exciting summer, seemed to have caught something of the undaunted spirit which he had aroused in the breasts of the people. They had eight million people in Ireland, he warned Peel, and another million Irish in the United States of America, and practically said to him: Come on if you dare! "We shall make no rebellion," O'Connell said. "We wish no civil war. We shall keep on the ground of the Constitution, as long as we are allowed; but if Peel

---

[1] He would have got a rude awakening had he lived to read in his noble heroine's private correspondence, when it came to be published, her letter written to Leopold of Belgium, after the subsidence of the '48 movement—in which she expressed her regret that the general uprising had not taken place as planned, "so that the Irish might be taught a lesson!" The little testimony to royal charity was carefully eliminated from the second and succeeding editions of the book.

forces a contest, if he invades the constitutional rights of the people—then *vae victis* between the contending parties! Where is the coward who would not die for such a land as Ireland! Let our enemies attack us if they dare. They shall never trample me under foot!"

And at the great Mallow meeting in June, where four hundred thousand people attended (just a few days after the Kilkenny meeting with its three hundred thousand) O'Connell waxed so militant as to quote with intense spirit Moore's words:

"Oh, where's the slave so lowly,
Condemned to chains unholy,
Who could he burst,
His bonds accurst,
Would pine beneath them slowly!"

And he thrilled his audience by thundering out, "I'm not that slave!"

Then also he launched the famous Mallow defiance, a characteristic O'Connell compound of independence and subserviency, sedition, and loyalty. "You may soon have the alternative to live as slaves," he shouted, "or die as freemen. . . . If they assailed us tomorrow, and we should conquer them—as conquer them we will, some day—our first use of that victory, would be to put the sceptre in the hands of Victoria. . . . They may trample on me, but it will be the dead body of me they will trample, not the living man!"

"Ah," said the pleased people, "Dan will now pass the word." And though the waiting host had not in sight any more effective arms than pitchforks and the like, they were willing with them to try and push the British army into the sea.

But when the Mallow defiance had roused the fighting spirit and the militant hopes of a million, Dan took the opportunity of the great Skibbereen meeting, ten days or so later, to lay the martial spirit he had evoked. "It is better," he counselled in Skibbereen, "to live for Ireland than to die for her." If O'Connell's inconsistencies this year confused the enemy as much as they did his own hosts, there might be something to be said in their favour.

Anyway, England was getting profoundly embarrassed, as well as frightened. Her enemies and the world were following every step of the Irish struggle. There was held in New York a great conference on Ireland, lasting a week—whereat it was counselled that if England plunged Ireland into civil war, Canada should be seized. President Tyler said that Ireland should have Repeal. Some of the French even came forward with offers of money and of arms and men. British regiments were thrown into Ireland. The

British navy circled it with a chain of warships. Feverish preparations for the worst were made by the Government.

Meantime the Monster meetings had gone forward, still increasing in numbers and in enthusiasm. One of the most wonderful things and one of the most pregnant, too, with alarm for England was, that Ireland, though rocking from shore to shore with excitement, became absolutely crimeless. This ominous fact frightened Ireland's governors infinitely more than if crime had raged over the land. The Monster meetings were signally characterised by an utter absence of both drink and disorder.[2] Father Mathew's Total Abstinence movement had swept the land, and secured this. The preaching, the teaching, and the drilling of the parish branches of the Repeal Association, had completed the good work. Thousands and tens of thousands of men marched to the meetings in military formation, quick to the word of command. And many, be it noted, marched a day and a night to the gathering place.

But the greatest and most memorable of all the great meetings was that at Tara—on Lady Day in August. To the historic place, crowds had been travelling for days and nights. Immense were the numbers that arrived at the Hill overnight. On the hillside were set up six altars, around which knelt multitudes to hear Mass in the morning. From daybreak the unending streams of humanity could be seen, riding, driving, walking—streaming to it from all points of the compass, every minute augmenting the sea of humanity that overspread the meeting place. An army of ten thousand Repeal cavalry rode out the Dublin road to meet O'Connell, and such was the extent and the crush of the great multitude that when they reached nigh the hill with him, it took them an hour and a half to steer him a mile through the living sea. Headed by bands and banners and marshalled by horsemen, no such gathering as that at Tara was ever seen before, and may never be seen again. While *The London Times* admitted a million as the number at the gathering, and the Repealers claimed twelve hundred thousand, if we, in skeptical mood, suppose that, by error, even the *Times* overestimated by even doubling the count, the number would still be so huge as to strain our imagination.[3]

When his eye swept over that human sea O'Connell himself must have marvelled at the spirit that animated the nation. "What," he said, "could

---

[2] Except once, when, it is told, an ardent English enthusiast, who came to help the work, lost his hat—and likewise his temper. "Damn you people!" he shouted. "I came here all the way from England to emancipate you, and you stole my hat." And he indignantly returned to England without emancipating them.

[3] Gavan Duffy would lead us to infer that all estimates of all the Monster meetings were about double the actual figures.

England effect against such a people so thoroughly aroused, if, provoked past endurance, they rose out in rebellion." The leader was not only elated by the wonderful things he saw and felt—but possibly alarmed. For he added: "While I live such an uprising will never occur."[4]

One of the last of the big meetings was that at Mullaghmast, the scene of the famous massacre of Irish chieftains in the time of Elizabeth of England. Four hundred thousand was the number said to have assembled there. Mullaghmast was the famous occasion of O'Connell's accepting a crown prepared for him, and presented to him by, the sculptor Hogan, the artist MacManus, and John Cornelius O'Callaghan the historian—an incident that naturally aroused wild enthusiasm, not only in the huge gathering that watched, but all over Ireland.

The Monster meetings of the year were to culminate and climax a week after Mullaghmast, on the battleplain of Clontarf, outside Dublin, where Brian Boru had broken the foreign invader and cast him into the sea. And now the Government, thoroughly aroused to its imminent danger, took desperate resolve. At the eleventh hour it forbade the Clontarf meeting. Sunday was to have been the meeting day. At three o'clock on Saturday afternoon—when already, from a hundred distant points, masses of marching men had started for the morrow's rendezvous—it papered Dublin with the proclamation. Five regiments of soldiers, with cannon and all the appliances of war, were stationed at vantage points in and around Clontarf. The gauntlet was thrown down to O'Connell.

An emergency meeting of the Repeal executive was instantly summoned. O'Connell, telling them that nothing would justify his permitting vast masses of unarmed men to be mowed down, pronounced that there was nothing to do but submit. They of course agreed. Mounted messengers were instantly sent flying out of Dublin along every road that led to the Capital. All bodies of marching men were turned back, and the word sent everywhere far and wide over the country that no meeting would be on the morrow.

The Government had taken a dangerous hazard and won.

And they quickly followed up their advantage. On Sunday morning they arrested O'Connell, his son John, Ray the Repeal Treasurer, Tom Steele, two priests, and the editors of three Nationalist papers, Gray of *The Freeman's Journal*, Barrett of *The Pilot*, and Duffy of *The Nation*. These were

---

[4] The spirit that raised up such a gathering will be all the more appreciated when it is remembered that on the same day, at less than a hundred miles' distance, in County Monaghan, was another gathering, estimated at a quarter of a million men.

charged with conspiring to change the Constitution by illegal methods, and to excite disaffection.

The country stood on tip-toe awaiting "the word" from O'Connell—whatever that word might be. And tens of thousands of eager ones prayed that it might be a bold one. But, Peace was the word given by the leader.

The people implicitly obeyed. The man who disobeyed the order would be a traitor to the cause and the country. Even *The Nation*, which after a little while was to condemn O'Connell for lack of boldness, and lead a revolt from him, sternly commanded that the captain's word must be unquestioningly obeyed.

The Traversers were tried by a packed jury of Tories and Orangemen. No Catholic was permitted on it. A whole file of the jury list, containing names of men who could not be welcomed to the jury by the prosecution, was, before the trial, "lost" from the sheriff's complete list. The spirit that sat in the British judgment seat then, as in most Irish political trials, was well and ludicrously exemplified by the presiding Chief Justice, Pennefather, when in giving an opinion upon a disputed point, he let slip: "I speak under the correction of the gentlemen of the other side!"

The Traversers were of course found guilty. O'Connell was sentenced to twelve months' imprisonment, to pay a fine of two thousand pounds, and give bail to be of good behaviour for seven years. The others were given nine months' imprisonment, fifty pounds' fine, and bail. Between the time of the verdict and the sentence, O'Connell, weakening, re-formed the Repeal Association so as to eliminate from it things that had now been established as unlawful—including his Arbitration Courts. And he set the example of closing every meeting by calling for cheers for England's Queen! It was upon this unwise retreat that *The Nation* and Young Ireland, violently opposing, began to break with him.

Yet he held the unhesitating loyalty of the country at large. And every tyrannical and unjust step of the Government, from the eve of Clontarf till they put the leader in prison, seemed to strengthen the people's fight—and, moreover, brought into the ranks many of the gentry who had hitherto stood outside—including Smith O'Brien. The Repeal rent went on increasing. When the final step of imprisoning him was taken, the Repeal rent bounded up with a great bound. In the quarter of a year after O'Connell went into prison, there was taken four times as much rent as in the quarter of a year preceding. Though the movement had undoubtedly got a rude check, the spirit of the country, strange to say, was not even feazed.

Yet time proved that on the day of Clontarf was dug the grave of O'Connell's Repeal.

CHAPTER LXVIII

The End of O'Connell

But the movement and the man had an Indian summer.

The great criminal in prison was as a mighty prince holding court. Deputations from all parts of Ireland, led by mayors of cities, bishops, and other dignitaries daily arrived to pay him court. Every word of O'Connell's, going out from his prison walls, had now double as much weight as had formerly the weightiest pronouncement of the free O'Connell, thundered from a platform.

After four months they were released by decision of the Law Lords of the House of Lords, when these heard the case on appeal. Two hundred thousand people frantic with joy, on the day of his release jammed the streets along which rode the Liberator from the prison to his home, throned in state on the high deck of a specially made triumphal car. It was one of the proudest days of a life that had been enriched with a plenitude of proud ones.

And on the second day after, great crowds crammed Conciliation Hall, and the streets surrounding it, to hear the message of the liberated leader, and get, as they thought, fresh inspiration for the still further speeding of the struggle.

But Clontarf and its sequel, the trial and imprisonment, had marked a great turning point in Dan's career; and he now disappointed the nation. While the speech rang as boldly as ever with denunciations of the Government that had perverted the laws to imprison him, and with threats of what he would do to them, and to all their minions, including Pennefather and the other mis-Judges on the Bench—all of which won the old wild plaudits from his hearers—he did not suggest a plan or lay a line for carrying the fight to fruition. He studiously avoided any statement of future policy—only emphasised, with an emphasis that did not decrease the people's disappointment, his too-oft reiterated single-drop-of-blood theory, boasting that he was the first apostle and founder of that noble political creed whose cardinal doctrine was that no human revolution was worth the effusion of one red drop.

And without giving the country a lead he went home to Derrynane to rest and recuperate—to forget politics for a period, stroll by the white strands of Kerry, and on its mountains hunt the hare. Afterwards, it was on all sides conceded that the softening of the brain which was to end his life, had set in during the months of his imprisonment. He was nevermore the old Dan, the bold Dan, whose magnetic power had gifted him, by the lifting of a little finger, to lead a nation.

In the course of a few months he courted Federalism—which a generation later came to be called Home Rule—and he compelled the Repeal Association to admit into its ranks the Federalists, a party of Whig country gentlemen for the most part, but having in their ranks a few progressive intellectual ones like William Smith O'Brien and the young poet Davis. But he soon found that Federalism fell flat on the country, even where, as amongst the thinking ones, it did not actually call up antagonism. And when he came up to Dublin in May for the great anniversary celebration of his imprisonment, the politician Dan confided to the people, who had spurned his Federalism, that after having now given the fullest consideration to Federalism, he considered—with a snap of the fingers—it wasn't worth *that!* And during the minutes of the multitude's frantic applause the astute Dan felt good reason for pluming himself that he was the peerless leader still.

And indeed in the hearts and thoughts of the vast body of the people he was. The homage paid him at that anniversary celebration was almost equal to anything he had before experienced. Let the bitterly antagonistic Tory *Mail* describe it, "While we write this," says the *Mail*, "Mr. O'Connell is sitting in autocratic state in the throne room of the Rotunda, surrounded by his peers, and receiving the addresses of the authorities, the corporate bodies, the nobility, clergy and gentry of his peculiar dominion. The business of the city is at a standstill. Professional duties are in suspense; tradesmen have closed their shops; the handicrafts have left their callings; and, save the great thoroughfares through which the ovation of the Autocrat is to pass, the streets are deserted, and as noiseless as a wilderness. In the latter, shops lie open, but without a customer; in the former the barricaded doors and windows scarce suffice to resist the pressure of the throng. A countless multitude, crowding all the avenues leading to the autocrat's presence, forms dense alleys for the passage of the public bodies, which, headed by their appointed leaders—some in military costume, some in their civic robes of office, and all in full dress—proceed to the music of the bands, with regimental uniformity, towards the chamber where their self-elected sovereign has appointed to receive their homage."

But alas, it was only in the warm hearts of a loving, worshipping people that their sovereign's greatness now lived. His old stamina gone, he could not evolve a new policy or face a fresh fight. Forgetful of his sad, sad lesson of the 'Thirties, he let himself again lean upon the Whigs—or, maybe it could be said, let the Whigs lean upon him. In '45 the Whig leader, Lord John Russell, had become so popular with the Irish leader that we find Dan threatening to transfer to his brows his own Mullaghmast crown. And a few months later, in May of '46—while Ireland staggered from the first bad blow of the '45 potato blight—we find the uncrowned king, Lord John, with his Whig following, trooping into the division lobby, shoulder to shoulder with the Tories, to vote comfort to England's suffering sister in the form of a vile Coercion Bill. This, on the Bill's first reading. Before the second reading was reached the Whigs found need for O'Connell and his fellows, enlisted again Dan's alliance to throw out the Tories—which he enabled them to do—and put their kind selves in power. And on the old, old and again implicitly believed promise of remedial measures for Ireland, O'Connell practically blotted out of his dictionary the word Repeal.

The *Nation* party, the Young Ireland party, which had its first serious difference with O'Connell on his Federal fad, led now by Duffy, Mitchel and Smith O'Brien, were rebelling against him and the Association (which was controlled by his son John); and, seeking an antidote to the Whigs' opiate, were preaching revolution to the country. The final split between the old and the new came when Dan ordered the Association to purge itself by passing the Peace Resolutions—which would pledge every man within the Association ranks to the single-drop-of-blood policy. The split at that meeting of the Association was immediately precipitated by young Meagher's Sword speech.

John O'Connell made immediate reply to Meagher, "These sentiments imperil the very existence of our association. Either Mr. Meagher or I must leave." Thereupon the Young Ireland leaders, Duffy, Mitchel, O'Brien and Meagher, marched out of the hall, and out of the Association.

And henceforward to the sincerely grieved Daniel O'Connell and his lieutenants in the Association, the Young Ireland party, more than England, were Ireland's enemy.[1]

---

[1] Mitchel (in after years) named O'Connell, "next to the British Government, the greatest enemy Ireland ever had." It was owing to his influence, Mitchel held, that the attempted insurrection of '48

And now, day by day, more ardently than ever Dan courted and flattered the new Whig friends who had come to him, and more bitterly than ever denounced the Irish friends who had left him.

Famine now fastened its clutch on the country. The potato crop of '46, which was eagerly expected to cure the acute distress produced by the '45 failure, was blighted—and proved a more overwhelming failure than that of the year before. And the harvest of '47 was yet to plunge the people in far deeper distress.

The dreadful sufferings of the poor people now helped to complete the Liberator's mental breakdown. The heart of him sank down into sadness. The Tribute which had been paid to him annually by his faithful people, and which, through recent years had amounted to about twenty thousand pounds annually, he now spurned. His friend Fitzpatrick, who had had charge of the Tribute, was rebuked by him for mentioning it in a time so pitiful. For though in his necessarily lavish way of living he needed money now, as always, and could command all he pleased whenever he pleased, he was never avaricious. And the suggestion of taking money from the people in these times cut him to the quick.

In the beginning of '47, though feeling sick and worn both in body and soul, he set out upon the sore week's journey to London to plead, this time, the material cause of the people. He made his last appearance, and last speech in Parliament, in February of that year. It was a pathetic scene, the pitifulness of which affected some of his bitterest enemies—who now saw and heard with pain the bent and broken giant, in tones weak, shaken, and indistinct, plead with them, beg of them, for sake of God and common humanity, to save his perishing people!

All the more heart-breaking for the giant was this trial, since he felt from sad, long, and bitter experience, that he spoke to ears that were officially deaf. Howsoever sympathetic they might have felt individually in response to his plea, these British members of Parliament were jealous

---

ended in failure. In his *Jail Journal* he, not without much of the exaggeration of prejudice, exclaims, "Poor old Dan! Wonderful, mighty, jovial, and mean old man! With silver tongue and smile of witchery and heart of unfathomable fraud! What a royal yet vulgar soul, with the keen eye and potent sweep of a generous eagle of Cairn Tuathal—with the base servility of a hound, and the cold cruelty of a spider! Think of his speech for John Magee, the most powerful forensic achievement since before Demosthenes, and then think of the 'gorgeous and gossamer' theory of moral and peaceful agitation, the most astounding organon of public swindling since first man bethought him of obtaining money under false pretence. And after one has thought of all this and more, what then can a man say? What but pray that Irish earth may lie light on O'Connell's breast, and that the good God who knew how to create so wondrous a creature may have mercy upon his soul?"

guardians of tradition. And British tradition always held that it was a serious mistake and setting unwise precedent ever to extend a helping hand to the perverse step-child of the Empire.

O'Connell went back to his hotel, and lay down, ill. "Take me home to Kerry!" No, it was ordered by the physicians—who diagnosed lingering congestion of the brain—that his only chance was to seek sunshine and distraction, under southern skies. He refused. But he soon compromised with them on the scheme of a pilgrimage to Rome.

He set out under charge of his youngest son, Daniel, and his chaplain, Dr. Miley. His sad, slow journey was yet relieved and made memorable by many proud things. The most noted men and Societies of the chief Continental cities through which they passed came to do homage to the famous invalid. Had he not been suffering from such deep depression, it would have been for him a truly triumphal journey. Not perhaps since the year Napoleon escaped from Elba had the journeying of any man through France been so widely chronicled on the Continent, so eagerly read of, caused such profound sensation.

He appeared to brighten, and the cloud over his mind to lighten, as he progressed south. But at Genoa he was severely stricken. He could go, would go, no farther. He took to his bed, there, and sank gradually. The sinking of an exiled monarch in their midst could not have moved and stirred the good citizens of Genoa as did that of the Irish Liberator—and certainly would not have evoked a tithe of the pleading prayers, deep and sincere, that from all classes, high and low, were daily going up for the dying man.

The great man's end came, calm and painless, on May 15th, 1847. In accordance with his dying wish, his heart, enshrined in a silver urn, was taken to Rome, where it was received with signal honours. The body was carried on the long journey to Ireland. And city vied with city in doing highest homage to it as it passed. To the funeral ship on the sea passages the ships of all nations lowered their flag. When a little Skerries fishing craft, accidentally encountering the funeral ship on the Irish sea, learnt that it bore O'Connell, it is recorded that all hands including the helmsman, let go everything, fell upon their knees, and while their little craft drifted, prayed toward the funeral ship till they were lost sight of. When the O'Connell ship was entering Dublin Bay they met, coming out, a big passenger ship, the *Birmingham*, crowded with poor emigrants leaving their beloved land behind—most of them, forever. The moment these creatures recognised the funeral ship, they spontaneously dropped on their knees on the deck, and with hands uplifted to heaven, raised the wildly sorrowful *caoine* (keen).

Having been accorded the greatest funeral that Dublin had ever witnessed, the remains of Daniel O'Connell were laid under the earth in Glasnevin cemetery on August 5th, 1847—while a whole nation wept the loss of a leader, than whom no Captain of any people was ever more widely, more deeply, and, let us say, on the whole more deservedly beloved.

By his intimate and personal friend, O'Neill Daunt, it was truly said of O'Connell: "Well may his countrymen feel pride in the extraordinary man, who, for a series of years, could assail and defy a hostile and powerful government, who could knit together a prostrate, divided, and dispirited nation into a resolute and invincible confederacy; who could lead his followers in safety through the traps and pitfalls that beset their path to freedom; who could baffle all the artifices of sectarian bigotry; and finally overthrow the last strongholds of anti-Catholic tyranny by the simple might of public opinion."

For O'Connell and the O'Connell Period read:
Lives of O'Connell by MacDonagh, Fagan, Luby.
Personal Recollections of O'Connell, O'Neill Daunt.
Leaders of Public Opinion, Lecky.

CHAPTER LXIX

Young Ireland

The Young Ireland movement developed naturally from the O'Connell movement. When any, the best, movement in the world grows old with its founder, it gradually loses its idealism, inspiration, and progressiveness, follows the line of least resistance and accepts men measures and methods that in its heyday it would have scorned.

The O'Connell movement, grown old, was no exception to the law. We have seen that during the 'Thirties O'Connell fell far from his earlier high aims, and dragging his movement, bound but willing, after the Whig chariot, lost it its respect, prestige and effectiveness. Its strength ebbed, and it was honeycombed with placehunters. The leader made a bold burst in the early 'Forties, resolved to put the movement in its high place again, but though he was a giant the effort needed more than a giant's strength. Besides he was now far from being the same moral giant who had pulled down the pillars of the enemy's temple twenty years before. True, the magic of his name and the memory of the dauntless O'Connell that had been, rallied behind him for a time the same nation in the same solid phalanx as of yore. But the giant leader now had not the same unflinching determination and unwavering vision which used to drive and draw him to victory over all obstacles. He did not now so surely feel the lofty ideals which he voiced, and consequently was not so irresistibly drawn on by them. In the olden days, in the fight for Emancipation, O'Connell was supereminently intolerant of any suggestion of compromise, and as a consequence won out. In these days, however, though he demanded as undauntedly and thundered as defiantly as before, he nursed in the back of his mind the wish to accept a part if he could not get the whole—occasionally too, let the wish thrust its head from its hiding-place. Consequently he failed.

The younger men whom he fired by his eloquence in the first forward move of the 'Forties, and who took his words at their face value, grew restive when at length they discovered that they had been deceived—and went out from his movement to found for themselves a more forward one, the Young Ireland movement.

The poet, Thomas Davis, was the founder of it. He was a young Protestant barrister from Cork. He was smitten by the enthusiasm in the air and drawn into the Repeal Movement. With a County Monaghan young man, Charles Gavan Duffy, then editing a national weekly in Belfast, and a young barrister, John Blake Dillon, he founded *The Nation*—to support the movement for Repeal, to propagate patriotism in the country, and to develop a love for Irish national literature. *The Nation* was destined to be a great power in the land, and to leave behind it a magnificent and inspiring tradition. The support of these intensely earnest and eminently able young men, and of their organ, which instantly leaped into powerful popularity, at first pleased O'Connell. But when, after a time, they showed that they had minds of their own, which exquisite blarney could not befog, he grew, first impatient with, and then resentful of, them. It was the O'Connellites, too, who in derision—because they failed to follow the Leader in every vagary in which he would indulge—first named them Young Irelanders. And that which was first applied to them in opprobrium came in course of time to be their pride.

With historical essays, patriotic ballads and poems, and virile national articles, they aroused and enthused the people—especially the young men, and quickly made for themselves a great following. They attracted and gathered around them the finest minds of the nation—till three patriot propagandists soon increased to thirty-three. Through the medium of the loved *Nation*, there blossomed upon Ireland poets, essayists, and patriots, the memory of most of whom has been an inspiration to succeeding generations of young Irish men and women, and will be cherished by generations yet to come. Duffy and Davis themselves gave to the country some of its most inspiring songs and ballads, and their efforts were well sustained by Denis Florence McCarthy, Samuel Ferguson, Michael Doheny, John Fisher Murray, Denny Lane, "Eva," "Mary," "Speranza" (Lady Wilde), Drennan, Brennan, Clarence Mangan, Devin Reilly, Barry and D'Arcy McGee.[1] And two of their greatest acquisitions undoubtedly were William Smith O'Brien and John Mitchel.

---

[1] Sad to say, in later days, Barry and also McGee who sang some noble strains and did, each, a man's work in the Young Ireland movement, lapsed and fell far from the ideal of their young manhood.

The death of Davis, young, brave, the hope of the country, in '45, was a sad blow, and probably a greater disaster than we can ever definitely realise, not only to Young Ireland but to Ireland. So loveable and so estimable was he, and so big with promise of a great future was his young life, that the whole nation wept—just as O'Connell wept when he learnt the sad news.

O'Brien, who eventually became one of the most prominent figures in the Young Ireland movement, was a Protestant country gentleman, studious of habit, who had not shown any national leanings until the O'Connell Repeal movement first won him to nationalism. The Young Ireland party gradually won him over from O'Connell. Their greatest acquisition was John Mitchel, son of a Unitarian minister, who was practising law in Banbridge when *The Nation* inspired him, drew him to Dublin, and into the whirl of national politics. In turn he drew in his brother-in-law the gentle but firm-willed John Martin.

The Nation gave fresh impetus to those who had already been inspired by O'Connell, and it awoke in their breasts a new spirit. O'Connell had deluded the multitude into giving awed respect to the foreign laws that bound them, marching to Repeal meetings in their many thousands, that they might cheer his speeches to the skies, and go home again without breach of law or order—leaving him and Providence to do the rest. *The Nation* and the Young Irelanders, while still giving heartiest help to O'Connell, managed, at first by suggestion, afterwards by plain precept, to stir the militant spirit in the people, and to impress on them that platform talk had to be backed by grim resolve, and that a nation's freedom was worth fighting and dying for. The militancy of the verse and prose that every week warmed the cold print, and enlivened the columns, of *The Nation*—and then the breasts of the people—hurt O'Connell, and alarmed him—and excited his jealousy, moreover. And when, in reply to a warning from the English press that the new Irish railway system afforded effective means for the quick movement of troops against Repealers grown bold, Mitchel, in *The Nation* wrote an article showing the people how easily railway lines could be rendered ineffective, O'Connell was thereby so deeply incensed that he held both the Repeal Association and himself silent while *The Nation* was now being prosecutèd for sedition.

Other causes of irritation to Dan were that they had opposed him on Federalism when he gave way for a time to that weakness—and upon the propriety of accepting the Queen's Colleges. On this latter issue he and his Repeal Association opposed them bitterly, going to such extravagant length as to accuse *The Nation* of being a school of infidelity.

While there was absolutely no ground for this accusation against the Young Irelanders, they had the best possible ground for being aggrieved against Dan and his Association for letting itself down from nationality to sectarianism. Young Ireland had set before it as one of its prime objects, the winning over to nationalism of the Protestant elements of the country; and they found the Repeal Association demonstrating that it was only a Catholic Association, thus driving the Orange element into its old anti-Irish shell. The breach between the Old and Young Irelanders widened when William Smith O'Brien, living up to O'Connell's command of '46, that the Repeal Members of Parliament should remain away from the British House to work for Ireland in Ireland, and refuse even to serve upon Special Committees to which Parliament commandeered them, went to prison in the House for disobedience—while O'Connell and his son, forsaking the principle, tamely obeyed the Parliamentary order. Young Ireland espoused the cause of O'Brien, commended him for his devotion to principle and Ireland—and thereby of course severely censured O'Connell.

Finally, when O'Connell, repeating his grave error of the 'Thirties, not only allied himself with the Whigs, but thus tacitly deserted Repeal, he was openly reprimanded by *The Nation* and Young Ireland. O'Connell, furious at such flagrant insubordination in the Repeal ranks resolved to rid it of all mutinous ones. For this purpose he directed the Repeal Association to reaffirm the constitutional and peace principles on which the Association was founded, and make every member subscribe to these principles. This would automatically rid the movement of the militants. The Peace Resolutions debate, which it came to be called, was a fierce one, lasting two days, and reaching its climax when Meagher burst into his famous sword speech—

> "The soldier is proof against an argument, but he is not proof against a bullet. The man who will listen to reason let him be reasoned with; but it is the weaponed arm of the patriot that can alone avail against battalioned despotism. I do not disclaim the use of arms as immoral, nor do I believe it is the truth to say that the God of Heaven withholds His sanction from the use of arms. From the day on which, in the valley of Bethulia, He nerved the arm of the Jewish girl to smite the drunken tyrant in his tent, down to the hour in which He blessed the insurgent chivalry of the Belgian priests, His Almighty hand hath been stretched forth from His throne of light, to consecrate the flag of freedom, to bless the patriots' sword. Be it for the defence, or be it for the assertion, of a nation's liberty, I look upon the sword as a sacred weapon. And if, my lord, it has sometimes

> reddened the shroud of the oppressor, like the anointed rod of the high priest, it has, at other times, blossomed into flower to deck the free man's brow. Abhor the sword, and stigmatise the sword? No, my lord, for in the cragged passes of the Tyrol it cut in pieces the banner of the Bavarian, and won an immortality for the peasant of Inspruck. Abhor the sword and stigmatise the sword? No, my lord, for at its blow a giant nation sprang from the waters of the Atlantic, and by its redeeming magic the fettered colony became a daring free republic. Abhor the sword and stigmatise the sword? No, my lord, for it scourged the Dutch marauders out of the fine towns of Belgium, back into their own phlegmatic swamps, and knocked their flag, and laws, and sceptre, and bayonets, into the sluggish waters of the Scheidt. My lord, I learnt that it was the right of a nation to govern itself, not in this Hall, but upon the ramparts of Antwerp."

O'Connell's son, John, who now always represented his father in the Repeal Association, arose from his seat on the platform, interrupting the speaker, and announcing that he could not sit there and listen to such sentiments. He would leave the hall and leave the Association if such a speech, in flagrant breach of the Association's Constitution, was permitted and approved.

Rather than have John O'Connell leave the Association that had been founded and fostered by his father, Meagher, Mitchell, Duffy, O'Brien, Reilly, Father Meehan, and other Young Irelanders present, got up and walked out—out of the hall and out of the Repeal Association.

Then the Young Irelanders founded the Confederacy—to work for Ireland's uplifting—at the very beginning of '47. And the two movements, the constitutional and the flagrantly unconstitutional, went side by side. *The Nation* had been driven from the Repeal reading rooms—which reading rooms, by the way, were mainly the fruits of Davis' work—and its circulation for a time materially injured. But the enthusiasm of its supporters soon widened its field, and compensated for the injury which the Association had done it. It now grew more militant than ever, with Mitchel ever in a militant lead.

Very great was the enthusiasm for *The Nation* throughout mountain and valley of all the land. At the cottage firesides, in the forge, in the churchyard, at the cross-roads—wherever the old men sat, and the young men met—*The Nation*, the news in *The Nation*, its rousing ballads, its stirring articles, were the inspiring constant theme. Though money was scarce and newspapers dear—*The Nation* costing fivepence—the people in the remotest mountains clubbed their pennies, and paid a smart boy to foot it far over the hills each Saturday and bring from distant town the coveted paper—which should be read in company on the day of rest. They gathered to the house of a farmer famed as a fine reader, or of a schoolmaster—oftentimes to the house of the tailor or shoemaker, whose smart daughter, seated on a chair on the table, read aloud for the delectation of the company the momentous happenings, the wonderful speeches of the week, the articles, the essays, the inspiring ballads. And the company afterwards dispersed, each to carry the great news to the group that waited for him at his own fireside.

Mitchel kept pushing so far ahead militantly of his fellows in *The Nation* group that he eventually parted with them—in February '48. He stood for action—and for precipitating action. He was impatient of temporising. His fellows on *The Nation*, and the general body of the Confederacy, felt, knew, that Ireland was not yet prepared to rise out against the mighty British Empire, that their people were neither trained nor equipped. They wanted to make the most of the Constitutional policy, at the same time that they proceeded with the ripening of the country for ultimate revolution, should revolution become necessary. Mitchel felt that so-called Constitutionalism had had its trial and failed despicably to do other than demoralise the people who used it—and also felt that since the famine was mowing down the people in hundreds of thousands it was infinitely better for Ireland, and nobler far for themselves, to sell their lives for their country than to throw them away without return—to fall on the field, facing their nation's foe, than to wait for the famine to drain their life from them in the ditches.

When he parted with his colleagues upon the matter of policy, he founded *The United Irishman* for purpose of propagating his principles. The little paper leaped into instant fame, and in widespread circulation soon far outstripped *The Nation*. He had Devin Reilly as his active coadjutor. And he had poor faithful Clarence Mangan, and "Mary" and "Eva" as his warm supporters and steady contributors. He preached open rebellion; and from week to week gave instructions in pike practice—which awaked such hearty response throughout the country that *The Nation* quickly felt itself called upon to follow suit.

The French Revolution now burst and quickly established the rule of the people in that nation. Europe was rocking with revolution. It had got into the people's blood. Their blood rose and thoughts of freedom fired their souls. All enslaved ones were bursting their bonds. Ireland was riper than most of them to nurture the new spirit. And nurture it Ireland did. The split in the Confederacy was closed by the new great dynamic impulse which reached Ireland's shores. Mitchel and Reilly again stood shoulder to shoulder with their former comrades—all followers of Young Ireland throughout the nation became as one. The wish to lift a pike or shoulder a gun nerved the young men. And to the labourers in the national field prospects were never before so promising. The good work strode forward magnificently—and it was foreseen that by the time the people had harvested their crops, the revolution would be ripe for bursting. '45, '46 and '47 had seen the great and progressive potato failure. In '47 the worst of all, the nation staggered at the mouth of a pit—not the most favourable condition for successful revolution. But things were more hopeful in '48. And a good harvest, safely gathered, would leave the country fit. The harvest was a necessity for the success of their plans. And the time that would elapse before harvest was also a necessity for the ripening of the plans, the training and equipping of an army.

But all this calculation was based on the foolish assumption that the British Government would accommodate them by waiting their time for rebelling. But the Government was not now grown any more accommodating to Irish revolutions and revolutionaries, than it had ever been. In the early summer it moved. It arrested O'Brien, Meagher and Mitchel on charges of sedition. At the trials of O'Brien and Meagher they failed to pack their juries with their usual care—one or two men of independent thought had, in each of those cases, been permitted to squeeze into the jury box—with the result that convictions could not be obtained. Before trying Mitchel the Government with its usual ingenuity invented and patented a new crime, treason-felony, under which an Irishman who uttered any revolutionary idea, was branded a felon, to be classed with the most despicable of criminals, and punished by many years' transportation. Mitchel was tried under the new Act. Moreover, the prosecution took care not to commit the same mistake it had made in the trials of O'Brien and Meagher. They did not let on the jury a single individual of whose verdict they were not certain. No Catholic, no independent-minded Protestant, was permitted in the box. Mitchel procured old Robert Holmes, one of the United Irish Revolutionaries of half a century before—brother-in-law to Robert Emmet—to defend him. Holmes was a ruggedly honest Irishman, in whom age had not dulled the edge of resolve, or smothered the fire of patriotism. In his youth he had taken the same bold stand that did John Mitchel now. And after fifty years of reflection upon the action of his youth, he now, in the winter of his days, stood up with Mitchel, and to the rage of the prosecution, and the horror of the court, instead of defending his client justified him. He told the judges his opinion and emphasised and repeated it, that Mitchel, statutably guilty, was not morally guilty.

"'Jailor, put forward John Mitchel,' said the official, whose duty is to make such orders.

"A grating of bolts, a clanging of chains, were heard. The low doorway at the back of the dock opened, and between turnkeys Mitchel entered.

"Ascending the steps to the front of the dock, and lifting, as he advanced, the glazed dark cap he wore through his imprisonment, as gracefully as if he entered a room, he took his stand in a firm but easy attitude. His appearance was equally removed from bravado and fear. His features, usually placid and pale, had a rigid clearness about them that day which we can never forget. They seemed, from their transparency and firmness, like some wondrous imagining of the artist's chisel, in which the marble, fancying itself human, had begun to breathe. The face was calm and bright—the mouth, the feature around which danger loves to play—though easy, motionless, and with lips apart, had about it an air of immobility and quiet scorn, which was not the effect of muscular action, but of nature in repose. And in his whole appearance, features, attitude and look, there was a conscious superiority over his opponents, which, though unpresuming and urbane, seemed to say louder than words—'I am victor here today.'"[2]

Mitchel, to be sure, for the crime of advocating the freedom of his country, was, under British law found guilty of treason-felony. And Baron Lefroy, after a hypocritical speech in which he said that he was indulging in a leniency which the magnitude of the crime did not countenance, sentenced Mitchel to fourteen years' transportation beyond the sea!

Then the prisoner, facing his judges, spoke—though to those present it seemed more like a noble judge in the dock lecturing miserable convicts on the bench. He defended his "crime," gloried in it, bade them and their laws an audacious defiance, and precipitated among his friends in the court such ringing avowal of "treason" as never before or since startled an English law court.[3]

---

[2] Doheny's description of Mitchel's arraignment.

[3] "'The law has now done its part, and the Queen of England, her crown and government in Ireland, are secure, pursuant to act of Parliament. I have done my part also. Three months ago I promised Lord Clarendon and his government, who holds this country for the English, that I would provoke him into his courts of justice, as places of this kind are called, and that I would force him publicly and notoriously, to pack a jury against me to convict me, or else that I would walk a free man out of

The Confederates' Club considered the advisability of letting the revolution burst, in attempt to rescue Mitchel from his jailers before they took him from Dublin. But the proposal was eventually and wisely voted down. For, the soldiery on the alert and equipped with all the paraphernalia of war, were in command of every strategic point; and thousands would have been mown down in the streets, and probably the incipient rising smothered in blood, had they decided to make the wild attempt. Mitchel himself in his *Jail Journal* reflects upon them for their decision. He considers that bloody slaughter would have been better than acquiescence. Under heavy

---

his court, and provoke him to a contest in another field. My lords, I knew that I was setting my life on that cast; but I knew that, in either event, victory should be with me—and it is with me. Neither the jury, nor the judges, nor any other man in this court presumes to imagine that it is a criminal who stands in this dock (murmurs of applause, which the police endeavoured to repress). I have kept my word. I have shown what the law is made of in Ireland. I have shown that her Majesty's government sustains itself in Ireland by packed juries—by partisan judges—by perjured sheriffs.

"'What I have now to add is simply this—I have acted all through this business, from the first, under a strong sense of duty. I do not repent anything I have done; and I believe that the course which I have opened is only commenced. The Roman who saw his hand burning to ashes before the tyrant, promised that three hundred should follow out his enterprise. Can I not promise for one, for two, for three?' He indicated as he spoke, Reilly, Martin, and Meagher.

"'Promise for me!' 'And me!' 'And me, Mitchel!' rose around him in commingled tones of earnest solemnity, passionate defiance, and fearless devotion, from his friends and followers.

"'Officer! officer! Remove Mr. Mitchel!' shouted Lefroy.

"A rush was made on the dock, and the foremost ranks sprang from the galleries with outstretched hands to vow with him too. The judges fled in terror from the benches—the turnkeys seized the hero, and in a scene of wild confusion he half walked, was half-dragged from the dock—and disappeared waving his hand in farewell. The bolts grated, the gate slammed, and he was seen no more.

"Men stood in affright, and looked in each other's faces wonderingly. They had seen a Roman sacrifice in this modern world and they were mute.

"An hour elapsed—the excited crowd had passed away; and the partisan judges, nervous and ill at ease, ventured upon the bench again.

"Then Holmes rose to his feet to add his defiance to that of the convict He said:

"'I think I had a perfect right to use the language I did yesterday. I now wish to state that what I said yesterday as an advocate, I adopt today as my own opinion. I here avow all I have said, and perhaps under late Act of Parliament, her majesty's Attorney-General, if I have violated the law in anything I said, may think it his first duty to proceed against me. But I must, with great respect to the court, assert that I had a perfect right to state what I stated; and now I say in respect to England and her treatment of this country, those are my sentiments, and I here openly avow them. The Attorney General is present—I retract nothing—these are my well judged sentiments—these are my opinions as to the relative position of England and Ireland; and if I have, as you seem to insinuate, violated the law by stating these things, I now deliberately do so again. Let her majesty's attorney-general do his duty to his government, I have done mine to my country.'

"Such was the conclusion of the trial of John Mitchel. The brother-in-law and friend of Robert Emmet, the Republican of our father's days, came to attest the justice of the republican of our own, and to vie with him in defying and scorning, the infamous laws of England."

escort, and by a roundabout route, he was secretly rushed off and conveyed to a ship which, in the Liffy, waited to carry him away.

John Martin, Mitchel's brother-in-law, a quiet Northern gentleman farmer, now felt called upon to step into the breach. To take the place of the suppressed *United Irishman*, Martin started *The Felon*. He had the assistance of Devin Reilly and of Fintan Lalor, the latter a Tipperary man, strange and lonely of nature, with powerful intellect and determination, and almost fanatically committed to ideas of land ownership far in advance of his time.

Another revolutionary paper, *The Tribune*, was founded by Kevin O'Doherty assisted by the poet Richard Dalton Williams. So the taking away of *The United Irishman* was almost compensated for. *The Felon*, *The Tribune*, and *The Nation* all three now worked with a will to rouse and to ripen the country with the harvest.

But still the English Government would not be accommodating. If there must be a revolution it must be forced before it is ready. Six weeks after Mitchel was convicted, the Government made a great swoop. The editors of all three papers were arrested, and, besides, O'Brien and Meagher were sought with warrants. The Young Irelanders instantly saw that they must at once strike or be struck. Although they knew that the country was not ready—neither the harvest ripe, nor the men equipped—they desperately resolved upon rising. O'Brien, Meagher, Doheny, O'Gorman, Terence Bellew MacManus, Reilly, Dillon and others, spread themselves over the south (chiefly). O'Brien, who was looked to as the leader, should give the signal by striking the first blow. Through want of preparedness, through O'Brien's exasperating punctiliousness about when, where, and how, he would strike the blow, and through the active opposition of the clergy[4]—part of whom were in principle against the rising, and part against it because circumstances were untoward, the people unprepared, and the harvest not gathered—the rising never materialised. O'Brien, Meagher, MacManus and others, were run down and arrested—while Doheny, Reilly, Dillon, O'Gorman escaped the country after long pursuit.

It was an unfortunate ending to a promising project. The various accounts of the times, written by the actors themselves, show that the people were ripe for revolution—full as anxious to take the field as in

---

[4] All of the clergy were not against the movement—evidently not all of the Hierarchy either. Bishop Maginn of Derry sent a messenger to Duffy, in prison, to say that if the Rising was deferred until the harvest was gathered, he would take the field himself, and have with him at least twenty officers in black.

'98—more anxious perhaps—even ready and anxious to go out unarmed, or with such homemade arms as they could procure on short notice. But, disastrous as might have been the fool-hardiness of facing the armies of the British Empire with pikes and scythes, even that forlorn hope was frustrated by the want of carefully prepared plans, unified direction, and a bold leader capable of sweeping aside the small considerations, grasping the big ones, and acting instantly, and with certitude.[5]

But consistent with the working of the strange fatality that through centuries dogged the steps of Ireland's liberators, the fierce desire of the people was not to eventuate in action.

The captured leaders were put through the usual farcical form of trial—found guilty of course—as Smith O'Brien convicted, and sentenced, and stepped out of the box put it to Meagher, "Guilty, Meagher, of not having sold our country." O'Doherty and Martin, whose offence was considered less gross since they had been imprisoned before putting in effect their rebellious purpose, were sentenced each to ten years' transportation.[6] Duffy, over whom a jury twice disagreed, was kept in prison a length of time, and eventually released because of his failing health. But the leaders who had been "out," O'Brien, Meagher, MacManus, and O'Donoghue got the same savage sentence—later commuted to life transportation, to Van Diemen's Land—"That sentence is that you, William Smith O'Brien,

---

[5] Meagher's description of the scene in the little town of Carrick-on-Suir when the news sped that the leaders had arrived "to give the word," well pictures for us the tremendous force of the long pent up desire now let loose: "A torrent of human beings, rushing through lanes and narrow streets, whirling in dizzy circles, and tossing up its dark waves with sounds of wrath, vengeance, and defiance . . . eyes red with rage and desperation . . . wild, half-stifled, passionate, frantic prayers of hope, curses on the red flag; scornful, exulting defiance of death. It was the Revolution, if we had accepted it."

[6] John Martin's speech upon being convicted is too beautiful to be omitted—"My lords, I have no imputation to cast upon the bench, neither have I anything of unfairness toward myself to charge the jury with. I think the judges desired to do their duty fairly, as upright judges and men, and that the twelve men who were put into the box, not to try but to convict me, voted honestly according to their prejudices. I have no personal enmity against the sheriff, sub-sheriff, or any other gentleman connected with the arrangements of the jury panel, nor against the attorney general, or any other person engaged in the proceedings called my trial. But, my lords, I consider I have not yet been tried! There have been certain formalities carried on here for three days, but I have not been put upon my country, according to the constitution said to exist in Ireland!

"Twelve of my countrymen, 'indifferently chosen' have not been put into the jury box to try me, but twelve men, who, I believe have been selected by the parties who represent the crown, for the purpose of convicting and not of trying me.

"Every person knows that what I have stated is the fact, and I would represent to the judges, most respectfully, that they, as honourable judges, and as upright citizens, ought to see that the administration of justice in this country is above suspicion. I have nothing more to say."

be taken from hence to the place from whence you came, and be thence drawn on a hurdle to the place of execution, and be there hanged by the neck until you are dead; and that afterwards your head shall be severed from your body, and your body divided into four quarters, to be disposed of as Her Majesty shall think fit. And may the Lord have mercy on your soul."

And so ended in gloom the short bright chapter of Ireland's history written by the gallant Young Irelanders.

After a period of joyful hope Ireland was prostrate once more under the conqueror's heel—to do what he would with. Some of the biggest English minds considered it was proper that it should be prostrate, that the iron heel should unmercifully be sunk into it. The great Carlyle, sad to relate, gave his British mind utterance on the subject thus, "When a mouse comes in the way of an elephant, what must the elephant do? Squelch it." Prime Minister Peel was evidently of a like mind: for, we are told that he considered the idea of another Cromwellian clearance of the troublesome Celt, and a new Plantation. Queen Victoria, in a letter to Leopold of Belgium expressed her regret that the Rising had not materialised and given chance for the British guns to mow down the young men of Ireland—"to teach the Irish a lesson," as the gentle lady put it.

Mitchel's Last Conquest.
Doheny's Felon's Track
Gavan Duffy's Young Ireland.
" " Four Years of Irish History.

CHAPTER LXX

The Great Famine

The Great Famine, usually known as the famine of '47, really began in '45, with the blighting and failure of the potato crop, the people's chief means of sustenance. The loss that year amounted to nine million pounds sterling. A worse failure occurred in '46. But by far the worst was in '47, when the suffering reached its climax. The terrible famine of '47 and '48 proved to be the most stunning blow that the Irish nation received in a century. It is calculated that about a million people died—either of direct starvation, or of the diseases introduced by the famine, and about another million fled to foreign lands between '46 and '50.[1]

The sufferings caused by the very first blight, that of '45, were such that Lord Brougham said: "They surpass anything on the page of Thucydides—on the canvass of Poussin—in the dismal chant of Dante." It was a catastrophe that demanded the immediate, energetic, most powerful, help of a country's government. And it is interesting to note just how those who insisted on governing this country met the terrible crisis.

Naturally, of course, the first thing that people in power should do, for a country facing starvation, was to forbid all export of foodstuffs from Ireland. But, as Englishmen, having this source of supply cut off, would then have to pay a higher price for their corn, the British Government, "could not interfere with the natural course of trade." "But," the Viceroy Lord Heytesbury, reassured the dying ones, "there is no cause for alarm—the Government is carefully watching the course of events!"

[1] The Government returns of emigration for those years are inaccurate. There were hundreds of little schooners sailing out of almost every bay on the west coast, weighted down with human cargo, of which no record was ever kept.

To relieve the acute situation, their first step was to send over a shipload of scientists to study the cause of the potato failure. Their second step was to bring in a new Coercion Bill for Ireland. The third step was—after they had voted two hundred thousand pounds to beautify London's Battersea Park—to vote one hundred thousand pounds for the relief of the two million Irish people (out of a total of eight million) who were suffering keen distress—which was the handsome help of twelve pence each person to tide a starving population over till the next harvest![2]

As they were this year unable to pay rack rent to the absentee landlord, thousands of the starving ones were thrown out, and other thousands threatened to be thrown out of their wretched homes, to perish on the roadside. In consequence frenzied poor men shot a few of the vilest of the land-agents and landlords. At the opening of the Parliament in January, '46, Queen Victoria, addressing her "Lords and Gentlemen" observed, with deep regret, the fearful situation in Ireland—adding—"It will be our duty to consider whether any measure can be devised, calculated to give peace and protection for life there."

The simple reader, who knows not the way of Britain with Ireland, would here naturally come to the conclusion that the tender-hearted gentlewoman, full of sympathy for the thousands who were dying of starvation, and for the hundreds of thousands who were daily in danger of dying, was directing her Parliament to try to save a multitude of lives. But this would be a mistaken conclusion. She was here referring to the handful of Anglo-Irish landlords and agents, whose lives must be solicitously protected whilst, in trying times, they were endeavouring to hack and hew their usual pound of flesh from the walking skeletons in the bogs and mountains of Ireland. Some of these thoughtless ones were in danger of slaying a landlord rather than see him slay their famished wife, or hollow-eyed children. Hence the good Queen advised her "Lords and Gentlemen" that a stringent Coercion Bill was needed, and must be provided to relieve the unfortunate conditions prevailing in Ireland.[3]

---

[2] When the Irish Parliamentary representatives presented the claim of their suffering country for assistance from the common Exchequer to which their country contributed millions ever year, the British view of their action was fairly well voiced by the *London Times:* "There would be something highly ludicrous in the impudence with which Irish legislators claim *English* assistance if the circumstances by which they enforced their claims were not of the most pitiable kind. The contrast between insolent menace and humble supplication reminds one forcibly of the Irish characters so popular with the dramatists of the last century who hectored through three acts of intermittent brogue, bullying the husband and making love to the wife."

[3] Among other benefits which this excellent Bill proposed to confer upon the suffering people, it rendered liable to fourteen years' transportation any one found out of his own house after the sun

In the following year, when the distress grew worse, the Government granted the Labour Rate Act to Ireland—permitting the Irish people to tax themselves to give employment to those of them who were worse off than the others. And over and above this, there was contributed from the Imperial Exchequer a hundred thousand pounds for districts that were too utterly destitute to raise any money under the Act. This Act and Government grant materially alleviated such polite poverty as existed among the Anglo-Irish class in Ireland—going chiefly in salaries to many thousands of these people employed as "Commissioners," "Superintendents of work," "Inspectors of work," and so forth—a huge staff who were paid a large part of the small fund for the purpose of administering the little that remained.[4]

What did remain was paid in half wages to starving men for doing work that was unprofitable. This latter was a specific Government condition embodied in the Act. The work must be unprofitable, non-productive. The money, for instance, could not be used to build Irish railways—

---

set in the evening and before it arose next morning. In the operation of this beneficial Act many things occurred, that to an outsider might seem strange. For instance, John Mitchel records such happenings as that of a quiet, respectable farmer, who on a summer evening, when the sun was near setting, strolled a short way down the road to pay his working-men, and walking back when the sun had just sunk—though it was still broad day light—was arrested for heinous crime against "the Queen and Constitution of this realm." At that time the tailor and the shoemaker would, in the late autumn and early winter, be taken by the big farmers to their houses, and kept there a week, to make shoes and clothes for the family. One of these tailors was arrested, on an evening, as he sat at his work in a big farmer's house—where of course he was spending his nights as well as his days. The villain had literally transgressed British law. He has been "out of his house" between sunset and sunrise! Fourteen years' transportation taught this dangerous criminal that British law was made to be respected.

Then, too, the Government was not only alert to guard the sacred rights of life—English landlords' lives, but also the sacred rights of property—English landlords' property. Mitchel, in his "Last Conquest," describes how he was called upon to defend poor starving creatures on charges of trespass because they had gone down to gather seaweed below high-water mark—and poor farmers who were indicted for robbery, because going forth into the sea's realm—where Britain decrees that the British landlords' rights reach—they had taken limestone from a rock that was uncovered at low-water only, and burnt it upon their lands, to try to force a little crop. The *Cork Examiner* of that period says: "Our town presents nothing but a moving mass of military and police, conveying to and from the court-house crowds of famine culprits. I attended the court for a few hours this day. The dock was crowded with the prisoners, not one of whom, when called up for trial, was able to support himself in front of the dock. The sentence of the court was received by each prisoner with apparent satisfaction. Even transportation appeared to many to be a relaxation from their sufferings."

[4] In the beginning of '47 there were ten thousand Government servants under salary for administering what portion of the relief fund their salaries did not consume. "Some of these gentlemen," says Mitchel, "got more pay than an American Secretary of State."

because that would be a discrimination against English railway builders. It could not be used either for seeding the lands, or reclaiming the millions of acres of bog—because that would be giving the Irish farmer an unfair advantage over his English brother, and might enable him to undersell the latter in the market. It could only be used—and only was used—for such benevolent purpose as cutting down roads where there was no hill, filling in roads where there was no hollow, building roads where nobody ever travelled—having them start anywhere and end nowhere—erecting bridges where no rivers flowed, and piers where a ship's sail was never seen. There are still to be viewed in various parts of Ireland, some of these monuments to British Government wisdom, and solicitude—roads that are only frequented by the daisy and harebell, and broken bridges and tumble-down piers that stood in solitude for years, before sinking in despair.

Public committees had been formed in various countries (including England) and hundreds of thousands of pounds were collected for the relief of Irish distress—even the Sultan of Turkey contributing to the starving Irish subjects that the great British Government could not afford to care for. With the money thus collected, shiploads of Indian corn were imported to Ireland from America. As there were in the country hundreds of thousands of people in want for food, who yet would not accept it in charity, it was proposed that imported corn should be sold to these people at reduced price—but the paternal Government forbade the irregular procedure. It was not in accordance with the laws of political economy, and "there must be no interference with the natural course of trade." For the same reason the Government still persistently refused to close the Irish ports against export of foodstuffs. And it was noted that a ship, laden with relief corn from America, sailing into an Irish harbour, would meet several ships laden with Irish foodstuffs, sailing out!

At length, when conditions reached their most fearful stage, in '47, and that the uncoffined dead were being buried in trenches,[5] and the world was expressing itself as appalled at the conditions, the Government advanced a loan of ten million pounds, one-half to be expended on public works, the other half for outdoor relief. And this carried with it the

[5] Some Poor Law Unions, unable to provide coffins for all who died destitute, hit on the expedient of using one coffin with a hinged bottom. Corpses were often simply wrapped in straw for burial. Some were buried even without the covering of straw. People driving after night sometimes drove over the dead who had dropped on the road and there lay unburied. Dogs, pigs, rats, were frequently found feasting on the neglected dead.

helpful proviso that no destitute farmer could benefit from that windfall unless he had first given up to the landlord all his farm except a quarter of an acre.

The extent of the want in Ireland, in the spring of '47, can be judged from the fact that in March there were no less than 730,000 heads of families engaged on relief works—almost three-quarters of a million men, who, for sake of earning about six-pence a day, forsook all work upon the land. Thus, the sagacious statesmanship of the English ruler in Ireland, sought to relieve want caused by shortage of crops, by paying men sixpence a day to refrain from raising further crops—and do work that was guaranteed by the Government expert not to produce anything for the country's aid.

But to relieve acute distress among the poor absentee landlords in the gambling hells of Europe, the Government gladly contributed troops to aid the Absentee's agent and bailiffs in seizing the sheep, the cow, the oats, the furniture, of the starving people. Sometimes to seize the potatoes that had been donated to them to seed their land.

But in these terrible times there were thousands of poor people who, having nothing left to seize, were by the landlord thrown out with their families on the roadside. These people had two resources open to them. Having no house of their own to be in between sunset and sunrise (for even the workhouses and hospitals were long since filled) they could take advantage of the Coercion Act, and get transported for their crime. Or, their cases were thoughtfully met by the Vagrancy Act which punished by imprisonment with hard labour any one found idly wandering without visible means of support.[6]

[6] To some who do not know the quaint ways of English laws with Irish people this will seem to be a joke. Alas, it is a grim truth. Many of the broken and broken-hearted creatures—of the half-million people evicted in one year—were sent to the prison stone-piles in punishment for vagrancy.

In this black year of '47 in which the potato crop failed a third time—a total failure this time—in which far more than half a million died of famine and of plague begotten by famine, and far more than a quarter million fled the country, Larcom (the Government Commissioner) estimated at forty-five million pounds the value of the food-crops produced. The greater portion of these crops crossed the channel—sold to satisfy the landlord and tax-gatherer. "Travellers were often appalled when they came upon some lonely village by the western coast, with the people all skeletons on their own hearths. . . . Priests, after going their rounds all day, administering Extreme Unction, often themselves went supperless to bed." And the Protestant clergy, too, be it noted, worked nobly for the sufferers. One brave Protestant minister took off his shirt, and put it on a fever patient. Some few signally noble-hearted ones among the landlords lived on Indian meal, in order to spare more for the starving—some of whom were eating grass and turf.

As the famine sufferings increased, the Government met the more acute situation by proposing a renewal of the Disarming Act, increase of police, and several other British remedies.

True, the Government now shipped in Indian corn. But there was more corn went out of the country in one month than the Government sent in, in a year. And during this time English traders were speculating in Irish corn, importing or exporting it, as called for by variations in the market. And while tens of thousands were dropping dead for want of food, in the fields, and on the roads, and in the streets of Irish cities, the shiploads of Irish corn in which these traders were speculating were crossing and recrossing the Channel, in furtherance of their gamble. It is recorded that, in the time of direst need, certain cargoes of corn crossed the Irish sea four times!

Things had now come to a dreadful pass. And the nation was in the throes of despair. Mitchel gives a harrowing account of the sights that he then saw on a journey to Galway through the fertile centre of a fertile island:

"We saw sights that will never wholly leave the eyes that beheld them, cowering wretches almost naked in the savage weather, prowling in turnip fields, and endeavouring to grub up roots which had been left, but running to hide as the mailcoach rolled by: groups and families, sitting or wandering on the highroad, with failing steps, and dim, patient eyes, gazing hopelessly into infinite darkness and despair; parties of tall, brawny men, once the flower of Meath and Galway, stalking by with a fierce but vacant scowl: as if they realised that all this ought not to be, but knew not whom to blame, saw none whom they could rend in their wrath. Sometimes, I could see, in front of the cottages, little children leaning against a fence when the sun shone out—for they could not stand—their limbs fleshless, their bodies half-naked, their faces bloated yet wrinkled, and of a pale greenish hue—children who would never, it was too plain, grow up to be men and women."[7]

---

[7] The Mayo Constitution in the month of March reported: "The land is one vast waste: a soul is not to be seen working on the holdings of the poor farmers throughout the country: and those who have had the prudence to plough or dig the ground are in fear of throwing in the seed."

The Dublin Evening Mail recorded: "A gentleman travelling from Borris-in-Ossory to Kilkenny one bright Spring morning, counts on both sides of the road, in a distance of twenty-four miles, 'nine men and four ploughs,' occupied in the fields; but sees multitudes of wan labourers, 'beyond the power of computation by a mail-car passenger,' labouring to destroy the road he was travelling upon. It was 'public work.'"

A sample report from an agent of a Society which, more than any other, deserves eternal gratitude from Irishmen for the great and noble work it did to mitigate the horrors of that horrible time—the Society of Friends—reads: "One poor woman whose cabin I had visited said, 'There will be nothing for us but to lie down and die.' I tried to give her hope in English aid. But alas! her prophecy has been too true. Out of a population of two hundred and forty I found thirteen already dead

Yet the Government and the law of the land were not remaining idle in this time of terror. Toward the end of that year, when hope seemed forever to have fled the country, the English Parliament, to meet the exigency, called for another Coercion Act!

In the summer of '47, when things were very bad indeed, and the living were trying—but oftentimes failing—to bury the dead, the Government, to relieve the distress, sent sixty agricultural lecturers over the country. Some of those who went into the West, came back reporting that they could find no one to lecture to. Others who found living people, could not lecture to them because there was not going to be any means of putting their wise principles into practice. One of the lecturers reports: "It is always the same excuse with them. They could not get seed, or anything to live on, meantime." Another reports: "All I met told me they were going to give up their land, for they had neither food nor strength to till it."[8]

In those terrible years the people began flocking from the stricken land in tens and hundreds of thousands—to America, and to the earth's ends. The little bays of Ireland were floating out human cargoes upon the bosom of every tide—till within five years' time a million despairing refugees had fled the land.[9]

---

from want. The survivors were like walking skeletons—the men gaunt and haggard, stamped with the livid mark of hunger, the children crying with pain—the women in some of the cabins too weak to stand. All the sheep were gone—all the cows—all the poultry killed—only one pig left—the very dogs which had barked at me before, had disappeared. No potatoes—no oats."

An item from a Dublin newspaper of '47—just a few lines casually set down in the ordinary way of news—nothing at all startling in a time when people could not any more be startled by anything so commonplace—reads: "Upwards of one hundred and fifty ass hides have been delivered in Dublin from the County Mayo, for exportation to Liverpool. The carcasses, owing to the scarcity of provisions, had been used as food."

[8] As a further means of helping the dread situation the Government, through its Lord Lieutenant, Lord Clarendon, hired a creature named Birch, publisher of a sheet that he called *The World*, to invent and print the foulest slanders the creature's filthy imagination could conceive, about the people's leaders, the Young Irelanders—and then gratuitously circulated, his lying sheet. It was only when Birch eventually sued his employer, Lord Clarendon, for more wages—black-mail, Clarendon called it—that the whole odious transaction came into the light of day.

[9] The great Exodus of the race, which then began, continued thence forward till, in a half a century, Ireland, which had almost nine million people in '46, lost one-half its population. On this sad subject Ethna Carbery penned her well known poem—

THE PASSING OF THE GAEL

They are going, going, going from the valleys and the hills,
They are leaving far behind them heathery moor and mountain rills,
All the wealth of hawthorn hedges where the brown thrush sways and thrills.

And in the famine exodus, thousands and thousands carried their load of famine fever with them aboard the little ships, or developed famine fever on the voyage. And thousands upon thousands, fleeing from Ireland, for the Promised Land beyond the Sea, never saw that land, but left their bones to whiten on the Ocean bed. And still other thousands and thousands reached the Promised Land only to see it, and die.

Along the Canadian shore, to which their little ships came, the famine-stricken ones were quarantined in droves, died in piles, and in heaps were buried.

They are going, shy-eyed *cailins*, and lads so straight and tall,
From the purple peaks of Kerry, from the crags of wild Imaal,
From the greening plains of Mayo, and the glens of Donegal.

They are leaving pleasant places, shores with snowy sands outspread;
Blue and lonely lakes a-stirring when the wind stirs overhead;
Tender living hearts that love them, and the graves of kindred dead.

They shall carry to the distant land a tear-drop in the eye
And some shall go uncomforted—their days an endless sigh
For Kathaleen Ni Houlihan's sad face, until they die.

Oh, Kathaleen Ni Houlihan, your road's a thorny way,
And 'tis a faithful soul would walk the flints with you for aye,
Would walk the sharp and cruel flints until his locks grew grey.

So some must wander to the East, and some must wander West;
Some seek the white wastes of the North, and some a Southern nest;
Yet never shall they sleep so sweet as on your mother breast.

Within the city streets, hot, hurried, full of care,
A sudden dream shall bring them a whiff of Irish air—
A cool air, faintly-scented, blown soft from otherwhere.

Oh, the cabins long-deserted!—Olden memories awake—
Oh, the pleasant, pleasant places!—Hush! the blackbird in the brake!
Oh, the dear and kindly voices!—Now their hearts are fain to ache.

They may win a golden store—sure the whins were golden too;
And no foreign skies hold beauty like the rainy skies they knew;
Nor any night-wind cool the brow as did the foggy dew.

. . . .

They are going, going, going, and we cannot bid the stay;
Their fields are now the stranger's, where the stranger's cattle stray.
Oh! Kathaleen Ni Houlihan, your way's a thorny way!

—From Ethna Carbery's "The Four Winds of Eirinn."

This writer once visited Patridge Island at the mouth of the St. John River, in the company of a very old man, a doctor, who as a boy saw the "coffin ships" arrive at St. John. He gave harrowing pictures of the appearance of the unfed, unclad creatures, who were dumped there by the shipload in those years—some of them clad only in straw—and showed the great furrows on the island, which mark the trenches wherein myriads were buried.

Six thousand of these poor creatures perished on Grosse Island, in the St. Lawrence—and other many thousands along its banks. A report of the Montreal Emigrant Society says: "From Grosse Island, the great charnel-house of victimised humanity, up to Port Sarnia, and along the borders of our magnificent river, upon the shores of Lakes Ontario and Erie—wherever the tide of emigration has extended—are to be found the final resting places of the sons and daughters of Erin, an unbroken chain of graves, where repose fathers and mothers, sisters and brothers, in one commingled heap, without a tear bedewing the soil, or a stone marking the spot. Twenty thousand and upwards thus went down to their graves."[10]

Of a certain ninety thousand only, of the emigrants to Canada in '47, of which accurate account was kept, it is recorded that 6,100 died on the voyage; 4,100 died on arrival; 5,200 died in hospitals, and 1,900 soon died in the towns to which they repaired.

Here is sample of the reports for a few of the individual ships in '47: *The Larch*, carrying 440 passengers, had 108 deaths; the *Queen*, carrying 493 passengers, had 137 deaths; the *Avon*, carrying 552 passengers, had 236 deaths; the *Virginius*, carrying 476 passengers, had 267 deaths. William Henry Smith, an English civil engineer, who was employed on public works in Connaught in '47, records that on one vessel carrying 600 emigrants not a hundred survived.

---

[10] One Englishman with a man's heart, the naturalist, Waterton, travelled from Quebec to Montreal on an American steamboat, on which there were five hundred Irish emigrants,—and in his "Wanderings" speaks thus beautifully of them:

"They were going, they hardly knew whither, far away from dear Ireland. It made one's heart ache to see them all huddled together, without expectation of ever revisiting their native soil. We feared that the sorrow of leaving home for ever, the miserable accommodation on board the ship which had brought them away, and the tossing of the angry ocean, in a long and dreary voyage, would have rendered them callous to good behaviour. But it was quite otherwise. They conducted themselves with great propriety. Every American on board seemed to feel for them. And, then, they were full of wretchedness. Need and oppression stared within their eyes; upon their backs hung ragged misery. The world was not their friend. 'Poor dear Ireland,' exclaimed an aged female, as I was talking to her, 'I shall never see it any more!'"

And thus was the flower of one of the finest nations on the face of the earth in swaths mowed down, and thus in wind-rows did they wither from off earth's face—under the ægis of British rule.[11]

John Mitchel, Last Conquest of Ireland (Perhaps).
O'Rorke's History of the Famine.
The Halliday Pamphlets.

---

[11] It was all for the advancement of civilisation, our wise and humane English rulers and friends assured us. Their mouthpiece, *The London Times*, which, when the exodus was most pitiful, screamed with delight in one of its editorials, "They are going! They are going! The Irish are going with a vengeance. Soon a Celt will be as rare in Ireland as a Red Indian on the shores of Manhattan"—this, their mouthpiece, comfortably informed the Imperial English world, "Law has ridden through Ireland: it has been taught with bayonets, and interpreted with ruin. Townships levelled with the ground, straggling columns of exiles, workhouses multiplied, and still crowded, express the determination of the legislature to rescue Ireland from its slovenly old barbarism, and to plant there the institutions of this more civilised land."

CHAPTER LXXI

The Fenians

When the day of the fiery and forward Young Irelanders had passed, the political reactionaries had their day. In 1850 reducing the issue from a national to a mere agrarian one, the Irish Tenant Right League was formed, to remedy the farmers' grievances. With this organisation as their instrument—though it had some good men in it, like Lucas, Gray, and even Gavan Duffy moderated in his Nationalism—and with another known as the Catholic Defence Association, the Whiggish element of the country took control of Irish affairs, and the time-servers jostled their way to the front. This deplorable state of affairs reached its climax when the Catholic Defence leaders, John Sadleir and William Keogh, trusted, honoured, lauded to the skies by both lay and ecclesiastical sponsors, and triumphantly contrasted with the base misleaders (Young Ireland) of the decade before—duped and betrayed their supporters, and sold the people and the cause for political place. Sadleir, later found to be a forger and swindler on a gigantic scale, fell with a sensational crash, leaving thousands of trusting poor Irish people financially ruined—and committed suicide. Keogh lived on, thinking that the Judge's ermine which was his price hid his shame.[1]

[1] Sadleir's price, when he sold out to the British Government, was the Lordship of the Treasury. Keogh's price was the Solicitor-Generalship. Sadleir was an able business man who had made much money. After he was made Lord of the Treasury, he soared into the dizziest realms of finance. All his ventures prospered. Everything he touched turned to gold. He became one of the very great ones in the London banking world. But, as his success, extraordinary and dazzling, was based upon rottenness and a people's betrayal, God's curse finally brought him down. Providence seemed to have helped him to a dizzy pinnacle in order that his fall might be the more tremendous. The corruption by which he felt it necessary to force himself upon the electors of Carlow, after he had betrayed

But however deeply it be buried, and however long it be covered by the snows of misfortune, the germ of nationality never expires in Ireland. Now it found its spring and woke again under the sun of Fenianism.

Fenianism began in Ireland at the end of the 'Fifties—and at the same time in America. James Stephens, who had been a very young man in the '48 movement, and who had since been a tutor both in Paris and in Kerry, was the founder and great organiser of Fenianism. On St. Patrick's Day, 1858, in a back room in Dublin, Stephens swore in his friend Thomas Clarke Luby, and Luby swore in Stephens.[2]

And from that modest beginning sprang, at first slowly, but after a few years with a rapidity that was magical, one of the greatest of Irish movements, with far reaching consequences. For, though to the near-sighted and superficial the movement seemed to end in disastrous failure, the spirit which got rebirth in that little back room on that fateful St. Patrick's Day, far from being broken by the so-called Fenian failure has ever since gone steadily marching onward, and been the motive power behind all various succeeding national organisations down to the present greatest Irish struggle.

---

them, was the means of setting his feet upon the downward path. Hurriedly upon the heels of this exposure, he had to resort to gigantic schemes of forgery, robbery, fraud, in vain endeavour to keep from toppling off his pinnacle. But he fell with a crash that shook the financial world. And finally a bottle of prussic acid taken on Hampstead Heath ended the betrayer's career.

Keogh, in his great days as joint leader (with Sadleir) of the Irish people, had again and again sworn in the most solemn and impressive manner—calling upon the Almighty God to witness his sincerity—that no bribe in the possession of the British Government would or could buy him. From the frequency with which he had invoked God to witness the sincerity of his oath, he was nicknamed "So-help-me-God Keogh." With Sadleir, he sold out at the very first opportunity that offered. And he was soon comfortably seated upon the Judges' bench, grinning at the dupes whom he had betrayed, and glad of the opportunity to send into transportation, or on to the gallows, the "foolish" ones who preferred to give up their lives in preference to giving up Liberty and Ireland. This scoundrel's name became a by-word for rottenness. He lived long to enjoy the place and pelf for which he sold his soul, and to be the despised and the scorned of his countrymen.

[2] The Fenian oath (as quoted by John O'Leary) ran: I, A B, do solemnly swear, in the presence of Almighty God, that I will do my utmost, at every risk, while life lasts, to make Ireland an independent democratic Republic; that I will yield implicit obedience, in all things not contrary to the law of God, to the commands of my superior officers, and that I shall preserve inviolable secrecy regarding all transactions of this secret society that may be confided to me. So help me God! Amen.

Fenianism was more strictly the American title of the movement. It was John O'Mahony, reader, scholar, poet, who conceived the title "Fenian" for the organisation which Stephens in Ireland called the Irish Republican Brotherhood. The Fenians, or Fianna, it will be remembered, were the famed national militia, commanded by Fionn MacCumhal. The title was at first resisted by O'Mahony's friends and followers, but he forced it on them. And it proved to be a happy one.

At the same time that it was started in Ireland by Stephens and Luby—with Charles Kickham[3] and John O'Leary as their co-workers, John O'Mahoney and Michael Doheny (both of them 'Forty-eighters also) gave it to America.

The American movement, from the beginning, affiliated with the movement at home. Stephens, immediately after starting the movement

---

[3] Kickham, one of the finest, ablest, noblest of the Fenian leaders, and certainly the most lovable, is best known today as the Irish novelist who wrote the finest story of Irish home life, "Knocknagow, or the Homes of Tipperary"—and the writer also who wrote a few of the finest of our ballads. Such as the beautiful Fenian ballad:

RORY OF THE HILLS

"That rake up near the rafters, why leave it there so long?
Its handle, of the best of ash, is smooth and straight and strong;
And, mother, will you tell me, why did my father frown
When to make the hay, in summertime I climbed to take it down?"
She looked into her husband's eyes, while her own with light did fill,
"You'll shortly know the reason, boy!" said Rory of the Hill.

The midnight moon is lighting up the slopes of Sliav-na-man,—
Whose foot affrights the startled hares so long before the dawn?
He stopped just where the Anner's stream winds up the woods, anear,
Then whistled low and looked around to see the coast was clear.
The shieling door flew open—in he stepped with right good-will—
"God save all here and bless your WORK!" said Rory of the Hill.

Right hearty was the welcome that greeted him, I ween,
For years gone by he fully proved how well he loved the Green;
And there was one amongst them who grasped him by the hand—
One who through all that weary time roamed on a foreign strand;
He brought them news from gallant friends that made their heart-strings thrill—
"My sowl! I never doubted them!" said Rory of the Hill.

They sat around the humble board till dawning of the day,
And yet not song nor shout I heard, no revelers were they;
Some brows flushed red with gladness, while some were grimly pale;
But pale or red, from out those eyes flashed souls that never quail!
"And sing us now about the vow, they swore for to fulfil"—
"You'll read it yet in history," said Rory of the Hill.

Next day the ashen handle he took down from where it hung,
The toothéd rake, full scornfully, into the fire he flung;
And in its stead a shining blade is gleaming once again—
(Oh! for a hundred thousand of such weapons and such men!)
Right soldierly he wielded it, and—going through his drill—
"Attention—charge—front point—advance!" cried Rory of the Hill.

in Ireland, went to the United States, travelled and successfully spread Fenianism there, collected £600 to carry on the work at home, and made O'Mahoney the American head of the movement. Strangely and unfortunately John Mitchel—and with him Meagher—refused to have anything to do with the new movement, which, except for O'Mahoney and Doheny, had to find its strength among new men. The same was the case at home, where Smith O'Brien, Dillon, and others of the Young Irelanders, resting on their now fading laurels, fairly set their faces against Fenianism.[4]

Stephens was a singularly strong and dominant character, a man who combined intellectual powers with high idealism, extraordinary self-confidence—which sometimes became intolerant egotism—and a hypnotic optimism. While he was commonplace as a writer and orator, he was great as an organiser, having a mesmeric power over men in the intimacy of personal discourse, and a wonderful faculty of infecting them with his own extraordinary optimism, inspiring them with his own extraordinary confidence, and winning them as enthusiastic disciples, and apostles. Now, especially, that he had the American money to finance him, he travelled east and west over Ireland, from town to town, from village to village, and it might be said, from farm to farm, laying the warp and weft of the organisation, winning men by the thousand, and swearing them in fealty to Ireland.

But the movement got its vastest impetus from the funeral of MacManus. Terence Bellew MacManus, one of the singularly noble and self-sacrificing of the Young Irelanders, sent into penal servitude in Australia, escaped therefrom to America, and in '61 died in San Francisco—living

She looked at him with woman's pride, with pride and woman's fears;
She flew to him, she clung to him, and dried away her tears;
He feels her pulse beat truly, while her arms around him twine—
"Now God be praised for your stout heart, brave little wife of mine."
He swung his first born in the air, while joy his heart did fill—
"You'll be a FREE MAN yet, my boy!" said Rory of the Hill.

Oh! knowledge is a wondrous power, and stronger than the wind;
And thrones shall fall, and despots bow, before the might of mind;
The poet and the orator the heart of man can sway,
And would to the kind heavens that Wolfe Tone were here today
Yet trust me, friends, dear Ireland's strength—her truest strength is still
The rough and ready roving boys, like Rory of the Hill!

[4] This strange attitude of many of the Young Ireland leaders was in part at least due to the natural jealousy of older leaders, grown stale, against the impetuous and virile young ones who come over the horizon threatening to fill the places which those elders long had graced.

and dying steadfast and true to his principles. The American Fenians, deciding that the body of this true man should rest in Irish earth, arranged to bring him home and lay him in Glasnevin. The funeral was one great demonstration all the way across the American Continent. In New York it assumed remarkable proportions. Wonderful was the reception given to it in Cork; and thence along the way to Dublin. It was not the funeral of a failure going to his grave, but the triumphal march of a conqueror coming to his own. The enthusiasm with which the triumphal coming of MacManus was hailed, grew and swelled across the country. At railway stations through which the funeral train passed vast crowds of reverent ones dropped upon their knees and prayed, while tears of mingled grief and joy rolled down their cheeks.

In Dublin (where the anti-national Archbishop Cullen[5] had closed all his church doors against the remains of the people's idol), the climax was reached. During the week that the body lay in the Mechanics' Institute, endless thousands of ardent ones, in continuous lines filed passed, praying for a patriot who lived and who died true to a true Irishman's ideal. And the day on which MacManus was to be laid under the earth witnessed such a funeral demonstration as perhaps Dublin never knew before or since. Following the hearse, through lanes of people numbering hundreds of thousands, marched fifty thousand men, who thereby consecrated themselves to live, and to strive, and to die as nobly as did he whose spirit brooded over and inspired the vast throng. And the great silent resolve of the marching myriads found just expression in a sentence of Captain Smith's oration at the grave side, "'Is there any hope?'" he said, quoting a question often asked about Ireland by MacManus in his last illness, "'Is there any hope?' That coffin speaks of more than hope today, for it gives us faith and firm resolve to do the work for which MacManus died."[6]

---

[5] Archbishop Cullen of Dublin banned the body, and blamed the life, of him whom Archbishop Hughes of New York only a few weeks before had blessed.

Once Archbishop Cullen, eulogising the British rule to which he commanded the docility of the Irish people, said that wherever the British flag floated there were to be found Irishmen lifting the standard of the church. He intimated that England deserved blessing rather than cursing for driving forth the Irish people over every country of the globe. This dispersal of the race was a dispensation of God for spreading the Faith. And he evidently desired it to be understood that England as the chosen instrument for the dispersal, was deserving of high credit!

[6] Thomas Clarke Luby, describing the funeral procession (in O'Leary's Recollections) says:

"But I had myself as yet no adequate notion of the magnitude of this unparalleled demonstration. It was only when about to turn into Britain Street that I first ventured to look back. Then, indeed, I was over-awed. I saw the whole of Gardiner Street filled with dense masses of men, and

That November day in '61, when MacManus made his last journey, was the greatest day for young Fenianism, conquering for it the hearts of hundreds of thousands of Irishmen whom, erstwhile it had not won.

Unfortunately, the great body of the Irish Bishops, and, in general, of the church in Ireland, conservatively following the Cullen lead denounced Fenians and Fenianism, and strove to stifle a movement which was sweeping Ireland like wildfire, and putting new hope in the hearts of the men of the country.[7]

The Irish People, the Fenian organ, was founded in '63 with John O'Leary as editor—assisted by Charles Kickham and Luby. Kickham, by far the finest and ablest writer of them all, did a lion's share of the virile writing which quickly popularised the paper.

The Irish People obtained a large circulation—but not so great as did *The Nation* of Young Ireland days. Its coming, every week, was longingly looked forward to by the folk in remote corners of the country, who eagerly bought and avidly read and digested it. And by its brightness and its virility the spread of the movement was vastly accelerated.

In autumn '65 the Government suddenly delivered a great *coup*—seizing *The Irish People*, its editors, Stephens, and many of the leading figures in the movement in various parts of the country.[8]

---

fresh masses, endlessly as it seemed still defiling into it from the direction of Abbey Street. I speak the truth when I tell you that I gasped for breath and felt my chest heave; I could have sobbed and cried. I felt as I never felt before or since the grandeur, the magnetism, of an immense crowd of human beings, when all are, for the time being, gloriously animated with one and the same noble aspiration and conviction. . . . At length the head of the procession reached Thomas Street; and now something truly impressive took place. Spontaneously as the foremost files passed by Catherine's Church (where Robert Emmet died on the scaffold) every man uncovered his head. As slowly the dense black column moves along in funeral pomp the generous impulse runs down the entire line. Not a man but passes the sacred spot bare-headed. . . I think it is no exaggeration to say that the funeral seems to me something in its kind unparalleled, or, at least, only to be compared with the second burial of the great Napoleon. But, in the last named pageant, the power and resources of a great nation were called into action, while the MacManus funeral was the unaided effort of a populace trampled on or expatriated."

O'Leary himself says that the funeral of Gambetta organised by a great nation, was probably the only funeral which in point of numbers and impressiveness surpassed MacManus's.

[7] It would be painful to set down here the intemperate, unpatriotic denunciations of Fenianism, by several Bishops and pastors who strove to array both heaven and hell on the side of Britain, against Fenianism and Ireland. Enough to record Bishop Moriarty's thundering against the Fenian organisers that Hell was not hot enough nor Eternity long enough to mete adequate punishment to such miscreants!

[8] After most of the other leaders were arrested Stephens, while the country was being searched for him, continued for more than a month living an easy and quiet existence, watering his flowers, and tending his garden, in the outskirts of Dublin.

This was truly a disaster, removing as it did from the direction of the movement some of the wisest heads that guided it. And every one of the hundreds of thousands of the rank and file severely felt the sad blow—from which indeed the movement never recovered—even though Stephens was given back to them.

For Stephens was given back. After defying the court before which he was arraigned—announcing to it, "I deliberately and conscientiously repudiate the existence of British law in Ireland, and I defy and despise any punishment it may inflict on me"—he was, with other leading prisoners, confined in Richmond jail—under special and careful guard. On an evening in November, the warders, going their rounds, saw that every man of the Fenian prisoners was safe in his cell—locked and double-locked. And early next morning the prison was in uproar. James Stephens' cell was open—and empty!

There were two tables, one on top of the other, against the yard-wall of the prison—and everything else was mystery absolute and complete! Locks had been opened, gates unbarred, walls surmounted—by a poor prisoner who had no instrument or implement left to him in his barred and bolted double-locked cell. The bird had flown. His jailers were dazed. The Government was frenzied. England was infuriated. The world was sensated. The extraordinary and mysterious escape of Stephens was the sensation of the decade.[9]

After remaining quiet for several weeks in a Dublin home, while almost every nook and cranny in England, Ireland, Scotland and Wales was being searched for him, every railway train and every ship and boat, Stephens one day entered a magnificent coach drawn by four spanking horses, a liveried

---

[9] Like many mysteries, that of Stephens' escape was, after all, one of the simplest. Fenianism had permeated not only every part of the country but also every class and every calling—including Government cohorts. The Government without knowing it, was placing Fenian prisoners in the hands of Fenian jailers. In Richmond jail, a hospitable superintendent, Jno. J. Breslin, and a night watchman, Joseph Byrne, two trusty Fenians, procured duplicate keys and made the other arrangements to convey their distinguished prisoner and Chief outside the walls. A decade later, Breslin, abroad in America, was a chief man in freeing from their Australian penal servitude the Fenian prisoners there.

The army in Ireland was honey-combed with Fenianism—and the police force likewise. The army was so Fenian that many regiments were entirely unreliable from the British point of view. Thousands of the men had taken the Fenian oath. The work was begun by O'Donovan Rossa who swore in a soldier named Sullivan, a native of his own Roscarbery—and this soldier swore in another, and so on. But it was the remarkable character, Pagan O'Leary, who, tackling the work some months after Rossa had begun it, made the big success of it. John Devoy and William Rowantree stepped into the gap and continued the work, when O'Leary, betrayed by a soldier at Athlone, was sent into penal servitude.

driver on the seat and liveried foot-men behind (each "flunkey" being an armed Fenian), and drove through the streets of Dublin to the sea-coast near Balbriggan, where he entered a boat that took him to a lugger in the offing, which in turn bore him safely to France. From thence the Chief made his way easily to America.

The other Fenian leaders were tried in December on a charge of high treason—by the usual bitterly biased judges and packed juries—found guilty, of course, and sentenced—O'Donovan Rossa for life, Kickham, Luby, O'Leary, and the others, to twenty years' penal servitude.[10]

---

[10] O'Donovan Rossa got a life sentence because it was his second conviction. In '58 he was convicted of treasonable conspiracy in his native Skibbereen. But, anyhow probably his judges would have considered him deserving of a double dose, by reason that, having insisted upon conducting his own defence, he gave judges, jury, and prosecutors many weary hours. As extracts from *The Irish People* were put in evidence against the prisoners, O'Donovan Rossa insisted that if any portion of the papers was placed before the Court, every word in every paper, for every week of the paper's existence, must be read. When the judges and prosecutors gasped at the fearful prospect, he sought to comfort them by a generous leniency—he would not insist upon reading the advertisements. Before he lifted from their hearts the load of dread he had placed there, he gave them upwards of eight hours' straight reading beginning with the first word at the top of the left-hand corner of the first number and continuing straight forward, conscientiously, without the omission of article or particle!

Fearful indeed was the life—the living death, rather—that Irish political prisoners had to face in English jails. O'Donovan Rossa, with hands chained behind his back for weeks together, had to feed himself as a dog would, by lapping it up. Michael Davitt tells how, when the keeper was not looking, prisoners would snatch a candle end out of the garbage, and save it to feast upon—also, how, to get a mouthful of air for which in their vile dungeons they were perishing, they would lie down upon the floor and through the crack at the bottom of the door, greedily suck in the already vitiated air of the corridor. In '77 O'Connor Power, in the House of Commons, demanding inquiry into the horrors to which Irish political prisoners were subjected, read a letter from Michael Davitt in Dartmoor prison, describing the sufferings of some of his fellow-prisoners there—from which is extracted a portion, about one of them: "In June or July 1868, Chambers received 'no grounds' as an answer to a petition that he had sent to the Secretary of State, begging to be allowed to attend his religious obligations, a privilege of which he was deprived, by a 'moral and religious' director for six months. At present he is daily driven in and out of chapel by officers brandishing bludgeons and shouting like cattle drovers. Even in chapel he is not free from their rudeness. Dozens of times those officers have stripped him naked in presence of thieves and subjected him to insults too disgusting to describe. He is made to open his clothes five times a day while an officer feels over his body. He has been several times separated from other political prisoners—although our being together was within the rules—and forced to associate with picked ruffians. He has been for six months in constant contact with lunatics. He has been forced to mop up filthy dens of dirt with a small piece of rag, to carry a portable water-closet on the public road and across the fields for the use of common malefactors. He has often been sick, but, except on a few occasions, was not taken to hospital. On one occasion he was sent to the dungeons for applying for relief after he had met with a severe hurt by falling from the gangway of a building. Last year while laid up with rheumatism, they kept him sixteen days on ten ounces of food daily, two months on half diet, and then put him out of hospital far worse than when he was taken in. He is weekly forced to act as charwoman

The movement had received a staggering blow—from which, however, it would have recovered were not further and greater misfortunes to follow. The country, eager for action, was disappointed that Stephens did not give the word in this year. They were infinitely more disappointed, discouraged, and embittered when, having solemnly pledged himself to give the word next year, he failed them again. Among their brethren in America—upon whose help great reliance had been placed—impatience gave way to criticism, and criticism to dissension. The great majority there set aside O'Mahony and Stephens, and their too long delayed (impossible) plan of invading Ireland, and chose Colonel Roberts for their leader, and an invasion of Canada for their plan.

The invasion of Canada, which would undoubtedly have been a successful move, and a severe blow to England, was stopped by the unexpected action of the American Government, which, having tacitly encouraged the scheme, and permitted the plans to be ripened, stepped in at the last moment to prevent it.

The American Government sold to the Fenians vast quantities of ammunition and other military supplies, winked at the gathering of the Fenian hosts from all corners of the country, and even permitted the crossing of the border (near Buffalo) by General John O'Neill at the head of the first body of Fenian soldiers. From over the British Fort Erie O'Neill hauled down the English colours and ran up the Irish, on the 31st May, '66.

And next morning, at Ridgeway, he encountered the enemy in numbers far superior to his own force, disastrously routed them, capturing standards and large supplies—to the frantic joy of the Irish race throughout the world. It was then that America stepped in, forbidding the passage of any more Fenian forces over the border, and completely cutting off O'Neill's supplies—thus stopping his victorious career, and compelling him to fall back upon American soil—where he and his forces were placed under technical arrest—and the ambitious scheme ended.

In Ireland, where Stephens had been superseded by Colonel John Kelly, the Rising, arranged for March 5th, '67, was frustrated by a combination of circumstances. The informer, Corydon, betrayed the plans; and, strangely, a great snow storm, one of the wildest and most protracted, with which the

---

to a lot of dirty creatures. He has had punishment diet (16 ounces of bread and water), penal class diet, and dungeons—dark, wet, cold and dirty in abundance. A smile, a movement of the lips—ay, even a glance of the eye—is often deemed a crime in Dartmoor. We have been frequently insulted by thieves and even struck by them. Chambers has been held by one jailer while another jailer was ill-using him. Worthy sons of worthy sires who once shot down the poor prisoners of war here!"

country was ever visited, beginning on the night of March 6th and abating not for twelve days and twelve nights, made absolutely impossible not only all communications, but all movements of men.

One of the greatest Irish movements of the century ended apparently in complete failure. Apparently only, for though there was not success of arms, other kinds of success began to show immediately. Within two years after, that terrible incubus upon Ireland, the Established (English) Church was disestablished, and within three years the first Land Act of the century, the Act of '70, was made law. And Prime Minister Gladstone afterwards confessed that it was the healthy fear instilled in him by the astonishing spirit of the Fenian movement, which forced him to these actions.

Moreover, the spirit begotten by Fenianism went forward, for future triumph.

John O'Leary, Recollections of Fenians and Fenianism.
Joseph Deneiffe, Personal Narrative.
A. M. Sullivan's New Ireland.

CHAPTER LXXII

Charles Stewart Parnell

From 1865–1870 the English Courts in Ireland were kept busy with the trial of the Fenian Prisoners. Courts-martial were also working at high pressure dealing with alleged sedition on the part of Irish soldiers. The barrack yards of Dublin ran red with the blood, and re-echoed the shrieks, of soldiers condemned to the lash. In many cases with all the breath left in their mangled bodies, these soldiers, after their inhuman torture raised a cheer for Ireland. The leading counsel for the defence of the prisoners was Isaac Butt, Q.C., one of the most able and eloquent lawyers at the Bar. In this capacity Butt had exceptional opportunities of learning a great deal about the ideals of the Fenians. He saw that they were men who had taken risks, and who were prepared to take punishment, be it the scaffold or the cell. He found none of them prepared for compromise, cowardice or surrender. The result was that the Tory M.P. for Trinity College, honest man that he was, became an advocate of the cause of Irish Independence.

True, Butt's definition of independence was not that of the Fenians. He invented a new term "Home Rule." The first meeting of the "Home Government Association," afterwards re-named the "Home Rule League," was held in a Dublin hotel in 1870. A resolution was passed "that the true remedy for the evils of Ireland is the establishment of an Irish Parliament with full control over our domestic affairs." Vague enough, in sooth, but probably as strong as Butt dared to make it in an assemblage comprised of landlords, Tories, "moderate" Nationalists, and some Fenians—the latter being present chiefly to take notes. The old demand for Repeal of the Union was dropped, and the demand for "Home Rule"—which might mean anything—took its place. Probably Butt could not have done better in the circumstances, and his action must be judged by his circumstances.

It was not then as clear as it now is that one of the chief devices for the consolidation of British power in Ireland is the exploitation of what is known as "moderate opinion."

In 1874 came a General Election, and to the surprise of the nation the Home Rulers carried thirty-nine seats, and later four Fenians were returned. The bulk of the members of "the Party," however, were Home Rulers in name, using their position for their own ends, pledged to vote right on Home Rule motions, but otherwise free to follow their own sweet will.

Charles Stewart Parnell was the squire of Avondale, County Wicklow. He was, on the paternal side, of English descent, one of his ancestors having purchased the Avondale property in the reign of Charles the Second. His great-grandfather was Sir John Parnell, Chancellor of the Irish Exchequer, who forfeited his position rather than vote for the Union. The poet, Thomas Parnell, was of his family. His mother was the daughter of Commodore Stewart of the U. S. Navy. During the war with England in the beginning of the nineteenth century the Commodore married, and almost immediately was detailed for active service. "What present shall I bring you home?" he asked his bride. Her reply was, "A British Frigate." "I shall bring you two," he said,—and he did. The mother of Charles Stewart Parnell hated England and the English and was probably a potent influence in determining his career and outlook on life.

Parnell was educated in English schools, finishing at the University of Cambridge. He gained some repute as a mathematician, but, generally speaking, he was neither very brilliant nor very assiduous. He left Cambridge without a degree, and not of his own volition. His biographers pass over the matter lightly—they generally refer to it as an ordinary Town and Gown row. His sister, Mrs. Monroe Dickinson, is more explicit. In "A Patriot's Mistake" she clearly brings out that Parnell, aged nineteen, had engaged the affections of a young girl in the neighbourhood, who was subsequently found drowned. Parnell was distracted over the affair, and only the care of his estate and his hunting saved him from a nervous collapse. His father, by his will, had made him master of Avondale, excluding his elder brother, John Howard, who was given the portion of a younger son. The explanation of this seems to be that Parnell's father was under the impression that John Howard was to be his uncle's heir, and, therefore, had allotted Avondale to Charles Stewart. John went to America, and was there visited by Charles Stewart, who promptly fell in love with a reigning beauty who had society at her feet. Tiring of American life she left for Rome. Parnell followed her, proposed and was accepted. Then one day she told him she could not marry him as "he had no name." "No name," exclaimed Parnell, "why I have one of the oldest in Ireland." The beauty explained that she wanted to marry a self-made man who had made his mark—"not a rusty old Irish name." Parnell promised to make a name, on condition that she married him when he had done so. He made his name, laid it at the feet of his beloved; in a short space she was married to another.

"He came forth," says his sister, "strengthened and ennobled by the fiery ordeal. . . . Thus, Ireland, for the devotion and sacrifice of Charles's life . . . had to thank the faithlessness and fickleness of a woman." "The work," continues Mrs. Dickinson, "which he had first undertaken for love of a woman he afterwards continued with unabated ardour from patriotic feeling."

To get elected to Parliament, he made two trials—one in Wicklow, another in Dublin, and was on both occasions defeated. Then in 1875 he replaced John Martin in Meath. He was regarded as a nice, gentlemanly fellow, who would create no sensation in the House of Commons,—who might make one speech, but never another.

The night that Parnell took his seat at Westminster he noted that there were two policies operating. One was that of Butt, who addressed the House of Commons as he might an impartial jury in the Four Courts, Dublin. Parnell missed the impartial jury. There was no such thing in the House of Commons, where everything seemed to be regulated by party interests. The other was that of Joseph Giles Biggar—called "Joe"—and this was to outrage the House of Commons in every possible way. It so happened that on the very night of Parnell's entry "Joe" had been told off to obstruct a coercion bill. He did. He was not a man of words, but he had provided himself with a copious stock of literature—Government Blue-books, newspapers and documents of all kinds from which he read extracts until he had thoroughly exhausted the patience of the House. The Speaker at his wit's end, at length declared that the orator was no longer heard at the chair. "Joe" declared that he was sorry that his ordinary position in the House placed him at a disadvantage, but, with permission, he would move up nearer to the chair. He then moved his file of documents up to the table and read from them for four hours in a tone and accent that might possibly be intelligible, even attractive in Belfast, but certainly not elsewhere.

Parnell remained a while a spectator, not quite sure which course to pursue. After consideration he decided to adopt Biggar's. But Parnell's obstruction was of a new brand. It was not just wanton like Biggar's; it was scientific. The system was this: propose an amendment to practically every clause of every measure introduced by the Government, and then discuss each amendment fully, his friends forming relays to keep the discussion going. But Parnell could hardly ever be accused of deliberate obstruction.

His amendments were generally worth consideration on their merits. Thus, he put an end to flogging in the British Army. He gained his end of obstructing the business of the House of Commons by amendments admittedly reasonable. In 1877 Isaac Butt was called into the House to reprove Parnell. He did so. Parnell disposed of him in one short sentence. Parnell and Butt were obviously coming to blows.

And the blows were going to be hard ones for Butt. Parnell intimated to his adherents that if he was to be of any use in Parliament something striking should be done. The hint was promptly taken. On September 1st, 1877, the Home Rule Federation of Great Britain held their annual meeting at Liverpool. Parnell was elected president instead of Butt. Butt was annoyed and made no secret of the fact. Everybody felt for him but in politics sympathy has no place. Parnell, an onlooker says, was there "looking like a piece of granite."

To understand the rise of Parnell to power and fame, certain popular misconceptions have to be removed. From the literature which has grown up about him it might be inferred that he was a poor speaker. While he was never an orator in the accepted sense of the word, while he was not a ready speaker, and often had trouble in finding the word that exactly expressed his meaning, he waited till he had found it, and then it was evident to his hearers that his hesitation was justified. He was never very keen on speaking, but when he had to speak he spoke in telling, and often in memorable phrases which sunk into the public mind and which are still on men's lips as part of the gospel of nationality. He was not a very original man; he often borrowed the ideas of others after due consideration; but once started on a certain line of action he worked to his goal with dogged persistence. Thus, the idea of obstruction did not originate in the brain of the most skilful of all the obstructionists; it was the suggestion of Joseph Ronayne of Cork and was already being operated by Biggar, when Parnell entered Parliament. He was a thoughtful rather than a learned man. But he was not ignorant and had a good knowledge of what interested him. His biographer, Mr. Barry O'Brien, records the opinion formed of him by careful and critical observers. The most remarkable thing about him was his silence. He let others do the talking. His main object was to unite all elements—Fenians, Constitutionalists, Clerics—all, in one grand rally for Ireland. He did not think that the struggle on constitutional lines could be a long one. It was to be "short, sharp and decisive." "Ireland," he said, "cannot afford to lose the services of a single man."

In 1880—after Mr. Shaw had temporarily succeeded Butt—he was elected leader of the Irish Party. Explanations of his rise to power are somewhat contradictory. There were clever men in the Party—orators like A. M. Sullivan, business-men like Thomas Sexton, literary men like

Justin McCarthy. There are two words common to all explanations of his selection—character and personality.

Parnell had only a limited belief in the efficiency of parliamentarianism. He was of opinion that without a well organised public opinion in Ireland his power in Parliament would be slight. He publicly advised the Irish people to keep a keen watch on the conduct of their representatives in the House of Commons. He publicly stated that long association with the House of Commons would destroy the integrity of any Irish Party. He saw nothing but disaster in the policy of conciliating the English. "We will never gain anything from England," he said, "unless we tread on her toes; we will never gain a sixpenny worth from her by conciliation."

Parnell's wish for an energetic movement at home was gratified in an unexpected manner. Michael Davitt was released from prison on the 19th December, 1877, on "ticket of leave" after serving seven years and seven months of a fifteen year sentence for Fenianism. Parnell and others met Davitt and his fellow-prisoners, Sergeant McCarthy, Chambers and O'Brien, at Kingstown, and on a later date entertained them to breakfast at Morrison's Hotel, Dublin. The rejoicing natural to such an occasion came to a tragic termination. Poor McCarthy had a wife and children down south to whom he was passionately attached and from whom he had been separated by an informer who had gained his confidence while enjoying his hospitality and playing with his little children. He was never to enjoy their embraces again. His heart collapsed and he died in Davitt's arms. He had taken the patriot's risk and consummated the patriot's sacrifice.

The name of Michael Davitt brings up the Land Question. Even in Ireland, today, it is difficult to understand the condition of affairs in bygone days. The Landlord was "the master." He could raise rents at will, he could evict, whether rent was paid or not; if the tenant improved his holding he could be taxed for doing so—the rent went up—if he defended the chastity of his daughters, or they did so, he was liable to eviction. The landlord owned his tenant, and his tenant's land, and his tenant's vote, and, as he thought, sometimes even his tenant's women-folk.[1] Michael Davitt had

---

[1] An old neighbour of my own told me that he was evicted from the land he and his fathers held, in return for which was given a piece of bog-land; that often when he opened the door of the cabin in which I found him the snipe and wild duck took wing from before his door. When, by the sweat of his brow, he had made something like land of the bog-holding, the landlord made him pay rent for it. He was fool enough to do so—with money obtained from relatives in America. One Christmas night, after paying the landlord, with money earned in another continent, his wife and children and himself sat hungry by the fireside.

good reason to know the conditions of land tenure in Ireland. At the age of five years he was thrown with his father, mother and two sisters on the roadside, and their little home, before their eyes, razed to the ground. The father was a hard-working, intelligent man who, having somehow survived the famine, and was hoping for a little comfort, was flung with his wife and babes on the world's highway while the landlord took over the fruit of years of toil without a cent of compensation. In time he crossed with his family to Lancashire and obtained employment as an Insurance Agent. Michael, while only a child, was sent to work in a mill. One day, when he was about twelve, he was told off to work on a machine which he was too young and inexperienced to manage. He protested, but in vain. His overseer thought more of output than of the danger to life or limb of an operative, and young Davitt was roughly hurled to his task. Soon his right arm got entangled in the machinery and was so severely injured that it had to be amputated. It can be imagined that he had very little schooling, but he was a bright, industrious lad, who, though self-taught, developed into an able writer, and an acute thinker with a good store of ready information. At an early age he joined the Irish Republican Brotherhood, but escaped the fate of so many of his comrades in the "Black Assize" of the later sixties. His turn came in 1870. He was an arms agent for the Irish Republican Brotherhood in the guise of a commercial traveller, and was caught in the toils by the too great secrecy of a fellow conspirator. A "centre" in Waterford was apprised of a consignment of arms to his order, and he alone knew the way the material was to be sent. He took fever and died. In the goods depot at Waterford was a box which was "to be kept till called for," but as time passed and no call was coming, the baggage-master, an ex-policeman, opened the box and informed the British Government of its contents. The arms were traced to a Birmingham manufacturer, Mr. Wilson. Davitt and Wilson were arrested. Davitt was sentenced to fifteen years' penal servitude, Wilson to seven years. Davitt, with true Irish pluck, asked to be allowed to serve both sentences. The request was not unnaturally refused, Wilson must have known where the arms were going. He was an Englishman and should have been as loyal to his country as Davitt to his own. But note the difference in the sentences! If Wilson was a traitor to England his crime was greater than that of Davitt. If not, he should have been acquitted. When Davitt emerged from prison there were various conjectures as to his future course of action. Of course, he rejoined the Fenians, but his object now was the conjunction of all bodies, Fenian and Home Ruler in a struggle to assert that the land of Ireland belonged to the Irish people. Landlordism should go for ever.

"But," said the extremist group, "make the farmers secure and they will throw over the National Movement altogether." "No!" said Davitt, and time has proved him right. The farmers of Ireland, fortunately, under better conditions, have not grown selfish. They were selfish only when they were fighting for their lives. In 1878 Davitt sailed for America where his mother now resided. He took up the Irish problem with the leaders of the advanced party. John Devoy, the Fenian leader, agreed with his policy, while Kickham and the great majority of the leaders opposed what had come to be called "the new departure." Finally, however, individual officers of the advanced organisation were left free to use their discretion. Devoy and Davitt came to Ireland, they met Parnell, who characteristically came to no terms, neither praised nor dispraised the revolutionary movement, but asked to be let alone to see what he could get out of the parliamentary machine, while admitting that the advanced party had a right to try out their own devices.

During the years '76–'79 the distress of the Irish tenantry touched the line of famine. The rents were not reduced. The landlord demanded payment for land which the land never earned. England's Parliament would do nothing to remedy matters. Every motion in that direction was rejected with scorn. Between 1870 and 1876 *fourteen* attempts to amend the Land Laws failed. What wonder that the Irish people got restive. By 1876 their patience was giving out. That year a land agent was shot at in County Cork. The shot, unfortunately, hit his driver. Joe Biggar afterwards remarked that he disapproved of shooting at landlords because *innocent people* were sometimes shot by accident. In 1878 Lord Leitrim, whose reputation for rack-renting—and worse—was notorious, was shot in Donegal. Donegal men were jealous of their women's honour. His slayers were never discovered, though the whole population was supposed to know who they were.

Rack-renting, however, went on, even for land that was literally the product of the tenant's labour. The evicted tenant who made his home on a strip of waste bog was rented, when with the sweat of his bones, he had converted it into land so called.

Mayo was one of the worst counties in respect of rack-rent and evictions. In Mayo, therefore, it was proper that the first organised assault on landlordism should be made. One Walter Burke bought a small estate, doubled the rent and put a fine of half a year's rent on the tenants. The terms were: pay or quit. Mr. Burke died, and his executor was the Reverend Canon Burke. The exaction of the last farthing of rent and arrears from the unfortunate tenants was insisted on. This was the case with which Michael Davitt chose to open his campaign. A great public meeting was held at

Irishtown, organised by P. W. Nally and other Mayo men, and addressed by Thomas Brennan of Dublin, O'Connor Power, John Ferguson of Glasgow and others.

The keynote of the speech was "the land for the people." The speakers in advocating peasant proprietary broke away notably from the more moderate land policy of Butt, "the three F's," viz.: Fixity of Tenure, Fair Rents, and Free Sale. A land revolution was in progress. The meeting was unprecedented. Seven thousand people were present; five hundred men on horseback acted as the bodyguard of the speakers. An immediate sequel was that the rents were reduced by twenty-five per cent. The Land Act of 1881 reduced them by a further forty per cent. What must they have been before 1879!

Parnell was, naturally, interested in this new movement. Here was a purely social revolution independent of parliamentary effort. He foresaw great risks. If he identified himself with the new agitation certain things would happen for which he would be held responsible. Butt had already warned him against the dangers latent in widespread organisations. He decided, however, to take the risk. He agreed to speak at a meeting in Westport. The risk was even greater than he had foreseen. The meeting—and the movement generally—were condemned by no less a man than John MacHale, Archbishop of Tuam, whose patriotism and public spirit none dared question. Parnell was not abashed. He had promised to attend and attend he would. That personal pride, which had such a part in his making and his undoing, sustained him. He attended. He spoke a few memorable sentences in his own peculiarly lucid style.

"A fair rent is a rent the tenant can pay according to the times, but in bad times a tenant cannot be expected to pay as much as he did in good times. . . . If such rents are insisted on . . . what must we do in order to induce the landlords to see the position? You must show them that you intend *to hold a firm grip of your homesteads and lands. . . .*"

That phrase stuck. "Hold a firm grip of your homesteads" became a rallying cry. Mayo was ablaze. The year 1879 vitalised the tenants. The crop of 1879 was a failure. Parnell's declaration was translated into "No Rent." Meeting succeeded meeting. There was a particularly successful one at Milltown, County Galway. The speeches were fairly violent. A question in regard to them was asked in the London House of Commons. Mr. James Lowther, then Tory Chief Secretary for Ireland, replied. He was inclined to be facetious. This is part of his reply: "One of the resolutions proposed at the meeting was moved by a clerk in a commercial house in Dublin (Mr. Brennan), and seconded by a person who was described as a discharged school-master (Mr. M. O'Sullivan). Another resolution was moved by a convict at large on ticket-of-leave (Mr. Davitt), (loud laughter and cheers), and the same resolution was seconded by a person who was stated to be the representative of a local newspaper." (Mr. James Daly.)

That was the spirit in which the English Government of the day regarded the land agitation in Ireland. The insinuation is obvious. The farmers were not in the movement at all: the whole thing was the work of landless agitators, criminals, and journalists. Mr. Lowther's jibes soon came home to roost. The "National Land League" was established at Castlebar. The imminent danger of famine supplied the movement with momentum. Two American journals, the *Irish World* edited by Patrick Ford, and the *Boston Pilot* edited by John Boyle O'Reilly, enlisted American sympathy and financial support. John Devoy granted aid from what was known as the "skirmishing fund," a collection in aid of revolutionary action against England, but Davitt paid all the money back when it had served its purpose.

Parnell finally agreed to recognise the "National Land League," and to become its president. Mr. Davitt, A. J. Kettle and Thomas Brennan were appointed honorary secretaries. Mr. Biggar, Patrick Egan and W. H. Sullivan were appointed treasurers. Parnell entered into no compact. He did not interfere in the plans of the Irish Republican Brotherhood, neither did he give himself away. He had espoused Parliamentarianism and was determined to see what could be got out of it. Any outside help was all to the good.

On Sunday, November 2nd, a great meeting was held at Gurteen, County Sligo. Davitt was there and John Dillon, Mr. Daly of Castlebar, Mr. Killeen, a Belfast Barrister, and others. There was also a Government reporter. Davitt, Daly, and Killeen were immediately lodged in Sligo jail. Parnell at once got active. He organised a great meeting of protest for the Rotunda, Dublin. He went down himself to Balla in the County Mayo, and addressed a great meeting there in connection with a threatened eviction, and was certainly as seditious as the others. Meanwhile, Davitt and his companions were returned for trial in Sligo.

CHAPTER LXXIII

The Land Struggle Begins

Davitt and his compatriots were duly arraigned in Sligo. The trial was a prolonged political meeting, with brass bands, fiery speeches, processions, and every manner of demonstration. The traversers were ordered to attend the Assizes in Carrick-on-Shannon. They turned up the day before their trial and held a public meeting at which they repeated all the language for which they were indicted. The trials were removed to Dublin, and subsequently dropped. For the moment the League had won.

Parnell and Dillon, having postponed their visit for the trials, set sail for America from Cove on the 27th December, 1879. They had a fine reception everywhere, and Parnell had the unusual distinction of addressing Congress, and delivered a cogent and striking address. Meanwhile relief money was coming from America and from other sources. The landlords ignored the distress. They wanted their rents, whether the land earned them or not. The League was just as determined. No process-server could travel without drawing a crowd; evicted families were a charge on the funds of the League; if a farm was evicted nobody dared to take it; if anybody did he was unfit for social intercourse; finally the League decided to defend cases in the English courts, thus piling expense on the landlord.

The first big battle with the process-server occurred at Carraroe, County Galway, on January 1st, 1880. The processes for the forthcoming sessions should be served before January 6th. The parties affected and their neighbours had made up their minds that they should not. Carraroe is in the heart of South Connemara where from any point of vantage nothing but moor and granite strikes the eye. Cuan an Fhir Mhoir (Great Man's Bay) divides this region into a number of islands now joined by the road, the creeks being so narrow that it is only gradually the traveller becomes aware of the fact that he is crossing from island to island. Not a tree or shrub relieves the desolation which is emphasised by the gaunt telegraph poles along the white winding road which links up the islands. As might be expected, the bulk of the populace—mostly the descendants of people who in former days took refuge from British extermination in this remote hinterland—are miserably poor. Their plight is a blot on the administration of any government of a civilised country.

A tenant's son in Carraroe made up his mind to marry without consulting the landlord or his agent. The rent of the holding was raised five pounds as a fine. Two sons of another tenant got married and were allotted an outhouse to live in. With perfect consistency the fine in this case was ten pounds. Another tenant—Andrew Conneely—paying five pounds a year had his rent doubled. His brother who had an adjoining holding was, through adverse circumstances, a defaulter for one year's rent; Andrew got the option of paying his brother's ten pounds in addition to his own or of being evicted. These and many other hardships, combined with bad harvests, maddened the flannel-coated men and women of Connemara to revolt.

Roads were cut up, barricades raised, and men, women and children massed. The process-server emerged from the barrack and the first intended victim was a Mrs. Maickle. As the official approached her house with his escort he was assailed by the women and children, his "process" was torn up, and he was in danger of bodily hurt. The "force" approached Mrs. Maickle's, who had prepared for them a big burning turf with which she hit the District Inspector of Police. A bayonet charge followed; many women and children were wounded; the men, who had up to now been spectators, joined in the fray, and the police were routed. This was on Friday. Extra forces were called in, totalling finally about two hundred and fifty. The people also exerted themselves, and on Monday some two thousand men were assembled, with others near by in reserve. The police were in a trap. Had they persisted in their effort to enable the process-server to deliver his notices the bridges would have been cut and return to their headquarters would have been impossible. Armed with weapons of precision, they might have done considerable slaughter of the unarmed peasantry before being annihilated, but, fortunately, matters were not forced to a bloody issue. While the "force" remained they had a hungry time of it. Needy as were the people, no sum of money could purchase food or service for the police.

Legal methods were adopted in other cases. The League supplied the funds for the defence of the tenants: the whole facts of the case—rent, valuation and other circumstances were brought out in public, and very often the landlord lost in law more than he could possibly gain in rent. The League saw to it that after an eviction took place the land would remain tenantless and profitless. The policy was to pay the rent for one holding in a district and on this consolidate the evicted, who would, thus, have some scanty subsistence and be near at hand to repel any attempt to grab their holdings.

An interesting meeting was held at Straide, County Mayo, on February 1st, 1880. The platform was erected on the very site of Davitt's home from which he was cast on the roadside at the age of five. In the course of a powerful address, Davitt said: "Can a more eloquent denunciation of an accursed land code be found than what is witnessed here in this depopulated district? In the memory of many now listening to my words that peaceful little stream which meanders by the outskirts of this multitude sang back the merry voices of happy children and wended its way through a once populous and prosperous village. Now, however, the merry sounds are gone, the busy hum of hamlet life is hushed in sad desolation, for the hands of the home-destroyers have been here and performed their hellish work, leaving Straide but a name to mark the place where happy homesteads once stood, and whence an inoffensive people were driven to the four corners of the earth by the ruthless decree of landlordism. How often in a strange land has my boyhood's ear drunk in the tale of outrage and wrong and infamy perpetrated here in the name of English laws, and in the interest of territorial greed; in listening to the accounts of famine and sorrow, of deaths by starvation, of coffinless graves, of scenes

"On highway side, where oft was seen
The wild dog and the vulture keen
Tug for the limbs and gnaw the face
Of some starved child of our Irish race.

. . . "It is no little consolation to know, however, that we are here today doing battle against a doomed monopoly, and that the power which has so long domineered over Ireland and its people is brought to its knees at last, and on the point of being crushed for ever, and if I am standing today upon a platform erected over the ruins of my levelled home, I may yet have the satisfaction of trampling on the ruins of Irish landlordism."

English statesmanship has never regarded any Irish question other than as a possible electioneering device. Disraeli wrote in 1874:

"Neither liberty of the press nor liberty of the person exists in Ireland. Arrests are at all times liable. It is a fact that at any time in Ireland the police may enter into your house, examine your papers to see if there is any resemblance between the writing and that of some anonymous letter that has been sent to a third person. In Ireland, if a man writes an article in a newspaper, and it offends the Government, he has a warning, and if he repeats the offence his paper may be suppressed. They say Ireland is peaceful. Yes, but she is so, not because she is contented, but because she is held under by coercive laws. These laws may be necessary. I am not here objecting to them. I am a Tory, and as such I might favour severer laws myself. But I say it isn't honest in the Liberals, while denouncing us, to imitate our ways."

Already he had written in 1844:

"I want to see a public man come forward and say what the Irish question is. One says it is a physical question; another a spiritual. Now it is the absence of the aristocracy; now the absence of railways. It is the Pope one day and potatoes the next. A dense population in extreme distress inhabit an island where there is an established church which is not their church; and a territorial aristocracy, the richest of whom live in a distant capital. Thus they have a starving population, an absentee aristocracy, an alien church, and in addition the weakest executive in the world. Well, what then would honourable gentlemen say if they were reading of a country in that position? They would say at once, 'The remedy is revolution.' But the Irish could not have a revolution, and why? Because Ireland is connected with another and more powerful country. Then what is the consequence? The connection with England became the cause of the present state of Ireland. If the connection with England prevented a revolution, and a revolution was the only remedy, England logically is in the odious position of being the cause of all the misery of Ireland. What, then, is the duty of an English minister? To effect by his policy all those changes which a revolution would do by force. That is the Irish question in its entirety."

Disraeli was twice premier in the meantime. In 1880 as Lord Beaconsfield he made Ireland, then more unsettled than ever, the basis of his appeal to the electorate. "The arts of agitators," he wrote, "which represented that England instead of being the generous and sympathising friend, was indifferent to the dangers and sufferings of Ireland, have been defeated by the measures, at once liberal and prudent, which Parliament have almost unanimously sanctioned."

Of a thousand answers to this manifesto we just pause to give one. Mulhall's Dictionary of Statistics gives the details year by year (taken from official British sources) of the number of Irish families evicted from 1849 to 1882; and the thirty-three years' total of officially reported evictions (which fall far short of the full number) is 482,000 families. Since a low average for each family in the mountain districts of Ireland would be father, mother and six children, this represents the appalling total of 3,856,000 creatures cast out to starve or die in a third of a century.

And the measures "at once liberal and prudent" during the half century from Catholic Emancipation 1829 to 1879 (the year before that in which Lord Beaconsfield spoke) are detailed in Michael Davitt's "Fall of Feudalism in Ireland." First are given the ameliorative measures offered in the British Parliament in Ireland's behalf—and next the measures that she received. Summing up the first it is shown that of the forty-nine ameliorative measures put forward in the fifty years, five were withdrawn, seven were rejected, twenty-one were dropped, fifteen proved abortive—and the grand total of one of the forty-nine was passed!

Then, the following is a list of acts "at once liberal and prudent" which the British Parliament, with "almost unanimous sanction," did bestow upon Ireland in those years:

1830 Importation of Arms Act.
1831 Whiteboy Act.
1831 Stanley's Arms Act.
1832 Arms and Gunpowder Act.
1833 Suppression of Disturbance.
1833 Change of Venue Act.
1834 Disturbances Amendment and Continuance.
1834 Arms and Gunpowder Act.
1835 Public Peace Act.
1836 Another Arms Act.
1838 Another Arms Act.
1839 Unlawful Oaths Act.
1840 Another Arms Act.
1841 Outrages Act.
1841 Another Arms Act.
1843 Another Arms Act.
1843 Act Consolidating all Previous Coercion Acts.
1844 Unlawful Oaths Act.
1845 Unlawful Oaths Act.
1846 Constabulary Enlargement.
1847 Crime and Outrage Act.
1848 Treason Amendment Act.
1848 Removal of Arms Act.
1848 Suspension of Habeas Corpus.
1848 Another Oaths Act.
1849 Suspension of Habeas Corpus.
1850 Crime and Outrage Act.
1851 Unlawful Oaths Act.
1853 Crime and Outrage Act.
1854 Crime and Outrage Act.
1855 Crime and Outrage Act.
1856 Peace Preservation Act.
1858 Peace Preservation Act.
1860 Peace Preservation Act.
1862 Peace Preservation Act.
1862 Unlawful Oaths Act.
1865 Peace Preservation Act.
1866 Suspension of Habeas Corpus Act (August).
1866 Suspension of Habeas Corpus.
1867 Suspension of Habeas Corpus.
1868 Suspension of Habeas Corpus.
1870 Peace Preservation Act.
1871 Protection of Life and Property.
1871 Peace Preservation Con.
1873 Peace Preservation Act.
1875 Peace Preservation Act.
1875 Unlawful Oaths Act (lasting until 1879).

CHAPTER LXXIV

The Land League

The funds of the Land League and of other organisations enabled the Western people to put in good seed in 1880, and there was every prospect of a good harvest. Suddenly, in March, the Tory Government resigned. Parnell hurried from America where he had founded the American Land League, leaving Dillon behind to attend to details. No man could have worked harder than Parnell during the elections. He was ubiquitous. The constituencies, Meath, Mayo and Cork City, vied for the honour of having him as representative. His nomination for Cork City was a piece of "political strategy." Parnell was wired to in the name of a friend asking him to accept nomination. Two hundred and fifty pounds was handed to his friend, Mr. Horgan, for expenses, and this sum was supposed to have been sent by Parnell. Mr. Horgan promptly paid fifty pounds of this sum to the sheriff. Parnell arrived in Cork. Then the plot was made manifest. The Tories wished to defeat the Whigs by a split vote. The tables were turned on them when Mr. T. M. Healy suggested that the two hundred pounds would go some way towards Parnell's election expenses. To the great disgust of the Tories Parnell was elected, and his election expenses defrayed in great part by their own money. He then got Mr. A. J. Kettle elected for Cork County, and followed up this triumph by success all over Ireland. Sixty-four Nationalists were elected. Of these Parnell was leader of thirty-six, who instead of joining the Liberals took their seats on the Opposition Benches. A Bill was introduced by Mr. O'Connor Power to compel landlords to compensate tenants for disturbance. This was taken up by Mr. Gladstone's new Liberal Chief Secretary, Mr. Forster, was watered down, made a Government measure, passed through the House of Commons, and contemptuously rejected by the Lords. Meanwhile, things had been moving in Ireland. "*Hold the Harvest*" had become a rallying cry. Mr. James Redpath, an American journalist, who had already risked life and fortune in the cause of human freedom, outlined at Claremorris the system afterwards known as Boycotting. The landlord who oppressed his tenants, the man who took a farm from which another tenant had been evicted, and all who had intercourse with the like, were to be made social outcasts. A little later Parnell preached the same doctrine. His sister, Fanny Parnell, sent a ringing song from America. A few verses will suffice to show its import:

"Keep the law, oh, keep it well—keep it as your rulers do!
Be not righteous overmuch—when they break it so can you!
As they rend their pledge and bond, rend you, too, their legal thongs;
When they crush your chartered rights, tread you down your chartered wrongs.
Help them on, and help them aye, help them as true brethren should, boys;
All that's right and good for them, sure for you is right and good, boys.

"Hold the rent and hold the crops, boys.
Pass the word from town to town,
Pull away the props, boys,
So you'll pull coercion down."

Mr. Forster, a well intentioned man, was entering on the ordeal of every Chief Secretary for Ireland. He felt that things were getting out of hand. An indictment of most of the prominent members of the League was prepared. The charge was that of conspiracy, under which any member could be found guilty of any utterance if any man definitely proved to be associated with the League. Meanwhile, the policy advocated by Redpath and Parnell was being carried out. The first victim was one Captain Boycott, agent for Lord Erne, who lived at Lough Mask House in County Mayo. He had dismissed his labourers owing to a dispute over wages. No others appeared to take their places. The Captain waxed angry. Thereafter he would grant no abatements of rent. Processes were duly obtained—there was no one to serve them. The blacksmith was too busy to shoe the Captain's horses. The herds found the climate unhealthy. The baker ran out of flour. The postman was liable to overlook Lough Mask House, unless his missives for the Captain were unmistakably bills. The Captain's crops were ripening with no one to reap them. But relief was coming.

Fifty northern Orangemen escorted by two thousand soldiers arrived in Mayo to assist Captain Boycott. There was not a car in Claremorris fit for the job of transporting any of them. There was not a horse that had not a loose shoe, spavins, rickets or housemaid's knee. The labourers and their escort had to walk from Claremorris—fifteen miles—and it *rained.* Somehow and sometime they reached Lough Mask House. The formidable force encamped on the Captain's lawn. They had not made provision for their subsistence; if they were doing the Captain's work they presumed that they were to be fed at the Captain's expense. They ate his turkeys, geese, piglings, goslings, ducklings and all other of the most succulent part of his possessions. It was estimated that—apart from the Captain's losses—it cost the country ten pounds for every pound's worth of crop reaped on his land.

At last they departed. An interested spectator of the scene was Father John O'Malley of the Neale. There was another, an old woman. She wished, as woman will, to see the passage of troops. Father John advanced on her with menace; "Did I not warn you to let the British Army alone? How dare you come here to intimidate Her Majesty's troops?"

Mr. Forster was on the whole about as unfortunate as any other Chief Secretary for Ireland. He meant well, so do they all. Mr. Forster on the second reading of O'Connor Power's Bill gave some interesting figures. In the *West Riding* of Galway alone he had employed the following forces for protecting process-servers and carrying out evictions 4,049 soldiers—all, in a single district, paid by the Irish people for their own extermination.

The Land League went ahead. Huts were erected for evicted tenants. Relief works were started. We cannot well say how many emigrated, and how many died on their way to a foreign shore; the dead do not talk. We know that there was a big toll of lives.[1]

A debate took place in 1880 on the conduct of the Royal Irish Constabulary at evictions. Mr. Forster was their champion. He admitted that ball

---

[1] John Mitchel in talking of the evicting horror, gives a terse and terrible summary of the happenings upon one estate as the result of one eviction crop:

"At an eviction in 1854, on a property under the management of Marcus Keane, James O'Gorman, one of the tenants evicted, died on the roadside. His wife and children were sent to the workhouse, where they died shortly afterwards.

"John Corbet, a tenant on another townland, was evicted by the same agent. He died on the roadside. His wife had died previous to the eviction; his ten children were sent into the workhouse and there died.

"Michael McMahon, evicted at the same time, was dragged out of bed, to the roadside, where he died of want the next day. His wife died of want previous to the eviction, and his children, eight in number, died in a few years in the workhouse."

cartridges should not be supplied to police in close contact with excited people—hence they should get buckshot. Even if loaded with only snipe-shot, a shotgun is more treacherous when discharged on a crowd than a rifle. His name in Ireland, first shouted across the floor of the House, has ever since been "Buckshot Forster."

Forster proceeded in the traditional way to pacify Ireland. All the leaders and organisers were arrested. The whole Irish nation was constituted by statute an illegal assembly. A conspiracy act was framed under which every individual in the League could be held accountable for the action or speech of any one.

The state trial opened in Dublin in December, 1880. There were three judges and a formidable array of counsel; seven for the Crown, nine for the traversers, exclusive of solicitors. One of the most interesting interludes was the production by Mr. Tom Brennan, the League's secretary, of some hundred evicted tenants from the Castlebar workhouse, who, however, were not heard, because of a change in tactics of the prosecution. They were *seen,* however, and were quite sufficient evidence of the necessity of the Land League organisation. Meanwhile Parnell and his colleagues crossed to London for the opening of the session of Parliament, letting the court do what it pleased. The jury disagreed after a trial of thirty days. There was a touch of farce about the whole proceeding. The Crown case broke down. Davitt's ticket-of-leave was immediately cancelled. He was sent back to prison. He had, however, laid his lines well. He had established the "Ladies' Land League." He had relied on the women of Ireland to carry on, even if all the leaders were in prison.[2]

---

[2] The following verses from a poem of Miss Fanny Parnell show the spirit of the women:

> "Now, are you men, or are you kine, ye tillers of the soil?
> Would you be free, or evermore the rich man's cattle toil?
> The shadow on the dial hangs that points the fatal hour—
> Now hold your own! or branded slaves, for ever cringe and cower.
>
> "The serpent's curse upon you lies—ye writhe within the dust,
> Ye fill your mouths with beggars' swill, ye grovel for a crust;
> Your lords have set their blood-stained heels upon your shameful heads,
> Yet they are kind—they leave you still their ditches for your beds!
>
> "Oh, by the God who made us all—the seignior and the serf—
> Rise up and swear this day to hold your own green Irish turf;
> Rise up and plant your feet as men where now you crawl as slaves,
> And make your harvest-fields your camps, or make of them your graves.

Miss Anna Parnell was president of the Ladies' Land League. When Miss Parnell and her associates took up work they did it in no half-hearted fashion. They were all that Davitt expected of them—and more. They were not very restrained or very scrupulous. There was no reason why they should. Davitt had been sent back to penal servitude on the 3rd February, 1881. Next day Parnell and all his followers were suspended, and forcibly ejected out of the London House of Commons. Gladstone introduced a measure which made, practically, an end of obstruction. But home in Irèland Parnell was a much more dangerous force than he had been in Westminster. Land League Courts were held before which offenders were arraigned. Boycotting went on effectually. How effectually is shown by the case of Jones of Clonakilty. He tried to sell grain at Bandon. The League picketted his produce. He tried to send cattle to England—no ship at a southern port would carry them. He sent them by rail to Dublin: the mariners would not sail with them; they were ultimately got to Liverpool in Liverpool boats: no Irish salesman would offer them for sale. At the end, a private sale of them, at a loss, was all Jones could effect.

Arrests were frequent. This fact intensified the agitation. A grabber was shot occasionally—showing Mr. Forster that two parties could operate outside the common law. The landlords welcomed coercion, and under its shield process-serving for rent went forward with a bound. Then, as now, forty years later, the idea was to rush matters, and have all the trouble over in a couple of months. Then, as now, an extension of time for the subjugation of the Irish was necessary. A bad conflict between civilians and police, guarding a process-server, occurred at Monasteraden, County Sligo, in April. The police fired on a crowd of people who blocked the way to the

---

"Three hundred years your crops have sprung, by murdered corpses fed:
Your butchered sires, your famished sires, your ghastly compost spread;
Their bones have fertilised your fields, their blood has fall'n like rain;
They died that ye might eat and live—God! have they died in vain?

"The hour has struck, Fate holds the dice, we stand with bated breath;
Now who shall have your harvests fair—'tis Life that plays with Death;
Now who shall have our Motherland? 'tis Right that plays with Might;
The peasant's arms were weak, indeed, in such unequal fight!

"But God is on the peasant's side, the God that loves the poor;
His angels stand with flaming swords on every mount and moor.
They guard the poor man's flocks and herds, they guard his ripening grain;
The robber sinks beneath their curse beside his ill-got gain."

houses of those on whom the notices were to be served. Two men were slain. Sergeant Armstrong, who gave the order to fire, was immediately steeped in gore and died. His men escaped a like fate by flight.

Then, at last, it began to dawn on the English Liberal Government that there must be something wrong in Ireland. There are two things that always go hand in hand in Ireland, coercion and benevolent legislation. Coercion is strong, harsh, ineffective. All English Governments—Liberal and Tory alike—come to us with a whip in one hand and a "concession" in the other.

Gladstone had to face facts and bring in a Land Bill for Ireland. It was considered at a convention of the Land League in Dublin in April, 1881. Parnell was for its acceptance with such amendments as might be possible; John Dillon and Secretary Brennan were opposed. The majority supported Parnell. Dillon was arrested on the 30th April and lodged in Kilmainham jail. Brennan was arrested soon after. It was hoped that this would create an atmosphere for the new Land Bill. It did. There were men forthcoming to fill all vacancies that Gladstone and Forster might create. And then there were the women.

Coercion bore its usual fruits: arrests, evictions, outrages. The people defied law that defied the people. The Irish have never been willing slaves.

The Gladstone Land Act of 1881 was the usual compromise. The tenants were allowed for their improvements—*if they could prove them in court of law*. It was well known that the landlords made no improvements. If a man bought a farm he had to pay for it as it stood, drains, fences and all. If a man inherited a farm he had to prove what improvements were made, and by whom, and when, and if he could not procure witnesses he was non-suited in claiming a fair rent. If the farm was at the seaside, the tenant was considered not to be entitled to normal reduction of rent because he could cut seaweed at the risk of his life; if he set up a mill, grew fruit or otherwise improved the holding, at his own expense, that was set against him. If he built "too good a house," again at his own expense, that prejudiced his claim to a fair rent. If he set up a shop, that also, in practice, went against him; the value of the holding went up.

The tenant was discouraged from doing anything to improve his place. The worse it looked the safer he was. Even though the Act was good in principle it proved to be what Dillon prophesied it would be: "a milch cow for the lawyers."

Forster succeeded in making Ireland what is called in official documents today "an appropriate hell" for those who disagreed with him. Men were imprisoned without trial, grabbers and other offenders were severely dealt with; men were shot dead: Priests were arrested, including Father Eugene Sheehy of Limerick, a veteran who lived to be present at the inauguration of the Irish Volunteers in 1913.

Parnell denounced the conduct of the English Government in Parliament. He was suspended for a vigorous attack on Gladstone, and immediately crossed to Ireland where his operations made the Government bitterly regret his suspension. He and his followers had shown that they had no responsibility for the Land Act, by leaving the House of Commons before the division on both the Second and Third Readings. He endeavoured to get the best Bill he could, but was anxious to make it clear that it was not his Bill, or one he approved of. One of his first actions in Ireland was to propose and carry at a Land League convention in Dublin a resolution that the Land Act be tested in Court by specially selected cases, and that other tenants should wait to see how things would go in these cases. This adroit move simply meant that the Land Act would be held up indefinitely, and that a chance, based on the results of proceedings in the courts might arise for its radical emendation. It was one of the most politic moves of Parnell's whole career. But it was foiled. Let Michael Davitt tell the story:

"A class of Ulster tenants who had given no help to the Land League movement rushed into the land courts and set an example, baited with an average twenty per cent reduction of old rents.... Those tenants, however, who acted thus precipitately and unwisely were to live to regret that they had not followed Mr. Parnell's advice."

Then came another of these little incidents which play such a part in the relations of the English Government with Ireland. A Parnellite candidate was beaten by a Liberal in Tyrone. Gladstone was delighted. He wrote Mr. Forster: "The unexpected victory in Tyrone is an event of importance, and I own it increases my desire to meet the remarkable Irish manifestation and discomfiture both of Parnell and the Tories with some initial act of clemency, *in view especially of the coming election for Monaghan.* I do not know whether the release of the priest (Father Sheehy) would be a reasonable beginning. . . . *To reduce the following of Parnell by drawing away from him all well inclined men seems to me the key of Irish politics for the moment. . . .*"

But Mr. Forster was adamant. Instead of inclining to an "act of clemency" he advised Gladstone, in a forthcoming speech at Leeds, to denounce Parnell's "action and policy." "Parnell's reply to you," he said, "may be a treasonable outburst." Mr. Gladstone took his secretary's advice. He denounced Parnell. He declared that "the resources of civilisation were not exhausted." Parnell's reply at Wexford, whether treasonable or not, was corrosive. He dissected the "Grand Old Man" mercilessly. He compared him to a schoolboy going past a graveyard, whistling to keep up his courage. And he concluded with the stinging phrases:

"I trust as the result of this great movement we shall see that, just as Gladstone by the Act of 1881 has eaten all his own words, has departed from all his formerly declared principles, now we shall see that these brave words of the English Prime Minister will be scattered like chaff before the united and advancing determination of the Irish people to regain for themselves their lost land and their legislative independence." His friends rightly felt that now his arrest was certain. At length one of them plucked up courage to ask him: "Suppose they arrest you, Mr. Parnell . . . who will take your place?" "Captain Moonlight,"[3] replied Parnell.

---

[3] The resolute ones who took guns and went after tyrannical landlords—and tyrants—were known as Moonlighters.

CHAPTER LXXV

THE LADIES' LAND LEAGUE

Meanwhile, *United Ireland* was founded on the ruins of a paper called the *Flag of Ireland* bought from one Richard Piggott, of which more will be heard later. William O'Brien became its editor and gave admirable service to the cause. The No Rent manifesto was issued, signed by Parnell, Kettle, Davitt, Brennan, Dillon, Sexton, Patrick Egan—all in prison except Egan who was in Paris to safeguard the funds. The purport was that no rents were to be paid under any circumstances until the Government abandoned terrorism and restored the constitutional rights of the people.

This was a bold and dangerous policy. Had it been tried earlier, as Davitt had suggested, it might have shaken the Government and secured a better Land Act. But now the leaders were all in prison. The Land Act would soon be law, and the harassed tenants were likely to accept any relief that it offered. The manifesto was written by William O'Brien, and only with much diffidence signed by Parnell, Dillon, and the others. Forster's counter-move was not delayed. Two days later the Land League was proclaimed an illegal association, and it was announced that all its meetings would be, if necessary, dispersed by force.

The Ladies' Land League took matters in hand and Mr. Forster began to realise that he had possibly blundered. He had some 1,083 men in prison,[1] including the most upright and sensible men in the movement, and how was he to rule a country directed by a few women in Dublin? They had plenty of money, partly supplied from America, partly from Paris by Mr. Patrick Egan. Relief and help were given according to the amount of activity

[1] These men were never faced with any charges. They were "suspects." Habeas corpus then—as often before and since—was suspended.

displayed in a district. Boycotting increased. Any agrarian crime was defended from the funds of the Ladies' Land League. If a grabber was left in quiet possession of a farm there was not a farthing available for the district in which he lived. Anybody going into the Land Courts was condemned and intimidated. Hunting by the "gentry" was stopped. The situation day by day became more and more chaotic.

Mr. Forster thought the matter over, and hoped that if he had some of these women arrested it might ease the situation. He had about half a dozen arrested and was not pleased with the result. He found he was only lashing public opinion into fury. He found that there was hardly a girl in Ireland who would not joyfully go to prison for the cause. In fact they were inviting arrest.

Needless to say, the "outrages" were not all on one side. Forster's Buckshot Brigade loyally and zealously carried out their master's orders. In addition to the buckshot, the peelers were provided with a more deadly type of bayonet. A few examples will suffice to show how the orders to break the spirit of the people were carried out. At Grawhill, near Belmullet in October 1881, a crowd assembled, chiefly composed of women and children. The officer in charge of the crown forces gave orders to fire a volley of buckshot into the crowd and then charge with the bayonet. Numbers were wounded; the crowd rushed away in shrieking panic, the police freely using their bayonets indiscriminately on all they came up with. Mrs. Mary Deane, a widowed mother, was shot dead; a young girl, Ellen McDonagh, was stabbed to death. On May 5th, 1882, a band of lads of twelve years and under paraded in Ballina, County Mayo, with tin whistles and cans to celebrate Parnell's release. They were assailed with a hail of buckshot, chased and stabbed. One poor lad, Patrick Melody, fell dead at his father's feet on the threshold of his home.

Poor Mr. Forster stuck it out bravely. He asked Gladstone for further powers, but Gladstone was getting nervous. Money was pouring in from America, where T. P. O'Connor, T. M. Healy and Father Sheehy were now operating, and the "Grand Old Man" was becoming alarmed. In his alarm he had recourse to Rome, conveniently forgetting a pamphlet he had written a short time previously on *Vaticanism.* He was successful—to a certain extent. Through diplomacy—which could also be called another name—he secured a condemnation of the Land League and its policy in January, 1882, though the League had passed out of legal existence by Mr. Forster's edict in October, 1881. This condemnation had no effect on the struggle.

The Ladies' Land League became daily more active in relieving distress and keeping up the agitation. Forster was being worsted. He was prepared to propose a system of provincial councils for Ireland with limited autonomy, hoping that a bribe might weaken the opposition. However, a dramatic change in the situation soon took place.

Parnell was released on parole to attend the funeral of a nephew in Paris. On his way through London he saw Justin McCarthy and explained to him a project he had in his mind for the amendment of the Land Act by the cancellation of arrears thereby bringing under its provisions a vast number of tenants who were at present excluded. The prisoners should be released, the *No-Rent* manifesto withdrawn, and the agitation, generally, slowed down. Captain O'Shea was selected as his envoy to break this to Gladstone and Chamberlain. The message was delivered. Gladstone was delighted. "On the whole," he wrote to Forster, "Parnell's letter is the most extraordinary I ever read. I cannot help feeling indebted to O'Shea."

Parnell returned to prison, but his release was now only a matter of time. Gladstone was sick of coercion. Chamberlain, on his own admission, would have liked to succeed Forster as Chief Secretary for Ireland. Rather than consent to Parnell's release, Earl Cowper and Forster resigned. The very day before Parnell's proposals reached Gladstone the latter had written to Forster giving dim outlines for Land reform and self-government. "It is liberty," he said, "that makes men fit for liberty. This proposition has its bounds but it is far safer than the counter-doctrine—wait till they are fit." Parnell's proposals contained no mention of self-government. Neither had he consulted his colleagues concerning them. A new and different Parnell was developing.

On May 4th, 1882, Forster was explaining his position to the House of Commons. He had had a bad time of it in Ireland; he had shown himself a plucky fighter and he had been beaten, beaten by the Irish, and that was sufficient to win him the sympathy of the house. He was in the middle of his speech, denouncing the League, denouncing Parnell, when suddenly he was interrupted by a storm of cheers from the Irish benches. Parnell, dignified and haughty as of old, triumph depicted on his handsome features, had entered the House. He went to his seat, folded his arms, and gazed with cold scorn at his jailer, now in disgrace. He could not but rejoice that he had done to England what English Governments have always sought to do in Ireland—divide the forces of the opposition. Here were Gladstone and Forster at loggerheads: Gladstone on his feet to answer his ex-Chief-Secretary at whose bidding he had invoked the "resources of civilisation," and defending the man against whom they had been invoked. Gladstone replied quietly that the circumstances which warranted the arrest no longer existed, and that he was assured that, if the Government settled the question of arrears, the three released members would be on the side of law and order.

This was open to the interpretation that Parnell had stipulated for the release as part of the treaty. Parnell, who next spoke, declared that never in speech or writing had he made the release of himself and his colleagues a condition of their action, but that the settlement of the arrears question—arrears through three bad seasons—would have a great effect on the restoration of law and order. He was not going to be fettered.

Davitt was released on the 6th May. He was met by Parnell, Dillon and O'Kelly and escorted to London. It was evident from Parnell's talk and demeanour that he meant to slow down the agitation, and was already making a beginning. He spoke of the amount of crime and outrage that had occurred during his imprisonment, and of the amount of money expended by the Ladies' Land League; Davitt drew his attention to the fact that the Ladies had broken Forster, killed coercion and released Parnell and his colleagues. However, expectations and discussions of policy faded into the background when the news came that night from Dublin that Lord Cavendish, who had only arrived that day, had been slain that evening in the Phoenix Park by members of a secret society called the "Invincibles." Parnell, ever so helpful in a crisis, collapsed. He wished to resign at once. He told his friends of his resolve to retire from public life for ever, and wrote to Gladstone and asking his opinion in relation to his leadership. All of them advised him to stay on. The *Arrears Act* was passed and Parnell was bent more than ever on slowing down the agitation. It transpired from O'Shea's evidence at the *Times* Commission that he was thinking of this as early as June 1881. The Ladies' Land League languished for lack of funds which Parnell refused to supply. On the other hand the landlords were as greedy for their pound of flesh as ever. Mr. George Trevelyan, the new Chief Secretary, admitted in Parliament that in three days one hundred and fifty families, numbering seven hundred and fifty persons, were evicted in one district alone, for arrears of the bad years—which they were no more able to pay than they were to pay the National Debt.

There was now no National Organisation, and so the "National League" was founded, with Home Rule, land reform, local self-government, parliamentary and municipal reform as the planks in its platform. As the new League was to pursue a parliamentary policy it followed that it would be under Parnell's control. The party could not quarrel with its leader in face of the enemy, and there was no question of any other leader. His dictatorship, about which so much ink has been spilled, was forced on him by his personality, by the admiration of his followers, and the circumstances of the fight. And until 1881, at least, he acted in consultation with his colleagues on matters of importance, and of his own initiative in matters of emergency, when none other could so thoroughly grasp the facts of a situation and act so promptly and effectively as himself.

The Phoenix Park tragedy led to further coercion. A Crimes Bill was introduced. Trial by Jury in certain specified cases was abolished. In proclaimed districts any dwelling might be entered and searched at any hour of day or night. Secret courts of enquiry were instituted, newspapers might be suppressed, meetings banned and dispersed by force.

There were many murders and other outrages in 1882, an exceptionally bad one at Maamtrasna on the borders of Mayo and Galway where a whole family, with the exception of one son, was destroyed. One of those accused of complicity in this crime, Myles Joyce, died protesting his innocence, and later the informer who swore his life away admitted to Doctor MacEvilly, Archbishop of Tuam, that Joyce was innocent. The Government, however, was deaf to all requests to grant an enquiry to clear the memory of an innocent man.

The arrest and trial, in the beginning of 1883, of persons supposed to have been implicated in the Phoenix Park murders gave Forster what he considered a fine opportunity of turning the tables on Parnell. They were arrested in January and the enquiry began in February. One of them, James Carey, was wiled by detective Mallon into turning Queen's evidence. He was given to think that others had given information. His wife helped to entrap him by some facts she communicated to Mallon in order to secure his release. Five of the conspirators were hanged and others sent into penal servitude. Carey was sent abroad, was identified on the high seas by a fellow-passenger, Patrick O'Donnell of Donegal, and shot dead. O'Donnell was taken to England and hanged.

Various details of the evidence gave hope that a case might be made convicting Parnell of complicity in the crime. Carey was a Home Ruler. An official of the National League of England, was implicated. The knives with which the deed was done had been secreted in the London office of the National League and brought to Dublin by this man's wife. These "revelations," exploited in the London press, gave Forster his chance which he was not slow to take.

In February, '83, there was a debate on Irish policy. Mr. Forster made an able speech showing that crime had followed the footsteps of the Land League and holding Parnell responsible for them, not for having personally planned or perpetrated outrage or murder but for having connived at them or at least for not having used his influence to stop them.

The House was agog with excitement to hear Parnell's reply to this terrible indictment. There was no reply. Parnell held his seat as if nothing had happened; he was the one unexcited man in the Assembly. He was called on loudly from all parts of the House; his own colleagues were amazed; and begged him to reply. Parnell refused. The debate was kept going by an English member's intervention. Grudgingly Parnell yielded at length to the entreaties of his followers and moved the adjournment.

The following day he replied to Forster in a memorable speech in which he scorned to defend himself to England and an English Parliament. In the course of it he said: "I have been accustomed during my political life to rely upon the public opinion of those whom I have desired to help, and with whose aid I have worked for the cause of prosperity and freedom in Ireland, and the utmost I desire to do in the very few words I shall address to the House is to make my position clear to the Irish people at home and abroad."

There spoke the real Parnell. He scorned to defend himself before an English tribunal. The Irish people and they alone should be the judges of his policy and of his actions. His sole power as leader was based on the driving force of organised Irish opinion. With that behind him he could deal independently with either Liberals or Tories.

From 1882 Parnell was frequently absent for long periods from the House of Commons, so much so as to mystify his followers who at times of great stress did not know where to find him. There were many reasons for this. One—the least powerful, perhaps—was failing health. Another was that events in Ireland and the increase in the number of outrages and the growth of secret societies made him feel that it was necessary that Ireland after her fierce struggle should be allowed to settle down. He was true to his plighted word given in the Kilmainham Treaty that he would help to "slow down" the agitation. But there was a third and incomparably more potent cause than either of these; the unhappy love entanglement which was to work the ruin of his career when he had attained the zenith of his power and triumphed over enemies who had used every endeavour open and occult to undermine his influence.

It is not necessary to go into the details of this intrigue except in so far as is necessary to illuminate some otherwise dark corners in Parnell's public life. Captain O'Shea, elected for Clare in 1880, had in that same year been introduced to Parnell. Soon after, Parnell met Mrs. O'Shea under circumstances about which accounts differ. A love affair soon developed between them which was sensed by O'Shea in '81. A challenge came from O'Shea and was accepted by Parnell, but Mrs. O'Shea intervened, and persuaded her husband that all was right, and the incident was apparently amicably settled.

In the beginning of '83 it became known that Parnell's property was heavily mortgaged. A subscription list was opened, and a grateful country subscribed generously. Once again English intrigue became busy at Rome. A letter was issued forbidding ecclesiastics to promote the Parnell Testimonial Fund. The testimonial, however, was a great success and reached a total of close on forty thousand pounds.

A Bill amending the Land Act of 1881 was introduced by Parnell soon after his duel with Forster, but was rejected by two hundred and fifty Liberal and Tory votes to sixty-three.

Invited to attend a convention in Philadelphia to establish the National League in America, he replied that his presence in the House of Commons was necessary just then, and respectfully asked that the platform of the American League should be so formed that help might be received from America without giving the English Government a pretext to suppress the League in Ireland.

The contest in Monaghan at which Gladstone had hoped a blow would be struck at Parnell's prestige took place in the summer of '83. Parnell put T. M. Healy forward for the seat. Mr. Healy won. It was not a tame election. The Orangemen arose in their might, there was much marching and drumming and the Orange leaders advised their followers to drive the rebel conspirators across the Boyne. "We are not an aggressive party," said Mr. Murray Ker, D.L. "Let there be no revolver practice. My advice to you about revolvers is, *never use a revolver except you are firing at someone.*"

At this time Parnell was much annoyed by the policy proclaimed in Patrick Ford's *Irish World* advocating the use of dynamite. Several public buildings, bridges, and railway stations were attacked. The Government and the English people were seriously alarmed. A less courageous leader, would, to save his reputation with the English, have dissociated himself from a policy he detested. He did nothing of the kind. He cared nothing about English opinion. Said Lord Randolph Churchill to him on one occasion, "I suppose you would object to having a bomb thrown into the House of Commons; you would not like to be blown up even by an Irishman." "I am not so sure of that," replied Parnell, "*if there were a call of the House.*"

In 1884 Parnell began to show occasional signs of his former activity and influence. After the Monaghan election he was in practical retirement until in April 1884 he attended a meeting at Drogheda where, without the slightest discourtesy to Davitt, he denounced his policy of Land Nationalisation, and disposed of any chance it might have of gaining a following.

In 1885 the General Election was imminent. Parnell became mildly active. At Cork in January he made the famous declaration which is inseparably connected with his name, and in part inscribed on his monument in O'Connell Street, Dublin:

"We cannot ask for less than the restitution of Grattan's Parliament, with its important privileges and wide, far-reaching constitution. We cannot, under the British constitution, ask for more than the restitution of Grattan's Parliament. But no man has a right to fix a boundary to the march of a nation. No man has a right to say, 'Thus far shalt thou go, and no further.' We have never attempted to fix the *ne plus ultra* to the progress of Ireland's nationhood, and we never shall."

He visited Cork, Ennis and a few other places in Ireland. In April the Prince and Princess of Wales were to visit Ireland. Parnell defined in *United Ireland* the duty of Nationalists with regard to the reception they should receive. It was to let them come and go without allowing the hospitable nature and cordial disposition of the Irish people to carry them into any attitude which might be taken as one of condonation for the past, or satisfaction for the present state, of Irish affairs. Nor did he fail to point out the indecency of using royalty as an electioneering dodge, not against a party but against the Irish nation. By sending over Wales it was sought to free whichever English party was returned to power from their obligations to Ireland. If Wales got an enthusiastic reception, then Ireland, apart from a few anarchists here and there, was contented; if a hostile, then the Irish were a people whom no measure would content; who after the settlement of the land question would dare to insult the future king, who, of course, is above politics. And so forth.

Parnell in 1885 had his powers as a politician taxed to the utmost. He decided to play three men against one another—Gladstone, Lord Randolph Churchill—a free-lance Tory—and Chamberlain—a free-lance Liberal. He hoped nothing from any English party or politician, except in so far as there was an axe to grind which could be ground only on the Irish question. He decided to beat the Liberals with the Irish vote and succeeded on a taxation question. Gladstone resigned. Without a dissolution of Parliament the Tories came into power, Lord Salisbury as Prime Minister.

The Tories, in their ticklish position, were like cooing doves toward the Irish question. The Crimes Act which was due for renewal, and which Gladstone had intended to renew, was dropped. A new Land Act was introduced by Lord Ashbourne in the House of Lords. It was a fairly good Act, providing £5,000,000 for advances to tenants to buy their holdings, principal and interest at 4% to be paid in forty-nine years. Lord Carnarvon, the newly appointed Lord Lieutenant, had private interviews with Parnell and Sir Charles Gavan Duffy in which he declared himself personally in favour of Irish self-government. Parnell assumed that this was the feeling, also, of the Tory Cabinet. In that, it transpired later, he was mistaken. While Carnarvon, personally, may have been sincere, he was the envoy of an English party with an election pending. The dissolution was fixed for November 1885.

On July 29th Lord Salisbury made overtures for the Irish vote. There was no further reason for coercion in Ireland. The voice of the people should be heard.

A week later Parnell opened his campaign in statesmanlike fashion, declaring for Home Rule and it alone. On August 24th at Dublin he said:

"I say that each and all of us have only looked upon the Acts we have been able to wring from an unwilling Parliament as a means to an end . . . I hope that it may not be necessary for us in the new Parliament to devote our attention to subsidiary measures, and that it may be possible for us to have a programme and a platform with only one plank, and that one plank National Independence."

It was a clever stroke. Now the rival statesmen must declare their colours. The first to do so was Lord Hartington, the Liberal. He declared that all England would unite to resist "so fatal and mischievous a proposal." Parnell replied that many similar mischievous proposals had become law, and that Ireland would have self-government or England would have to govern her as a Crown Colony. Lord Randolph Churchill spoke soon after. He was mute regarding Parnell's ultimatum. Next came Chamberlain, "Speaking for myself," he said, "if these and these alone are the terms on which Mr. Parnell's support is to be obtained, I will not enter into competition for it." John Morley followed with a suggestion of Home Rule on the Canadian system. Gladstone then came along with the Hawarden manifesto:

"In my opinion, not now for the first time delivered, the limit is clear within which the desires of Ireland, constitutionally ascertained, may, and beyond which they cannot, receive the assent of Parliament. To maintain the supremacy of the Crown, the unity of the Empire, and all the authority of Parliament necessary for the conservation of that unity, is the first duty of every representative of the people. Subject to this governing principle, every grant to portions of the country of enlarged powers for the management of their own affairs is, in my view, not a source of danger, but a means of averting it, and is in the nature of a new guarantee for increased cohesion, happiness and strength. I believe history and posterity will consign to disgrace the memory of every man, be he who he may, on whichever side of the channel he may dwell, that, having the power to aid in an equitable arrangement between Ireland and Great Britain, shall use the power, not to aid, but to prevent or retard it."

Lord Salisbury was next with an ambiguous statement which left one wondering what his attitude was. Then Mr. Childers, Gladstone's friend, gave his views:

"He was ready, he said, to give Ireland a large measure of local self-government. He would have her to legislate for herself, reserving Imperial rights over foreign policy, military organisation, external trade (including customs duties), the post office, the currency, the national debt, and the court of ultimate appeal."

Parnell felt that this last statement represented Gladstone's views. He resolved to make sure. But Gladstone refused to be drawn. So Parnell, having listened long enough to the bidding, brought down the hammer in favour of the Tories.

The result of the election was:

Liberals	335
Tories	249
Liberal Majority	86

Parnell had a following of 86. He could give the Liberals a majority of 172 if they did his bidding. If not they went out of power. He had won.

The Parliament of 1886 opened with the Tories still in power. The Queen's speech showed how hollow had been the Tory professions of sympathy with Ireland's aspirations. There was not a word in the speech about Home Rule, but there was a promise of further coercion. Lord Salisbury in 1885 sang a hymn of peace; now, having gained Parnell's support at the recent elections he intoned a note of menace. This was a shortsighted policy. That very night Parnell drove him from office.

Mr. Gladstone assumed power once more. Allied with the Irish party he would have a possible one hundred and seventy-two majority. But it was evident also that there would be dissension in his own ranks on the Home Rule question. Hope was mingled with doubt.

John Morley became Chief Secretary for Ireland. A consistent opponent of coercion, his appointment was welcome, and he was a Home Ruler in conviction, the Irish demand having been made overwhelmingly clear.

Gladstone lost no time in framing his Home Rule Bill. It was anything but a satisfactory solution of the Irish question. The financial clauses in particular were unjust to Ireland. There were frequent negotiations between Parnell and Gladstone on this point, but Gladstone held his ground. Chamberlain was a possible danger. Gladstone had frequent discussions with him but neither could Chamberlain convert Gladstone to his scheme of local councils nor could Gladstone be persuaded to depart from the principle of an Irish Government. Parnell was not enthusiastic about the measure, but finally the Irish party decided to support it.

While the negotiations were in progress an event occurred which shows us the might of Parnell's personality and the mean subterfuge to which a guilty secret may reduce a proud and haughty character.

At the election of 1885 Parnell had taken the extraordinary step of running candidates for three seats in Liverpool. Only in one could he hope to win, in the Scotland division which was T. P. O'Connor's preserve. He nominated John Redmond for a second division, and he, himself, offered to contest a third. At the last moment Parnell retired, and so, for reasons unexplained, did the Liberal candidate. Captain O'Shea was nominated for the seat, and lost by a few votes. Parnell who had just denounced the Liberals in vitriolic terms, had worked might and main for this particular Liberal. But stranger things were to follow. T. P. O'Connor had been elected for Galway, as well as for the Liverpool seat, and had resigned his seat in Galway. Parnell's nominee was Captain O'Shea!

A Whig for an Irish constituency! O'Connor, whom Parnell had interviewed, and who knew of his intentions, rushed across to Ireland hoping to have a local candidate nominated before Parnell had taken action. On reaching Dublin he found to his consternation that Parnell had forestalled him. What was he to do? He consulted the other members then in Dublin, and all agreed with him that it would be treachery to Ireland, at that moment of crisis, to oppose Parnell. Healy and Biggar, however, believed in straight dealing, and had taken the first train to Galway. A local candidate was put up—a Mr. Lynch—and during the following week the two members lashed the temper of Galway into fury. With Northern directness, and in the plainest of language, Biggar laid bare the sordid secret supposed to underlie Parnell's action. Parnell all this time made no move. Wires to his parliamentary rooms remained unanswered. Nobody knew his private address. When it pleased him he came over.

Accompanied by O'Connor, O'Kelly and Sexton he set out for Galway. All except himself were in a fever of apprehension. He showed no feeling. Galway elections have always been pretty hot affairs, and this occasion was exceptional. The scene at the Galway station exceeded the worst anticipations. A howling, groaning populace crowded all the approaches to the

Station. Mr. Lynch was delivering an impassioned address from the steps of the Railway Hotel. Parnell coolly went to his room, washed and dressed. Then he met Healy, Biggar and the others. Healy, not without passion, explained his position. Parnell listened quietly. Some reference to Parnell's leadership had been raised. "I have no intention of resigning my position," he said. "I would not resign it if the people of Galway were to kick me through the streets today." Healy capitulated. Biggar then felt he had been badly let down. Healy had deserted him. The local candidate was called in, and told what had happened. A public meeting was held. Parnell faced an audience whose hostility was unmistakable. In the course of a powerful speech he said: "I have a parliament for College Green within the hollow of my hand." He referred to the possible rejection of O'Shea: "There will rise a shout," he said, "from all the enemies of Ireland: 'Parnell is beaten, Ireland has no longer a leader.'" The day was won; O'Shea was elected.

Parnell, however, was mistaken. Gladstone's Home Rule Bill was defeated by three hundred and forty-three to three hundred and thirteen votes, and once more a general election followed. Parnell and the Liberals, who were at daggers drawn in December, 1885, were now going forward hand in hand. The election was soon over giving the Tories a majority over Irish and Liberals of one hundred and eighteen.

Lord Salisbury was again in power and would like to score over the Liberals by showing that where Gladstone had failed he could rule Ireland without coercion.

In the end of 1886 the Plan of Campaign was launched by William O'Brien and John Dillon. Parnell was ill, and was not consulted about it; when it was expounded to him he did not like it. The basis of the plan was as follows: A Managing Committee was to be elected for each district. The tenants should offer the landlord a fair rent: if this was refused the total fair rents should be banked with the Committee, and the Committee should deal with the landlords. If the landlords refused to come to terms the money should be used to support evicted tenants, and for general purposes of the agitation.

All the turmoil of the early 'eighties was renewed and continued during 1887, 1888, 1889. Lord Salisbury was convinced in 1886 that revision of judicial rents fixed under the Act of 1881 would be "neither honest nor expedient." In 1887 he passed a Land Act allowing the revision of these judicial rents. Parnell was present and enjoyed this somersault of the Tory party. His own Bill on similar lines had been contemptuously rejected the previous year. His sensible and moderate measure had been rejected; then came the Plan of Campaign; and then the Tories began to take notice.

Herein we have an epitome of the history of all ameliorative legislation by England for Ireland.

But, of course, the Land Bill only came after a stringent Coercion Bill. This gave Gladstone and the Liberals a fine opportunity of poking fun at Salisbury, the pacifist of 1885. Mr. Arthur Balfour, nephew of the Prime Minister, had by this time become Chief Secretary. He ably supported the Bill which became law, and made himself responsible for carrying it out, and right loyally did he execute his task. He proclaimed the National League a month after the Act was passed. League rooms were entered, literature and accounts carried away, meetings and newspapers suppressed. Resident Magistrates alone sat on the bench, political prisoners were treated as ordinary criminals, police and military in enormous numbers were disposed through the country, with orders "not to hesitate to shoot." Priests identified with the movement could not go on a sick call without being tracked by police spies. Collisions occurred in all parts of the country, with casualties on both sides, but naturally the unarmed people were at a disadvantage, and there were several civilian deaths from stabbing and gunshot. A boy was sent to prison for grinning at a policeman; a girl of twelve for conspiracy to obstruct the sheriff's officers; a man for winking in the market place, at the pig of a boycotted one. The worst case was that of Mitchelstown in September, 1887. A public meeting was held. English as well as Irish speakers, including Mr. Dillon, were present. A Government reporter arriving late, with a police escort, tried to force his way through the crowd. The peaceful people were jostled about, and exasperated by this attack on free speech, attacked their assailants with sticks. The latter retired to barracks and from this vantage ground deliberately fired on the multitude. Three men were killed and a verdict of wilful murder was returned against the police at the coroner's inquest, but no action was taken. John Mandeville of Mitchelstown died as a result of brutal treatment in prison. Thus, in Ireland, was celebrated the Jubilee Year of the Queen of England's reign.

United Ireland in those days was spicy reading. Those of us who were children at the time enjoyed weekly the cartoons of Balfour, who was presented to us spider-legged, malevolent, and waspish in appearance. It came as a surprise to us in later years to learn that Balfour, brutal as he proved himself in practice, was a philosopher of parts and had written books!

Balfour, having imprisoned at least three distinguished priests—Canon Keller of Youghal, Father Matt Ryan of Tipperary, and Father McFadden of Gweedore, appealed for assistance to the Pope. Cardinal Persico was sent to Ireland. In 1888 was issued a Papal Rescript condemning the Plan of

Campaign. Cardinal Persico was, of course, blamed for this; but truth will out. The Persico letters have been since published, and it is now known that he was blameless. The Rescript was the result of English diplomacy at Rome.

But worse things were coming. A sinister plot to ruin Parnell was started in England. In the spring of 1887 a series of articles in the London Times appeared under the heading *Parnellism and Crime.* Alleged letters of Parnell were used for the purpose of connecting him with the Phoenix Park murders, and the physical force movement generally. Parnell at last demanded a select committee of the House of Commons to inquire into the matter. Instead, the Government appointed a special commission of three judges to make the enquiry. The commission was given *carte blanche* to open up the whole conduct of the agitation in Ireland. Not Parnell alone but all Ireland was in the dock.

Witnesses came in droves. Spies, policemen, officials, farmers, agents, informers—all were baited with gold into the net of the *Times.*

Time dragged wearily on until in February 1889 Richard Piggott entered the witness chair. He was well known as an impecunious journalist, always "on the make." In 1888 he applied to Forster offering to assist the Government for a trifle of £1,500 down, and then to Patrick Egan offering to assist the League on similar terms. But let his variegated career pass. He went into the witness-box, gave his evidence, and then Sir Charles Russell, Parnell's Counsel, took him in hands. Handing him pen and paper Russell put him through a spelling exercise. The last word dictated was "hesitancy." Piggott spelled it "hesitency." So was it spelled in one of the alleged *fac-simile* letters! But Russell had another rod in pickle. Four days before the letters appeared in the *Times* Piggott had written to Doctor Walsh, Archbishop of Dublin, saying that a plot was laid for Parnell, that certain incriminatory letters were to be published, and how should he warn the National leaders? Piggott fell to pieces. He contradicted himself hopelessly. Everything was clear. Copies of Archbishop Walsh's replies to him were produced in Court.

The unfortunate man cleared the country at once and was traced to Madrid. Here at his hotel a Spanish Inspector of Police called. Piggott retired to his room, took up a pistol and blew out his brains. Interest in the commission was now at an end. When it resumed its adjourned session Mr. Biggar addressed the judges. He spoke for some twenty minutes, not wishing to occupy their time as his friend, Mr. Davitt, wished to make a few observations. Mr. Davitt's remarks only occupied five days!

One interesting question remains. It is this. Who paid for Piggott's passage and expenses to Madrid?

CHAPTER LXXVI

Fall of Parnell and of Parliamentarianism

Parnell was now the man of the hour. He had triumphed over all who had crossed his path. He had broken Forster; he had humbled even Gladstone. He had beaten the most elaborate conspiracy ever launched against a politician and supported by one of the greatest newspaper syndicates in the world. Again and again he had changed the tune of the Government from "the Government will" to "the Government must." He was *fêted* and lionised; he was entertained by exclusive clubs, and was the guest of honour at such society functions as he would attend. He was presented with the freedom of the city of Edinburgh. His reception in the House of Commons was flattering in the extreme, and on one occasion when some murmurs arose from the Tory benches against the assertion of a member that the case against him was based on forgery, he rose in his place and dared any member of that body in the House to indicate by word, or nod, or gesture that he did not believe this to be the case. There was no response. He seemed absolutely master of the situation, the dictator of policy, the ruling force in the House of Commons, unquestioned chief of his own party by dint of his personality, and master of other parties by reason of his magnificent and seemingly instinctive diplomacy. And then the blow fell!

Captain O'Shea, who had given what was meant to be damaging proof against him at the *Times* Commission, filed a petition for divorce against his wife, naming Parnell as co-respondent. There was no defence, and no appearance for the defence. Parnell ignored the whole business as if it were of no importance, whatever. When the decree was made absolute he promptly married Mrs. O'Shea.

If others had taken matters as coolly as Parnell, it might have been better. But a meeting of the party was called at the Leinster Hall, Dublin, and a resolution of confidence in Parnell's leadership was passed. The delegates at the time in America—O'Connor, O'Kelly, O'Brien, Dillon and others were asked to cable a resolution of confidence in Parnell, and this was in due course done. Mr. T. D. Sullivan alone, of those in contact with each other, reserved judgment. He was sharply criticised for his reticence, but he had this consolation: that while the others went back on their words later, he had nothing to retract.

A meeting of the Irish Party was held, and Parnell was re-elected sessional chairman without a dissentient voice. It was known to Justin McCarthy, and must also have been known to Parnell, that Gladstone had prepared a letter in which he stated that Parnell's continuance in the leadership of the Irish Party would be productive of consequences disastrous in the highest degree to the cause of Ireland and would render his retention of the leadership of the Liberal party almost a nullity.

This was the letter of a political strategist. Gladstone did not say that he would resign his leadership. He did not say that he would wash his hands of legislation for Ireland. In plain fact he said nothing tangible at all, except that Parnell's leadership pleased him no longer.

Parnell replied in a long manifesto which he submitted to a number of members of his party—the Redmonds, O'Kelly, Leamy, Col. Nalan, Justin McCarthy. He asked not to be thrown to the "English wolves," now howling for his destruction. He disclosed all his negotiations with the Liberals, and showed that his chairmanship from the Liberal point of view did not matter in the least; that Liberals would proceed on their pre-arranged plans whether he was leader or not, but that as leader he might be able to counter them. Bribes offered him by the Liberals he disclosed: the Chief Secretaryship for himself; one of the law-officerships of the Crown for a colleague, and so forth. He had rejected all these offers valuing the independence of his party more than anything else. He lifted a corner of the veil which had screened his negotiations with the Liberals, and pointed out that his leadership had nothing to do with Liberal policy which was settled and in gear, though possibly it might interfere with its smooth working if he was continued in power.

There was a moment of tension. Then Justin McCarthy spoke. He disapproved of the manifesto from beginning to end. Parnell urged him for particulars. He objected to it all especially the words "English wolves." "I will not change them," Parnell said, *"whatever goes out, these words shall not go out."* The "split" was thenceforward in being.

In the heart of the controversy which followed the truth was submerged under *ex-parte* pleadings on either side. Gladstone was accused of sacrificing Parnell, though for years he had been well aware of the relations between Parnell and Mrs. O'Shea. Mrs. O'Shea had in fact acted as envoy to him, again and again, from Parnell. But in fair play it must be said that whatever Gladstone suspected he had no proof. When the matter became public he had to consider the attitude of his party and electorate and was not really one of the "English wolves," though for aught we know he may have been glad of Parnell's downfall. Morley was asked if Parnell would retire if found guilty. "He will not," said Morley, "he will remain where he is, and he is quite right."

The Irish Party met. Parnell simply asked them not to sell him without getting his value. "Gentlemen," said Parnell, "it is not for you to act in this matter. You are dealing with a man who is an unrivalled sophist. You are dealing with a man to whom it is as impossible to give a direct answer to a plain and simple question, as it is for me impossible to give an indirect answer to a plain and simple question. You are dealing with a man who is capable of appealing to the constituencies for a majority which would make him independent of the Irish Party. And if I surrender to him, if I give up my position to him—if you throw me to him, I say, gentlemen, that it is your bounden duty to see that you secure value for the sacrifice. How can you secure this value? You can secure this value by making up your minds as to what these provisions in the next Home Rule Bill should be."

Envoys of the party called on Mr. Gladstone and they learned the nothing which deputations learn of Cabinet Ministers. It was a duel between Parnell and Gladstone. The latter won. On December 6th, 1890, Mr. Justin McCarthy withdrew with forty-four followers; Parnell was left with twenty-six.

Then came the Kilkenny election and Parnell crossed over to Ireland. But before going to Kilkenny there was work to be done in Dublin. *United Ireland* bought by Parnell, and for long brilliantly edited by William O'Brien, had, under the direction of Mathias McD. Bodkin, gone over to the enemy! On the morning of December 18th, 1890, a call was made at the office. A Fenian, a follower of Parnell, approached the acting editor and said: "Matty, will you walk out, or would you like to be thrown out?" Matty decided for the less exciting manner of exit.

That night, at a wonderful meeting in the Rotunda, Parnell spoke a sentence that lived for ever in the hearts of those who heard it, and ought to live in the hearts of their descendants. He said:

"I don't pretend that I had not moments of trial and of temptation, but I do claim that never in thought, word, or deed, have I been false to the trust which Irishmen have confided in me."

Next morning before setting out for Cork he had to re-conquer *United Ireland* which had been re-captured by the enemy. With the assistance of a vast crowd he did so, and then drove to Kingsbridge and took his train for Cork. An immense crowd followed him to the terminus at Kingsbridge and Parnell made a royal departure declaring that what Dublin said today all Ireland would say tomorrow.

There were disappointments ahead, however. His candidate for a by-election in Kilkenny was beaten by two to one, and a little later in North Sligo the Parnellite candidate met with a similar fate. Later his candidate was defeated in Carlow. It was obvious that Parnell either miscalculated the forces against him, or was determined to fight to the last even if he fought alone.

By the end of the year Mr. William O'Brien had returned from America to France. There was a whitewashed cell awaiting him in Ireland, and he decided to remain, for the time being, in Boulogne. Here Parnell, in the interests of peace, agreed to meet him. O'Brien, however, found Parnell unyielding. This is not surprising, inasmuch as the terms of peace suggested by Mr. O'Brien were such, and involved so many people—the Bishops, Gladstone, and both sections of the divided Irish Party—that Parnell saw at once that a peace by negotiation was impossible and thenceforward devoted his great gifts of strategy to sowing the seeds of dissension among his opponents. Ostensibly he was trying to get his opponents and the peacemakers to extract promises from Gladstone and the Liberals regarding details relating to land and the police in any forthcoming Home Rule Bill—a re-assertion of his attitude that he should not be sold for less than his price. He and William O'Brien were to be the judges of the value of the promises made by the Liberals. As was to be expected, they disagreed. Mr. O'Brien seemed to be satisfied with a memorandum containing the points of a letter which Gladstone was prepared to publish. Parnell was not. It is not now, and it was not then, an easy matter to decide whether Parnell in the course of these negotiations was really striving for peace, or waging diplomatic war. In either case he was forcing O'Brien and the others to exact conditions from the Liberals. In the midst of much mischief he was to this extent doing good, although it has to be admitted that he openly mocked at the chance of one of his former colleagues getting any reliable guarantee from Gladstone, the unrivalled sophist. Still he said: "Some good may come of these negotiations. We may pin the Liberals to something definite yet."

O'Brien and Dillon came across to England and were promptly dispatched to Galway jail. On their release, some months later they both declared against Parnell. On this account they came in for a good deal of criticism, mostly undeserved. Parnell's jibe at them summarised and concentrated it. "Some of the seceders," he said, "the majority of them—have changed only twice. Mr. Dillon and Mr. O'Brien have changed four times." It was not fair; men who are working for peace may be forced by circumstances to make many changes, and Parnell himself had not been as consistent as he pretended. In fact it was only after "the split" that he discovered the cloven hoof of the Liberal party; up to the date of his "manifesto" he had been exploiting Gladstone and the alliance with the Liberals. It is true that his strictures on Gladstone's propositions had reference to the end of the year 1889. But it is fairly evident that if Gladstone's letter to Morley had not been published, if dissension had not been fomented in the Irish party, there would have been no question of Gladstone's sincerity.

Parnell worked very hard during these few years of strife. He was far from well; his medical advisers counselled rest and quiet; but Parnell was ubiquitous. He put into this personal conflict more energy in one year than he had expended in the House of Commons in the preceding eight. His friends told him that he was killing himself—but in vain.

In the meantime, the Tory Government was giving, along with plenty of coercion, some "ameliorative" legislation. Measures were adopted to cope with the failure of the potato crop. Irish railway development was taken in hand; a Bill for Land Purchase was introduced, and the *Congested Districts* Act was an enactment that contained a good deal of promise which has been realised only in part. A new Board was constituted, but its powers of transfer of tenants from congested areas were so limited that even today we have families living in absolute poverty in parts of Ireland while over the rich plains of the midlands the low of the bullock has replaced the merry prattle of children, the whistle of the ploughman behind his team, the swish of the caman on the hurling field and the song of the girls scutching flax or feeding the quaint and beautiful little *tuirne.*[1] Landlordism had claimed the land. The law allowed it and the courts awarded it. The people had to go, and the palatial bawn represents scores of vanished homesteads. On the outskirts of huge, unpeopled ranches we still find a hardy and industrious race cultivating marsh and moor, hoping, often in vain, to take out a crop before the substance of the soil is again claimed for the support of the rush and of the heather.

Irishmen are kind to the memory of Parnell. He sinned, and he was punished. No other man—not even O'Connell—always excepting men

---

[1] Spinning wheel.

who had sealed their allegiance to Dark Rosaleen with their blood—was more dearly beloved by the Irish Catholic people than this Protestant. The people of Ireland were all Parnellite at heart. They did not wish to oppose him. If he had only bowed for a time before the storm he would have come back in triumph. But Parnell was too proud for compromise. He would lead or break the Irish Party. He tried diplomacy. But, in Ireland, at least, there is a greater force, which sometimes becomes powerful. It is truth.[2]

Parnell's last meeting was at Creggs, County Galway. He was warned by his medical advisers not to go. He had promised to go, and he went. This was on September 27th, 1891. There was death in his face, as he delivered his speech. On October 6th, he died at Brighton. He was buried in Glasnevin Cemetery, Dublin, close beside O'Connell. His funeral cortège was magnificent, and on the Sunday nearest his anniversary, a pilgrimage is made annually to his grave, which is always adorned by flowers, the gift of many nameless friends.

Parnell was adored by the Irish and feared by the English. Nobody, even among his followers, could foretell his attitude towards a measure in Parliament. He often seemed to make up his mind in a moment. He seemed to have what we may call political instinct, an instinct dangerous to the stability of Governments. Gladstone, the one statesman who could be compared with him, regarded him as an "intellectual phenomenon."

And now Parnell passes from the scene for ever, and there is a vacancy that no member of his followers is able or willing to fill. Sexton was out of the ordinary in many ways; but he had practically retired. Healy was brilliant, "the one political brain amongst them," said Parnell, but he had not the gifts requisite in a leader. Parnell professed to be willing to hand over his leadership to Healy, but the sincerity of the proposal is open to doubt. The rents and rifts in the party made it impossible to select a leader of the whole.

Shortly after Parnell's death there was a General Election. Gladstone had a working majority of about forty-two. The Home Rule Bill of 1893 was passed in the House of Commons by a majority of forty-three. It was rejected by the House of Lords. Next year the "Grand Old Man" resigned and was succeeded by Lord Rosebery.

John Redmond's party (the Parnellites), Dillon's party, O'Brien's party and Healy's party, floundered rather hopelessly for years, disputing plenty, achieving little.

---

[2] It is hardly necessary to say that sincere Irishmen still hold opposite opinions upon the right or wrong of Parnell's stand.

In 1897 the Report of a Commission temporarily re-united the various shades of Irish opinion. The Royal Commission on taxation discovered, among other things, that Ireland was being taxed at over £3,000,000 a year beyond her obligations under the enforced Act of Union. The report of the Commission was put on the shelf along with many other reports, and in the face of it, Mr. Balfour announced in the House of Commons that Ireland was really a financial loss to the Empire! Restitution to Ireland of the vast sum of which she had been robbed (in 50 years £150 million) was, of course, point blank refused.

A Land Act had been introduced in 1896. It gave a good bribe to the landlords and substantial relief to the tenants. The Local Government Act of 1898 displaced the Grand Juries and transferred control of local affairs to popularly elected bodies. In 1899 the Department of Agriculture and Technical Instruction was instituted owing chiefly to the work and influence of Mr. Horace Plunket.

Meanwhile, the Parnellites, led by Mr. John Redmond, though a poor minority, held their ground, and resisted all attempts at compromise. In 1898 Mr. Dillon effected a compromise and agreed to resign in behalf of a Parnellite leader. John Redmond, supported by a handful of followers, accepted the office and became leader of the united party in 1900. The United Irish League formed by Mr. William O'Brien in 1898 gave the united party an organisation at their back. The League was a good effort to get the seat of agitation transferred from Westminster to Ireland. But its new heads, hypnotised by Westminster, did not develop it in its natural way. And it never became a great force.

During the Boer war which broke out in 1899 the sympathies of the Irish people were, of course, on the side of the Boers, and no attempt was made to dissemble the delight in Ireland when the Boers scored a victory over the English. Major John MacBride held command of an Irish Brigade fighting with the Boer forces.

In 1902 on the initiative of Captain Shawe-Taylor, a Galway landlord, representatives of landlords and tenants met in conference to investigate the possibility of an agreed solution of the Land Question. An agreement was reached on the basis of long term purchase which would secure the landlords against loss, and while making the purchase money of their farms higher to the tenants would enable them to secure money at a low rate of interest, and secure them their land at a fixed annuity which would be lower than the actual rent.

Mr. George Wyndham, Chief Secretary, proceeded to give effect to these recommendations and the result was the Land Act of 1903. It was a measure welcomed by the tenants who wished to be rid of the landlords at all costs, and by the landlords who got a very good bargain by the sale of their estates *for cash* that in many instances was very urgently needed.

A move by Lord Dunraven and others to bring about by conference a solution of the question of self-government for Ireland by means of an enlargement of local government was not so successful. The Orange element was alarmed. They pointed out that a Tory government had placed a papist—Sir Anthony (now Lord) McDonnell, Under Secretary, in virtual control of Ireland.

In 1906 Mr. Davitt passed away. He lies in his native Straide close to the home from which, as a child, English aggression drove him in support of the landlordism whose power it was his manhood's task to break. He succeeded; and dear to Irish hearts is that grave in Mayo which encloses the mortal remains of a man whose spirit could not be broken.

In 1906, also, the Liberals returned to power. Mr. Birrell was appointed Chief Secretary for Ireland. His first legislative effort was an Irish Councils Bill, a sort of enlargement of the Local Government Act. Mr. Redmond favoured the measure; but having learned the temper of Ireland, he had to reject it.

In 1914 a so-called "Home Rule" Act was passed—empowering the Irish people to play at a "Parliament" in Dublin, whose enactments could be vetoed by either the British Lord Lieutenant or the British Parliament—or ruled illegal by the High Court of Justice! Also it provided that Ireland's finances should chiefly remain in England's hands! The Irish Parliamentary Party, grasping at any straw that might save it from being finally engulfed, begged Ireland to believe that this was the nation's "great charter of liberty." (Such was the phrase actually in daily use by the Party.) And Mr. John Dillon in the House of Commons solemnly pledged, for Ireland and the Irish Parliamentary Party, that the Act would be accepted as a full and final settlement of Ireland's claims![3] When the "Home Rule" Bill became

[3] The Party had been rapidly sinking in self-respect for a quarter of a century—but in the last nine years of this time had gone down hill with accelerated velocity. It became the official "tail" of the British Liberals, and obediently wagged as the dog willed. For the older, wise, and well proved maxim, "England's difficulty is Ireland's opportunity," the Party adopted as its slogan: "Don't embarrass the Government!"—till the slogan and its users passed into a joke. In reward for the unworthy services rendered to the Liberals, the members of the Party were permitted to scramble for the crumbs that fell from their masters' table. For although they still went through the form of gravely subscribing to the pledge that Parnell had seen it necessary to prescribe—the solemn pledge that no one of them would accept, or ask, from an English Government, office or favour for himself or friends—there was furious scramble among them for the offices and favours—oftentimes ludicrously petty ones—that Dublin Castle had in its gift.

law, it was postponed on the plea that the war was on—in reality because Sir Edward Carson forbade its application. The British Government kept postponing it period after period, till eventually it never went into force. The Irish people, most of whom had at first been deceived into regarding it as a desirable step toward larger liberty, eventually disillusioned, would not in the end accept it.

The dreary years from 1892 onwards, characterised by strife and bitterness and the growth of dictatorial management of Irish affairs by the Parliamentarians, were not without some good results. Honest and patriotic men and women in Ireland grew tired of the squabbles of rival politicians, of the manipulation of parliamentary and local elections, of the general corruption of public life, and, falling back on first principles, endeavoured to plan a future for Ireland far different from that in the dreams of the provincialist politicians. National consciousness was awakening, and the intellect of Ireland found expression, first in the *Sean Bhean Bhocht* of Belfast edited by Ethna Carbery and Alice Milligan, and afterwards in the *United Irishman* of Dublin edited by Arthur Griffith and contributed to by William Rooney. The Gaelic League had been established, and by slow degrees the Irish people were taught to rely on themselves, to rebuild their ancient, though shattered civilisation, to rediscover their soul as a people, and confront the world as an ancient, cultured and dignified race, and no longer an obscure beggar seeking for English doles. And worthily did the best of the Irish race respond to this appeal. No greater sacrifice of personal interests can be recorded in the world than the work expended in Ireland during the past three decades. Father O'Growney gave his life for the language; William Rooney for the national cause generally; Pearse, McDonagh and their comrades have faced the firing squad; and among the host of those who have given up their lives for the preservation of an Irish Ireland are numbers of unnamed and forgotten men and women who were prepared to work in obscurity and neglect, that Ireland might live.

This remarkable resurgence of national self-respect was looked on askance by the political leaders whose vision was limited to action in the English House of Commons. The intellectual phase of the Irish movement they heartily disliked. Criticism of "the Party" was speedily suppressed. The Party controlled nearly all the newspapers of Ireland and woe betide the journalist who took any liberties in criticism of the Kings. They would not trust the intellect of Young Ireland. And thus for thirty years and more the Party sat on a mine which was certain to explode someday. They, themselves, provided the fuse. In the English House of Commons John Redmond, in 1914, unreservedly offered the services of the manhood of Ireland in one of England's wars. Earl Grey was happy to announce that Ireland was "the one bright spot" on the horizon. Then, Mr. Redmond, having gone so far was forced to go further; and when at Woodenbridge, County Wicklow, he advised the Irish Volunteers to go to war for England, he, fortunately, sounded the final knell of the "Party."

The Parliamentary leaders, Redmond, Dillon, Davitt, Devlin, O'Connor, came out openly as England's recruiting sergeants—and their followers in the country, the scales at length fallen from their eyes, began a wholesale desertion—which in startlingly short time left the leaders looking in vain to find any followers. They were to be formally wiped out at the next general election. The Irish Parliamentary Party, having compromised Ireland's every claim to nationhood, and touched the depths of disgrace, then disappeared from history. And Ireland severed itself from the bad tradition of British Parliamentarianism.

William O'Brien's Recollections and Evening Memories.
T. P. O'Connor's Parnell Movement.
Michael Davitt's Fall of Feudalism.
Mrs. Dickenson's A Patriot's Mistake.
Barry O'Brien's Life of Parnell.

CHAPTER LXXVII

The Modern Literature of Ireland

I. *Modern Gaelic Literature*

The last writers in the ancient bardic dialect, the three O'Clerys and O'Mulconry, four friars who have been immortalised as the Four Masters, in the early 17th century collected all the old manuscripts they could find, and in Donegal Abbey wrote their mighty Annals that, though the nation, as they feared, should perish, the names of the great ones at least should be preserved. They praised and dispraised Gael and Englishman with perfect impartiality—evidence that their minds were still untuned to the new world of warring states. "They belonged to the old, individual, poetic life, and spoke a language even, in which it was all but impossible to think an abstract thought."[1]

---

[1] THE FOUR MASTERS

BY THOMAS D'ARCY MC GEE

Many altars are in Banba, many chancels hung in white,
Many schools and many abbeys, glorious in our fathers' sight;
Yet whene'er I go a pilgrim back, dear Native Isle, to thee,
May my filial footsteps bear me to that Abbey by the sea—
To that Abbey—roofless, doorless, shrineless, monkless, though it be!

. . . .

I still hear them in my musings, still see them as I gaze,—
Four meek men around the dresset, reading scrolls of other days;
Four unwearied scribes who treasure every word and every line—
Saving every ancient sentence as if writ by hands divine.

After the disastrous Elizabethan wars, Ireland was stripped of her forests. Partly this was done for plunder, but chiefly to destroy all refuges and cover. From being an island Lebanon, Ireland became the gaunt, naked, shelterless expanse that it is today. "The wandering companies that keep the wood" were gone, and the modern period set in. With the sweeping away of the proud, aristocratic order of Gaeldom, Irish literature became impoverished, and yet, by an accident, the greatest of all Irish writers, Goeffrey Keating, was the first eminent "popular" writer.

Returning from Spain a doctor of divinity, Keating won fame as a preacher in County Tipperary. On a certain occasion, he preached in the presence of a lady whose name was associated with that of Carew, the Lord President of Munster, a sermon calculated to give as much offence as John the Baptist's reproof of Herod. The anti-popery laws were put in motion

---

Not of fame, and not of fortune, do these eager penmen dream;
Darkness shrouds the hills of Banba, sorrow sits by every stream;
One by one the lights that lead her, hour by hour, are quenched in gloom;
But the patient, sad, Four Masters toil on in their lonely room—
  Duty still defying Doom.

As the breathing of the west winds over bound and bearded sheaves—
As the murmur in the bee-hives softly heard on summer eves—
So the rustle of the vellum,—so the anxious voices sound;—
While a deep expectant silence seems to listen all around.

Brightly on the Abbey gable shines the full moon thro' the night,
While afar to westward glances all the bay in waves of light:
Tufted isle and splinter'd headland smile and soften in her ray;
Yet within their dusky chamber the meek Masters toil away,
  Finding all too short the day.

Now they kneel! oh, list the accents, from the soul of mourners wrung;
Hear the soaring aspirations in the old ancestral tongue;
For the houseless sons of chieftains, for their brethren near and far,
For the mourning Mother Island these their aspirations are.

And they say before up-rising: "Father! grant one other pray'r.
Bless the Lord of Moy—O'Gara! Bless his lady and his heir!
Send the generous Chief, whose bounty cheers, sustains us, in our task,
Health, success, renown, salvation: Father! grant the prayer we ask."

Oh, that we, who now inherit the great bequest of their toil,—
Were but fit to trace their footsteps through the annals of the Isle;
Oh, that the same angel, Duty, guardian of our tasks might be;
Teach us, as she taught our Masters, faithful, grateful, just, to be:—
As she taught the old Four Masters in the Abbey by the sea!

through Carew's personal spite, and Keating had to fly. Hiding in the Glen of Aherlow, he composed his celebrated *Forus Feasa ar Eirinn,* or History of Ireland, which was and is the standard work of Irish prose. Hundreds of manuscript copies were made. Several English translations exist, one by John O'Mahony, the Fenian Head Centre in America. Keating also composed religious works, one of which, the *Three Shafts of Death,* is full of spirited moral tales told with the story-telling zest that makes the *History* so readable. Thus Keating writes of a wild and ignorant kern of Munster who went exploring and landing in England, was sumptuously entertained at the first great house he came to. When, at last, sated with good living, he and his company made to depart, the keeper of the house cried to his accountant: *Make reckoning*—English words that the kern did not understand. The accountant therewith stripped the visitors of their goods, sending them bare away: for the house was an Inn. The kern was much puzzled, for never before had he known food bought or sold. Coming home, he told his friends that England was a wonderful country for food and drink and hospitality, only when strangers were leaving their entertainer, a violent fellow called MacRaicin was called down to despoil them. Keating adds that "England is the earth; the innkeepers, the world, the flesh and the devil; the Kern, people in general, and MacRaicin—death!"

Keating attended some of the last bardic schools, but he chose to write in a style to be "understanded of the people." His poetry is in the new lyrical style then coming in, breaking away from the severe old metres that only the learned could compose—or perhaps enjoy. He was a genuine poet, too. Witness this exile-song, of the typical Gaelic "catalogue" order:

MO BHEANNACHT LEAT A SGRIBHINN

My blessing with thee, letter
To the delightful isle of Eire,
My pity that I see not her hilltops
Though oft their beacons blaze!

Farewell to her nobles and her people,
Fond, fond farewell to her clergy,
Farewell to her gentle womenkind,
Farewell to her learned in letters!

Farewell to her smooth plains,
A thousand farewells to her hills,

Hail to him who dwells there,
Farewell to her pools and lakes!

Farewell to her fruity woods,
Farewell to her fishing weirs,
Farewell to her bogs and lawns,
Farewell to her raths and moors!

Farewell from my heart to her harbours,
Farewell, too, to her heavy pastures,
Good-bye to her hillocks of fairs,
Farewell to her bowed branches!

Though battle-wrath be frequent
In the holy heaven-favoured isle,
Westward o'er the ocean's ridge,
Bear, O writing, my blessing!

The difference between the old classical metres—used in Old and Middle Irish verse—and the free metres of modern Irish may briefly be explained by an imitation of a classical verse. Here is the original:

Do chuadar as rinn mo ruisg
Do tholcha is áluinn éaguisg,
Is tuar orcra dá n-éisi
Dromla fhuar na h-aibheisi.

Dr. Hyde gives an imitation of this, as follows:

Slowly pass my aching eye
Her holy hills of beauty;
Neath me tossing to and fro
Hoarse cries the crossing billow.

Now those used to English verse can make little of this, beyond the fact that there are seven syllables in each line. Note, however, that there is an intricate system of internal assonances and alliterations (slowly and holy, tossing and crossing, etc.) while the chief peculiarity is that the rhyming and syllables are not, as in English verse, equally stressed. *Fro* is stressed, but its rhyme is unstressed—"low" in *billow*. Further than this, it must be mentioned that certain groups of letters were held to rhyme, so that "maid" rhymed with MacCabe, these groups being distinct and rigidly observed. From this it will be seen that classic Gaelic verse could not live as a popular art. Keating gave the popular forms of versification—already common in Scotland—a standing that they could not achieve while they were confined to folk-compositions, and soon after his days, the old metres disappeared.

Daithi O'Bruadair, a poet of the Williamite wars, was the last aristocratic poet, but Egan O'Rahilly, who lived in the first half of the 18th century—the century of the Penal Laws, when Catholics, i.e., the nation, were forbidden the rudiments of education, had much of the austere dignity of the past in his style. He it was who composed *"Gile na Gile,"* the most refined and melodious of all those multi-rhyming songs in which, during the 18th century, Ireland was sung of as a discrowned maiden, Cathleen-ny-Houlihan, Shiela-ny-Gara, or Moirin-ny-Chuillenain, awaiting the King's son who should free her and enthrone her once more.

> Brightness of brightness came, in loneliness, advancing
> Crystal of crystal, her clear grey eyes were glancing,
> Sweetness of sweetness, her soft words flowed entrancing,
> Redness and whiteness her cheek's fair form enhancing.

A curious story, probably untrue, but quite typical of the times, tells that poor O'Rahilly was once standing by when a planter minister ordered a certain tree to be hewed down. The workers (Catholic hewers of wood and drawers of water) refused to lay axe to the trunk on account of some historic associations. The minister's son climbed the tree and began to hew branches, but fell, and was caught in a cleft and hanged. O'Rahilly at once made a verse beginning *Is maith do thoradh a chrainn,* viz., "Good is your fruit, O tree; may it flourish on every branch. My grief that the trees of Eire are not loaded with the same fruit every day!"

Seán O'Neachtain of Meath, contemporary, composed sparkling lyrics comparable to nothing in English but Herrick, and wrote humorous tales satirising the Gaels of the day who talked broken English under the impression that they were speaking Shakespeare's tongue. Tarlach O'Carolan—best known as Carolan—lived about the same time. His meeting with Goldsmith has been written of as a meeting of the dying Gaelic and the new-born Anglo-Irish literatures, but the conceit is scarcely justified, for Carolan was more musician than poet, merely writing words for tunes. His music was such that we may believe that, had Ireland been free to cultivate national art, he would have exalted the wonderful traditional music into a lofty art, as Chopin did with the national music of Poland.

Séan Clárach MacDonnell, at whose house in Co. Cork the "bardic sessions" of the southern poets, i.e., literary evenings assisted with good fare, were held, was more exuberant, more popular, than any who had gone before him, and his passionate, joyous, rollicking songs are sung to this day. Sometimes, in serious mood, he drew terrible pictures of the plight of the Gael under the brutal foreign planters. Of one such usurper he declares that "he has tethered the famine in a cleft of the mountains to prey upon the people"—an image terrible enough for Æschylus.

Donacha Rua Macnamara is chiefly remembered for his poem, "The Fair Hills of Eire O," which is so exquisite an exile-song, that a score of translations into English have been made:

> Take my heart's blessing over to dear Eire's strand
>   And the fair hills of Eire O!
> To the Remnant that love her—our forefather's land—
>   Fair hills of Eire O!
>
> How sweet sing the birds, o'er mount there and vale
> Like soft sounding chords, that lament for the Gael—
> And I o'er the surge, far, far away must wail
>   The fair hills of Eire O!

It is particularly interesting to note, in the numerous popular poets, how the ancient heroic names occur in their songs. O'Tuama, keeper of a tavern, laments the passing of the Gaelic aristocracy, comparing them to "Warlike MacMorna, tremendous in the chase; gallant Oscar, spear-shatterer of legions; young, generous Conall, bringer of help"—and in a final line that Virgil might envy, he cries: *"Nior clos dom Gall ba dheallrach leo"* [I never heard of Englishmen of their like!]. Thus did the heroic figures remain through the centuries symbols of the ideal, enriching the speech and thought of the people with beautiful allusions. Towards the end of the 18th century we meet Eoghan Rua O'Sullivan, the most wonderful maker of adjectival symphonies who ever composed Gaelic verse. His songs are mighty rushes of melodious language, sense sometimes failing under sheer loveliness of sound. Swinburne is his faint reflex in modern English poetry. Yet this remarkable man worked as a farm labourer. It is recorded that his employer's son, puzzled by some passage of Greek set him by his tutor, was astonished to find O'Sullivan able to assist him!

Merriman, author of *The Midnight Court,* may be mentioned as closing the 18th century. This lengthy and richly-phrased poem is a Rabelaisian skit on the contemporary shortage of marriageable young men, and it stands unique in the Gaelic literature of that age in originality. Save the mannerism of their style, there was scarcely anything to distinguish one of the 18th century singers from another—all sang of love, of wine, of repentance and of Cathleen-ny-Houlihan in much the same style and even the same phrases; only Merriman stood apart, a man of piquant personality, daring wit and conscious literary artistry.

Though the Munster poets were the most exuberant and are today the most famous, there was an important Northern school of song, of which MacCuarta, O'Doirnín, MacAlendon and MacCooey are famous names. It is said, with some aptness, that the North had matter without style and the South style without matter. At least, the Northern writers, now being edited, display much strength and vigour of thought that is lacking in O'Sullivan. On the whole, the course of modern Irish poetry may be compared to the descent of a river from the first trickles at the frozen heights of classicism (O'Bruadair and O'Rahilly) to a growing stream (O'Neachtain) which at last becomes a rushing torrent in the low country (O'Sullivan and his popular contemporaries).

The Ulster school lived longest. In 1795 Belfast had a Gaelic magazine. Many of the Northern leaders in '98 were students of Gaelic, and a nascent revival was proceeding. Some of Maria Edgeworth's writings were done into Irish and printed in Belfast in 1833. A bardic session was held in Dundalk in 1820. Art Bennett, a Gaelic scribe, scholar and poet, was still living in Co. Armagh in 1879, and since men still living knew him, we may truly claim that Gaelic literature is, in the North, an unbroken continuity to this day.

Early in the 19th century, the first gleams of the new dawn appeared. In the Penal night, Ireland had almost grown ashamed or forgetful of her past. But Petrie, O'Curry and O'Donovan, following some preliminary work by O'Reilly, the lexicographer, and Hardiman, the collector of songs, performed the great work which restored Ireland's traditions. These three giants unveiled the forgotten past in their researches into Gaelic typography and editing of Gaelic annals. O'Curry and O'Donovan were both poor and one might say despised labourers, but no men ever did such mighty nation-building as they. Tom Moore, writing an Irish history, one day saw O'Curry working at the huge manuscripts of the Annals, and listened with amazement at the scholar's account of the sealed Gaelic literature. At last he said: "I ought never to have undertaken an Irish history. These great works were not written by fools, and I know nothing of them." He had sung of "the long-faded glories" of Eirinn, taking them all on trust. He and his generation knew nothing of the Irish past save what was revealed by hostile English historians and vague native tradition. O'Curry and O'Donovan gave Ireland back her national memory.

Several academic societies did good work during the century in printing Gaelic classics—notably the Ossianic Society and the Society for the Preservation of the Irish Language. Standish Hayes O'Grady, the most prominent figure in these societies, was the greatest Gaelic *litterateur* after O'Donovan and O'Curry. In "Silva Gadelica," two huge volumes, he edited a large number of Fenian and other texts, with a spirited translation that did more to revive appreciation of classic Irish than is generally realised. It is not every man who can read English who can appreciate Shakespeare, and a knowledge of Irish does not imply an understanding of the subtle humour and delicate beauty of its literature. O'Grady had a liver appreciation of the *nuances* of Irish prose than any other of his day—he was himself able to write a richly humorous Irish style—and so his translations, with their wondrous, reckless, imaginative language reveal the richness of classic Irish with the power of brilliant criticism.

O'Grady's influence was great on Mr. W. B. Yeats, Dr. Douglas Hyde, Padraic Pearse, and others who have taken prominent parts in the Gaelic and Anglo-Irish literary movement of today. Dr. Douglas Hyde's "Literary History of Ireland" (1898) was the bible of the Gaelic League. It is a treasury of wonders. His pen, as it were a magic wand, transformed the Ireland of late Parnell days from being a sordid hovel to a regal palace in the eyes of the living Gael. He, Father Dineen, and others began to edit the classics of Irish letters and to compose a new literature in Gaelic. Dr. Hyde's playlets were the earliest fruits of the revival. Most of what was written in the new Irish was, however, of small literary value. Writers quite reasonably concentrated attention on developing a modern idiomatic style, and so a piece of good reporting from "the speech of the people," useful as a text for students, was more valued than a tale or poem of originality written in an indifferent or artificial style. Nine-tenths or more of the copious Gaelic publishing of the last 25 years has been of linguistic rather than literary value, and the attempt to produce a Gaelic drama has failed, save in *translations* from Anglo-Irish artists, such as the Irish versions of W. B. Yeats's "Cathleen-ny-Houlihan, Seumas MacManus's "Lad from Largymore" and Corkery's "Clan Falvey."

The search for a modern Gaelic style reached success in the epoch-making work of Canon Peter O'Leary (died 1920). *An t-Athair Peadar,* as we call him, wrote exactly as the good speakers of the old generation talked. He poured scorn—too much scorn, perhaps—on the "scholars" who fabricated a book-style. He broke away from the stately long sentences of classic Irish as Macaulay broke away from the Gibbonesque long English sentence, and like Macaulay, he coined a short-sentence style that is, above all else, lucid. His "Séadna," a folk-story told with much elaboration, descriptive of the life of the country side, is his great masterpiece. It ranks as pure literature, and may be read in an English translation. His Irish translation of "The Imitation of Christ" goes out of print as fast as it can be printed. A dozen or so other books from his pen are modern renderings of classic Irish romances, etc.

Next to Canon O'Leary, Padraic O'Conaire is the most successful modern Irish writer. His novels and short tales in Irish are the "best-sellers" printed in Ireland. He has not so rich a style as the master of modern Irish prose, but he is the most "modern" of Irish or Anglo-Irish writers. A grim and gloomy realism, combined with a skill in story-telling not excelled by Maupassant, make him a writer whose works cannot be put down or ignored, even if they be distasteful to the reader. His influence is seen in Liam O'Rinn, the most promising of younger writers, who has written wonderfully realistic, if drab, tales of modern Dublin, and, having perfected a style based partly on the O'Leary tradition and partly on the classic literature that O'Leary neglected, has given us a standard work in translating Mickiewicz's "Book of the Polish Pilgrimage," a holy book of nationalism that has not yet appeared in English.

"An Seabhac" and "Conan Maol" are two other writers of short tales whose work cannot be overlooked. The former has written a volume of humorous stories that are classic records of country humour and models of a racy style. The latter is severely dignified in style and will live, though not winning great popularity.

Padraic Pearse's Gaelic works are varied. His short tales, done in the colloquial manner, lack idiomatic finish, but have the strength of French short stories. They may be read in translation. They mark a departure in our literature by introducing the "explosive opening" and other modernisms which were cried out against by Gaelic purists, but have been established by O'Conaire's highly modern art. Pearse stands almost alone in understanding—as O'Grady understood—the dignity of the artificial classic style, and he used this style very beautifully in some Gaelic political essays which yet await appreciation. His poetry was classic in metre, but highly individual in matter. Old fashioned critics who objected to the individuality of Pearse's verse did not realise that he was harking back to the personal richness of the Golden Age.

There are living other Irish writers who excel O'Leary, O'Conaire and Pearse in scholarship, in beauty of style, and perhaps in potentiality, but they have yet to do their best work, and it would be invidious to attempt comparisons. In the Gaelic quarterly, *An Branar,* their work may be seen. But the three names here quoted are names that stand for personalities, each strongly original and all dissimilar. Between the idyllic ruralism of O'Leary, the modernism of O'Conaire, the passion, the vision, the splendour of Pearse, there is room for a very notable literature to grow up. There are many most encouraging signs of its early appearance.

II. *The Literature of Anglo-Ireland*

Gaelic Ireland is the real Ireland, the secret Ireland. Only in the last twenty-five years has this been realised. Up to 1893 (when the Gaelic League was founded) Irish-Ireland was contemned, even by Irish patriots, and the pseudo-Ireland, the superficial, historically insignificant English-speaking Ireland, was accepted as the true reality. Up to the date of the Great Famine, the bulk of the nation was Irish speaking. Even down till the end of the last century, English-writing authors in Ireland mostly came of a caste partly separated from the mass of the people. Only in our own days has Ireland been genuinely articulate in the English language, and the best of modern Anglo-Irish literature owes something to English literature, while failing to express certain untranslatable elements of Irish-Ireland thought and feeling. Still, Anglo-Irish literature is a not undistinguished body of work. It falls into two chief divisions.

The first of these is the 18th century group. Molyneux was the first, famous for his "Case of Ireland," ordered to be burnt by the hangman because it contained such passages as this: "To tax me without my consent is little better than downright robbing me" and "There may be ill consequences if the Irish come to think of their rights and liberties left to depend on the will of a legislature wherein they are not parties." This spirited work played its part later in inspiring the American revolutionaries, but Molyneux' brave words in favour of liberty were intended to apply to the colonists only: the authentic nation, the Gaelic race, the Catholic population, he feared and detested as much as any of his political opponents.

Similarly Bishop Berkeley, whose pamphlet, *The Querist,* is often quoted as Nationalist propaganda, exhibits in his political writings the same narrow colonial, or ascendancy, vision. *The Querist* is directed against the ill economy of the wasteful Ascendancy:

> Whether an Irish lady, set out with French silks and Flanders lace, may not be said to consume more beef and butter than a hundred of our labouring peasants?
>
> Whether nine-tenths of our foreign trade be not carried on singly to support the article of vanity?
>
> Whether it is not madness for a poor nation to imitate a rich one?
>
> Whether a woman of fashion ought not to be declared a public enemy?
>
> Whether as seed equally scattered produceth a goodly harvest, even so an equal distribution of wealth doth not cause a nation to flourish?

But when Berkeley goes on to ask whether Ireland could not support her population in full comfort even were a brass wall built around the island, he is but the settler discussing the potentialities of captured land. He asks whether "the upper parts of this people" are not "English by blood, language, religion, manners, inclination and interest." The evils he inveighed against did not touch the Gaelic masses, for their trouble was not uneven distribution of wealth, but political and economic annihilation.

Berkeley's celebrated works on philosophy belong to another field than pure literature, but their English is esteemed as ranking with the finest in lucidity and eloquence. We may note that he is often written of as being, in philosophy, as Irish as Locke was English and Hume Scottish. This is as just as it is plausible, for Berkeley's thought was on the Platonic side of that line which is said to divide all men into Platonists and Aristoteleans; and from the Druids and Duns Scotus down, Irish speculators have been found on the Platonic side.

Swift was the most notable of the colonial writers, and the nearest to a national figure, for his personality is inseparable from the traditions of Dublin. He was an Englishman born and educated in Ireland, but hating his life in that country. Some instinct in his nature made him unusually sensitive to environment, for despite his English blood, he is a true Irish type of the line Shane O'Neill, Parnell, G. B. Shaw. The humbug-piercing cynicism, the cold-blooded satire, the love of overthrowing other people's idols that characterise that line of Irishmen were supremely represented in him. So mercilessly, so truthfully, did he satirise the feuds of sects, that he was suspected by the dense of intending to ridicule all religion. When he solemnly proposed that Irish poverty be cured by using babies as food, he was quite in the Irish tradition of solemnly shocking criminal indifference with the logical, if absurd, working out of its principles. He was Irish, too, in his feminism. In the 18th century, a Turkish attitude to women prevailed, and it needed courage in a man of his creed and class, to declare that "the same virtues equally become both sexes."

Goldsmith, who resembled Swift in wit and chivalry, was of a tenderer nature, and perhaps came nearer to expressing the Irish spirit in his writings, though they were not directly associated with Ireland. Like Swift, he came into contact with Gaelic Ireland, for if Swift did an Irish poem (O'Rourke's feast) into English and (perhaps) derived the plot of "Gulliver's Travels" from the Gaelic story "Eisirt," Goldsmith met Carolan in the flesh. Had Goldsmith been born in a cottier's hut, had he frequented the humble bardic courts, he might have assumed Keating's mantle, and bent Irish prose to the range of modern thought. In "The Deserted Village" we feel we are touching Ireland. In 1740 (when Goldsmith was aged 12) Ireland was desolated by a famine that dispeopled whole villages—400,000 people perished. Hence the gloomy colours of the famous poem. The lament contains some sound Irish political economy, and the whole is a vignette of 18th century Ireland.

> Ill fares the land, to hastening ills a prey
> Where wealth accumulates and men decay:
> Princes or lords may flourish or may fade,
> A breath could make them as a breath has made;
> But a bold peasantry, their country's pride
> When once destroyed can never be supplied.

Goldsmith and Sheridan hold high places in English drama, ranking only below Shakespeare. Something more than a thread connects these 18th century Anglo-Irish dramatists with Wilde and Bernard Shaw, masters of social comedy in our own days. The satiric trait in the Irish temperament (strengthened by Irish history!) finds congenial expression in the drama; verbal wit, flashing dialogue, colloquial prose, all vital elements of a dramatic style, come easily to the Irish pen. The flexibility of style which marks Anglo-Irish prose writers, particularly the dramatists, is traceable to the animation of Irish conversation, which in turn is attributable to our bilingual conditions. The grammatic opulence of the Gaelic tongue makes Irish use of the English language lively and apt; and authors ignorant of Gaelic itself may reap benefit from the vitality of popular speech. To this day in Ireland an expressive, rhythmic English is spoken such as the English Elizabethans heard around them, though it died in England not long after their great days. Anglo-Irish prose offers the most imitative worthy models, the bright, easy, clear and forceful English of Berkeley, Goldsmith and Swift contrasting with the stilted and laborious prose of Johnson or Gibbon.

The cause to which we attribute this flexibility of style is also accountable for Anglo-Irish writers' eminence in translation. Francis' "Horace," Cary's "Dante," Mangan's renderings from Irish, German and Oriental tongues, Fitzgerald's "Omar"—these are but a few examples.

Mentio must not be omitted of Grattan's orations—ornate, eloquent, unsurpassable rhetoric. But a contemporary of the great parliamentarian calls for more particular notice—Wolfe Tone. Tone's "Autobiogaphy" is one of the very greatest works of Anglo-Irish literature, little as it is appreciated by the critics. Padraic Pearse used to carry it about with him like a Gospel, and indeed, it is one of the gospels of Irish nationality. It reveals the most lovable personality who ever set pen to paper in Ireland. We cannot read it today without tears for his wistful memories of his runaway marriage on "one beautiful morning in June," thrills for his patriotic ideals, bitterness for his defeat, and heartfelt enthusiasm for his heroic example.

Thomas Moore was accused by Hazlitt of "turning the wild harp of Erin into a musical snuff-box"—a criticism worthy of a man with a satiric Irish strain. It corrects the idolisation of Moore which prevailed in the anglicised 19th century. But while we do right to remember that Moore's prettiness is not the majesty and passion of the authentic Gael, yet he should be honoured because, in however artificial a manner, he did keep alive a belief in "the days of old"

> . . . ere the emerald gem of the western world
> Was set in the crown of a stranger.

He was of the prevailing "romantic" school: but romance was better than darkness, in the absence of certainty.

The second division of Anglo-Irish literature comprises the writers of the "Nation," the men of '48 and their immediate successors. These energetic young men set out to create a national literature in English. They owed nothing to the 18th century school. Belonging to the Ascendancy class, they knew nothing of the Gael, save what was being introduced to the scholars' attention by O'Curry and O'Donovan. Their rousing national ballads were mostly composed on foreign models, and John Mitchel's mighty prose was marred by imitation of rhetorical Carlyle. The greatest by far was Thomas Davis. His was a mind of encyclopedic range, though not very deep learning. Ardently and persuadingly he pleaded in his glowing essays for a national art, for reading-rooms, for historical studies, for industrial development. His poems have never been excelled as patriotic verse. "The West's Awake" will never lose popularity, but his songs of rural life, praising sturdy country manners and simple joys, were equally part of his prophetic message to his people. His supreme teaching was—the return of Gaelicism. "Ireland free," he said, "yes, but at all hazards, Ireland Gaelic." Laughed at by the superficial, he preached revival of the Gaelic tongue, and set about its study himself. He died with but three crowded years of work to his credit. The Famine came and struck down all the national energies. It was left to our own days for men to take up Davis's work, and his essays are the program of the Irish-Ireland movement today.

Though Davis was greatest as a national teacher, Clarence Mangan was greatest as a literary artist. He differed from Davis, too, in being immersed in Gaelic style; his poetry is full of Gaelic imagery and music. He is to Irish what Chapman is to Homer. His Gaelicism renders him strange and difficult to English critics; otherwise he would be recognised as one of the greatest poets using English in his days. He was capable of magnificent symbolism as in this lament for the Irish princes:

> Theirs were not souls wherein dull Time
> Could domicile decay, or house Decrepitude,

and of unforgettable passionate imagery, as in *Dark Rosaleen, Meehal Dhu MacGiolla Keerin* and *Cathleen-ny-Houlihan.*

Sir Samuel Ferguson must be mentioned with Mangan because, though his style was less racily Gaelic, and derived more from classical study, he aided in presenting Gaelic tradition through English verse. He was more scholarly and more artistic than the political writers of the *Nation,* but his patriotism was less from the heart. His poem describing *The Burial of King Cormac*—telling how the Boyne water carried away the corpse of the King who wished not to be buried with his pagan sires—gives us both the atmosphere of the Boyne country and a true picture of the splendid and barbaric pre-patrician age. His *Lays of the Western Gael* bring up a vivid pageant of the Red Branch figures.

The reader who possesses Mitchel's *Jail Journal* (the second gospel of Irish nationality), the *Spirit of the Nation* (an anthology of the *Nation* poets), the *Essays* of Davis, and the poems of Mangan and Ferguson, has a fairly complete collection of Anglo-Irish literature of this group.

We have thus far made no allusion to fiction, for the reason that it is in poetry and the essay that Ireland found some degree of national expression, while fiction is a more external or impressionist matter. Maria Edgeworth's name is a great one in English literature, and her brilliant tales of 18th century Ascendancy life in Ireland deserve attention, though they cannot be described as an expression of the nation. Carleton's tales contain a rich gallery of pictures of the people's life in the early 19th century, but their anti-Irish bias renders them displeasing to modern readers. Love and Lever wrote rollicking tales which are similarly disapproved of because they distorted Irish life to please the prejudices of a contemptuous English market. The judicious reader, of course, can peruse these works with interest and profit, but they are intrinsically unnational. Kickham's *Knocknagow* is the one outstanding Irish novel of the age that is national, inoffensive and historic.

CHAPTER LXXVIII

SINN FEIN

The world is witnessing in Ireland an extraordinary national renaissance, which expresses itself in literature, art, industry, social idealism, religious fervour and personal self-sacrifice. Deprived of the means of learning, impoverished and ground down, the Irish people for 200 years have not known culture or freedom, and their history for that period is gloomy reading.

The country in these long years lay fallow, but the soil was good. In the closing years of the 9th century the untilled field was ploughed up and sown in by the Gaelic League. From this educational movement which began in 1893 the whole revival of Irish-Ireland may be dated.[1]

---

[1] At the very beginning of the Gaelic League movement a Gaelic song, sung from the gallery of a Dublin theatre by William Rooney and some fellow enthusiasts (the first of its kind ever heard in such place) had thrilling effect upon many of the hearers—especially upon Ethna Carbery who commemorated the event in her poem:

A GAELIC SONG

A murmurous tangle of voices,
  Laughter to left and right,
We waited the curtain's rising,
  In a glare of electric light;
When down through the din came, slowly,
  Softly, then clear and strong,
The mournful minor cadence
  Of a sweet old Gaelic song.

Like the trill of a lark new-risen,
  It trembled upon the air,

Recovering some measure of strength at last after the exhaustion of the famine years, but disheartened and confused by the collapse of the Parnell movement, Ireland welcomed the Gaelic League as a new and hopeful means of exerting her national energies. The League spread like fire. With its pageants, its countryside "feiseanna" or festivals, its Gaelic

---

And wondering eyes were lifted
To seek for the singer there;
Some dreamed of the thrush at noontide,
Some fancied a linnet's wail,
While the notes went sobbing, sighing,
O'er the heartstrings of the Gael.

The lights grew blurred, and a vision
Fell upon all who heard—
The purple of moorland heather
By a wonderful wind was stirred;
Green rings of rushes went swaying,
Gaunt boughs of Winter made moan;
One saw the glory of Life go by,
And one saw Death alone.

A river twined through its shallows,
Cool waves crept up on a strand,
Or fierce, like a mighty army,
Swept wide on a conquered land;
The Dead left cairn and barrow,
And passed in noble train,
With sheltering shield, and slender spear—
Ere the curtain rose again.

The four great seas of Eire
Heaved under fierce ships of war,
The God of Battles befriended,
We saw the Star! the Star!
We nerved us for deeds of daring,
For Right we stood against Wrong;
We heard the prayer of our mothers,
In that sweet old Gaelic song.

It was the soul of Eire
Awaking in speech she knew,
When the clans held the glens and the mountains,
And the hearts of her chiefs were true:
She hath stirred at last in her sleeping,
She is folding her dreams away,
The hour of her destiny neareth—
And it may be today—today!

song and music, rich with memories, its lectures on the forgotten glories of the Gael, it roused the whole mind of the country. *Thainig anam in Eirinn*—a soul came into Ireland. The popular imagination recovered a vision of historic Ireland, that traditional nation whose heroes were not the orators of College Green but the O'Neills and the Fianna and the chivalry of the Red Branch. Twenty-five years ago, the multitude were stark ignorant of the names of Conall Cearnach, Luke Wadding, Céitinn, Raftery: today the traditional lore is at least as familiar as the English lore which had threatened utterly to usurp it. Today, too, Gaelic education has its numerous summer colleges and diocesan colleges; it has assumed something like its proper national position in all the better seminaries, and no scholar can enter the National University without a knowledge of the Irish tongue.

The centre of gravity in national life changed from the anglicised towns to the rural population, sturdy, unspoilt, patriotic, virile, the offspring and living representatives of the traditional Gael. Hence Irish politics began forthwith to reflect the mind of the real Irish race.

We now see Ireland, in the new century new-awakened to self-consciousness, a stout rural nation, filled with new pride in its past, and feeling after means to achieve a worthy future. Throughout the country, a band of enthusiasts toils at an intellectual movement—studies a difficult and educative language, reads history and all manner of books on national construction, and acts as a ferment to the whole people.

Extraordinary little newspapers and magazines, written voluntarily by enthusiasts, began to appear. The most important was the *United Irishman*,[2] edited by Mr. Arthur Griffith (the Hamlet of the whole story) and contributed to by scores of brilliant writers of verse, drama, tale, essay and research-work. This weekly, voluntary, paper, published work that has since taken rank among the immortal things of Irish literature. Parallel to this journalistic movement, a dramatic movement, led by W. B. Yeats and Lady Gregory, was proceeding in the Abbey Theatre.

This intellectual ferment called for a political expression. You could not have all young Ireland brimful with enthusiasm for the glories of the Gael, primed with ambition to see again on Irish soil a hale and lovely polity like that of old, eager to use hand and brain in patriot work, and yet rest content to mark time behind a (Parliamentary) political movement that

[2] Preceded by the *Shan Van Vocht*, which, edited by Ethna Carbery and Alice Milligan, first awaked the new national enthusiasm, and did splendid pioneer work.

seemed to have lost momentum, and which certainly gave no promise that it was seeking an Ireland such as was now envisioned.

In 1905 Mr. Griffith and his friends put before the nation a new political movement. In Dublin on Nov. 28, 1905, a National Council[3] was called into being for the purpose of organising the nation with a view to withdrawing the representatives sitting at Westminster and setting up a provisional Irish Parliament made up of these members and representatives of public bodies. This *de facto* Parliament would call upon the people to cooperate with it voluntarily in the administration of Ireland. In a newly-founded weekly, *Sinn Fein* (succeeding the *United Irishman*), Mr. Griffith proceeded to show how the nation could thus conduct its own affairs even while the national parliament was denied recognition by outside powers.

Thus, through the Harbour Boards, difficulties could be imposed in the "dumping" of foreign goods, which would amount to a system of protection for Irish industries. The public could be organised for the support of native industry, and capital could be encouraged by the offer of rate-free sites, etc. Arbitration Courts could be set up everywhere, superseding the British courts in civil matters. National insurance could be undertaken. National banks could divert from foreign fields the Irish money which could so much more profitably be invested in buying up Irish land, financing Irish developments and extending Irish control of home resources. A national mercantile marine could be cooperatively bought and set to carrying Irish produce to those Continental markets which offered so much better prices than the English markets to which English ships carried Irish cattle and manufactured goods. Irish commercial agents—consuls—could be sent to the great foreign trade centres.[4]

It was this policy of boycotting foreign institutions, and of "non-cooperation" with the usurping power, which, under Deak's leadership, won Hungary the status of an independent nation in the struggle with Austria

---

[3] For sake of historical record it may be stated that those who first met and formed this National Council were: Arthur Griffith, Maud Gonne MacBride, Alderman Tom Kelly, Henry Dixon, Seumas MacManus, and Edward Martyn.

[4] This policy was not wholly a novel one. Daniel O'Connell once contemplated summoning a Council of Three Hundred, withdrawing representation at Westminster, and proceeding to legislate for the country. The idea had been enthusiastically taken up by the Young Irelanders, but when O'Connell found he had a militant and united nation behind him, he abandoned the scheme. That it had frightened the British supremacy is clear from Lord John Russell's dictum: "In six months the power and function of government will be wrested from our hands, and the Lord Lieutenant will sit powerless in Dublin Castle." The Arbitration Courts which had been prepared with a view to superseding the English courts, were surrendered as well as the Council, and Ireland heard no more of the proposal until it was brought to mind by Griffith.

that culminated in 1867. Griffith's personality is in ways reminiscent of Deak's. In Hungarian history you will read that Deak was above all other things, inflexible. He was not an "extremist," but he was trusted by those who went farther than he did because they knew that he would never be betrayed into standing for a party instead of for a nation. He would do nothing to help Austria govern Hungary. He preached the pure doctrine of nationality. The blandishments of the Emperor, paper promises of a constitution, the actual setting-up of a subordinate Home-Rule parliament; all failed to extort one sign of recognition from this iron leader. When even all his demands were promised him if he would promise in return Hungarian military aid, he refused to be moved. Freedom was a right, not a thing to be bargained for. Only when the free Hungarian constitution was brought into being did he extend the hand of friendship.

That has been Arthur Griffith's attitude, and the fact that his policy has made such remarkable progress is due to his iron refusal to compromise on any point, or to parley, until liberty is brought into being. A pen-portrait thus describes him: . . . "A small man, very sturdily built, nothing remarkable about his appearance except his eyes, which are impenetrable and steely; taciturn, deliberate, speaking when he does speak with the authority and finality of genius, totally without rhetoric, under complete self-control, and the coolest and best brain in Ireland." And: "He believes intensely in himself, and he has no real faith in anybody else, so that he is always more or less cold towards anybody who tries to do any political work in or about his own particular sphere. . . . Once he has made up his mind on anything he never changes. In controversy he is like a bull-dog: he is always the last to let go, and by that time there isn't much left of the other man's case. As a controversialist he is able and . . . unscrupulous,[5] but he is nearly always right." The same writer adds that "he is naturally a believer in evolutionary methods in politics rather than in revolutionary methods, and, in a free Ireland, would I think be found on the side of what *The Times* would call 'stability.' He is no great believer in the rights of man, and modern radical catch-cries leave him cold; his creed being rather the rights of nations and the duties of man, the rights of a nation being freedom and the allegiance and service of all its children, and the rights of man being to fear God and serve his nation. He believes in the State as against the individual."

We give this extended account of Arthur Griffith, because it may justly be said that his personality *is* the Sinn Fein movement. Though he alone

---

[5] It is just to say, here, that the writer of this foot-note, long intimate with Griffith's work, can recall nothing to justify this surprising charge.—S. M. M.

could not have made Sinn Fein the power in Ireland that it is, yet those brilliant minds, those fighters and doers, who brought his movement to its present position, would without him have been disunited and perhaps conflicting forces. In particular, the Volunteer movement, had it stood as a Physical Force movement alone, would have resulted in a disastrous and disheartening failure such as took the heart out of former generations in Ireland. When Easter Week was over, and the insurgents were crushed, the country was not broken as after '98 or '48 or '67, because the large fabric of the comprehensive Sinn Fein policy remained, and the sacrifice of Pearse and his comrades served but as a stimulus to the masses to carry on the work of industrial revival, language-restoration, etc.

Griffith, in his long years of propaganda, had taught the rising generation that nationality was to be served in every act of life. The pages of Sinn Fein teemed with ideas, represented every phase of national existence. Art, literature, the drama, economics, industry, sociology; all such topics were discussed by enthusiasts, and plans were even laid for a national decimal coinage of which the unit was to be the *Gael* (equivalent to the Franc). When in 1910 Mr. Redmond secured the Balance of Power in the British Parliament, Mr. Griffith suspended the organising of Sinn Fein as a political party, giving the Parliamentary leader a free hand to achieve whatever he could achieve for Ireland with the parliamentary weapon. For years, then, Sinn Fein was apparently dormant, its only large activity being the publication of the weekly with its constructive and critical articles. Mr. Griffith believed that the parliamentary dice was weighted against Ireland, and that at the critical moment, the rival British parties would coalesce, rather than be played off against each other to yield Irish freedom. So he bided his time. It may here be remarked that one man could have wielded the weapon of Abstention with force at that time. Mr. Redmond had the leadership of the nation and could have secured its approval of a dramatic leaving of the House of Commons when the Liberals played Ireland false. It is a tragedy that (for whatever cause) he was not able to cooperate with Arthur Griffith in this way. Much blood and sorrow might have been spared.

Unhappily Redmond allowed himself to be coerced by the threats of Sir Edward Carson, and early in 1914, accepted the principle of Partition. Weakness, and perhaps anglicisation led him to almost abject surrender, and ever since, English politicians have used the authority of an Irish leader for a policy of dividing the Irish nation. In Ireland, there was horror and almost despair. Meanwhile, Nationalists had organised a Volunteer force numbering up to 200,000 to repel the threat of Sir Edward Carson's Volunteers, who were armed with the connivance of English military authorities and at the expense of English Unionists. There was even talk of Civil War on the eve of the Great War: but this must be largely discounted as journalistic sensationalism, since the Ulster Volunteer, who would not even subscribe for his own equipment, not parade without the free gift of a bowler-hat, was not likely to play the hero in the field against men fighting for a real cause. Indeed, when the Great War came, only one in ten of these loyal warriors enlisted for the defence of the Empire which they professed to love so dearly.

But the Great War found the Irish situation under the influence of another element than Unionism, Parliamentarianism and Sinn Fein—an element which we have not yet referred to, to wit, Fenianism, or Republicanism. A Physical Force party, aiming at an independent Irish Republic, owned a monthly paper, *Irish Freedom,* and through a series of "Wolfe Tone Clubs," exerted an influence on public opinion that was far from being negligible. This party enjoyed the allegiance of several of the best brains of modern Ireland: in particular, it numbered among its leading adherents, Padraic Pearse, one of the most remarkable men of his age.

Parnell had said that Fenianism was the backbone of the nation. Though not a Physical Force man himself, he did nothing to check the activities of those who believed in freeing Ireland by armed conflict: he refused to be "England's policeman." And so his own movement was the stronger because his opponents knew that if it were withdrawn they would have to deal with the desperate men who stood behind. Even so, Grattan once had used the menace of the Volunteers of 1782. But Fenianism appeared to the outer world to have perished in our own days. A few old Fenians here and there, "embers" kept the fire of freedom aflame in the country, and some, like the venerable John O'Leary, preached that Physical Force was needed, not because it was capable of winning against England, but because sacrifice alone would keep Nationality alive.

How far Fenianism survived as *an organisation* only the initiates could tell; but it is a known fact that Fenianism definitely took up arms again some years before the war.

The Fenians adopted from Fintan Lalor the motto: "Repeal not the Union, but the Conquest." These were lean years for Sinn Fein, but these two small parties of enthusiasts worked side by side without acrimony. Each was equally devoted to the full Irish-Ireland program of a Gaelicised nation. The Fenians were the active element in the Volunteers when that extraordinary armed movement came into being: but they did not at first control the new development.

Such, then, were the factors in the Irish situation on which the Great War descended in August, 1914.

CHAPTER LXXIX

Easter Rising

'Tis said that the first shots in the Great War were fired in Ireland. This happened on July 26th, 1914, a beautiful summer Sunday. It came about thus:

Early in 1914 the Carsonite Volunteers, with the connivance of British sympathisers in high places, ran a big cargo of arms ashore at Larne, and distributed them over Ulster by motors flying through the night. The exploit was carried out with excellent generalship, and one life, that of an over-excited official, was lost. Those were dull days in world affairs—the calm before the storm—and the press received the news with voracious joy. Every newspaper published thrilling (often imaginative) accounts, garnished with maps and war-artists' pictures. The public enjoyed a sensation bigger than anything since the Boer War. Forthwith, the British Government prohibited the importation of arms into Ireland, lest the Nationalists should secure weapons too.

On Sunday, July 19th, the Dublin Volunteers were mobilised for a route march. A big column assembled at the Volunteer grounds at Clontarf after Mass, and received orders to march towards Howth. Only one or two officers knew what the day's program was, and the section commanders and rank and file obediently tramped out along the side of Dublin Bay, turning off to the left, according to orders, where a bye-road leads to Baldoyle, a little village near a racecourse. The Volunteers were, as usual, watched by police. This being the first big muster of Volunteers, perhaps a suspicion passed through the minds of both the Volunteers and the police, that some *coup* was being planned. However, arrived at Baldoyle, the column was dismissed and allowed to take refreshments. After an hour or so, the whistles sounded, and the men were marched back to Dublin. Nothing remarkable had happened.

There was talk that at the next route march there would probably be some drill in field operations. . . .

On the following Sunday, the volunteers were again mobilised. Nearly a thousand paraded. As they hurried from all parts of Dublin to the parade ground, they saw announcements on the Sunday paper placards of a serious international crisis that had been brought about through Austria's quarrel with Serbia. The very sensitive minds felt, perhaps, the first tremors of the coming cataclysm.

Out towards Howth they marched once more, singing their marchings songs, "Clare's Dragoons," "Step Together," and the "Soldiers' Song." Only a few knew the words of this last and none guessed that in less than three years it would be as popular with the Irish race as "God Save Ireland." Out the Howth Road they swung along and past Kilbarrack churchyard; but instead of turning to the left for Baldoyle, they were led past Sutton on towards the great hill of Howth itself.

When the column reached the narrow isthmus which links Howth to the mainland, the island of Ireland's Eye could be seen to the left across the sunny green waters. Past it, making for Howth Harbour, a small yacht was sailing. None of the Volunteers, save perhaps three men, knew what that yacht was carrying in her hold. When the Volunteers reached the foot of Howth pier, they were halted. The yacht was then nearing the mouth of the harbour. Suddenly, as the white sails dropped and the little craft ran under the lighthouse, and around the pierhead, the order was passed along the line to double down the pier. Vaguely sensing that something notable was afoot, the Volunteers ran. Small contingents of picked men appeared from no one knew where and guarded the foot of the pier with automatic pistols. Coast guards venturing to interfere found themselves looking into the muzzles of lethal weapons and desisted. Police, going to barracks to telephone to Dublin discovered that wires had been cut and that Howth was isolated. And then—

The column had been halted along the pier. The little yacht was moored at the pierhead. Heavy batons of wood with leather wrist-straps were dealt out and a hundred or so Volunteers were armed therewith. Suddenly it was noticed that in the summer sunlight straw-bound objects were being handed up from the boat to those Volunteers who held the pierhead. Straining eyes saw the straw torn away, and the Irish Volunteers' first rifles appearing!

An indescribable shriek of cheers went up. The column broke, and men dashed forward, eager to get arms. For a few minutes the officers had difficulty in restoring order. "Have patience," they said. "Don't fear—there's enough to go 'round."

And so, in a few minutes, every Volunteer held a heavy rifle in his hands, while motors shot away with further stands and boxes of ammunition.

Loudly were the armed men cheered by holiday makers at Howth, people on tramtops and by roadside, as they marched back to the city, their rifles on their shoulders. Word of their approach was carried ahead of them, by, it may be assumed, a police motor. Bodies of police marched behind them, and when, after 9 miles' tramping, they neared Clontarf, the Volunteer cycle scouts rode back to the column with word that a detachment of British soldiers blocked the way into the city. The marching column drew up a few score feet from the sinister khaki line. Their officers received from a police official the intimation that they must surrender their arms. The officers temporised. The police official, on some technical point, was acting beyond his powers, though in the spirit of his authorities. The discussion between the two parties was accordingly prolonged. While the argument over technicalities lasted the Volunteers quietly dispersed and got away across fields to safe hiding places for their guns. And so battle was avoided. Yet it was touch-and-go, and had ammunition been served out instead of prudently held back by the Volunteer leaders, there would undoubtedly have ensued a bloody episode with huge casualties.[1]

But though the armed men thus got their weapons away without a clash of arms, the day was not to end in peace. The khaki forces marching back to barracks were hooted by a mob that resented an attempt to disarm Nationalists while Carsonites were encouraged to arm. The soldiers fired two volleys into the crowd. Four people were in cold blood shot dead and about fifty wounded.

This tragic occurrence shocked the whole country. Mr. Asquith's efforts to gloze over the shooting of civilians infuriated the insulted nation. The victims' funeral was one of the most impressive events ever witnessed in Dublin. Hundreds of thousands participated. Volunteers kept order and fired a military salute over the graves. There was a breath of revolution in the air.

---

[1] One body of worthy ones, who materially aided in the saving of the guns—as well as in other good projects—was the fine, and well-trained body of patriotic Irish lads, the Fianna na hEireann. They were a body of brave boys enrolled by a brave Irishwoman, who fought gallantly, and suffered sorely for Ireland, the Countess Markievicz. The admirable Con Colbert, who smilingly met the martyr death dealt to the patriot leaders of the Easter Rising, was one of the Fian—and had become a chief trainer of them. He had an able assistant in another lovable Fian graduate, and rebel leader, Liam Mellowes.

And then the Great War began. Everyone felt that those shots at civilians in Dublin had been the first blows in the conflict. Appeals were now made to Irishmen to rally to the defence of England! Mr. Asquith, visiting Dublin to address a great ticket meeting, had to approach the hall through armed guards, and the demonstration secured, it is said, only six recruits.[2]

When Mr. Redmond, who had promised unreserved Irish aid in the war without even stipulating that national freedom should first be ensured, went farther, and declared that the Irish Volunteers' duty was to enlist en masse under England's flag, the founders of the Volunteer organisation revolted, and the movement was split. The original Volunteers were a minority, but they were a determined body of men, and as Irish nationality received one rebuff after another, and coercion was used against Irishmen of independent standing, an increasing body of discontented or disillusioned people passed over to the "extreme" camp. In 1914 the majority was with Mr. Redmond. By the beginning of 1916 his Volunteers had melted away and he was a lonely, disappointed, failing man. On St. Patrick's Day of that year, a wonderful demonstration took place, a vast body of Volunteers parading in College Green before the old Parliament House, and saluting Eoin MacNeill, recognised leader of the recalcitrants. It was then clear that the Volunteer movement was definitely in the opposite camp to Mr. Redmond, and was both powerful and determined. Nobody doubted now that an armed conflict between this well-organised body and the forces of the Crown was something more than a lively possibility.

Professor MacNeill, however, was known to be a cautious and moderate man, who then followed a policy far short of the republican. He was in favour of accepting and defending Home Rule. He wished to see the Volunteers' organisation brought to a pitch of completeness that would enable the leaders, at the war's end, to confront England with an armed nation demanding its promised freedom. He was not in favour of striking for a republic to be achieved by force of arms, though it is, of course, impossible to say whether he would not have agreed to an insurrection had Germany been able to send forces and arms that would render such action seriously formidable to British power.

[2] The meeting was attended by Mr. Redmond's faithful "loyalists" and the Anglo-Irish. Admission by ticket was arranged, to prevent the real Irish from smashing it up.

How came it, then, that insurrection without German aid ultimately came about? The answer is found in the personality of two men—Padraic Pearse and James Connolly.

Without doubt, Pearse was one of the most remarkable men ever born in Ireland. His curious and powerful writings expound a philosophy that sets the Irish cause in the light of a tremendous religious mission. As an educationalist alone, Pearse came with a message destined to work profound revolution in the nation's intellectual life. Starting, as it were, where the Gaelic League left off, to wit: at the conviction that Irish must be restored to the position it enjoyed in Gaelic days if the nation is to preserve its apostolicity, he went farther, and showed that the whole system of education in Ireland, and the intellectual standards of the educated, must be utterly changed. He advocated bilingualism on the ground that it made for rich intellectual development, and having studied bilingual education in Belgium, he expounded it in the press and in practice. Irish was made the school language at St. Enda's, his school, only the sciences in which a Gaelic vocabulary is lacking being taught in English. But his educational ideals went far farther than bilingualism. He held that heroic literature, the national sagas, should take a prime place in school curricula. At St. Enda's every boy was made as familiar with Cuchulainn and Fionn as in other schools he would be with Macaulay. Heroic pageants and Passion Plays were enacted while lectures from eminent literati introduced the lads to realms of modern culture. Further, the common relation of master and pupil was changed for that of teacher and disciple. Pearse held that Our Lord, moving with the Twelve about the countryside and feeding them on the richness of His wisdom, was the ideal type towards which education should aspire.

Pearse held that English commercialism was the wickedest thing that ever corrupted the hearts of great nations. Irish nationality, on the other hand, he saw as a sacred trust, committed to the race by God, who spoke through Tone and Mitchel and Davis and Labor as the Four Evangelists of Ireland, and was crucified in Robert Emmet, who made the supreme sacrifice to keep the spirit of the nation alive. Every generation, Pearse said, must make protest in blood against foreign dominion; otherwise Ireland's claim to independent nationhood would be annulled. He quoted the inspired utterance that "without blood there is no remission of sins," and both in his school and in his writings preached ceaselessly the beauty of sacrifice. In one of his most typical school plays, a saintly youth takes the place of the king at the head of a failing army, and by the gift of his young life wins a victory. "Let me do this *little* thing, O King," says the boy as he goes forth to death. That was Pearse's most typical and most actually personal line.

When the war came, Pearse brooded even more seriously on the need of an armed rising. When every other subject people rose for freedom, was Ireland alone to make no sign? She must fight, if not with hope of success, then in the spirit of a blood sacrifice to demonstrate her undying resolve to win ultimate freedom. This Pearse preached to the people, speaking at meetings where, with a religious solemnity, he made his hearers stand as for the recitation of the Creed in Church, and repeat after him: "I believe in One Irish Nation, and that Free."

And yet Pearse was slow to consent to the Rising. Undoubtedly he expected and relied on an armed conflict in Ireland before the Great War should end, but he was resolved to strike when the blow should have best chance of success. It is generally believed, and is probably the case, that James Connolly was responsible for the hurrying of things to an issue.

Connolly was a Socialist, and the Socialist Republican Party which he founded before the '98 Centenary was an active force in the revival of separation. He believed in the Marxian doctrine of Social Revolution with more earnestness than the Socialists of other countries, who professed to be revolutionaries, but feared revolution no less than other classes of the community. Connolly worked at all times to bring about that violent revolt against the Capitalist system from which the new order was expected to rise. Pearse, no less than Connolly, was opposed to the Capitalist order and looked to see new Ireland blossom as a cooperative commonwealth; but he did not share Connolly's reliance on Class War: he hoped to see patriotism, by inspiring all classes with a lofty ideal, direct the nation to a nobler order than the present. Connolly, however, was no doctrinaire Socialist: he was not pledged to a communistic future, and would have supported any program which made for democracy in industry and equitable distribution of wealth and power. He was as intensely patriotic as any anti-socialist, and when awaiting execution said to his daughter: "Other socialists will not understand why I am here—they forget that I am an Irishman."

Connolly is said to have told his friends in 1914 that he would not let the war end without striking a blow for revolution. In the early part of 1916, his paper preached revolt in unmistakable terms. Undoubtedly his propaganda hastened the ultimate decision. During the Lent preceding the Rising he published such fiercely rebellious matter that no reader could doubt his intention. It was expected that the Castle would raid Liberty Hall and destroy the revolutionary printing press. So, to defend liberty of utterance, a Citizen Army guard stood with loaded rifles, day and night, prepared to resist to the end. Just a week before Easter, the Irish Tricolour was hoisted over the Hall as if the Republic were already in being. The atmosphere was tense. Various raids, captures of arms, strange threats and rumours, filled the public mind with the impression that something sensational was afoot. It was thought that an attempt might soon be made to disarm the Volunteers, and people vaguely wondered what resistance could be offered.

On Easter Sunday two mysterious items in the papers sent a thrill of sensation through the country. The first was a report of how a motor carrying unknown persons, driving furiously in the dark towards the Kerry coast, had taken a wrong turn and plunged into an arm of the sea. The second was this note, signed by Eoin MacNeill, chairman of the Volunteers:

> "Owing to the very critical position, all orders given to Irish Volunteers for tomorrow, Easter Sunday, are hereby rescinded, and no parades, marches, or other movements of Irish Volunteers will take place. Each individual Volunteer will obey this order strictly in every particular."

It needed little imagination to guess that the motor car accident had been in connection with some landing of arms or persons, and Professor MacNeill's order clearly showed that some stupendous crisis had just been passed.

What had happened was, that Roger Casement had landed in Kerry, had failed to be met by those who were to take him to his destination, and had been captured by police, identified, and hurried away, a prisoner, to London. Simultaneously, a liner, now named the *Aud,* which accompanied Casement's submarine, disguised as a Norwegian timber ship, but really carrying 20,000 rifles, millions of rounds of ammunition, with machine guns and explosives, had been stopped by a British patrol boat near Tralee, where the arms were to be landed. Flying the German flag, the *Aud* was scuttled by its own crew.

A Rising had been planned for Easter Sunday. The news of Casement's arrest and the loss of the cargo of arms had reached the Volunteer headquarters, and it is believed that Casement at the last moment got an appeal through to abandon the project. It is not known whether the Volunteer council as a whole had decided on insurrection, or whether it was the secret intention of the Fenian section only. But in any case, the proposal was negatived and Eoin MacNeill sent the Countermanding

Order broadcast through the land. The manœuvres arranged for Easter Sunday—which from drill were to have been transformed into action—were abandoned, and the Insurrection appeared to be definitely and finally "off."

But on Easter Monday, soon after noon, the Irish Republic was proclaimed in Dublin, and the insurgent Tricolour suddenly broke on startled eyes from the flagstaff above the General Post Office in the heart of the Irish capital.

What caused the change of plan? This.—The British government learnt from the sinking of the *Aud* how nearly insurrection had come to pass, and the decision was made to seize the Volunteer executive and break up the organisation. No sooner was the decision made than it was communicated to the threatened parties by their Secret Service. On Easter Sunday the Volunteer council sat to consider a situation which was in substance this: a simultaneous rising throughout the country had been rendered impracticable by the Countermanding Order. But if no blow was struck there and then, the possibility of striking a blow at any time would be lost, for the Castle was to arrest all the leaders during the coming week. Should they submit to disarmament thus, or should they strike in Dublin with whatever sporadic support might be rendered through the country?

It is said that the decision to strike was reached by only a majority of one. Eoin MacNeill and those who felt with him consistently opposed unaided insurrection. Sean MacDiarmada, Tom Clarke and Thomas MacDonagh were, on the other hand, committed to the insurgent policy. Pearse is believed to have favoured the moderate counsel, but Connolly declared that the Citizen Army at any cost would strike before it was disarmed, and so, having preached at all times the duty of Irishmen to vindicate their national faith by sacrifice, Pearse gave the vote for insurrection which turned the course of Irish history.

It seemed a forlorn hope. Did the insurgents think to win on the field of battle? When all was over, people gasped at the apparent madness of a few ill-armed youths in throwing down the gage to an empire. But a week before, the Rising was by no means an extravagant proposal. Had the *Aud* safely landed its cargo, to be followed by further consignments at some point on the coast held by the now-equipped insurgents, then a certain belt or area of the country could have been captured, entrenched, and held for an indefinite period. Some 100,000 men could have been secured for the fighting line. To crush an insurrection of such magnitude—supported perhaps by German air and naval raids on the English coast and by the establishment of German submarine bases in ports seized by the rebels—England would have needed practically to withdraw her forces on the Western Front. It is not too much to say that the issue of the war in the West might have been wholly changed had a well-armed, all-Ireland insurrection taken place.

The Easter Monday Rising, however, had no such military prospects of success. There was always, of course, the chance that a German success on the Western Front would break England's defences and allow substantial help to be sent before the Rising was crushed, but this proved a vain hope. A small ineffectual shelling of the English coast was all that Germany performed in Ireland's aid. The insurgents put little reliance on German succour: they went out fully prepared to meet defeat and death, believing the Rising to be an honourable necessity, and hoping that it would ultimately prove successful by rousing the spirit of the nation and making the Irish cause once more an international question.

On the morning of Easter Monday, April 24th, 1916, the Dublin battalions paraded, bearing full arms and one day's rations. Shortly after noon, the General Post Office, the Four Courts, three of the railway termini, and other important points circling the centre of Dublin, were rushed and occupied. The Proclamation of the Irish Republic was published in big placards:

Poblacht na hEireann

The Provisional Government of the Irish Republic To the People of Ireland:

Irishmen and Irishwomen! In the name of God and of the dead generations from which she receives the old tradition of nationhood, Ireland, through us, summons her children to her flag, and strikes for her freedom. . . .

We declare the right of the people of Ireland to the ownership of Ireland, and to the unfettered control of Irish destinies, to be sovereign and indefeasible. . . . In every generation the Irish people have asserted their right to National freedom and sovereignty; six times during the past three hundred years they have asserted it in arms. Standing on that fundamental right and again asserting it in arms in the face of the world, we hereby proclaim the Irish Republic as a Sovereign Independent State, and we pledge our lives and the lives of our comrades to the cause of its freedom, of its welfare, and of its exaltation among the nations. . . .

The Republic guarantees civil and religious liberty, equal rights and equal opportunities to all its citizens, and declares its resolve to pursue the happiness and prosperity of the whole nation and of all its parts, cherishing all the children of the nation equally, and oblivious of the differences carefully fostered by an alien government, which have divided a minority from the majority in the past. . . .

We place the cause of the Irish Republic under the protection of the Most High God, whose blessing we invoke upon our arms. . . . In this supreme hour the Irish nation must, by its valour and discipline, and by the readiness of its children, to sacrifice themselves for the common good, prove itself worthy of the august destiny to which it is called.

Signed on behalf of the Provisional Government,
Thomas J. Clarke,

Sean MacDiarmada,	*Thomas MacDonagh,*
P. H. Pearse,	*Eamonn Ceannt,*
James Connolly,	*Joseph Plunkett.*

There was little fighting on the first day of the Rising. Wholly unprepared, since it was believed that the Volunteers had abandoned the project, the British authorities were taken by surprise and could not immediately muster forces to attack the insurgents before they had "dug themselves in." Two important points within the Dublin war area were, however, held by the British, namely, Trinity College, which was defended by the Officers' Training Corps, and Dublin Castle. The former dominated the old Parliament House and two leading thoroughfares. The latter could have been taken easily enough, but the Volunteers suspected it to be more strongly garrisoned than it actually was, and abstained from attack until troops were got in, and it was too late. It was on the Tuesday that a British force of some 4,500 men, with artillery, attacked the rebel strongholds, and secured the Castle. Fierce fighting with rifle, bomb and bayonet went on in buildings near the Castle, these being cleared of insurgents after desperate hand-to-hand battles. A cordon was then drawn around the north of the city, some of the rebel outposts being attacked and broken with rifle or artillery.

Meanwhile large reinforcements were being hurried into Ireland, via Kingstown, and on Wednesday, the south side of the city was brought within the cordon, which then began to be tightened, while the insurgents, receiving no addition of strength to fortify their somewhat loose hold of a large area, consolidated their position. The British forces marching in from Kingstown had, however, to fight their way. At Mount Street, the canal was covered by a Volunteer force in corner houses. The invading column was fired on, and a ferocious battle ensued. The rebels—who were but a few men—were ultimately dislodged or destroyed by waves of bombing raids. The British casualties were: officers killed 4, wounded 14; men, 216 killed or wounded.

On the Thursday the encircling forces pressed closer and penetrated to the central scene of operations, though every inch of the advance was contested by snipers and little bodies of desperate, daring men. Liberty

Hall had been shattered by gunfire from the river, and now shells ignited great buildings in O'Connell Street. On Thursday night, the city was under a canopy of crimson smoke, while rifle, machine gun and cannon contested in a furious crescendo. The lines of communication between the insurgent strongholds were broken, and the British forces concentrated on reducing headquarters, the General Post Office, over which the Republican flag still flew.

Meanwhile what was happening in the rest of Ireland?

When news reached the country battalions that, despite the Countermanding Order, a Rising had begun, there were necessarily divided counsels. All over Ireland, the thought of a few hundred youths, ill-armed, standing their ground against the might of Britain, sent an unforgettable thrill. Men knew that the circle of fire and steel was contracting 'round the daring insurgents, and everywhere they wrung their hands, saying: "Can we do nothing?" What could they do? The very best organised counties had not munitions for an hour's fight. Still, here and there, the cast was made. The Co. Dublin Volunteers, acting from Swords, pierced into Co. Meath, taking R. I. C. barracks, and fighting a pitched battle at Ashbourne with a constabulary force that was defeated at the cost of heavy casualties. Dr. Hayes, later elected to the Dáil, was the leading figure in this smaller campaign.

In Co. Galway Liam Mellows led a large body of insurgents on Galway city. A gunboat in Galway Bay dispersed them by shellfire. At Athenry, the insurgent camp was surrounded, and dispersed when the hopelessness of resistance became clear. Liam Mellows escaped capture by that remarkable resourcefulness which enabled him to make Galway so formidable.

In Co. Wexford Enniscorthy was seized on the Thursday morning, and the Republican flag was hoisted over the Athenæum. The greater part of northern Co. Wexford was also taken. Great administrative skill was shown, order being maintained, not by the armed Volunteers, but by a civil force, the Irish Republican Police. A large military force with artillery was sent to capture Enniscorthy, but happily the extremely bloody struggle that might have taken place was avoided. News came on Saturday that Dublin had surrendered and that Pearse had ordered all Volunteers to lay down their arms. As with the force at Swords, representatives of the insurgents were motored to Dublin under a safe conduct and the white flag, to see Pearse in person. Heartbroken, the delegates returned from the prison to the rebel town. Their impulse to fight a despairing fight to a finish was overcome by the good offices of an inter-denominational Peace Committee, and they, too, joined in the surrender.

How had the surrender come about?

On Friday, a terrific bombardment had set the centre of Dublin city wholly ablaze. Banks, churches and business places were aflame and tottering. The loss of life among non-combatants was appalling. Amid the carnage, Pearse wrote his final manifesto. Connolly lay wounded with a bullet through the thigh, still directing the defence.

> "I desire now" [Pearse wrote] "lest I may not have an opportunity later, to pay homage to the gallantry of the Soldiers of Irish Freedom who have during the past four days been writing with fire and steel the most glorious chapter in the later history of Ireland. . . .
>
> "For four days they have fought and toiled almost without cessation, almost without sleep, and in the intervals of fighting, they have sung songs of the freedom of Ireland. No man has complained, no man has asked 'why?' Each individual has spent himself, happy to pour out his strength for Ireland and for freedom. If they do not win this fight, they will at least have deserved to win it. But win it they will, though they may win it in death. . . .
>
> "If we accomplish no more than we have accomplished, I am satisfied. I am satisfied that we have saved Ireland's honour . . . of the fatal countermanding order which prevented those plans from being carried out, I shall not speak further. Both Eoin MacNeill and we have acted in the best interests of Ireland.
>
> "For my part, as to anything I have done in this, I am not afraid to face either the judgment of God or the judgment of posterity."

Here we see Pearse facing impending defeat. His reference to Eoin MacNeill suggests that he felt it was well that a Rising had been made, and also well that the whole country had not come into it. A localised rising was enough to give Ireland her blood sacrifice: MacNeill's order had spared many who would otherwise have been lost. If military victory was impossible, it was well that the necessary sacrifice was limited.

Commandant Daly had destroyed the Linen Hall Barracks but was now surrounded at the Four Courts. Countess Markievicz, after being driven out of trenches in Stephens' Green, was defending the College of Surgeons. Commandant McDonagh was surrounded in Jacob's factory. Commandant de Valera, whose men had so tenaciously resisted the advance from the south, was now holding Boland's Mills, while Commandant Ceannt held part of the South Dublin Union.

On Saturday, the General Post Office was set aflame, and the Republican Provisional government had to evacuate its so-bravely defended headquarters. In the dash to Moore Street—a neighbouring bye-way—The. O'Rahilly, who had opposed the Rising with MacNeill, but had gone out in it because he felt himself committed to that course, was shot dead. From the new headquarters soon after noon, a message was sent by Pearse, by the hand of a Red Cross nurse, asking for terms. These were refused, and at 2 o'clock, Pearse surrendered to Sir John Maxwell unconditionally. He then sent out notices to the Commandants of surviving Volunteer bodies, ordering arms to be laid down:

> "In order to prevent the further slaughter of unarmed people, and in the hope of saving the lives of our followers, now surrendered and hopelessly outnumbered."

And so the Rising ended, the outstanding forces laying down arms on the Sunday.

But the tragic story was as yet only beginning.

Arms had not been laid down, sniping had not died into silence, the smoke of the terrific conflagration in the heart of Dublin had not settled, before a huge roundup of Irish Irelanders began all over Ireland. In every village there were arrests. To have been heard speaking Irish was in some cases cause enough for the breadwinner to be torn from the family. The horrors of the congested prisons are too disgusting to narrate. Soon the hundreds and hundreds of prisoners were sent to rat-ridden internment camps across the water.

In ones and twos fifteen leaders[3] of the Rising were shot after secret military trial. Many of the executed prisoners were mere boys. All the signatories of the Republican declaration were put to death. Some death

---

[3] The leaders shot were:—Padraic Pearse and his brother William, James Connolly, Eamonn Kent, Michael O'Hanrahan, Sean MacDermott, Con Colbert, J. J. Houston, Thomas Kent (shot in Cork), Joseph Mary Plunkett, Edward Daly, Michael Mallon, Thomas MacDonagh, Tom Clark and John MacBride.

Sir John Maxwell, in command of the British Army in Dublin, deserves having his name transmitted to posterity in conjunction with the names of the martyred ones. In response to the cry of the British nation for the blood of "scoundrels" guilty of the fearful crime of fighting their land's invader, Sir John, with an expedition that won him praise, blotted out the lives of fifteen of Ireland's noblest—of the world's noblest. The manful Connolly was lying in hospital, helpless, and possibly dying from the wounds got in the fight. But the blood of the vanquished and dying was necessary to the victor's complete and happy satisfaction. So, the helpless one was borne on a stretcher to the place of execution, solicitously propped up against a support and shot dead. The rebel's foul crime was expiated. The Just One, the Owner of Ireland, was temporarily appeased.—S. M. M.

sentences, however, were commuted to sentences of imprisonment for life, happily for Ireland, Commandant de Valera escaping thus.

The callous shooting of the boy prisoners, most of all, roused in Ireland a terrific storm of indignation. The remarkable spirit of religious devotion displayed by the doomed men stirred the depths of Irish emotion. Sinn Fein became at once the creed of all Nationalist Ireland. The British had dubbed the rebel movement "Sinn Fein." And in the furnace of national suffering, all parties who stood for the nation were welded into one, and the name "Sinn Fein" was accepted.

After a year the prisoners were released for the purpose of English propaganda in America. During their imprisonment a man hitherto known only as an obscure mathematical professor, a silent Gaelic League and Volunteer worker, had been strangely recognised as the national leader. This was Eamon de Valera. At the Release, he shot, as it were, to the nation's lead in a flash. One week, his name was scarcely known; the next he was recognised as the man on the bridge. Character alone was the cause of this remarkable ascendancy. Cool, resolved, gentle, masterly, humble, firm: Eamon de Valera impressed all. He is no great orator like Pearse; he does not pretend to have Griffith's marvellous mastery of political science, and indeed, talks always of Griffith as his teacher: but he combines the idealism of one with the statesmanship of the other. Pearse performed the revolutionary task he set himself, but we cannot imagine him as counsellor in days of peace or negotiation; Griffith alone could not win the nation's adherence. The stars were lucky when Ireland was given three men so remarkable in one generation. But where in political history is there a finer spectacle than the superb self-sacrifice with which Griffith handed the leadership of Sinn Fein to his young disciple, saying: "The people of Ireland now have a leader who is both soldier and statesman"?

When, one year later again, that is, in 1918, England decreed the conscription of Ireland's manhood to save her from the great German advance, it was 'round de Valera that the whole nation rallied. His coolness and wisdom saved Ireland from a bloody defeat, and secured a moral victory. Very nearly was Ireland plunged into a life-and-death struggle, but de Valera's resolved bearing, and the splendid succour offered by the Church, held the whole people firm and calm. Before the determined nation, fortified with spiritual strength, those who had planned a desperate onslaught hesitated, and at last withdrew. Irish conscription was, at the last moment, abandoned, and Ireland for the first time in many centuries escaped the scourge prepared for her.

In December, at the General Election, all Nationalist Ireland declared its allegiance to the Republican ideal, and the Sinn Fein policy of abstention from Westminster was adopted. In January, the republican representatives assembled in Dublin and founded *Dáil Eireann,* the Irish Constituent Assembly, proclaiming the Republic once again. A message was sent to the nations of the world requesting the recognition of the free Irish State, and a national government was erected.

The best history of the Sinn Fein movement is *The Evolution of Sinn Fein,* by Prof. R. M. Henry of Belfast University [Talbot Press]. A useful companion is P. S. O'Hegarty's small brochure *Sinn Fein: An Illumination* [Maunsel]. Also Aodh de Blacam's *Towards the Republic,* which deals with Sinn Fein social ideals as well as history.

Griffith's *Resurrection of Hungary* is important. Francis P. Jones' *History of Sinn Fein* [Kenedy] is fine.

CHAPTER LXXX

THE LAST WAR?

No sooner had the new Government begun to function, established its Courts, appointed Consuls, started a stock-taking of the country's undeveloped natural resources, and put a hundred constructive schemes to work, than Britain stepped in, with her army of Soldiers and Constabulary, to counter the work, harassing and imprisoning the workers. This move of England's called forth a secretly built-up Irish Republican Army (developed from The Irish Volunteers), which, early in 1920, began a guerilla warfare, and quickly succeeded in clearing vast districts of the Constabulary who were ever England's right arm in Ireland.

Lloyd George met this not only by pouring into Ireland regiments of soldiers with tanks, armored cars, aeroplanes, and all the other terrorising paraphernalia that had been found useful in the European War, but also by organising and turning loose upon Ireland an irregular force of Britons, among the most vicious and bloodthirsty known to history—the force which quickly became notorious to the world under the title of the Black and Tans. And then, with carefully planned purpose to quickly break the Irish spirit and subdue the nation, was waged upon the Irish people—alike combatants and non-combatants, Irish women as well as men, toddling child and tottering aged—a war of vengeance, unparalleled for blind fury and fearful cruelty by any war in any civilised country of the world since the seventeenth century. The wholesale burning of a hundred villages, towns, cities, the looting, the spoliation of the inhabitants, though in themselves appalling, were as nothing compared with the cold-blooded murders perpetrated by the British, and the elaborate refinement of torture, worse far than death, which they visited on non-combatants as well as combatants—fearful tortures that frequently only ended when slow death snatched from them their prey.

It was intended that the job of "settling Ireland" should, like Cromwell's campaign on which it was modelled, be sharp, short, and decisive. It should be over and done with ere the outside world awoke to the fearful reality of what was happening. And the English press, with a bare two or three honourable exceptions, the English correspondents of foreign newspapers, and the English cable service, well did their part to back the British army in the field. They saw to it that not only was the hideousness of their campaign in Ireland concealed from the world, but that instead, the brave Irish boys, fighting for freedom a fearfully unequal fight, were lied about and painted to the world as corner boy ruffians. And, loyally doing their bit in the disgraceful campaign of hoodwinking the world, the highest, most "Honourable" Government officials, from Premier Lloyd George down to Irish Secretary Sir Hamar Greenwood, from their places in the British House of Commons deliberately and persistently falsified the accounts of occurrences in Ireland, denied, without wincing, the barbarous crimes of the British which they knew and approved of, and unblushingly fathered upon the clean-fighting Irish boys callous and diabolical cruelties that were native alone to the breasts of their own—even to insinuating that the murders, by disguised and masked British ruffians, of Mayor MacCurtain of Cork and Mayor Clancy of Limerick were perpetrated by their own Republican comrades, who slew them as traitors. Thus did the Honourable British gentlemen blacken the dead as well as the living.

Yet the well-planned campaign for the quick wasting of Ireland, and breaking of Ireland's spirit did not come off on schedule. The atrocities which were meant to frighten and subdue, only stimulated the outraged nation to more vigour: and by the time the fight was expected to end it was found to be only well begun. And, carefully as the army of falsifiers guarded every gate by which the truth might escape to the world, tricklings of truth had begun to find their way out, and the world was beginning to whisper of strange British doings in Ireland. More than by anything else, probably, the world was awakened to the truth of the situation in Ireland through the extraordinary heroism of Terence MacSwiney (Mayor of Cork in succession to the martyred MacCurtain), who in protest against the foreign tyranny which seized and jailed him as a criminal for the guilt of working for his country, refused to eat in British dungeon, till, after three months of slow and painful starving to death, with the wondering world literally by his bedside watching his death agonies, he at length went to join the joyful company of martyrs who had died that Ireland might live.

The world was stirred. The terrible truth about Britain's rape of Ireland began to be realised—and began to call forth muttered foreign protest.

Only then, when they realised that they were found out, an appreciable portion of the Britons themselves began to protest—chiefly, not to save Ireland, but to save Britain's face.[1]

The general aspect of the British Campaign in Ireland is best summarised, perhaps, in the findings of the American Commission on Conditions in Ireland—a Commission whose members were selected by the American Committee of One Hundred—this latter being composed of many of the most representative men and women in America, Protestant, Catholic, Methodist, Presbyterian and Jew—including Governors of States, Senators,

[1] The Protestant Archbishop of Canterbury speaking in the House of Lords (Feb. 22nd, 1921) said, with just indignation, "What is being done in Ireland is exactly what we condemned the Germans for doing in Belgium."

The Moderator of the Presbyterian Church in England, Rev. Duncan MacGregor, said, "The result of the present policy is that British rule has become a by-word and a scoff in every country in Europe, and across the Atlantic. . . . I wonder whether the whole Church of God cannot speak with united voice on so clear and crying a moral issue."

Ex-Prime Minister Asquith declared, "Things are being done in Ireland with the knowledge and approval, if not under the direction of, Government officials, which would disgrace the blackest annals of the lowest despotism of Europe."

The British Labor Party found themselves forced to send a Commission to Ireland to investigate. After journeying to the various parts of Ireland most affected by the war machine, and interviewing witnesses to some of the most terrible of the occurrences, as well as leading men and officials of both sides, they found themselves forced to give a report that made myriads of their British people gasp. The gist of their findings may be conveyed in one sentence taken from the closing paragraph of their report: "Things are being done in Ireland, in the name of Britain, which must make her name stink in the nostrils of the whole world."

Hon. C. F. G. Masterman at Macclesfield: "Speaking with a full sense of my responsibility as former Cabinet Minister, I declare the evidence is overwhelming that a systematic policy of terror is being pursued in Ireland—defended by Lloyd George, backed up by the flagrant lies of Sir Hamar Greenwood, and organised by officials in high places in Dublin. The attempt is not merely to punish the guilty, but to break the whole spirit of Ireland by inflicting punishment upon people who are as innocent as babes unborn. That was the system which, under the German invasion of Belgium, turned the whole world against Germany. Yet in every particular the things going on in Ireland today are a replica—in some cases they are worse than—the things the Germans did in Belgium."

Lord Hugh Cecil (in the House of Commons, on March 1st, 1921): "The methods adopted in Ireland have no precedent whatever in the story of the restoration of law and order by previous governments in the nineteenth century."

General Gough, formerly of the British Army—one of the Army leaders who, when a follower of Carson, in 1914, threatened to mutiny if "Home Rule" was forced upon the Orangemen—now wrote a letter to the press (March 1st, 1921) in the course of which he said: "Law and order has given place to a bloody and brutal anarchy, in which the armed agents of the Crown violate every law in aimless and vindictive and insolent savagery. England has departed further from her own standards, and further from the standards even of any nation in the world, not excepting the Turk and the Zulu, than has ever been known in history before."

Congressmen, Protestant, Catholic and Methodist Bishops, College Presidents, Editors, Business men, Labor men. Following are the most remarkable of their findings:

> "1. The Imperial British Government has created and introduced into Ireland a force of at least 78,000 men, many of them youthful and inexperienced, and some of them convicts; and has incited that force to unbridled violence.
>
> 2. The Imperial British forces in Ireland have indiscriminately killed innocent men, women, and children; have discriminately assassinated persons suspected of being republicans; have tortured and shot prisoners while in custody, adopting the subterfuges of 'refusal to halt' and 'attempting to escape'; and have attributed to alleged 'Sinn Fein extremists' the British assassination of prominent Irish Republicans.
>
> 3. House burning and wanton destruction of villages and cities by Imperial British forces under Imperial British officers have been countenanced and ordered by officials of the British Government, and elaborate provision by gasoline sprays and bombs has been made in a number of instances for systematic incendiarism as part of a plan of terrorism.
>
> 4. A campaign for the destruction of the means of existence of the Irish people has been conducted by the burning of factories, creameries, crops, and farm implements, and the shooting of farm animals. This campaign is carried on regardless of the political views of their owners, and results in widespread and acute suffering among women and children.
>
> 5. Acting under a series of proclamations issued by the competent military authorities of the Imperial British forces hostages are carried by forces exposed to the fire of the Republican Army; fines are levied upon towns and villages as punishment for alleged offenses of individuals; private property is destroyed in reprisal for acts with which the owners have no connection; and the civilian population is subjected to an inquisition upon the theory that individuals are in possession of information valuable to the military forces of Great Britain. These acts of the Imperial British forces are contrary to the laws of peace or war among modern civilised nations."

In the spring of 1921 there was galloped through the English Parliament a "Home Rule Bill" for Ireland—whose object was, by giving the eastern part of Ulster, the Orange corner, a Parliament of its own, to detach it from the rest of Ireland, thus dividing the nation on sectarian lines, and by the

Orangemen's aid strengthening the foreign grip on the whole country. The Orangemen (all British in blood)—ever the Ascendancy in Ireland treading on the necks of the real Irish—had professed that they feared to trust themselves to the certain intolerance of an Irish Parliament—though the true fact was well known to English statesmen: even Sir Hamar Greenwood, who blackened Nationalist Ireland by every device in his power, having had to state in the British House of Commons, "I am constrained to confess that the North is the only part of Ireland where people are interfered with on account of their religion." These Northeasterners in July, 1920, celebrated their coming freedom from an intolerant Irish Parliament by instituting a series of pogroms against the minority among them—in the course of which in twelve months more than one hundred of the minority were killed by being beaten, stabbed, kicked, or shot to death, and more than one thousand injured, while the homes and belongings of several hundreds were burnt, and six thousand Nationalists driven out of employment. It is to be remembered in this connection that the motto of these noble Orangemen is "Civil and Religious Liberty."

Premier Lloyd George, having ignored the rising tide of world indignation until Britain's hold on Ireland's northeastern corner was well secured and clamped, then had King George go to Belfast to open Britain's branch Parliament there, and speak a prepared piece, calling for union among the people he was dividing, and asking also for peace between England and Ireland. And then in deference to his King's pious wish (so he informed the world) the Prime Minister invited Sinn Fein to a parley. Ireland had proved unconquerable by any other means.

President De Valera, for the Irish Republic, accepted the invitation. A truce was arranged between the invader's army and the army of the Republic in July, 1921. And the English Prime Minister received with honour the head of that body which he had with long and faithful persistence denounced to the world as "the Irish murder gang."

To De Valera, in this parley, offer was made to give Ireland what George called "Dominion status"—supposedly that amount of freedom under the British Crown which is the lot of Canada and Australia—but less the control by Britain of the Irish harbours, seas, skies, and some other such perquisites—which offer was promptly and unanimously rejected by An Dail Eireann. Rather than sanction Britain's covetous and dishonest grab of anything that was Ireland's the Irish representatives preferred that their people should return to the wilderness.

Then, after resorting to threat of a renewed war upon Ireland far more fierce than had gone before—which threat caused no weakening of the

Irish resolve—the English Prime Minister invited Ireland to send delegates to a peace conference, on the understanding that the idea of separating Ireland from the British Crown should not be considered. De Valera, for An Dail Eireann, refused such condition. And, beaten from one position after another, Premier Lloyd George finally called for a conference, free of conditions, to be held in London on October 11th, 1921. And President De Valera accepted the invitation.

* * * * * * * *

An Irish delegation, headed by Arthur Griffith and Michael Collins, met representatives of the British Cabinet in London, and, after six weeks' conference, the Irish delegates, compelled by threat of renewed ruthless warfare on their prostrate land, signed a compromise treaty—at two a. m. December 6th.

This treaty would affect four-fifths of Ireland. Nominally it embraced all Ireland—but provided that the Northeastern corner of the country, which had already been given over to Orange sway, was free to withdraw from the compact.

The Treaty provided—

> That such part of the country (presumably four-fifths) as acquiesced, should be named the Irish Free State; should have the same status as Canada; should acknowledge the English king, and enjoy a British Governor-General—
>
> That the people of the Free State portion of Ireland should elect representatives who, having sworn allegiance to the King of England, should then be empowered to make the laws for their territory, rule it, direct its trade, and maintain a small army—
>
> That the Free State should be privileged to shoulder its share of Britain's tremendous national debt (incurred chiefly in British wars of conquest)—
>
> And that Britain should retain control of the Irish seas, and of strategic harbours in Ireland, and "other facilities" (happy phrase) needed by her—in plain words, that her right should be acknowledged forever to hold the sword suspended over Ireland.

The British Parliament almost unanimously ratified the treaty for Britain. But in Ireland De Valera fought for a change in the treaty terms—and a change in the form of oath. He would "externally associate" Ireland with the British Empire, and would have the elected Irish representatives swear to "recognize" the English king as the head of the association of British nations with which Ireland now joined.

An important group of the Irish workers and fighters held out for the Irish Republic, which had been consecrated by the blood of Pearse, Connolly, Clarke, and their gallant companions, and by a thousand martyrs since.

After long and hot debate, the Dail Eireann, on January 7th, 1922, ratified the treaty by a narrow majority.

And, seemingly, an end was put to one phase of Ireland's struggle.

But *the* end was not yet.

CHAPTER LXXXI

The Dawning

The final chapter of the story of the Irish Race will not be written till, please God, many a long and glorious Irish day shall yet have come and gone. The final chapter of our partial story cannot be better written than in the words of Ethna Carbery, who shortly before her early death saw with her spirit eyes the radiant Dawn dethroning Eire's dark Night of Sorrow—and in beautiful words pictured for us her vision—

MO CHRAOIBHIN CNO.[1]

A Sword of Light hath pierced the dark! Our eyes have seen the Star!
Oh, Eire, leave the ways of sleep now days of promise are!
The rusty spears upon your walls are stirring to and fro,
In dreams they front uplifted shields—Then wake,
Mo Chraoibhin Cno!

The little waves creep whispering where sedges fold you in,
And round you are the barrows of your buried kith and kin;
Oh! famine-wasted, fever-burnt, they faded like the snow
Or set their hearts to meet the steel—for you,
Mo Chraoibhin Cno!

[1] Pronounced *mo chreeveen no*, "My cluster of nuts"—my brown-haired girl, *i.e.*, Ireland. During our many dark ages when it was treason for our singers to sing of Ireland, the olden poets sang of, and to, their beloved, under many such endearing and figurative titles.

Their names are blest, their *caoine* sung, our bitter tears are dried;
We bury Sorrow in their graves, Patience we cast aside;
Within the gloom we hear a voice that once was ours to know—
'Tis Freedom—Freedom calling loud, Arise,
Mo Chraoibhin Cno!
Afar beyond that empty sea, on many a battle-place,
Your sons have stretched brave hands to Death before the foeman's face—
Down the sad silence of your rest their war-notes faintly blow,
And bear an echo of your name—of yours,
Mo Chraoibhin Cno!

Then wake, *a gradh!* We yet shall win a gold crown for your head,
Strong wine to make a royal feast—the white wine and the red—
And in your oaken mether the yellow mead shall flow
What day you rise in all men's eyes—a Queen,
Mo Chraoibhin Cno!

The silver speech our fathers knew shall once again be heard;
The fire-lit story, crooning song, sweeter than lilt of bird;
Your quicken-tree shall break in flower, its ruddy fruit shall glow,
And the Gentle People dance beneath its shade—
Mo Chraoibhin Cno!

There shall be peace and plenty—the kindly open door;
Blessings on all who come and go—the prosperous or the poor—
The misty glens and purple hills a fairer tint shall show,
When your splendid Sun shall ride the skies again—
Mo Chraoibhin Cno!